BRITISH ECONOMIC DEVELOPMENT IN
SOUTH EAST ASIA, 1880–1939

CONTENTS OF THE EDITION

BRITISH ECONOMIC DEVELOPMENT IN SOUTH EAST ASIA, 1880–1939

Volume 2
Mining, Trade and Industry

Edited by
David Sunderland

Routledge
Taylor & Francis Group

LONDON AND NEW YORK

First published 2014 by Pickering & Chatto (Publishers) Limited

2 Park Square, Milton Park, Abingdon, Oxon, OX14 4RN
605 Third Avenue, New York, NY 10017

Routledge is an imprint of the Taylor & Francis Group, an informa business

First issued in paperback 2020

BRITISH LIBRARY CATALOGUING IN PUBLICATION DATA

British economic development in South East Asia, 1880–1939.
1. Great Britain – Commerce – Southeast Asia – History – 19th century – Sources.
2. Great Britain – Commerce – Southeast Asia – History – 20th century – Sources.
3. Southeast Asia – Commerce – Great Britain – History – 19th century – Sources.
4. Southeast Asia – Commerce – Great Britain – History – 20th century – Sources.
5. Economic development – Southeast Asia – History – 19th century – Sources.
6. Economic development – Southeast Asia – History – 20th century – Sources.
7. Agriculture – Economic aspects – Southeast Asia – History – 19th century –
Sources. 8. Agriculture – Economic aspects – Southeast Asia – History – 20th
century – Sources. 9. Great Britain – Colonies – Asia – Economic policy – Sources.
I. Sunderland, David, 1958– editor of compilation.
330.9'5904-dc23

ISBN-13: 978-1-138-75069-2 (hbk)
ISBN-13: 978-0-367-74001-6 (pbk)

CONTENTS

MINING

Mining in Malaya

e most important metal extracted in Malaya was tin, discussed in the General Introduction. Other minerals included iron ore, coal, granite, tungsten, bauxite, gold and oil. The iron ore sector was controlled by the Japanese. Japan's iron and steel industry had an insatiable need for ore, which could not be met by its domestic mines, and British administrators welcomed Japanese investment, aware that there was little interest in the industry in the UK and that it would generate useful revenue. The proximity of Malaya and the dearth of home cargos for ships returning to Japan also minimized transport costs. The first mine was opened near Batu Pahat in Johore in 1921, and, as these deposits became exhausted, shifted to Trengganu, Pahang and, from 1935, to the Temangan district of Kelantan. In 1937, of the 2.438m tons extracted (1.4 per cent of world output), 620,000 tons came from Johore, 827,000 tons from Kelantan and 991,000 tons from Trengganu. The industry was dominated by four companies. Ishihara Sangyo Koshi Ltd established the first mine in Johore, obtaining from the Sultan a twenty-one-year concession. High returns prompted the firm to open two further mines at Machang Satahun near Kemaman, Trengganu and, when the Johore workings became depleted, to sink a shaft at Sri Medan, Johore and begin prospecting at Ulu Rompin and Sungei Bebar in Pahang. Unfortunately, the outcrop at Trengganu proved limited and inaccessible and the exploitation of the Sri Medan mine was delayed by the International Tin Scheme, the iron being inter-bedded with tin, and by labour problems sparked by the Sino-Japanese war, which in 1937 led to the entire Chinese workforce walking out. Other important miners were Shigeru Iizuka, who sank a shaft at Bukit Langkap, Endau in Johore and obtained concessions at Sambang and Tanjong Tuan; the Nippon Mining Co., which in 1930 took over the Kuhara mine at Bukit Besi, Trengganu; and the South Seas Iron Mining Co. floated in Tokyo with a capital of 1m yen to take over a Kenantan concession developed by a syndicate of six firms.[1]

Coal was discovered at Batu Arang in Selangor in 1913. The deposits were

square miles. To exploit the seam, in the same year Malayan Colleries Ltd was founded, raising $1.5m from British and Chinese shareholders, some of which was used to purchase leases covering 9,000 acres of land. Its mine was opened in 1915 after a seven-mile $1m branch line had been constructed by the Federated Malay States Railway (FMSR) to link Batu Arang to Kuang, the closest mainline junction. The company used the latest technology in the form of coal cutters, hammer drills and air compressors; owned a brick and cement factory and a saw mill, which supplied the colliery and sold their goods locally; and employed in 1918 and 1937 respectively 1,000 and 5,000 Chinese miners. Workers were difficult to recruit, rubber planting offering a lighter workload and higher wages, and, in the late 1930s, there was significant labour unrest, supposedly incited by Communists. Output rose from 10,725 tons in 1915 to 781,509 tons in 1940, most of which was bought by the FMSR (450 tons per day in 1937), tin mines (700 tons per day), the Bangsar Power Station in Selangor and the Perak River Hydro-Electric Co. (700 tons per day) and local steamers.[2]

Of the other minerals mined, the most important were probably gold and bauxite. Gold had been extracted on the east coast of the Malayan peninsula from the early nineteenth century by Chinese miners. During the colonial period, Chinese entrepreneurs, encouraged by British administrators, established lode mines in Pahang, Negeri Sembilan and Kelantan, extracting 15,070 ounces in Pahang/Negeri Sembilan (1903) and 40,000 ounces in Kelantan (1906/12). There was also an Australian mine at Raub, West of Pahang, operated by Australian Syndicate Ltd (1889), later to become Australian Gold Mining Co. Ltd (1912). Bauxite, by comparison was only exploited in the early 1930s when the metal, smelted to produce aluminium, began to be used in the manufacture of aeroplanes. The sector produced 66,700 tons in 1939 and again was controlled by the Japanese, the majority of the output coming from Ishihara Sangyo Koashi Ltd's Sri Medan mine at Johore. Other minerals excavated include granite and limestone at the FMSR-owned quarries at Segamat (Johore), Ipoh (Perak), Kodiang (Kedah) and Kuala Lipis (Pahang); Tungston, much of the 673,000 metric tons produced in 1938 coming from a British-owned mine at Pulai, Perak; and oil from the Royal Dutch Shell wells in Miri, Sarawak.[3]

Mining Elsewhere in British South East Asia

The two most important Burmese mining sectors were oil and rubies. The country also produced 18,000 tons (1885) of salt, extracted through the boiling of sea water and largely used in the manufacture of fish paste, and respectable quantities of tin, lead, zinc, tungston and silver, mainly at the Bowdwin mine, forty miles north-east of Lashio. The mine went through a number of owners

smelted at Mandalay and, as production increased, at smelters constructed at Namtu, connected to the mine and the Lashio–Mandalay railway by privately owned branch lines.[4]

Oil had a long history. Hand dug wells existed in Twingon and Beme long before the arrival of the British, the oil extracted used as a wood preservative and as a source of light and for the caulking of boats. The industry was commercialized from the turn of the century, mainly due to the construction by the Admiralty of oil powered destroyers and submarines and the 1911 decision to convert the Fleet to oil, and was dominated by the Burmah Oil Co., which drilled 75 per cent of the country's output. Founded in 1886 as the Rangoon Oil Co., the firm benefitted from the exclusion for strategic reasons of non-British companies from the sector; the government turning down requests for prospecting licences from Royal Dutch Shell and two subsidiaries of Standard Oil. It sank its first well in the Yenangyaun oil field in 1887 and in the Singu field in 1902, initially buying sites, and, from 1906, leasing them from the Twinzayo and Twinza, the owners of the reserves. To increase margins, a fleet of oil tankers was purchased, storage tanks constructed at the main Indian ports and, in 1909, a nery built at Syrium (close to Rangoon) connected to the Yenangyaung and Singu fields by a 325-mile pipeline. Other major players in the sector included the British Burmah Oil Co. (1910), which took over the Rangoon Oil Co.'s operations in Singu and the assets of the Rangoon Refinery Co. and the Aungban Oil Co., and the Indo-Burma Petroleum Co. The latter's first well (1918) at Indow in Lower Chindwin proved disappointing, producing only 3m gallons by 1930. Luckily its facilities at Lanywa were more successful, supplying 13m gallons in their first year of operation.

Of the two fields, the Yenangyaun reserves were the most productive, yielding 2.3m gallons in 1887, 10m gallons in 1893, 57m gallons in 1903 and 200m gallons in 1913. Output then fell to 130m gallons in the late 1920s, by which time the Singu oil field was fully on-stream, supplying 23m gallons in 1904, 50m gallons in 1911 and 100m gallons in 1921. Eighty per cent of the $55m of oil produced in 1939 was exported tariff free to India, increasingly as kerosene – Burma by 1900/1 supplying 10 per cent of the sub-continent's requirements, and, by 1938/9, 58 per cent. The remainder was mainly shipped to the UK.[5]

e award of the Burmese ruby concession was the subject of some controversy. The outcry that followed the award of a temporary lease on generous terms to Gillanders, Arbuthnot & Co., a long established Calcutta-based Agency house with a large share of the oriental ruby market, forced the Burmese government to put the concession up for tender, which was won by a syndicate led by Edwin Streeker, a Bond Street Jeweller. Claims by Motitz Unger, a French jewel seller, who secretly represented the Exploration Co., a Rothschilds backed concern, that was won by a combined bid from Streeker and the Exploration Co., which agreed to pay the government Rs 40,000 plus one sixth of all profits in return for a five-year lease. To raise the necessary capital, in 1889 the Burma Ruby Mine Co. was floated on the London Stock Exchange raising £300,000. So successful was the company that on the expiration of the first lease it agreed to pay $800,000 plus one fifth of all profits for a second fourteen-year contract. Alas, soon afterwards it encountered serious flooding and, despite the expenditure of £200,000 in an attempt to alleviate the problem, in 1922 it halted all operations.[6]

Elsewhere in British South East Asia, oil was mined in Brunei, oil, gold, coal, antimony and cinnabar (mercury sulphate) in Sarawak and coal at Silimpopon, British North Borneo and in Labuan. In addition, in 1914, the Renong Dredging Co. (1908), a subsidiary of Guthrie & Co., plus two other firms registered in the UK, operated Siam tin mines and 40 per cent of the capital of the Batavian Co. and the Anglo-Saxon Petroleum Co., major players in the Sumatran oil industry, was held by Britons. The exploration for oil in Brunei began in 1899 when a well was sunk at Bandar Seri Begawan. Although no oil was discovered, many remained convinced that the country possessed significant deposits and over the following twenty-five years seven companies searched for the elusive mineral, drilling wells in Labi and Bukit Puan in Belait (1911) and in Tutong (1923). In 1925, exploration switched to Seria, and, four years later, the British Malayan Petroleum Co., a subsidiary of Royal Dutch Shell, discovered the first commercial field, sinking a well at Padang Berawa on the west bank of the Seria river, which went on-stream in 1931.[7]

Oil was discovered in Sarawak by the Anglo-Saxon Petroleum Co., which in 1907 obtained from the Brooke family a seventy-five-year exploration concession in return for a pledge to pay a royalty of just 1*s* on every ton of oil extracted. The company sank its first well at Miri Kampong in the Miri district in 1910 and later constructed a refinery at Lutong, between the Baram and Miri rivers, from where the drummed refined oil was transported by lighters and thence by submarine oil pipelines to tankers anchored off shore. In 1921, the concession was sold to Sarawak Oilfields Ltd, by which time the Miri oilfields were producing 2,000 barrels per day, output peaking eight years later at 15,000 barrels per day worth $45m.[8] Coal was mined in two locations: at Simunjan on the Sadong River by the Borneo Co. and on the Brunei island of Muara. C.C. Cowie & Sons had obtained the latter concession from the Sultan of Brunei and, in 1888, this was purchased by the Brooke family, partly to gain greater control of the Sultanate. From 1873 to 1931, when mining ceased, the Simunjan mine produced 876,345 tons of coal, most of which was exported to Singapore where it fuelled the ships of the Peninsular & Oriental Steam Navigation Co. The Muara mine, renamed Brooketon by Brookes, turned out 582,412 tons from 1888 to 1924, all

e Borneo Co. also had interests in the country's other mining sectors. By 1884, it had taken over most of the Chinese gold mines partly because it possessed superior technology and capital resources, but largely due to the preferential treatment it received from the Brookes family – in 1879 it was given the right to work all Sarawak's gold mines and, prior to 1895, paid no royalties. Between 1899 and 1921, its Bau and Bidi operations produced 983,255 troy ounces of gold, worth $25.9m. Unfortunately, by the early 1920s the seams of both mines had become exhausted and the company withdrew from the sector, its place taken by Chinese miners, despite the harsh conditions placed upon them by the Brookes family – land grants were small, a 10 per cent royalty was imposed and none were permitted to take out exclusive prospecting licences. As for cinnabar and antimony, the company extracted the former at Tegora, Gading and Gambang, excavating $1.159m worth of the metal between 1870 and 1899 when seams became exhausted. Antimony was mined at Jambusan and Buso, workings being abandoned in 1916 by which time $1.905m had been extracted.[9]

Note: Information on mining can also be found in the following sources/themes:

Topic	Source	Volume/Theme
Malayan and Sarawak mining	Anon., *The Manufacturing Industries of the British Empire*	Volume 2/Industry
Malayan mining	W. L. Blythe, *Methods and Conditions of Employment of Chinese Labour in the Federated Malay States*	Volume 3/Human Capital

1. Y. C. Leng, 'Japanese Rubber and Iron Investments in Malaya, 1900–1941', *Journal of Southeast Asian Studies*, 5:1 (1974), pp. 18–36, on pp. 26–9, 31–2; A. Barber, 'British Malaya as a Leading Source for Japanese Iron', *Far Eastern Survey*, 8:6 (1939), pp. 66–8. The British halted development of only one mine and then only because it was in an area of air and naval importance (A. Linden, 'The British Commonwealth and Colonial Rivalry in Southeast Asia', *Pacific Historical Review*, 11:1 (1942), pp. 19–27, on p. 22).
2. A. Kaur, 'Hewers and Haulers: A History of Coal Miners and Coal Mining in Malaya', *Modern Asian Studies*, 24:1 (1990), pp. 75–113, on pp. 76–7, 80–3, 85–6, 89, 91.
3. N. Dodge, 'Mineral Production on the East Coast of Malaya in the Nineteenth Century', *Journal of the Malaysian Branch of the Royal Asiatic Society*, 50:2 (1977), pp. 89–110; K. S. Ariffin, 'Mesothermal Lode Gold Deposit Central Belt Peninsular Malaysia', available online at http://www.intechopen.com/download/get/type/pdfs/id/27599 [accessed 12 December 2013], pp. 1, 4; V. Thompson, 'Japan Frozen Out of British Malaya', *Far Eastern Survey*, 10:20 (1941), p. 238; Leng, 'Japanese Rubber', pp. 28, 32; A. Kaur, 'The Impact of Railroads on The Malayan Economy, 1874–1941', *Journal of Asian Studies*, 39:4 (1980), pp. 693–710, on p. 698; Anon., 'Malaya and its Communications', *Bulletin of International News*, 18:26 (1941), pp. 2003–7, on p. 2004; H. G. Callis, 'Capital Investment in Southeastern Asia and the Philippines', *Annals of the American Academy of Political and Social Science*, 226 (1943), pp. 22–31, on p. 25; Anon., 'The History of Shell in Malaysia', available online at http://www.shell.com.my/aboutshell/who-we-are/

4.   S. A. Resnick, 'The Decline of Rural Industry Under Export Expansion: A Comparison among Burma, Philippines, and Thailand, 1870–1938', *Journal of Economic History*, 30:1 (1970), pp. 51–73, on pp. 57–8; N. Nishizawa, 'Economic Development of Burma', *Institute of Peace Studies, Hiroshima University, Japan, Research Report*, 16 (1991), pp. 1–155, on p. 68; L. D. Stamp, 'Burma: An Undeveloped Monsoon Country', *Geographical Review*, 20:1 (1930), pp. 86–109, on pp. 92, 97. See also J. Hillman, 'Capitalism and the Development of the Tin Industry in Burma', *Journal of Burma Studies*, 15 (2011), pp. 119–51.

5.   M. Ehrmann, 'Gem Mining In Burma', *Gems & Gemology* (Spring 1957), pp. 1–28; M. V. Longmuir, 'Oil in Burma: The Extraction of "Earth-Oil" to 1914' (PhD dissertation, University of Queensland, 1999); Callis, 'Capital Investment', p. 25; D. Sunderland, *Managing the British Empire: The Crown Agents for the Colonies 1833–1914* (London: Royal Historical Society/Boydell & Brewer, 2004), p. 240; R. L. Clifford, 'The Rise and Fall of British Investment in Burma', *Asian Affairs*, 6:2 (1975), pp. 196–204; Anon., 'The Coloured History of the Burmah Oil Company. Footnote to Burmese Economic History: The Rise and Decline of the Arakan Oil Fields', *Myanmar Times*, 20–26 August 2007; Nishizawa, 'Economic Development ', pp. 66–8.

6.   R. V. Turrell, 'Conquest and Concession: The Case of the Burma Ruby Mines', *Modern Asian Studies*, 22:1 (1988), pp. 141–63, on pp. 141–2, 148, 150–3, 157, 159–60; G. P. Means, 'Special Rights as a Strategy for Development: The Case of Malaysia', *Comparative Politics*, 5:1 (1972), pp. 29–61, on pp. 43–4.

7.   R. Ibbotson, *Silimpopon – A Borneo Coal Mine* (London: Opus Publications, 2010); J. F. Hennart, 'Transaction Costs and the Multinational Enterprise: The Case of Tin', *Business and Economic History*, 16 (1987), pp. 1–13, on p. 7; G. C. Allen and A. G. Donnithorne, *Western Enterprise in Indonesia and Malaya: A Study in Economic Development* (London: Routledge, 2003), pp. 54–5; Callis, 'Capital Investment', p. 26; G. C. Harper, *The Discovery and Development of the Seria Oil Field* (Bandar Seri Begawan, Brunei: Jabatan Muzium-Muzium, 1975), p. 200; Anon., 'History of Oil & Gas', available online at https://www.bsp.com.bn/main/aboutbsp/about_oil_gas.asp [accessed 28 December 2013]. The companies that searched for Brunei oil were the British Borneo Petroleum Syndicate Limited, the Shanghai Langkat Company (a Singapore consortium), Nederlandsche Koloniale Petroleum Maatschappij (a Dutch firm), the Anglo-Saxon Petroleum Company Limited, Asiatic Petroleum Company (Federated Malay States) Limited and the British Malayan Petroleum Company Ltd (Harper, *The Discovery*).

8.   A barrel held 42 gallons of oil.

9.   A. Kaur, 'The Babbling Brookes: Economic Change in Sarawak 1841–1941', *Modern Asian Studies*, 29:1 (1995), pp. 76–82; A. V. M. Horton, 'Rajah Charles Brooke and Mining Concessions in Brunei 1888–1924', *Journal of the Malaysian Branch of the Royal Asiatic Society*, 59:1 (1986), pp. 49–72; M. C. Cleary, 'Indigenous Trade and European Economic Intervention in North-West Borneo c. 1860–1930', *Modern Asian Studies*, 30:2 (1996), pp. 301–24, on p. 319; G. Jones, *Merchants to Multinationals: British Trading Companies in the Nineteenth and Twentieth Centuries* (Oxford: Oxford University

WRAY JR, *NOTES ON PERAK WITH A SKETCH OF ITS VEGETABLE, ANIMAL AND MINERAL PRODUCTS* (1886)

L. Wray Jr, *Notes on Perak with a Sketch of its Vegetable, Animal and Mineral Products* (London: W. Clowes & Sons, 1886), pp. 23–8.

is relatively early summary of Perak's mining sector concentrates on the tin industry, but also surveys the other minerals mined/available. In 1887, a year er the extract was written, Larut had eighty mines employing 6,843 labourers. The main mine owners were Cheng Ah Kwi, responsible for 18 per cent of output, Goh Siu Swen (10 per cent), Chan Thai (8 per cent), Khoo Onn Keong (8 per cent) and Thai Lee (5 per cent). As discussed in the General Introduction, from the late 1880s the Larut tin fields gradually became exhausted and miners moved inland to Kinta.[1]

---

1.   T. Tojo, 'Chinese-Operated Tin Mining in Perak during the Late Nineteenth Century: A New Style of Labour Employment and the Problem of Absconding', *Chinese Southern Diaspora Studies*, 3 (2009), pp. 204–15, on pp. 206, 207.

L. Wray Jr, *Notes on Perak with a Sketch of its Vegetable, Animal and Mineral Products* (1886), extract

ECONOMIC MINERALS.

TIN. – The principal product by Perak is tin, and it was the presence of this metal which first attracted Chinese to the State. Disputes with reference to the possession of mines ensued, followed by bloodshed and failure of the Malay chief to preserve his authority. An appeal was then made to the British Government for assistance, and the present system of Protection established by treaty. Since that time (January 1874) the revenue has increased seven-fold; the export duty on tin contributing most largely to that result. The ore is found in the form of "stream tin." /

e output of tin from Larut, the principal field, has risen from a monthly average of 54 tons, in 1874, to 629 tons, in 1884. The total output in the latter year for the whole State being 10,190 tons, valued at $3,640,924.

Almost all the tin has been raised by Chinese miners with most primitive appliances, and although, no doubt, much metal has been and is still lost by the imperfection of their methods of working, yet at the same time, owing to their inexpensive system and the lowness of the wages paid to the overseers, &c., land, which would not pay Europeans to work, has given Chinese a profitable return.

e tin fields of Larut, which may be taken as typical of those of the rest of Perak, form a strip of land of from two to three miles broad along the base of a range of granite mountains.

ese alluvial flats are composed of layers of clays, sands, and gravels, with beds of peat, containing the stumps of trees and fallen tree trunks, marking former swamps and the plain.

e tin-bearing stratum rests on a stiff gray or white clay bottom, and varies in thickness from a few inches to six or eight feet, and even more. Sometimes the stratum is divided by a layer of clay.

e whole of the plains are composed of the detritus of the granite and the

The tin is not evenly distributed over the plains, but is found to follow the lowest parts of the clay bed, or, in other words, the beds of the ancient rivers. The tin-sand is, as a rule, coarse-grained near the hills, and finer as it recedes from them.

No lodes have as yet been discovered in the State, but specimens have been found which show that there must be large and rich veins near some of the present workings; one block of tin ore now in the Perak Museum weighing 184 lbs., and larger ones have been found in the same mine.

The method of working the mines is to remove the earth covering the tin-bearing stratum. This is what is called the "over burden" or "stripping," and varies from three or four to thirty feet in thickness.

The work is usually done by contract in the Chinese mines. / The tin-bearing layer called the "wash dirt" is then raised to the surface and washed with a stream of water in long wooden coffin-shaped boxes. The tin-sand being more than twice as heavy as the clay and gravel with which it is mixed, stops in the upper part of the box, while the lighter parts are carried away by the stream of water.

The tin-sand is re-washed by hand in large wooden dishes, and is then sold to the smelters.

The wash contains about one to two per cent. of ore as an average. There are portions of it which contain sometimes as much as twenty-five per cent., and on the other hand, very poor parts which hardly pay for the trouble of washing.

The shifting and raising of the earth in the mines is all done by digging with large hoes called *changkuls*, and the earth is then filled into baskets, two of which are carried by each man by means of a yoke or stick over his shoulder. The water is pumped from most of the mines by Chinese overshot water-wheels, and endless chain pumps.

In the larger mines steam-engines are used in conjunction with centrifugal pumps.

The Chinese mines are worked on the truck system: all food and other necessaries being supplied by the mine owners or money advancers. Some mines are carried on which could not pay if the profits from the sale of food, &c., to the coolies did not come into the advancer's hands. The commonest arrangement is called the co-operative system, where all the coolies have a share in whatever profit is made after repaying the advancers' loans, and settling with him for the value of food and other supplies.

The tin-sand after being re-washed is smelted in rude wind furnaces,[1] charcoal being used as fuel.

The loss of tin is rather high in the poorer class of ores when treated in these Chinese furnaces, and the slag is several times re-smelted; but it seems very problematical whether this loss is sufficient to ensure success to European smelters, when the cost and working expenses of both systems are taken into consideration.

is question is now being tested, as costly smelting works have been erected in Larut and Kinta, but it is too early to form any definite idea of what will be the result. Should the / European methods be found to pay, the Chinese are too keen as men of business not to adopt them, and they will always be able to work at cheaper rates than Europeans can. The real difficulty, however, is that a large quantity of ore is required to keep this expensive machinery working, and in the purchase of that ore the European will find himself heavily handicapped.

GOLD. – Upper Perak and Bâtang Padang produce a limited quantity of gold. It is associated with the tin-sand in the alluvial drifts, as a rule, and the tin-sand is re-washed to separate it. There are no statistics to show the amount of gold that has been raised up to the present time; some of the tin-sand gives as much as 6 ozs. to the ton, some "wash" recently examined gave 7 dwts.[2] per ton. Some quartz leaders showed as much as 132 ozs. of gold per ton of rock, but nothing has been done to prove the extent of the lode.

It would be undoubtedly a calamity to the State if a rich gold field were discovered, because it would cause an influx of the most dissolute and lawless class of Europeans, and the effect would be, as it has always been in other countries, moralizing on the native population.

LEAD. – Galena[3] of very good quality has been found and worked in Petani, and should the territory which is claimed Perak be restored, a large amount of lead may be confidently expected to be raised.

Carbonate and phosphate of lead are also found in considerable quantities.

e galena is said to carry a paying percentage of silver.

IRON. – Ores of this metal are to be had in many parts of the State, but would not pay to work, as there is no coal, notwithstanding what has been stated to the contrary by writers of books of travels.

No diamonds, rubies, sapphires, or other precious stones, have yet been discovered in Perak.

MARBLE. – There is an abundance of fine marble scattered over the State, some of it very handsomely veined with grey, red, and black, some again is nearly black, veined with white, / while other kinds are mottled with different shades of greys and olive greens, and in Kinta there is some pure white marble.

In many places the limestone mountains are near navigable streams, and there would be no difficulty in rafting down any quantity of the stone to the coast for shipment, if a market for it could be obtained.

In Penang and Singapore, the houses of the wealthier classes are largely decorated with marble, which is now all imported from China.

At present the only use which is made of the inexhaustible supply of this handsome and valuable material, is the conversion of a small quantity of it into lime at Gunong Pondok. The lime is of good quality, but, like all lime made from

to transport, though not more so than the shell lime, which is generally used in the Straits Settlements for building purposes.

When quarries are opened, as they are sure to be sooner or later, it will be possible, with a liberal use of this beautiful and lasting material, to vastly improve at moderate cost, not only in Perak, but in Penang and Singapore, the present class of unattractive buildings.

GRANITE. – The granitic ranges of which so large a portion of Perak consists afford an unlimited store of this useful stone. The granite that is worked near Thaipeng and at Bukit Gantang is of a grey colour, and rather large grained. It is quarried for road-making, Blake's crusher being used to reduce it; blocks are also cut for building purposes, culverts, and landmarks. The work is principally carried on by convicts, a quarry having been opened near the gaol at Thaipeng, with a tramway running into the gaol yard, where the rough blocks of stone are dressed.

CHINA CLAY. – In most of the tin fields of Perak the stratum underlying the "wash" or tin-bearing deposit, is pure white China clay or kaolin.

There must be many millions of tons of this material in Perak, but it is doubtful if it could be worked with profit, on account of the cost of transport to Europe. If Chinese potters could be induced to start works here, a large trade might be carried on with / such fine material to work upon, and white fire-bricks could be made of the refuse.

Bricks are made from the same stuff in Cornwall, in the China clay works, and sell for a high price, being used both as fire and as ornamental building bricks.

BRICK EARTH. – Plenty of good brick clay is scattered over the country, and the material for making fire-bricks is also to be had in abundance, as mentioned above.

Very fair bricks are now made in Perak, and sell for about $7 per 1,000; but they are small, and like everything of Chinese manufacture, they are susceptible of great improvement; and when the clay is weathered, well mixed, and moulded, and the bricks are equally burned, they will be of excellent quality.

Tiles have not yet been made here, but there is no reason why they should not be.

POTTERY. – The manufacture of pottery is confined to the Malays, and is only carried on in a small way in two or three districts. It is mostly unglazed, or only glazed on the lower part. Some of the shapes are very graceful. The patterns are pressed into the work by means of stamps, and tools are used to produce dots and lines. Raised work is also employed in decorating the ware, being put on in strips after the vessels are formed.

Stamped raised work does not seem to be employed.

ANON., *GOLDEN RAUB: A SERIES OF ARTICLES ON THE RAUB GOLD MINES AND THEIR PROSPECTS* (1897)

Anon., *Golden Raub: A Series of Articles on the Raub Gold Mines and their Prospects* (Singapore: Straits Times Press, 1897), pp. 11–30.

Although West Pahang had produced gold for centuries, systematic mining only began in 1889 when William Bibby (1837–1900), a Liverpool-born Australian gold miner employed by the Australian Syndicate Ltd, sank a shaft at Raub. After detailing the difficulties faced by Bibby, the anonymous author of this pamphlet describes his own descent into the mine, extraction methods, the workforce, the on-site processing of ore and the returns enjoyed by the Syndicate. Underground mining continued at the site until 1985 when open pit methods were adopted. From 1889 to 1985, the mine produced nearly 1m ounces of gold, 85 per cent of Peninsular Malaysia's total output.[1]

1. P. J. Henney et al., 'Characterisation of Gold from the Raub Area, Pahang, Malaysia', *British Geological Survey, Technical Report*, WC/95/20 [1995], p. 8.

Anon., *Golden Raub: A Series of Articles on the Raub Gold Mines and their Prospects* (1897), extract

(3.) – EARLY DEVELOPMENT WORK.

[...] Raub is being developed, to-day, with more vigour than ever. But the opening-up of to-day is as naught compared with the work performed at a time when obstacles were great, knowledge small, and money extremely scarce. The miner, with a fair field, knowledge of his property, and plenty of money behind him, nds development a comparatively easy business. All these favourable conditions were wanting when the work was first begun in October, 1889.

It will be remembered that the route through Selangor was impossible for the transport of mining machinery, or for the thousand and one other requisites needed before the work could be commenced. It was decided, therefore, that the machinery and stores should be brought to Raub by the river route. A glance at the map of the Malay Peninsula will show the River Semantan, which joins the Pahang River on its south bank about midway between Kuala Lipis and Pekan.

e River Bilut, a tributary of the Semantan, passes Raub about three miles and a half to the south, and it was by way of these rivers that stores were brought to the mines from the sea on the east side of the Malay Peninsula. Until the Trunk Road from Selangor is completed, these rivers must still remain the principal means of traffic between Raub and the outside world.

e first thing Mr. Bibby had to do was to cut a road from Raub through the swamps to the Bilut. He enlisted for this work Chinese, Malays, and, in fact, anybody whom he could get. He / had a lot of trouble with the men to start with, owing to their demand for advances. Mr. Bibby is greatly opposed to this custom; and he refused to grant a single advance. "I have never," he said to me, "advanced a single dollar to any of my men, with the result, of course, that I have never lost a cent in this way yet." In the meantime, the stores had been conveyed from Singapore to Pekan, a port on the east side of the Peninsula, and had been got up as far as Lubok Tua, on the Semantan River, about a hundred miles from Raub, following the windings of the streams. The difficulty, then, was to get boats and boatmen to bring the goods the remainder of the journey.

Mr. Bibby had the misfortune to be boycotted by the Orang Kayah Pahlawan of Semantan, a powerful Malay Chief, who afterwards headed what was called the Pahang Rising. This Chief wanted "chukei," a sort of royalty on every transaction between Mr. Bibby and the natives. Mr. Bibby, quite ignorant of the means by which these Chiefs raised their revenue, flatly refused to pay. "He would see the Orang Kayah in a particularly warm place first!" This was a mistake, as Mr. Bibby is quite prepared to admit. "Had I known," he remarked to me, "as much of the Malay character as I know now, I should certainly have made a pensioner of him, and it would have paid me." Nevertheless, after a considerable amount of trouble, boatmen were obtained in spite of the Orang Kayah; and, once having defeated that individual, Mr. Bibby had no further difficulty in this direction. In the last week of December 1889, thirteen boats, laden with machinery, arrived at the landing place on the Bilut. It says much for the careful supervision of Mr. Bibby's staff that not a single thing was lost on the way. The boilers, the engine, and the ten head battery were all brought up in sections, and they were conveyed from the river to Raub by means of sleighs and rollers. There was no vehicle of any kind to be had. The road was very soft and swampy; and the goods had to be dragged over it by sheer brute force.

Having put the boilers together, Mr. Bibby started pumping the water out of the Raub Hole, where all the gold was supposed to be. By this time he had several conversations with Rajah Impi, and was by no means sanguine as to the result of the work. It was not until after several months of pumping that the bottom of the hole, sixty feet down, was reached. The hole was sunk to a depth of eighty feet, and then Mr. Bibby opened out levels, and met with a number of small rich leaders carrying very good gold. But they were able to turn out very little stuff. Exactly twelve months from the day the party left Brisbane, August 7th, 1890, the mill was set going, and the first crushing was performed. Work was continued upon these small leaders with varying success. But there was / nothing permanent about them, and the crushings, though sometimes fair, were generally unsatisfactory. Meanwhile, prospecting work was being pushed forward in different parts of the concession, though the work was mainly confined to the Raub Hole. It was during that time Mr. Bibby discovered the Western Lode, hitherto unknown. Crushing was continued with varying success. Sometimes, the outlook was fairly promising, and at other times things were very black. No ore could be accumulated; the work was always of a hand to mouth character.

In 1891, the struggling venture met with a sad disaster. The whole of the Raub workings were destroyed by a great flood, which the pumping arrangements were powerless to combat. In three hours seven inches of rain had fallen, and the whole country was flooded. The water rose two feet above the surface of the Raub Hole, put out the fires, and ruined all the workings. In those days, Mr.

ood, many improvements and precautions have been carried out. The pumps, such as they were, were lost, and Mr. Bibby borrowed a pump from the Malay Peninsula Prospecting Company, which had a small working adjoining. It took two months of solid pumping to get clear to the original pumps, but these workings have never since been re-opened. Mr. Bibby had to begin all over again, and sink a new shaft close to the old workings. As a result of these and other difficulties, the market value of the shares of the "Raub Australian Syndicate (Ltd.)" fell to a nominal value; and the adventure was reconstructed in November of 1892 into the "Raub Australian Gold Mining Company (Ltd.)" In the reconstruction of the Company, the shares – one pound shares – were cut down in number from one million to two hundred thousand. Fifty thousand were classed as paid up, one hundred and forty thousand were liable to calls of six shillings and eight pence each, and ten thousand were held in reserve unissued.

But the fates continued to be cruel. It was in December, 1892, that there broke out certain local troubles, known in local history as the Pahang Rising.

e leader in the Rising was the same Orang Kayah Pahlawan of Semantan, who had previously given Mr. Bibby some trouble. After the flood, and while the new was being sunk, crushing stuff was being obtained from the Western Lode. But it was very poor stuff, obtained by tunneling into the hill. The Rising seriously interefered with all the operations. For eight months, Raub was in a state of siege. Mr. Bibby's house was turned into a fort, and was stockaded with huge timbers. The mining staff left their houses, and joined Mr. Bibby in his stronghold on the hill, and every man slept with rifle and ammunition by his side.

erwards, Colonel Walker, of the Perak / Sikhs, arrived, and controlled the arrangements for the defence of the place. Looking back to these exciting times, Mr. Bibby laughs at the precautions that they took. But it was no laughing matter then. It was believed, at first, that the rebellion was going to be general all over the State. During this time few coolies would work, for all around the district Chinamen were being murdered. The morning that Colonel Walker arrived, he stumbled over the bodies of two dead Chinamen, lying in the path not far from the mines. The coolies lived all together in a *kongsie* house. The danger at Raub, as it afterwards transpired, was more imaginary than real; but, in the disturbed state of the country, it was impossible to get accurate information. For twelve months almost nothing was done, except to crush a little of the ore from the Western Lode. This might just as well have been left alone, for the results were very poor. Numerous other troubles arose. Twelve thousand dollars' worth of new machinery was being brought up the river when the Rising broke out. The rebels seized it and threw it into the water, or otherwise destroyed it. They also appropriated various stores, while the Government seized, for their own use, one hundred and thirty-eight bags of rice, which they never acknowledged! That is

the actual money needed to replace the machinery and stores that were lost, all the satisfaction they got was a letter requiring them to prove who were the actual perpetators of the damage before the Government could consider the matter! That was an impossibility; and so there the matter still stands. "That," said Mr. Bibby to me, "is the protection and assistance we got out of the Government. If they had left us to go for the Sultan himself, we could very soon have settled the matter." After the disaster to the new machinery and stores, the river was for months no longer available for the Company's traffic, and the only inlet into the country was by the bridle path from Selangor.

In 1893 the fortunes of the Company began to turn. The first ray of hope proceeded from the new Raub Hole. At a depth of seventy feet, a chute of ore was stuck, running north and south with the strata of the country. I used the word "country" in the mining sense. They were following small leaders in when they came upon the chute, and, up to date, that chute has been followed for twelve hundred feet to a depth of one hundred and sixty feet, dipping at the rate of one in five to the south. This chute, thus accidentally stumbled upon, was enormously rich when it was first cut. If the ore had been taken by itself where it was first cut, it would have realised five or six ounces to the ton. This piece of good luck occurred in the middle of 1893, and it provided / the necessary funds to begin to develop the mines to what they are now. The first crushing from the new chute gave thirteen hundred ounces, and the second two thousand five hundred ounces. These fine crushings relieved the manager of financial trouble, and, now, having plenty of money at this disposal, Mr. Bibby began to prospect in various portions of the concession. Eventually, he settled upon Bukit Koman, as the principal place for development work, and the wonderful success of this mine is a fact now known to everybody. The shaft was sunk to a depth of one hundred and forty-eight feet in 1894. The sinking occupied nine months, and it was twelve months from the time of starting before any gold was got. But the lode, having once been struck, has yielded payable ore ever since. I will describe the working of this mine, and its results up to date, in another article. Bukit Jalis, half a mile north of the Bukit Koman mine, was investigated at an early period of the Company's existence. A tunnel was driven into the hill for a distance of three hundred and ninety-six feet, exposing a large body of ore; but at that time, there being no road or railway, it was impossible to get the ore to the mill. A considerable amount of work has been done at Bukit Malacca, some four or five hundred yards off Bukit Jalis, but further work there is for the present suspended. /

(4.) – DOWN THE MINES.

[...]

On the third day of my visit to Raub, Sunday having intervened, I accompanied Mr. Bibby down the Raub Hole. Gold-mining, to judge by Raub, is a very comfortable business. I have been down one of the deepest coal mines in England, and I found it a very disagreeable experience. The air, laden with fine dust, was hot and foul; and to have to crawl through long galleries, with a Davy lamp in one's teeth, was not nice. At Raub, both in the Raub Hole and elsewhere, the air is uniformly good, and the galleries high and broad, while candles may be carried without the slightest danger. The only inconvenience is the water, which requires the pumps to be constantly going. The water carries with it in suspense enormous quantities of iron oxide, and that is not a good thing to get upon one's clothes. Encased, as it were, in an old khaki suit with a cap on my head, and a candle in my / hand, I was completely equipped to descend to where the gold comes from. The work at present going on at the Raub Hole, as I was able to see for myself, is almost entirely of a development and prospecting character. Down below, in the bottom level, Chinamen were busily engaged on the face of the hard black slate, extending the feelers which the manager is throwing out to ascertain the directions of the ore chutes. Driving is proceeding north and south along the course of the lode. The drive going north was in for one hundred and eighty feet on the morning of my visit, and the other drive about four hundred feet. There is also a crosscut going in a westerly direction, and this had been carried a distance of one hundred and seventy feet. The manager expects to go some five hundred feet before getting any definite result. The southern drive, before-mentioned, offers an excellent illustration of the changes and chances of the miner's work. As Mr. Bibby explained in his last report, he expected to reach the main ore chute long before. But four hundred feet have not sufficed to reach it, and it is highly probable that some geological fault has abruptly cut it off in that neighbourhood. At the present time, as I previously remarked, there is not much ore being taken from this mine; but, in a short time, Mr. Bibby expects to be turning out a fair quantity of high grade ore, there being still a large extent of ground ready for stoping between the bottom and the intermediate levels. Just now, the only stoping that is proceeding is that in the No. 2 or bottom level. I wonder how many people there are, who have anything like an accurate idea as to what stoping means. I will endeavour to explain this and other terms. To begin with, it should be understood that the level or drive is, in the main, merely a road running to the face of the lode. Steel rails along it serve for the passage of the little cars, which bring to the bottom of the shaft the ore that has been shot down through the chutes from the stopes above. Having got the drive up to the lode, the next thing is to extract the ore overhead, and this is done by running up stopes, or small galleries, into the lode. The ore is taken out, and shot down into the level, by means of chutes, as the Americans spell the word, and then the space so emptied is filled up with mullock and strongly timbered, to secure the ground, and another stope is made at the most favourable place for working. This stoping work is largely facilitated by the winzes, or shafts, that are put down between the various levels. These winzes are extremely useful, also, for the purpose of ven-tilation. The large extent of ground between Raub and Bukit Koman is as yet untouched; but Mr. Bibby thinks there is every reason to believe that this district will prove highly auriferous. The new workings at Bukit Itam will dispose of the question before very long.

Bukit Koman, as most people interested / in Raub know, has rapidly devel-oped into a great mine. The quality of the ore, fair at first, has steadily improved, and it has continued to improve as the mine has been opened up. As mines go, this mine, judging by existing indications, would appear to be almost inexhaust-ible. It has been the principal source of supply for the battery for twelve months past; but the battery is quite unable to cope with the enormous quantities of ore the mine can supply. In consequence, the reserves of ore have steadily increased until, at the present time, the manager estimates the quantity of ore actually in sight at a quarter of a million tons! Everyday, the pushing on of the levels adds a huge number of tons to this total. I was able to see ample evidence of these things during my visit to the mine, the day after my visit to Raub. The first level is one hundred and forty-eight feet from the surface, and has been carried a total distance of a thousand feet, running north and south. The lode, I noticed, varied considerably in width. It runs from twelve feet in the south up to the enormous width of forty-six feet in the north. Of the ore actually cut through at the time of my visit, according to Mr. Bibby, only one-fifth has as yet been taken, the other four-fifths being left standing. The lode travels right down to the second level, a distance of a hundred feet; and time alone will show how much further it can be followed. The present depth of the mine is two hundred and fifty feet, and the shaft is to be sunk deeper at an early date. In the south level, four stopes are being worked, and there are two in the north. In the bottom level, nothing but driving is being done. The ore is being left standing in its entirety, and so it must remain until more battery power is available for dealing with it. This level was, at the time of my visit, two hundred and thirty-eight feet long from face to face – one hundred and six feet to the north and one hundred and thirty-two feet to the south. The average width of the lode, which is to be seen all the way along showing much gold, is about ten feet. A winze is just now in process of sinking between the two levels, which will add materially to the facilities for working. The existing winding and pumping machinery is in good order, and is quite pow-

Preliminary prospecting work is all that is being done at present at Bukit Jalis. No stoping has yet been performed, but the prospecting is being pushed forward with a view to permanent development later on. The work consists, first, of a tunnel driven three hundred and ninety-six feet into the hill, exposing, I was informed, a large body of ore the whole way. This ore carries gold estimated at from ten to twelve pennyweights to the ton. At the mouth of the tunnel, a prospecting shaft has been sunk a distance of seventy-three feet. A drive has been driven, in a / southerly direction from the shaft, and, up to date, a lode has been revealed averaging five feet in width. The prospects are considered fair, but not so good as those in the tunnel.

Bukit Malacca is four or five hundred yards north of Bukit Jalis, and on the same line of lode. Last year, a shaft was sunk here to a depth of one hundred and forty-five feet, and a level was opened at one hundred and forty feet. A crosscut was put in seventy feet to the west, and a large body of stone was passed through carrying a little gold, but not sufficient to be payable. Some very good ore was cut sixty-seven feet to the eastward, but it appeared to be limited in extent. The is a tremendously wet one, and two eight-inch pumps have had to be kept constantly going to keep the water down. Owing to this fact and to the difficulty of getting forward during the wet monsoon, this mine has been closed for the present, and is now full of water. Bukit Malacca is half way along the Company's lease, a little over three miles. Beyond this, nothing has been done in the way of exploration; but it is intended, as soon as the new batteries are erected, to push on the development work, further north, on the line of the lode.

e shaft at the western lode is two hundred and forty-nine feet deep, and the ground between the two levels is practically worked out. Mr. Bibby has just nished sinking down an additional seventy feet, and driving is being conducted preparatory to opening up fresh stopes.

e railway connecting the mines with each other, and with the mill, which has a gauge of 2ft. 6ins., was laid down by the Company and is its property. The iron cars are drawn by a locomotive, and the cost of bringing the ore to the mill is something under 10 cents per ton. Transport by bullock carts costs five times as much, with the risk of heavy mortality amongst the bullocks. Mr. Bibby once used as many as eighty bullocks, and half of them died, on one occasion, within three months. /

(5.) – DETAILS OF WORKING.

[...]. There is much to interest even the most casual observer in the important operations of crushing and cleaning-up; and, in the course of several visits to the mill, I was able to get an accurate idea of the various operations. The existing mill or battery is near the south end of the concession at the foot of the hill, leading up to the manager's residence. The rise of Bukit Koman, and the large quantities of ore turned out there, two miles away, have made the present position of the mill an inconvenient one. When the forty new stampers that are to be erected arrive, and when the electric power, now being arranged for, has been installed, the mill will, accordingly, be moved to Bukit Koman, which, thereafter, will be the head and centre of the whole of the Company's operations. The railway now brings the ore in trucks to the mill, and it is emptied into an excavation close up to the crushers.

Malays, standing in this pit, shovel the ore into the mortars, and it is crushed into a fine powder by means of a twenty-head steam driven battery of iron revolving stampers, each of which, weighing seven hundredweight, comes down upon the stone with tremendous force, seventy times a minute. The Battery is, also, fitted with the requisite grinding machinery, and the whole will crush twelve hundred tons per month. The noise caused by these stampers can be heard afar off. Stamping away day and night, week in and week out, they make music sweet to the ear of the miner. Like the rumbling of the railway train in the ears of a rumbling of the railway train in the ears of a sleepy traveler, they hum over to his imagination all his favourite airs; and in the night, should the engineer in charge have occasion to shut off steam, and the tumult cease, the sleeper wakes up with a start. This, it is needless to say, is not the experience of the unaccustomed visitor. To return to the mill. At intervals of two hours, while this process of pounding is going on, small quantities of mercury are run into the mortars, and this, getting mixed up with the ore, arrests and coats over / any gold with which it comes in contact. Masses of amalgam are thus formed about the mortars. Constant streams of water are, also, flowing, and all the powdered quartz which is fine enough runs away with the water through fine enough runs away with the water through fine screens of soft Russian iron. But it is impossible for all the gold to be captured by the mercury in the mortars or on the screens, and elaborate arrangements have, therefore, to be made for catching as much as possible of the precious metal, which rushes through the screens with the sand. The mixture has first to run through the mercury wells, a number of troughs containing mercury, and after that it passes over tables or plates of copper, coated with mercury. By this time the major portion of the gold has been secured, but the stream has yet to pass over long narrow channels, along which blankets are laid. This is the last precaution taken at Raub, for the residuum then runs away to the low-lying ground behind, where many thousands of tons of it are now lying. There is still some gold in it which, someday, may be treated by the cyanide process. The mortars, it should be noted, would soon be worn out by the perpetual stamping, were it not for the loose dies which are fixed inside to receive the blow. The additional forty head of stamps, each weighing a thousand pounds, which the Company recently decided to purchase, will enable the manager to put more

e screens are changed every Sunday, and all the amalgam on them, in the quicksilver wells, and on the copper plates is taken away, and, having been separated from extraneous matter, is weighed and locked up until the general clean-up takes places. There is a rough clean-up once every month, when the mortars and the loose dies are dealt with, and then, every two months, there is what is called the general clean-up. The mortars, the dies, the screens, the wells, the tables, and the blankets are all deprived of their amalgam, which is washed in water with extreme care, in order to get rid, as much as possible, of foreign mineral matter and dirt. Then the amalgam, made up into shining silvery spheres, is retorted. The retort, hermetically sealed, is placed in a furnace, and the retort tube, issuing from the top, has a stream of water running down it into an enameled vessel beneath. Two hours in the retort suffice to drive off the mercury, which, finding, an outlet in the tube, is condensed by the cold water, and falls into the vessel beneath in its original form. A large ill-formed, and still impure lump of gold is left at the bottom of the retort, and this is smelted in a furnace, and is run out finally in the form of ingots. Taken to the Bank at Singapore, it eventually finds its way to the Bank of England, the great and recognised market for gold. It is all re-smelted there, and assayed, and, on the basis of that assay, it is sold, the Bank acting as / the agent for the Company. The gold realises the excellent price of about three pounds and seventeen shillings per ounce, and I will refer to this point again in a comparison with other mines, which I propose to make in a future article.

[...]

e mines of Raub afford employment, in one way or another, to some seven or eight hundred people. Fully five hundred are directly employed at the mines, while the remainder is made up of wood-cutters, boatmen on the river, and other classes of workmen. Twenty-two boats come up the river with stores for Raub, and each boat employs five men. The European staff at Raub numbers twelve, including the manager; "and," said Mr. Bibby to me, "we have not a spare man in the place." All the ordinary mining work is done by Chinamen under supervision of the European Miners. The Malay will not work underground. He is useful, however, for jungle and surface work, "We have always," remarked Mr. Bibby, "paid the highest rates for our labour, and, in consequence, have had the pick of it. We have never had any difficulty in getting all the labour that we require, and have never had to go far from our doors for it." Chinese Miners are paid sixty cents a day, and the mandores or headmen one dollar. All the surface men get fifty cents per day, and tradesmen – fitters, blacksmiths, carpenters, and others – from one dollar to one dollar and three quarters. The payment of sawyers and for firewood cutting is arranged by contract, and, wherever possible, all the mining is, also, done by contract. Everything at Bukit Koman, for instance, is being done by contract. All contracts are settled monthly. The Chinamen form a "kongsie," and they appoint one of their number, with whom the manager deals. These contractors are watched, and, if they are detected in any attempt to "chisel" the coolies, they are promptly ousted. The contract amount paid / varies, of course, according to the nature of the work to be performed. Driving levels is paid for at an arranged price per foot, and the ore is raised at so much per ton. Three truckloads go to the ton.

[…] The following figures will show the yield of gold at Raub since the first trashing in 1890: –

		Yield.		
Year.	Tons milled.	Ozs.	Dwts.	Grs.
1890	840	1,625	4	12
1891	2,380	2,917	1	17
1892	3,010	957	15	00
1893	4,560	4,887	3	00
1894	5,400	3,092	10	00
1895	11,766	5,755	17	00
1896	14,069	8,144	3	00
1897	4,650	4,389	7	12
Total	46,675	31,769	1	17

*   1890 5 months work only.
* 1 897 4   do.   do.   do.

The year 1892, it should be noted, was the year of the Rising. All that was done in that year was to crush a little poor stuff from the Western Lode. The following year witnessed the discovery, in the Rabu Hole, of a chute of ore of exceptional richness.

The following figures will show the rise and fall of the shares since the commencement. The shares were first quoted, on the 28th of November, 1889, as "Raub Syndicate, 10s. 6d. sellers." In January, 1890, they were 9s.; and in June, (the price now being quoted in dollars,) they were down to $2.30. In January, 1891, they had descended ominously to 90 cents, only to fall in June, still further, to 67½ cents (17s. 11d paid). In January, 1892, they were 60 cents (18s. 1d. paid); and the fully paid shares were at 95 cents. In June, they dropped to 40 cents. At the end of 1892, the Company was re-organised, and became the Raub Australian Gold Mining Company. Its capital was cut down, from £1,000,000, to £200,000, so that in January of 1893, with the shares (13s. 4d. paid) quoted at $1 , the shareholder was slightly worse off than he was in June, 1892. In the following June, the shares (13s. 10d. paid) were at $4.40. The following are the figures for January and June of the next 3 years. – 1894, $4.50, $4.50; 1895, $4.90, $4.10; 1896, $4.10, $5.10. On January 2nd, this year, they had gone up to $9; in February, they were $10; in March, $11 on April 1st, $13; on May 1st,

GREIG, *MINING IN MALAYA* (1924)

G. E. Greig, *Mining in Malaya* (London: Malayan Information Agency, 1924), pp. 5–14, 16, 18–22, 24, 26, 28–30, 32–40, 42–4, 46–8, 50–2, 54, 56–8.

e extracts reproduced here discuss mining methods, the mechanization of the sector, the nature of the labour force, mining legislation, export duties/charges, transportation and the living conditions of European managers and engineers, adding a great deal to the secondary literature, which is reviewed in the General Introduction and thematic introductions. G. E. Greig (b. 1879) became an Inspector of Mines in the Straits Settlements in 1902 and ended his career as Senior Warden of Mines in 1934, a position he gained in 1922.[1]

Straits Times, 4 June 1934, p. 11.

G. E. Greig, *Mining in Malaya* (1924), extract

Tin-mining at the present day may be divided into the following various forms:
  (i) Open-cast mining (*a*) with trucks and rails (*b*) by hand labour only.
  (ii) Gravel pumping (*a*) with water under pressure, (*b*) with water without pressure. /
  (iii) Hydraulicing, (*a*) using water under natural pressure, (*b*) using water under artificial pressure, (*c*) using water without pressure.
  (iv) Dredging by (*a*) buckets, (*b*) suction cutters.
  (v) Shafting (*a*) in lodes,[1] (*b*) in alluvial ground.
  (vi) "Dulang" or panning.

) With trucks and rails. Some enormous excavations have been made in this way. Lahat Mines Ltd. has two open-east mines adjoining each other of a total area of 37 acres and a depth of 200 feet. A further depth of 130 feet has been reached by shafts. Nearly 4,000,000 cubic yards have been excavated by hand since 1912. Tronoh Mines' open-cast before it was finished had a length of 1,850 feet, a width of 520 feet, and a depth of 150 feet, showing that about 4,000,000 cubic yards had been cut and lifted into trucks by hand labour. The Sungei Besi Mine is larger, being 2,180 feet long, 794 feet / wide, with a depth of about 100 feet; about 5,500,000 cubic yards of ground have been taken out of it.
   All the ground is cut by hand labour using the changkol (a form of hoe.) The tin-bearing ground cut is either lifted by baskets or allowed to fall into trucks, which are either run by hand or by a light locomotive to inclines up which they are hauled in trains of two or more to the surface. The contents of the trucks are dumped into puddlers, which may be either of the open circular description, using harrows hauled round by arms mounted on a vertical axis, or of the enclosed type, where the ground is broken up by a series of knives mounted on a horizontal axis. The resultant mixture, with water added, is then sent down sluices in which the ore is caught. Before reaching the tin-bearing ground, or "karang," as it is called, the overburden has to be stripped, and this work continues as the mine deepens. This is treated in a similar way to the "karang," viz. by hand labour and trucks, the contents of which (if value-less) are dumped

beyond the limits of the open-cast. Considerable pumping machinery has to be employed at times, especially in the vicinity of limestone near the contact. The various forms of prime mover will be described under "Machinery."

The method described above is used both by Europeans and Chinese.

(*b*) By hand labour only. This is a purely Chinese method. The ground cut is put into flat baskets, which are hung on either side of a pole and so carried by coolies up a notched log to the surface. [...]

Another method of raising the tin-bearing gravel is to churn it into a mud and lift that mud from one ledge to another by means of a tin bucket at the end of a long pole till the surface is reached. Wet mines are dewatered by means of an ingenious chain pump made of wood, in which boards set at right angles to a wooden chain lie close fitting / in a wooden trough set so that its base is in the sump and its upper end high enough for the water to flow away. On revolving the chain, either by a tread-mill or by a water-wheel, the mine water is brought to the surface. In other mines a portable steam engine or an oil engine is used in conjunction with a turbine pump to dewater the mine. Pulsometers[2] are sometimes employed.

The "karang," having been brought to the surface, is, if necessary, puddled in a square pit by hand and then carried to the cleaning sluices called "landshutes." These are coffin-shaped boxes. Water is brought into the head of the box and the "karang" is introduced by a coolie at the side. A coolie stands in the water and rakes the concentrates up with a changkol. The waste matter is dug out and carried away by other coolies, often female. [...]

(ii) (*a*) Using water under pressure. There are only one or two mines now working under this once very popular method. On a pontoon are mounted two large pumps, one for pumping water through a monitor or jet, and the other for lifting the resulting gravel, sands and water. The necessary machinery for driving these pumps is also installed on the pontoon. The monitor or jet cuts away the ground and the gravel pump lifts it to the surface, where the ore is concentrated in the usual sluices. When it is desired to move the pontoon, the paddock is allowed to fill with water and the pontoon is floated and so moved with ease to another place. The paddock is then pumped out by the gravel pump. This method has lost its popularity owing to its cost and the advent of the more efficient bucket dredge, though a very up-to-date steam electric plant is working successfully at Rawang. Its use is confined to Europeans.

(*b*) With water without pressure. In this method water is allowed to fall down the face of the excavation and the ground is churned up with it by coolies, who lead the resulting mud to the sump of a gravel pump, which lifts the mixture to the surface whence it flows down concentrating / sluices. The waste material is confined within the limits of a dumping-ground and the water is frequently returned to the mine for further use. The gravel pumps vary in size from 6 inches, a popular size among the Chinese, to 14 inches for the larger mines. The power used is either steam, oil, or, where available, electricity.

a) Using water under natural pressure. A dam is made in a suitable place   Hydraulicing. in a stream-bed and elevated as much as is necessary above the level of the mine.

e impounded water is then either sent down pipes direct to the mine or is led by means of ditches to a box known as the pressure-box, whence it flows down pipes to the mine. The water, which is now under pressure, the amount of which depends on the height of the pressure-box above the mine, is allowed to emerge from a monitor which is like a fireman's jet on a large scale. This jet, playing upon the face of the mine, cuts it down with ease, and the resulting mixtures ows down a ditch or wooden sluice where the tin ore is concentrated, usually by women using a round, shallow, wooden dish called "dulang."

When conditions are such that there is not sufficient fall for the mixture, an elevator is employed to lift it to such a height that the requisite fall is procured.

e usual form of elevator consists of a jet of water issuing under pressure from a nozzle, which is set in a cast-iron frame and has a pipe erected above it in such a manner that the jet shoots straight up the pipe. Orifices are connected by an annular[3] pipe to a pipe leading to the sump, and the material brought down by the monitor is sucked up and lifted to the head of the sluice-boxes.

Gravel pumps are sometimes employed to do this work. An instance of the latter is that of the Société Française des Mines d'Etain de Tekkah (usually known as French Tekka), which uses the first 300 feet of fall for the purpose of developing electrical power and the remainder for procuring water under pressure on the mine.

e quantities of water used and the pressure obtained vary very considerably, from installations using only 100 cubic feet a minute under a pressure of 50 lb. to the / big pipe line of Gopeng Consolidated and Kinta Tin-mines, which carries 6,000 cubic feet of water a minute and produces a pressure of 170 lb. per square inch on the mine. The size of the jets used varies from 1 inch diameter to 3 inched. The power produced by these larger-sized monitors working under high pressures is considerable, and the ground is cut extremely quickly by them. A 3-inch jet working under a pressure of 170 lb. would have a potential energy at the jet of about 340 h.p. Compared with some installations in America they are, however, small. [...].

An adaption of the process described above has just been introduced by Mr. Powell, of New Zealand. The main departure of this method from the usual consists in taking the intake pipe of the elevator, which normally extends only to the sump, right up to the face. The result is that / the ground cut enters the suction pipe at once and the necessity for maintaining levels or blowing the cut ground into the sump is done away with. Cutting can therefore be carried out continuously, resulting in a much greater output for the amount of water consumed. The wear on the suction pipes and elevator detracts somewhat from the advantages of their process, which is, however, at the present only in the trial stage.

(*b*) Using water under artificial pressure. This method is similar to that described above, except that the pressure water is supplied by a pump, either turbine or reciprocal, driven by any suitable form of power.

(*c*) Using water without pressure. This is known locally as "lampan" working. Water is led through a ditch cut at the foot of a face. The face is cut in steps, starting from the top, and when the foot of the face is reached, the steps are cut away working upwards. The ground so barred down falls into the ditch, where the waste earth is washed away and the tin ore remains. This is cleaned up and concentrated later.

It will be seen that hydraulicing produces considerable quantities of waste material, or tailings, the proper retention / of which is a matter of anxiety both to the Government and the miners, and, in certain cases, of considerable expense to the latter. Where no great volume of flood-water is to be allowed for, or where there is no large natural stream to contend with, the problem resolves itself into the construction of suitable impounding earthworks and a masonry spillway, so designed as to take the maximum estimated flow of water. The spillway should also be capable of being raised quickly and easily.

(iv) (*a*) By buckets. All the bucket dredges used in this country conform more or less to standard but vary considerably in size and age. A number are considerably in size and age. A number are converted gold-dredges obtained from Australia and New Zealand, but the majority are new. In the latest construction the tendency is to increase both the size and the power. The principle is simple. A number of steel buckets of capacities varying between 5 and 12 cubic feet are joined together by a chain made of steel plates or are linked up close together. The latter is the more modern practice. In one instance of the former kind an apron of steel is placed between each bucket to catch and so save loose ground which may spill from the buckets. The chain of buckets is mounted on a steel ladder, at the upper end of which is placed the receiving hopper. The lower end is hung by a steel rope and by means of shieves[4] can be raised or lowered as required. On revolving the upper wheel or tumbler on which the chain of buckets is mounted, the chain is caused to move, and so by suitably adjusting the lower end, usually at an angle of 45°, the buckets scrape along the face, fill themselves with ground and are carried up to the hopper into which they drop their contents, and so down to repeat the process over again. The ground cut drops from the hopper into a revolving cylinder, or trammel, of steel plates with suitably sized holes punched in them. Water under pressure is fed into the interior of the cylinder by means of

which, and aided by the revolving motion, the ground is broken up. Any ground that is not so broken is usually run off / down a shoot, though it is sometimes carried off by a belt conveyor. The broken ground is sent into a series of sluices in which the tin is concentrated.

e whole machinery is mounted on a steel or wooden pontoon which floats in the working paddock. Reinforced concrete is used for the hull in one instance. With three exceptions the power employed is steam, the exceptions being two dredges driven electrically by a steam electric plant and another operated by a hydro-electric plant. The dredge is held up to its work by means of head ropes controlled by winches, and it is pulled backwards and forwards against the face by means of side ropes.

is method of mining has proved most successful in this country. It is cheap, and much ground of low value which would otherwise have been left untouched is being worked profitably. Where the bed-rock is soft, the whole of the tin-bearing ground can be excavated, but losses appear when the bed-rock consists of limestone pinnacles, amid the interstices of which a certain amount of ground is lost at present owing to its inaccessibility.

At the end of 1922 the number of bucket dredges working in Malaya was forty-one. There were also two under construction. Twenty-seven more had been proposed, but their construction was delayed owing to the existing trade depression. The flat country round Taiping is now almost entirely given over to bucket dredging, and there are fourteen dredges at work there.

is method of mining produced 4,656 tons of tin in 1921, out of a total production of the Federated Malay States of 34,489 tons.

) By suction cutters. There is at present only one example of this method, which is employed extensively elsewhere for dredging harbours. It is, however, attracting considerable attention. A large wheel or cutter, bearing a considerable resemblance to that type of electric fan which exhausts the air from a room, is mounted on a revolving steel shaft. Beneath the shaft is a pipe, the end of which is turned up so as to form a shell round the cutter. The / upper end of the pipe is connected with powerful gravel pumps. The revolving cutter breaks up the ground, the pumps suck it and water up the pipe, whence the mixture flows into sluice-boxes, where tin ore is saved. The pioneers of this method are very hopeful of success, but in the absence of longer experience it is as yet impossible to say whether it is likely in the end to prove a more efficient method than that of dredging by buckets.

) In lodes. One of the largest tin-producing mines in the world is that of the Pahang Consolidated on the east coast of Pahang. As already explained under the head of Modes of Occurrence, the mine consists of a series of lodes in sedimentary rocks which bear a strong resemblance to the Cornish Kellas, and these lodes continue through to the granite. At least forty of such lodes have been

Shafting.

worked, and some are of considerable size. The method of exploitation employed is the usual one for mining in hard ground, viz. levels and stopes; but, thanks to the configuration of the ground, adit levels can be used to a considerable extent. Other ores besides cassiterite are found, and a certain amount of copper is recovered by passing the concentrates through hot sulphuric-acid vats. The ore has to be roasted and the arsenic is recovered in flues and put on the market. This mine has now reached a depth of 1,218 feet, and produces an average of 1,600 tons of metallic tin a year. There are a few other lode-mines in hard rock working for tin, but some have been closed down owing to the low price of the metal.

(*b*) In alluvial ground. Where the ore-bearing gravel is either very deep or is a thin deposit, it is extracted by means of numerous small shafts. Formerly some of the larger mines used to take out the ore by means of shafts, but that practice was given up in favour of the more efficient open-cast method. The shafting under discussion is done almost entirely by Chinese. The shafts vary from small circular holes, just large enough to take a man squatting, to double-compartment shafts properly timbered from top to bottom. The shafts lie about 30 feet from each other / and the ore-bearing gravel is excavated between them. Artificial ventilation is seldom employed, and then only in the form of a wind-shoot of canvas, possibly aided by a coolie with a palm-leaf fan.

Water is removed by buckets and a winch or by a pulsometer pump if in any quantity. This method of mining is unsound, as it is apt to leave good ore in the ground.

(vi) This is a method which, though by no means peculiar to this country, is extensively employed for winning tin ore, owing to the enormous tracks of tin-ore-bearing alluvium scattered about the country. Women do most of this work, and are either employed by miners to concentrate the ore in the sluices, or work on their own in streams and rivers. They also do some business in conveying stolen ore to the ore buyers. The method employed is simple, but requires some skill. A shallow wooden dish about 30 inches in diameter and 3½ inches deep is dug into sluice or stream-bed and a quantity of sand and water is thus put into the dish. The dish is now subjected to a peculiar motion more or less of the nature known as vanning, by means of which the waste material is washed over the edge and the ore remains. / It is arduous work in the heat of the day, entailing as it does continual standing in water with the back bent. Those women employed in the large hydraulic mines are, however, sheltered by a roof. Tin ore to the extent of 42,716 pikuls was sold by licensed dulang women working individually during 1921. This represents 5 per cent. of the total ore won in that year.

The following figures will convey some idea of the amount of ore won by these various methods and the part it has taken in supplying the world's needs for the various uses to which tin is put, such as tin and terne[5] plates, alloys such as bronzes, gunmetal, fusible alloys, babbit metal and other similar "bearing" alloys, type-metal and pewter, tinfoil, collapsible tubes and block-tin articles. In addition, compounds of tin are used in dyeing and calico printing, and the chloride is used for weighting silk before dyeing.

EXPORT OF TIN FROM THE F.M.S.
SHOWING PERCENTAGE OF WORLD'S OUTPUT.

REVISED STATISTICS

Malayan imports of Tin Ore in 1926: 36,890 tons valued at £7,303,194.
Malayan exports of Tin in 1926: 76,334 tons valued at £21,644,754.
Federated Malay States Tin exports in 1926: 45,946 tons.
World production of Tin in 1926: (estimated) 142,581 tons.

Year	Output in tons.	Percentage.
1910	43,862	42
1911	44,148	40
1912	48,420	39
1913	50,126	37
1914	49,042	40
1915	46,766	37
1916	43,870	36 /
1917	39,833	32
1918	37,370	31
1919	36,934	31
1920	34,934	30
1921	34,490	33
1922	35,286	30

e world's output of tin was increased considerably from 1900 owing to Bolivia entering the field as a serious competitor to the Federated Malay States as a tin producer. The output from this country, according to the most reliable figures available, increased from 10,000 tons in 1900 to 22,750 tons in 1910 and 29,000 tons in 1920.

e only coal now being mined is at Rantau Panjang, in Selangor, 25 miles distant from Kuala Lumpur. There lie the remains of the Triassic beds that once covered the country, and in them is found the coal. It is thus described: "It has a pitch-black colour and breaks with a conchoidal[6] fracture. It is fairly hard, and has a specific gravity of 1·2 – 1·3. It does not coke and burns with a long flame." Its great characteristic, however, is its tendency to spontaneous combustion due to oxidization. About 10,000,000 tons have been proved.

Coal-mining.

e two seams are worked in two ways. Originally an incline was sunk on the upper seam, which averages 40 feet in thickness, and the coal was worked by pillar and stall. It was found, however, that the liability to spontaneous fires was too great, and whole sections of the mine had to be bricked off in consequence. Recently a most successful method of sand filling was introduced, which enables the whole of the coal to be won by the long-wall method and eliminates all chance of fires. There is no gas in the coal. Where the seams outcrop, the coal has been worked open-cast with success. The lower seam is 25 feet thick. The output from the mine has risen from 170,000 tons in 1918 / to 300,000 tons in 1921. The whole of the coal is consumed locally and proved a godsend to consumers of power during the war, when foreign coal was either unobtainable or procurable only at a prohibitive cost.

Gold is now only mined on an extensive scale on the Raub Australian Gold Mining Company's Concession. The deposit is in the nature of a lode in calcareous rocks of the Raub Series. It is the only gold-mine, as such, that remains of many, though it is quite conceivable that others may be reopened when transport facilities improve, and interest has already awakened in one or two of the other gold deposits in Pahang. The Raub mine has now been working for thirty years and has reached a depth of 940 feet. It produces about 14,000 oz, of gold a year. The average content of the rock is between 3 and 4 dwt. to the ton. The power is obtained from a hydro-electric power-station on some falls seven and a half miles off. About 16,000 h.p. are developed. The method of mining is the usual one of shafts and levels and the ground is taken out by stoping. The ore treated in the usual mill. New plant to treat the ore by the cyanide process is in process of erection.

Alluvial gold is recovered, mixed with the tin, from several other localities, such as Kenaboi and other places in the Negri Sembilan, Bentong in Pahang, and Bidor in Perak, where about 1,000 oz. a year are won. Gold is also recovered by primitive methods by Malays in the Lipis area. The total output of gold for the last twenty years has been about 313,000 oz.

Wolfram is usually mined as a by-product with tin ore, though in certain places it is mined for its own worth, as in Trengganu and Kedah. It is found in veins and in mass and is usually mined by open-cast methods.

Scheelite, calcium tungstate, is found usually associated with limestone. Where found in quantity, it is mined by open-cast methods.

Like many other industries, the mining of tungsten ores / has suffered its ups and downs. During the war period the output from the Federated Malay States rose to 650 tons a year owing to the high price, but it has now fallen to about 60 tons a year.

Transport has improved enormously in the last twenty years. A main railway line (metre gauge) from Penang to Singapore provides accessibility for machinery, fuel, etc., to most of the main mining centres. Subsidiary feeders, such as Port Weld to Taiping (mainly used for transporting mangrove firewood), Teluk

amount of machinery enters the country this way), Port Dickson to Seremban and Malacca to Tampin all help to make the transport problem easier. Another line in course of construction from Gemas in the Negri Sembilan through Pahang to join the East Coast Siamese line is already helping and will, as it extends, help more towards the same desirable object as well as opening up the country. Another line from Bukit Mertajam, near Penang, goes north through Kedah and Perlis and connects with the Siamese line to Bangkok. Fed by the railways, of which there are 1,021 miles, including the Johore line, is a very large system of metalled roads, in all 2,446 miles, which connects all the more important mining centres. There is now hardly a mine of any importance that cannot be reached by road. In addition there are 177 miles of unmetalled cart-roads and 1,800 miles of bridle-roads and paths.

Transport of supplies from the railways is carried out by motor-lorries, steam-tractors and bullock-carts. The lorries take a load up to three tons, and the bullock-carts up to 15 cwt. Officially, but can and do carry up to 1y ton. In addition heavy machinery transported on trucks drawn by teams of bullocks or by some form of tractor.

Passenger traffic outside the railways is now catered for almost entirely by motor-cars, mostly of American make, motor-buses. Rickshaws in the towns are still used, and gharries are seen in some of the outlying places and / for short connections. The individual gets about in his car, on a motor-cycle with or without a sidecar, by a "Push bike," or, where these cannot be used, on foot. A few people ride horses or ponies.

In certain places where the conditions call for it, elephants and sometimes cattle are used for the transport of supplies. The average load for an elephant is about 800 lb., depending on the bulk of the load. Where elephants are not obtainable and in very hilly areas, all supplies are carried by coolies. They are capable of carrying as much as 150 lb., but the average load is about 100 lb. They sometimes travel very fast.

e cost of transport at the present time (1922) is as / given below ($1 = 100 cents = 2*s*. 4*d*. 1 pikul = 100 katis = 133⅓ lb. 1 kati = 100 1⅓ lb.):

By rail. Passenger fares are:

First class, 6¼ cents per miles =	about 1¾*d*.
Second " 3¾ " " " =	" 1¼*d*.
Third " 2½ " " " =	" ¾*d*.

Luggage is carried free up to 100 katis, first class.

Goods are carried at rated varying from a minimum of ⁵⁄₃₂ cent per pikul per mile (equal to ·75*d*. per ton per mile), according to the class of the goods. These charges are subject to considerable reduction for long distances. Machinery is scheduled as Class 4, and costs ¹⁵⁄₁₆ cent per pikul per mile, which is equivalent

Petrol at present (1922) cost $1·20 (2*s.* 9½*d.*) a galloon, and is obtainable nearly everywhere. Motors-cars can be hired at the rates of about a shilling a mile or 2½*yd.* per mile per passenger.

(b) Coolie hire. When camping, coolies are paid by the day; but when on the march, they are paid as a rule at so much per kati (1⅓ lb.). The rates vary according to the distance, but 5 cents per kati up to 15 miles a day and 6 to 7 cents per kati above 15 miles a day is the average cost. This is equivalent to about 8*s* a day.

This mainstay of the mining industry and of many other industries in this country is the Chinese. He has done and is doing most of the work. He is extremely industrious. He is prepared, if need be, to work the whole day to obtain what he considers necessary to meet his requirements. On the other hand, if he is working for himself and has made that daily amount he is disinclined to do any more work that day. He very seldom gives any trouble, and on the whole is most tractable and obedient. In times of high prices and much profit, he takes what he can get; but when the slump comes, he comes down with it and carries on in a most admirable / way. If a Chinese mine-owner can convince his coolies that his mine has lost money, they are often willing to accept as little as 20 per cent of their wages with very little demur.

The various clans of Chinese that come to Malaya include Cantonese, Hakka or Khehs, Hokkiens, Teochews, Kwangsais and Hylams. Work by shafting is almost entirely confined to Hakkas or khehs, while Hylams usually work as domestic servants, but become miners or rubber planters when the occasion seems profitable. Hokkiens from most of the shopkeepers. There are now very few Teochews engaged in mining. In 1921 there were 92,000 Chinese employed as miners, including 12,000 "dulang" women, who are mostly of the redoubtable Kheh clan.

Chinese methods are best shown when dealing with water, with water, with which they are exceedingly clever. They are capable of bringing water from any distance by ditches or bamboo pipes and of distributing it without any survey except of the order of what they would call "look-see." They also show to great advantage in open-cast working and "lampan." They make most admirable labour underground. Their houses are, in large mines airy, clean, and / tidily kept. The "dulang" women are out all day standing in water, working their "dulangs" or pans, and are frequently to be seen carrying a baby on their backs. In the evening they cut up the firewood, cook the food and do the housework.

Recruiting is done in china, and the coolies arrive and depart according to the demand. Indentured labour was abolished in 1914. The Chinese coolie is employed in one of three ways. He may work for a daily wage, or by contract or on what is called the tribute system. At present (1922) conditions are the reverse of flourishing, and the coolie works for a very moderate wage. It amounts to about 30 cents a day, which is equivalent to 8½*d.* In addition to this, he is housed

said that the average coolie working on wages receives about 50 – 60 cents a day, equivalent to 1s. 2d. to 1s. 5d.

e working hours are usually eight, with extra payment for overtime. The contract coolie works under a contractor, who receives as a general rules from $15 – $20 (35s. to 47s.) / for each "chang," or 50 cubic yards of ground, cut and carried away. The tribute coolie usually forms one of a gang who, having had their supplies advanced to them by a mining speculator, work the ground and share all profits that are lefts after the lessor has had his tribute paid to him. The head of the gang and any foremen receive a slightly larger share than the rest.

e coolies are housed admirably on the large mines in big, airy structures with high roofs. These houses are made of poles and the walls and roofs. These houses are made of poles and the walls and roof are made of "attap." Attaps are usually made from the leaf of the leaf of the nipah palm. Each frond is cut off and bent over a stick, and other fronds are added until the stick is full. The ends of the fronds are tied, and the result is a kind of board made of these fronds.

ese attaps are placed one on top of the other from the top of the roof down, each stick being about two inches below its upper neighbor. The whole is plaited together and makes a perfectly watertight roof for a year to two, when the attaps begin to give way to the destructive climate. Inside, the building will have an ce where the accounts are kept, a store for keeping the tools and tin ore, and a kitchen, which consists of fires under enormous iron dishes in which the rice is boiled, while a small shop to provide simple needs, such as matches and tobacco, en included. The remainder of the house will be devoted to the beds of the coolies. These beds consist of planks laid on a framework about two had a feet high, and usually hold two coolies. Mosquito curtains are invariably used, and a grass mat, but not mattresses. At the head of the bed are the coolie's personal belongings in a box, and he uses a blanket, usually a red one. Pillows take the curious and, one would have thought, most uncomfortable form of a lump of wood, a square piece of earthenware, or a rattan framework covered with black oil-cloth. These pillows are placed under the head about the levels of the ear, so that there is a space under the nape of the neck while the head is supported. It is therefore cooler than a soft pillow. /

e coolies' staple food is rice, prepared according to the custom of their clan. The majority boil the rice with very little water and eat it in a dry condition, but the Hokkiens and Teochews prefer to eat he watery rice that is obtained by boiling a little rice in a lot of water. In addition to rice, vegetables and sometimes meat and fish both fresh and dried are added. The amount and frequency of this addition depends on the prosperity or otherwise of the industry. As a rule three meals are taken a day, the first at dawn, the second at 10.30, and the third about 5 p.m. Tea without sugar or milk is mostly drunk, but water when thirsty. Very

female relations remain in China, and he is very good in remitting money for their sustenance. Certain Chinese firms undertake to forward these remittances for a small charge, and the undertaking is carried out so satisfactorily that there are few, if any, complaints.

The above description applies to the bigger and more flourishing mines. When conditions reach the stages of a struggle for a bare existence, the coolies, who will be / tributers, live in hovels made of anything handy, such as old kerosene tins beaten out, leaves, etc. etc.

Under all circumstances, however, their neatness and cleanliness are remarkable.

Malays seldom live on the mines, but have their houses elsewhere, generally on their own piece of land. A typical Malay house is raised on wooden posts a few feet above the ground and is approached by a ladder. The floor is usually of large bamboo, split and hammered out flat after the joints or partitions have been removed. The walls are either "attap" or the same flattened bamboo interwoven. Their food consists of rice as a staple with curry added. Meat, fruit and vegetables are also eaten.

The Malay does not as a rule indulge in mining himself, being generally content to hold the land and sublease the mining rights to a Chinese. There are, however certain functions in mining rights to a Chinese. There are, however, certain functions in mining which a Malay fulfils admirably, such as engine driving, overseering pipe-lines, managing hydraulic monitors, electrical work, surveying, etc. The women are largely employed in concentrating the ore by "dulangs" in the big sluice-boxes, and in their bright sarongs are a very attractive sight. In 1921 there were 2,307 Malays and Javanese employed in mining.

Of natives of India, South Indians such as Tamils, Telegus and Malayalis predominate. They are very good at moving earth, which they carry in baskets on their heads, unlike the Chinese, who carry it in baskets slung at either end of a pole over the shoulder. Some of them make very fair engine drivers.

The other races of India are grouped together, irrespective of their origin as "Bengalis." Most of the so-called "Bengalis" come from the Punjab. As far as actual mining is concerned they do but little, but can, if occasion arises, shift ground with considerable they efficiency. They are mostly employed indirectly as bullock-cart drives. In 1921, 3,525 Indians of all kinds were employed in mining. Recruiting in India is under Government controls and an / assessment per coolie is charged, the money going to a fund for assisting immigration to Malaya.

Of other eastern races there are very few. Occasionally Japanese, Siamese and Sakais are found working, but their numbers only amounted to 70 in all in 1921.

Western races are represented in the Malayan tin-mining industry by British (both home and colonial), French in some number, and a few Italians, Austrians,

Alaska and elsewhere, and is now busily engaged in erecting dredges and Europeans actively engaged in mining has increased considerably in the last few years, as the following figures show:

1913	195
1919	225
1920	274
1921	327

e advent of the bucket dredge is largely responsible for this increase.

e machinery employed in the Federated Malay States for mining pur‑ Machinery. poses is driven by most of the usual sources of energy. The machines themselves vary from the comparatively humble but useful 12 n.h.p. portable steam boiler and engine, which is so extensively used for driving water and gravel pumps, to the most elaborate batteries of Babcock and Wilcox boilers fitted with every known device for economising. Water-tube boilers have become very popular. Diesels engines in sets up to 200 b.h.p. and in batteries of 3 sets are fairly / extensively employed, usually to drive dynamos. Other forms of oil engines, such as semi-Diesel, are used for various purposes, but generally for driving pumps. Suction-gas plants are similarly employed both for pumping and electrical work. Water under pressure is employed on Pelton wheels[7] for driving dynamos and gravel-pumps. Wire-rope ways are used in one case for conveying the ore from one hill to the mill on the adjoining hill. The Chinese use a primitive form for lowering their ore-bearing ground from the limestone cliffs to the valleys below. It consists of a pair of heavy wires strung taut between the cliff and the ground and a light rope which passes round a pulley on the top. The full baskets are slung on the upper end of the rope and by their fall pull up the empty ones. Water is pumped out of the mines by the Chinese chain pumps worked by foot or by a waterwheel, by turbine pumps actuated by steam, by hydraulic elevators, by Cornish pumps in the deep mines and by reciprocating pumps electrically driven, as in the Malayan collieries. Lighting is done by electricity, or one or other of the various forms of incandescent-mantle lamps. In small mines, where required, and in underground workings, candles are used, except on inspection, when occasionally an acetylene lamp is employed. The bucket dredges are mostly driven by steam, using wood fuel.

e following table shows the extent to which the various forms of machinery were employed in 1921:

Nature of Power.	No.	Horse-power.
Steam	894	46,182 i.h.p.
Oil	649	19,553 b.h.p.
Gas	258	13,892 b.h.p.

Steam engines use either the local coal known as Rawang coal, or firewood, the latter being to a large extent obtained from the extensive mangrove swamps near the coast. The Diesel engine use the oil produced for their use, and the gas plants imported anthracite or / local charcoal. The supply of Rawang coal is equal to the demand, but in many cases it is found that more economy results from the use of mangrove firewood, where the mines are near the source of supply as at Taiping. The local coal does not keep very well. It is apt to heat up and can only be prevented from igniting by being kept in water. It costs now from $7 to $11 (16*s.* 4*d.* – 25*s.* 8*d.)* a ton free on rail, the price varying with the quality. The present (1922) price of foreign coal is $25 (58*s.* 4*d.)* a ton. Anthracite costs about $40 (93*s.* 4*d.*) a ton, firewood $8 (18*s.* 10*d.*) a ton and diesel oil $16.50 (38*s.* 6*d.*) per drum of 65 gallons. The possibility of using liquid fuel in bucket-dredge boilers has lately been discussed and a trial has been made.

Mining land can be acquired in any of three ways:

(i) By purchase from the lessee.

(ii) By applying for and obtaining a prospecting licence, and subsequently selecting an area for lease.

(iii) By direct application to Government for a lease.

As a rule nowadays, unless the land is obviously required to form part of a scheme of work, mining land, unless purchased under (i), is obtained by means of a prospecting licence. Application for this is made through the local District officer, and sufficient detail must be given to enable the latter to know within reasonable limits the situation of the land. A report is called for from the Mines Department, and final approval is in the jurisdiction of the British Resident. The fee for a prospecting licence is not less than $100, equivalent to about 11 guineas. It entitles the holder to prospect for the mineral or minerals described in the licence and to dispose of such minerals as he may find during his prospecting. If his prospecting work has been sufficient to satisfy the Resident, he is entitled to select such areas to be leased to him as were described in the licence. Unless he does sufficient prospecting, this right of selection is denied him.

A mining lease is acquired by application must show the position of / the land and such details as will enable the land officer to find it accurately and the surveyor to survey it. At the same time a cash deposit must be made. On the application being approved by the Resident, the land is surveyed and a lease is issued. If the applicant wishes to commence mining operations without delay or before survey can be completed, a mining certificate may be issued. This certificate shows the boundaries of the lease. Premium is charged for the lease at rates from $10 (£1 3*s.* 4*d.*) per acre upwards. A mining lease conveys the following rights to the lessee:

(i) The right to work and win all minerals described in the lease and to dispose of them.

(ii) The right to put such building on the land as may be necessary and to grow such vegetables and keep such live stock as are required for the labour force employed.

(iii) The exclusive right to all jungle produce found on the land for this own use, but such produce cannot be removed beyond the boundaries of the land.

e following is a brief summary of the conditions by which the lease is gov-

(i) Rent must be paid. It is usually $1 (2*s. 4d.*) an acre per annum.

(ii) Boundaries must be kept open.

(iii) Work must start within six months of date of issue of lease.

(iv) Within a further six months the requisite number of coolies must be employed. This number is usually one coolie per acre, and power-producing machinery is allowed for at the rate of eight coolies per horse-power.

(v) There must not be a lapse from these labour conditions of more than twelve months.

(vi) The lessee may be required to work any lodes found on his land.

(vii) The work must be done in an orderly, skilful and workmanlike manner. /

(viii) Government officers shall have free access to the land.

(ix) Such notices as are required shall be exhibited.

(x) Material such as stone, gravel, etc., may be removed without payment, if required by the State for a public purpose.

(xi) Proper account books must be kept.

(xii) Reasonable access to adjoining land must be allowed.

(xiii) Proper precautions shall be taken to ensure the health and safety of all labour employed on the land.

Breach of conditions numbered (i), (iii), (iv) or (v) render the lease liable to forfeiture. The leases may be sublet, in which case the conditions described above are still binding on the lessee as well as on the sub-lessee. Leases may be renewed if the conditions have been carried out to the satisfaction of the Resident.

e control of all water is in the hands of the State. Licences to use water for mining purposes, if for over twelve months, are issued by the Resident under the Mining Enactment, Licences up to twelve months may be issued by the Warden, while the Inspector has powers to distribute water in minor cases.

Mining is subject to the following regulations, which may be found in detail in the Mining Enactment of 1912:

(1) The use and storage of explosives are governed by rules.

(2) Accidents involving death or serious bodily injury must be reported. The circumstances are investigated by the Mines Department and, if carelessness or blame is attributable to anyone, the matter is taken into court.

(3) A mine manager may draw up a code of rules for the local government of the mine, and these, if approved, have all the force of law.

(4) Overburden can only be deposited on unworked land by permission of an Inspector who may issue directions as to where overburden or tailings shall be deposited. Mines producing tailings, as nearly all mines do, have to control them in dams and so forth, in such a way that the effluent / water does not carry more than 800 grains of solid matter per gallon. This entails in some cases tailings-retention works of very considerable magnitude, especially on mines using water under pressure through monitors. It is difficult in some cases to effect the necessary control, especially where the mining is in the hills, where there are no suitable sites of sufficient capacity to hold the tailings. The result is that the dam has to enclose the whole of the river in the valley and has be capable of passing safely any flood water that may come down owing to excessive rains.

(5) Shafting can only be carried out under licence. There are also various rules governing the control of mining underground.

(6) Hydraulic mining of any kind also can only be carried out under licence.

The industry is controlled by the Mines Department, which consists of a Senior Warden of Mines, Wardens of Perak and Selangor, Assistant Wardens of Negri Sembilan and Palang and a number of Inspectors, who, when qualified, become Assistant Wardens. All these officers are recruited from approved Schools of Mines and furthermore must have served for at least three years on some mine. Control over the ore-buying business is exercised by an Inspector under the Mineral Ores Enactment, and the use and safety of machinery is controlled by Inspectors under the Machinery Enactment. Electrical machinery is similarly governed by an Inspector under the Electricity Enactment. All these Enactments and the officer under them are under the administrative control of the Senior Warden of Mines.

After the tin ore in the form of a dark-coloured sand has been won from the mine and cleaned up, it is put into canvas bags and sold to one of the local tin-ore buyers, who may be Chinese or a branch of one of the two smelting companies, the Straits Trading Company and the Eastern Smelting Company. The parcel of ore is weighted and assayed for its metallic contents, and the price offered is in accordance with that result and the current price of tin, less export duty, smelting charges / and transport. The assay is usually done by cyanide in the English houses, but, strange though it may appear, the Chinese can approximate to the true contents within 1 per cent. by a process of careful cleaning, weighing and keen observation.

Eventually all the ore with the exception of about 12 per cent. which is smelted locally finds its way to the big smelteries of the two companies in Singapore and Penang. The result is what is known as "Straits Tin," and is refined up to as high as 99.939 per cent., but averages 99.9 per cent. Apart from its fineness, it possesses peculiarly liquid properties when melted, which make it more suitable for the tin-plate industry than other tin, which may possibly be even finer. The locally smelted Chinese tin is refined in Singapore and finds a market in India, China and Japan.

e charges the miner has to pay are, as has been said, three:

Export Duty and Charges.

(1)   Export duty.
(2)   Smelting charges.
(3)   Transport.

If the ore is of low grade or is contaminated with other minerals, which have to be separated before the ore can be smelted, a further cut in price is made.

e export duty now in force is on a sliding scale. It represents the following percentages *ad valorem* at the various prices per ton of metallic tin:

Price per ton of Tin. £	Duty per cent.
100	10.0
120	11.0
140	11.9
160	12.5
180	12.9
200	13.3
220	13.6
240	13.8 /
260	14.0
280	14.1
300	14.3
320	14.4
340	14.5
360	14.6
380	14.8
400	14.9

is duty is deducted by the ore buyer when he makes the purchase and is collected by Government at the various ports. Provided the ore is to be smelted in the Straits Settlements, Australia or England, this is the only duty charged. If the ore is shipped elsewhere, an additional duty of $30 a bhara (3 pikuls), equal to £3 . per 400 lb., is charged. The smelting charges average about $2.20 per pikul, equivalent to £4 6s. a ton. Transport charges vary, but average about $1.60 per pikul, equivalent to £3 12s. 8d. a ton.

[...]

The climate being hot and damp, the lightest clothes are worn and the least exercise induces profuse perspiration, so that as far as possible such clothes should be washable. After sun-down the heat is less and it is quite possible to wear thin tweed suits. For anyone who has much outdoor work to do, khaki drill is the most suitable material. A thin flannel or cotton shirt with or without a cotton vest is usually worn. A coat, also of khaki drill, is useful for the carrying capacity of its pockets. The cost of a suit of khaki is about 17*s*. 6*d*. Excellent canvas boots can be obtained locally from the Chinese boot makers at a cost of about $5 (11*s*. 8*d*.) a pair. /

The most important part of wearing apparel is the hat. Owing to the humidity of the atmosphere the effect of the sun is very strong, in fact much stronger at a temperature of 95° in Malaya, than, for instance, in the drier parts of Australia at 120°, where a straw hat is sufficient. The most suitable sun-hat for much outdoor work is that which takes the form of a large helmet. It is made of pith and is covered with khaki drill. It is very light, and gives great protection to the sensitive back of the neck and at the same time ventilates the head well. It is preferable to wear a large size, which rests on the top of the head by straps, than to wear a helmet which fits closely round the head. Such a hat is generally known as a "pig-sticker." It costs from 10*s*. 6*d*. to 15*s*. For ordinary use in towns and offices, a hat made of cork and covered with white cloth is used. The double felt hat known as a double terai is also very suitable. People vary a great deal in the degree in which the sun affects them, but it is always advisable to take no risks whatever between 7 a.m. and 5 p.m. The length of the day varies but slightly, the greatest difference being about half an hour, darkness setting in between 6.15 and 6.45 p.m. Similarly the dawn varies between 5.30 and 6 a.m.

In the daytime in offices white suits are usually worn. Tunic coats buttoning up to the collar and worn with a vest are still popular in some places, but coats and shirts have largely replaced them. A white suit – coat and trousers – costs about 14*s*. All possible clothing requirements can be supplied by the local shops, though many consider it better and cheaper to order from home.

The usual houses built on mines are of wood and are sometimes bungalows, in other words one-story houses, and sometimes two-story houses. The latter form of house is preferable if the occupier is married, as it engenders a feeling of security in the chatelaine. The typical house consists of a living-room, a dining-room and two or more bedrooms with bathrooms attached. Verandahs are essential to keep out both the glare and heat. The walls are of / wooden and should be, but seldom are, double. The roof is generally of "attap," already described. The bathroom is of course constantly used, and the method is novel to anyone straight from home. A large wooden tub, or much better a Shanghai jar, is filled with water. The bather stands outside the tub and pours cold water over himself by aid of a tin pail. It is an extremely refreshing form of bath. Some, however, who are

e quality of the food-supply varies considerably with the distance from the main towns. When transport is available, supplies of excellent meat, butter, etc., can be obtained from the Cold Storage Company, which has depots in Kuala Lumpur, Ipoh, Taiping and Seremban. These are supplied from Singapore, and most of the meat and butter comes from Australia and New Zealand. Potatoes are obtained from India, but the rest of the vegetables are supplied locally, and are unfortunately rather tasteless. Salads such as lettuces, etc., if grown by Chinese vegetable gardeners should not be eaten, as they may induce typhoid. Chickens, ducks and eggs are easily obtainable, and local meat in the form of pork and buffalo can be eaten but is unpalatable. With the present transport facilities, however, it is seldom necessary to rely on these latter.

e cost of living of course varies greatly with the locality, the tastes of the individual and the conditions on the mine. In the towns there is much more scope for spending money, but the following figures, which have been obtained from mines situated in every part of the Federated Malay States, will give an idea of what it costs an Assistant on a mine to live quietly.

It may be taken the management of a mine will supply the following free: houses, furniture (sometimes necessities only), firewood, lighting (usually electric), medical attendance (sometimes for employee only, not his wife), and generally a rough servant or water-carrier, and sometimes a gardener as well.

Figures have been received stating that a single man / can live quietly at an inclusive cost on a mine of from \$125 to \$250 a month. This is equivalent to £175 to £350 a year. By inclusive cost is meant all food and reasonable liquor, clothes and amusements. The first figure is very low, but if the individual combines with others to live in a mess, the cost of living is largely reduced. Married people as Assistants on mines would need about \$350 to \$450 a month (say from £500 to £600 a year) at least. These figures represent the minimum, and do not allow for anything except living in a very quiet way, nor do they allow for the expenses of illness of the wife or children.

ANON., 'REPORT ON MINING IN MALAYA, 1939' (1939)

Anon., 'Report on Mining in Malaya, 1939', National Archives, CO 717/132/9, pp. 47–81, 103–5, 107.

is report was completed in 1939, but not published owing to the outbreak of the Second World War. In the extracts included here, the author calculates the value and quantity of all the mineral classes mined in Malaya from 1898 to 1937 obtaining the data from the *Annual Report on the Administration of the Mines Department and on the Mining Industries*, published from 1919; the monthly and quarterly *Bulletin of Statistics Relating to the Mining Industry*; annual Reports of the Residents of the Federated Malay States, of the British Advisers to the Unfederated States and of the General Adviser to Johore; the annual *Summary of Monthly Malayan Statistic*s; the *Statistical Year Book of the International Tin Research and Development Council*; and from mining companies operating in Malaya. Statistics relating to each mineral are then presented in alphabetical order.

Anon., 'Report on Mining in Malaya, 1939' (1939), extract

IV. – MINERAL PRODUCTION OF MALAYA – 1898 to 1937.

[...]

Tons throughout this report are long tons of 2,240 lbs. For the non-Malayan readers it is desirable to mention that 1 pikul – 100 katis – 133 ⅓rd lbs. Consequently 16.8 pikuls – 1 ton. The Straits dollar is worth 2– 8d. sterling. /

3. [...]/

Summary of forty years' data of production.

TABLE 2. Value and Quantity of Mineral Output of Malaya from 1898 to 1937 expressed in Quinquennial Averages.

	1898–1903	1904–1908	1909–1913	1914–1918	1919–1923
Tin: £ tons	5,208,729	7,319,155	8,346,994	8,766,317	8,042,074
	43,925	49,633	48,166	46,100	38,138
Iron ore: £ tons					120,709(c)
					113,257(c)
Petrol: £ cubic metres					
Coal: £ tons	20,336	19,424	26,359	88,234	284,591
	28,453	21,401	38,127	113,573	285,304
Phosphates: £ tons	101,118(a)	257,370	371,200	131,461	171,234
	40,920(a)	96,826	141,457	60,424	80,347
Gold: £ ozs	86,428	57,553	68,875	68,718	57,585
	19,378	14,390	17,392	17,741	13,620
Tungsten ore: £ tons	1,124	471	14,773	150,529	41,766
			175	857	499
Building stone: £ tons			52,566(b)	50,432	44,200
			450,567(b)	432,278	378,861
Petrol gas: £ cubic metres					
Manganese ore: £ tons					
Aluminium ore: £ tons.					
Ilmenite[1] £ tons					
China clay: £ tons					1,750(e)
					501(e)
Total value:	5,417,735	7,653,973	8,880,767	9,255,691	8,763,910

(a) 1899–1903.
(b) 1911–1913.
(c) 1921–1923
(d) 1928 only.
(e) 1923 only.
(f) 1931–1933. /

1924–1928	1929–1933	1934	1935	1936	1937	1938	1934–1937
13,451,368	7,601,124	7,584,124	9,193,978	13,134,051	17,901,544		11,953,424
52,462	47,624	33,919	42,319	66,703	77,192		55,034
230,690	510,581	582,519	696,042	752,837	851,702		720,775
375,735	752,322	1,135,648	1,411,635	1,654,996	1,560,828		1,440,777
	120,626	289,380	347,942	368,804	495,033		375,289
	173,921	419,171	510,330	509,070	653,590		523,040
370,622	286,796	180,650	223,326	302,700	387,443		273,530
456,558	426,252	321,888	392,178	520,799	628,951		465,954
263,579	210,215	235,515	293,393	320,189	322,427		297,881
120,047	96,902	128,831	147,929	161,440	162,568		150,192
59,705	139,254	218,548	215,026	248,513	222,789		226,219
14,818	29,364	32,822	30,644	38,610	34,653		34,182
15,093	42,164	194,294	215,279	212,392	193,354		203,980
280	716	1,603	1,634	1,639	1,099		1,494
68,432	46,611	63,614	83,735	96,808	124,011		92,043
586,801	399,527	545,263	717,728	829,785	1,062,951		788,932
	37,338(f)	42,349	48,854	40,812	79,440		82,864
	3,719,068(f)	11,951,030	83,004,750	69,339,780	134,970,374		89,816,434
45,245(d)	15,611	21,325	30,561	39,511	34,085		31,371
48,852(d)	16,948	18,649	28,045	36,777	32,793		
				21	7,366	18,090(gm)	1,847
				36	12,627	31,012	3,166
			860	3,127	1,566		1,388
			2,431	10,331	6,252		4,753
1,948	915	812	277	353	838		570
614	384	307	96	121	293		204
14,496,862	9,011,434	9,433,730	11,349,273	15,520,118	20,621,598		14,231,181

The story told by this table is one of increase in the total value for all minerals produced in Malaya from an annual average of £5.4 millions in 1898–1903 to £14.5 millions in 1924–1928, followed by a tremendous fall to £9.0 millions in 1929–1933. In the following four years the annual value has increased rapidly to £20.6 millions in 1937, with an average for the four years of £14.2 millions, a figure close to that for the period 1924–1928. These violent fluctuations in total value are largely due to the predominant part played by tin. Other minerals are, however, accounting for an increasing proportion of the total. Thus in the first quinquennium[2] the total value of minerals other than tin averaged only £190,000 or 3.5 per cent of the total; in 1924–1928, this value had risen to £1.03 millions or 7.1 per cent; in the depression period of 1929–1933 the total value of minerals other than tin had <u>increased</u> to £1.39 millions or 15.5 per cent. In the first four years of the present quinquennium the value of these other minerals has increased to £2.72 millions or 13.2 per cent by 1937, with an average for the four years of £2.28 or 16.0 per cent. This steadily increasing production of minerals other than tin tends to smooth out the curve of total values and to reduce the violent fluctuations therein caused by tin. Unfortunately the tin fluctuations are mainly due to the Federated Malay States, whilst the increasing values of minerals other than tin are largely due to minerals outside the F.M.S., chiefly iron-ore in the Unfederated States, oil and natural gas in Brunei, and phosphates in Christmas Island. But coal and gold and tungsten-ores in the F.M.S. also play their part.

4. [...]

ALUMINIUM-ORE (BAUXITE)

5. The only State in Malaya in which bauxite or aluminium ore is produced is Johore, where an industry for the export of this ore to Japan has sprung up recently, the first exports being in 1936. At present bauxite is being quarried at two places – namely, at Kim Kim, to the east of Johore Bharu, and at Bukit Pasir near Batu Pahat; but other deposits are known to occur. The figures of exports are as follows:

YEAR	BUKIT PASIR		KIM KIM		TOTAL		
	Tons	$	Tons	$	Tons	$	£.
1936	36	180	Nil	Nil	36	180	21
1937	12,531	62,655	96	480	12,627	63,135	7,366
1938	23,857˙	119,285	7,155˙	35,775	31,012˙	155,060	12,627

□ Figures of exports up to the end of September, 1938, only.

e composition of the Johore bauxite is indicated by the following figures:

	BUKIT PASIR Per Cent	KIM KIM Per Cent
Al2O3	52.6 to 61.5	54.57
Fe2O3	15.6 to 5.8	9.12
SiO2	4.0 to 1.6	6.52
TiO2	0.8 to 1.0	0.25
Loss on ignition	27.3 to 30.2	29.20
		99.66 /

BUILDING STONE AND ROAD METAL

6. Because the stone required for building purposes and road metal is not as a rule produced under mining leases, stone for this purpose being commonly extracted by the Public Works Department, or by Municipalities and other public bodies, and because the quarries that thus result are frequently not made an object of inspection by the Mines Department of a country, the figures of production of such materials are not infrequently omitted from statements of mineral statistics. To omit such figures, however, is to overlook an important form of contribution by the rocks of country to its welfare, and it is desirable that such data should be collected and used. Owing to the fact that many stone quarries are small enterprises lying outside the purview of the Mines or other department responsible for the collection of mineral statistics, such figures as may be obtained for building stones must necessarily be below the truth. Nevertheless, data representing an important proportion of the total production are not without value. As an example, the average annual output in India of granite, gneiss,[3] sandstone, limestone and laterite, for the last quinquennial period for which the data have been compiled – namely, 1929–1933 – was 4,896,553 tons, valued at RS. 73,04,705 or £544,808. This figure is, of course, much below the real truth, but it gives an indication of the important part that the output of stone plays in the economics of India. It should be mentioned here that a considerable proportion of the production of limestone is for fluxing in the iron and steel industry.

For Malaya, the Chief Inspector of Mines has been able to provide me with gures of the quantity of stone quarried by the Public Works Department in each of the four Federated States from the year 1911 onwards. These figures are shown in Table 3: /

No figures of value have been given, and as stone produced by the Public Works Department is not sold, any value must necessarily be arbitrary. It must at least equal the cost of production. The average value allotted to the stone produced in India, based on the figures given above, is about Rs. 1.49 per ton, or almost 2s. 3d. As this is close to the value of the Straits dollar, I have assumed for

For the Unfederated States, data are available only from 1933. These are given in the Table 4, whilst data for 1936–1937 for Malacca are given in Table 3. The method of valuation is the same.

There is, of course, a considerable production of stone in Singapore, but no figures have been received.

Combining the data from the foregoing tables, the quinquennial average figures for Malaya are shown in Table 5.

There are also imports into Malaya of substances that would come under this head, the items imported in 1937 beings:

	Tons	$
Marble	196	22,895
Other sorts of stone	133	6,285
Lime	1	28 /

TABLE 3. Building Stone Quarried by the P.W.D. in the F.M.S.

PRODUCTION IN TONS.

YEAR	FEDERATED MALAY STATES					UNPEDERATED MALAY STATES	MALACCA	TOTAL MALAYA	VALUE IN $ MALAYA
	Negri Sombilan	Pahang	Perak	Selanger	Total				
1911	47,387	102,787	101,410	138,634	390,218	–	–	390,218	390,218
1912	48,590	110,265	108,907	165,717	433,479	–	–	433,479	433,479
1913	87,831	112,311	102,384	225,478	528,004	–	–	528,004	528,004
1914	109,562	73,740	158,782	199,434	541,518	–	–	541,518	541,518
1915	113,800	65,956	118,995	162,401	461,152	–	–	461,152	461,152
1916	89,938	55,050	111,772	149,060	405,820	–	–	405,820	405,820
1917	73,421	48,999	104,226	152,940	379,586	–	–	379,586	379,586
1918	71,792	34,322	125,924	141,276	373,314	–	–	373,314	373,314
1919	83,478	37,079	114,574	143,633	378,764	–	–	378,764	378,764
1920	38,119	40,167	105,976	158,294	342,556	–	–	342,556	342,556
1921	71,952	40,809	158,893	154,098	425,752	–	–	425,752	425,752
1922	60,657	50,302	95,744	161,635	368,338	–	–	368,338	368,338
1923	66,102	32,000	114,299	166,495	378,896	–	–	378,896	378,896
1924	61,318	69,025	142,983	167,721	441,047	–	–	441,047	441,047
1925	100,930	55,982	137,004	174,622	468,538	–	–	468,538	468,538
1926	80,286	80,068	112,878	211,147	384,379	–	–	384,379	384,379
1927	86,491	142,053	189,436	221,983	639,963	–	–	639,963	639,963
1928	153,740	171,250	355,210	319,876	1,000,076"	–	–	1,000,076	1,000,076
1929	84,053	115,331	134,008	355,852	689,244	–	–	689,244	689,244
1930	79,630	101,472	189,456	181,540	552,098	–	–	552,098	552,098
1931	72,881	50,755	169,134	142,637	435,407	–	–	435,407	435,407
1932	21,519	16,095	52,093	64,985	154,692	–	–	154,692	154,692

PRODUCTION IN TONS.

YEAR	FEDERATED MALAY STATES					UNPEDER-ATED MALAY STATES	MALACCA	TOTAL MALAYA	VALUE IN $ MALAYA
	Negri Sombilan	Pahang	Perak	Selanger	Total				
1933	18,964	21,500	54,654	52,150	147,268	18,924	–	166,192	166,192
1934	26,905	17,253	41,790	–	85,948	459,315	–	545,263	545,263
1935	43,726	15,568	111,756	76,041	246,091	471,637	–	717,728	717,728
1936	64,705	25,779	142,755	86,709	322,948	459,323	47,414	829,765	829,765
1937	63,937	30,005	180,267	114,606	388,815	579,812	94,324	1,062,951	1,062,951

N.B. Stone was also quarried for railway purposes.

x Details of these figures given below in Table 4.

is figure is based on the P.W.D. returns of cubes of 100 cubic feet in the solid. Figure in the loose is 660,000 tons. /

TABLE 4. Production of Building Stone in the Unfederated Malay States

PRODUCTION IN TONS

YEAR	UNFEDERATED MALAY STATES						VALUE IN $ U.M.S.
	Johore	Kedah	Kelantan	Perlis	Trengganu	Total	
1933	–	–	170	11,584	40,005	18,924	18,924
1934	438,740	–	5,320	7,243	42,387	459,315	459,315
1935	437,838	–	6,730	8,112	18,957	471,637	471,637
1936	345,336	53,760	11,140	6,700	8,012	459,323	459,323
1937	407,315	70,866	32,300	29,326	7,170	579,812	579,812
1938							

TABLE 5. Production of Building Stone in Malaya, Quinquennial Averages.

QUINQUENNIAL AVERAGES, F.M.S. and U.M.S.

PERIOD	AVERAGE ANNUAL PRODUCTION	VALUE IN $	VALUE IN £ STERLING
1911–1913	450,567	450,567	52,566
1914–1918	432,278	432,278	50,432
1919–1923	378,861	378,861	44,200
1924–1928	586,801	586,801	68,460
1929–1933	399,527	399,527	46,611
1934–1937	788,932	788,932	92,043 /

CHINA CLAY.

ere is a small industry for the production of china clay, for use in the rubber industry, based on a quarry in kaolinised granite[4] near Tapah in Perak State. As most of this is utilized within the State, export figures are of no value, but only figures of production. In addition, there has been a small export of china clay from Johore State. Such figures as are available are assembled in the following table.

TABLE 6. Production of China Clay in Malaya. 1923 to 1937

YEAR	FEDERATED MALAY STATES								UNFEDER-ATED MALAY STATES		TOTAL – MALAYA	
	Pahang		Perak		Selanger		Total		Johore[a]			
	Tons	$	Tons	$	Tons	$	Tons	$	Tons	$	Tons	$
1923	–	–	–	–	–	–	451	13,556	50	1,492	501	15,048
1924	–	–	–	–	–	–	830	36,335	80	2,400	910	38,735
1925	–	–	–	–	–	–	8.8	508	–	–	8.8	508
1926	–	–	–	–	–	–	–	–	337	7,747	337	7,747
1927	–	–	–	–	–	–	6.8	308	824	16,481	830.8	16,789
1928	–	–	–	–	–	–	–	–	985	19,700	985	19,700
1929	–	–	–	–	–	–	–	–	741	14,820	741	14,820
1930	–	–	–	–	–	–	–	–	410	8,200	410	8,200
1931	–	–	–	–	.22	4	.22	4	396	7,920	396.22	7,924
1932	–	–	–	–	–	–	5	125	186	3,720	191	3,845
1933	–	–	153		–	–	153	3,825[c]	30	600	183	4,425
1934	–	–	164		–	–	164	4,100[c]	143	2,860	307	6,960
1935	–	–	91		–	–	91	2,275[c]	5	100	96	2,375
1936	–	–	121				121	3,025[c]	–	–	121	3,025
1937	.12	2	177		86		263.2	6,580[c]	30	602	293.2	7,182
1938			115[b]		172[b]							

☐ The figures for 1923 to 1932 are for exports, and therefore are much below the truth, as a large proportion of the china clay produced in Perak State is consumed within the State.

a.   Export figures.

b   1938 figures Jan.–Sept. only

c.   Valued at $.25 per ton, this being rate used for exports of 5 tons in 1932, 65.1 tons in 1933 and 60 tons in 1934.

QUINQUENNIAL AVERAGES

Period	Tons	$	£s.
1923	501	15,048	1,750
1924–1928	614	16,696	1,948
1929–1933	384	7,843	915
1934–1937	204	4,885	570 /

In addition, there are sometimes imports of china clay into Malaya, the imports for 1937 being 188 tons valued at $5,299. In the same year there was an import of fireclay amounting to 490 tons valued at $20,397.

COAL.

8. In the Peninsula of Malaya coal-bearing rocks have been identified at no less   Coal in Selangor. than five localities, but only two of these have been proved to possess seams of coal of economic value. The less important of these is at Enggor, in Perak State, from which coal was produced from 1925–1928 by the Enggor Coalfields Limited. The only important field in Malaya is, however, the Batu Arang Goalfield, in Selangor State, worked by Malayan Collieries Limited since 1915. The figures of both quantity of production and of value are show in Table 7. From 1920 onwards the output of this company has ranged between 218,247 tons in 1933 and a maximum of 661,514 tons in 1929 as show in Table 7. The output for 1937 was but little less at 628,948 tons. Almost the whole of this coal is used in Malaya. Although less than half this output is used by the mining companies, the extent to which general industrial activity in Malaya runs parallel with the fortunes of the tin industry can be seen by comparing the figures of coal output from 1929 to 1937 with those of tin for the same period. The degree of correlation is in fact remarkable, the ratio of coal output to tin output during the ten years 1928 to 1937 averaging 8.6 with limits of 7.3 to 9.5 As the permissible production of tin for Malaya for 1938 is 42,973 tons one might even hazard a prediction that the coal output of Malaya for this year will be about $370,000 \pm 40,000$ tons.

With this intimate relationship between the output of coal and that of tin, it is of interest to show the distribution of coal in 1937 (Mines Report, 1937, page 16), amongst various consumers: /

TABLE 7. Production of Coal in Malaya, 1898 to 1937

YEAR	BRUNEI.+		LABUAN.X		PERAK.		SELANGOR.
	Tons	$	Tons	$	Tons.	$	Tons.
1898	–	–	46,829	329,781	–	–	–
1899	–	–	45,747	276,861	–	–	–
1900	–	–	22,090	154,920	–	–	–
1901	–	–	18,119	172,122	–	–	–
1902	–	–	19,093	181,381	–	–	–
1903	–	–	18,844	183,051	–	–	–
1904	–	–	12,460	112,971	–	–	–
1905	–	–	15,047	127,900	–	–	–
1906	–	–	13,758	106,131	–	–	–
1907	–	–	32,233	257,863	–	–	–
1908	–	–	33,508	268,063	–	–	–
1909	–	–	61,855	309,274	–	–	–
1910	–	–	86,689	476,786	–	–	–
1911	–	–	5,625	28,123	–	–	–
1912	12,724	80,248	–	–	–	–	–
1913	23,743	145,686	–	–	–	–	–
1914	25,378	161,583	–	–	–	–	–
1915	22,633	148,730	–	–	–	–	10,725
1916	27,447^x	206,077	–	–	–	–	100,921
1917	27,621^x	295,800	–	–	–	–	142,084
1918	29,565^x	413,910	–	–	–	–	181,493
1919	17,363	296,621	–	–	–	–	186,170
1920	17,000	296,000	–	–	–	–	260,222
1921	16,210	275,570	–	–	–	–	310,445
1922	7,440	104,160	–	–	–	–	282,727
1923	8,941	102,920	–	–	–	–	320,000
1924	10,337	98,202	–	–	–	–	372,796
1925	676	6,760	–	–	350	2,430^a	407,734
1926	–	–	–	–	7,762	54,334^a	456,522
1927	52	624	–	–	13,421	93,947^a	449,681
1928	25	300	–	–	6,944	48,608^a	556,590
1929	–	–	–	–	–	–	661,514
1930	–	–	–	–	–	–	567,166
1931	57	330	–	–	–	–	401,172
1932	168	1,750	–	–	–	–	282,860
1933	78	618	–	–	–	–	218,246
1934	28	298	–	–	–	–	321,860
1935	25	200	–	–	–	–	392,153
1936	49	392	–	–	–	–	520,750
1937	3	27	–	–	–	–	628,948
1938							

+   Export figures, except for those marked x (output figures)

a)   estimated at $7.00 per ton.

SELANGOR.	TOTAL.		QUINQUENNIAL AVERAGES.		
$	Tons.	$	Tons.	$	£
–	46,829	329,781			
–	45,747	276,861			
–	22,090	154,920	28,453	216,353	20,336
–	18,119	172,122			
–	19,093	181,381			
–	18,844	183,051			
–	12,460	112,971			
–	15,047	127,900			
–	13,758	106,131	21,401	174,586	19,424
–	32,233	257,853			
–	33,508	268,063			
–	61,855	309,274			
–	86,689	476,786			
–	5,625	28,123	38,127	208,023	26,359
–	12,724	80,248			
–	23,743	145,686			
–	25,378	161,583			
53,046	33,358	201,776			
482,374	128,368	688,451	113,573	756,288	88,234
762,445	169,705	1,058,245			
1,257,473	211,058	1,671,383			
1,500,434	203,533	1,797,055			
2,247,080	277,222	2,543,080			
2,767,072	326,655	3,042,642	285,304	2,439,352	284,591
2,230,122	290,167	2,334,282			
2,376,779	328,941	2,479,699			
2,698,645	383,133	2,794,847			
2,958,764	408,760	2,967,954			
3,327,792	464,284	3,382,126	456,558	3,178,472	370,822
3,107,216	463,054	3,201,787			
3,496,737	563,559	3,545,645			
3,902,662	661,514	3,902,662			
3,272,121	567,166	3,272,121			
2,317,064	401,229	2,317,394	426,252	2,458,239	286,795
1,588,398	283,028	1,590,148			
1,208,250	218,324	1,208,868			
1,548,127	321,888	1,548,425			
1,914,022	392,178	1,914,222			
2,594,179	520,799	2,594,571	465,954	2,344,539	273,530
3,320,909	628,951	3,320,936			

	Tons
Sold to F.M.S. Railways	193,450
Sold to mines in the F.M.S.	189,313
Sold to other consumers in the F.M.S.	212,050
Sold to other consumers outside the F.M.S.	89
Coal used at Collieries	29,406
Coal dumped	3,582
	627,890

9. Coal is also worked in the State of Brunei, the most important production having been during the years 1913–1918. The exports of Brunei have now fallen to an insignificant figure. It is not known whether there is any internal consumption. Coal has been produced in Labuan also, up till 1911, as shown in Table 7, the quantity varying during this period from a minimum of 12,460 tons in 1904 to a maximum of 86,689 tons in 1910, the year before the cessation of work.

10. The imports of coal into Malaya during 1937 were:

	Tons
Japan	314,953
Netherlands Indies	193,712
British Possessions and Protectorates	140,314
United Kingdom	14,008
Continent of Europe	3,530
Other countries	60,389
	726,906

These imports were valued at $6,435,515. It will be noticed that the imports exceed the internal production of Malaya by about 100,000 tons, whilst the value is almost double.

Malayan exports of coal in the same year amounted to 4,443 tons valued at $45,321. Thus the Malayan coal as exported is valued at about twice its value in Malaya. /

GOLD.

11. The principal source of gold in Malaya is of course the Raub Australian Gold Mines Limited in Pahang, producing from lodes in the Raub series of rocks, thought to be Carboniferous in age. In addition, there is in Pahang a production of gold from lodes on the same belt by small producers and elsewhere in the State, especially in the headwaters of the Sungei Tembeling of alluvial gold by gold washers. There is also a small but steady production of gold from Perak State, especially in the Tapah-Bidor area, where gold is found with tin in alluvial deposits. A certain amount of gold is now being recovered on tin dredges in Selangor State by a slight modification in the cone entreating plant. In addi-

Chin Tin Mine near the Johore boundary. Both the gold and the tin occur there in veinlets in decomposed shales, presumably of Carboniferous age, overlain by alluvial clays. A certain quantity of gold is also won in the States of Johore and Kelantan, but the figures are very imperfect.

12. Gold is an example of a mineral for which it is essential to secure figures of pro- Production. duction and not merely of export, if a correct idea is to be obtained of the full value of gold to the country. Consequently the figures in Table No. 8 are as far as possible production figures. For some years the figures for the F.M.S. originally secured were of imports, from which it was seen that, taking the figures from 1929 only, the annual consumption within the F.M.S. amounted to some 4,000 to 7,000 ozs. annually. The data supplied contained no indication of the fineness of the gold, nor is it recorded that the ounces are ounces Troy, though this is presumed to be the case. Certain of the figures for Kelantan were given in terms of tahils, which have been converted to ounces Troy by / multiplying by the factor 1.4628.

13. The total gold production of Malaya is, of course, but a small proportion of Imports and her requirements, as is shown by the fact that during 1937 the imports of gold Exports.

Bullion	$7,271,538
Coin	4,370,434
	$11,641,972

During the same year the exports of gold were:

Bullion	$3,631,758
Coin	1,642,155
	$5,273,913

Such of the Malayan gold output as is exported is presumably included under gold bullion.

e Malayan statistics also record imports and exports of silver bullion and coin, but there is no indigenous production of this metal. /

TABLE 8. Production of Gold from Malaya, 1898 to 1937

YEAR	FEDERATED MALAY STATES							UNFEDERATED	
	Negri Sembilan	Pahang	Perak	Selanger	Total.			Johore	
	Ozs.	Ozs.	Ozs.	Ozs.	Ozs.	$	£	Ozs.	$
1898	–	22,200	–	–	22,200	830,660		–	–
1899	–	18,507	–	–	18,507	740,280		–	–
1900	–	17,048	–	–	17,048	681,920		–	–
1901	–	23,948	–	–	23,948	786,503		–	–
1902	199	19,554	–	–	19,753	742,131		–	–
1903	2,370	12,441	–	–	14,811	663,366		–	–
1904	–	–	–	–	20,157	690,857		–	–
1905	–	–	–	–	9,972	341,840	39,838	–	–
1906	434	10,089	1,057	–	11,580	397,028	46,320	–	–
1907	35	14,386	1,032	–	15,353	526,388	61,412	–	–
1908	–	13,653"	1,234	–	14,887	510,398	59,546	–	–
1909	77"	14,886"	1,279a	–	16,244	556,923	64,974	–	–
1910	–	15,868"	899a	–	16,767	574,868	67,068	–	–
1911	242x	7,677x	1,309x	–	9,228	306,514	35,760	–	–
1912	92x	12,441x	1,888x	–	14,421	478,983	55,881	–	–
1913	50x	13,083x	1,842x	–	14,975	497,391	58,029	–	–
1914	64x	13,273x	935x	–	14,272	474,034	55,304	–	–
1915	142x	17,214x	1,285x	–	18,641	619,149	72,234	–	–
1916	120x	16,181x	1,085x	–	17,386	577,483	67,373	–	–
1917	128x	16,817x	1,209x	–	18,154	602,965	70,346	–	–
1918	38x	17,034x	1,237x	–	18,309	608,124	70,948	–	–
1919	33x	15,278x	1,091x	–	16,402	626,600	73,100	–	–
1920	9x	11,476x	1,338x	–	12,823	422,522	51,627	–	–
1921	–	13,236x	1,438x	–	14,674	506,546	59,097	–	–
1922	81x	13,781x	1,143x	–	15,005	578,763	67,525	–	–
1923	83x	8,227x	883x	–	9,193		36,550	–	–
1924	–	12,848	2,112	–	14,960		59,466	–	–
1925	–	12,526	1,659	–	14,185		56,385	–	–
1926	–	13,042	1,433	–	14,475		57,538	–	–
1927	–	9,919	1,839	–	11,758		45,660	–	–
1928	–	16,815	1,878	–	18,693		79,389	–	–
1929	–	23,383	3,399	–	26,782		113,743	–	–
1930	–	24,012	5,585	–	29,597		125,698	–	–
1931	–	26,941	2,521	–	29,462		141,112	–	–
1932	–	27,755	1,541	–	29,296		135,617	20	903
1933	–	26,358	2,678	–	29,036		169,498	71	3,539
1934	–	26,015	4,118	88	30,221		208,084	76	3,779
1935	–	22,909	6,527	335	29,771		211,506	8	420
1936	–	29,449	7,789	541	37,779		246,823	33.5	1,895
1937	25	26,175	7,043	585	33,828		221,009	2.8	154

FOOTNOTES

MALAY STATES.				TOTAL – MALAYA QUINQUENNIAL AVERAGES					
Kelantan		Total		Ozs	$	£.	Tons	£.	$
Ozs.	$	Ozs.	$						
–	–	–	–	22,200	830,660				
–	–	–	–	18,507	740,280				
–	–	–	–	17,048	681,920				
–	–	–	–	23,943	786,503		19,378	86,428	740,810
–	–	–	–	19,753	742,131				
–	–	–	–	14,811	683,366				
–	–	–	–	20,157	690,857				
–	–	–	–	9,972	341,840	39,888			
–	–	–	–	11,580	397,028	46,320	14,390	57,553	493,313
–	–	–	–	15,353	526,388	61,412			
–	–	–	–	14,887	510,398	59,546			
–	–	–	–	24,752	846,195	–			
8,508	289,272	8,508	289,272	20,463	704,333	82,172			
3,699	129,465	3,699	129,465	9,228	306,514	35,760	17,392	68,875	590,356
–	–	–	–	17,398	592,771	69,156			
2,976.5	113,788	2,976.5	113,788	15,117	501,969	58,563			
142.4	4,578	142.4	4,578	15,193	503,986	58,798			
920.9	29,952	920.9	29,952	19,661	652,490	76,124			
1,020.3	33,341	1,020.3	33,341	17,386	577,483	67,373	17,741	68,718	589,010
–	–	–	–	18,154	602,965	70,346			
–	–	–	–	18,309	608,124	70,948			
–	–	–	–	16,402	626,600	73,100			
–	–	–	–	12,823	422,522	51,627			
–	–	–	–	14,674	506,546	59,097	13,620	57,585	493,585
–	–	–	–	15,005	578,763	67,525			
–	–	–	–	9,198		36,574			
5 b.	206	5	206	14,980		59,352			
20 b.	740	20	740	14,185		56,385			
–	–	–	–	14,475		57,538	14,818	59,705	511,757
–	–	–	–	11,758		45,660			
–	–	–	–	18,693		79,389			
–	–	–	–	26,782		113,743			
–	–	–	–	29,597		125,698			
–	–	–	–	29,462		141,112	29,364	139,254	1,193,608
–	–	–	–	29,612		136,806			
295.5	9,289	315.5	10,192	31,366		178,912			
2,259.6	77,154	2,329.6	80,693						
2524.8	85,913	2,600.8	89,692	32,822		218,548			
864.5	29,752	872.5	30,172	30,644		215,026	34,182	226,219	1,939,020
797.2	12,590	830.7	14,485	38,610		248,513			
822.1	15,107	824.9	15,261	34,853		222,789			

ILMENITE

14. The crude concentrates obtained from dredging and other operations of the tin industry consist of tinstone, or cassiterite, mixed with other heavy minerals. The final stage of the concentrating operations is the washing of these concentrates in the tin sheds by skilled Chinese labour, using their time-honoured methods, with the resultant production of tin-ore concentrates fit for smelting and of refuse known as <u>amang</u>, containing but a trivial quantity of tin-ore. This refuse consists in many mines very largely of ilmenite, which of recent years has acquired a considerable market value, due principally to the development of the use of titanium oxide in the manufacture of white paints. This industry, based upon the black sands of the seashore of Travancore, has been developed of recent years, so that India is now the chief world's producer of limonite, the average annual output in the last quinquennial period – namely, 1929–1933 – being 38,329 tons valued at £44,741, whilst the output for 1937 was 181,047 tons valued at £84,606.

The value of the Malayan ilmenite has only recently been recognised, and first considerable exports appear to have taken place in 1935, when this mineral was grouped under exports of 'other sorts of ore.' The available data are collected in the Table 9, the recorded value of the ilmenite varying from about 1 to 3 dollars per ton. If this is compared with the value allotted to the Indian production (£ 0.47 or $4 a ton in 1937) it will be seen that the Malayan ilmenite has been somewhat undervalued, and the presumption is that with better marketing facilities a higher price might be obtained.

According to the Annual Report of the Chief Inspector of Mines, that Department is making a rough survey of <u>amang</u> head – a survey that has been in progress since March, 1936. According / to the Quarterly Bulletin for September 1938, stocks of <u>amang</u> surveyed by that date amounted to 358,700 tons. It is not known how many years' accumulation this stock represents, and what is the annual addition to the stocks resulting from new operations.

Magnetic concentrating is used in cleaning the amang and freeing the ilmenite from other minerals. /

As an example of the destination of the exported ilmenite, the following figures of distribution of exports in 1937 are of interest:

	Tons
United Kingdom	4,569.27
Germany	1,271.40
Japan	339.44
Singapore	.06
Penang	72.05
	6,252.22

The percentage of tin in this amang ranged from 0.09 to 0.19 per cent. With the

IRON-ORE.

15. I have discussed the general mode of occurrence of the iron-ore deposits of Malaya in the Geological Outline forming Section II [not included]. From this it will the seen that, with the exception of the haematite deposit near Ipoh in Perak State, used not as a source of iron, but as ragging in jigs on dredges, the valuable iron-ore deposits of Malaya, as at present known, are confined to the eastern States – namely, in order from north to south, Kelantan, Trengganu, Pahang, and Johore. No production has yet taken place from Pahang. The output of the other three States is show in Table 10, together with that from Perak, the figures for the eastern states being export figures. It will be seen that operations commenced in Johore State in 1921, in Trengganu in 1925, and in Kelantan in 1937. In all cases the operating Companies are Japanese, and the iron-ore is being exported to Japan for use in the Japanese iron and steel industry. The export duty charged is on a 10 per cent. basis, being 50 cents a ton in Johore, 40 cents in Kelantan, and 40 cents in Trengganu. Although the Sri Modan iron mine at Batu Pahat in Jahore, has already passed its prime, yet with the discovery of /

Production.

TABLE 10. Production of Iron-ore in Malaya, 1921 to 1937. ø

YEAR.	FEDERATED MALAY STATES Perak.[+]		UNFEDERATED MALAY STATES					
			Johore.		Kelanban.		Trengganu.	
	Tons.	$.	Tons.	$	Tons.	$	Tons.	$
1921	–	–	74,250	742,500	–	–	–	–
1922	–	–	111,367	1,113,670	–	–	–	–
1923	–	–	184,161	1,248,378	–	–	–	–
1924	–	–	235,118	1,641,161	–	–	–	–
1925	–	–	≠ 271,992	a 1,359,960	–	–	7,690	69,204
1926	–	–	250,100	1,250,498	–	–	45,511	349,864
1927	–	–	409,242	2,046,205	–	–	48,505	372,012
1928	–	–	584,588	2,658,193	–	–	25,927	139,639
1929	–	–	743,209	7,432,090	–	–	55,150	278,143
1930	–	–	729,251	3,646,254	–	–	87,364	374,920
1931	–	–	488,877	2,444,387	–	–	203,109	870,995
1932	–	–	485,067	2,425,339	–	–	203,105	855,839
1933	–	–	408,644	2,043,220	–	–	357,833	1,510,867
1934	–	–	578,180	2,890,900	–	–	557,468	2,102,124
1935	–	–	594,891	2,974,453	–	–	816,744	2,991,623
1936	449	″ 4,490	590,288	2,951,445	–	–	1,064,259	3,496,955
1937	1,147	″ 11,470	519,339	2,596,696	49,223	196,892	991,119	4,495,245
1938	554 †							

ø   The figures for Perak are figures of production, and of the other States of exports.

+   This ore is haematite, used as 'ragging' for jigs on dredges, and not for iron-smelting.

≠   Iron-ore figure for 1925 represents amount produced.

a   Estimated at $5.00 per ton.

□   Estimated at $10.00 per ton.

†   Figures from January – August only. /

TOTAL, MALAYA   QUINQUENNIAL AVERAGES.

Tons.	$	Tons.	$	£
74,250	742,500			
111,367	1,113,670	113,257	1,034,647	120,709
154,161	1,248,378			
235,118	1,641,161			
279,682	1,429,164			
295,611	1,600,362	375,735	1,977,347	230,690
457,747	2,418,217			
610,515	2,797,832			
798,359	7,710,233			
816,615	4,021,174			
691,986	3,315,382	752,322	4,376,411	510,581
688,172	3,281,178			
766,477	3,554,087			
1,135,648	4,993,024			
1,411,635	5,966,076			
1,654,996	6,452,890	1,440,777	6,178,073	720,775
1,560,828	7,300,303			

other deposits in Johore, and, it is stated, of a large deposit in Pahang, the annual production of iron-ore found in Malaya is not likely to decrease in the near future.

16. The general composition of the iron-ores of Malaya may be judged from the following table:

| | JOHORE | | KELANTAN | TRENGGANU |
	Sri Medan, (Ishihara Sangyo Koshi Ltd.)	Bukit Langkap (S. Iisuka)	Bukit Besi Temangan (Southern Mining Co.)	Bukit Besi dungun (Nippon Mug Co. Ltd.)
	Range of three analyses. %	Average analysis %	Average analysis %	Average for 1936 %
Iron	61.8 to 63.0	56.00	50	61
Manganese	0.12 to 0.17	3.21	2 to 3	0.23
Silica	5.7 to 3.9	3.51	5 to 8	2.91
Phosphorus	0.303 to 0.346	0.02	Trace to 0.08	0.061
Sulphur	Trace to 0.22	–	–	0.019
Copper	0.008 to 0.014	–	–	0.01
Combined Water	–	–	–	5.38

☐ The quality of the iron-ore produced from Bukit Besi in Trengganu has since fallen to 59 to 60%

17. A complication has arisen in the iron-mining industry in both Johore and Trengganu, in that certain portion of the iron have been found to be stanniferous, rendering it necessary to restrain the extraction and export of those portions of deposits containing tin in economically extractable quantities until it has been possible to provide an assessment with corresponding quota out of the total international standard tonnage allotted to Malaya. The mines thus affected are the Pelepah Kanan iron mine in Johore State and the iron mine at Machang Satahum in Trengganu. At the latter mine, since the discovery of the presence of tin, an assay plan has been prepared, showing the distribution of tin values according to/ the following limits:

%
0.0 to 0.10
0.10 to 0.25
0.25 to 0.5
over 0.5 (up to 4%)

A dressing plant is in course of construction, and all ore assaying 0.2% of tin or over is to be put through this dressing plant.

Geologically, this occurrence of tin in some of the Malayan iron-ores, though interesting, is not surprising. There is no reason to suppose that the tin and iron have been deposited contemporaneously. Elsewhere in the Peninsula tin-ores have been in many cases introduced into Triassic rocks from the intruding granites, and there is no reason why, where these Triassic rocks contain deposits of iron-ore, the tin-bearing solutions should confine their activities to the accompanying rocks and refrain from impregnating the iron-ores.

18. There is, of course, no import of iron-ore into Malaya, but there is a considerable trade in scrap iron. The imports for 1937 were 8,123 tons valued at $197,100 the chief supplying country being the Netherlands Indies. The exports were on a considerably larger scale, amounting in 1937 to 26,594 tons valued at $705,398, nearly the whole of this going to Japan, doubtless for use in the manufacture of steel.

Imports & exports of scrap iron.

MANGANESE-ORE.

19. Manganese-ore deposits of economic value, as at present known, are conned to the two eastern States of Kelantan and Trengganu. [...] These ores are worked solely for export to Japan, and the relevant figures are summarised in Table 11. Compared / with Indian ores, the Malayan manganese-ores are of low grade, being usually various forms of psilomelane, with some pyrolusite and wad, and very often limonite. The general composition of these ores can be judged from the following figures:

	KELANTAN		TRENGGANU	
	Bukit Tandok Manganese Mine (Nippon Mining Co., Ltd.)		Garu, (Nippon Mining Co. Ltd.)	Machang Sata-hun (Ishihata Sangyo Koshi Ltd.)
	Lump ore, 1936 output	Washed ore		
	%	%	%	%
Manganese	45.56	28	34	15 to 25
Iron	3.31	–	8 to 9	About 30
Silica	5.87	–	Very high	
Phosphorus	0.063	–		
Sulphur	0.003	–		
Copper	0.008	–		
Combined Water	4.9	–		

As with the iron mine at Machang Satahun, the working of manganese-ore at the same locality is complicated by the discovery that some of the ores carry tin. Again a detailed assay plan has been made, showing the presence of tin associated with limonite on the north-east wall of the North Mine and on the south-west of the Central Mine.

TABLE 11. Exports of Manganese-ore from Malaya, 1928 to 1937

YEAR	KELANTAN		TRENGGANU		TOTAL MALAYA		QUINQUENNIAL AVERAGES	
	Tons.	$.	Tons.	$	Tons.	$	Tons.	$
1928	–	–	48,852	387,815	48,852	387,815	–	–
1929	–	–	32,726	257,781	32,726	257,781		
1930	–	–	20,696	165,568	20,696	165,568		
1931	–	–	8,848	70,784	8,848	70,784	16,948	135,519
1932	50	420	9,228	73,824	9,278	74,244		
1933	2,866	26,716	10,327	82,500	13,193	109,216		
1934	8,968	103,338	9,681	77,451	18,649	162,789		
1935	10,678	132,260	17,367	129,691	28,045	261,951		268,891
1936	10,006	124,571	26,771	214,097	36,777	336,668	116,264	/
1937	9,667	120,827	23,128	171,328	32,793	292,155		
1938								

PETROLEUM AND NATURAL GAS.

20. There has been a regular production of petroleum and natural gas since July, 1931, in the Seria oil field, Brunei State, by the British Malayan Petroleum Co. Ltd. I am indebted to the Company for the statement of production of crude oil and natural gas given in Tables 12 and 12a.

This production has resulted in substantial annual royalty payments to Brunei State, which have risen to £55,810 for crude oil in the year 1st March, 1937 to 28th February, 1938, and £1,842 for natural gas.

TABLE 12. Production of Crude Oil, Brunei State, 1931–1938.

Year	Production Cubic Metres	Value £.	Averages Cubic Metres	£.
1931	15,917	10,675		
1932	188,812	133,659	173,921	120,626
1933	317,033	217,543		
1934	419,171	289,380)		
1935	510,330	347,942)		
1936	509,070	368,804)	523,040	375,289
1937	653,590	495,033)		
1938″	743,127	633,464		

‥   To November 30th.

TABLE 12a. Production of Natural Gas, Brunei State, 1931 to 1938

Year	Production Cubic Metres	Value £.	Averages Cubic Metres	£.
1931	–	–		
1932	22,453,956	13,216	31,719,088	37,338
1933	40,984,220	24,122		
1934	71,951,030	42,349)		
1935	83,004,750	48,854)		
1936	69,339,780	40,812)	89,816,484	52,864
1937	134,970,374	79,440)		
1938¨	124,783,670	73,445		

¨   To November 30th. /

PHOSPHATE OF LIME.

21. Deposits of rock phosphate, or phosphate of lime, occur at Christmas Island, which is one of the Straits Settlements and lies in the Indian Ocean about 190 miles south of the western extremity of Java. This phosphate results from interaction between solutions derived from guano deposits and the underlying limestone. These deposits have been worked since 1899 by the Christmas Island Phosphate Company Limited, registered in London. Annual production may be regarded as represented by the exports, which are show for each year since 1899 in Table 13, and for the provision of which for the years 1899 to 1930 I am indebted to the producing company.

From this table it will be seen that the exports have varied from 4,855 tons in the first year of working to 162,568 tons in 1937. The growth, however, has not been continuous, and the exports reached as high a figure as 156,781 tons as long age as 1912, falling to a figure of 25,908 tons in 1915, during the Great War.

Whilst Japan has been the principal importer of these phosphates, other large importers at intervals have been Australia, Germany, Hungary, Denmark and Sweden. The destination of the exported phosphates for the last four years, 1934 to 1937, is shown in the following table:

Countries to which exported	1934 Tons	1935 Tons	1936 Tons	1937 Tons
Union of South Africa	5,500	5,170	5,200	5,900
British India	–	–	50	–
Finland	11,480	–	–	–
Germany	–	–	5,550	–
Netherlands	–	–	5,600	–
Hungary	–	23,050	11,825	11,800
Other Foreign Countries in Europe	5,500	–	–	–
Japan	105,060	116,678	124,550	127,617
Java	–	2,084	2,300	6,510

Of the values given in Table 13, those for the years 1901 to 1930 were received from the Christmas Island Phosphate Company Limited, London, and for the years 1931 to 1937 from the Registrar General of Statistics, Singapore.

The following analysis of Christmas Island phosphate by H. Gilbert is taken from the article on Phosphates for the War Period published by the Imperial Mineral Resources Bureau in 1921 (page 17).

	%
$Ca_3(PO_4)_2$	83.53
$CaCO_3$	4.82
CaF_2	3.44
MgO	0.26
Al_2O_3	1.22
Oxide of iron (?Fe_2O_3)	0.72
H_2O	3.05
Total	97.04
P_2O_5	39.18 /

TABLE 13. Exports of Phosphate of Lime from Christmas Island, 1899–1937

Year				QUINQUENNIAL AVERAGES.		
	Tons	£	$	Tons	£	$
1899	4,855	12,107[x]				
1900	29,682	74,205[x]				
1901	45,347	111,842		40,920	101,118	866,726
1902	55,935	128,171				
1903	68,781	179,267				
1904	75,694	186,124				
1905	92,783	223,080				
1906	100,290	248,061		96,826	257,370	2,206,029
1907	105,719	300,345				
1908	109,643	329,242				
1909	105,793	317,756				
1910	139,005	349,879				
1911	153,153	393,455		141,457	371,200	3,181,714
1912	156,781	404,373				
1913	152,554	390,537				
1914	84,621	221,197				
1915	25,908	56,474				
1916	45,304	116,926		60,424	131,461	1,126,809
1917	91,932	179,911				
1918	54,355	82,798				
1919	70,156	113,232				
1920	71,085	126,284				
1921	87,217	184,544		80,347	171,234	1,467,720
1923	70,926	166,547				
1924	125,940	269,734				

Year				QUINQUENNIAL AVERAGES.		
	Tons	£	$	Tons	£	$
1928	116,703	262,365				
1929	120,403	278,155				
1930	122,580	293,894				
1931	65,849	130,601	1,119,433	96,902	210,215	1,801,843
1932	84,197	166,991	1,431,349			
1933	91,480	181,435	1,555,160			
1934	128,831	255,515	2,190,127			
1935	147,929	293,393	2,514,793			
1936	161,440	320,189	2,744,480	180,192	297,881	2,553,264
1937	162,568	322,427	2,763,656			
1938						

x   Estimated from figures for 1901 at £2 5s. per ton. /

TIN-ORE.

22. From the Geological Outline forming Section II it will be realised that there are two principal mode of occurrence of tin-ore in Malaya, normally as primary deposits in situ, in veins or lodes, stock-works or impregnations in granite or in the rocks into which granite is intruded; and, secondary deposits consisting (a) partly of detrital or eluvial deposits overlying the stanniferous lodes and rocks, but chiefly (b) of alluvial deposits formed by the rivers of Malaya as a result of the decomposition and erosion of the rocks and lodes in which the primary tin-ore is contained, and of the eluvial deposits formed therefrom as an intermediate stage.

Distribution in Malaya

Owing to the wide extension of the tin-bearing granites of Malaya, tin-ore at one time or another has been found in every one of the States, except Brunei, and in every section of the Straits Settlements, except Penang, and, of course, the island settlements of Labuan and Christmas Island. At the present tin-ore is being produced in each of the four Federated States, in each of the five Unfederated States, and from Malacca amongst the Straits Settlements.

23. Strictly speaking, the crude tin-ore is the rock containing the crystals or granules of tinstone or cassiterite in the case of primary deposits and the stanniferous eluvium and alluvium in the case of secondary deposits. No attempt is of course made to record the volumes or weights of such tin-ore in its unconcentrated condition, and it is only after the production of tin concentrates by the various methods in vogue that measurement of quantity of production becomes feasible, so that when one speaks of production or exports or sales of tin-ore one is referring to tin concentrates. Pure cassiterite or tinstone contains 78.6% of metallic tin, and the object of washing and milling operations is to produce concentrates with / a percentage of tin as near this figure as possible. In practice, of

Figures of production of tin-ore

concentrates from each property, and thereafter from each State during a calendar year, especially as by comparing such true production figures with figures of exports it would be possible to ascertain the stocks remaining on the mines at the end of each year. Such figures, however, do not appear to have been recorded in the past, although now that mines are allowed to accumulate stocks up to 25 per cent of the allotted quota under the International Tin Control Scheme some procedure has now presumably been introduced, requiring the record of actual production as distinct from experts. From figures received from the Chief Inspector of Mines for the years 1935–1937 it appears that there is now a record of production as ascertained by sales, together with a statement of stocks on mines, and that by allowing for a change in stocks it is possible to arrive at figures of actual production; as an example I give below the figures for the years 1935–1937, which relate to the F.M.S. only:

1.	2.	3.			4.	5.
Year	Production of tin-in-ore as ascertained by sales	Stock on Mines				Actual production for the year
		Current Year	Previous Year	Difference or –		Total of Col. 2 & 4.
	Pikuls	Pikuls	Pikuls	Pikuls		Pikuls
1934	547,112	28,507	–	–		–
1935	685,222	54,016	28,507	+25,509		710,731
1936	1,086,663[1]	67,583	54,016	+13,567		1,090,230
1937	1,261,986[1]	41,626	67,583	–25,957		1,236,029

(1) As an example of the difficulty of understanding the mineral statistics of Malaya, I must point out that the totals for the years 1936 & 1937 given above disagree radically with those given in Table 13, entitled, "Method of Recovery and Sales of Ore in Individual States," of the issue for September, 1938 of the Quarterly Bulletin of Statistics Relating to the Mining Industry. In that table, showing the data separately for each State in F.M.S., the total for 1936 is given as 1,439,288 pikuls against 1,086,663 pikuls in the statement given above, and 1,671,508 pikuls for 1937 against 1,261,986 in the foregoing statement. /

Whilst stocks on mines have been recorded by the Mines Department for 4 years only, the Department has been able to supply me with data of production as ascertained by sales, with values estimated on the average market-price of the year, for 8 years, namely 1930 to 1937. These data are show in the following table:

Year	Pikuls	$
1930	1,041,117	76,464,113
1931	850,979	50,644,547
1932	445,839	30,732,530
1933	401,411	40,137,085
1934	547,112	42,593,476
1935	685,222	72,215,424

ese date are not, however, as has been show above, true figures of production as they have not been corrected for changes of stocks on the mines.

For the years prior to 1930 there are no available figures of production, and consequently it is necessary in a general statement of the output of tin in Malaya to make use of the export statistics, the weights and values of which are recorded by the Customs Department of the F.M.S. and are utilised by Mines Department in their Statistical Bulletins. It should be explained that all the tin-ore production in the Federated Malay States and the Unfederated States is exported for smelting, either to the Straits Smelting Company in Singapore, or the Eastern Smelting Company in Penang, with the exception of the small quantity smelted by the Chinese smelting firm, the Tan Ban Joo Company at Pudu, near Kuala Lumpur, which is exported in the form of block tin. The exports from the Federated Malay States therefore consists of two section – namely block tin and concentrates, which are recorded as tin-in-ore on the assumption of an assay value of 75.5% of tin. As / an example, the figure for the three years 1935–1937 are recorded below:

Exports of tin-ore and tin.

YEAR	BLOCK TIN		TIN-IN-ORE		TOTAL TIN	
	Pikuls	Tons	Pikuls	Tons	Pikuls	Tons
1935	3,184¼	189½	681,384	40,559	684,569	40,749
1936	5,624	334	1,081,649	64,385	1,087,273	64,719
1937	5,307	316	1,261,291	75,077	1,266,598	75,393

It will be realised from this that the only satisfactory way in which we can study the production in Malaya for so long a period as forty years is by making use of the exports in terms of metal. This is done in Table 14 for the F.M.S., the figures for 1931 to 1937 being production as ascertained by sales. I found it necessary to use these figures rather than exports in order to show production by separate states. The same table also shows the data for Malacca and the totals for the U.M.S. The details of the exports by Unfederated States are shown in Tabel 15#. Table 16 gives the totals and quinquennial averages for Malaya as a whole. These totals differ throughout from those given in Statistical Year Book 1938 of the International Tin Research & Development Council. The latter are presumably based on total exports from Malaya without allowing for inter-State trade.

I am indebted to the Statistical section of the Colonial Office Library for much help in the compilation of Tables 14, 15 and 17.

25. In the case of other metals we have been content with a statement of production in terms of separate states. Tin, however, is of such viral importance to Malaya that the distribution of activities from district to district within the various States is of much interest. In the F.M.S. the Mines Department has been able to provide me with data of output as determined by sales in pikuls, district by district, from the years 1904 in the case of Pahang, 1910 in the case of Selangor, and 1911 in the

District Sales of Tin-ore F.M.S.

TABLE 14 – Exports (1898 to 1930) and Production (1931 to 1937) of Tin from the Federated Malay States.

YEAR	Negri Sembilan Tons.	£	Pahang. Tons.	£	Perak Tons.	£	Selangor Tons.	£
1898	2,746	204,291	631	46,943	19,703	1,465,914	16,489	1,226,818
1899	3,410	431,751	803	101,684	18,960	2,400,311	15,180	1,921,801
1900	4,301	592,193	936	128,949	21,166	2,914,544	16,041	2,208,846
1901	4,479	541,911	1,330	160,887	22,921	2,773,375	18,012	2,179,421
1902	4,376	530,322	1,376	166,741	24,159	2,928,107	15,569	2,008,218
1903	5,089	643,771	1,504	189,282	25,949	3,282,605	17,420	2,203,687
1904	5,051	642,680	1,635	208,644	26,399	3,359,302	17,882	2,276,441
1905	5,067	701,945	2,076	287,587	26,594	3,683,837	17,254	2,390,038
1906	4,629	815,984	1,605	356,879	24,718	4,343,979	15,989	2,780,310
1907	4,473	747,737	1,976	330,266	25,678	4,292,008	16,304	2,725,122
1908	3,823	500,347	2,352	307,897	27,844	3,644,504	16,818	2,201,269
1909	2,861	381,794	2,568	339,970	27,480	3,606,082	15,834	2,073,416
1910	2,065	313,224	2,421	368,773	25,079	3,807,968	14,297	2,172,590
1911	1,740	320,845	2,616	481,829	26,032	4,795,679	13,760	2,534,516
1912	1,730	349,769	2,890	628,597	28,407	5,757,793	15,201	3,079,388
1913	1,884	368,189	3,433	667,057	29,403	5,725,704	15,406	2,997,471
1914	1,697	244,986	3,685	509,460	28,557	4,138,593	15,103	2,167,531
1915	1,244	189,699	3,808	584,430	27,771	4,255,603	13,938	2,135,236
1916	907	155,887	3,480	596,228	27,241	4,675,379	12,241	2,099,072
1917	733	157,349	3,498	744,508	24,643	5,264,215	10,960	2,323,541
1918	625	181,969	3,017	883,517	22,983	6,794,986	10,744	3,171,762
1919	879	207,825	3,299	780,375	22,126	6,233,598	10,631	2,514,682
1920	697	205,840	3,252	960,330	22,134	6,536,406	8,852	2,614,137
1921	851	141,766	3,357	559,474	21,041	3,507,052	9,242	1,540,456
1922	959	151,619	3,207	506,931	21,848	3,453,216	9,271	1,465,352
1923	1,072	213,864	2,953	588,959	24,772	4,940,332	8,852	1,765,347
1924	956	232,633	3,155	767,865	29,840	7,263,310	10,093	2,456,814
1925	1,004	259,263	3,014	778,465	30,734	7,937,944	11,174	2,886,099
1926	697	197,585	2,871	813,685	30,702	8,700,843	11,677	3,309,091
1927	806	228,975	2,339	664,352	36,319	10,316,840	12,716	3,612,163
1928	1,739	389,093	2,762	618,121	41,031	9,182,485	16,403	3,670,855
1929	1,883	385,125	2,910	595,350	42,751	8,745,703	19,499	3,988,920
1930	1,554	221,967	2,726	389,493	39,825	5,689,566	17,960	2,565,845
1931	1,535	178,960	2,332	272,524	32,506	3,787,641	14,281	1,669,416
1932	865	117,234	1,245	167,510	16,453	2,221,448	7,975	1,079,269
1933	658	128,939	1,069	209,431	15,034	2,946,273	7,133	1,398,017
1934	980	220,016	1,443	323,799	20,203	4,530,270	9,941	2,228,487
1935	1,279	279,541	1,771	388,589	25,048	5,458,342	12,689	2,767,327
1936	1,769	349,016	2,760	542,140	39,038	7,700,627	21,115	4,169,353
1937	2,510	578,705	3,158	723,342	44,874	10,390,259	24,576	5,722,151
1938								

Footnotes to Table 14.

Total., F.M.S.		Quinquennial Averages.			
Tons.	£	Tons.	£	$	YEAR.
39,569	2,943,966				1898
38,353	4,855,547				1899
42,444	5,844,532				1900
46,742	5,655,594	43,925	5,208,729	44,646,249	1901
46,480	5,633,388				1902
49,962	6,319,346				1903
50,967	6,486,067				1904
50,991	7,063,407				1905
46,941	8,297,152	49,633	7,319,155	62,735,614	1906
48,431	8,095,133				1907
50,837	6,656,017				1908
48,743	6,401,262				1909
43,862	6,662,555				1910
44,148	8,132,869	47,021	8,154,130	69,892,543	1911
48,228	9,815,547				1912
50,126	9,758,421				1913
49,042	7,080,570				1914
46,761	7,164,968				1915
43,869	7,526,566	43,375	8,258,790	70,789,629	1916
39,832	8,489,613				1917
37,369	11,032,234				1918
36,935	8,736,480				1919
34,935	10,316,713				1920
34,491	5,748,748	35,859	7,577,512	64,950,103	1921
35,285	5,577,118				1922
37,649	7,508,502				1923
44,044	10,720,622				1924
45,926	11,861,771				1925
45,947	13,021,204	50,006	12,857,296	110,205,394	1926
52,180	14,822,330				1927
61,935	13,860,554				1928
67,043	13,715,098				1929
62,065	8,866,871				1930
50,654	5,908,531	46,039	7,351,724	63,014,777	1931
26,538	3,585,461				1932
23,894	4,682,660				1933
32,567	7,302,572				1934
40,787	8,891,799				1935
64,682	12,761,136	53,289	11,592,491	99,364,209	1936
75,118	17,414,457				1937
					1938 /

TABLE 15 – Exports of Tin from the Unfederated Malay States, 1909–1937

YEAR	JOHORE Tons	£.	KEDAH Tons	£.	KELANTAN Tons	£.	PERLIS Tons	£.
1909			536	64,078[e]	3	395	98	13,230[c]
1910	245[a]	50,548[d]	505	75,936	17	3,381	113	17,515[c]
1911	198	33,223[d]	546	91,553	20	3,796	77	12,475
1912	222	42,000	609	111,338	14	2,710	142	26,407[d]
1913	332	61,833	608	112,472	4	1,011	82	15,363[d]
1914	608	84,000	619	84,504	6	804	141	19,250
1915	2,046	301,933	625	83,238	4	637	173	24,525
1916	2,453	415,158	489	75,502	–	–	158	24,563[d]
1917	2,355	485,450	343	80,615	–	–	148	24,563[d]
1918	1,689	491,283	X	x	–	–	117	29,968[d]
1919	1,329	307,790	518	110,529[d]	1.4	588[d]	85	17,347[d]
1920	1,586[f]	466,200	372	101,416[d]	2	686	195	50,904[d]
1921	1,493[f]	244,654	115	17,696	2.8	459	180	24,186[d]
1922	1,490[f]	237,836	276	37,022[d]	1.7	297	347	44,349[d]
1923	957	214,486	435	71,983	.6	97	270	44,457[d]
1924	1,015	274,037	265	55,533[d]	–	–	393	78,622[d]
1925	1,400[b]	354,669	278	88,868	.9	204	253	45,062[d]
1926	1,039[f]	293,843	243	79,606	.4	89	301	71,244[d]
1927	975[f]	272,924	289	55,766	2.5	758	249	66,267[d]
1928	1,097[f]	237,741	285	66,766	3	702	415	86,793[d]
1929	672	137,630	268	53,555[d]	1.2	208	421	84,134[d]
1930	516	73,692	342	49,030[d]	2.4	443	419	60,073[d]
1931	426	47,602[d]	148	16,538[d]	2	223[d]	321	35,869[d]
1932	305	39,499[d]	119	15,411[d]	–	–	483	62,551[d]
1933	219	40,920[d]	113	21,114[d]	1	187[d]	312	58,297[d]
1934	393	81,842[d]	158	32,903[d]	3	625[d]	432	89,963[d]
1935	604	119,136[d]	200	39,449[d]	6	1,183[d]	323	63,710[d]
1936	755	138,690[d]	308	56,578[d]	20	3,674[d]	458	85,799[d]
1937	814	191,129[d]	341	80,096[d]	34	7,986[d]	456	107,109[d]
1938								

Source of data: Figures of quantity of metal, Perlis, 1909–1937, received direct from British Adviser, Perlis; and of quantity and value of tin-ore, Trengganu, 1909–1937, direct from British Adviser, Trengganu; other data obtained for Johore, 1910–1925, for Kedah & Kelantan, 1909–1917, and Perlis, 1911,–1914, 1915, from Dominions and Colonial Statistical Abstracts, supplemented for later years up to 1930 by data from State Annual Reports. 1931–1932 exports of tin obtained from Malaya Foreign Exports Annual Summaries. 1933–1937 from Annual Reports, Mines Dept. In many cases values are not given and have been estimated as stated in notes below:

(a) Quantity figures in italics calculated from weights of tin-ore on assumption of 72% metallic contents up to 1933, and thereafter 75.5%

(b) Quantity of metal calculated from value at £252 per ton in 1925.

(c) Values given in Statistical Abstracts is an obvious overstatement. Valued at £135 per ton for 1909 and £155 per ton for 1910.

TRENGGANU TOTAL – U.M.S. QUINQUENNIAL AVERAGES

Tons	£.	Tons	£.	Tons	£.	$
261	31,500	898	109,203			
257	36,537	1,137	183,917			
307	53,324	1,148	194,371	1,145	192,864	1,653,120
290	56,607	1,277	239,062			
238	47,086	1,264	237,765			
273	39,667	1,647	228,225			
287	44,256	3,135	454,589			
342	55,825	3,442	571,048	2,725	507,527	4,350,231
310	54,535	3,156	645,163			
437	117,357	2,243	638,608			
454	96,713	2,387.4	532,967			
348	94,930	2,503	714,136			
287	40,378	2,077.8	327,373	2,279	464,562	3,981,960
310	41,553	2,424.7	361,057			
341	56,253	2,003.6	387,276			
427	89,489	2,100	497,681			
842	157,379	2,773.9	646,182			
549	136,238	2,132.4	581,020	2,456	594,072	5,092,076
839	223,944	2,354.5	619,659			
1,118	233,817	2,918	625,819			
952	190,241	2,341.2	465,768			
738	105,808	2,017.4	289,046			
493	55,089	1,390	155,321	1,585	249,400	2,139,000
400	51,802	1,307	169,263			
252	47,086	897	167,604			
366	76,219	1,352	281,552			
399	78,701	1,532	302,179			
480	88,174	2,021	372,915	1,745	360,933	3,093,711
429	100,767	2,074	487,087			

(e) Values from 1909–1917 stated to include value of wolfram produced: but values per ton approximately similar to those of Trengganu for tin-ore in same years: hence no deduction made for value of wolfram.

(f) Given as tin-ore: but value shows that it must be metal.

x. Figures not available. /

TABLE 16 – Production of Tin from Malaya, 1898 to 1937, as represented by Exports from 1898 to 1930, and Sales (F.M.S.) and Exports (U.M.S.) from 1931 to 1937

Year	Tons	£.	Tons	£.	$
			Quinquennial Averages.		
1898	39,589	2,943,966			
1899	38,353	4,855,547			
1900	42,444	5,844,532	43,925	5,208,729	44,646,249
1901	46,742	5,655,594			
1902	46,480	5,633,388			
1903	49,962	6,319,345			
1904	50,967	6,486,067			
1905	50,991	7,063,407			
1906	46,941	8,297,152	49,633	7,319,155	62,735,614
1907	48,431	8,095,133			
1908	50,837	6,654,017			
1909	49,641	6,510,465			
1910	44,999	6,846,472			
1911	45,296	8,327,240	48,166	8,346,994	71,545,663
1912	49,505	10,054,609			
1913	51,390	9,996,186			
1914	50,689	7,308,795			
1915	49,896	7,619,557			
1916	47,311	8,097,614	46,100	8,766,317	75,139,860
1917	42,988	9,134,776			
1918	39,612	11,670,842			
1919	39,322	9,269,447			
1920	37,438	11,030,849			
1921	36,569	6,076,121	38,138	8,042,074	68,932,063
1922	37,710	5,938,175			
1923	39,653	7,895,778			
1924	46,144	11,218,303			
1925	48,700	12,507,953			
1926	48,079	13,602,224	52,462	13,451,368	115,297,470
1927	54,535	15,441,989			
1928	64,853	14,486,373			
1929	69,357	14,180,866			
1930	64,082	9,155,917			
1931	52,044	6,063,852	47,684	7,601,124	65,153,777
1932	27,845	3,754,724			
1933	24,791	4,850,264			
1934	33,919	7,584,124			
1935	42,319	9,193,978			
1936	66,703	13,134,051	55,034	11,953,424	102,457,920
1937	77,192	17,901,544			
1938					/

		1904–1908 Pikuls	1909–1913 Pikuls	1914–1918 Pikuls	1919–1923 Pikuls	1924–1928 Pikuls	1929–1933 Pikuls	1934–1937 Pikuls
Negri Sembilan	(Jelobu	—	15,008 ø	11,090	8,322	3,538	3,613	6,146
	(Kuala Pilah	—	1,234 ø	1,810	910	140	–	–
	(Port Dickson	—	184 ø	1,181	638	945	2,648	2,377
	(Seramban	—	26,949 ø	12,699	11,357	18,010	23,856	27,848
	Totals:	—	43,375 ø	26,780	21,227	22,633	30,117	36,371
Pahang	(Coast	17,046	29,133	35,047+	32,857	32,912	26,904	37,451
	(Ulu Pahang	16,856	18,313	23,711+	20,353	15,321	8,856	13,351
	Totals:	33,902	47,446	58,758	53,210	48,233	35,760	50,802
Perak	(Batang Padang		25,049 ø	23,193	12,735	22,181	66,638	69,510
	(Kinta Valley		553,940 ø	516,847	398,478	638,038	542,047	567,777
	(Kuala Kangsar		23,017 ø	15,379	11,517	13,476	14,041	19,467
	(Larut		38,175 ø	59,375	54,182	92,823	41,265	48,548
	(Upper Perak	—	–	13,686 x	16,049	19,998	15,615	13,222
	Totals:	—	640,181	617,531	492,961	786,516	679,606	718,524
Selangor	(Kuala Lumpur		204,426	156,689	121,764	174,673	208,102	267,074
	(Ulu Langat		17,876 xx	14,842	6,543	12,995	27,371	41,929
	(Ulu Selangor		56,850 xxx	85,925	62,514	84,641	74,479	71,058
	Totals:		279,152	257,456	190,821	272,309	309,952	380,061

The Pahang figures refer to metal from 1904 to 1927. The data for 1928 to 1937 have also been converted to metal on a basis of 75% tin.
ø Average of three years 1911–1913.
Average of four years, the 1917 figures by districts being unavailable.
x Quantity for 1918
xx Average of four years 1910–1913.
Xxx Based on the average of 119, 868 tons for 1913, and outputs for 1910, 1911, 1912, of 18,832, 30,274 and 58,432 tons tin-ore deduced from totals of ore plus metal for Selangor on the assumption of 75% metal recovery. /

From a study of these data it will be seen that by far the most important district is the Kinta Valley in Perak State, which appears to be the richest stanniferous tract in the world. The next most important district is Kuala Lumpur, shown in three section in the statistics, followed at a long distance by Batang Padang in Perak and Ulu Selangor in Selangor. The production of Batang Padang is probably much less than it may be in the future, for at present a large portion of the district is closed to mining on account of priority given to other interests. The Larut district in Perak is of much historical importance, because it is in this district that Chinese activity first became manifest many decades ago, leading to British intervention in Perak. The importance of the coast district in Pahang lies mainly in the presence therein of the Pahang Consolidated Company's mine at Sungei Lembing.

26. [...] Anyone who has had any contact with the Chinese mining community of Malaya must be filled with unbounded admiration at the ingenuity of their methods of winning tin, both in the hills and in the plains, and with the assiduity with which they work; and no one will contradict the statement that from the earliest times in which there has been a mining industry in Malaya, the Chinese with their labour have been the backbone. Owing to their individualism, however, they appear to find combination into units of any size a difficulty, and the consequence is that Chinese enterprises are normally on a smaller scale than those of Europeans (the Hong Fatt Mine is a notable exception). The Chinese methods are eminently / suitable for many types of occurrences of tin-ore in this country, and especially for those for which any very considerable capital outlay is unnecessary. Certain types of deposits in Malaya are, however, suitable only for treatment by large-scale methods employing a considerable capital. I refer principally to dredging propositions, particularly to those dealing with considerable thicknesses of tin-bearing alluvium, in which dredging can be resorted to profitably only if the largest and most up-to-date types of dredge are used. With the progressive exhaustion of the more easily won deposits and the closure of much of Malaya to prospecting of recent years it is not surprising, therefore, that the balance of relative importance of Chinese activity to that of Europeans' in the tin-mining industry of Malaya should have changed during recent years. This is shown by Table 18, from which it will be seen that, whereas in 1910 only 22 per cent. of the output was derived from mines owned, managed or financed by European capital, and 78 per cent. from these owned and managed exclusively by Chinese, by 1937 the European proportion had risen to 68 per cent. and the Chinese proportion had fallen to 32 per cent.

TABLE 18. Percentage Output of European and Chinese Mines.

Year.	European Mines	Chinese Mines
1910	22%	78%
1911	23%	77%
1912	20%	80%
1913	26%	74%
1914	24%	76%
1915	28%	72%
1916	32%	68%
1917	29%	71%
1918	32%	68%
1919	32%	68%
1920	36%	64%
1921	39%	61%
1922	38%	62%
1923	44%	56%
1924	45%	55%
1925	44%	56%
1926	44%	56%
1927	41%	59%
1928	49%	51%
1929	61%	39%
1930	63%	37%
1931	65%	35%
1932	66%	34%
1933	66%	34%
1934	66%	34%
1935	66%	34%
1936	67%	33%
1937	68%	32% /

ese figures do not, however, mean such a drastic decline in Chinese activity as they seem at first to suggest, for they must be viewed in relationship to the actual production of Malaya. This was 45,918 tons in 1910 and 77,542 tons in 1937, corresponding to the production by Chinese mines of about 35,700 in 1910 and 24,700 tons in 1937. It must not be overlooked, however, that in the worst year this century for the Malayan tin industry, namely 1933, when the production was only 24,904 tons, the Chinese proportion could only have been about 8,500 tons.

27. Of much interest in a study of the Malayan tin industry is the relative importance of the various methods of winning tin. This is show in Table 19, relating to the year 1937. As this year is the year of maximum output in Malaya it perhaps gives the best idea of the potentialities of the different methods available for winning tin-ore as applicable to the Malayan deposits at present being worked.

gures of 1936 are included in the table, but only in total and not by sepa-

Relative importance of various methods of recovery.

of course show the great change that has been produced by the introduction of dredging, which in its application to Malaya dates from 1913. Whilst dredging has been undertaken only by European enterprises, the Chinese are engaged in working by all the other methods listed:

TABLE 19. Production of Tin-ore, Federated Malay States, 1936 and 1937, as judged by sales, according to Method of Recovery.
Pikuls of Tin-ore

Year	State	Dredging	Gravel Pumping	Hydrau- licing	Open cast	Lode	Alluvial shafting	Dulang washers	Samples & sweepings	Total
1936	Total F.M.S.	677,675	552,591	70,074	56,923	56,903	906	22,866	1,350	1,439,288
	Perak	445,753	460,709	64,569	8,668	1,768	649	15,326	1,097	998,539
	Selangor	310,843	168,861	448	57,393	3,394	187	5,352	358	546,836
1937	Negri Sembilam	44,475	7,569	2,185	507	–	21	1,095	4	55,856
	Pehang	3,488	1,768	5,063	636	58,725	–	590	7	70,277
	Total F.M.S.	804,559	638,907	72,265	67,204	63,887	857	22,363	1,466	1,671,508 /

36. In Table 29 [not included] I have put together for the period 1926–1937 the data of world's production, world's apparent tin consumption, the annual excess of production over consumption or the reverse, with cumulative totals, and also the average annual price of tin. From this Table it will be seen that the continuous fall in the price of tin from 1926 to 1931 can be correlated with a continuous surplus of production over consumption during this period from a figure of – 2,700 tons in 1926 to a cumulative total of 41,100 tons in 1931.

It was in this year that the first International Tin Control Scheme was introduced; and it is interesting to notice that it took five years for an annual excess of production over consumption to convert the minus of 1926 into the maximum plus figure of 1931, but that two years of control with production below consumption were sufficient to reduce the running total in column five to a minus figure again, a figure which continued to increase to – 15,800 tons in 1935. This reversal from 1931 resulted in a steady increase in the annual average price of tin from £118.4 in 1931 to £230.4 in 1934. In 1935 a close balance between consumption and production was effected, production being 147,100 tons and consumption 149,200 tons, with an average price for the year of £225.7. Thereafter tin consumption rose rapidly to a maximum of 198,300 tons in 1937, which must be the highest consumption hitherto recorded; and although the world's production increased to a still larger figure – namely 208,400 tons, also the highest ever recorded – the price rose to an average of £242.3, the highest since 1927.

[...]

TUNGSTEN-ORES.

Occurrence.

e two principal sources of tungsten of commercial value are the tungstate of iron and manganese, known as wolfram or wolframite, and the tungstate of calcium, known as scheelite, the latter mineral being much the less common. Both minerals are found in Malaya, and their distribution and geological relationship are alluded to briefly in the Geological Outline forming Section II. Malaya is perhaps fortunate in that the tungsten deposits of the country usually occur separately from the tin-ores, so that regulation of the output of tin under the International Control Scheme has not also involved regulation of the output of tungsten. In Burma, where a much larger proportion of tin is derived from lodes, almost all such occurrences consist of mixed tin and wolfram ores, so that it is not practicable to control the production of tin from Burma without also controlling the production of wolfram. This is the principal reason why Burma has not adhered to the International Control Scheme for tin.

Production.

42. The facts of production of tungsten-ores in Malaya, both of quantity and values, in so far as they are obtainable, are shown in Table 32. Beginning with the initial production of one ton in 1901, which happened to be from Negri Sembilan, the output gradually expanded, showing a sudden and marked increase in the War quinquennium when the output of these ores became so important for munitions purposes, a time when also the wolfram of Tavoy in Lower Burma showed such a great expansion. The Malayan maximum production at that time was 1,494 tons in 1918. This fell to 1,206 tons in 1919, and thereafter the industry rapidly subsided to much smaller figures, so that the quinquennial average for 1924–1928 was only 280 tons as compared with the average of 857 tons for the quinquennium 1914–1918. With the discovery, however, of the large scheelite deposit of / Kramat Pulai in Perak, the industry has once more blossomed forth, with the result that the quinquennial average for the period 1928–1933 increased to 716 tons, while for the four years, 1934–1937, of the present quinquennium, the average has been 1,494 tons, the same as the maximum production of the War period, the actual peak production of tungsten-ores in Malaya being 1,639 tons in 1936. This recent large increase in the Malayan production of tungsten-ores has, of course, been encouraged by the high prices due to the revived demand for these ores for munitions purposes. The output must, however, fall off in the near future, unless there are discoveries of fresh sources of supply, because the remarkable scheelite deposit at Kramat Pulai, according to the last annual report of the operating Company, has only a further life of one or two years, exploratory operations to prove further extensions of the deposit having been disappointing.

ere was a trivial import of Scheelite during 1937, amounting to 1.02 tons

TABLE 32. Production of Tungsten Ores in Malaya, 1901 to 1937

| | SCHEELITE | | | | | | WOLFRAM | | | | TOTAL WOLFRAM, F.M.S | | TOTAL TUNGSTEN-ORE F.M.S. | | Johore | |
| | Perak | | Negri Sembilan | | Pahang | | Perak | | Selangor | | | | | | | |
YEAR	Tons	$	Tons	$	Tons	$	Tons	$	Tons	$	Tons	$	Tons	$	Tons	$
	–	–	1	300a	–	–	–	–	–	–	1	300	1	300	–	–
1902	–	–	3	945	–	–	–	–	–	–	3	945	3	945	–	–
1903	–	–			–	–	x	27,663	–	–	X	27,663	x	27,663	–	–
1904	–	–				–	x	11,556	–	–	X	11,556	x	11,556	–	–
1905	–	–	–	–	–	–	–	–	4	846	4	846	4	846	–	–
1906	–	–	–	–	–	–	–	–	15	4,541	15	4,541	15	4,541	–	–
1907	–	–	–	–			–	–	–	–	–	–	–	–	–	–
1908	–	–	–	–		–	–	–	10	3,241	10	3,241	10	3,241	–	–
1909	1	346	1	278	–	–	56	34,174	31	14,603	87	49,055	88	49,401	–	–
1910	2	700a	–	–	–	–	60	x	34	x	94	47,400	96	48,100	–	–
1911	1.5	1,368d	2	X	2	x	71	x	93	x	168	84,500	169.5	85,868	–	–
1912	3	1,796d	–	–	–	–	134	x	90	x	224	140,217	227	142,013	–	–
1913	18	16,776d	34	X	5	x	53	x	114	x	206	138,824	224	155,600	–	–
1914	29	25,213d	3	X	–	–	36	x	193	x	232	155,904	261	181,117	–	–
1915	57	70,945d	x	X	–	–	x	x	x	x	235	275,779	292	346,724	2@	x
1916	204	312,557d	x	X	–	–	x	x	x	x	311	476,496d	515	789,053	23	21,600
1917	340	568,286d	x	X	–	–	–	–	x	x	421	703,671d	761	1,271,957	2	2,200
1918	112	187,200d	4	X	–	–	20	x	220	x	244	407,829d	356	595,029	.65	800
1919	228	227,571d	1	X	–	–	6	x	200	x	207	206,611d	435	434,182	.3	400
1920	120	97,143d	–	–	–	–	–	–	113	x	113	34,815d	233	131,958	–	–
1921	–	–	–	–	–	–	–	–	55	x	55	20,684d	55	20,684	–	–
1922	.4	138d	39	X	–	–	–	–	56	x	95	32,842d	95.4	32,980	–	–
1923	–	–	38	10,367	–	–	–	–	–	–	38	10,367	38	10,367	–	–
1924S	89S	69,944	8	2,390	–	–	–	–	–	–	8	2,390	97	72,334	–	–
1925S	27S	8,973	17	X	–	–	8	x	106	x	131	56,869	158	65,842	–	–
1926x	40	27,727	–	–	–	–	4	1,120	55	19,270	59	20,390	99	48,117	–	–
1927	–	–	x	X	–	–	x	x	x	x	20	7,384	20	7,384	–	–
1928	–	–	–	–	–	–	5	800	–	–	5	800	5	800	–	–
1929	275	214,010	30	7,664	–	–	2	3,088	12	5,307	44	16,059	319	230,069	–	–
1930	792	521,741	–	–	–	–	55	x	10	x	65	34,196	857	555,937	–	–
1931	368	190,051	–	–	–	–	–	–	–	–	–	–	368	190,051	–	–
1932	302	96,350	–	–	–	–	–	–	–	–	–	–	302	96,350	–	–
1933	918	340,760	–	–	–	–	25	10,808	8	3,900	33	14,708	951	355,468	–	–
1934	1,508	1,594,754	.49	380	–	–	15	13,000	13	6,660	28	20,040	1,536	1,614,794	–	–
1935	1,365	1,608,714	2	1,121	–	–	3	2,000	3	1,860	8	4,981	1,373	1,613,695	–	–
1936	1,364	1,592,838	1	461	–	–	–	–	2	1,198	3	1,659	1,367	1,594,497	–	–
1937	836	1,238,065	1	1,064	3	3,926	19	5,214	4	2,760	27	12,964	863	1,251,029	.13	32

The figures for 1909 to 1922 are the total exports of scheelite from F.M.S.

S includes 15 tons of scheelite value not known, exported from Selangor in 1924 and 1925.

includes 26 tons of scheelite valued at $ 14,079, exported from Selangor in 1926.

a. Crude estimate based on figures for adjoining years.

b. Export figures.

c. Estimated at same value per ton as F.M.S. production.

	UNFEDERATED MALAY STATES WOLFRAM					TOTAL TUNGESTEN-ORE MALAYA		QUINQUENNIAL AVERAGES, MALAYA.			YEAR
Kedah		Trengganu		Total U.M.S.							
Tons	$	Tons	$	Tons	$	Tons	$	Tons	$	£	
–	–	–	–	–	–	1	300				1901
–	–	–	–	–	–	3	945	9,636	1,124		1902
–	–	–	–	–	–	–	27,663				1903
–	–	–	–	–	–	–	11,556				1904
–	–	–	–	–	–	4	846				1905
–	–	–	–	–	–	15	4,541	4,037	471		1906
–	–	–	–	–	–	–	–				1907
–	–	–	–	–	–	10	3,241				1908
.25b	x	–	–	.25c	140	88.25	49,541				1909
12b	x	–	–	12c	6,048d	108	54,148				1910
16b	x	–	–	16	14,614d	185.5	100,482	175.5	126,622	14,773	1911
22b	x	12	53,384	34	27,865d	161	169,878				1912
28b	x	83	67,215	111	103,463d	335	259,063				1913
25b	x	143	109,389	168	146,063d	429	327,180				1914
13b	x	143	147,561	158	196,656d	450	543,380				1915
17b	x	271	366,573	311	476,496d	826	1,265,549	857.13	1,290,246	150,529	1916
124b	x	201	270,227	327	546,543d	1,087	1,818,590				1917
520b	x	617	832,288	1,137.66	1,901,501d	1,493.65	2,496,530				1918
211	x	580	611,670	771.3	769,851d	1,206.3	1,204,033				1919
42	x	153	102,582	195	157,858d	428	289,816				1920
48	x	1	3,600	49	2,633d	104	23,317	498.74	367,997	41,766	1921
106	50,149	174	44,400	280	94,549	375.4	127,529				1922
62	49,815	280	85,110	342	134,925	380	145,292				1923
153	90,775	173	43,050	326	133,825	423	206,159				1924
117	76,689	77	20,326	194	97,015	352	162,857				1925
90	59,916	119	40,369	209	100,285	308	148,402	280.4	129,367	15,093	1926
70	35,526	58	18,592	128	54,118	148	61,502				1927
64	32,933	102	34,182	166	67,115	171	67,915				1928
108	114,959	71	23,882	179	138,841	498	368,910				1929
165	77,056	43	14,013	208	91,069	1,065	647,006				1930
167	64,417	23	7,608	190	72,225	558	262,278	718.4	361,402	42,164	1931
98	30,465	31	10,423	129	40,906	431	137,256				1932
55	26,937	24	9,159	79	36,096	1,030	391,564				1933
44	48,002	23	7,727	67	55,729	1,603	1,670,523				1934
168	160,891	93	70,662	261	231,553	1,634	1,845,248	1,493.78	1,748,400	203,980	1935
160	138,059	112	87,948	272	226,007	1,639	1,820,504				1936
138	231,653	98	174,641	236.13	406,294	1,099.13	1,657,323				1937
											1938

IMPORTS AND EXPORTS OF MINERAL PRODUCTS.

44. In addition to the minerals and metals dealt with in their respective section, the following statistics of imports or exports during 1937 have been recorded:–

TABLE 33. Imports and Exports of Mineral Products, Malaya, 1937

	IMPORTS		EXPORTS	
	Tons.	$	Tons.	$
Asphalt & bitumen	20,917	928,413	798	52,971
Precious stones	–	1,439	–	29
Sulphur (crude)	334	27,810	26	2,285
Scraps of tin plates	159	5,208	1,973	76,700
Scrap and old metal (non-ferrous)	2,186	446,777	2,302	658,371
Crude petroleum	78	8,034	0.04	4
Kerosene	125,258	13,174,255	88,647	9,771,271
Liquid fuel	701,311	22,482,555	227,154	7,875,897
Motor spirit	433,989	49,152,335	332,320	37,780,084
Paraffin wax	1,598	295,670	101	20,633
Lubricating oil (gallons)	4,800,867	2,978,904	617,127	478,574

Other mineral products for which the Annual Summaries contain import and export data, but for which I have not thought it necessary to reproduce the data here, are, taking them in their order of record: salt, coal tar and pitch, asbestos, bricks, chalk, crockery and porcelain, cement, earthenware, glass, tiles, flints, iron and steel and manufactories thereof, non-ferrous metals (including, in decreasing order of value, aluminium, brass, copper, lead, zinc, mercury and platinum, and inorganic chemicals, dyes, paints and colours).

NOETLING, *REPORT ON THE PETROLEUM INDUSTRY IN UPPER BURMA FROM THE END OF THE LAST CENTURY UP TO THE BEGINNING OF 1891* (1892)

F. Noetling, *Report on the Petroleum Industry in Upper Burma from the End of the Last Century up to the Beginning of 1891* (Rangoon: Government Printing Office, 1892), pp. 51–67, 72–3.

Friedrich Wilhelm Noetling (1857–1928) worked as a geologist for the Geological Survey of India. His report describes the relatively ignored early history of the Burmese oil industry. Its broad findings are that previous estimates of the number of wells and outputs are incorrect and that production probably steadily increased from 1795 to approximately 1873, after which there was a continuous decline until 1885 when output again rose. Towards the end of the report, Noe-

writes, 'Burma will in the close future rank amongst the most important oil-bearing countries'; a prediction that was more than fulfilled. As discussed in the thematic introduction, the sector grew rapidly from the turn of the century and, by 1913, was producing approximately 250m gallons pa.[1]

1. N. Nishizawa, 'Economic Development of Burma', *Institute of Peace Studies, Hiroshima University, Japan, Research Report*, 16 (1991), pp. 1–55, on p. 66.

F. Noetling, *Report on the Petroleum Industry in Upper Burma from the End of the Last Century up to the Beginning of 1891* (1892), extract

Table No. 58 showing the number of wells, their average daily yield, and the monthly production of the Yenangyaung oil-field as estimated for different periods in the past.

Year.	Total number of wells.	Number of productive wells.	Number of unproductive wells.	Average daily yield per well in viss.	Monthly production.	
1795 – 97	130	70	60	171	359,100	Estimate of the
1826	200	107	93	142	455,820	monthly production
1855	243	130	113	113	440,700	probably too low.
1873	280	150	130	98	441,000	Ditto.
1874	400	214	186	91		
1885	538	245	289	51	375,000	
1890	602	373	229	78	563,452	

As regards the figures of the Table No. 58 I believe that the estimate for 1855 is too low probably on account of too small a number of productive wells. The estimate for 1873 is perhaps a little too low; but if we, however, take the same average yield for the productive wells in 1874 we arrive at a monthly production of over 6 lakhs of viss per month, an estimate which is certainly too high. The average yield per well must therefore be somewhat lower.

[...]

e following table will show the annual production of the oil-fields in Upper Burma during the last 13 financial years: –

Table No. 59 showing the production of the oil-fields in Upper Burma in

Financial year.	Viss at lbs. 3·65.	Gallons at lbs 8·83.	Barrels at 35 gallons.	Remarks.
1878 – 79	1,916,769	792,053	22,630	Estimated, the year being one of political disturbance it is rather doubtful whether these figures even approximately represent the actual output; it is more likely that they are below the mark.
1879 – 80	3,724,128	1,538,896	43,968	Estimated, the estimated, is based on the statement
1880 – 81	4,434,865	1,832,588	52,379	of a late Burmese minister, that about 15·6 lakhs of viss or 32·5 per cent. of the annual production were consumed in Upper Burma, the rest was exported to Lower Burma. The import of crude oil was registered at Thayetmyo and this quantity was accordingly estimated at 67·5 per cent. of the total production. The production of Yenangyat is estimated at viss 100,000.
1881 – 82	3,416,234	1,411,666	40,333	Estimated, see note above, the import has, however, decreased, and it only amounts to 61·5 per
1882 – 83	4,221,630	1,744,475	49,842	cent. of the total production. It is supposed that
1883 – 84	3,980,528	1,644,846	46,995	during these three years the proportion between consumption in Upper Burma and export into Lower Burma has not changed; production of Yenangyat as before. /
1884 – 85	4,577,556	1,891,552	54,044	Estimated, if however the same proportion of con
1885 – 86	4,528,667	1,871,350	53,467	sumption and import (38·5, 61·5) would have been used for the calculation of the production, the result of 62 and 63 lakhs of viss would apparently be too high. The rate of imported oil must therefore be necessarily higher, and it is supposed that it is the same as in 1886 – 87, namely, 82·2 per cent. of the total production; this may be too much, and the actual production may therefore be a little higher than the estimate. Production of Yenangyat as before.
1886 – 87	4,982,900	2,059,049	58,829	For this year the production of Yenangyat cannot
1887 – 88	5,685,710	2,349,467	67,127	be estimated higher than 90,000 viss.
1888 – 89	6,433,330	2,650,136	75,718	Actual production.
1889 – 90	7,242,260	2,992,669	85,505	
1890 – 91	11,577,621	4,784,140	136,690	Estimated, the actuals up to end of December 1890 amounted to –

	Viss.
(*a*) Native wells, Yenangyaung	7,062,901
(*b*) Drilled wells, Yenangyaung	3,235,950
(*c*) Native wells, Yenangyat	79,500
Total	10,398,351

gures in this table may be considered as fairly correct, as they are based on the returns about the import of crude oil into Lower Burma during this period. As there was only one highway on which the oil could be transported to Lower Burma, namely, the Irrawaddy, the figures about the quantity of import must be as correct as possible provided the records were kept properly. As we further know that previous to the influx of kerosine-oil from America about one-third of the production was consumed in Upper Burma we are enabled to conclude from the amount of imported oil to the amount of the production, and I dare say that the figures thus obtained will be pretty near the mark. We see that from till 1884 the production fluctuates between 34 and 44 lakhs of viss per year; the statememt of the Burmese Minister, that the production has declined since 1881, is therefore strongly supported. From 1884 the production steadily rises, and has risen to the unprecedented maximum of 115 lakhs of viss in the nancial year. As records about the monthly production are kept since April the figures for the last five years are accurate. Now we see that since the last ve years the production has increased at the rate of 133 per cent. of its amount in 1885 – 86. If a similar rise could be predicted with certainty for the years to come the future of the Burmese oil-fields would be very rosy.

Annual production during the last five years. – We might finish here this section, but as the last five years are the period of the largest revolution the Burmese oil production has ever gone through, it will be interesting to dwell a little longer on the subject of production.

e following table will show the annual production of the pit and drilled wells in the Magwe district during the last five calendar years: – /

Table No. 60 showing the production of the oil-fields in the Magwe district from 1886 to 1890.

	PRODUCTION OF NATIVE WELLS.			PRODUCTION OF DRILLED WELLS.			TOTAL.		
	Viss at lbs. 3·65.	Gallons at lbs.8·83.	Barrels at 35 gallons.	Viss at lbs. 3·65.	Gallons at lbs. 8·83.	Barrels at 35 gallons.	Viss at lbs. 3·65.	Gallons at lbs. 8·83.	Barrels at 35 gallons.
1886	3,418,090	1,412,433	40,355				3,418,090	1,412,443	40,355
1887	5,651,200	2,335,205	66,720				5,651,200	2,335,205	66,720
1888	6,125,430	2,531,169	72,319	41,590	17,186	491	6,167,020	2,548,355	72,810
1889	6,408,650	2,648,202	75,662	427,130	176,500	5,042	6,835,780	2,824,702	80,705
1890	6,761,430	2,793,980	79,828	3,671,080	1,516,975	43·342	10,432,510	4,310,955	123,170
Total	28,364,800	11,720,991	334,884	4,139,800	1,710,661	48,875	32,404,600	12,931,652	383,759

We see that the production of the pit-wells shows the considerable increase of nearly 100 per cent. within four years. Much more striking is, however, the increase in the production of the drilled wells, which show an increase of 900 per cent. from 1889 to 1890.

The following table will show the production of the oil-fields in Upper Burma during the last five years: –

Table No. 61 showing the production of the oil-fields
in Upper Burma from 1886 to 1890.

Year.	PRODUCTION OF THE OIL-FIELDS IN THE MAGWE DISTRICT.			PRODUCTION OF THE OIL FIELDS IN THE PAKÔKKU DISTRICT.			TOTAL.		
	Viss at lbs. 3·65.	Gallons at lbs. 8·83.	Barrels at 35 gallons.	Viss at lbs. 3·65.	Gallons at lbs. 8·83.	Barrels at 35 gallons.	Viss at lbs. 3·65.	Gallons at lbs. 8·83.	Barrels at 35 gallons.
1886	3,41,090	1,412,433	40,355	No record.	No record.	No record.	3,518,090	1,453,752	41,536
1887	5,651,200	2,335,205	66,720	90,010	37,194	1,062	5,741,210	2,372,400	67,783
1888	6,167,020	2,548,355	72,810	104,100	43,016	1,229	6,271,120	2,591,372	74,039
1889	6,835,780	2,824,702	80,705	105,100	43,430	1,241	6,940,880	2,868,132	81,947
1890	10,432,510	4,310,955	123,170	105,900	43,760	1,249	10,538,410	4,354,714	124,420
Total	32,504,600	10,931,652	383,759	405,110	167,401	4,782	33,009,710	13,640,317	389,723

From the figures of Table No. 59 we may form an estimate as to the total production of the Burmese oil-fields since the end of the last century. Supposing that the average production per year up to 1826 amounted to 43·2 lakhs of viss (3·6 lakhs of viss per month), from 1826 to 1873 54 lakhs of viss per year (4·5 lakhs of viss per month), from 1873 to 1885 48 lakhs of viss per year (4 lakhs of viss per month), and that from 1885 up to the end of 1890 the / total production amounted to 330 lakhs, the following represents the total production since 1795 –

From 1795 to 1826, 31 years, at 43·2 lakhs of viss	1,339·2 lakhs of viss.
From 1826 to 1873, 47 years, at 54 lakhs of viss	2,538 lakhs of viss.
From 1873 to 1885, 12 years, at 48 lakhs of viss	576 lakhs of viss.
From 1885 to 1890	330 lakhs of viss.
Total	4,783·2 lakhs of viss.

One lakh of viss being equal to 41,323 gallons the above amount is equal to 197,647,909 gallons = 5,647,082 barrels, or if we suppose that in round figures the total production since 1795 amounted to 200 millions of gallons equal to 5·7 millions of barrels we are not likely to go above than below the mark.

[...]

Part 3. – The Petroleum Trade.

[...]

A. – Import of crude oil from Upper into Lower Burma. – The following table will show the import of crude oil into Lower Burma during the period from 1880 –

imported during 1889 – 90 and 1890 – 91 is estimated, as since April 1889 the import was no longer registered at Thayetmyo.

Table No. 63 showing the import of crude oil from Upper into
Lower Burma during the period 1880 – 81 to 1890 – 91.

Financial year.	In maunds at lbs. 82·28.	In viss at lbs. 3·65.	In gallons at lbs. 8·83.	In barrels at 35 gallons.
1880 – 81	1,29,801	2,926,034	1,209,105	34,546
1881 – 82	90,473	2,039,484	842,762	24,079
1882 – 83	1,12,451	2,534,923	1,047,489	29,928
1883 – 84	1,05,868	2,386,525	987,820	28,223
1884 – 85	1,69,230	3,814,861	1,576,389	45,039
1885 – 86	1,67,383	3,773,225	1,559,184	44,548
1886 – 87	1,88,372	4,246,369	1,755,524	50,158
1887 – 88	1,89,197	4,264,967	1,762,300	50,351
1888 – 89	2,74,352	6,184,570	2,547,343	72,781
1889 – 90	No record.	5,499,598*	12,272,47	64,928
1890 – 91	No record.	9,074,343*	3,749,728	107,135

*   Estimated. /

If Colonel Yule's[1] statement about the quantity of oil passing the Custom-house ayetmyo in 1855 is correct, there seems to be hardly any increase in the quantity of oil imported into Lower Burma up to 1884. During the year 1884 – 85 a considerable rise took place, which has lasted since, the quantity imported during 1890 – 91 being more than the double of its amount at the end of 1884 – 85.

B. Local consumption of crude oil. – It is much more difficult to form an idea about the probable quantity of the local consumption, as there are no data available referring to it previous to the annexation. During the three years following the annexation we may form an estimate by deducting the oil exported into Lower Burma from the production of the oil-fields, the quantity of both being known. But even the figures thus obtained are not quite correct, as under the arrangement presently referred to this quantity only represents the offtake[2] of the local contractor who had the monopoly of supplying the whole of Burma and India with crude oil; that part of his offtake which went to Lower Burma and India is therefore included in the quantity of oil imported into Lower Burma. The consumption of oil in Upper Burma must therefore be considerably less than the gures represented by the following table. I arrived at the amount representing the local consumption from 1880 – 81 to 1885 – 86 by taking the statement of the Burmese Minister that about one-third of the total production was consumed locally as the basis of my calculation. As I received the actual figures from May 1889 till December 1890, the figures representing the offtake of the local contractor during those years are nearly correct. /

Table No. 64 showing the local consumption of crude oil
from 1880 – 81 to 1890 – 91.

Financial year.	Viss at lbs. 3·65.	Gallons at lbs. 8·83.	Barrels at 35 gallons.
1880 – 81	1,508,831*	623,484	17,814
1881 – 82	1,376,750*	568,905	16,254
1882 – 83	1,686,707*	696,986	19,914
1883 – 84	1,594,003*	658,679	18,819
1884 – 85	762,695*	315,463	9,005
1885 – 86	755,442*	312,166	8,862
1886 – 87	736,831	304,175	8,699
1887 – 88	1,420,743	587,084	16,774
1888 – 89	248,760	102,876	2,939
1889 – 90	1,742,662*	720,198	20,577
1890 – 91	2,503,278*	1,034,412	29,555

*   Estimated. /

We see that up to 1885 the local consumption was something like 1 lakh of viss per month. During the years following the annexation it has greatly fallen off, being a little more than ½ lakh of viss per month. There is, however, a consider-able rise in 1887 – 88, which is followed by an equally considerable decline in the following year. This fluctuation is not easily explained, but it is probable that the contractor provided himself for reasons of his own with a large quantity of crude oil in 1887 – 88, of which a large stock remained in his hands, so that in 1888 – 89 his offtake was much smaller. The large quantity of 1889 – 90 and 1890 – 91 it is easily explained by the fact that in April 1891 the arrangement made with the native well-owners came to an end and that the contractor expect-ing a rise in the selling price of the oil provided himself with as large a quantity as possible at the cheap rate to be able to meet the demand for the next two years.

C. Export of petroleum and its products from Rangoon. – The following table will show the export of mineral oil, including crude and refined petroleum and par-affine wax obtained by refining the crude oil from Rangoon. As all oil, whether in its crude state or refined, has to pass Rangoon, the following table will show the total foreign trade in Burmese petroleum, &c., except of course those small quantities which went overland to China.

Table No. 65 showing the export of Burmese petroleum and other products derived therefrom from Rangoon during the period 1880 – 81 to 1889 – 90.

Financial year.	EXPORT OF MINERAL OIL (CRUDE AND REFINED).			EXPORT OF PARAFFINE WAX.	
	Viss at lbs. 3·65.	Gallons at lbs. 8·83.	Barrels at 35 gallons.	Viss at lbs. 3·65.	Cwts.
1880 – 81	525,877	217,625	6,218	Nil.	Nil.
1881 – 82	573,786	237,440	6,784	398	13
1882 – 83	878,350	363,490	10,387	Nil.	Nil.
1883 – 84	859,114	355,529	10,158	Nil.	Nil.
1884 – 85	1,197,980	495,763	14,164	9,849	321
1885 – 86	1,211,635	547,200	15,634	117,368	3,825
1886 – 87	1,189,537	492,269	14,065	133,141	4,339
1887 – 88	1,518,069	626,216	17,949	176,651	5,757
1888 – 89	1,732,221	716,849	20,481	185,273	6,038
1889 – 90	2,226,499	921,397	26,325	243,023	7,920

From this table we see that the export of petroleum has steadily increased, having risen from a little over 5 lakhs of viss of 1880 – 81 to 22¼ lakhs of viss in 1889 – 90, that is to say, an increase of over 400 per cent, within 9 years. Much / more considerably still has been the increase in the export of paraffine wax, which has risen from 321 cwts. in 1884 – 85 to 7,920 cwts. in 1889 – 90, that is to say, within five years the enormous increase of about 2,000 per cent. of the production in 1884 – 85 took place. This increase is probably chiefly due to the improved methods in the manufacture of the paraffine wax, which being of better quality found a better market in Europe than before. It may hardly be expected that the same rate of increase will last during the next years to come, although Burmese paraffine wax will always be in good demand. Having arrived at the conclusion that the foreign trade in Burmese petroleum is in a very prosperous condition and is rapidly increasing we shall have to examine the question about the ratio between the quantity of crude oil imported into Lower Burma, the total production of petroleum, and the quantity of oil exported. The following table will show the annual export of mineral oil and the total quantity of petroleum and its products from Rangoon if the quantity of crude oil imported into Lower Burma is taken as 100.

Table No. 66 showing the ratio between the quantity of petroleum imported and exported into and from Rangoon.

Financial year.	Export of mineral oil from Rangoon.	Total export of mineral oil, paraffine wax, &c., from Rangoon.	Unaccounted for.	Remarks.
1880 – 81	18·0	18·0	82	The figures of columns 2 and 3 are based on the statements of
1881 – 82	28·1	28·1	71·9	export and import of Burmese oil from and into Rangoon fur-
1882 – 83	34·6	34·6	65·4	nished by the Chief Collector of Customs, Burma. There was no
1883 – 84	36·0	36·0	74·0	export of paraffine wax or other products derived from Crude
1884 – 85	31·1	31·6	68·4	oil during 1880 – 81, 1881 – 82, 1882 – 83, and 1883 – 84.
1885 – 86	32·1	34·1	65·9	
1886 – 87	28·0	31·1	68·9	
1887 – 88	35·5	39·7	60·3	
1888 – 89	28·0	31·0	69·0	
1889 – 90	31·5*	34·8*	65·2	* Approximately only; the actuals are likely to be higher.

We see that the total export forms only a small part of the oil imported being not more than 18 per cent, in 1880 – 81, but having risen since, forming, however, not more than 34·8 per cent. in 1889 – 90. What has become of the remainder? This is a problem which has puzzled me all this time without finding an explanation. The data about import and export must be considered as correct, being supplied by the Custom-house. There remain therefore as much as 65·2 per cent. of the quantity of oil imported into Rangoon in 1889 – 90 which cannot be accounted for. It would be absurd to assume that this large share represents the waste and refuse lost in refining the crude oil. If the refinery were conducted on such principles to result in two-thirds of loss of the imported quantity, for which a considerable freight for carrying from the oil-fields to Rangoon had to be paid, it would hardly be astonishing if it did not work at a large profit. But such a supposition would be more than absurd. We must either assume that the figures representing the quantity of export and import are wrong or that a large quantity of petroleum has flown off into a channel hitherto unknown. Now as there is no reason to suppose that the statistics of the Custom-house are wrong, the remarkable concordance with the figures for the different years seems even to prove that the statistics a very reliable, we are bound to believe that a large quantity of the crude oil imported into Lower Burma from the oil-fields of Upper Burma has found its way into a direction which we may only guess. /

e following table will show the ratio between the production of the oil-elds, the local consumption, the import into Lower Burma, and the export from Rangoon, the total amount of production being taken as 100: –

Table No. 67 showing the ratio between the production of petroleum, local consumption, and export from Rangoon.

Financial year.	Local consumption of crude oil.	Import of crude oil into Lower Burma.	Export of mineral oil from Rangoon.	Total export of mineral oil, paraffine wax, &c., from Rangoon.	Remarks.
1880 – 81	32·5	67·5	11·8	11·8	The figure in column 2 is based on the statement of a late Burmese Minister; no export of paraffine wax.
1881 – 82	38·5	61·5	16·7	16·7	Ditto
1882 – 83	38·5	61·5	20·8	20·8	Ditto
1883 – 84	38·5	61·5	21·5	21·5	Ditto
1884 – 85	14·8	85·2	26·1	26·3	The figure in column 2 is estimated; it may be lower, but it is not likely that it is higher.
1885 – 86	14·8	85·2	26·7	29·3	Ditto
1886 – 87	14·8	85·2	23·9	26·5	As during three years the actual production
1887 – 88	25·0	75·0	26·7	29·8	of crude oil has been recorded, the figures
1888 – 89	3·9	96·1	26·9	29·8	in column 2 could have been obtained by deducting the import into Lower Burma from the total production of crude oil.
1889 – 90	24·0*	75·9*	30·7	34	* Approximately only; probably the percentage of imported oil is too low.

We see that till quite lately the export has been hardly more than one-fourth of the annual production; it is only during the last year that it has risen to about one-third. It is therefore quite clear that the local petroleum industry is capable of further development with a view of utilizing the crude material more than it has been done hitherto.

Part 4. – The value and cost price of the oil.

[...]

From 1879 to 1891 the price was Rs. 25 per 100 viss of oil brought up the river and Rs. 15 per 100 viss brought down the river. Afterwards the price for up-country oil rose to Rs. 25, that for Lower Burma fell to Rs. 7 per 100 viss, but it recovered afterwards and till April 1891 the ordinary selling price of crude oil delivered at the river bank was Rs. 15. The local Government having given back the right of free sale to the native well-owners the price of the crude oil dropped at once owing to the competition of the oil from the drilled wells, and it now (May 1891) sells for Rs. 2-12-0 per 100 viss delivered at the river bank.

ANON., *REPORT ON THE MINERAL PRODUCTION OF BURMA 1939* (1939)

Anon., *Report on the Mineral Production of Burma 1939* (Rangoon: Government Printing Office, 1939), pp. 3–11, 17–25, 34–41.

e excerpts from Part I of the report give details of all the mines operating in Burma at the end of the period under review, plus the mining methods adopted, the labour employed and the number and causes of accidents. Part II extracts comprise statistics relating to output, taxation, exports/imports and processing. The report was compiled by K. W. Foster, Secretary to the Financial Commissioner.

Anon., *Report on the Mineral Production of Burma 1939* (1939), extract

PART I

CHAPTER I.

[...] Methods of Working.

4. Working by (*a*) Hill sluicing, (*b*) Hydraulicing, (*c*) Gravel pumping, (*d*) Dredging, (*e*) Quarrying and (*f*) Underground methods continued as in previous years.

In Table III appended, mines are classified according to the derivation of the major part of their output in cases in which more than one of these methods are employed. The Table shows no notable changes. Another tin dredge commenced operations in Mergui during the year, and in general underground mining increased together with the use of monitors. [...]

In hydraulicing, the mineralised ground is broken up and excavated by jets of water under pressure. Water must be impounded by dams or diverted from streams and conducted by ditches or pipes to a tank above the working place. From this tank it is piped down to the working place and the issuing jets of water are controlled and directed by means of monitors. The ore-bearing ground is broken down, not only by the direct impact of the water, but also by under-cutting the banks and causing them to cave by gravity. Where high banks are being under-cut in this way, skill and a knowledge of ground must be exercised in order to prevent the occurrence of large landslides that may overwhelm the monitors and the men working in the ditches or de-stoning some distance back from the face. As the water flows away from the face the broken ground is carried with it to the sluice ditches. Boulders and rocks, too heavy to be transported by the ordinary ow of water remain on the bedrock or in the ditches. If the rocks are large they may require sledging or blasting before removal is possible by the de-stoning gang.

From time to time the bedrock is cleared up by the monitors to prevent the loss of the larger mineral particles and to clear space for stacking waste boulders.

As the working face is cut back by the monitors so the ditches and feed pipes must be advanced to maintain the necessary contact. /

In the sluices the ground is further disintegrated by stream action and the mineral particles freed. The lightest particles remain in suspension and are carried away by the flow of water while the larger particles of gangue[1] and the heavier minerals tend to settle and become concentrated in the ditches. In order to recover as high a percentage as possible of the mineral worked, additional wood sluice boxes are used following the ground ditches. In these the finer heavy minerals are trapped. The use however in Burma of a long series of sluice boxes is noticeably absent. Except on the largest mines, one 6-foot box generally terminates the ditches and such "fines" as may exist are allowed to escape into the streams. The simple principle that sluice boxes should be lengthened until the recovery from the lowest box does not pay for the cost of its installation appears to be practised by few.

The principal technical problems therefore of hydraulicing are connected with the adequate supply of pressure water for working, the proper grading of the sluices for concentrating and the provision of dump area for waste. This entails building of dams, construction of flumes,[2] ditches, pipe lines and sluices, and the purchase of pipes and monitors, and requires a considerable capital outlay.

The size and richness of the deposit must be sufficient to amortize the invested capital required and pay a profit commensurate with the risk of the proposition. The minimum mineral content of ore that will supply these requirements varies with the locality, the geological character of the ground to be worked, the rate of working and estimated life of the property, the working costs, recovery of mineral obtainable and, not least, the price of the final product on the market.

The proper evaluation of these variables is a science, and with few exceptions, mining in Burma is not conducted on such a basis. Systematic prospecting is rarely carried out except by the large European companies. The mining risk rate in the case of tin and wolfram is higher in Burma than in other countries, largely due to local geological factors. As a result the individual owner or small partnership is loth to risk capital and prefers to work a concession on a hand to mouth system. Similarly, the larger limited companies do not find it easy to attract capital.

Permanent and Seasonal Workings.

5. There was a marked tendency to more intensified working during the monsoon period in order to extract the maximum output possible while water was available. This was obtained mainly by systems of continuous working. During the dry season numbers of small mines are temporarily closed down, and simple underground operations are commenced. [...]. /

Machinery and Electrical Power Used.

6. [...] Owing to war conditions the commercial cost of machinery increased considerably towards the end of the year, offering a further check to advancement in this direction.

e statement of Electrical Power used as detailed in Table VI shows however that advances have been effected. A further 2,332 Horse Power has roughly been utilised in the industry mainly in connection with the mining of tin and wolfram. The use of electrical power underground has slightly declined but increases are shown in surface haulage, ore-dressing and miscellaneous on surface.

Explosives.

7. Table V gives details of the quantities of explosives and detonators used in mines classified according to the minerals worked.

e total number of mines using explosives was 191 (166), an increase of 25 on the previous year.

e total quantity of the gelatinised dynamite type of explosives used was 273,742 (280,241) pounds, a decrease of 6,499 pounds. The use of gunpowder also decreased from 2,199 pounds to 40 pounds.

e number of detonators used was 1,559,305 (1,230,188), an increase of 329,117. Less blasting was carried out in quarries working road metal and limestone and mines working silver-lead ore and antimony ore, while a 45 per cent increase occurred in mines working tin and wolfram.

Mines in Burma continued the practice of blasting shallow holes with a single stick of explosive, the average charge of explosives per detonator used being 0·134 pounds.

e average charge underground in the Northern Shan States was 0·62 pounds per detonator.

CHAPTER II.

LABOUR CONDITIONS.

Types of Labour employed.

8. [...] The majority of permanent labour in quarries and mines continues to be Indian. Chinese labour is employed chiefly in the Northern Shan States and to a lesser extent in Tavoy and Mergui. In the more isolated localities it is generally found that only Gurkha labour will remain for any length of time. Labour employed in Government quarries is almost entirely Burman. /

Sources of Labour.

9. Mines attempt to encourage the local inhabitants to work on the mines in order to stabilise their labour turnover. In most cases the mines are situated in

sparsely populated areas, unsuitable for agricultural settlement. Most of the mine labour therefore must be recruited outside Burma and comes mainly from Southern India and Chittagong. A special Commission is at present examining the question of Indian immigration.

Number employed.

10. Table IV shows the number of workers employed in various districts and system of working. The total reported number of persons employed in mines during the year was 40,348 (37,195).

The total increase of over 3,000 persons includes 851 men underground 2,656 men and 152 women in open workings. This increase was to a certain extent off set by a decrease in the number of persons employed on surface workings.

The main increases occurred in Tavoy District with small increases in Kyauksè, Mandalay, Thatôn, Yamèthin and the Federated Shan States.

The most notable decrease is recorded in Amherst District.

The percentage of labour employed underground was 69 (69˙5) in the Federated Shan States, 25˙8 (24˙1) in Tavoy, 14˙1 (23˙3) in Yamèthin, 1˙9 (5˙6) in Thatón and 0˙7 (1˙2) in Mergui. These figures form some basis in estimating the relative degree of importance of underground mining in the different districts.

Employment of Women and Children.

11. The employment of persons under 15 years of age on mines is prohibited by section 26 of the Act. No case of infringement of this provision came to light during the year. The total number of women employed was 1,016 (886) showing an increase of 130. These women are employed in open workings, as dump and ore pickers; in de-stoning paddocks and in removing waste and rock in quarries. On the smaller mines the women assist in the drying and cleaning of concentrates. The employment of women underground in mines has been prohibited since 1st July 1937 by Notification under section 29, and none were found so working during the year. Section 26A provides that no person who has not completed his seventeenth year of age shall be allowed below ground in a mine unless he has a prescribed certificate of fitness. The employment of such young persons underground appears to be rare however, and none has been observed in the course of inspections. /

Hours of Work.

12. The last column in Table IV shows by districts the average number of hours worked per week in mines. Persons employed on the tribute system are exempted from the sections of the Act restricting hours of work. It is apparent however from visits of inspection that many mine owners are beginning to realise the advantage of controlling the working hours of tribute labour in order to attain greater production by a more regular and rhythmic flow of work.

e average number of hours worked per week in mines for all districts was 47, a figure well below the statutory limit of 54. Although enforcement of hours of work restrictions is one of the most difficult problems in the administration of all industrial enactments of this kind, there appears at present no tendency to excessive hours in the mining industry generally.

Wages.

ere are no standard rates or fixed scales of wages. Wages vary considerably not only from district to district but also on different mines in the same district. Wages are naturally controlled by supply and demand and are not unfavourable to labour, as the supply does not fulfil the constant demand.

e following daily rates represent approximate maxima and minima for erent types of labour: –

Skilled	Rs. 3 to Rs. 4.
Semi-skilled	Rs. 1/8 to Rs. 3.
Unskilled (male)	Annas 8 to Re 1.
Unskilled (female)	Annas 5 to Annas 10.

e rates paid per viss of cleaned concentrate to tributors also vary considerably.

gure of Rs 1-8 per viss is a rough average. The actual daily earnings of tributors vary according to the prevailing rate and the amount of concentrate they can bring in. The tribute system as applied to tin and wolfram mining in Burma was discussed at some length in the report for 1938, and the position remains very much the same.

Relations between Employer and Employee.

14. Relations continued generally satisfactory throughout the year. Minor dissatisfaction was shown by labour on two dredges in Mergui but conditions speedily returned to normal. /

[...]

CHAPTER III.

ACCIDENTS AND SAFETY.

Accidents.

16. Fatal and serious accidents occurring in mines during the year have been analysed in Tables VII, VIII and IX appended.

Table VII shows the accidents affecting workers underground, in open workings and on surface by districts. 46 (31) separate fatal occurrences were reported resulting in the deaths of 53 persons, 2 men underground, 27 men and 2 women in open workings and 22 men on surface. The fatal accidents rate per 1,000 workers as shown in Table VIII shows a decrease from 0˙75 to 0˙23 underground, and increases from 0˙96 to 1˙05 in open working and from 1˙59 to 5˙63 on surface and a resulting total rate of 1˙31 (1˙00).

The total number of occurrences resulting in serious injuries was 195 (180) involving 207 persons, 116 men underground, 20 men and 1 woman in open workings and 69 men and 1 woman on surface. The serious accident rate per 1,000 workers shows a decrease in the total from 5˙38 to 5˙13 resulting from a fall in the underground rate to 13˙10 from 13˙49, in open working to 0˙76 from 1˙45 and an increase on surface to 17˙93 from 12˙7. Table VIII which shows this has been amplified this year to give district figures.

In the districts the fatal accident rate per 1,000 rose in Mergui to 1˙89 (0˙49) and also in Tavoy to 1˙20 (0˙89) while the serious accident rate for the latter declined to 2˙69 (3. ˙24).

The rates of deaths and serious injury per 1,000 workers for the other districts were respectively as follows: – Thatôn 1˙72 and 2˙21, Yamèthin 1˙86 and 0˙93 and Federated Shan States 0˙43 (1˙37) and 27˙97 (27˙82).

Causation.

17. The causation of accidents is analysed in Table IX. The percentage of total fatalities to the total fatal and serious accidents shows an increase for the year from 15˙6 to 20˙4. Examining in the / first place the totals of fatal and serious accidents shown in column 6 it is seen that sundry accidents underground are, as is to be expected, the most numerous, being 96 (79). Such accidents seldom result in death however and no deaths under this classification resulted during the year. 90 (68) are classified as miscellaneous on surface of which 24˙4 (10˙3) per cent were fatal. 36 (31) were caused in open workings by falls of ground, 72˙2 (70˙9) per cent of these resulting fatally. 21 (34) were due to falls of roof and side underground and 4˙8 (11˙8) per cent of these were fatal. Accidents caused by explosives follow in order of frequency being 4˙2 (5˙1) per cent of all accidents while the percentage of deaths resulting was 18˙2 (16˙7).

In general an improvement is noted in the handling of explosives as the average number of blasts per death was 779,652 as against 615,094 in 1938 and the average per person injured was 151,023 (123,019).

Accidents in shafts, by underground haulage, surface machinery, surface haulage and by electricity each provided less than 1 per cent of total accidents.

With regard to fatalities, 49 (59) per cent were caused in open workings by falls of ground, 41˙5 (19˙0) per cent occurred on surface. 3˙8 (5˙4) per cent were due to explosives and 1˙9 per cent each to falls of roof and sides underground, miscellaneous in shafts and electricity.

e relatively large number of accidents classified as miscellaneous on surface have been further analysed below: –

Caused by.	Number of persons injured.	
	Fatally.	Seriously.
1. Slipping and falling down	10	7
2. Falling trees (in mine workings)	2	
3. Falling trees in Mine Area	7	
4. Winches		3
5. Materials dropped, flying splinters, jammed fingers, toes, etc.		40
6. Drowning	1	3
7. Other causes	2	15
	22	68

e number of fatalities caused by persons slipping and falling down are abnormal. In most cases the occurrences appear to be purely accidental in character but there is generally an element of / carelessness in such cases. To prevent the occurrence of accidents of this kind, proper graded paths must be maintained and safety ropes supplied to the men working on steep faces. The legislation exists; clear cases for prosecution are seldom encountered however owing to the element of carelessness which is usually shown by the worker.

Amongst accidents classed under falling trees, one serious occurrence resulted in the death of the three men cutting down a tree. Two other persons were also killed by the trees they were felling. Other deaths were caused by the fall of dead branches during strong winds. The other figures in the list require no special comment.

Investigation of the accidents due to falls of side in open workings showed that out of 28 occurrences involving fatal or serious injuries to persons only one occurrence appeared to have been unavoidably accidental. In 13 cases, involving the deaths of 16 persons and serious injury to one person, it appeared that the accident occurred while workers were undercutting steep banks, in most cases in areas closed down on account of the danger from falls of ground. That a man will disobey warnings and risk his life for a small quantity of mineral in this way appears incomprehensible but remains nevertheless a tragic fact which must be realised and the practice prevented. Managers appear loth to take action against persons contravening Mines Regulations 89, 91 and 93. Such action together with the strictest possible supervision would seem to offer the best means of preventing this annual loss of life.

Six cases resulting in 2 deaths and 5 serious injuries were caused by the fall of rocks, boulders and loose material from steep faces. The workman must often be held to be careless for not cleaning down the face before commencing work and the management are not free of blame and show negligence in the inspection of the working places. This is unfortunately a far too common cause for complaint

The remaining 9 cases, with one exception of which there were no witnesses, appear to be due either to lack of mining knowledge and experience on the part of the manager as to the safe angle of slope permissible in the workings, or to workmen taking risks and working without skill and judgment. These cases resulted in the deaths of 6 persons and serious injury to 4 others. As a result of the numbers of accidents caused by landslips it has been the practice lately of the Inspector to lay down the maximum degree of slope permissible in a working place where this seemed necessary for the safety of the workers.

Safety precautions and accident prevention.

18. It has been stated that although legislation must be given a substantial share of the credit for the reduction of accident hazards / and improvement in health conditions, it is not so much the punitive provisions of the law that make it constructively effective as the fact that regulations are progressively moulded by the results of enquiries into accidents and by increased knowledge of their causes. The cooperation of the industry is essential to combat the dangers encountered and it is generally recognized that, whilst one of the main preoccupations of inspectors is the prevention of accidents and the study of such accidents as do occur with a view to preventing their recurrence, the promotion of health and safety is even more important outside than within the statutory frame-work.

In applying these remarks to conditions in Burma it is felt that in general the owners of small mines are not sufficiently conscious of their responsibilities towards the health and safety of their workmen. As was pointed out in last year's report, the tribute system under which so large a proportion of the men work and the general fatalistic outlook on life of these workers does not tend to a reduction in accidents. Many of the accidents reported during the year were caused by carelessness and lack of experience. Owing to the widely scattered position of mines throughout Burma it is rarely possible for the Inspector to visit the scene even of a very serious accident within a day or so of its occurrence. This is an unfortunate handicap in the prevention of accidents and can be satisfactorily overcome only by an increase in the inspecting staff. As a temporary expedient and an aid in this direction the Mines Department has devised a form of questionnaire for the use of local Magistrates deputed to hold inquests in cases of fatalities on mines. The form, if adequately followed, should provide such information as will enable the Inspectorate to judge whether the setting aside of other work is justified in order to make an immediate visit of inspection and enquiry into any particular accident.

[...]

TABLE I. – *Mines by Districts.*

Mines working.

District	Total 1939. (2)	Total 1938. (3)	Total 1937. (4)	Under Mining Lease. (5)	Under Prospecting License (6)	Under Quarrying Lease (LR IV). (7)	Native Mining Lease. (8)	Returns not available. (9)	Mines closed during the year. (10)
	601			195	320	27	59	48	48
		585		193	310	24	58	8	45
			437	158	279			20	54
1. Amherst	9	17	9	4	4	1		3	6
2. Bassein	1	1	1			1			
3. Chindwin (Lower).	1	1	1			1			
	8	9	9	8					1
5. Kyauksè	3	1			1	2			
6. Mandalay	2	1	1	1		1			
7. Meiktila	1	2	1			1		1	
8. Mergui	263	256	186	86	117	1	59	26	17
9. Myikyina	1				1				
10. Slaween	1	1	1			1			
11. Tavoy	239	224	164	79	155	5		11	23
atôn	34	34	29	5	19	10			
ayetmyo	1	1				1			
14. Toungoo	1	1	2			1			
15. Yamèthin	20	22	23	6	13	1		6	
16. Federated Shan States.	16	14	10	5	10	1		1	1 /

TABLE II. – *Mines by Mineral Worked.*

District. (1)	Total. (2)	Roadstone. (3)	Iron Ore. (4)	Limestone. (5)	Tin and Tungsten Ore. (6)	Lead, Zinc and Copper Ore. (7)	Antimonial Ore. (8)	Gold. (9)	Gem Stones. (10)	Manganese. (11)
1939	601	23	3	2	552	4	6	2	8	1
1938	585	20	4	4	533	2	13		9	
1937	437	20	3	3	390	5	7		9	
1. Amherst	9	1			6		2			
2. Bassein	1	1								
3. Chindwin (Lower).	1	1								
4. Katha	8								8	
5. Kyauksè	3	2			1					
6. Mandalay	2	1	1							

District.	Total.	Roadstone.	Iron Ore.	Limestone.	Tin and Tungsten Ore.	Lead, Zinc and Copper Ore.	Antimonial Ore.	Gold.	Gem Stones.	Manganese.
8. Mergui	263	1			261				1	
9. Myitkyina	1								1	
10. Salween	1						1			
11. Tavoy	239	5			234					
12. Thatôn	34	8			23	1	2			
13. Thayetmyo	1			1						
14. Toungoo	1	1								
15. Yamèthin	20	1			18	1				
16. Federated Shan States.	16		2	1	9	2	1			1 /

TABLE III. — *Mines by method of Working.*

District.	Total.			No underground working. Open Working by				Underground working throughout the year.	Dry season working underground and open working in wet season by			
	1939.	1938.	1937.	Hill Sluicing.	Gravel Pumping.	Hydraulicing.	Quarrying.		Hill Sluicing.	Gravel Pumping.	Hydraulicing.	Dredging.
	(2)	(3)	(4)	(5)	(6)	(7)	(8)	(9)	(10)	(11)	(12)	(13)
1939	601			435	11	10	25	13	93	2	4	8
1938		585		418	12	10	22	22	88	1	5	7
1937			437	357	20	7	20	2	23	2	3	3
1. Amherst	9	17	9	7				1		1		
2. Bassein	1	1	1					1				
3. Chindwin (Lower).	1	1	1					1				
4. Katha	8	9	9		8							
5. Kyauksè	3	1		1				2				
6. Mandalay	2	1	1	1				1				
7. Meiktila	1	2	1					1				
8. Mergui	263	256	186	247	2	2	1			6		5
9. Myitkyina	1				1							
10. Salween	1	1	1	1								
11. Tavoy	239	224	164	151		8	5	12	55	2	3	3
12. Thatôn	34	34	29	10			8		15		1	
13. Thayetmyo	1	1						1				
14. Toungoo	1	1	2					1				

TABLE IV. – *Workers.*

(1)	Total.		Under-ground.	In Open workings		On Surface.		Average number of hours worked per week.
	Men.	Women	Men.	Men.	Women	Men.	Women.	
	(2)	(3)	(4)	(5)	(6)	(7)	(8)	(9)
1939	39,332	1,016	8,858	26,591	994	3,883	22	
1938	36,309	886	8,007	23,935	842	4,367	44	
1937	29,063	948	6,968	19,069	859	3,026	89	
1. Amherst	214	27		194	27	20		41·6
2. Bassein	16			13		3		42·0
3. Chindwin (Lower).	334			318		16		45·0
4. Katha	114			109		5		49·8
5. Kyauksè	121	13		108	13	13		48·0
6. Mandalay	52	17		23	17	29		52·0
7. Meiktila	15	4		15	4			48·0
8. Mergui	7,807	112	56	6,921	111	830	1	49·8
9. Myitkyina	14					14		54·0
10. Salween	12			12				36·0
11. Tavoy	9,464	605	5,180	12,823	600	1,461	5	47·4
atòn	3,905	162	77	3,425	154	403	8	48·3
ayetmyo	354	15		279	15	75		46·0
14. Toungoo	89	50		89	50			48·0
15. Yamèthin	2,146	1	302	1,567	1	277		46·3
16. Federated Shan States.	4,675	10	3,243	695	2	737	8	51·9 /

TABLE V. – *Statement of Explosives Used.*

Name of Explosives.	Total.			Minerals Worked.				Pre-cious Metal.			Gem-stone.
	1939.	1938.	1937.	Road-stone.	Iron Ore.	Lime-stone.	Tin and Wolfram.		Lead Zinc And Copper.	Antimony.	
	(2)	(3)	(4)	(5)	(6)	(7)	(8)	(9)	(10)	(11)	(12)
Gelignite (in pounds)	254,303	252,259	213,806	37,801	1,025	7,308	108,011		100,024	60	74
Gelatine Dynamite (in pounds).	19,439	27,982	14,786	913			18,517				9
Gun Powder (in pounds).	40	2,199	140	40							
Number of Detonators used.	1,559,305	1,230,188	889,402	195,863	5,530	35,452	1,161,175		160,168	600	517
Number of Mines,1939	191			18	1	1	162		3	1	5
Number of Mines,1938		166		20		3	130		2	5	6
Number of Mines,1937			147	16		7	116		3	1	4 /

TABLE VI. – *Statement of Electrical Power Used.*

(1)	Total Horse Power. (2)	Roadstone. (3)	Iron Ore. (4)	Limestone. (5)	Tin and Wolfram. (6)	Precious Metal. (7)	Lead, Zinc and Copper. (8)	Antimonial Ore. (9)	Gem Stone. (10)
1939 Grand Total	9,212	28			4,326		4,506		316
Number of Mines.	25	1			15		1		8
1938 Grand Total	6,880				2,088		4,485		307
Number of Mines.	22				13		1		8
1937 Grand Total	7,186				2,182		4,485		519
Number of Mines.	18				9		1		8
Surface. Winding	1,416				250		1,166		
Ventilation	195						195		
Haulage	888				650		238		
Dressing	525				462		63		
Miscellaneous	5,287	28			3,000		1,943		316
Surface Total	8,311	28			4,362		3,605		316
Underground Haulage	355						355		
Pumping	466						466		
Portable Miscellaneous	80						80		
Underground	901						901		/

TABLE VII. – *Statement of Fatal and Serious Occurrences in or about Mines.*

		Deaths.							Persons seriously injured.			
	Number of separate Occurrences.	Underground.	Open working.		Surface workings.		Number of separate Occurrences.	Underground.	Open workings.		Surface workings.	
		Men.	Men.	Women.	Men.	Women.		Men.	Men.	Women.	Men.	Women.
(1)	(2)	(3)	(4)	(5)	(6)	(7)	(8)	(9)	(10)	(11)	(12)	(13)
1939	46	2	27	2	22		195	116	20	1	69	1
1938	31	6	23	1	7		180	108	25	1	54	2
1937	29	4	20		8	1	171	108	22		47	1
1. Amherst	1			1								

6. Mandalay				1							1	

District.	Number of separate Occurrences.	Deaths.					Number of separate Occurrences.	Persons seriously injured.				
		Under-ground.	Open working.		Surface workings.			Under-ground.	Open work-ings.		Surface workings.	
		Men.	Men.	Women.	Men.	Women.		Men.	Men.	Women.	Men.	Women.
(1)	(2)	(3)	(4)	(5)	(6)	(7)	(8)	(9)	(10)	(11)	(12)	(13)
8. Mergui	10		5	1	9		6				7	
9. Myitkyina												
10. Salween												
11. Tavoy	23	1	14		9		47	4	13		36	1
atôn	6		5		2		6		3	1	5	
ayet-							3		1		2	
14. Toungoo												
Yamèthin	4		3		1		1		2			
16. Feder-ated Shan States.	2	1			1		131	112	1		18	/

TABLE VIII. – *Incidence of Accident Rate according to district and Nature of Workings.*

A. – By Districts.

		Fatal Accident.		Serious Accident.	
	Number of	Actual	Per 1,000	Actual	Per 1,000
District	Workers.	Number.	Workers.	Number.	Workers.
(1)	(2)	(3)	(4)	(5)	(6)
Total 1939	40,348	53	1·31	207	5·13
Total 1938	37,195	37	1·00	200	5·38
Total 1937	30,011	33	1·10	178	5·93
1. Amherst	241	1	4·15		
2. Bassein	16				
3. Chindwin (Lower)	334				
4. Katha	114				
5. Kyauksè	134				
6. Mandalay	69			1	14·50
7. Meiktila	19				
8. Mergui	7,919	15	1·89	7	0·88
9. Myitkyina	14				
10. Salween	12				
11. Tavoy	20,069	24	1·20	54	2·69
12. Thatón	4,067	7	1·72	9	2·21
13. Thayetmyo	369			3	8·13

A. – By Districts.

District	Number of Workers.	Fatal Accident. Actual Number.	Fatal Accident. Per 1,000 Workers.	Serious Accident. Actual Number.	Serious Accident. Per 1,000 Workers.
(1)	(2)	(3)	(4)	(5)	(6)
14. Toungoo	139				
15. Yamèthin	2,147	4	1·86	2	0·93
16. Federated Shan States	4,685	2	0·43	131	27·97

B. – By Nature of Workings.

Underground	1939	8,858	2	0·23	116	13·10
	1938	8,007	6	0·75	108	13·49
Open workings	1939	27,585	29	1·05	21	0·76
	1938	24,777	24	0·96	36	1·45
Surface	1939	3,905	22	5·63	70	17·93
	1938	4,411	7	1·59	56	12·70 /

TABLE IX. – *Accidents by Causation.*

Causes of Accidents.	Fatal Accidents. Actual Number	Fatal Accidents. Percentage of Fatal and Serious Accidents.	Fatal Accidents. Percentage of all Fatal Accidents.	Serious. Actual Number.	Serious And Fatal Accidents. Total Number.	Serious And Fatal Accidents. Percentage of total Accidents.
	(2)	(3)	(4)	(5)	(6)	(7)
Total 1939	53	20·4		207	260	
Total 1938	37	15·6		200	237	
Total 1937	33	15·7		178	211	
1. Explosions and ignitions of fire damp.						
2. Falls of roof and side (underground).	1	4·8	1·9	20	21	8·1
3. Falls of sides (open workings).	26	72·2	49·0	10	36	13.8
4. In shafts (over winding).						
5. In shafts (ropes and chains breaking).						
6. In shafts (while ascending or descending by machinery).						
7. In shafts (falling down shafts).						
8. In shafts (things falling down shafts).						
9. In shafts (miscellaneous)	1	100·0	1·9		1	0·4
10. Suffocation by gases						
11. By explosives	2	18·2	3·8	9	11	4·2
12. Irruptions of water						

Causes of Accidents.	Fatal Accidents.			Serious.	Serious And Fatal Accidents.	
	Actual Number	Percentage of Fatal and Serious Accidents.	Percentage of all Fatal Accidents.	Actual Number.	Total Number.	Percentage of total Accidents.
(1)	(2)	(3)	(4)	(5)	(6)	(7)
14. By underground machinery.						
15. Sundries underground				96	96	36.9
16. By surface machinery				1	1	0.4
17. Boilers or pipes bursting						
18. On surface railway or tramways belonging to the mine.				2	2	0.8
19. By electricity	1	100.0	1.9		1	0.4
20. Miscellaneous on surface	22	24.4	41.5	68	90	34.6 /

PART II

[...]

CHAPTER III.

OUTPUT OF MINERALS.

Statement III shows the output of various minerals during the past six years. The notes below explain the increase or decrease so far as the reasons are known: –

TABLE I. – *Building Materials, Road metal, Clay for Pottery and Soap-sand.*

	Output during 1939.					
	Building stone and road metal.		Clay for pottery.		Soap-sand.	
District.	Quantity.	Value.	Quantity.	Value.	Quantity.	Value.
(1)	(2)	(3)	(4)	(5)	(6)	(7)
	Tons.	Rs.	Tons.	Rs.	Tons.	Rs.
Akyab	15,677	40,140				
Kyaukpyu	10,770	3,714				
Sandoway	9,687	6,030	240	120		
Hanthawaddy	951	238				
Insein	6,904	6,664				
Prome	34,413	26,042	13,502	13,898		
Bassein	13,665	14,607				

Output during 1939.

District.	Building stone and road metal.		Clay for pottery.		Soap-sand.	
	Quantity.	Value.	Quantity.	Value.	Quantity.	Value.
(1)	(2)	(3)	(4)	(5)	(6)	(7)
	Tons.	Rs.	Tons.	Rs.	Tons.	Rs.
Henzada	22,352	37,370				
Myaungmya	16,150	17,848	117	15		
Salween	8,505	2,126				
Thatôn	660,579	9,20,796				
Amherst	69,701	63,978				
Tavoy	24,115	41,331				
Mergui	41,129	38,548				
Toungoo	9,961	10,001				
Thayetmyo	143,468	84,229				
Minbu	30,299	19,930				
Magwe	41,159	6,174	39	752		
Pakokku	119,241	1,55,292				
Mandalay	52,101	*30,445				
Kyaukse	55,593	74,929				
Meiktila	14,013	5,856			1,397	5,399 /
Myingyan	53,041	54,730	136	468	177	999
Yamèthin	56,217	78,202				
Bhamo	16,149	16,840				
Myitkyina	37,849	30,931				
Shwebo	17,447	10,477	1,720	884		
Sagaing	42,705	15,201			304	1,931
Katha	39,733	39,438				
Upper Chind-win	8,413	8,754	284	852		
Lower Chind-win	39,997	11,987	305	1,485		
Northern Shan States	397,455	2,78,425				
Southern Shan States	455,002	2,96,613				
Total for 1939	2,564,441	*24,47,886	16,343	18,474	1,878	8,329
Total for 1938	2,545,098	†24,54,636	18,066	19,792	2,749	10,731

* Excludes the value of 17,549 tons of building stone and road metal as it is not ascertainable.

† Excludes the value of 15,973 tons of building stone and road metal.

e production of building stone and road metal increased slightly owing to greater demand by the Public Works Department and Local Bodies. The production of clay for pottery decreased owing to fewer persons taking to pottery manufacture in the Prome and Shwebo Districts. The decrease in the production of soap-sand is ascribed to heavy rainfall during the earlier part of the year in the Meiktila District which washed away the accumulations of soap-sand before they were collected.

TABLE II. – *Gold.*

District.	Output during 1939.	
	Quantity.	Value.
	Oz.	Rs.
Myitkyina	6	630
Katha	28	2,289
Upper Chindwin	61	8,106
Northern Shan States	1,111	1,04,206
Total for 1939	1,206	1,15,231
Total for 1938	1,209	1,05,144

The decrease in the Katha District is attributed to insufficient labour, while the decrease in the Upper Chindwin District is ascribed to floods.

TABLE III. – *Jadeite.*

District.	Output during 1939.	
	Quantity.	Value.
	Cwt.	Rs.
Myitkyina	767	65,532
Total for 1939	767	65,532
Total for 1938	1,303	57,891

The stones extracted during the year were more valuable than the stones extracted in the previous year.

TABLE IV. – *Amber.*

District.	Output during 1939.	
	Quantity.	Value.
	Cwt.	Rs.
Myitkyina	6	900
Total for 1939	6	900
Total for 1938	*Nil*	*Nil*

The mineral is reported to have been imported from the Hukawng Valley.

TABLE V. – *Petroleum.*

District. (1)		Output during 1939. (2) Gallons.	Maximum annual output since 1920.	
			Year. (3)	Amount. (4) Gallons.
Kyaukpyu		11,076 (11,189)	1920	30,075
Magwe	1) Yenangyaung drilled wells.	106,089,250 (112,185,673)	1921	184,420,141
	(2) Chauk drilled wells	139,792,004 (120,769,811)q	1939	139,792,004
	(3) Hand-dug wells	825,293 (831,841)	1924	2,498,941 /
Minbu		2,818,228 (2,929,940)	1928	6,101,822
Thayetmyo		1,996,376 (2,712,800)	1938	2,712,800
Upper Chindwin		2,014,072 (2,359,568)	1932	4,040,690
Pakôkku	(1) Drilled wells	22,072,236 (21,958,864)	1935	30,338,043
	(2) Hand-dug wells	54,829 (63,579)	1934	78,429
	Total for 1939	275,673,364		
	Total for 1938	263,823,263		

NOTE. – Figures in brackets immediately below the figures for the year of report are the previ-ous year's figures.

e variations in output as compared with the preceding year were: –

District.		Decrease. (2) Gallons.	District. (3)	Increase. (4) Gallons.
Kyaukpyu			Magwe – Chauk drilled wells	19,022,193
		113		
Magwe	(1) Yenangyaung drilled wells	6,096,423	Pakôkku – Drilled wells	113,372
	(2) Hand-dug wells	6,548		
Minbu		111,712		
ayetmyo		716,424		
Upper Chindwin		345,496		
Pakôkku – Hand-dug wells		8,750		

The decrease in output in the Yenangyaung Oil-field and in Upper Chindwin is attributed to natural decline in production while the decrease in Thayetmyo is ascribed to less activity.

Increased drilling activity contributed to the increased output in the Chauk Oil-field. The increase in the Pakôkku District is attributed to greater activity of Messrs. The Burmah Oil Company, Limited.

The production of petrol from natural gas increased from 10,587,291 gallons to 11,269,626 gallons. /

TABLE VI. – *Tin Concentrates.*

District.	Output during 1939.	
	Quantity.	Value.
	Tons.	Rs.
Amherst	42	58,629
Thatôn	14	17,157
Tavoy	3,360	64,37,554
Mergui	2,017	36,68,366
Yamèthin	6	5,396
Southern Shan States	2	1,580
Total for 1939	5,441	1,01,88,682
Total for 1938	4,519	56,59,146

TABLE VII. – *Tungsten Concentrates.*

District.	Output during 1939.	
	Quantity.	Value.
	Tons.	Rs.
Thatôn	213	2,22,357
Tavoy	3,373	55,40,292
Mergui	343	3,91,944
Yamèthin	407	6,15,518
Southern Shan States	6	8,050
Total for 1939	4,342	67,78,161
Total for 1938	3,849	58,63,572

There was an output of 5,564 tons of mixed tin and wolfram concentrates from the Mawchi Mines, valued at Rs. 96,11,347, the metallic contents of which were approximately 2,155 tons tin and 1,807 tons wolfram. There was also an output of 29 tons of mixed tin and wolfram concentrates from Yamèthin District valued at Rs. 49,890 the metallic contents of which are not known. /

TABLE VIII. – *Lead, Silver, Zinc, Copper, etc.*

District.	Output during 1939.	
	Quantity.	Value.
	Tons.	Rs.
Northern Shan States	486,876	87,24,997
Total for 1939	486,876	87,24,997
Total for 1938	472,100	63,14,092

e production of ore by the Burma Corporation, Limited, from the Bawdwin Mines, shows an increase of 14,776 tons as compared with the previous year.

e Corporation's smelting and refinery operations resulted in the production of 76,000 tons lead; 1,180 tons antimonial lead; 59,347 tons zinc concentrates; 7,935 tons copper matte; 2,896 tons nickel speiss; 6,175,000 troy ounces silver and 1,111 troy ounces gold.*

TABLE IX. – *Iron Ore.*

District.	Output during 1939.	
	Quantity.	Value.
	Tons.	Rs.
Northern Shan States	26,259	70,175
Total for 1939	26,259	70,175
Total for 1938	18,050	58,663

TABLE X. – *Rubies and Sapphires.*

District.	Output during 1939.		
	Kind of precious stones.	Quantity.	Value.
(1)	(2)	(3)	(4)
Katha	Rubies	211,570	1,30,805
	Sapphires	10,532	24,783
Total for 1939		222,102	1,55,588
Total for 1938		212,827	1,47,476

NOTE. – Figures relate only to a limited class of mines.
* This is also shown separately in Table II. /

CHAPTER IV.

TAXATION OF MINERALS.

e amount of revenue collected from minerals during the year was Rs. 51,78,615 against Rs. 52,59,443 in the preceding year, showing a decrease of Rs. 80,828.

e decrease is principally due to the decline in collections of acreage fees in the Lower Chindwin District; of dead rents in the Tavoy District; of royalties in the

Statements IV and V.

cellaneous fees in the Katha District and also to a security deposit of Rs. 54,400 in the Hanthawaddy District being wrongly shown as ·acreage fee in the previous year's report. The decrease has to a certain extent been set off by larger collections of acreage fees in the Thayetmyo, Magwe, Shwebo and Upper Chindwin Districts; of dead-rents in the Magwe and Pakôkku Districts; and of royalties in the Mergui and Tavoy Districts.

Details as regards the royalty collected on different minerals are given below: –
(1) Petroleum, Rs. 33,00,096 of which a sum of Rs. 29,75,835 was collected on the output from the oil-fields in the Magwe District.
(2) Tin, Rs. 2,54,387.
(3) Wolfram, Rs. 1,97,326.
(4) Amber and Jade, Rs. 10,875.
(5) Gold, Rs. 2,822.
(6) Iron ore, Rs. 646.
(7) Rubies, Sapphires, Spinels and Quartz, Rs. 3,828.
(8) Lead and Silver, Rs. 1,90,979.
(9) Other Minerals, Rs. 1,75,987.

CHAPTER V.

EXPORTS AND IMPORTS OF MINERALS.

The total value of all minerals exported during the year was Rs. 17,53,26,015 (Rs. 17,40,71,756), of which Rs. 12,03,40,078 (Rs. 11,82,83,387) were exports to India and Rs. 5,49,85,937 (Rs.5,57,88,369) were exports to foreign countries. Minerals worth Rs. 1,19,34,093 (Rs. 1,43,22,386) were imported into Burma during the year under report. Of the minerals imported Rs. 49,39,416 (Rs. 62,77,296) worth were imported from India and the balance from abroad. The principal minerals exported to foreign countries were silver, copper matte, lead, tin, wolfram and zinc concentrates and mineral oils of all kinds. The principal minerals exported to India were gold, silver, lead, tin blocks and mineral oils of various kinds.

The principal minerals imported from foreign countries were precious stones, silver, coal, clay, tin blocks, zinc blocks and mineral oils of various kinds. The principal imports from India were precious stones, clay, coal, copper, iron and mineral oils of various kinds.

The kinds and quantities of mineral oils imported during the year are set out below: –

Kinds of mineral oil.	From foreign countries. Gallons.	From India. Gallons.
Fuel oil	25,530,712	148,090
Kerosene oil in tins	7	131,676

Kinds of mineral oil.	From foreign countries. Gallons.	From India. Gallons.
Petroleum	26,121	11,546
Paint oil	3,479	158
White oil		234
Other kinds	6,335	42,557

NOTE. – Figure in brackets immediately following the figures for the year of report are the previous year's figures.

CHAPTER VI.

MINERALS REFINED.

67,892,652 gallons of dangerous and 193,429,214 gallons of non-dangerous   Statement VI
petroleum, 2,056 tons of wolfram concentrates, 557 tons of tin concentrates,
1,579 tons of mixed tin and wolfram concentrates, 175 tons of tin concentrates
carrying a little wolfram, 280 tons of tin carrying sand and 7 cwt. of bismuth
were refined during the year of report.

CHHIBBER, 'THE SALT INDUSTRY OF AMHERST DISTRICT', *JOURNAL OF THE BURMA RESEARCH SOCIETY* (1929)

H. L. Chhibber, 'The Salt Industry of Amherst District', *Journal of the Burma Research Society*, 19:2 (1929), pp. 47–56.

From 1926 to 1928, Harbans Lal Chhibber (1899–1955) was Head of the Geography and Geology Department at the University of Rangoon. He then joined the Geological Survey of India as Assistant Superintendent, before returning to the University of Rangoon in 1939. His article describes the extraction of salt from sea water in the Amherst district of Burma. Salt distillation also occurred in the Kyaukpyu, Sandoway, Bassein, Hanthawaddy, Tavoy and Mergui districts, where similar extraction methods were adopted.[1]

1. Anon., 'Our Past Masters: Obituaries', available online at http://www.bhu.ac.in/science/geography/OurPastMasters.pdf [accessed 28 March 2014].

H. L. Chhibber, 'The Salt Industry of Amherst District', *Journal of the Burma Research Society* (1929)

I. Introduction and previous Observers.

e writer had an opportunity of studying the salt industry at Amherst during October 1927, and since the industry was carried on, on a very extensive scale (in fact the output in the Amherst District is the largest in Burma), it was considered advisable to place these observations on record to show the present landmark in the development of the industry, since the Government are taking steps to place the manufacture on a more economical basis by introducing modern scientific methods in place of the existing wasteful system. However, it is unfortunate that the salt boilers as a class are very conservative and are most reluctant to accept suggestions which they regard as amateur interference. However, it is a matter of great satisfaction that improvements in certain directions have taken place, first, in the size of their cauldrons and secondly in the design of their furnaces. Not very long ago they boiled salt in small earthen pots, having the capacity of not more than a few gallons, while the capacity of the iron pans used at present varies from 70 to 150 gallons. Their furnaces have also undergone considerable modification and they can now get over 50 per cent. additional salt with the same amount of fuel, they used before.

Manufacture of salt in Burma is of ancient origin and so far as the British records go, salt was manufactured at Amherst when the provinces of Tenasserim and Martaban came under British rule. But it would be almost impossible to trace the earliest date for as is recorded by Dr. Ratton (7) 1921 "a history of salt is to some extent a history of civilisation. We can trace salt back in the past as far as the pages of / history extend." A report by Mr. G. Plowden submitted to the Government of India in 1856 contained the following information regarding the then Tenasserim and Martaban provinces which included Amherst. "Salt is manufactured in the districts of Amherst and Tavoy but not with any regularity, or in any great quantities. In some seasons numerous persons undertake the

of the article in the markets, and the consequent prices they may obtain for the produce. The quality of the salt produced is styled by the Commissioner in one of his letters as 'superb'. In the Tenasserim province the manufacture of salt is absolutely free subject only to an excise, levied in the shape of a license of annas 4 on every earthen pot, and Re. 1 per iron boiler employed in manufacture. The average annual revenue of 10 years (1844-54) is only Rs. 2,638." With regard to the extent of the salt industry in Burma the following was placed on record by Wingate and Thurley: (2) "The largest number of hired labourers is employed in the districts of the Tenasserim division of which Amherst takes the lead with 417, Tavoy comes next with 289 and Thaton with 52. Including owners and working members of the family of owners the numbers are 520, 348, 208 respectively for the three districts or 1076 persons in all. Except in the Thaton district each licensee employs from four to five labourers who do not always receive regular wages, but are sometimes given lump sums in advance. For instance at the Panga works in Amherst District a labourer and his wife received 150 rupees for a season of five months, fifty rupees being paid in advance when starting and the balance in June when manufacture closes or a monthly wage of Rs. 15 per head. In 1908 the main salt producing districts in order named." It will be noted that Amherst then also led all the other salt manufacturing districts. [...]

II. Concentration of Brine.

Reservoirs are filled with sea-water run through a channel or creek connected with the sea and the flow of water in the channel depends upon the level of the locality in relation to that of the sea. If the place is on a lower level than the sea, then the water replenishes the reservoir / at every high tide, but Amherst being situated at a higher level than that reached by normal tides, sea water only flows through the channel during spring tides. In any case a sluice gate is erected at the entrance to reservoirs and is opened at high tides and closed again before the ebb commences. The sea water stored in the reservoir mentioned above, is pumped by a very ingenious contrivance called a "Persian wheel" up to the beds, or "solar pans" where it is concentrated by solar evaporation. This Persian wheel appears to be a Chinese idea, as a similar contrivance is portrayed by Richardson (4), 1916, and designated as a "dragon bone-lift wood chain pump worked on an incline by a tread mill." This is supported by the fact that a number of Chinese are also engaged in the industry at Amherst. It is remarkable that this contrivance works fairly rapidly, about 40,000 (1 gallon) of brine can be pumped up 6 feet in one hour. The beds or "solar pans" are merely level fields separated by low ridges of mud, and the size of these beds is variable, depending upon the topography and amount of land available. However, those at Amherst were fairly extensive, some of them measured about 850 × 200 ft. The soil of these beds must not be porous.

In the first bed the depth of water is about 4 ins. and the evaporation goes on for 3 days,* when it is passed on to the second bed, till the process has been repeated 4 times when the depth of the concentrated brine remains only one inch and by this time it has almost reached the point of saturation, which is 25° Beaume.[1]

A table of suitable relative areas for each series of beds suggested by the Salt Department is as follows: –

Beds.	Degrees, Beaume.	Area, Square Metres.	Depth of Brine. Metres.	Inches.	Contents, Cubic Metres.
1st Condenser	3.5°	5.960	.168	6.6	1.000
2nd "	7°	4.708	.113	4.4	.533
3rd "	12°	4.514	.070	2.7	.316
4th "	20°	2.774	.054	2.1	.144

e depths being constant but the areas varying in accordance with the magnitude of the works.

But the concentrated brine is boiled generally at a density of 22.23°B. The primitive method of finding the density before Beaume's hydrometer[2] came into use, was by throwing some boiled rice in the brine. If the grains of rice floated, the brine was considered fit for / boiling. It has been noted in the report by Wingate and Thurley, 1908, "In some localities the test whether a handful of boiled rice or the twigs of *Khayon* tree will float on the brine is used to ascertain whether the brine in the last condenser is sufficiently concentrated for admission into the brine tank. Mr. Ashton states "that it was found by test with the hydrometer that grains of boiled rice float upon the surface of brine when it has about reached the saturation point of chloride of sodium (25 degrees Beaume = 1.208 sp. gr.)", but on several trials we found that the tests worked with brine of any density from 16 degrees upwards. The test such as it is, does not seem to be much used or relied on. In many places no test at all or that of taste only is employed". I was told by Mr. Robertson that the concentration of brine to 22 is rather to be preferred as at the higher density of 25°B certain organic matter (algae) is held in suspension and tends to discolour salt during the boiling process. The concentrated brine is led finally into a storage tank, by means of bamboo pipes and the depth and dimensions of this tank must be again variable but the average depth is about 4-5 . while the dimensions are a little over 70 × 100 ft.

e final stage of evaporation is conducted inside a hut in which there is a small well hollowed out of the stem of a large tree into which the brine flows automatically to a depth of about 4 ½ ft., by means of a bamboo pipe connected with the storage tank.

---

* These periods are, however, approximate only as the time it takes a charge to pass through the beds varies in accordance with the amount of solar heat and moisture or humidity of

III. Description of the Furnaces.

The furnace in vogue comprises a platform made up of bricks about 3 ft. 9 ins. high and about 18 ft. long and about 12 ft. wide and contains three furnaces. About half way high in front are three crescent-shaped holes about 2 ft. wide and 18 inches high and these represent the mouths of the furnaces and are lined with iron sheets. The fuel or fire wood is burnt inside to heat the iron pans placed above. [...] There are two pans in front which measure 7 ft. 6 ins. by 5 ft. 3 ins. and are about 4 to 5 ins. in depth. There is a third pan, the length of which is double the combined width of the first two pans. The third pan receives less heat than the front pans and consequently it takes about twice the time for the complete evaporation of brine in this pan. [...]

Brine is transferred from the well into the pans by means of a bucket which works by a kind of lever arrangement. There is a semi-circular trunk of wood, dug out and connected by means of a bamboo pipe to a long hollowed out tree-trunk, about 25 ft. long, by 15 ins. wide in which the brine remains up to a depth of 9 to 8 inches In the centre of this wooden cistern there are two / holes, by means of which brine pours into the iron pans. In the pans, all the brine is evaporated away in approximately three hours. A spoonful of cocoanut oil, or a little kerosine oil, or a little rice water is added to prevent the coarse crystallisation of salt and to refine it. The addition of oil retards evaporation and increases the temperature of brine and hence produces finer grain. On inquiry the writer was told by a salt boiler that 25 viss (one viss = 36 lbs.) of salt is obtained from one pan; while the quantity is double during the dry season. This fall in the yield is attributed to the dilute brine in the rainy reason, though it is remarkable that rain water in the tank remains at the top of the heavy brine below and there is no marked diffusion between the two layers. The brine in these storage tanks remains very much as it is stored, *i.e*, in distinct layers varying in accordance with local conditions at the time of storage. For instance a slight shower of rain may reduce the density of an inch or two of brine and over this a fresh supply of denser brine may be stored later. Another cause of the fall in yield during the rainy weather is the greater humidity and saturated S. W. winds which tend to retard evaporation during salt boiling. Also at the end of the season when the concentrated brine is really finished surface brine which is diluted with rain water is naturally of lower density and contains less salt.

The salt boilers work day and night and get about 200 viss of salt from each pan. Three men work at the furnace, by shifts one at a time, and the men in turn add fuel and scrape the salt when evaporation is complete. The labourers are paid at the rate of Rs. 17-20 a month with board and lodging free. Rs. 25 p.m. is the maximum during the dry season.

When salt is ready it is drawn from the pans on to a wooden platform (4 ×
.) from which it is transferred to the godown through a wooden grating. The
salt godown is kept locked both by the owner and the Excise Department and
cer of the Excise Department visits the godown every day during the dry
season and on alternate days during the rainy season.

Fuel used in the furnaces is obtained from the neighbouring jungle and the
salt boilers have to pay Rs. 4 – in dry weather for a stack 6 ft. long, 2 to 2½
. wide and 6 ft. high while the price rises 50 per cent. – during the rainy season. The question of fuel supply is an important problem and it must ultimately
ect the industry a great deal. Steps are being taken by the salt department in
conjunction with the forest department to provide suitable plots of forest land,
which will be divided into compartments to be worked in rotation.

e salt manufactured in Amherst compares very favourably with that of
Liverpool, both are obtained by evaporation. The quality of Burmese salt however could be further improved by a better system of placing it on the market. At
present it is not sufficiently protected from / dust and deteriorates very much in
appearance while in transit from factory to market. It is purchased by Burmese,
Chinese and Indian merchants and taken to Moulmein, Rangoon, Mergui and
aton. The price of the salt per 1000 viss varies from Rs. 75 (minimum) to Rs.
90 (maximum) out of which Rs. 54-11-0 represents the Government duty. It is
a pity that the industry is declining at Amherst. The writer was told that there
were 24 factories working about eight years ago while at the time of the visit
of the author there were only 9. On inquiry the cause of decline was said to
be heavy taxation, on account of which they did not find it paying to continue
their operations. There may be some truth in their statement but another potent
factor may be that they cannot compete with the foreign cheaper salt. A third
factor, as already remarked is the scarcity of fuel, as a result of which continuous
work for longer hours is not possible.

V. Output.

It is noteworthy that Amherst district produces the largest amount of salt in
Burma. [...] During 1926–27 338,210 maunds[3] of salt were produced which
brought in a revenue of Rs. 425,352 to the Government. The output was considerably increased from 1915–19 and since then there was an abrupt fall. This
must have been due to the War, when the import of salt from abroad would
have been stopped and every effort must have been made to meet the demand
of the country. The lack of shipping, the high rate of freight and the restrictions
on trade in countries which had hitherto exported salt to Burma gave a great
impetus to the industry and the local manufacturers did make the most of a good
market. In 1918, the output of salt of Amherst district was 52 per cent. of the

total for Burma. It may be noted in passing that it was only in those prosperous days that the methods of manufacture were considerably improved.

There is one important feature which considerably affects the output of salt in the area visited by the writer. The season during which brine can be concentrated by solar heat is limited and in Amherst fresh water drainage *via* the Salween River dilutes the initial brine, consequently relatively larger concentrating beds are necessary here than is the case further South beyond the influence of the Salween River. Ignoring this fact the Amherst salt boiler provides a storage tank equal in capacity to concentrating season is far advanced he succumbs to the temptation of storing brine of a low density in order to fill the tank before the advent of the rains and then finds to his cost that he has considerably increased his cost of production on account of the extra fuel required to convert his brine to salt. /

VI. By-Products.

Below are given the results of analyses of salt from Amherst district as given in Wingate and Thurley's report.

		I	II	III	IV
	Moisture	6.15	18.72	5.50	4.88
Insoluble matter	Inorganic	6.092	0.017	0.056	0.117
	Organic	0.041	0.0002	0.058	0.056
	Sodium chloride	88.52	72.67	91.91	92.64
	Magnesium chloride	1.86	3.99	0.16	0.47
	Magnesium sulphate	0.45	1.17		0.35
	Calcium sulphate	2 07	2.14	1.71	0.98
	Calcium chloride			0.42	

I. Amherst (Amherst District).
II. Panga (Amherst District).
III. Panga (Second sample), (Amherst District).
IV. Karokpi (Amherst District).

A glance at the figures will show that apart from sodium chloride other salts, *viz.*, magnesium chloride, magnesium sulphate and potassium are also present. Mr. Robertson (6), 1920 has suggested a fairly simple and effective method of obtaining these compounds as by-products, but the salt boilers as a class, as remarked above, are very conservative and would not soon adopt a suggestion to improve their primitive and wasteful processes. With regard to the recovery of magnesium sulphate alone, the following was stated by the Deputy Commissioner, Amherst in 1916. "Incidentally I would remark that sufficent Epsom salts (magnesium sulphate) to supply the whole of the requirements of the province can be produced as a waste-product in the salt fields of Amherst district." The large percentage of magnesium chloride accounts for such a high percentage of moisture as the former is one of the most deliquescent[4] substances known. It not only imparts an unpleasant taste to the salt, but is responsible for the considerable wastage on account of the draining of salt. During the year 1926-27 there was a wastage of 28,572 maunds of salt in Amherst district alone. It has been suggested to eliminate magnesium chloride, which is the last product of evaporation, by washing the salt with a saturated solution of brine.

Pan-scale: – As the brine in the pans is evaporated "all out," calcium sulphate in the form of anhydrite is deposited on the bottom and sides / of pans and is known as pan-scale.[1] As already noted by Robertson (6) it is a source of great annoyance as it contributes towards loss of both salt and fuel and causes damage to pans. It has been suggested by Ratton (7) 1921 that it can be eliminated by boiling the brine when it has reached 5° B., as at that density all calcium sulphate is precipitated in the brine the tank from which brine can be gradually drawn off without stirring the precipitate at the bottom.

e composition of the pan-scale varies as its following analyses from other parts of Burma reproduced from Wingate and Thurley's report (2) will show.

	– –	I	II
	Moisture	4.94	3.22
Insoluble matter	{Inorganic	0.505	0.051
	Organic	0.069	0.019
	Sodium chloride	21.02	96.97
	Magnesium chloride	–	
	Magnesium sulphate	0.70	
	Calcium sulphate	1.02	0.34
	Sodium sulphate	72.09	

I. Pan-scale (Yego, Sagaing District).
II. Pan-scale (Sagyin, Myaungmya District). /

VII. Conclusion.

In conclusion, a word about the development and expansion of the industry may not be out of place. The industry has a bright future, the only requisites being capital and more economical methods of working. The first is not only a very serious obstacle in the way of development of the industry, but is also the chief cause of its decline as shown below. About Rs. 2,000 are required to start a salt factory, the necessary land is provided free of any tax by the Government. This amount is borrowed from the money-lender at a rate of 36 per cent. per annum, while the net yield from the industry is only about 25 per cent. A profit of 25 per cent. is considered to be fairly good in other industrial countries but in this case all the profit goes to the money-lender moreover there is an accumulating

cit of 11 per cent. per annum. After a few years of working the money lender takes possession of the factory and invites the overseer of the factory to take up the control on writing "On demand pronote" for the original capital plus the unpaid interest. This story goes on repeating. So at present the money-lender is sweating the whole industry. Another serious disadvantage is that at present the whole business is in the hands of absolutely illiterate people, who not only cannot think of any improvement or economy in the methods of working but would not be prepared to take any suggestions, from the competent authorities. Though their furnaces have considerably improved of late and capacity of the boiling pans also increased yet they are far from being what they ought to be and considerable improvement can still be / effected. It must be remembered that in order that an industry may thrive, the article must be manufactured on the minimum cost so that it can compete with the foreign imported salt and this can be only done when none of the bye-products are wasted. Further, salt-manufacture as a cottage industry will be difficult to survive and in order that Burmese salt may be able to compete with the foreign salt, manufacture must be carried out on a commercial scale, but then again the difficulty of capital would come in. In passing it may be mentioned that as early as 1856 Burma was able to export some of its surplus salt to Chittagong and to Calcutta as well, but now it cannot even meet its own demand. Nearly two-thirds of the imported salt valued at Rs. 16,33,169, exclusive of the salt tax comes from foreign countries *viz.* Spain, Germany and Port Said. Would it not be worthwhile to make an effort to at least keep that wealth within the country and within the Empire? That would also provide some work to those who are unemployed at present, bringing contentment to the country. Finally, the writer feels confident that if the same factories were in the hands of educated classes with some capital the state of affairs would be far better and if this short article can attract their attention, its aim is served.

COWIE HARBOUR COAL CO. LTD, 'REPORT ON THE SILIMPOPON COAL MINES AND PROPERTY, 1926' (1926)

Cowie Harbour Coal Co. Ltd, 'Report on the Silimpopon Coal Mines and Property, 1926', National Archives, CO 874/160, pp. 1–2, 9–12, 14–15.

e following extract provides a 1926 description of the coal mine at Silimpopon (Kalabakan), British North Borneo. The coal seam was discovered by the Sandakan Bay Coalfield Ltd, which in 1904 obtained a ninety-nine-year concession to mine for coal over an area of 2,331 squ. km in return for a royalty d per tonne. Before the company could develop its concession, it ran out of funds and was forced to sell its assets to the newly formed Cowie Harbour Coal Co. Mining commenced in 1906. Unfortunately, the mine was blighted by numerous problems – flooding, its remote location, shortage of labour and poor quality coal. Production peaked in 1924 at 90,000 tons, but in 1929 the firm went out of business, passing the works onto the British North Borneo Company, which operated the mine until 1930 when it was finally closed down.

Cowie Harbour Coal Co. Ltd, 'Report on the Silimpopon Coal Mines and Property, 1926' (1926), extract

13th February 1926.

Dear Sirs,

In accordance with instructions, our Representative has visited and inspected the above property, and we now beg to submit our Report thereon.

e Property in question is situate in British North Borneo, latitude 4° 18' North; longitude 117° 27' East.

e present Mines lie about 21 miles distant from the Coaling Station on Sebattik Island, and are reached by means of steam launch up the Rivers Serudong and Silimpopon, to a point known as the No. 2 Wharf, which is 17 miles distant, and from thence by a narrow gauge railway for a further distance of 4½ miles.

e nearest Government Post is at Tawau, a small Port in St. Lucia Bay, 17 miles East of the Sebattik Coaling Station, and is the Headquarters of the East Coast Residency.

e general character of the country may be described as hilly, intersected by the Silimpopon River and a number of smaller streams. The surface of the higher ground is covered with dense jungle, whilst the lowlands near the rivers are hidden by mangrove swamps.

We do not propose to set out in detail herein the particulars of the Tenure under which the Company hold the Concession, but, shortly, they are as follows: – /

e Cowie Harbour Coal Company Ld possess the rights, by Agreements dated 4th March 1904, and 14th December 1921, made with the British North Borneo Company, of winning and working the Seams and Beds of Coal under an area of four square miles in the Serudong District, for a Term of 99 years from 1st October 1903, with the Option of Leasing a further sixteen square miles within 15 years of 15th January 1920.

The Royalty is 2½d per ton, with a Consumption Allowance not exceeding 10 per cent, although during the years 1923 and 1924 15 per cent has been allowed.

The Minimum amount of Rents payable is based on an increasing output of saleable Coal, as follows: –

For the year 1908	£250	0	0
do. 1909 to 1913 inclusive, total	£1458	6	8
do. 1914 to 1918 " "	£2343	15	0
do. 1919 to 1923 " "	£3750	0	0
Each period of 5 years afterwards	£5208	6	8

which at the above mentioned Royalty would represent an average output of 100,000 tons per annum, for the residue of the Term of the Letting.

GEOLOGY

The whole of the surface of the Company's Property is covered with dense jungle, and there are few outcrops by which the strata can be examined.

The geological formation is believed to be Tertiary, but no fossils have been discovered so far as we know. The strata consist principally of Sandstones and Shales.

Within the area of four square miles only one Seam of Coal of importance (known as the Queen Seam) has so far /

TRANSPORTATION.

The output from the Mines, after being tipped into trucks, with a capacity of 3½ tons, is conveyed to No 2 Wharf on the Silimpopon River, a distance of 4½ miles, by a light 2-feet gauge Railway, constructed with flat-bottomed rails, section 30 lbs per yard, fishplated and dogged to wooden sleepers.

There are three Locomotives used, one being kept at the Mines for stunting purposes, the others running between the Mines and the Wharf. These Locomotives take a train of seven trucks.

At No 2 Wharf the Coal is tipped from the truck direct into Lighters, in which it is taken to the Coaling Station on Sebattik Island by Steam Launches.

Two Launches, the "Maud" and "Doris", are employed for towing the Lighters the 17 miles to Sebattik.

When the Lighters reach Sebattik those not required for Sandakan are unloaded by means of a crane and grab into a small hopper, from which the Coal is tipped into small side – tipping wagons of 15 cwts capacity, which convey the Coal to the storage dump for stock. These wagons are hauled by a small stationary engine and rope.

Only the larger Lighters are sent from Sebattik to Sandakan, and these are towed to the latter place by one of the Sabah Steamship Company's vessels.

At Sandakan the Lighters are unloaded by means of baskets carried by hand to the stocking ground, or in many instances the Lighters remain loaded in harbour so that the Coal can be transferred direct into the bunkers of steamers by means of baskets. /

All materials and stores for the Mines are sent via Sandakan, and from thence by the Sabah Steamship Co's vessels to Sebattik, or in the Colliery Company's Lighters to the latter place, from whence they are towed up the River to the No 2 Wharf, and so by Railway to the Mines.

HOUSING.

e Camp or Settlement for the Staff and Employees at the Mines is situated at Silimpopon. It consists chiefly of seven Bungalows for the European Staff, including a Rest House for the use of Government Officials when visiting the Mines; Storehouses, Smiths', Fitters', and Carpenters' Shops, Offices etc.

ere are several other Bungalows occupied by Clerks and Native Officials, together with six Kongsies or Barracks accommodating about 550 single men, whilst there are a number of Married Quarters for families, in addition to which there are a number of houses built by the natives themselves.

e Hospital is situated about two miles from the Camp, with Dispenser's House, Dispensary, one European Ward, and four Wards for natives, each of the latter having accommodation for fourteen beds.

At the No 2 Wharf, 4½ miles south of the Mine Camp, there are three Company's Houses, also Kongsies and Store, together with several privately owned Houses

At the Sebattik Coaling Station there is a Loading Superintendent's Bungalow, and Stores, together with a number of Kongsies and Houses for the Employees. /

WATER SUPPLY.

MINE CAMP.

Two steam-driven Pumps are installed on the up-stream side of the No 1 Bridge on the Silimpopon River, above the Mining Camp. These Pumps supply water to the Camp, and also to Nos 1 and 6 Inclines and Water Shaft Boilers.

NO 2 WHARF.

Water is obtained from small wells, and carried by hand to meet the requirements of the Houses.

SEBATTIK.

Here the water is collected in a catchment or service Reservoir, about 500 yards from the Wharf, and runs by gravitation through 4-inch Pipes, for the requirements of the Coaling Station. This supply cannot be considered satisfactory owing to its inferior quality.

OUTPUTS.

The following are the outputs obtained from the Mines since 1909: –

Year.	Tons.
1909	28,480
1910	35,200
1911	38,900
1912	46,562
1913	56,091
1914	66,487
1915	57,809
1916	62,876
1917	85,545
1918	72,148 /
1919	75,642
1920	66,756
1921	82,869
1922	87,544
1923	62,671
1924	90,012
January to August 1925	55,663

The Colliery Consumption since 1922 has been as follows: –

Year.	Tons.
1922	12,586 or 14·37% of output.
1923	12,213 or 19·48% do.
1924	10,579 or 11·75% do.
January to August 1925	6;272 or 11·27% do. /

The average number of Days Worked at the Mines during the past five years equals 335, including Sundays, during which the Mines continue to work. The chief stoppages are the Pinjam or Paydays, which take place twice per calendar month, and the Chinese Festivals and New Year.

LABOUR.

Practically the whole of the underground employees are Chinese. On the surface Chinese are employed for all labouring work, and Malays are engaged on skilled work.

The total number of employees at the time of our visit were as follows: –

	Chinese.	Malay.
Underground	552	4
Surface, including Workshops &c	70	24
" General	157	62
" Clerks, Messengers, Water – carriers, Hospital &c	32	11
" Contractors (Timber)	93	60
No 2 Wharf	21	6
Launches and Lighters	8	41
Sebattik	70	32
	1003	240
	Total	1,243

e Chinese are recruited chiefly from the Hong Kong District.

Two methods of recruiting are employed –

    1. By Coal Company's Recruiter

    2. By Company's Agents, Sandakan. /

Examination of the figures relating to the last batches of recruits by these two methods produced the following results: –

	Dollars
1. Cost per Coolie per Coal Co's Recruiter	70·50
2. do. Sandakan Agents	115·64

In the case of No 2 Method we understand that coolies recruited by the Agents are entitled to repatriation to Hong Kong after the expiration of the term of 300 working days, which is estimated to cost 63 dollars each. Hence the cost of the second method is 178·64 as against 70·50 by the Coal Company's Recruiter. It would therefore seem very desirable that all further supplies of this class of labour should if possible be obtained by the Coal Co's Recruiter.

WAGES.

At the present time the majority of the underground employees are paid by Contractors. Repairers on the Mechanical Haulage roads and return airways[1] are paid piece work rates. General underground labourers are paid 50 cents per day.

    e Contractors to produce Coal and deliver same at the mouth of the Incline, repair, timber, and keep the working places in a safe condition; find oil, explosives, timber and stores; pay the Haulage-men and their own Talley-men

RATES: –

Nos 2 & 6 Inclines, 3·10 per ton.

No 1 Incline, 2·50; 2·70; and 3·10 per ton.

'LABUAN. LEASE OF COAL MINES IN THE ISLAND OF LABUAN DATED 14TH NOVEMBER, 1889' (1889)

'Labuan. Lease of Coal Mines in the Island of Labuan dated 14th November, 1889', National Archives, CAOG 14/162, pp. 1–15.

Between 1847 and 1911, when mining ceased owing to a string of accidents, several companies attempted to mine the coal reserves located at Tanjong Kubong on the northern tip of Labuan. After the British North Borneo Company had abandoned its works in 1882, the Central Borneo Co. was given the concession. Its lease, part of which is reproduced here, is typical of all such legal agreements.

e company constructed a railway line to transport coal to the port of Victoria, but halted operations in 1898. The concession was then worked by the Labuan & Borneo Co. Ltd until 1900, and, from 1902 to 1911, by the Labuan Coalfields Ltd, which in 1903 produced 50,000 tons of coal. In February 1890, the Central Borneo Co. also leased 50,000 acres for the cultivation of tobacco and another 50,000 acres for the growth of other crops from the British North Borneo Company in return for £20,000 in cash and 10,000 fully paid up shares of £1 each.[1]

1. D. A. Thomas, 'The Growth and Direction of Our Foreign Trade in Coal During the Last Half Century', *Journal of the Royal Statistical Society*, 66:3 (1903), pp. 439–533, on p. 496; D. W. John and J. C. Jackson, 'The Tobacco Industry of North Borneo: A Distinctive Form of Plantation Agriculture', *Journal of Southeast Asian Studies*, 4:1 (1973), pp. 88–106, on p. 98.

'Labuan. Lease of Coal Mines in the Island of Labuan dated 14th November, 1889' (1889)

is Indenture made the Fourteenth day of November One thousand eight hundred and eighty-nine BETWEEN the GOVERNOR OF THE COLONY OF LABUAN acting for and on behalf of HER MOST GRACIOUS MAJESTY ALEXANDRINA VICTORIA Queen of the United Kingdom of Great Britain and Ireland and Empress of India of the one part and the CENTRAL BOR-NEO COMPANY LIMITED whose registered Office is at Winchester House Old Broad Street in the City of London hereinafter called "the Lessees" of the other part [...] To have hold use exercise and enjoy all and singular the mines beds seams and strata of coal springs of petroleum and other mineral oils powers authorities liberties licenses and premises hereby respectively demised and granted unto and by the Lessees from the 24th day of June 1889 for the term of 99 years thence next ensuing and fully to be complete and ended subject to determination in manner hereinafter mentioned

Yielding and paying therefore during the said term unto the Crown Agents for the Colonies for the time being at their Office in London for and on behalf of Her Majesty and her successors or to such other person or persons as Her Majesty's Secretary of State for the Colonics for the time being / shall from time to time appoint in writing to receive the several royalties rents and sums of money following that is to say first the fixed or minimum annual rent of £1 for and in respect of the premises hereby demised to be paid half and first payment thereof to be made on the 25th day of December 1889

And secondly the following tonnage royalties over and above and in addition to the said fixed or minimum rent that is to say in the second third and fourth of the term hereby granted the sum of one penny sterling for each and every ton of 2240 lbs. avoirdupois of all coal whether large or small raised and sold by the Lessees or their assigns under the powers aforesaid and in the fifth and every succeeding year of the said term until the expiration or determination thereof for and in respect of all coal raised and sold as aforesaid royalty or sum of 3d. per ton on clean coal and 1d. per ton on all small coal screenings coal dust &c. sold

And also yielding and paying for each and every ton of 20 cwt. of ironstone iron ore fireclay or firestone which shall be smelted manufactured sold or disposed of in any shape for value by the Lessees or their assigns the sum of 4d. sterling

And also yielding and paying for petroleum or other mineral oil except oil extracted from coal on which royalty shall have been said Gotten and sold by the Lessees or their assigns during the first seven years of the term hereby granted the following royalties – 3d. for every hundred imperial gallons up to one million gallons 6d. for every hundred imperial gallons over one million gallons up to five million gallons 9d. for every hundred imperial gallons over five million up to ten million gallons 1s. for every hundred imperial gallons over such last-named quantity and for every hundred imperial gallons gotten and sold during the remainder of the term hereby granted such royalty not exceeding 2s. 6d. as may be agreed upon or as failing agreement shall on the application of either party hereto be settled by arbitration pursuant to the provisions of "The Common Law Procedure Act 1854"or any statutory modification thereof [...]

And that all the said royalties and sums of money hereinbefore reserved other than the said fixed rent shall be deemed to have accrued due half-yearly on the 24th day of June and the 25th day of December in each year and shall be paid as follows that is to say the royalties and sums of which shall have accrued due on the 24th day of June in any year shall be paid on or before the 25th day of December next following and the royalties and sums of money which shall have / accrued due on the 25th day of December in any year shall be paid on or before the 24th day of June next following and that the first of such last-mentioned half-yearly payments in respect of the half-year ending on the 25th day of December 1890 shall be made on or before the 24th day of June 1891 and that all such payments whether for rents royalties or sums of money shall he made without any deduction or abatement whatsoever

And it is hereby agreed and declared that such coal only shall be deemed slack or screenings for the purposes of these presents as will pass through a screen the bars of which shall be not more than 1½ inches apart in either direction

And the Lessees hereby for themselves and their assigns covenant with Her Majesty and her successors in manner following that is to say that the Lessees and their assigns shall during the term hereby granted within thirty days after every 24th day of June and 25th day of December in every year after the first year of the said term settle and make up full true and accurate accounts of all the coal ironstone iron ore firestone and petroleum and other oils which shall have been raised and gotten melted manufactured and refined by the Lessees or their assigns out of and from the said mines pits and other premises hereby demised or authorized to be wrought as aforesaid and sold within and during the half-year ending on every such 24th day of June and 25th day of December as aforesaid [...]

And also that the Lessees and their assigns shall half yearly and within three calendar months next after every 24th day of June and 25th day of December during the said terra deliver unto the said Governor or Chief Officer of the Government for the time being within the said Island a true and faithful written account in duplicate of the weights and quantities of all such coal and other minerals and substances as the said Lessees or their assigns shall have raised and gotten out of the said mines and premises / and sold during the half-year next preceding such 24th day of June or 25th day of December respectively in every year [...]

And Her Majesty for herself her heirs and successors hereby agrees with the Lessees that the said Governor or other Chief Officer of Government for the time being in the said Island shall from time to time examine the accounts aforesaid as and when they shall be rendered to him by or on behalf of the Lessees and affix to such accounts when so examined by him a certificate under his hand setting forth whether the same accounts in his judgment are or are not true and correct [...]

And the Lessees do hereby for themselves and their assigns further covenant with Her Majesty and her successors in manner following that is to say That they the Lessees or their assigns shall at the end or other sooner determination of the said term hereby granted leave and deliver up all and singular the said premises hereinbefore expressed to be hereby demised or which shall have been taken possession of under the powers aforesaid subject nevertheless to the provisions as to the removal of machinery and fixtures hereinafter contained

And also shall work and get the said mines and pits of coal and other the premises hereinbefore expressed to be hereby demised and authorized to wrought respectively or such part or parts thereof a shall be enter / upon and worked by the Lessees at any time or times during the said term in a proper and workmanlike manner and without any unnecessary waste and according to the best mode and course of working mines of the same or the like description as those already demised

And also shall if and when the same shall be practicable leave substantial walls and pillars of coal or rock to support the roofs of each coal and other mine and pit and also shall not do or knowingly suffer to be done any negligent or wilful act matter or thing which shall or may hazard or endanger the drowning or setting on fire of the mines and premises hereinbefore described and demised or authorized to be wrought as aforesaid or occasion any loss or damage thereto but shall keep the headways levels and drifts for the time being clear and free and the necessary passages for air and water for the time being clear and in good repair during the said term hereby granted or until in each or any ease the mine pit vein bed or scam in question shall be worked out or abandoned

And also shall from time to time during the said term hereby granted at their own costs and charges erect and supply and keep in good and substantial order convenient house or houses for such machine or machines in and upon some convenient spot or spots in the said Island and will cause and procure all the coal and other minerals or substances other than oil that shall be raised or gotten from and out of the said mines and premises to be brought upon and weighed by and at such machine or machines before the same shall be taken or carried away or be consumed converted or disposed of

And shall also cause and procure the weights of all coal and other minerals and substances other than oil and the quantities of all oil raised and gotten out of the said mines and premises to be from time to time entered in a book or books to be provided for that purpose by the Lessees and also shall cause all such books as last aforesaid and also accurate plans and diallings of the workings of the said mines to be carefully kept at an office on some part of the said Island to which office and book or books of accounts and to all entries and accounts touching or relating to the said mines and premises and the produce thereof and to which plans and diallings the Governor or other the Chief Officer of the Government in the said Island for the time being on behalf of Her Majesty and her successors and his agents or bailiffs or any of them shall at all seasonable times have free access and be at liberty to inspect, cast up and examine the same books entries and accounts plans and diallings and to take extracts from or copies of the same respectively

And also that the said Governor or / other Chief Officer of the Government for the time being in the said Island and his agents bailiffs workmen or other persons employed by him for the purpose shall at all seasonable times during the said term hereby granted have free access to the weighing machines so to be erected and supplied as aforesaid and make use of prove and at the expense of the Lessees or their assigns repair the same as often as occasion shall require and if he shall think fit to direct the same to weigh measure and take account of all the coal and other minerals and substances that shall be raised or gotten from or out of the premises hereby demised

And also that the Lessees shall permit such Governor or Chief Officer for the time being as aforesaid on behalf of Her Majesty and her successors and his agents bailiffs inspectors and surveyors and other proper persons authored by him to go down into and return out of all and every or any of the shafts mines pits collieries or works to be sunk made opened or worked by or on behalf of the Lessees under the provisions of these presents and to enter into go through survey and inspect the said mines collieries and works and the state and condition thereof and of every part thereof and to latch inspect examine and measure the workings thereof and the quantity of the coal and other materials and substances above specified made sold consumed or converted worked or gotten therein or thereout and see that the same mines and every part thereof are worked and carried on in a fair proper and workman-like manner and for all or any of the

requiring any satisfaction or compensation therefor the Lessees or their assigns shall permit such Governor or other officer and his agents bailiffs inspectors and surveyors and other proper persons authorized as aforesaid to make use of the engines gins machinery ropes tackle and all other articles and things used and employed at upon or in the said mines pits collieries and works and to have the help and assistance of any of the colliers and workmen employed in or about the said mines collieries and also that the Lessees and their assigns shall at their own cost and charges from time to time during the term hereby granted supply and provide and also keep in good order and repair an adequate supply of suitable lighters for the purpose of coaling any ships of Her Majesty's Navy or under charter to any department of Her Majesty's Government pursuant to the said covenant in that behalf hereinafter contained

And that the said Lessees and their assigns shall and will during the continuance of the said term hereby granted supply for the use of Her Majesty any coal which she may by notice in writing signified under / the hand of such Governor or Chief Officer as aforesaid in the said Island and left at the place of business in the said Island of the Lessees or the place of abode of their Resident Manager or principal agent there require for the use of any vessels or ships of Her Majesty's Navy or of any other ships under charter to any department of Her Majesty's Government at the actual cost of cutting raising hauling and delivering the same including a fair proportion of the standing charges of the collieries for management drainage ventilation stores and other incidental expenses with the addition by way of profit of 5 per cent. on such total cost and so that the price so to be charged shall in no case exceed the current market price or rate for the time being charged by the Lessees for similar clean coal delivered free on board and that such coal shall be by the Lessees or their assigns delivered immediately and in preference to all existing or other demands should the same be so required by such notice and such coal shall be delivered free of charge for delivery on board any and every such vessel or ship as aforesaid which may be lying alongside of any wharf or jetty erected or to be erected in the said Island but if the said vessel or ship shall not be lying alongside of any such wharf or jetty then free on board of proper lighters to be supplied as aforesaid by the Lessees or their assigns and which lighters shall be placed as conveniently as may be in every case with reference to the position of the vessel or ship required to be coaled and so that such lighters may most conveniently be navigated or towed off to the same vessel or ship by and at the expense of Her Majesty or her successors or of the captain or owner of the ship or vessel requiring such coal [...]

TRADE

Development of Singapore

Malaya's three ocean going ports were Port Swettenham at the mouth of the Klang River, Penang, lying at the north end of the Malacca straits, and Singapore, which by 1914 in terms of shipping tonnage handled was the seventh busiest in the world. Although Port Swettenham possessed a landlocked harbour and both it and Penang had good wharves and warehouses and railway connections, they were not on world shipping routes. They thus largely acted as a landing place for Indian immigrants and as *entrepôts*, sending local produce to Singapore, where it was sometimes processed and shipped to the West, Japan and East Asia. As for the lesser ports, those on the east coast were almost inaccessible during the north-east monsoon season and were constrained by sand bars, which made navigation difcult. Nonetheless, much local produce was moved through Kelantan, Tumpat, Bachok, Semark, Kuala Trengganu, Chuckai, Kuantan, Pekan, Endau and Mersing. On the south and west coasts, Johore possessed Muar and Batu Pahat, the port through which Japanese miners exported iron ore; Perak had Teluk Anson, Sitiawan, Port Weld and Kuala Kurau; Negri Sembilan had Port Dickson; Selanger had Kuala Selangor; and Kedah had Sungei Patani and Alor Star.[1]

Singapore possessed a number of advantages as a port. It had a natural sheltered deep water harbour and, positioned at the tip of the Malaya Peninsula and at the southernmost extremity of continental Asia, it controlled the straits of Malacca, the shortest of two international trade routes between the Indian Ocean and the South China Sea. It thus attracted the trade of Malaya, Borneo and Sumatra, plus that of countries to the east of the Peninsula, such as French Indo-China, the Philippines, China and Japan. Moreover, goods moving through its docks were not subject to custom duties or charges, and, unlike its Dutch counterparts, it was free from government interference regarding the nationalities of traders and ships.[2]

Over time, the port became a centre for Malayan and Chinese *entrepôt* trade, but only experienced rapid growth from the early 1870s. Between 1871/3 and

to reach £1,832m in 1940 (Table 1). By 1935, it was one of the busiest ports in the world, dealing with 13,595 merchant vessels and 30.255m tons of freight per year. The genesis of the expansion was the opening of the Suez Canal and the European industrial revolution. The Canal shortened the distance and the cost of transporting goods between Malaya and Europe and opened Eastern waters to steamships, which had little option but to use Singapore as the second gateway between the Indian Ocean and the South China Sea – the Sunda straits – provided few landing places where they could take on coal and fresh water. European industrialisation, meanwhile, increased the demand for primary products from the Malayan region and the resultant concentration of Western shipping at the port initially reduced freight rates and attracted exports from the surrounding region. Further growth was then stimulated by the development of the Peninsula's internal transport system, which converged on Singapore; the construction of the Panama Canal and the creation of a round-the-world route that passed through South East Asia; the laying of a submarine cable between Singapore and Madras in 1871 and the establishment of direct telegraphic communication via India with Europe; the relatively low charges of the Singapore Harbour Board; and the development of a naval base.[3]

Table 1: Trade of Singapore ($m).

Year	Imports	Exports	Total
1880	60.7	54.6	115.3
1900	251.8	205.5	457.3
1920	1005.6	695.7	1701.3
1930	528.3	405.9	934.2
1938	369.6	320.3	689.9

Source: Adapted from W. L. Ken, 'Singapore: Its Growth as an Entrepot Port, 1819–1941', *Journal of Southeast Asian Studies*, 9:1 (1978), pp. 50–84, on pp. 63, 72.

In order to handle the ever-growing volume of trade, the port extended its harbour facilities. In the early days, most shipping anchored in the pool or at Boat Quay constructed in 1823 along the northern and southern banks of the Singapore River. Too small and shallow for steamships and with inadequate coal wharfage, the quay was superseded for trans-ocean shipping by a new deep water harbour built in 1852 at Tanjong Pagar, imaginatively named New Harbour, and, in 1900, renamed Keppel Harbour. Jardine Matheson, the Borneo Co. and John Purvis & Son established wharves, warehouses and coal stores in the new quay, in 1859 the Bon Accord Dock was opened by the firm of Buyers & Robb, and, in 1870, the Patent Slip & Dock Co. constructed a dry dock at Pantai. A more important development, however, was the arrival of the Tanjong Pagar Dock Co. Established by a group of Singapore merchants in 1864 with a capital of

respectively the Victoria and Albert Docks, in 1874 introduced steam winches and cranes, more than doubling the amount of cargo that could be handled each day, and, from the early 1880s, began to expand into its competitors' territories. In 1884 it leased Jardine Matheson's wharf, the following year bought the Borneo Co.'s and John Purvis & Son's wharfs, and, with the Patent Slip & Dock Co., leased the Bon Accord Dock. With the takeover of the Patent Slip & Dock Co. in 1899, it controlled virtually all the shipping business of the harbour – operat-

ve dry docks, managing 1.25 miles of wharf and owning warehouses capable of storing 200,000 tons of cargo and 250,000 tons of coal.

e company's downfall was rapid. Opponents claimed that it operated in an inefficient manner, had failed to invest in new facilities and was vulnerable to a German takeover. Threatened with government expropriation, its directors hatched a plan to invest $12m in the expansion and modernization of its facilities. Alas, these plans were rejected by its London Consulting Committee, which according to its articles of association had final veto over all expenditure, and, in 1905 after a great deal of negotiation, the company was compulsorily purchased by the government at a price of $880 per share. Unfortunately, the organization set up to run the harbour, the Tanjong Pagar Board, comprised most of the company's former directors and staff and performed equally poorly, and, in 1913, it was absorbed into the Singapore Harbour Board formed the previous year. The Board constructed the 40,000 dwt King Dock (1913), replaced the wooden wharfage with concrete structures, introduced electric cranes, elevating platforms and forklift trucks for the handling of cargo, built facilities for cold storage and the bulk storage of vegetable oils and latex, permitted the establishment of a British naval base serving the Eastern Fleet at Sembawang on the northern shores of the island, and, in 1932, took charge of a new harbour, the Telok Ayer Basin. By 1939, the port was one of the most advanced in the world and possessed a wharfage of 12,744 feet and a land area of 36.5 square miles (23,168 acres).[4]

Trade of Singapore

Singapore's trading activities can be split into trade with the West, with East Asia and with the surrounding region. Singapore's trade with the West grew from $21.1m in 1870 to $608.9m in 1920 and then fell to $380.6m in 1937 (Table 2) and comprised both imports and exports. Volumes of Western imports rose from the late nineteenth century. Rising incomes brought about by the expanding tin and rubber industries increased the demand for manufactured products and the development of the rail and road network facilitated distribution. Throughout the period the goods largely came from the UK, which in 1939 accounted for 14 per cent of the port's total imports, and initially comprised textiles, iron and

Table 2: Trade with the West and East Asia (percentages of trade and total trade).

Year	Trade with West				Trade with East Asia				
	Continental Europe (% of Western trade)	UK (% of Western trade)	North America (% of Western trade)	Total trade with West ($m)	China (% of East Asian trade)	Hong Kong (% of East Asian trade)	Japan (% of East Asian trade)	Total trade with East Asia ($m)
1870	10	76	14	21.1	20	79	1	9
1900	29	53	18	124.2	15	69	16	56.1
1920	12	38	50	608.4	19	71	10	206.4
1937	19	27	54	380.6	22	11	67	166.1

Source: Adapted from Ken, 'Singapore', pp. 64, 71, 77.

The main exports to the West were tin and palm oil, and, after the First World War, rubber and mineral oil. During the inter-war period, the port's importance as an outlet for such goods diminished. Malayan tin was increasingly shipped from Penang, Singapore concentrating on ore from elsewhere and particularly the Dutch East Indies. Sheet rubber began to be exported from Port Swettenham and again Penang, though Singapore became the main outlet for latex rubber and remained the centre of the rubber market. Goods from French Indo-China and the Dutch East Indies started to be shipped direct; the barter and credit system described below by which Singapore Chinese merchants bought these products broke down, ocean-going wharves were constructed at Saigon, Batavia, Sourabaya, Macassar and Belawan and direct shipping services established between Saigon and the major French ports. Exports of other Malayan produce, meanwhile, were damaged by the fall in gambier, pepper and tapioca acreages, the deterioration in the quality of gambier, and the cultivation of flake and pearl tapioca in Java.

Over time, there was also a shift in the direction of Western exports from the UK to continental Europe and, increasingly, the United States; Britain in 1939 accounting for just 11 per cent of exports as compared to the US's 33 per cent. Reasons for the change include the UK's relative industrial deterioration; the growing world dominance of the American tin-plate and rubber tyre industries; and the waning of London's *entrepôt* trade, goods being exported direct to continental Europe rather than via the port of London. The establishment of the Straits Homeward Conference, which controlled shipping to Europe and the UK, also played a part. Its better connections with continental ports encouraged direct shipment to Europe and, until the 1905 formation of the New York Freights Conference, it tended to charge higher rates than ships bound for America.[6]

Singapore's trade with East Asia rose from $9m in 1870 to $206.4m in 1920,

67 per cent of the total and that with China, either directly or through Hong Kong, fell to 33 per cent (Table 2). Exports to Japan comprised tin, rubber, palm oil and petroleum and its main import was cheap cotton piece goods, which vigorously competed with similar textiles from the UK and Europe. The most
 cant product despatched to China was opium, which in 1889 accounted by value for 22 per cent of the goods exported, followed by sandalwood (5.89 per cent), woollen cloth (5.82 per cent), rattans (4.94 per cent) and sea cucumbers (4.75 per cent). The main imports in 1889 were fresh vegetables, accounting for 10 per cent of the goods imported, tea (6.55 per cent), salted goods (5.9 per cent), joss sticks (5.61 per cent) and silk piece goods (5.3 per cent). Reasons for the decline in Chinese exports and imports included the failure of China to develop either its agriculture or industry; in the early 1930s, the introduction of quotas on Chinese textile imports; and, in the case of tea, the appearance of black tea produced in Ceylon, Java and Sumatra and competition in the green tea market from Taiwan. Chinese government inter-war attempts to promote its goods through 'buy Chinese' campaigns aimed at the Malayan Chinese community and exhibitions failed to reverse the downward trend.[7]
 e port's trade with South East Asia (Table 3) remained buoyant until the early 1920s when the development of local ports and the collapse of the barter-credit system prompted French Indo-China, Siam and the Dutch East Indies to ship more of their goods direct rather than via Singapore. Imports came from the Dutch East Indies, Siam, French Indo-China, Burma and British North Borneo. The Dutch East Indies supplied rubber, petroleum, sugar, copra, pepper,
 ee and areca-nuts, 24 per cent of the goods in 1939 coming from Sumatra. Siam imports largely comprised rice and dried/salted fish, the country accounting in 1897/8 for respectively 51.5 per cent and 28.8 per cent of the port's rice and dried/salted fish imports, and from the turn of the century included tin ore and rubber. Of the other countries, French Indo-China was again a source of rice and dried/salted fish, providing in 1897/8 respectively 14.8 per cent and 43.5 per cent of Singapore's imports of these foodstuffs; Burma sent largely rice (28.4 per cent of total rice imports); British North Borneo rubber and petroleum; and Java sugar. The majority of the rubber, tin and petroleum imports were re-exported to the West and Japan, sugar went mainly to China, areca-nuts to India and rice and dried/salted fish to other regions in South East Asia, along with Western imports. On arrival in Singapore, rice was packed into 224 lb gunny bags and distributed to mines and plantations in Malaya and the Dutch East Indies, which together took four-fifths of the port's rice imports. Dried/salted
 sh, after it had been cleaned, sorted and re-died, was re-exported to the Dutch East Indies and Burma and Western manufactures, largely textiles, were shipped

Table 3: Trade with S. E. Asia ($m).

Year	Dutch East Indies	French Indo-China	Malaya	Siam
1870	12.3	3.8	9.4	4.6
	(i = 6.6. e = 5.7)	(i = 1.6. e = 2.2)	(i = 5.6. e = 3.8)	(i = 1.7. e = 2.9)
1915	110.8	21.4	160	51.4
	(i = 60.1.e = 50.7)	(i = 18.5. e – 2.9)	(i = 104.1. e = 55.9)	(i = 40.1. e = 11.3)
1920	251.9	98.5	386	39.9
	(i = 150.4. e = 50.7)	(i = 78.5. e = 20)	(i = 229.5. e – 157.1)	(i = 20. e = 19.9)
1937	230.9	13.9	-	38.4
	(i = 199. e = 31.9)	(i = 12.8. e = 1.1)		(i = 29. e = 9.4)

Notes: i = Import; e = exports.
Source: Adapted from Ken, 'Singapore', pp. 66, 73.

Singapore Merchants

Singapore's trade with the West and Japan was dominated by the British Agency Houses described in the General Introduction in Volume 1, though during the inter-war period imports were increasingly handled by Chinese merchants, who had developed direct links with Western and Japanese manufacturers, and rubber began to be exported to the US through the American companies Goodyear Orient Co. and the Firestone Tyre & Rubber Co.[9] Until the early 1920s, almost all the trade with East Asia and South East Asia was managed by Chinese merchants, originally from Fujian and Guangdong, who from the 1900s formed trading associations such as the Singapore Rice Traders Association, the Siam Traders Association and the Rangoon Traders Association. The merchants had a long history of trading in China, French Indo-China, the Dutch East Indies and Siam, but in Sarawak and British North Borneo they supplanted Malay merchants.[10]

Chinese merchants retained their dominance of the sector until the inter-war period largely because of the use of barter and credit. In return for the following year's crop, the Chinese merchant would provide an indigenous farmer with a cash advance, used to finance the cultivation of the crop, and provisions, such as dried fish or rice, used to feed the farmer's family and workers. On receiving the harvested produce, he would then pay the farmer the remainder of the agreed sum, minus the cost of the supplies, and sell the crop or use it or a portion for further barter. Rice, for example, would be purchased in Burma in part-exchange for dried/salted fish, perhaps obtained by credit/barter in Siam, and, in turn, would be exchanged in the Dutch East Indies for rubber. The system flourished because indigenous farmers lacked access to alternate sources of finance, there was often a scarcity of currency and no unified monetary standard in these countries and the merchant could make two-way profits – on the imported provisions, which he valued at more than their cost, and on the bartered goods, sold

specialize as importers or re-exporters and intermediary traders appeared, buying from importers and selling to re-exporters, often sharing the cost of purchases in order to spread risk. The system waned from the early 1920s when currency nance became more widely available and farmers became less willing to sell their future crops for bartered goods and credit, well aware that they could obtain far higher prices by marketing their produce immediately after it had been harvested. Singapore's Chinese merchants were thus increasingly bypassed and trade with South East Asia fell. Burmese, Siamese and French Indo-Chinese rice and dried fish were increasingly purchased by indigenous traders and shipped directly to the consuming countries from local ports.[11]

Burma

Burma's trade comprised the movement of goods between Upper and Lower Burma and exports/imports to/from other countries. The main exports from Lower to Upper Burma were textiles, which made up 30 per cent of the total, and rice and other foodstuffs – these accounted for 50 per cent of exports in the early 1890s, but then fell as Upper Burma's rice acreages and yields rose. The main goods moving in the opposite direction were timber, crude oil, cutch and rice, which represented nearly 70 per cent of Lower Burma's imports. The country's primary export was rice. From the early 1870s to 1929, the value of rice exported increased fifteen fold from Rs 45m pa to Rs 350m pa, and, by the late 1890s, the crop accounted for 70 per cent of all exports, later falling to 50 per cent in 1914. Other goods sold overseas include teak, 10 per cent of total exports in the late nineteenth century, before falling to 6 per cent; oil products, the value of which rose from Rs 4m pa (2 per cent of total exports) in the late 1890s to Rs 115m pa (17 per cent of total exports) in the late 1920s; and, from the First World War, non-ferrous metals such as lead and tin. The most important destination for these goods was India, the recipient of 41.6 per cent of exports in 1883/4, 43.1 per cent in 1903/4, and 50.6 per cent in 1931/2. The UK was a close second, though its proportion of exports fell over time from 31.8 per cent in 1883/4 to 12.3 per cent in 1903/4 and just 8.1 per cent in 1931/2. Other destinations included Germany, Austria-Hungary, Holland, Japan and the Straits.

As for the country's imports, values more than doubled from Rs 100m pa in the later 1890s to Rs 216m pa in the mid-1930s. The main goods delivered were textiles, Rs 26m worth in 1898/9 (26.7 per cent of total imports), and food-s, which accounted for 25 per cent of all imports in 1870 and 45 to 52 per cent at the end of the period and included edible oils, salted fish, wheat, pulses, salt, alcohol and biscuits. Other important imports were porcelain, lacquerware, boots and shoes, and, from the turn of the century, cigarettes. In 1883/4, 43 per

in 1903/4 and 20.1 per cent in 1931/2, despite the introduction of Imperial preference. In comparison, imports from India rose – from just 17.8 per cent in 1883/4 to 23.2 per cent in 1903/4 and 48.7 per cent in 1931/2. Other import-ing countries included the Straits, Germany, Belgium, France, the US and Japan, imports from which rose to 11.6 per cent of the total in 1932 and remained at this level, despite the 1933 introduction of high tariffs on the country's textiles.[12]

The majority of Burma's trade went through Rangoon, though until the early 1900s significant amounts of teak were handled by Moulmein, situated at the mouth of the Thanlwin River and some rice by Bassein and Akyab. Rangoon was established in 1853, largely because of its geographic position. At the con-fluence of the Hlaing and Pegu rivers, it had access to the Irrawaddy Delta and Sittang valley, and, 21 miles from the sea, avoided the silting and strong currents of the main stream of the Rangoon River, though two training walls had to be constructed to maintain the channel, which was constantly dredged. The port handled 80 to 90 per cent of Burma's trade, and, by 1939/40, 1,513 ships with a combined tonnage of 4.237m were using its wharves (874 ships with a tonnage of 598,303 in 1880/1). The main cargo was rice, 2.095m tons of which were exported in 1937/9. The rice trade with Europe and Cuba was controlled by European companies, principally Bulloch Bros and Steel Bros, and, to a lesser extent, Todd Findlay & Co. Exports to India, Ceylon, Java and East Africa were largely in the hands of Indian Hindu traders and the South East Asia market was controlled by Chinese merchants, largely Cantonese, Hokkien/Fukien from Amoy and Teochieu/Chaochow from Swatow. All bought rice from millers, and, by 1900, a futures market had developed, based in Mogul Street. Other signifi-cant exports in 1937/8 were mineral oil, 840,463 tons of which were exported, 98 per cent to India; timber, 208,598 tons, 76 per cent bound for India; bran, 269,712 tons; non-ferrous metals (pig lead, zinc concentrate, copper matte and wolfram), 171,945 tons; and tea. The latter cargo was grown in China in Xish-uangbanna and transported from Bhamo down the Irrawaddy to Rangoon from whence it was shipped to India and then moved overland to Tibet, a circuitous route necessitated by hostilities on the Sino-Tibetan border that blocked the northern route to Tibet. Imports mainly comprised manufactured goods from Europe, India, Japan, China and the United States.[13]

Note: Information on trade can also be found in the following sources/ themes:

Topic	Source	Volume/Theme
Burmese rice exports	F. Noel-Paton, *Burma Rice*	Volume 1/Agriculture
Malayan mineral exports/imports	'Report on Mining in Malaya'	Volume 2/Mining

Data relating to Malayan manufactured goods imports (1929),
Sarawak exports/imports
(1928–30), Brunei imports
(1928–30), British North Borneo
exports (1929–30) and imports
(1928–30) and Labuan imports/
exports (1928)

Anon., *The Manufacturing
Industries of the British
Empire*

Volume 2/Industry

1. G. Jones, *Merchants to Multinationals: British Trading Companies in the Nineteenth and Twentieth Centuries* (Oxford: Oxford University Press, 2000), p. 69; Anon., 'Malaya and its Communications', p. 2007; W. G. Huff, *The Economic Growth of Singapore: Trade and Development in the Twentieth Century* (Cambridge: Cambridge University Press, 1994), p. 11.
2. G. Huff, 'Gateway Cities and Urbanisation in Southeast Asia before World War II', *University of Oxford Discussion Papers in Economic and Social History*, 96 (2012), pp. 1–45, on p. 9; S. Dobbs, 'The Singapore River/Port in a Global Context', in D. Heng and S. M. K. Aljunied (eds), *Singapore in Global History* (Amsterdam: Amsterdam University Press, 2011), pp. 40–69, on p. 58; W. L. Ken, 'Singapore: Its Growth as an Entrepot Port, 1819–1941', *Journal of Southeast Asian Studies*, 9:1 (1978), pp. 50–84, on p. 56.
3. Huff, 'Gateway Cities', p. 5; Huff, *The Economic Growth*, pp. 8, 10, 11; V. Ponko, 'The Colonial Office and British Business before World War I: A Case Study', *Business History Review*, 43:1 (1969), pp. 39–58, on p. 45; A. W. King, 'Plantation and Agriculture in Malaya, with Notes on the Trade of Singapore', *Geographical Journal*, 93:2 (1939), pp. 134–48, on p. 145; N. C. Parkinson, 'The Pre-1942 Singapore Naval Base', *U.S. Naval Institute Proceedings*, 82:9 (1956), pp. 939–53.
4. J. Hon, *Tidal Fortunes: A Story of Change: The Singapore River and Kallang Basin* (Singapore: Landmark Books, 1990), pp. 9–13, 50; Ken, 'Singapore', p. 69; Ponko, 'The Colonial Office', pp. 42–3, 45–6, 49, 52–6; L. K. Khiun, 'Labour Formation, Identity and Resistance in HM Dockyard, Singapore (1921–1971)', *International Review of Social History*, 51:3 (2006), pp. 415–39. The King Dock was then the second largest dock in the world.
5. Huff, *The Economic Growth*, pp. 54, 108, 114–15; King, 'Plantation and Agriculture', p. 147.
6. Ken, 'Singapore', pp. 64, 71–2; King, 'Plantation and Agriculture', pp. 139, 143, 147–8; C. H. Ding, 'The Early Shipping Conference System of Singapore, 1897–1911', *Journal of Southeast Asian History*, 10:1 (1969), pp. 64–5; Huff, *The Economic Growth*, p. 54; Huff, 'Gateway Cities', p. 13. See also W. G. Huff, 'The Development of the Rubber Market in Pre-World War II', *Journal of Southeast Asian Studies*, 24:2 (1993), pp. 285–306. The Straits Homeward Conference is described in the Transport thematic introduction.
7. King, 'Plantation and Agriculture', p. 148; J. Lim, 'Chinese Merchants in Singapore and the China Trade, 1819–1959', *Chinese Southern Diaspora Studies*, 5 (2011–12), pp. 79–115, on pp. 91–2, 96–7; H. Kuo, 'Chinese Bourgeois Nationalism in Hong Kong and Singapore in the 1930s', *Journal of Contemporary Asia*, 36:3 (2006), pp. 385–405, on

8. Ken, 'Singapore', pp. 55, 65; Huff, *The Economic Growth*, pp. 54–5, 57, 93, 97, 103, 110; King, 'Plantation and Agriculture', pp. 146–7.
9. G. Jones and J. Wale, 'Merchants as Business Groups: British Trading Companies in Asia before 1945', *Business History Review*, 72:3 (1998), pp. 367–408, on p. 383; G. A. Wood (ed.), *American Association of Singapore 50th anniversary 1917–1967* (Singapore: American Association of Singapore, 1967), pp. 297–8.
10. Lim, 'Chinese Merchants', p 79; M. C. Cleary, 'Indigenous Trade and European Economic Intervention in North-West Borneo c. 1860–1930', *Modern Asian Studies*, 30:2 (1996), pp. 301–14, on pp. 308–9.
11. W. G. Huff, 'Monetization and Financial Development in Southeast Asia before the Second World War', *Economic History Review*, 56:2 (2003), pp. 300–45, on pp. 309, 329; Huff, *The Economic Growth*, p. 97; Ken, 'Singapore', p. 74.
12. N. Nishizawa, 'Economic Development of Burma', *Institute of Peace Studies, Hiroshima University, Japan, Research Report*, 16 (1991), pp. 1–155, on pp. 78–92; S. A. Resnick, 'The Decline of Rural Industry Under Export Expansion: A Comparison among Burma, Philippines, and Thailand, 1870–1938', *Journal of Economic History*, 30:1 (1970), pp. 51–73, on p. 57; A. Booth, 'Four Colonies and a Kingdom: A Comparison of Fiscal, Trade and Exchange Rate Policies in South East Asia in the 1930s', *Modern Asian Studies*, 37:2 (2003), pp. 429–102, on pp. 442, 449.
13. Nishizawa, 'Economic Development', pp. 35, 78–90; K. M. Kyi et al., *A Vision and A Strategy. Economic Development of Burma* (Stockholm: Olof Palme International Centre, 2000), p. 175; O. H. K. Spate and L. W. Trueblood, 'Rangoon: A Study in Urban Geography', *Geographical Review*, 32:1 (1942), pp. 56–73, on pp. 57, 68–9; Huff, 'Gateway Cities', p. 8; A. J. H. Latham and L. Neal, 'The International Market in Rice and Wheat, 1868–1914', *Economic History Review*, 36:2 (1983), pp. 260–80, on p. 274; A. J. H. Latham, 'From Competition to Constraint: The International Rice Trade in the Nineteenth and Twentieth Centuries', *Business and Economic History*, 17 (1988), pp. 91–102, on p. 95; Jones, *Merchants to Multinationals*, p. 69; A. M. Hill, 'Chinese Dominance of the Xishuangbanna Tea Trade: An Interregional Perspective', *Modern China*, 15:3 (1989), pp. 321–45, on pp. 321, 325–6.

ANON., *RETURN OF IMPORTS AND EXPORTS, STRAITS SETTLEMENTS, 1889* (1890)

Anon., *Return of Imports and Exports, Straits Settlements, 1889* (Singapore: Government Printer, 1890), pp. 199–229.

e extract contains detailed lists of the articles imported to and exported from Singapore, Penang and Malacca by value and by origins/destinations during 1888 and 1889. Comparisons with the source that follows reveal some of the changes in the region's trade described in the thematic introduction, for example, the rise of tin exports, the decline in the importance of Britain as a trading partner etc.

Anon., *Return of Imports and Exports, Straits Settlements, 1889* (1890), extract

COMPARATIVE STATEMENT OF THE VALUE IN DOLLARS OF
THE PRINCIPAL ARTICLES OF IMPORT.
SETTLEMENT OF SINGAPORE.
FROM THE UNITED KINGDOM.

	1888.	1889.	*Increase.*	*Decrease.*
	$	$	$	$
Millinery and Hosiery,	417,583	446,748	29,165	
Cabinetware,	74,112	44,838		29,274
Coals,	3,031,251	2,852,761		178,490
Cement,	90,553	122,091	31,538	
Cotton Goods,	7,288,441	5,958,946		1,329,495
Handkerchiefs, Coloured and Plain,	41,841	286,313	244,472	
Sarongs and Slendangs,[1]	73,434	169,960	96,526	
Cotton Blankets,	142,074	81,816		60,258
read,	281,072	286,313	5,241	
Do. Twist,	56,332	132,041	75,709	
Do. Dyed Yarn,	709,120	840,477	131,351	
Earthenware,	89,437	92,557	3,120	
Drugs,	36,663	43,890	7,227	
Glass and Glassware,	47,539	77,814	30,275	
Hats and Caps,	125,521	34,673		90,848
Machinery,	313,422	383,541	70,119	
Malt Liquor,	136,790	149,057	12,267	
Matches,	97,738	139,395	41,657	
Ironware,	70,100	194,276	124,176	
Hardware and Cutlery,	279,811	329,274	49,463	
Iron Nails and Rod,	35,118	145,193	110,075	
Iron Bars and Bolt,	138,048	38,600		99,448
Iron, Corrugated,	61,498	120,722	59,224	
Naval Stores,	116,862	119,956	3,094	
Linen Cloth,	38,694	42,655	3,961	
Paints,	91,069	96,348	5,252	
Paper,	22,359	22,857	498	

Articles.	1888.	1889.	Increase.	Decrease.
	$	$	$	$
Provisions,	336,844	306,733		30,111
Gunpowder,	31,452	42,073	10,621	
Dynamite,	90,900	58,950		31,950
Books and Maps,	20,844	27,968	7,124	
Butter and Cheese,	19,055	5,933		13,122
Canvas,	32,415	48,990	16,575	
Clocks and Watches,	22,942	13,285		9,657
Bread and Biscuits,	70,510	48,225		22,285
Specie,[2]	2,186,605	3,972,413	1,785,808	
Umbrellas, Cotton & Silk,	209,865	157,828		52,037
Woollen Goods,	303,574	397,311	93,737	
Blankets,	112,680	79,397		33,291
Brandy,	137,106	192,078	54,972	
Oilman's Stores,	116,862	92,792		24,070
Gin,	74,835	92,071	17,236	
Whisky,	75,152	121,524	46,372	
Tobacco,	44,528	55,129	10,601	
FROM AMERICA.				
Petroleum,	624,328	666,472	42,144	
FROM AUSTRIA.				
Millinery and Hosiery,	47,789	16,353		31,436
Cotton Goods,	86,513	22,486		64,027
Sarongs and Slendangs,	253,021	39,745		213,276 /
Glass and Glassware,	14,222	14,867	645	
Wheat Flour,	6,688	7,699	1,011	
Hardware and Cutlery,	14,688	24,228	9,540	
FROM AUSTRALIA.				
Horses,	26,000	20,105		5,895
Sheep,	14,717	22,823	8,106	
Coals,	184,773	490,836	306,063	
Provisions,	1,360	365		995
Sandal Wood,	69,661	252,258	182,597	
FROM BRITISH INDIA.				
Cattle,	24,480	32,410	7,930	
Sheep and Goats,	58,945	94,522	35,577	
Horses,	17,600	27,100	9,500	
Apparel,	3,275	49,494	46,219	
Bees' Wax,	108,901	75,397		33,504
Twist,	143,505	140,109		3,396
Dates,	51,904	84,747	32,843	
Ghee,	36,336	75,674	39,338	
Rice,	115,278	149,393	34,115	
Gunnies,	1,127,710	2,070,690	942,980	
Opium, Benares,	4,301,120	5,795,876	1,494,756	
Do., Patna,	37,500	228,597	191,697	

	1888.	1889.	*Increase.*	*Decrease.*
	$	$	$	$
Oil, Castor,	104,470	120,908	16,438	

FROM BRITISH BURMA.

	1888.	1889.	*Increase.*	*Decrease.*
Cotton,	88,612	18,451		70,161
Bran,	64,741	58,381		6,360
and Dholl,[4]	2,894	7,247	4,353	
Rice,	764,827	2,808,674	2,043,847	
Cutch,	20,414	3,575		16,839
Hides,	284,769	184,754		100,015
Horns,	51,407	79,656	28,249	
Precious Stones	121,649	1,022,370	600,730	

FROM CHINA.

	1888.	1889.	*Increase.*	*Decrease.*
Earthenware,	128,617	96,354		32,263
Joss Sticks and Joss Paper,	182,575	187,424	4,849	
Paper,	139,138	285,238	146,100	
Provisions,	286,028	197,237		88,791
Raw Silk,	153,178	109,360		43,818
Silk Piece Goods,	137,999	177,012	39,013	
Specie,	2,243,150	480,540		1,762,610
Tea,	202,536	218,829	16,293	
Salted Vegetables,	220,863	335,360	114,497	

FROM COCHIN CHINA.

	1888.	1889.	*Increase.*	*Decrease.*
Swine,	162,540	128,785		33,755
Salt,	38,021	17,713		20,308
Rice,	39,285	33,080		6,205
Hides,	28,895	12,480		16,410
Oil, Kachang,	10,724		10,724	
Provisions,	9,331	3,305		6,005
Raw Silk,	9,800	2,200		7,600 /

FROM EAST MALAY PENINSULA.

	1888.	1889.	*Increase.*	*Decrease.*
Poultry,	40,887	11,879		29,008
Swine,	64,750	29,042		35,708
Salted Fish,	191,443	167,133		24,310
Gutta Percha,	32,622	50,210	17,588	
Hides,	8,973	7,773		1,200
Rattans,	105,509	141,608	36,099	
Specie,	109,470	57,000		52,470

FROM FRANCE.

	1888.	1889.	*Increase.*	*Decrease.*
Apparel,	110,658	97,011		13,647
Butter and Cheese,	13,095	22,415	9,320	
Cotton Goods,	143,874	107,271		36,603
Sarongs and Slendangs,	312,223	409,187	96,964	
Brandy,	56,587	53,131		3,456
Champagne,	53,080	33,982		19,098
Claret,	29,846	30,692	846	
Sherry,	350	990	640	

Articles.	1888.	1889.	Increase.	Decrease.
	$	$	$	$
Provision,	25,314	25,926	612	
Silk Piece Goods,	131,693	119,670		12,023
Woollen Cloth,	12,385	21,455	9,070	
FROM BELGIUM.				
Arms and Ammunition,	55,396	50,213		5,183
Apparel,	62,550	51,844		10,706
Candles,	42,829	59,800	16,971	
Sarongs and Slendangs,	42,082	47,974	5,892	
Earthenware,	76,921	55,010		21,911
Glassware,	76,169	46,848		29,321
Hardware and Cutlery,	54,491	95,796		41,305
Gin,	66,333	20,824		45,509
Champagne,	13,171	20,697	7,526	
Woollen Goods,	15,473	11,374		4,099
Mineral Waters,	16,955	18,861	1,906	
Paints,	18,148	19,495	1,347	
FROM GERMANY.				
Apparel,	168,687	147,362		21,361
Gunpowder,	24,220	35,495	11,275	
Bread and Biscuits,	25,352	36,646	11,294	
Cabinetware,	37,613	11,390		26,223
Cotton Goods,	64,117	66,858	2,741	
Glassware,	140,837	76,635		64,202
Malt Liquor,	146,966	199,930	52,964	
Matches,	30,420	26,550		3,870
Hardware and Cutlery,	116,123	104,822		11,301
Ironware,	30,291	49,905	19,614	
Woollen Goods,	258,118	118,833		139,285
Provision,	23,853	34,154	10,301	
Brandy,	30,945	38,068	7,123	
FROM FRENCH COCHIN CHINA.				
Salted Fish,	938,011	1,177,163	239,152	
Padi,	2,843	13,484	10,641	
Peas,	58,256	93,682	35,426	
Rice,	1,182,747	1,317,946	135,199 /	
Copra,	141,234	55,328		85,906
Hides,	241,213	79,417		161,796
Horns,	29,918	30,595	677	
Lard,	122,520	139,079	16,559	
Raw Silk,	226,829	246,110	19,281	
Specie,	549,705	74,227		475,478
FROM HONGKONG.				
Apparel.	416,499	175,473		241,026
Bees' Wax,	7,955	21,612	13,657	
Bullion, Gold,	220,240	96,230		124,010

	1888.	1889.	Increase.	Decrease.
	$	$	$	$
Earthenware,	365,363	195,516		169,847
Cabinetware,	26,135	37,251	11,116	
Fireworks,	293,311	321,802	28,491	
Salted Fish,	339,983	217,916		122,067
Fishmaws,[5]	39,810	53,335	13,525	
Wheat Flour,	584,299	656,210	71,911	
Peas,	175,818	162,969		12,849
Sewing Thread,	33,510	32,640		10,870
Fruits, Dried, of Sorts,	24,746	40,066	15,320	
Do., Fresh, of Sorts,	54,983	52,873		2,110
Hides,	239,968	134,760		105,208
Horns,	74,882	86,652	11,770	
Joss Sticks and Joss Paper,	650,276	138,142		512,134
Boots and Shoes,	282,522	234,337		48,185
Medicines,	472,971	535,055	62,084	
Matches,	252,112	325,035	72,923	
Paper,	319,894	577,838	257,944	
Provisions,	673,038	645,399		207,639
Raw Silk,	481,316	642,382	161,066	
Silk Piece Goods,	990,692	1,272,896	282,204	
Specie,	2,142,270	882,890		1,259,380
Gold Bullion,	220,240	96,230		124,010
	62,102	201,248	139,346	
	357,580	383,503	26,004	
Tobacco,	745,582	1,117,732	372,150	
Umbrellas, Paper,	178,877	161,269		17,608
Preserved Vegetables,	104,605	84,982		19,693
Woodenware,	79,934	52,641		27,229
Copperware,	44,826	101,964	57,138	
Onions and Garlic,	89,699	105,850	16,181	
FROM JAPAN.				
Japanware,	83,077	75,937		7,140
	3,873,700	1,088,000		2,785,700
	505,089	271,193		233,896
Carriages and Carriage Materials,	78,338	22,776		55,562
FROM LABUAN.				
Birds' Nests,	4,345	5,365	1,020	
Gum Dammar,	1,360	90		1,270
Gutta Percha,	10,805	12,507	1,702	
Rattans,	57,680	18,922		38,758
Sago Flour,	129,333	165,366	36,033	
Mother-o'-Pearl Shells,	200			200 /
FROM NETHERLANDS INDIA.				
Beche-de-mer,[6]	457,344	227,455		229,889
Bees' Wax,	32,597	29,706		2,891

Articles.	1888.	1889.	Increase.	Decrease.
	$	$	$	$
Birds' Nests,	91,770	176,079	84,309	
Charcoal,	57,015	51,822		5,193
Coffee,	683,009	1,586,996	903,987	
Copra,	1,254,519	671,907		582,612
Cotton,	145,508	156,096	10,588	
Salted Fish,	167,289	164,896		2,393
Gambier,	2,172,278	2,838,033	665,755	
Gum Benjamin,	202,029	195,656		6,373
Gum Copal,	296,548	243,750		52,798
Gum Dammar,	63,990	77,973	13,983	
Gutta Percha,	177,141	2,262,949	485,808	
India Rubber,	27,705	22,467		5,238
Borneo Rubber,	600,330	242,152		358,178
Hides,	131,804	86,290		45,514
Lime,	105,068	137,517	32,449	
Coco-nut Oil,	202,509	346,883	144,374	
Mats and Matting,	22,871	77,832	54,961	
Rattans,	1,335,233	1,446,745	111,512	
Tin,	241,313	134,135		107,178
Raw Sago,	278,531	335,079	56,548	
Sago Flour,	129,181	103,824		25,357
Specie,	431,971	314,567		117,404
Areca-nuts,	136,576	232,004	95,428	
Nutmegs,	390,946	270,316		120,630
Black Pepper,	2,364,149	1,061,767		1,302,382
White Pepper,	1,282,459	1,120,869		161,590
Cubebs,[7]	38,738	89,880	51,142	
Sugar,	439,687	892,016	452,329	
Tobacco,	142,055	386,839	244,784	
Planks,	198,109	236,208	38,099	
Timber,	182,200	291,600	109,400	
Rice,	1,270,221	502,531		767,690
FROM NATUNAS ISLANDS.				
Copra,	295,390	196,307		99,083
Coco-nut Oil,	12,260	10,000		2,260
Raw Sago,	12,372	26,697	14,325	
FROM PHILIPPINES.				
Coffee,	29,376	31,368	1,992	
Hides,	221,530	35,377		186,153
Indigo,	37,186	22,635		14,551
Cigars,	173,765	203,409	29,644	
Copra,	210,021	139,810		70,211
FROM SIAM PROPER.				
Cattle,	601,835	604,260	2,425	
Salted Fish,	515,572	1,133,217	617,645	

	1888.	1889.	*Increase.*	*Decrease.*
	$	$	$	$
Sticklac,	45,273	36,777		8,496
Hides,	204,070	199,392		4,678
Teelseed,	19,942	98,660	78,718	
Specie,	391,910	1,343,650	951,740	
Sapan Wood,	11,350	14,611	3,261	
Horns,	30,605	48,930	18,325 /	

FROM SARAWAK.

	1888.	1889.	*Increase.*	*Decrease.*
Birds' Nests,	17,136	49,828	32,692	
Bees' Wax,	15,098	9,670		5,428
Coal,	23,858	35,439	11,581	
Salted Fish,	38,113	12,522		25,591
Gambier,	103,762	103,302		460
Gutta Percha,	82,632	130,246	47,614	
India Rubber,	17,574	26,176	8,602	
Rattans,	283,785	216,443		67,342
Sago Flour,	309,001	318,559	9,558	
Black Pepper,	126,326	325,261	198,935	

FROM HOLLAND.

	1888.	1889.	*Increase.*	*Decrease.*
Cotton Goods,	14,612	10,178		4,434
Candles,	800	30		770
Sarongs and Slendangs,	65,337	86,216	20,879	
Gin,	33,639	26,450		7,189

FROM MALACCA.

	1888.	1889.	*Increase.*	*Decrease.*
Bricks and Tiles,	8,489	3,219		5,270
Coco-nuts,	1,370	4,420	3,050	
Copra,	19,033	4,037		14,996
Salted Fish,	22,233	5,978		16,255
Gambier,	19,233	69,016	49,783	
Gutta Percha,	1,570	1,200		370
Tin Ore,		15,300	15,300	
Tin,	3,337,172	475,936		2,861,236
Sago Flour,	13,134	47,269	34,135	
Areca-nuts,	3,500	8,154	4,654	
Sago Pearl,	9,587	77,520	67,933	
Black Pepper,	9,858	20,546	10,688	
Tapioca Flour,	243,720	238,373		5,347
Do. Pearl,	572,381	587,305	14,024	
Do. Flake,	327,351	103,008		102,283
Specie,	32,390	51,400	19,010	

FROM PENANG.

	1888.	1889.	*Increase.*	*Decrease.*
Cotton Goods,	141,565	100,673		40,895
Salted Fish,	73,980	101,311	27,331	
Rice,	50,403	33,170		17,233
Gutta Percha,		25,622	25,622	
Tin,	1,863,342	2,677,237	813,895	

Articles.	1888.	1889.	Increase.	Decrease.
	$	$	$	$
Sugar,	172,435	153,484		18,951
FROM SULU ARCHIPELAGO.				
Beche-de-mer,	6,020	16,675	10,655	
Copra,	56,403	53,716		2,687
Gutta Percha,	2,130	2,150	20	
Mother-o'-Pearl Shells,	84,387	65,070		19,317 /
FROM WEST MALAY PENINSULA.				
Bark, Mangrove,	2,604	2,411		193
Bricks and Tiles,				
Coffee,	44,573	94,460	49,887	
Copra,	50,663	29,248		21,415
Salted Fish,	57,747	85,169	27,422	
Gambier,	2,555,358	3,019,568	464,210	
Gutta Percha,	180	20,110	19,930	
Indigo,	2,097	6,177	4,080	
Tin,	4,027,978	4,291,982	264,004	
Tin Ore,		1,192,419	1,192,419	
Rattans,	5,475	29,547	24,072	
Sago Flour,	2,128	16,177	14,049	
Specie,	15,650	90,226	74,576	
Areca-nuts,	68,909	180,059	111,150	
Black Pepper,	3,650,352	2,361,101		1,289,251
White Pepper,	13,448	126,448	113,000	
Tapioca Flour,	20,329	28,719	8,390	
Do. Flake,	125,855	98,872		26,983
Do. Pearl,	60,896	67,505	6,609	
FROM MADRAS.				
Cattle,	14,136	3,185		10,951
Bees' Wax,	11,010	4,350		6,660
Cotton Goods,	75,634	64,915		10,719
Dyed Yarn,	5,480	14,242	8,762	
Sarongs and Slendangs,	15,608	5,196		10,412
Curry Stuffs,	3,160	2,640		520
Sharks' Fins,	4,190	4,275	85	
Hides, Tanned,	70,001	51,875		18,126
Goats' Skin,	74,675	136,100	61,425	
Tamarind,[9]	2,715	685		2,030
Ghee,	2,460	2,665	205	
Rice,	1,024	2,254	1,230	
FROM SIAM WEST COAST.				
Tin,	52,710	133,131	80,421	
Salt,	1,626	9,158	7,532	
Specie,	6,700	39,100	32,400	
Planks,	5,300			5,300 /

COMPARATIVE STATEMENT OF THE VALUE IN DOLLARS OF THE PRINCIPAL ARTICLES OF EXPORT.
SETTLEMENT OF SINGAPORE.
To the United Kingdom.

Articles.	1888.	1889.	Increase.	Decrease.
		$	$	$
ee,	319,000	448,733	129,733	
	758,278	311,880		446,398
Fishmaws,	32,172	38,635	6,463	
Gambier,	2,101,205	2,555,575	454,370	
Gamboge,	15,150	12,782		2,368
Gum Benjamin,	68,753	107,384	38,631	
Gum Copal,	69,316	76,667	7,351	
Gum Dammar,	35,675	64,207	28,532	
Gutta Percha,	872,177	2,615,935	1,743,758	
India Rubber,	68,437	12,179		56,258
Borneo Rubber,	131,044	217,596	86,552	
Sticklac,	21,985	3,882		18,103
	1,350,626	866,625		484,001
	37,960	40,610	2,650	
Rattans,	321,965	553,879	231,914	
Sago Flour,	981,397	1,192,106	210,709	
Sago Pearl,	106,022	160,286	54,264	
Mother-o'-Pearl Shells,	159,087	142,411		16,676
Tortoise Shells,	21,500	25,494	3,994	
Green Snail Shells,	29,500	16,099		13,401
Cloves,	16,200	59,213	43,013	
Cubebs,	10,800	29,595	18,795	
Nutmegs,	55,638	58,381		254,298
Black Pepper,	1,799,731	1,545,433		254,298
White Pepper,	843,815	703,814		140,001
Long Pepper,		10,115	10,115	
Fruits, Preserved,	135,176	161,229	26,053	
	7,963,534	5,852,657		2,110,877
Tapioca Flour,	202,418	187,344		15,074
Do. Pearl,	328,284	282,655		45,629
Do. Flake,	367,922	464,252	96,330	
Bullion, Gold,	35,600	15,336		20,264
To Austria.				
ee,	32,162	333,603	301,441	
Gambier,	58,531	34,220		24,311
	22,463	11,230		11,233
	13,700	8,250		5,450
Shells, of Sorts,	7,479	6,251		1,228
	17,025	89,400	72,375	
Black Pepper,	490,020	488,347		1,673

Articles.	1888.	1889.	Increase.	Decrease.
	$	$	$	$
White Pepper,	11,500	18,947	7,447	
Rice,	17,963			17,963
Green Snail Shells,	3,190	6,514	3,324	
Fruits, Preserved,	830	5,160	4,330	

To Arabia.

Coffee,	47,862	54,041	6,179	
Fireworks,	908	500		408
Gum Benjamin,	17,516	3,092		14,424
Tin,	2,922	320		2,602
Black Pepper,	1,378	470		908
Garroo Wood,	5,622	3,095		2,527
Planks,		7,200	7,200 /	

To Australia.

Coffee,	7,830	29,241	21,411	
Fishmaws,	5,198	933		4,265
Rice,	60,291	78,551	18,260	
Rattans,	480	12,071	11,591	
Sago Flour,	1,523	2,238	715	
Sago Pearl,	2,921	2,895		26
Nutmegs,	61,622	29,857		31,765
Black Pepper,	83,650	40,037		43,613
White Pepper,	172,803	123,988		48,815
Gin,	22,331	22,888	557	
Tapioca Flour,	4,399	3,314		1,085
Do. Pearl,	189,951	252,557		37,394
Do. Flake,	58,978	40,273		18,705
Sugar,	3,953	9,699	5,746	
Whisky,	3,025	1,659		1,366
Mace,[10]	8,992	5,401		3,591
Cloves,	10,640	6,409		4,231
Provisions, Fresh & Salted,	6,631	5,005		1,626
Fruits, Preserved,	4,499	5,391	892	

To British India.

Coffee,	141,932	185,810	43,878	
Gambier,	81,791	120,608	38,817	
Gum Benjamin,	88,157	117,962	29,805	
Camphor,	20,926	22,311	1,385	
Gum Dammar,	11,689	22,704	11,015	
Sticklac,	3,003	6,945	3,942	
Tin,	35,459	32,743		2,716
Rattans,	24,783	32,414	7,631	
Sago Flour,	8,880	21,780	12,900	
Sago Pearl,	30,744	59,142	28,398	
Tapioca Flour,	9,155	8,273		882
Do. Pearl,	36,734	14,782		21,952

Articles.	1888.	1889.	Increase.	Decrease.
		$	$	$
Do. Flake,	2,097	2,357	260	
Areca-nuts,	71,430	157,998	86,568	
	45,407	33,720		11,681
Nutmegs,	50,847	65,138	14,291	
Black Pepper,	74,091	333,616	259,525	
White Pepper,	3,500	4,261	761	
Long Pepper,	39,998	38,141		1,857
	49,772	33,981		15,791
	41,500	15,400		26,100
	To British Burma.			
ee,	22,245	27,372	5,127	
Cotton Goods,	150,512	79,334		71,178
Salted Fish,	666,698	479,771		186,927
Teel Seeds,	78,490	233,211	154,721	
Raw Silk,	663,079	700,977	37,898	
Silk Piece Goods,	193,781	121,148		72,633
Oil, Kachang,	257,924	4,762		253,162
	11,177	3,900		7,277
Earthenware,	47,390	45,361		2,029
Tobacco,	12,013	19,948	7,935	
	17,940	19,333	1,393 /	
Umbrellas, Paper,	65,335	50,380		14,955
Provisions, Fresh & Salted,	127,522	83,642		43,880
Oil, Coco-nut,	22,026			22,026
Matches,	33,776	59,746	25,970	
	To America.			
ee,	33,981	37,601	3,620	
Gambier,	1,197,403	1,181,807		15,596
Gum Benjamin,	4,800	2,721		2,079
Gum Copal,	213,333	446,392	233,059	
Gum Dammar,	14,680	8,334		6,346
Dragon's Blood,[11]	8,200	2,700		5,500
Gutta Percha,	1,072,276	165,747		906,529
Borneo Rubber,	175,640	79,298		96,342
	57,542	26,700		30,842
	2,107,942	3,247,603	1,139,661	
Rattans,	1,060,792	942,330		118,462
Sago Flour,	67,377	95,142	27,765	
Sago Pearl,	2,300	700		1,600
Cloves,	3,529	12,623	9,094	
Cubebs,	17,135	39,565	22,430	
	26,405	6,505		19,900
Nutmegs,		278,507	278,507	
Black Pepper,	605,481	650,518	45,037	
White Pepper,	67,560	79,563	12,003	

Articles.	1888.	1889.	Increase.	Decrease.
	$	$	$	$
Tapioca Flour,	31,096	37,714	6,618	
Do. Pearl,	176,395	138,995		37,400
Do. Flake,	107,978	127,632	19,654	

TO COCHIN CHINA.

Gunpowder,	4,462	750		3,712
Cotton Goods,	104,124	63,871		40,253
Iron, Old,	8,115	4,629	4,486	
Opium, Benares,	398,751	155,863		242,888
Specie,	163,310	165,670	2,360	
Areca-nuts,	4,750	1,466		3,284

TO CHINA.

Mangrove Bark,	17,967	18,395	428	
Beche-de-mer,	79,159	122,685	43,526	
Birds' Nests,	50,885	88,180	37,295	
Cotton,	7,525	32,985	25,460	
Cotton Goods,	285,575	68,305		217,270
Fish, Salted,	95,998	62,863		33,135
Gunnies,	32,793	73,303	40,510	
Tin,	50,947	46,732		4,215
Opium, Benares,	175,430	522,332	346,902	
Rattans,	48,288	127,585	79,297	
Seaweed,	21,958	25,408	3,450	
Garoo Wood,	4,256	2,178		2,078
Sandal Wood,	31,252	152,251	120,999	
Planks,	29,373	48,384	19,011	
Timber,	39,924	54,826	14,902 /	

TO FRENCH COCHIN CHINA.

Apparel,	71,907	55,201		16,706
Bees' Wax,	28,032	27,787		245
Bread & Biscuits,	9,265	3,420		5,845
Coffee,	11,219	20,237	9,018	
Cotton Goods,	1,642,983	899,219		743,764
Cotton Thread,	24,811	28,190	3,379	
Dyed Yarn,	23,220	10,175		13,045
Gunnies,	238,444	165,135		73,309
Matches,	8,650	7,420		1,230
Hardware & Cutlery,	53,117	51,290		1,827
Ironware,	9,893	4,059		5,834
Iron Bars and Bolt,	10,187	2,472		7,715
Specie,	272,872	147,300		125,572
Areca-nuts,	40,106	48,461	8,355	
Umbrellas Cotton,	48,192	8,255		39,937
Do. Paper,	942	6,405	5,463	
Woollen Goods,	129,851	18,294		111,557
Blankets,	14,110	4,890		9,220

Articles.	1888.	1889.	Increase.	Decrease.
		$	$	$
To Hongkong.				
Beche-de-mer,	273,479	316,749	43,270	
Birds' Nests,	95,262	115,423	20,161	
Cotton,	157,179	95,195		61,984
Cotton Goods,	235,658	92,252		143,406
Fish, Salted,	67,159	43,499		23,660
Sharks' Fins,	32,883	34,176	1,293	
	288,798	11,855		276,943
Camphor,	11,750	6,010		5,740
	116,591	93,653		22,938
Goats' Skins,	238,487	210,873		27,614
	89,748	98,607	8,859	
Opium, Benares,	727,802	653,860		73,942
Precious Stones,	440,900	403,750		37,150
Rattans,	346,345	326,110		20,235
	380,500	251,800		128,700
Areca-nuts,	66,191	37,590		
Black Pepper,	58,311	55,553		2,758
	165,421	329,289	163,868	
Sandal Wood,	121,933	148,002	26,069	
Timber,	189,692	219,094	29,402	
	35,090	50,865	15,775	
To Germany.				
	22,569	26,619	4,050	
ee,	73,979	433,292	359,313	
	329,717	378,374	48,657	
Gambier,	457,561	449,364		8,197
	25,914	300,392	274,478	
Gutta Percha,	2,562	107,444	104,882	
Gum Copal,	7,550	3,740		3,810
Sticklac,	13,392	18,786	5,394	
	11,952	570		11,382
	17,080			17,080
Rattans,	566,387	510,778		55,609
	29,150	15,264		13,886
Black Pepper,	708,305	774,412	66,107 /	
White Pepper,	70,190	102,320	32,130	
Borneo Rubber,	112,135	64,475		47,660
Illipi-nuts,	12,850	18,100	5,250	
Sago Flour,	13,154	8,894		4,260
Sago Pearl,	11,263	50,167	38,904	
Tortoise Shells,	16,664	8,478		8,186
Tapioca Pearl,	21,250	57,671	36,421	
Do. Flake,	7,506	18,473	10,967	

Articles.	1888.	1889.	Increase.	Decrease.
		$	$	$
To France.				
Canes,	3,988	18,465	14,477	
Coffee,	39,411	176,361	136,950	
Copra,	963,798	801,015		162,783
Gambier,	447,128	549,182	102,054	
Gum Benjamin,	17,645	18,801	1,156	
Gum Copal,	38,585	28,424		10,161
Gum Dammar,	28,393	26,396		1,997
Gutta Percha,	37,310	217,720	180,410	
Borneo Rubber,	220,988	161,125		59,863
Hides,	27,142	39,764	12,622	
Horns,	178,226	235,686	57,460	
Tin,	790,996	1,941,098	1,150,102	
Rattans,	60,507	166,307	105,800	
Black Pepper,	162,602	337,640	175,038	
White Pepper,	215,688	250,150	34,462	
Illipi-nuts,	19,550	1,000		18,550
Tapioca Flake,	63,106	171,099	107,993	
Green Snail Shells,	17,724	25,828	8,104	
To Italy.				
Gambier,	93,411	48,411		45,000
Nutmegs,	2,970	1,790		1,180
Hides,	13,500	1,918		11,582
Tin,	56,778	43,890		12,888
Black Pepper,	129,701	240,962	111,261	
Sago Flour,	70,533	123,262	52,729	
To Labuan.				
Cotton Goods,	18,700	14,644		4,056
Sugar,	4,331	4,689	358	
Rice,	27,052	23,883		3,169
Silk Piece Goods,	13,400	60		13,340
Opium, Benares,	11,139	13,054	1,915	
Brandy,	1,709	3,186	1,477	
Gin,	2,427	2,145		282
To Mauritius.				
Rattans,	8,916	9,389	473	
Black Pepper,	5,675	6,609	934	
Tea,	1,598	1,260		338
Tobacco,	3,409	2,231		1,178
Planks,	37,393	71,186	33,793	
Timber,	4,190	1,073		3,117 /
Coffee,	27,155	23,675		3,480
Fireworks,	3,945	1,170		2,775
Lard,	35,704	104,320	68,616	

Articles.	1888.	1889.	Increase.	Decrease.
		$	$	$
To Natunas Islands.				
Cotton Goods,	45,462	15,827		29,635
Sarongs & Slendangs,	27,385	10,808		16,577
	79,153	71,382		7,771
Opium, Benares,	6,216	6,826	610	
Petroleum,	1,800	3,557	1,757	
	113,695	82,620		31,075
Provisions,	13,195	11,407		1,788
Tobacco,	6,251	4,119		2,132
Earthenware,	3,675	724		2,951
	2,897	2,314		583
To Netherlands India,				
	47,290	62,727	15,437	
	9,719	15,849	6,130	
Apparel,	262,571	243,038		19,533
Medicines,	135,682	78,462		57,220
Brassware,	12,616	19,381	6,765	
Copperware,	18,448	19,675	1,227	
Hardware and Cutlery,	179,790	235,213	55,423	
Ironware,	46,667	57,067	10,400	
Opium, Benares,	1,902,964	1,618,976		283,988
Do., Patna,	30,500	18,850		11,650
Do., Turkey,	57,850	34,700		23,150
Onions and Garlic,	43,807	51,704	7,897	
	136,338	211,354	75,016	
Petroleum,	252,429	286,853	34,424	
Provisions,	294,183	228,171		66,012
	38,847	44,214	5,367	
Raw Silk,	16,071	32,830	16,759	
Silk Piece Goods,	322,631	431,005	108,374	
	2,475,387	2,613,384	137,997	
Brandy,	22,499	37,229	14,730	
	55,261	54,726		535
	81,525	92,925	11,400	
	174,811	145,539		29,272
Tobacco,	188,261	196,370	8,109	
	68,336	65,063		3,273
Umbrellas, Cotton & Silk,	50,751	19,392		31,359
	6,592	13,328	6,736	
Bees' Wax,	38,802	30,063		8,739
Books & Maps,	21,845	22,395	550	
Bread & Biscuits,	18,919	18,897		22
Cabinetware,	46,750	32,719		14,031
Cotton Goods,	1,726,942	1,148,155		578,787
Cotton Twist,	58,952	65,587	6,635	

Articles.	1888.	1889.	Increase.	Decrease.
		$	$	$
Dyed Yarn,	58,113	71,465	18,352	
Cotton Thread,	96,932	59,471		37,461
Sarongs & Slendangs,	232,101	294,193	62,092	
Earthenware,	237,457	158,404		79,053
Fireworks,	100,525	108,639	8,114 /	
Salted Fish,	1,363,634	2,042,954	679,320	
Dates,	12,646	21,523	8,877	
Gambier,	714,485	793,727	79,242	
Glass & Glassware,	116,179	35,810		80,369
Gold Thread,	13,091	24,592	11,501	
Rice,	1,751,028	2,454,289	703,261	
Beans & Peas,	41,764	32,507		9,257
Wheat Flour,	108,812	146,386	37,574	
Gunnies,	295,527	219,355		76,162
Joss Sticks & Joss Papers,	218,048	92,058		125,990
Boots & Shoes,	136,930	45,576		91,354
Matches,	154,890	201,030	46,140	
Umbrellas, Paper,	53,799	41,817		11,982
Salted Vegetables,	90,514	49,149		41,365
TO PHILIPPINES.				
Hardware & Cutlery,	3,498	1,651		1,847
Rice,	428,759	362,391		66,368
Chocolate & Cocoa,	69,870	104,983	35,113	
Onions & Garlic,	13,533	6,851		6,682
Fish, Salted,	8,657	7,581		1,076
Opium, Benares,	1,080	12,569	11,489	
Do., Patna,	2,500	114,595	112,095	
Specie,	63,030	40,482		22,548
Woollen Cloth,	8,835	220		8,615
Black Pepper,	8,121	4,347		3,774
Gin,	8,308	62,009	53,701	
Mats & Matting,	6,922	11,219	4,297	
TO EAST MALAY PENINSULA.				
Apparel,	17,000	9,537		7,463
Cotton Goods,	163,148	137,741		25,407
Cotton Twist,	32,115	54,633	22,518	
Dyed Yarn,	66,001	100,255	34,254	
Sarongs & Slendangs,	24,025	17,514		6,511
Cotton Thread,	26,927	15,120		11,807
Earthenware,	21,897	4,033		17,864
Rice,	260,799	136,292		124,507
Hardware & Cutlery,	10,195	4,405		5,790
Opium, Benares,	135,578	101,188		34,390
Ironware,	3,194	9,862	6,668	
Provisions,	40,733	36,688		4,045

Articles.	1888.	1889.	Increase.	Decrease.
	$	$	$	$
Raw Silk,	27,095	30,599	3,504	
	362,682	423,454	60,772	
Silk Thread,	17,480	3,270		14,210
Tobacco,	30,728	25,480		5,248
To West Malay Peninsula.				
Apparel,	22,158	57,528	35,370	
Cotton Goods,	27,842	15,620		12,222
Earthenware,	22,278	11,212		11,066
Sarongs & Slendangs,	1,470	332		1,138
	1,450,078	2,365,232	915,154	
Joss Sticks & Joss Paper,	138,468	19,684		118,784
Hardware & Cutlery,	4,010	4,351	341 /	
Opium, Benares,	720,755	669,894		50,861
Provisions,	1,174,202	595,674		578,528
Petroleum,	10,634	31,595	20,961	
	1,985,670	1,965,595		20,075
Tobacco,	30,458	35,447	4,989	
To Holland.				
ee,	50,020	52,587	2,567	
	3,579	6,792	3,213	
Rattans,	11,398	41,654	3,256	
Gum Copal,	24,520	16,211		8,309
Gum Dammar,	1,260	1,896	636	
Gutta Percha,		1,200	1,200	
	5,100			5,100
Gambier,	174,114	259,099	84,985	
	330			330
To Malacca.				
	15,774	29,040	13,266	
Cotton Goods,	13,354	7,740		5,614
Earthenware,	15,763	9,344		6,419
Fish, Salted,	2,526	9,503	6,977	
	213,057	398,650	185,593	
Oil, Kachang,	3,096	3,923	827	
Petroleum,	17,537	38,519	20,982	
Opium, Benares,	69,531	5,716		63,815
Provisions,	78,900	63,138		15,762
	236,765	95,585		141,180
Tobacco,	17,386	25,031	7,645	
To Penang.				
Cotton Goods,	79,973	47,834		32,139
Earthenware,	3,980	3,934		46
Beans & Peas,	6,546	17,198	10,052	
	19,861	42,733	22,872	
	367,469	246,235		121,234

Articles.	1888.	1889.	Increase.	Decrease.
	$	$	$	$
Oil, Kachang,	112,288	143,337	31,049	
Opium, Benares,	20,320	45,732	25,412	
Provisions,	87,243	29,945		57,298
Specie,	922,510	236,750		685,760
Sugar,	11,208	21,968	10,760	
Tobacco,	110,260	91,134		19,126

To Siam Proper.

Articles.	1888.	1889.	Increase.	Decrease.
Bread & Biscuits,	32,303	30,903		1,400
Cotton Goods,	2,311,033	1,643,605		667,428
Do. Twist,	101,562	48,517		53,045
Do. Thread,	59,197	31,208		27,989
Dyed Yarn,	234,393	271,911	37,518	
Sarongs & Slendangs,	272,197	508,876	236,679	
Glassware,	50,770	39,287		11,483
Gunnies,	390,915	357,210		33,705
Hats,	61,848	32,559		29,289 /
Matches,	1,350	19,032	17,682	
Mats & Mattings,	45,938	58,777	12,839	
Iron Nails & Rod,	21,730	41,843	20,113	
Iron Bars & Bolt,	29,265	4,704		24,561
Ironware,	17,454	30,850	13,396	
Hardware & Cutlery,	45,685	19,454		26,231
Oil, Coco-nut,	106,438	140,769	34,331	
Oil, Kachang,	17,832	8,954		8,878
Petroleum,	135,068	55,898		79,170
Opium, Benares,	365,170	556,270	191,100	
Specie,	1,883,655	358,200		1,525,455
Areca-nuts,	56,733	125,383	68,650	
Woollen Goods,	107,491	9,840		97,651
Blankets,	34,900	7,591		27,309

To Sarawak.

Articles.	1888.	1889.	Increase.	Decrease.
Apparel,	34,789	12,182		22,607
Cotton Goods,	255,047	344,149	89,102	
Earthenware,	12,727	15,431	2,704	
Fish, Dry & Salted,	42,053	45,964	3,901	
Rice,	160,860	210,664	49,804	
Brassware,	24,637	21,502		3,135
Opium, Benares,	73,781	81,163	7,382	
Petroleum,	36,985	38,066	1,081	
Provisions,	23,346	23,893	547	
Silk Piece Goods,	57,460	77,421	19,961	
Specie,	55,970	74,069	18,099	
Sugar,	18,577	35,321	16,744	
Tobacco,	55,185	55,636	451	
Preserved Vegetables,	18,833	11,468		7,365

Articles.	1888.	1889.	*Increase.*	*Decrease.*
	$	$	$	$
To Madras.				
Fireworks,	11,195	7,250		3,945
Gum Benjamin,	21,150	5,114		16,036
Nutmegs,	4,501	305		4,130
	2,070	416		1,654
Sugar Candy,	1,655	1,645		10
Camphor,	62,535	23,595		38,940
Rattans,	2,174	1,988		186
To Siam West Coast.				
Cotton,	2,150	1,000		1,150
White Twist,	1,436	31,760	30,324	
Dyed Yarn,	11,270	75,435	64,165	
Sewing Thread,	3,300	4,136	836	
Sarongs & Slendangs,	18,255	11,695		6,560
Opium, Benares,	39,647	78,864	39,217	
	8,759	7,350		1,409
Provisions,	5,840	6,402	542	
	19,350	40,354	21,004 /	

COMPARATIVE STATEMENT OF THE VALUE IN DOLLARS OF THE PRINCIPAL ARTICLES OF IMPORT.
SETTLEMENT OF PENANG.
From the United Kingdom.

	1888.	1889.	*Increase.*	*Decrease.*
	$	$	$	$
Cabinetware,	2,939	10,524	7,585	
Coals,	41,446	91,596	50,150	
Cement,	52,135	65,300	9,165	
Cotton Goods,	1,576,262	1,327,812		248,450
Sarongs and Slendangs,	57,462	38,133		19,329
Cotton Thread,	31,293	29,552		1,741
Do. Twist,	5,010	3,250		1,760
Do. Dyed Yarn,	5,950	13,962	8,012	
Earthenware,	26,817	32,901	6,084	
Glass and Glassware,	50,193	56,754	6,561	
Machinery,	192,395	175,592		16,803
Malt Liquor,	103,553	96,635		6,918
Matches,	102,989	53,117		49,872
Iron Bars and Bolts,	63,379	62,539		840
Paints,	28,360	29,871	1,511	
Provisions,	176,561	129,342		47,219
Gunpowder,	4,638	365		4,273
Dynamite,	3,950	4,605	655	

Articles.	1888.	1889.	Increase.	Decrease.
	$	$	$	$
Specie,	2,105,346	2,103,086		2,260
Cotton & Silk Umbrellas,	24,993	25,050	57	
Woollen Goods,	65,531	39,825		25,706
Brandy,	84,644	94,428	9,784	
Oilman's Stores,	29,263	20,745		8,518
FROM AMERICA.				
Petroleum,	251,000	386,525	135,525	
FROM AUSTRIA.				
Gunpowder,	4,500			4,500
Cabinetware,	2,723	5,611	2,888	
Cotton Goods,	108,466	11,665		96,801
Do. Yarn,	6,140	760		5,380
Sarongs and Slendangs,	30,705	3,080		27,625
Glass and Glassware,	7,021	3,564		3,457
Gold Thread,	2,670	360		2,310
Machinery,	2,780	850		1,930
Malt Liquor,	19,711	25,331	5,620	
Hardware and Cutlery,	11,653	1,940		9,713
Paper,	19,965	11,702		8,263
FROM BRITISH INDIA.				
Cattle,	71,548	19,360		52,188
Sheep and Goats,	78,710	83,639	4,929	
Horses and Ponies,	52,058	20,433		31,625
Apparel,	32,074	18,060		14,014
Cotton Goods,	567,035	256,423		310,612
Twist,	5,494	11,903	6,409	
Dates,	17,121	12,400		4,721
Ghee,	58,319	43,854		14,465
Rice,	284,742	150,046		134,696
Gunnies,	86,588	79,461		7,127
Opium, Benares,	2,035,245	2,013,671		21,574
Oil, Castor,	32,076	38,748	6,672	
Onions and Garlic,	55,361	55,025		336 /
Cotton,	158,536	96,874		61,662
Gram and Dholl,	3,021	4,174	1,153	
Rice,	3,081,919	3,929,090	847,171	
Hides,	220	50,054	49,834	
Horns,	2,665	320		2,345
FROM CHINA.				
Earthenware,	23,727	17,916		5,811
Joss Sticks and Joss Paper,	25,019	30,391	5,372	
Paper,	64,555	67,563	3,008	
Provisions,	69,698	70,609	911	
Silk, Raw,	32,250	21,166		11,084
Specie,	365,000	7,835		357,165

	1888.	1889.	*Increase.*	*Decrease.*
	$	$	$	$
Tea,	11,247	8,357		2,890
Salted Vegetables,	14,482	20,429	5,947	
FROM FRANCE.				
Apparel,	6,055	14,006	7,951	
Cotton Goods,	20,395	34,759	14,364	
Sarongs and Slendangs,	10,330	17,837	7,507	
Brandy,	49,929	40,738		9,191
Champagne,	1,440	11,745	10,305	
Claret,	32,901	22,326		10,575
Port,	6,680	1,988		4,692
FROM BELGIUM.				
Apparel,	4,130	340		3,790
Arms and Ammunition,	58,224	17,420		40,804
Candles,	1,275	2,250	975	
Earthenware,	13,880	22,500	8,620	
Glass and Glassware,	16,514	24,221	7,707	
Hardware and Cutlery,	14,104	17,710	3,606	
Gin,	23,795	5,630		18,165
Brandy,	30,287	1,000		29,287
Woollen Goods,	2,000	2,156	136	
FROM GERMANY.				
Apparel,	9,306	12,157	2,851	
Bread and Biscuits,	10,300	16,400	6,100	
Cabinetware,	2,125	2,100		25
Cotton Goods,	67,938	28,270		39,668
Glass and Glassware,	45,673	29,141		16,532
Malt Liquor,	132,903	160,470	27,567	
Matches,	39,264	107,915	68,651	
Hardware and Cutlery,	30,477	18,311		12,166
Woollen Goods,	30,974	10,429		20,545
FROM HONGKONG.				
Apparel,	1,062,092	852,270		209,822
Bees' Wax,	9,333	6,838		2,495
Earthenware,	74,934	62,265		12,669
Fireworks,	138,119	143,645	5,526	
Salted Fish,	124,638	122,162		2,476
Fishmaws,	4,755	550		4,205
Wheat Flour,	237,693	292,224	54,531	
Peas,	130,658	132,694	2,036 /	
Hides, Raw and Tanned,	40,853	29,728		11,125
Joss Sticks & Joss Paper,	52,848	59,499	6,651	
Medicines,	139,393	143,496	4,103	
Paper,	276,503	238,099		38,404
Provisions,	512,175	552,333	40,158	
Raw Silk,	127,860	101,419		26,441

Articles.	1888.	1889.	Increase.	Decrease.
	$	$	$	$
Silk Piece Goods,	32,250	42,790	10,540	
Specie,	2,172,095	438,908		1,733,187
Bullion, Gold,	1,295,182	507,237		787,945
Sugar,	59,197	90,571	31,374	
Tea,	203,557	204,708	1,151	
Tobacco,	143,287	236,024	92,737	
Paper Umbrellas,	99,577	97,081		2,496
Woodenware,	37,440	34,366		3,074
Gold Coin,	1,500	33,095	31,595	
FROM JAPAN.				
Bullion, Gold,	42,535			42,535
Japanware,	8,116	1,100		7,016
Specie,	853,150	360,000		493,150
FROM MALACCA.				
Brick and Tiles,	6,060	2,920		3,140
Fish, Dry and Salted,	4,999	3,380		1,619
Gambier,	14,934	11,130		3,804
Gutta Percha,	1,150	85		1,065
Tin,	4,025	24,030	20,005	
Areca-nuts,	46,109	20,482		25,627
Tapioca Flour,	18,531	3,660		14,871
Do. Flake,		1,100	1,100	
FROM SINGAPORE.				
Fish, Dry and Salted,	42,583	19,120		23,463
Lard,	68,182	58,691		9,491
Rice,	352,535	196,654		155,881
Rachang Oil,	103,024	127,190	23,574	
Opium, Benares,	5,050	24,938		19,888
Provisions,	73,092	68,450		4,642
Specie,	967,006	643,665		323,341
Sugar,	19,723	18,406		1,317
Tobacco,	148,232	173,018	24,786	
FROM CEYLON.				
Cordage Coir,	5,328	12,300	6,972	
Fish, Dry and Salted,	11,423	67,125	55,702	
Specie,	2,175	990		1,185
Tea,	1,325	2,305	980	
FROM MADRAS.				
Cattle,	106,950	60,741		46,209
Carriages and Carriage Materials,	6,870	4,102		2,768
Cotton Goods,	45,124	25,051		20,073
Yarn,	5,290	875		4,415
Sarongs and Slendangs,	28,642	4,750		23,892
Onions and Garlic,	5,368	9,074	3,706	/

	1888. $	1889. $	*Increase.* $	*Decrease.* $
FROM ARABIA.				
Fish, Dry and Salted,	4,646	2,448		2,198
Onions and Garlic,	6,720			6,720
	34,100	49,166	15,066	
FROM SUMATRA.				
Horses and Ponies,	30,081	13,965		16,116
Poultry,	32,329			32,329
Bees' Wax,	2,825	999		1,826
	34,422	35,881	1,459	
Fish, Dry and Salted,	144,714	115,674		29,040
Fishmaws,	55,875	32,585		23,290
Sharks' Fins,	11,133	10,639		494
Gambier,	26,103	56,147	30,044	
Gum Benjamin,	46,959	47,918	959	
Camphor,	55,505	48,225		7,280
Gutta Percha,	18,327	30,977	12,650	
India Rubber,	12,285	1,840		10,445
Hides, Raw,	13,585	14,581	996	
	246,029	101,849		144,180
	31,067	13,300		17,767
Nutmegs,	129,799	149,818	20,019	
Black Pepper,	2,958,006	2,169,571		788,435
Tobacco,	720,055	208,249		511,806
FROM RUSSIA.				
Petroleum,	175,000	302,000	127,000	
FROM JAVA.				
Bullion, Gold,	13,597			13,597
FROM SIAM WEST COAST.				
	54,595	78,090	23,495	
	74,857	94,798	10,941	
Bark, Mangrove,	23,402	37,291	11,889	
Beche-de-mer,	3,552	2,340		1,212
Fish, Dry and Salted,	16,261	21,164	4,903	
	32,695	54,221	21,526	
	36,580	148,868	112,288	
	2,920	13,875	10,955	
Mats and Mattings,	12,484	5,085		7,399
	3,005,592	2,967,489		38,103
Rattans,	3,554	2,900		654
Green Snail Shells,	2,389	315		2,074
	33,700	30,200		3,500
Areca-nuts,	4,680	4,210		470
Black Pepper,	124,846	332,300	207,454	
FROM HOLLAND.				
Cotton Goods,	35,220	21,190		14,030

Articles.	1888.	1889.	Increase.	Decrease.
	$	$	$	$
Sarongs and Slendangs,	6,150	2,225		3,925
Malt Liquor,	16,879	18,029	1,150	
Provisions,	44,711	72,612	27,901	
Gin,	26,647	58,483	31,836	
Cigars,	9,585	13,478	3,893	/

FROM PERAK.

Fish, Dry and Salted,	22,271			22,271
Fishmaws,	5,215			5,215
Tin,	8,785,775	7,977,096		808,679
Rattans,	7,439	22,243	14,804	
Tapioca Flour,	5,300	3,350		1,950
Tobacco,	3,210			3,210
Wood, Planks,	29,349	19,919		9,430
Firewood,	83,533	74,679		8,854
Timber,	48,234	51,797	3,563	

FROM SELANGOR.

Fish, Dry and Salted,	3,124	24,590	21,460	
Tin,	51,406	279,444	228,038	

FROM FRENCH INDIA.

Cattle,	49,595			49,595
Sheep,	3,708	129		3,579
Cotton Goods,	94,555	62,410		32,145
Curry Stuffs,	1,548	260		1,288
Tamarind,	3,438	1,791		1,647
Ghee,	3,288	4,120	832	
Rice,	87,281	81,518		5,763
Oil Cakes,	58,063	49,014		9,049
Nuts, Ground,	24,205	25,696	1,491 /	

COMPARATIVE STATEMENT OF THE VALUE IN DOLLARS OF THE PRINCIPAL ARTICLES OF EXPORT.
SETTLEMENT OF PENANG.
To The United Kingdom.

Articles.	1888.	1889.	Increase.	Decrease.
	$	$	$	$
Coffee,	3,272			3,272
Copra,	94,877			94,877
Fishmaws,	182,268	142,330		39,938
Gum Benjamin,	20,424	45,790	25,366	
Gutta Percha,		490	490	
India Rubber,	48,363	40,401		7,962
Borneo Rubber,	2,404	515		1,889
Hides,	19,060	63,430	44,370	

Articles.	1888.	1889.	Increase.	Decrease.
	$	$	$	$
Rattans,	1,116	6,939	5,823	
Green Snail Shells,	12,687	24,483	11,796	
Cloves,	18,175	79,885	61,710	
Nutmegs,	242,239	242,054		185
Black Pepper,	1,491,248	1,185,551		305,697
White Pepper,	419,103	892,420	473,317	
Tin,	6,523,477	4,258,239		2,265,238
Tapioca Flour,	139,305	290,125	150,820	
Do. Flake,	74,009	140,333	66,324	
Sugar,	176,206	674,617	498,411	
Putch Leaf,	1,345	3,160	1,815	
Mace,	12,237	91,563	79,326	
To America.				
Tin,	417,280	1,406,193	988,913	
Black Pepper,	26,550	39,010	12,460	
White do.,		112,510	112,510	
Nutmegs,	97,651	144,991	47,340	
Mace,	12,237	4,916		7,321
To Austria.				
Black Pepper,	31,690			31,690
To British India.				
Gum Benjamin,	6,503	7,482	919	
Camphor,	7,110	9,630	2,520	
Tin,	888,320	770,977		117,343
Rattans,	9,490	18,516	9,026	
Sago Flour,	1,850	6,916	5,066	
Do. Pearl,	2,800	2,390		410
Areca-nuts,	467,832	396,243		71,589
Mace,	29,432	25,660		3,772
Nutmegs,	51,880	44,360		7,520
Black Pepper,	75,291	336,228	260,937	
White do.,	2,655	6,149	3,494	
To British Burma.				
Fish, Dry and Salted,	44,776	58,526	13,750	
Raw Silk,	130,270	158,850	28,580	
Silk Piece Goods,	149,351	85,213		64,138
Sugar,	1,090	85,618	84,528	
Tobacco,	11,916	8,338		3,578
Tin,	14,003	36,018	22,015	
Areca-nuts,	38,376	82,808	44,432	
Nutmegs,	6,396	4,384		2,012
Black Pepper,	11,450	22,730	11,280 /	
To China.				
Mangrove Bark,	25,855	13,844		12,011
Cotton,	85,801	40,155		45,646

Articles.	1888.	1889.	Increase.	Decrease.
	$	$	$	$
Fish, Salted,	7,031	4,252		2,779
Tin,		1,093,026	1,093,026	
Opium, Benares,	37,285	28,680		8,605
Black Pepper,	156,419	69,772		86,647
To FRANCE				
Tin,	19,621	43,816	24,195	
Black Pepper,	75,492	165,537	90,045	
White do.,	3,085	86,313	83,228	
Tapioca Flake,	14,764	13,749		1,015
Putch Leaf,	3,633	2,100		1,533
Copra,	31,691			31,691
Hides,	4,035		4,035	
To GERMANY.				
Black Pepper,	18,820	3,000		15,820
White do.,	5,537	10,010	4,473	
Tapioca Flake,	2,430		2,430	
Gum Benjamin,	3,953	475		3,478
To ITALY.				
Hides,	5,204			5,204
Black Pepper,	23,327	29,423	6,096	
White do.,	8,859	10,850	1,991	
To MADRAS.				
Gum Benjamin,	3,090	160		2,930
Tin,	36,845	26,025		10,820
Tobacco,	10,800	12,250	1,450	
To CEYLON				
Coffee,	4,766	7,075	2,309	
Areca-nuts,	3,866			3,866
To HONGKONG.				
Beche-de-mer	12,132	22,836	10,704	
Birds' Nests,	16,050	7,310		8,740
Cotton,	90,295	72,595		17,700
Cotton Goods,	78,590	76,725		1,865
Fish, Dry and Salted,	46,267	33,574		12,693
Sharks' Fins,	80,685	84,910	4,235	
Rice,	33,462	76,200	42,738	
Camphor,	47,560	49,100	1,540	
Hides, Raw and Tanned,	19,460	24,112	4,652	
Tin,	1,157,967	567,243		590,724
Opium, Benares,	8,550			8,550
Precious Stones,	219,630	163,170		56,460
Rattans,	25,714	12,302		13,416
Specie,	45,100	10,450		34,650
Areca-nuts,	114,869	36,944		77,925
Black Pepper,	649,069	242,752		406,317

Articles.	1888.	1889.	Increase.	Decrease.
	$	$	$	$
White do.,	28,980	18,977		10,003
Bark, Mangrove,	50,745	57,314	6,569 /	
Cloves,	3,270	975		2,295
Nutmegs,	16,085	24,557	8,472	
Sugar,	262,611	135,039		127,572
Tapioca Flour,	26,119	25,313		806
Fishmaws,	10,221	38,045	27,824	
To French India.				
Cotton Goods,	2,300	750		1,550
Fireworks,	2,522	5,288	2,766	
Areca-nuts,	33,291	17,620		15,671
To Siam West Coast				
Cotton Goods,	112,442	83,940		28,502
Sarongs & Slendangs,	18,707	14,928		3,779
Fish, Dry & Salted,	24,723	29,530	4,807	
Bran,	14,374	15,858	1,484	
Rice,	246,733	240,831		5,902
Flour,	17,279	15,343		1,936
Joss Sticks & Joss Paper,	11,145	9,783		1,362
Lard,	23,660	28,160	4,500	
Matches,	6,549	5,600		949
Hardware & Cutlery,	5,071	1,372		3,499
Ground Nuts,	9,198	9,653	455	
Oil, Coco-nut,	8,388	16,294	7,906	
Oil, Kachang,	11,056	20,044	8,988	
Onions & Garlic,	10,125	10,452	327	
Opium, Benares,	417,816	368,283		49,533
Petroleum,	19,273	27,756	8,483	
Provisions,	47,864	60,984	13,120	
Salt,	8,826	10,208	1,382	
Specie,	1,002,529	627,318		375,211
Arrack & Samsoo,	24,223	18,220		6,003
Tea,	5,212	16,869	11,657	
Tobacco,	37,570	38,152	582	
Vegetables, Preserved,	5,587	7,427	1,840	
TO SIAM PROPER				
Fish, Dry & Salted,	18,140,	22,098	3,958	
Rice,	58,488	131,131	72,643	
Opium, Benares,	42,676	73,971	31,295	
Petroleum,	12,783	15,808	3,025	
Arrack & Samsoo,	7,092	3,890		3,202
Brandy,	6,246	3,591		2,655
Sugar,	12,843	21,333	8,490	
To Perak.				
Cattle,	24,872	42,916	18,044	

Articles.	1888.	1889.	Increase.	Decrease.
	$	$	$	$
Horses & Ponies,	24,209	14,000		10,209
Poultry,	69,768	61,345		8,423
Swine,	148,790	170,641	21,851	
Apparel,	11,636	9,364		2,272
Bricks & Tiles,	11,392	14,696	3,304	
Candles,	5,094	2,365		2,729
Carriages and Carriage Materials,	7,202	8,487	1,285	
Cement,	9,672	19,358	9,686	
Cotton Goods,	30,283	47,103	16,820	
Earthenware,	24,466	8,549		15,917
Fireworks	33,658	21,743		11,915 /
Fish, Dry & Salted,	21,874	29,318	7,444	
Bran,	21,132	36,176	15,044	
Rice,	1,257,428	1,203,264		54,164
Padi,	6,811	12,244	5,433	
Beans & Peas,	51,266	51,084		182
Flour,	34,540	127,160	92,620	
Joss Sticks & Joss Paper,	8,207	12,428	4,221	
Machinery,	17,970	17,148		822
Malt Liquor,	13,076	20,759	7,683	
Matches,	14,376	8,379		5,997
Medicines,	10,012	13,946	3,934	
Metals, Corrugated,	12,401	5,142		7,259
Hardware & Cutlery,	19,795	2,996		16,799
Ironware,	24,305	32,498	8,193	
Oil, Coco-nut,	17,259	33,560	16,301	
Oil, Kachang,	131,335	102,660		28,675
Oilman's Stores,	6,620	16,261	9,641	
Onions & Garlic,	6,680	11,785	5,105	
Opium, Benares,	781,733	753,614		28,119
Paper,	5,240	13,142	7,902	
Petroleum,	53,743	56,215	2,472	
Provisions,	203,971	118,715		85,256
Salt,	7,562	14,926	7,364	
Specie,	950,062	1,961,325	1,011,263	
Arrack & Samsoo,	10,990	16,477	5,487	
Brandy,	22,239	28,368	6,129	
Gin,	9,003	11,953	2,950	
Whisky,	7,281	12,390	5,109	
Sugar,	86,029	91,096	5,067	
Tea,	22,765	16,086		6,679
Tobacco,	69,972	88,298	18,326	
Vegetable, Fresh & Salted,	26,265	29,449	3,184	
To SUMATRA.				
Cattle,	309,947	325,387	15,440	

Articles.	1888.	1889.	Increase.	Decrease.
	$	$	$	$
Medicines,	9,255	15,688	6,433	
Opium, Benares,	515,336	496,649		18,687
Onions & Garlic,	28,234	29,920	1,686	
Petroleum,	167,203	192,816	25,613	
Provisions,	481,164	485,815	4,651	
Salt,	17,975	13,393		4,582
Specie,	2,988,463	2,537,270		451,193
Brandy,	47,776	59,773	11,997	
Gin,	52,472	46,507		5,965
Sugar,	177,314	178,098	784	
Tea,	33,622	51,839	18,217	
Tobacco,	67,902	80,951	13,049	
Bread & Biscuits,	14,866	16,928	2,062	
Cotton Goods,	745,957	594,626		151,331
Sarongs & Slendangs,	6,328	11,003	4,675	
Earthenware,	33,872	43,786	9,914	
Fiereworks,	30,060	34,444	4,384	
Fish, Dry & Salted,	172,518	196,877	24,359 /	
Dates,	7,973	4,195		3,778
Glass & Glassware,	12,902	21,626	8,724	
Gold Thread,		1,045	1,045	
Rice,	1,969,547	1,751,085		218,462
Flour,	42,961	58,095	15,134	
Gunnies,	14,884	11,726		3,158
Joss Sticks & Joss Paper,	17,289	29,611	12,322	
Boots & Shoes,	6,892	10,687	3,795	
Matches,	64,423	62,345		2,078
Paper Umbrellas,	7,478	7,208		270
Vegetables, Fresh & Salted,	14,443	23,753	9,310	
Bamboo & Rattanware,	14,226	10,133		4,093
Bricks & Tiles,	16,617	14,991		1,626
Butter & Cheese,	17,430	13,915		3,515
Cabinetware,	11,258	5,202		6,056
Carriages and Carriage Materials,	21,421	25,377	3,956	
Cement,	13,762	13,492		270
Cordage, Coir,	22,068	20,805		1,263
Ghee,	9,766	7,953		1,813
Bran,	13,422	22,798	9,376	
Beans & Peas,	25,056	30,269	5,213	
Gram,	10,696	4,804		5,892
Lime,	19,557	21,941	2,384	
Malt Liquor,	166,844	196,411	29,567	
Manure, Guano,	291,397	406,280	114,883	
Do., Other kinds,	60,037	3,820		56,217
Mats and Mattings,	34,509	21,811		12,698

Articles.	1888.	1889.	Increase.	Decrease.
	$	$	$	$
Oil, Kachang,	48,071	33,546		14,525
Oilman's Stores,	13,641	17,084	3,443	
Paper,	17,177	33,552	16,375	
Arrack & Samsoo,	17,115	31,056		16,050
Twine,	17,815	12,014		5,801
Champagne,	6,457	3,755		2,702
Claret,	26,443	23,910		2,533
Wine, Port,	5,403	6,546	1,143	
Do., Other kinds,	20,380	24,034	3,654	
Wood Timber,	59,449	42,776		16,673
Do. Planks,	112,742	99,903		12,839
Firewood,	10,578	14,828	4,250	
Woodenware,	19,599	55,699	36,100	
To MALACCA.				
Cotton Goods,	18,116	13,015		5,101
Curry Stuffs,	5,933	8,361	2,428	
Fish, Dry &-Salted,	7,304	8,745	1,441	
Bran,	3,803	6,935	3,132	
Rice,	78,171	99,105	20,934	
Petroleum,	4,894	19,852	14,958	
Provisions,	5,572	7,679	2,107	
Sugar,	14,388	9,027		5,361 /
To SINGAPORE.				
Bark, Mangrove,	8,718	8,437		281
Coals,	12,500			12,500
Copra,	9,252			9,252
Cotton,	10,000			10,000
Cotton Goods,	201,081	215,140	14,059	
Curry Stuffs,	12,509	3,597		8,912
Fish, Dry & Salted,	24,219	77,179	52,960	
Rice,	40,742	45,015	4,273	
Gunnies,	8,907	4,142		4,765
Tin,	3,890,414	3,694,572	195,842	
Specie,	206,086	235,676	29,590	
Sugar,	197,900	161,773		36,127
Tapioca Flour,	10,790	60		10,730 /

COMPARATIVE STATEMENT OF THE VALUE IN DOLLARS OF
THE ARTICLES OF IMPORT.
SETTLEMENT OF MALACCA.

Articles.	1888.	1889.	Increase.	Decrease.
	$	$	$	$
Animals,	175,735	104,886		70,849
Apparel,	700			700

	1888.	1889.	*Increase.*	*Decrease.*
	$	$	$	$
Arms, &c.,	760	695		65
Bamboo and Rattanware,		93	93	
Bark,	79	4,500	4,421	
Bees' Wax,	967	550		417
Books and Maps,	331	628	297	
Bread Stuffs,	974	1,804	830	
Bricks and Tiles,	2,863	3,110	247	
Butter and Cheese,	8	115	107	
Candles,		60	60	
Carriages and Carriage Materials,	2,545	3,111	566	
Canes and Sticks,	46	28		18
Cement,	505	2,005	1,500	
Charcoal,	1,098	1,335	237	
Clocks and Watches,		200	200	
Coal,	775	962	187	
Coco-nuts,	201	54		147
ee,	150	6,405	6,255	
Copra,	1,728	315		1,413
Cotton,	719	649		70
Cotton Goods,	10,759	17,879	7,120	
Cordage,	334	10		324
Curry Stuffs,	5,347	1,309		4,038
Earthenware,	8,012	9,787	1,775	
Fireworks,	548			548
Fish,	80,358	134,743	54,385	
Fruits,	5,815	4,204		1,611
Gambier,	17,429	36,647	19,218	
Ghee,	5	80	75	
Glassware,		40	40	
Gunnies,	21			21
Grain,	571,536	759,523	187,987	
Gum,	1,373	905		468
Hats & Caps,		15	15	
Hides,	49	87	38	
Ice,	4	10	6	
Indigo,	130	48		82
Jewellery,		800	800	
Joss Sticks, &c.,	2,647	5,225	2,578	
Leather,	30	225	195	
Lime,	1,761	3,153	1,392	
Lard,	38	280	242	
Machinery,	6,000	6,272	272	
Malt Liquor,	355	1,674	1,319	
Manure,	5,398	5,226		172
Matches,	939	1,646	707	

Articles.	1888.	1889.	Increase.	Decrease.
	$	$	$	$
Mattings,	2,913	2,634		279
Medicines,	160	730	570	
Metals Unmanufactured,	814,785	332,446		482,339
Manufactured Metals,	38,863	17,101		21,762
Nuts,	899	3,004	2,105	
Oil,	14,044	13,567		477
Onions & Garlic,	4,190	4,478	288	
Opium,	71,335	246,985	175,650	
Paints,		239	239	
Paper,	418	315		103 /
Perfumery,		129	129	
Petroleum,	53,164	52,430		734
Provisions,	1,907	4,949	3,042	
Rattans,	5,971	9,109	3,138	
Sago,	3,145	180		2,965
Salt,	11,126	11,448	322	
Seeds,		18	18	
Shells,		65	65	
Silk,		150	150	
Soap,	20	188	168	
Specie,	274,365	113,627		160,738
Spices,	37,623	19,467		18,156
Spirits,	22,018	27,918	5,900	
Stones,	1,672	314		1,358
Sugar,	24,294	25,444	1,150	
Tallow,	48	24		24
Tapioca,	29,339	75,416	46,077	
Tar,	17	12		5
Tea,	2,204	2,913	709	
Twine,	78			78
Tobacco,	46,310	57,594	11,284	
Umbrellas,	38			38
Vegetables,	13,385	16,648	3,263	
Wood,	29,595	27,947		1,648
Wine,	717	3,891	3,174	
Sundries,	48,427	78,401	29,974 /	

COMPARATIVE STATEMENT OF THE VALUE IN DOLLARS OF
THE ARTICLES OF EXPORT.
SETTLEMENT OF MALACCA.

Articles.	1888.	1889.	Increase.	Decrease.
	$	$	$	$
Animals,	80,394	67,923		12,471
Apparel,	708			708

	1888.	1889.	*Increase.*	*Decrease.*
	$	$	$	$
Arms and Ammunition,		700	700	
Bark, Mangrove,		4,500	4,500	
Birds,		260	260	
Books and Maps,	758	25		733
Bread and Biscuits,	213			213
Bricks and Tiles,	17,128	12,886		4,242
Candles,	67	144	77	
Canes and Sticks,	400	63		335
Carriages and Carriage Materials,	7,137	5,079		2,058
Cement,	75	50		25
Charcoal,	6	230	224	
Coco-nuts,	959	22,751	21,792	
ee,	210	6,102	5,892	
Copra,	45,427	8,415		37,012
Cotton Goods,	2,618	2,291		327
Curry Stuffs,	70			70
Earthenware,	68	153	85	
Fish,	11,599	10,036		1,563
Fruits,	7,226	2,322		4,904
Gambier,	64,973	100,376	35,403	
Glass and Glassware,		5	5	
Grain,	171,749	146,319		25,430
Gum, Dyes and Rosin,	2,710	17,976	15,266	
Gunnies,	351	200		151
Hides,	3,509	4,995	1,486	
Joss Sticks, &c.,	5	48	43	
Indigo,	120			120
Leather,		766	766	
Lard,	447	651	204	
Lime,	352	1,318	966	
Machinery,	1,000	1,000		
Matches,	23	20		3
Mats and Mattings,	6,979	6,104		875
Medicines,	121	5		116
Metals, Unmanufactured,	883,621	401,603		482,018
Metals, Manufactured,	184	378	194	
Nuts,	90	75		15
Oil,	5,916	7,590	1,674	
Onions and Garlic,	91	97	6	
Opium,	57,619	44,064		13,555
Petroleum,	2,436	3,154	718	
Provisions,	3,089	5,596	2,507	
Rattans,	2,265	1,543		722
Sago,	3,558	2,453		1,105
Salt,	5,318	4,789		529

Articles.	1888.	1889.	Increase.	Decrease.
	$	$	$	$
Soap,	1,965	17		1,948
Specie,	247,873	296,441	48,568	
Spices,	77,967	36,323		41,644
Spirits,	2,930	7,291	4,361	
Stones,	333	503	170	
Sugar,	15,415	24,858	9,443 /	
Tapioca,	1,425,486	1,378,446		47,040
Tar,	20			20
Tea,	11	73	62	
Twine,	16	30	14	
Tobacco,	2,752	1,560		1,192
Vegetables,	9,954	17,303	7,349	
Wine,	66	5		61
Wood,	372	1,546	1,174	
Sundries,	31,857	43,035	11,178	

ALEXANDER, *BRITISH MALAYA: MALAYAN STATISTICS* (1928)

C. S. Alexander, *British Malaya: Malayan Statistics* (London: Malayan Information Agency, 1928), pp. 13–70.

is extract provides a cornucopia of Malayan statistics analysing shipping data (1913–28) and imports and exports by good (value and quantity) and origin/destination (1923–8). The trade statistics were compiled from the *Annual Summary of Monthly Returns of Foreign Imports and Exports of British Malaya* for the year ended 31 December 1928 and from the *Returns of Imports and Exports of British Malaya* for previous years. The values of the Imports are CIF and that of exports FOB. The shipping data was extracted from the *Annual Reports of the Trade and Customs Department, FMS*. Manufactured goods import data (1929) and other trade statistics can be found below in the extract from *The Manufacturing Industries of the British Empire Overseas* on pp. 373–402.

C. S. Alexander, *British Malaya: Malayan Statistics* (1928), extract

EXTERNAL TRADE OF BRITISH MALAYA.

[...]

IMPORTS AND EXPORTS OF MERCHANDISE AND OF COIN AND BULLION, 1921 TO 1928. TOTAL ANNUAL VALUES.

	MERCHANDISE.			COIN AND BULLION.		
	Imports.	Exports.	Excess of Exports (+)or Imports (–)	Imports.	Exports.	Excess of Exports (+) or Imports (–)
	$'000.	$'000.	$'000.	$'000.	$'000.	$'000.
1921	482,474 (*a*)	417,605 (*a*)	– 64,869	19,592	16,001	– 3,591
	455,396 (*a*)	489,100 (*a*)	+ 33,704	15,587	11,020	– 4,567
1923	577,568 (*a*)	669,738 (*a*)	+ 92,170	15,846	4,956	– 10,890
1924	658,894	722,630	+ 63,736	13,381	4,635	– 8,746
1925	975,709	1,284,388	+ 308,679	40,109	8,110	– 31,999
1926	1,016,553	1,265,124	+ 248,571	46,263	10,878	– 35,385
1927	1,004,559	1,066,322	+ 61,763	27,251	6,965	– 20,286
1928	867,637	847,014	– 20,623	18,862	6,962	– 11,900 /

) Exclusive of Parcel Post. /

IMPORTS AND EXPORTS OF MERCHANDISE DETAILED 1924 TO 1928. IMPORTANT AND OTHER ARTICLES. VALUES.
(In thousands of dollars.)

Particulars.	1924.	1925.	1926.	1927.	1928.
	IMPORTS.				
	Class I. – Animals,.				
Food, Drink					

Particulars.	1924.	1925.	1926.	1927.	1928.
and Tobacco					
Beans	2,083	2,765	3,481	4,020	3,843
Rice	72,606	80,650	98,378	104,355	95,473
Wheat Flour	5,671	7,632	7,740	8,091	6,984
Sago Flour	4,716	3,927	3,001	3,506	2,538
Tapioca, Flour and Pearl	1,090	760	872	804	787
Other Grain and Flour	2,876	3,342	3,956	4,382	3,609
Rice Meal (Bran)	5,921	5,686	6,254	6,185	6,463
Other Feeding Stuffs for Animals	1,022	1,161	1,585	1,629	1,986
Meat	2,327	2,761	3,298	3,446	3,438
Cattle	2,590	3,258	3,639	3,314	3,714
Swine	3,205	4,329	5,715	5,836	5,388
Other Animals for Food	743	844	1,197	1,458	1,303
Birds' Nests	1,080	1,148	1,293	1,078	980
Biscuits	872	1,429	2,067	1,841	1,388
Butter, Tinned and Frozen	1,026	1,011	1,180	1,172	1,408
Coffee, Raw	4,973	6,470	6,084	5,145	4,137
Curry Stuffs	1,410	1,548	1,929	1,746	1,609
Eggs, Fresh and Salted	548	789	1,099	1,487	1,176
Fish, Dried and Salted	12,471	13,889	15,731	15,460	13,966
Fish, Fresh	643	646	813	1,034	1,082
Sardines	1,710	2,109	2,502	2,218	1,541
Fish, Other Kinds of	957	1,129	1,405	1,640	1,228
Fruits, Fresh	1,321	1,382	1,926	2,809	2,181
Fruits, Dried and Preserved	2,442	2,686	3,234	3,528	2,967
Fruits, Canned	528	713	1,028	804	586
Ghee[1]	1,391	1,519	1,735	1,726	1,682
Lard	791	1,067	859	818	925
Carried forward	137,013	154,550	182,001	189,532	172,382 /
Brought forward	137,013	154,550	182,001	189,532	172,382
Milk, Condensed and Sterilized	10,035	13,780	15,857	15,141	15,491
Salt	974	890	897	988	973
Arecanuts[2]	7,706	10,009	9,399	5,878	6,981
Cloves	1,110	1,434	1,050	1,089	581
Nutmegs	1,159	1,396	1,492	1,277	1,232
Pepper, Black, Long and White	7,820	9,391	12,225	15,028	16,378
Other Spices	923	1,104	1,500	1,921	2,158
Sugar	18,156	15,808	15,169	15,367	12,905
Tea	3,247	3,634	4,539	4,542	4,285
Potatoes	709	794	935	1,154	996
Vegetables, Preserved	2,516	3,409	4,834	4,654	4,191
Vegetables, Other Kinds of	3,167	3,293	4,108	4,416	4,654
Other Provisions	5,228	6,182	7,909	7,475	6,724
Brandy	2,681	3,485	4,488	4,163	3,348
Whisky	1,502	1,454	1,586	1,612	1,541
Arrack[3] and Samsoo[4]	1,167	1,497	1,714	1,503	1,306

Particulars.	1924.	1925.	1926.	1927.	1928.
Beer and Ale	969	1,378	1,934	2,201	2,130
Porter and Stout	932	1,409	2,567	2,135	2,005
Other Spirituous Liquors	854	1,168	1,622	1,833	1,379
	315	424	507	549	443
Cigarettes	22,358	29,129	27,102	26,334	26,636
Tobacco, Manufactured	1,263	6,508	6,017	6,009	5,610
Tobacco, Native, Unmanufactured	[illeg.]	1,759	1,973	2,137	2,267
Animals, Living, not for Food	166	217	285	347	350
Total, Class I	237,945	274,102	311,710	317,285	296,946

Class II. – Raw Materials and Articles Mainly Unmanufactured.

	9,912	8,052	9,545	10,972	9,766
Asphalt and Bitumen	1,351	1,200	1,080	1,280	1,553
	55,359	60,984	62,598	73,362	66,950
Carried forward	66,622	70,236	73,223	85,614	78,269 /
Brought forward	66,622	70,236	73,223	85,614	78,269
Firewood	1,019	1,031	1,094	1,089	1,037
	2,583	2,602	3,844	4,747	3,799
Other Wood	1,009	1,073	1,405	1,509	1,868
	12,929	13,036	15,178	10,040	15,418
Ground Nuts	1,154	1,737	1,551	1,905	4,148
Benjamin	697	803	918	1,022	1,007
	1,220	1,034	1,308	1,575	1,384
	1,140	751	719	1,569	1,156
Other Gums and Resins	1,184	903	1,029	1,159	845
Kachang Oil	3,689	4,307	4,760	5,095	5,758
Hides and Skins	2,386	2,214	2,000	1,806	1,626
Gutta Percha (over $840 per ton)	2,251	2,350	1,878	1,115	365
Gutta, Inferior (under $840 per ton)				628	789
Jelutong	1,569	1,773	4,876	2,307	1,659
Para Rubber	76,298	237,617	170,497	171,913	88,218
Rattans	3,663	3,547	4,468	3,990	3,722
Gambier, in Bales and Cube	1,464	1,206	687	471	435
Other Articles	7,207	8,527	9,099	7,745	8,417
Total, Class II	188,084	354,747	298,534	305,299	219,920

Class III. – Articles Wholly or Mainly Manufactured.

Asbestos Manufactures	233	350	690	1,155	1,224
Crockery and Porcelain	1,519	2,949	3,080	1,686	1,395
Cement	2,558	3,822	4,564	6,771	8,785
Glass and Glassware	1,136	1,906	2,592	2,088	1,659
Tiles	505	492	716	1,015	1,441
Steel Bars, Rods, Angles, Shapes and Sections	1,432	1,347	1,762	1,752	2,026
Hollow-ware (Cooking and Household Utensils)	1,795	2,534	2,661	2,115	1,723
Iron, Galvanized (Corrugated and Sheet)	2,126	3,560	5,267	4,877	3,219

Particulars.	1924.	1925.	1926.	1927.	1928.
Tin Plates	3,666	3,247	2,989	3,561	3,337
Carried forward	14,970	20,207	24,321	25,020	24,809 /
Brought forward	14,970	20,207	24,321	25,020	24,809
Tubes, Pipes and Fittings	2,231	3,978	2,963	3,309	3,443
Other Iron and Steel Goods	9,787	9,141	13,182	13,478	13,975
Brass and Brassware	740	1,015	1,440	1,257	1,260
Other Metals and Manufactures thereof	2,339	2,560	3,032	2,543	2,656
Cutlery, Hardware, Implements and Instruments	3,860	5,614	7,027	6,095	5,081
Electrical Goods and Apparatus	2,282	3,320	4,230	5,444	6,869
Electrical Machinery	996	1,361	1,930	1,955	3,102
Dredging Materials	–	–	–	766	13,133
Sewing Machines	957	952	2,271	1,601	724
Other Machines and Machinery	6,778	10,701	15,457	18,593	10,619
Cotton Piece Goods, Plain, Dyed and Printed	30,431	46,009	41,254	36,887	29,473
Cotton Sarongs, Slendangs and Kains	13,144	17,243	17,361	14,148	12,847
Other Cotton Goods	5,183	7,375	7,387	5,142	5,128
Woollen Goods	1,712	2,722	3,921	2,596	1,876
Silk Piece Goods	3,035	5,564	7,995	6,303	3,817
Other Silk Goods	832	1,869	1,853	881	1,286
Artificial Silk Piece Goods	–	–	–	–	2,351
Cordage	1,975	2,425	2,767	2,678	2,698
Gunnies[7]	4,328	7,721	6,548	6,569	5,199
Other Textile Goods	2,295	2,207	2,475	2,630	2,287
Boots and Shoes (Leather and other sorts)	426	658	1,093	1,186	1,168
Haberdashery and Millinery (including Hats, Caps, etc.)	1,726	4,243	5,194	3,450	2,325
Other Apparel	3,810	4,262	6,453	4,425	3,849
Acetic Acid	792	1,342	1,001	747	639
Other Chemicals	1,697	2,478	2,899	3,080	3,234
Opium, Raw	4,865	4,821	10,001	7,308	7,134
Other Drugs and Medicienes	3,600	4,351	5,086	5,901	5,234
Paints and Dyes	2,739	2,637	2,675	2,851	2,922
Kerosene	15,023	18,095	15,114	18,951	15,640
Liquid Fuel	10,445	11,992	13,057	18,986	21,046
Lubricating Oils	3,422	4,184	5,067	5,150	4,528
Motor Spirit	29,210	62,546	75,269	65,426	55,310
Carried forward	185,630	273,593	310,923	295,350	275,662 /
Brought forward	185,630	273,593	310,923	295,356	275,662
Soap (Toilet and Other Sorts)	2,045	2,736	2,833	2,961	3,082
Other Manufactured Oils, Fats and Resins	1,163	1,688	1,513	1,529	1,729
Leather and Leather Manufactures	1,321	1,681	2,113	1,660	1,462

Particulars.	1924.	1925.	1926.	1927.	1928.
Paper and Paperware	4,030	4,832	6,057	6,463	6,185
Motor Cars, Passenger	4,615	12,534	14,782	10,283	7,435
Motor Cars, Commercial	668	2,214	3,329	2,848	2,486
Cycles and Motor Cycles	608	2,016	1,846	786	575
Parts and Accessories, Motor Cars and					
	1,747	1,997	2,810	2,593	2,552
Parts and Accessories, Cycles	845	2,281	1,682	1,013	869
Pneumatic Tyres and Tubes:					
Motor Car, Motor Truck and Motor					
Cycle Covers	1,767	2,963	3,736	4,348	3,189
Motor Car, Motor Truck and Motor					
Cycle Tubes	334	510	557	648	408
Cycle Covers and Tubes	246	265	690	678	577
Fireworks	959	1,184	2,007	1,289	1,149
Cabinetware	410	564	1,326	1,064	1,050
Fancy Goods and Toys	914	1,561	2,566	2,113	1,325
Joss Sticks and Joss Paper	2,089	2,217	2,658	2,227	2,196
	1,643	1,590	1,413	1,502	1,639
Mats and Matting	1,001	1,256	1,377	1,165	926
Perfumery and Cosmetics	1,597	2,616	2,899	2,632	2,078
Woodenware – Rubber Cases	2,212	3,175	5,050	3,450	3,172
Other Articles	11,439	15,621	21,437	21,370	23,217
Total, Class III	227,283	339,094	393,604	367,978	342,963
Class IV. – Parcel Post.					
Total, Class IV	5,582	7,766	12,705	13,997	7,808
I. Animals, Food, Drink and Tobacco	237,945	274,102	311,710	317,285	296,946
II. Raw Materials and Articles Mainly					
Unmanufactured	188,084	354,747	298,534	305,299	219,920
III. Articles Wholly or Mainly Manu-					
factured	227,283	339,094	393,604	367,978	342,963
IV. Parcel Post	5,582	7,766	12,705	13,997	7,808
Total Imports	658,894	975,709	1,016,553	1,004,559	867,637 /

EXPORTS.

Class I. – Animals, Food, Drink and Tobacco.

	1924.	1925.	1926.	1927.	1928.
	23,712	31,212	36,613	35,992	32,304
Sago Flour	6,191	5,328	4,220	4,351	3,716
Tapioca, Flake, Flour and Pearl	7,119	4,819	4,376	4,244	3,834
Other Grain and Flour	3,182	3,751	3,781	3,786	3,592
Feeding Stuffs for Animals	880	1,163	1,122	1,191	1,458
Meat and Animals for Food	213	285	462	381	331
	564	864	1,102	921	1,358
ee, Raw	3,412	4,137	3,348	2,794	2,029
Fish, Dried and Salted	14,512	14,105	15,161	14,309	14,458
	1,080	1,237	1,462	1,103	676
Fruits, Dried and Preserved	1,016	1,050	1,180	1,228	1,023
Pineapples, Canned	8,874	8,237	7,670	8,297	8,421

Particulars.	1924.	1925.	1926.	1927.	1928.
Milk, Condensed and Sterilized	1,958	2,744	3,251	2,710	2,503
Arecanuts	14,983	18,293	17,288	10, 300	12,196
Pepper, Black, Long and While	8,296	10,143	13,292	16,762	18,413
Other Spices	3,293	3,818	3,609	3,817	3,555
Sugar	5,048	3,692	2,984	2,534	2,421
Sugar Candy	3,096	2,540	1,570	1,109	1,504
Vegetables	1,958	2,210	2,727	2,891	2,955
Other Provisions	6,665	7,352	8,412	7,948	7,841
Wines, Spirits and Malt Liquors	1,254	1,766	1,866	1,848	1,331
Cigarettes	10,929	12,348	9,988	8,598	7,886
Tobacco, Manufactured	910	2,326	1,998	1,753	1,789
Other Articles	1,555	356	318	366	270
Total, Class I	130,700	143,776	147,800	139,233	135,864

Class II. – Raw Materials and Articles Mainly Unmanufactured.

	1924.	1925.	1926.	1927.	1928.
Phosphates of Lime	1,915	1,684	1,973	1,999	– (a)
Iron Ore	1,510	1,361	1,383	2,116	3,324
Wood and Timber	3,488	2,267	1,667	1,645	1,572
Copra	32,668	32,110	36,988	26,578	34,165
Carried forward	39,581	37,422	42,011	32,338	39,061 /
Brought forward	39,581	37,422	42,011	32,338	39,061
Ground Nuts	169	436	333	511	2,689
Benjamin	752	727	832	900	897
Copal	995	1,052	786	781	591
Damar	1,950	1,789	1,773	2,127	2,072
Sticklac	1,136	1,028	663	1,837	1,094
Coconut Oil	2,204	2,836	3,144	3,479	3,174
Palm Oil	–	–	–	270	392
Other Oils, Nuts and Seeds for Oils, Gums, etc.	2,344	2,183	3,096	1,673	2,800
Hides and Skins	1,554	1,849	1,130	1,367	1,358
Gutta Percha	3,560	3,227	2,881	937	388
Gutta, Inferior	1,954	2,935	6,173	1,078	1,231
Jelutong				3,164	2,638
Para Rubber	264,940	746,228	711,302	519,465	329,790
Para Rubber Latex	1,252	10,413	6,650	3,523	1,297
Rattans	5,582	4,821	4,729	4,321	4,335
Gambier, in Bales and Cube	3,453	2,544	1,501	1,142	1,008
Rubber Seeds	–	1	14	8	235
Other Articles	3,344	3,574	3,694	3,642	4,013
Total, Class II	334,770	823,065	790,712	582,563	399,063

Class III. – Articles Wholly or Mainly Manufactured.

	1924.	1925.	1926.	1927.	1928.
Crockery and Porcelain	919	1,476	1,158	941	599
Glass and Glassware	570	716	754	783	683
Iron and Steel Goods	3,219	4,858	4,999	3,988	4,435
Tin	169,147	175,202	185,526	206,571	191,279

Particulars.	1924.	1925.	1926.	1927.	1928.
Cutlery, Hardware, Implements and Instruments	1,167	1,285	1,271	1,293	1,272
Electrical Goods and Apparatus	168	310	361	571	697
Machinery	1,874	1,938	2,169	2,226	4,586
Cotton Piece Goods, Plain, Dyed and Printed	12,427	14,994	12,429	11,772	9,565
Cotton Sarongs, Slendangs and Kains	7,434	7,941	7,751	7,779	6,549
Other Cotton Goods	3,059	3,851	2,639	2,312	[illeg.]
Silk Goods	751	1,286	993	959	1,102
Carried forward	200,735	213,857	220,050	239,195	222,440 /
Brought forward	200,735	213,857	220,050	239,195	222,440
	3,638	6,840	6,000	6,682	5,272
Other Textile Goods	2,122	1,894	1,943	1,939	2,021
Boots and Shoes, Leather and other	698	1,711	1,837	3,001	3,203
Other Apparel	1,568	2,139	2,042	1,880	1,608
Chemicals and Drugs	1,686	2,455	2,160	2,390	2,408
Paints and Dyes	1,346	1,101	838	841	828
Kerosene	8,208	10,076	9,283	12,587	11,974
Liquid Fuel	1,217	1,413	1,856	2,289	2,682
Lubricating Oils	1,478	1,850	1,767	1,687	1,200
Motor Spirit	17,257	53,175	57,486	48,834	34,937
Other Manufactured Oils, Fats and	1,252	1,347	1,230	1,384	1,405
Leather and Leather Manufactures	2,747	2,355	2,546	2,506	2,179
Paper and Paperware	702	723	785	586	559
Motor Cars and Parts and Accessories thereof	1,036	1,837	1,660	1,565	1,614
Cycles and Parts and Accessories thereof	347	1,381	854	562	396
Pneumatic Tyres and Tubes: Motor Cars, Motor Trucks and Motor Cycles, Covers and Tubes	454	714	1,013	1,456	1,689
Rubber Manufactures (other than Tyres and Tubes)	1,235	1,053	1,103	1,246	1,341
Other Articles	7,254	9,013	9,630	9,353	8,886
Total, Class III	254,980	314,934	324,083	339,933	306,642
Class IV – Parcel Post.					
Total, Class IV	2,181	2,613	2,529	4,593	5,445
I. Animals, Food, Drink and Tobacco	130,700	143,776	147,800	139,233	135,864
II. Raw Materials and Articles Mainly Unmanufactured	334,770	823,065	790,712	582,563	399,063
III. Articles Wholly or Mainly Manufactured	254,980	314,934	324,083	339,933	306,642
IV. Parcel Post	2.180	2,613	2,529	4,5933	5,445
Total Exports of Merchandise	722,630	1,284,388	1,265,124	1,066,322	847,014 /

IMPORTS AND EXPORTS OF MERCHANDISE DETAILED.
IMPORTANT ARTICLES.
QUANTITIES.

Particulars.	Unit.	1924.	1925.	1926.	1927.	1928.
		IMPORTS.				
Beans	Tons	17,077	22,844	28,522	35,250	34,527
Rice	Tons	580,735	650,007	755,380	839,959	803,914
Wheat Flour	Tons	42,572	48,380	49,544	57,061	52,955
Sago Flour	Tons	48,847	39,629	31,332	36,958	32,614
Tapioca Flour	Tons	6,303	5,724	7,375	6,869	5,457
Other Grain and Flour	Tons	24,013	24,387	23,895	28,276	26,296
Rice Meal (Bran)	Tons	113,100	114,844	129,792	132,878	127,591
Meat (except Live Poultry and Game)	Tons	2,420	2,644	3,032	3,391	3,748
Cattle	Number	38,455	46,071	46,118	38,053	43,937
Swine	Number	139,469	183,343	226,951	220,645	198,927
Biscuits	Cwts.	14,256	21,526	32,069	27,842	19,482
Butter, Tinned	Cwts.	7,688	6,565	9,853	10,100	12,403
Butter, Frozen	Cwts.	4,422	6,280	5,562	5,644	7,207
Coffee, Raw	Thous. lbs.	16,470	18,879	18,515	18,613	14,074
Curry Stuffs	Cwts.	75,738	89,686	104,011	94,803	111,791
Eggs, Fresh and Salted	Thous.	21,531	28,957	38,312	52,288	43,417
Fish, Dried and Salted	Tons.	47,917	56,172	56,535	52,609	50,995
Fish, Fresh	Tons.	1,566	1,359	1,635	2,086	2,203
Sardines	Tons.	5,381	6,592	7,743	6,802	4,769
Fruits, Fresh	Tons.	8,311	7,808	9,238	12,722	9,912
Fruits, Dried and Preserved	Tons.	11,733	10,870	12,326	13,998	12,615
Ghee	Tons.	1,197	1,298	1,393	1,404	1,346
Milk, Condensed	Thous. cases.	720·4	1,004·5	1,178·8	1,225·0	1,312·3
Arecanuts	Tons.	40,021	39,977	40,525	32,132	45,185
Cloves	Tons.	973	1,533	1,270	1,702	835
Nutmegs	Tons.	1,772	1,697	2,257	2,436	2,492
Pepper, Black and White	Tons.	18,814	14,025	14,068	11,712	12,504
Other Spices	Tons.	3,524	3,682	4,950	5,444	6,013
Sugar	Tons.	91,112	112,919	108,829	110,683	111,731
Tea	Thous. lbs.	8,424	9,127	11,198	10,778	9,973
Vegetables, Preserved	Tons.	13,037	17,419	22,906	21,429	18,120
Onions and Garlic	Tons.	22,172	24,004	23,978	28,856	30,913 /
Arrack and Samsoo	Thous. gallons	545·2	608·7	702·2	650·1	616·1
Brandy	"	312·6	423·2	541·3	448·9	357·8
Beer and Ale	"	461·9	612·3	849·3	954·6	935·2
Porter and Stout	"	279·4	438·0	809·0	702·4	675·7
Other Spirituous Liquors	"	246·4	289·1	374·1	375·8	332·3
Cigarettes	Thous. lbs.	12,698	15,398	12,436	11,383	11,131

Particulars.	Unit.	1924.	1925.	1926.	1927.	1928.
Tobacco, Native						
Unmanufactured	Thous. lbs.	12,939	6,101	6,452	6,588	6,677
	Tons	673,962	627,482	793,301	876,348	811,929
Asphalt and Bitumen	Tons	14,063	12,734	12,607	16,016	20,058
	Tons	37,909	39,489	36,891	42,254	44,389
	Cub. [illeg.] of					
	50 [illeg.].	150,803	127,421	103,752	102,702	103,708
	Cub. [illeg.] of					
	50 [illeg.].	183,057	162,577	151,666	190,654	179,852
	Tons	67,314	66,815	81,010	56,538	87,763
Ground Nuts	Tons	6,682	10,597	8,721	11,548	24,195
	Tons	1,444	1,586	1,567	1,626	1,444
	Tons	6,567	5,457	6,805	8,967	7,374
	Tons	1,004	699	904	1,566	1,305
Other Gums and Resins	Tons	2,266	1,721	1,974	2,067	1,615
Kachang Oil	Cwts.	190,385	188,074	229,530	241,464	263,883
Cow Hides	Tons	2,139	1,665	1,860	1,534	953
	Tons	2,316	2,378	1,441	875	345
Gutta Inferior	Tons	}7,089	6,598	10,072	{1,017	1,357
	Tons				7,397	5,140
Para Rubber	Tons	108,524	158,931	151,511	183,250	149,787
	Tons	21,951	19,852	21,077	20,786	20,771
Gambier (in Bales and Cube)	Tons	2,853	2,599	2,230	1,883	1,710
Asbestos Manufactures	Tons	1,850	2,759	5,840	9,901	11,048
	Tons	86,323	136,387	161,579	239,335	313,054
Steel Bars, Rods, Angles,						
Shapes and Sections	Tons	13,353	15,562	21,811	22,687	27,243
Hollow-ware (Cooking and						
Household Utensils)	Tons	3,582	4,713	4,786	4,023	3,964 /
Iron, Galvanized (Corru-						
gated and Sheet)	Tons.	8,849	24,667	23,793	23,255	17,261
	Tons.	15,645	14,367	14,814	17,422	17,757
Tubes, Pipes and Fittings	Tons.	10,409	18,380	21,818	21,739	25,545
Brass and Brassware	Tons.	615	832	1,120	1,062	1,117
Wire and Cables, Insulated	Tons.	2,154	2,203	1,732	1,760	3,143
Sewing Machines	Number	16,210	19,458	47,626	30,681	15,956
Cotton Piece Goods, Plain,						
Dyed and Printed	Thous. yds.	112,532	169,463	150,266	154,400	124,682
Cotton Sarongs, Slendangs						
and Kains	Thous.	9,510	12,493	12,325	10,673	9,618
Silk Piece Goods	Thous. yds.	2,612	4,503	6,772	6,220	3,409
	Tons.	2,052	2,260	2,594	2,494	2,520
	Bales of 100					
	pieces	111,469	155,771	142,239	171,897	134,340
Boots and Shoes (other than						
	Doz. pairs	33,413	39,505	56,848	78,631	73,680

Particulars.	Unit.	1924.	1925.	1926.	1927.	1928.
Acetic Acid	Tons	1,387	2,620	1,965	1,508	1,290
Opium, Raw	Thous. lbs.	426·4	358·9	625·6	450·9	388·0
Other Drugs and Medicines	Thous. Lbs.	6,689	7,782	9,692	9,258	9,202
Paints	Cwts.	52,561	69,909	66,842	78,241	82,239
Kerosene	Tons	93,704	110,070	91,316	134,994	147,074
Liquid Fuel	Tons	298,710	303,533	346,611	475,044	524,858
Lubricating Oils	Thou, galls.	4,665	6,227	6,243	5,929	5,683
Motor Spirit	Tons	107,112	225,840	273,270	269,319	290,886
Soap (other than Toilet)	Cwts.	106,363	131,007	142,430	147,963	152,304(a)
Stationery (including MS. and Account Books)	Cwts.	22,085	22,102	29,041	26,259	22,170
Motor Cars, Passenger	Number	2,361	7,761	9,138	6,196	4,291
Motor Cars, Commercial	Number	368	1,135	2,125	1,857	1,438
Pneumatic Tyres & Tubes: Motor Cars, Motor Trucks and Motor Cycles – Covers	Thous.	87·3	156·3	178·1	273·5	192·6
Motor Cars, Motor Trucks and Motor Cycles – Tubes	Thous.	208·4	349·0	108·9	185·4	125·2
Matches	Millions	24,923	29,071	25,953	26,600	29,243 /
EXPORTS.						
Rice	Tons	186,354	246,949	280,533	294,241	276,581
Sago Flour	Tons	56,558	49,018	39,785	42,022	42,346
Tapioca, Flake, Flour and Pearl	Tons	37,878	37,003	36,707	35,140	28,223
Other Grain and Flour	Tons	22,697	21,304	21,703	24,540	23,085
Feeding Stuff for Animals	Tons	14,142	18,503	19,075	20,573	22,372
Biscuits	Cwts.	21,634	37,067	45,528	41,766	71,189
Coffee, Raw	Thous. lbs.	10,927	11,849	10,011	10,143	6,782
Fish, Dried and Salted	Tons	55,020	59,021	60,220	58,577	57,521
Sardines	Tons	2,714	3,338	3,851	3,209	2,080
Fruits, Dried and Preserved	Tons	5,164	4,300	4,331	4,918	4,635
Pineapples, Canned	Tons	39,204	43,208	40,634	40,134	46,400
Milk, Condensed	Thous. cases	137·0	191·3	225·3	204·2	197·4
Arecanuts	Tons	62,195	58,908	63,021	49,879	69,303
Cloves	Tons	926	1,465	1,244	1,641	913
Nutmegs	Tons	1,265	1,146	1,397	1,670	1,779
Pepper, Black and White	Tons	19,295	15,548	14,196	13,275	13,262
Other Spices	Tons	2,063	1,773	2,212	2,515	3,166
Sugar	Tons	24,585	26,049	20,218	18,065	19,529
Sugar Candy	Tons	11,534	12,507	8,416	5,732	8,464
Tea	Thous. Lbs.	1,248	1,301	1,533	1,238	1,317
Vegetables, Preserved	Tons	2,351	2,612	3,132	3,197	2,998
Onions and Garlic	Tons	8,814	11,408	13,084	15,361	17,071
Cigarettes	Thous. lbs.	7,295	7,958	5,411	4,280	3,927
Tobacco, Manufactured	Thous. lbs.	537	2,993	2,457	2,156	2,103

Particulars.	Unit.	1924.	1925.	1926.	1927.	1928.
Phosphates of Lime	Tons	125,157	110,068	128,981	116,652	– (b)
	Tons	236,119	272,001	276,444	423,264	664,703
	Cub. tons of 50					
	c.ft.	89,060	52,832	22,926	27,724	28,901
	Tons	159,049	153,236	185,404	143,042	182,854
Ground Nuts	Tons	912	2,794	1,753	2,898	15,716
	Tons	1,583	1,445	1,436	1,402	1,284
	Tons	2,074	2,301	1,764	1,843	1,432
	Tons	8,709	7,928	6,641	8,900	8,973 /
	Tons	963	847	793	1,832	1,185
Coconut Oil	Tons	6,093	7,685	8,586	10,300	9,842
alo Hides	Tons	2,306	2,743	1,414	2,116	1,985
Gutta Percha	Tons	2,866	1,807	1,467	701	274
Gutta Inferior	Tons	}5,843	6,622	8,257	{1,581	1,840
	Tons				5,989	5,119
Para Rubber	Tons	259,706	316,826	391,337	371,309	408,693
Para Rubber Latex	Thou. gals.	804	2,316	2,088	1,561	920
	Tons	22,777	18,349	16,715	15,960	16,432
Gambier (in Bales and Cube)	Tons	6,297	5,721	4,989	5,001	4,803
Rubber Seeds	Thous. lbs.	3	17	105	32	17,655
	Tons	80,674	79,082	76,334	83,773	99,052
Cotton Piece Goods, Plain,						
Dyed and Printed	Thous. yds.	50,637	57,666	49,124	47,992	39,245
Sarongs, Slendangs and Kains	Thous.	5,380	5,636	5,511	6,089	5,190
	Bales of 100					
	pieces	109,220	153,696	144,305	187,496	158,152
Boots and Shoes (other than						
	Doz. pairs	36,233	88,862	102,680	190,013	203,663
Drugs and Medicines	Thous. lbs.	2,607	2,794	2,537	2,417	2,817
	Tons	50,446	63,518	61,649	92,538	111,243
Liquid Fuel	Tons	33,854	34,701	45,961	55,383	62,309
Lubricating Oils	Thous. gals.	2,267	2,977	2,458	2,128	1,554
Motor Spirit	Tons	62,309	189,912	205,455	202,439	184,310
Hides, Tanned	Tons	2,548	2,142	2,145	2,023	1,700
Motor Cars, Passenger	Number	365	909	750	575	568 /

) Household and washing soap. /
) Not included in the "Annual Summary," see page 13. /

TRADE WITH DIFFERENT COUNTRIES
OR GROUPS OF COUNTRIES.
IMPORTS AND EXPORTS OF MERCHANDISE (EXCLUSIVE OF
PARCEL POST).
TOTAL VALUES – 1922 TO 1928. Imports.
(In thousands of dollars.)

Country.	1922.	1923.	1924.	1925.	1926.	1927.	1928.
United Kingdom	70,728	79,231	87,904	121,855	136,913	132,609	138,896
British India and Burma	47,282	54,206	67,384	77,386	88,257	81,220	70,040
Sarawak	8,783	16,545	22,598	48,751	42,357	39,703	32,625
Hongkong	31,612	29,407	28,401	28,577	27,054	35,847	33,283
Australia	15,119	14,102	14,920	18,201	15,206	17,072	16,847
Other British Countries (*a*)	6,926	10,689	13,296	15,938	17,712	20,641	15,496
Total, British Countries	180,450	203,659	234,503	310,708	327,499	327,092	307,187
France	3,306	4,639	6,583	7,942	13,301	11,173	8,093
Germany	2,651	5,820	5,764	8,537	13,715	13,705	14,443
Italy	3,772	4,386	5,440	9,469	15,947	9,672	7,499
Netherlands	3,620	3,916	5,431	9,487	10,859	11,583	10,905
Other European Countries	2,526	5,281	5,538	5,628	7,889	13,422	15,656
Japan	18,147	18,123	16,556	29,957	34,900	30,215	20,147
United States	17,118	18,422	22,712	30,726	34,866	31,799	27,566
Netherlands Indies	117,278	198,135	231,644	403,000	367,979	363,614	287,006
China	21,078	25,109	26,678	34,996	48,251	35,114	29,691
French Indo - China	16,170	11,679	15,196	16,725	20,265	24,053	22,014
Siam & Siamese States	64,135	70,160	72,023	93,972	100,431	113,144	102,918
Other Foreign Countries	5,145	8,801	5,244	6,796	7,947	5,976	6,704
Total, Foreign Countries	274,946	374,068	418,809	657,235	676,350	663,470	552,642
Total Imports	455,396	577,594	653,312	967,943	1,003,849	990,562	859,829 /

Exports.
(In thousands of dollars.)

United Kingdom	54,364	93,296	94,894	178,160	205,931	158,632	98,246
British India and Burma	22,133	27,810	32,233	36,899	35,983	32,965	29,179
Sarawak	5,560	7,615	7,070	9,198	9,808	10,848	10,915
Hongkong	12,738	15,114	16,326	9,996	9,973	10,139	15,717

Country.	1922.	1923.	1924.	1925.	1926.	1927.	1928.
Other British							
Countries (*a*)	12,788	28,727	23,692	43,196	39,823	37,724	26,947
Total, British							
Countries	110,243	176,161	182,018	300,418	339,901	285,968	206,548
	17,701	25,311	29,843	44,132	40,912	34,060	26,260
Germany	16,017	11,775	12,534	29,697	18,576	16,818	18,290
	6,882	10,629	12,647	18,410	15,245	13,046	10,023
Netherlands	9,058	12,028	17,076	29,543	29,673	41,575	35,535
Other European							
Countries	6,088	10,459	10,425	10,612	11,454	8,290	10,292
	16,419	29,554	26,487	36,987	39,966	38,628	(*b*)32,183
United States	187,141	273,243	298,555	643,129	597,875	466,998	353,371
Netherlands Indies	81,808	79,572	83,805	113,378	112,451	101,280	91,494
	8,534	7,540	7,316	8,503	9,213	8,589	12,410
French Indo -							
China	3,897	6,260	7,106	7,978	10,195	10,368	9,327
Siam & Siamese							
States	21,015	22,845	24,777	28,986	28,082	29,442	28,906
Other Foreign							
Countries	4,297	4,361	7,861	10,002	9,053	6,667	6,930
Total, Foreign							
Countries	378,857	493,577	538,432	981,357	922,695	775,761	635,021
Total Exports	489,100	669,738	720,450	1,281,775	1,262,596	1,061,729	841,569 /

) Including Egypt in 1922 ($1,150,000) and 1923 ($8,012,000).

) Excluding export of Phosphates of Lime, see page 50. /

TRADE WITH DIFFERENT COUNTRIES – PERCENTAGE DISTRIBUTION – 1924–1928.

IMPORTS.	1924.	1925.	1926.	1927.	1928.
United Kingdom	13·45	12·59	13·64	13·39	16·15
British India and Burma	10·31	7·99	8·79	8·20	8·15
Sarawak	3·46	5·04	4·22	4·01	3·80
Hongkong	4·32	2·95	2·69	3·62	3·87
Other British Countries	4·32	3·53	3·28	3·80	3·76
Total. British Countries	35·89	32·10	32·62	33·02	35·73
Continent of Europe	4.4	4·24	6·15	6·01	6·58
Japan	2·53	3·10	3·48	3·05	2·34
United States	3·48	3·17	3·47	3·21	3·21
Netherlands Indies	35·46	41·63	36·66	36·71	33·38
China	4·08	3·62	4·81	3·54	3·45
Siam and Siamese States	11·03	9·71	10·00	11·42	11·97
Other Foreign Countries	3·13	2·43	2·81	3·04	3·34
Total, Foreign Countries	64·11	67·90	67·38	66·98	64·27

	1924.	1925.	1926.	1927.	1928.
EXPORTS.					
United Kingdom	13·17	13·90	16·31	14·94	11·67
British India and Burma	4·47	2·88	2·85	3·10	3·47
Australia	1·08	1·79	3·04	3·36	3·03
Other British Countries	6·54	4·87	4·72	5·53	6·37
Total, British Countries	25·20	23·44	26·92	26·93	24·54
France	4·14	3·44	3·24	3·21	3·12
Netherlands	2·37	2·30	2·35	3·92	4·22
Other European Countries. .	4·94	4·58	3·59	3·59	4·59
Japan	3·68	2·89	3·17	3·64	3·82
United States	41·44	50·17	47·35	43·99	41·99
Netherlands Indies	11·63	8·85	8·91	9·54	10·87
Siam and Siamese States	3·44	2·26	2·22	2·77	3·44
Other Foreign Countries	3·10	2·07	2·25	2·41	3·41
Total, Foreign Countries	74·74	76·56	73·08	73·07	75·46 /
IMPORTS OF MANUFACTURES (CLASS III).					
United Kingdom	30·5	28·4	27 0	27·4	31·2
British India and Burma	} 20·2	19·5{	8·2	7·8	7·3
Sarawak			5·4	5·4	}11·0
Hongkong			2·8	4·2	
Other British Countries			1·2	1·8	
Total, British Countries	50·7	47·9	44·6	46·6	49·5
Continent of Europe	8·8	8·9	11·1	11·3	11·7
Japan	6·0	7·4	6·8	6·2	4·5
United States	6·0	6·1	6·5	6·3	5·7
Netherlands Indies	} 28·5	29·7 {	23·3	24·6	23·3
China			5·6	3·6	} 5·3
Other Foreign Countries			2·1	1·4	
Total, Foreign Countries	49·3	52·1	55·4	53·4	50·5 /

TRADE WITH DIFFERENT COUNTRIES OR GROUPS OF COUNTRIES.
IMPORTS AND EXPORTS OF MERCHANDISE (EXCLUSIVE OF PARCEL POST) DETAILED 1926 TO 1928.
IMPORTANT AND OTHER ARTICLES.

Particulars.					Values (In thousands of dollars).		
		Quantities.					
	Unit.	1926.	1927.	1928.	1926.	1927.	1928.
UNITED KINGDOM IMPORTS.							
I. – Animals, Food, Drink and Tobacco.							
Meat	Tons.	477	469	487	687	630	642
Biscuits	Cwts.	5,834	23,754	16,822	1,826	1,666	1,269
Milk, Condensed	Th. Cases	66·5	102·0	98·9	787	1,172	1,063

Particulars.		Quantities.			Values (In thousands of dollars).		
	Unit.	1926.	1927.	1928.	1926.	1927.	1928.
Brandy	Th. galls.	110·2	82·1	52·7	997	833	518
Whisky	Th. galls.	134·7	138·9	136·9	1,578	1,607	1,538
Beer and Ale	Th. galls.	261·7	333·7	329·1	535	719	687
Porter and Stout	Th. galls.	807·1	701·8	675·3	2,560	2,133	2,004
Other Spirituous Liquors	Th. galls.	82·8	81·4	69·3	672	685	549
Cigarettes	Th. lbs.	5,491	5,487	5,957	16,869	7,547	19,176
Tobacco, Manufactured	Th. lbs.	359	345	317	821	767	587
Other Articles	–	–	–	–	177	202	232
Total, Class I	–	–	–	–	29,862	30,152	30,314
II. – Raw Materials and Articles Mainly Unmanufactured.							
	Tons	52,288	59,594	56,467	217	963	849
Asphalt and Bitumen	Tons	353	875	1,277	53	104	141
Linseed Oil (Boiled & ned)	Th. galls.	118.9	133·4	181·1	237	259	327
Coal Tar	Tons	1,456	1,645	1,740	123	142	140
Other Articles	–	–	–	–	276	259	255
Total, Class II	–	–	–	–	906	1,727	1,712
III. – Articles Wholly or Mainly Manufactured.							
Asbestos Manufactures	Tons	1,182	2,036	3,378	210	337	516
Crockery and Porcelain	–	–	–	–	362	261	179
Cement	Tons	36.098	56,183	109,639	1,139	1,785	3,338
Glass and Glassware	–	–	–	–	291	442	400
Steel Bars, Rods, Angles, Shapes and Sections	Tons	8,855	8,454	9,307	735	804	870
Hollow-ware (Cooking and Household Utensils)	Tons	1,246	1,021	950	611	526	430
Iron, Galvanized (Corrugated and Sheet)	Tons	18,183	17,171	13,183	3,999	3,502	2,383
Carried forward	–	–	–	–	7,347	7,657	8,116 /
Brought forward	–	–	–	–	7,347	7,657	8,116
Tin Plates	Tons	12,851	13,560	16,566	2,535	2,731	3,053
Tubes, Pipes and Fittings	Tons	20,100	19,367	23,797	2,622	2,729	3,012
Other Iron and Steel Goods	–	–	–	–	7,276	8,076	9,232
Brass and Brassware	Tons	471	283	304	625	444	531
Copperwire (including Uninsulated Electric Wire)	Tons	436	797	993	344	588	702
Other Metals and Manufactures thereof	–	–	–	–	1,247	1,059	1,109
Cutlery, Hardware, Implements and Instruments	–	–	–	–	2,169	2,122	1,891

Particulars.	Unit.	Quantities.			Values (In thousands of dollars).		
		1926.	1927.	1928.	1926.	1927.	1928.
Wire and Cables, Insulated	Tons	1,627	1,725	3,113	1,233	1,549	2,124
Other Electrical Goods and Apparatus	–	–	–	–	1,668	2,292	3,027
Electrical Machinery	–	–	–	–	1,609	1,357	2,727
Dredging Materials	–	–	–	–	–	304	9,424
Sewing Machines	No.	34,159	27,456	12,828	1,791	1,460	612
Other Machines and Machinery	–	–	–	–	9,500	10,522	6,877
Cotton Piece Goods, Plain, Dyed and Printed	Th. yds.	80,610	80,856	65,587	23,900	20,859	16,762
Cotton Sarongs, Slen-dangs and Kains	Ths.	996	904	786	717	619	580
Sewing Thread (Reels)	Gross	86,310	72,910	81,255	1,423	1,027	1,191
Other Cotton Goods	–	–	–	–	2,545	1,404	1,638
Woollen Goods	–	–	–	–	2,588	1,564	1,123
Silk Piece Goods	Th. yds.	630	855	76	614	659	90
Manufactures of other Textile Materials	–	–	–	–	1,108	1,151	1,590
Boots and Shoes (Leather and other sorts)	Doz. pairs	10,033	9,753	7,263	430	397	350
Haberdashery and Mil-linery (including Hats, Caps, etc.)	–	–	–	–	1,631	1,232	965
Other Apparel	–	–	–	–	1,472	997	870
Chemicals	–	–	–	–	1,147	1,239	1,040
Drugs and Medicines, Manufactured and Prepared	Th. lbs.	942	1,075	1,054	1,044	1,135	1,038
Paints	Cwts.	53,211	60,212	65,246	1,362	1,494	1,484
Lubricating Oils	Th. galls.	165	254	290	302	455	432
Soap, Toilet and other	–	–	–	–	2,227	2,378	2,366
Paper and Paperware	–	–	–	–	2,336	2,570	2,371
Motor Cars, Passenger	No.	2,151	2,014	1,433	4,911	4,153	2,761
Motor Cars, Commercial	No.	470	481	371	1,357	1,215	1,193
Carried forward		–	–	–	91,080	87,438	90,281 /
Brought forward		–	–	–	91,080	87,438	90,281
Parts and Accessories – Motor Cars and Trucks	–	–	–	–	802	720	626
Other Road Vehicles and Parts and Accessories thereof	–	–	–	–	2,957	626	1,468

Particulars.	Unit.	Quantities.			Values (In thousands of dollars).		
		1926.	1927.	1928.	1926.	1927.	1928.
Pneumatic Tyres – Motor Car, Motor Truck and Motor Cycle Covers	Ths.	54·8	46·1	37·4	1,001	641	689
Plated and Silverware	–	–	–	–	434	521	418
Perfumery and Cosmetics	–	–	–	–	649	612	468
Wooden ware – Rubber Cases	Ths.	857	905	1,039	1,339	1,144	1,165
Other Articles	–	–	–	–	7,883	8,028	11,755
Total, Class III		–	–	–	106,145	100,730	106,870
Total Imports		–	–	–	136,913	132,609	138,896

EXPORTS.

I. – Animals, Food, Drink and Tobacco.

Particulars.	Unit.	1926.	1927.	1928.	1926.	1927.	1928.
Sago, Flour and Pearl	Tons	22,852	25,828	25,294	2,448	2,720	2,322
Tapioca, Flake and Pearl	Tons	[illeg.]	1,254	388	300	167	54
Fishmaws	Tons	30	38	35	268	401	279
Pineapples, Canned	Tons	31,100	30,952	33,453	5,852	6,373	6,036
Nutmegs	Tons	146	265	247	214	303	257
Pepper, Black and White	–	5,530	6,601	5,498	5,985	8,531	8,327
Other Articles	–	–	–	–	201	174	128
Total, Class I		–	–	–	15,268	18,669	17,403

II. – Raw Materials and Articles Mainly Unmanufactured.

Particulars.	Unit.	1926.	1927.	1928.	1926.	1927.	1928.
	Tons	17,065	12,078	10,554	3,302	2,215	1,937
	Tons	158	255	210	98	121	101
	Tons	540	878	668	190	290	184
Palm Oil and Palm Kernals	Tons	–	386	2,792	–	104	657
alo Hides	Tons	1,040	1,611	1,470	472	579	605
Gutta Percha, Gutta Inferior and Jelutong	Tons	619	172	120	1,884	328	182
Para Rubber	Tons	83,998	76,398	60,996	155,493	111,234	50,311
Para Rubber Latex	Th. galls.	55	76	67	151	178	86
Carried forward		–	–	–	161,590	115,049	54,063 /
Brought forward		–	–	–	161,590	115,049	54,063
Rattans	Tons	786	1,241	666	180	249	156
Gambier (in Bales and Cube)	Tons	613	701	392	134	114	56
Other Articles	–	–	–	–	1,247	684	663
Total, Class II		–	–	–	163,151	116,096	54,938

III. – Articles Wholly or Mainly Manufactured.

Particulars.	Unit.	1926.	1927.	1928.	1926.	1927.	1928.
	Tons	11,101	9,453	12,908	26,785	22,986	24,843
Other Articles	–	–	–	–	727	881	1,062
Total, Class III		–	–	–	27,512	23,867	25,905
Total Exports		–	–	–	205,931	158,632	98,246

BRITISH INDIA AND BURMA. IMPORTS.

Particulars.	Unit.	Quantities. 1926.	1927.	1928.	Values (In thousands of dollars). 1926.	1927.	1928.
		I. – Animals, Food, Drink and Tobacco.					
Rice	Tons	258,953	218,363	209,647	31,429	25,581	22,447
Pepper, Black, Long and White	Tons	446	1,430	155	503	1,396	213
Wheat Flour	Tons	2,933	3,162	3,665	486	497	548
Other Grain and Flour	Tons	5,351	6,426	–	737	924	}12,847
Rice Meal	Tons	38,902	27,667	–	1,765	1,300	
Other Feeding Stuffs for Animals	Tons	10,623	9,403	–	1,367	1,269	
Cattle	No.	5,321	5,969	–	728	774	
Goats	No.	24,334	24,722	–	419	456	
Sheep	No.	23,534	16,916	–	350	271	
Curry Stuffs	Cwts.	73,891	53,193	–	1,301	947	
Fruits, Dried and Preserved	Tons.	7,000	7,697	–	1,296	1,327	
Ghee	Tons.	1,272	1,315	–	1,577	1,627	
Coriander Seeds	Tons.	2,774	2,745	–	489	746	
Tea	Th. lbs.	434	363	–	252	223	
Carried forward		–	–	–	42,699	37,338	36,055 /
Brought forward		–	–	–	42,699	37,338	36,055
Onions and Garlic	Tons	13,379	18,866	–	1,648	2,072	
Tobacco, Native Unmanufactured	Th. lbs.	5,418	5,543	–	1,629	1,799	
Other Articles	–	–	–	–	1,501	1,344	
Total, Class I		–	–	–	47,477	42,553	36,055
		II. – Raw Materials and Articles Mainly Unmanufactured.					
Coal	Tons	111,913	138,501	75,963	1,181	1,524	827
Tin Ore	Tons	1,802	2,226	2,307	2,967	3,614	3,033
Para Rubber	Tons	1,717	2,625	2,053	2,802	3,505	1,816
Goat Skins	Tons	90	124	–	332	399	}3,299
Other Articles	–	–	–	–	1,054	887	
Total, Class II		–	–	–	8,336	9,929	8,975
		III. – Articles Wholly or Mainly Manufactured.					
Cotton Piece Goods, Plain, Dyed, Printed and Woven Coloured	Th. lbs.	3,945	4,174	3,400	1,710	1,671	1,230
Cotton Sarongs, Slendangs and Kains	Ths.	4,358	4,025	3,593	9,086	7,889	7,010
Cotton Yarns, Grey Unbleached	Th. lbs.	1,185	1,095	–	501	419	}16,770
Other Cotton Goods	–	–	–	–	246	211	
Silk Goods	–	–	–	–	80	160	
Coir	Tons	1,406	1,705	–	467	522	
Twine	Tons	2,233	2,094	–	999	738	

Particulars.		Quantities.			Values (In thousands of dollars).		
	Unit.	1926.	1927.	1928.	1926.	1927.	1928.
Gunnies	Bales of 100 pieces	139,240	169,525	–	6,463	6,511	
Apparel	–	–	–	–	752	357	
Opium Raw	Th. lbs.	552·0	450·9	–	9,032	7,308	
Other Articles	–	–	–	–	3,108	2,952	
Total, Class III	–	–	–	–	32,444	28,738	25,010
Total Imports	–	–	–	–	88,257	81,220	70,040 /

Exports.

I. – Animals, Food, Drink and Tobacco.

Particulars.	Unit.	1926.	1927.	1928.	1926.	1927.	1928.
	Tons	205	17,105	13,960	26	1,434	1,162
Sago, Flour and Pearl	Tons	6,804	9,044	0,834	710	904	566
Tapioca, Flake, Flour and	Tons	9,533	10,143	7,284	1,171	1,233	994
ee, Raw	Th. lbs.	3,053	2,840	1,640	1,011	757	494
Fish, Dried and Salted	Tons	5,287	4,907	3,815	2,272	2,100	1,511
Arecanuts	Tons	51,490	37,349	59,487	13,896	7,181	9,895
Pepper, Black, Long and White	Tons	1,479	308	629	1,179	370	732
Other Spices	Tons	831	826	–	736	541	} 2,463
Coconuts, Fresh	Cwts.	178,667	208,237	–	371	481	
Other Articles	–	–	–	–	1,887	1,354	
Total, Class I	–	–	–	–	23,259	16,355	17,817

II. – Raw Materials and Articles Mainly Unmanufactured.

Particulars.	Unit.	1926.	1927.	1928.	1926.	1927.	1928.
Rattans	Tons	742	625	1,100	150	155	237
	Tons	2,615	3,555	3,311	233	269	243
Benjamin	Tons	913	956	–	538	623	} 2,017
Camphor, Crude	Tons	97	203	–	133	284	
Sticklac	Tons	398	1,241	–	332	1,263	
Gambier, Cube	Tons	1,794	1,717	–	504	387	
Other Articles	–	–	–	–	447	477	
Total, Class II	–	–	–	–	2,337	3,458	2,497

III. – Articles Wholly or Mainly Manufactured.

Particulars.	Unit.	1926.	1927.	1928.	1926.	1927.	1928.
	Tons	2,632	3,546	2,871	6,447	8,838	5,655
Kerosene	Tons	1,902	6,792	7,104	306	1,092	666
Cotton Sarongs, Slendangs and Kains	Ths.	1,424	1,384	819	1,435	1,192	647
Other Cotton Goods	–	–	–	–	293	199	} 1,897
Other Articles	–	–	–	–	1,906	1,831	
Total, Class III	–	–	–	–	10,387	13,152	8,865
Total Exports	–	–	–	–	35,983	32,965	29,179 /

Particulars.	Unit.	Quantities. 1926.	1927.	1928.	Values (In thousands of dollars). 1926.	1927.	1928.
		OTHER BRITISH COUNTRIES.					
		Imports.					
		I. – Animals, Food, Drink and Tobacco.					
Wheat Flour	Tons	38,932	46,735	42,878	6,146	6,624	6,432
Sago, Flour and Pearl	Tons	16,862	16,585	14,192	1,571	1,527	1,081
Fish, Dried and Salted	Tons	2,564	2,857	2,772	1,443	1,548	1,436
Pepper, Black, Long and White	Tons	858	981	875	935	1,502	1,275
Milk, Condensed and Sterilized	Th. cases	334·1	300·1	361·3	4,426	3,701	4,264
Cigarettes	Th. lbs.	957	432	1,017	1,586	579	1,425
Tobacco, manufactured	Th. lbs.	1,249	4,310	3,784	880	3,322	2,802
Vegetables, Preserved	Tons	3,157	4,110	4,066	1,185	1,446	1,623
Vegetables, Other kinds	Tons	5,476	9,337	–	681	1,085	} 17,056
Beans	Tons	15,007	17,516	–	1,936	2,082	
Grain and Flour not specified above	Tons	5,659	4,055	–	1,415	1,450	
Meat	–	–	–	–	1,760	2,147	
Sheep	No.	28,219	38,401	–	381	538	
Butter, Tinned and Frozen	Cwts.	14,583	14,764	–	1,086	1,080	
Fruits, Fresh	Tons	1,128	1,812	–	381	625	
Fruits, Dried, Preserved and Canned	Tons	2,064	3,719	–	810	1405	
Cloves	Tons	497	1,453	–	380	918	
Tea	Th. lbs.	5,275	7,060	–	1,900	2,434	
Samsoo	Th. galls.	145	116	–	362	327	
Horses and Ponies	No.	163	161	–	146	164	
Other Articles	–	–	–	–	3,288	3,540	
Total, Class I		–	–	–	32,698	38,044	37,394
		II. – Raw Materials and Articles Mainly Unmanufactured.					
Coal	Tons	178.831	212,356	254,642	2,405	2,987	3,192
Tin Ore	Tons	1,562	1,862	1,839	2,463	2,993	2,225
Copra	Tons	5,766	4,214	6,852	1,103	768	1,213
Para Rubber	Tons	12,216	14,891	13,480	19,542	19,643	10,496
Carried forward		–	–	–	25,513	26,391	17,126 /
Brought forward		–	–	–	25,513	26,391	17,126
Timber	Tons of 50 c. ft.	672	19,543	–	56	1,123	} 5,957
Damar	Tons	2,263	3,880	–	231	401	
Kachang Oil	Cwts.	72,232	81,663	–	1,484	1,731	
Cow Hides	Tons	758	869	–	495	599	
Gutta, Inferior and Jelutong..	Tons	5,565	4,821	–	3,144	1,690	

Particulars.	Unit.	Quantities. 1926.	1927.	1928.	Values (In thousands of dollars). 1926.	1927.	1928.
Other Articles	–	–	–	–	1,666	1,436	
Total, Class II		–	–	–	32,589	33,371	23,083
III. – Articles Wholly or Mainly Manufactured.							
Kerosene	Tons	34,756	49,743	40,797	5,558	6,550	3,829
Liquid Fuel	Tons	83,571	44,343	4,727	2,970	1,614	183
Motor Spirit	Tons	44,006	47,542	83,146	12,158	11,000	15,160
Motor Cars, Passenger	No.	1,850	1,715	860	1,593	2,060	1,341
Silk Piece Goods	Th. yds.	870	533	210	858	568	210
Cotton Piece Goods, Plain, Dyed, Printed and Woven Coloured	Th. yds.	3,018	6,185	6,686	1,061	1,674	1,545
Other Cotton Goods	–	–	–	–	174	223	} 15,506
Cement	Tons	10,857	8,988	–	318	292	
Iron and Steel Goods	–	–	–	–	381	540	
Brass and Brassware	Tons	58	140	–	89	217	
Machines and Machinery	–	–	–	–	309	244	
Woollen Goods	–	–	–	–	500	492	
Cordage	Tons	1,163	1,173	–	264	290	
Apparel	–	–	–	–	989	1,150	
Drugs and Medicines	Th. lbs.	3,758	5,820	–	2,021	3,171	
	Tons	3,820	3,523	–	565	529	
Soap (other than toilet)	Cwts.	28,181	23,203	–	352	290	
Leather and Leather Manufactures	–	–	–	–	399	332	
Paper and Paperware	–	–	–	–	512	825	
Motor Cars, Commercial	No.	799	712	–	813	688	
Carried forward		–	–	–	31,884	32,749	37,774 /
Brought forward		–	–	–	31,884	32,749	37,774
Parts and Accessories – Motor Cars and Trucks	–	–	–	–	90	406	
Pneumatic Tyres and Tubes – Motor Vehicles – Covers	Ths.	11·1	80·1	–	176	1,051	
Fireworks	Cwts.	35,484	44,517	–	937	1,253	
Bamboo and Rattan ware	–	–	–	–	178	390	
Cabinetware	–	–	–	–	110	236	
Imitation Gold & Silver Leaves	–	–	–	–	14	1,036	
Joss Sticks and Joss Paper	Th.	3,136	3,358	–	672	776	
Perfumery and Cosmetics	–	–	–	–	285	458	
Other Articles	–	–	–	–	2,696	3,493	
Total, Class III		–	–	–	37,042	41,848	37,774
Total Imports		–	–	–	102,329	113,263	98,251 /

Particulars.	Unit.	Quantities.			Values (In thousands of dollars).		
		1926.	1927.	1928.	1926.	1927.	1928.
		Exports.					
I. – Animals, Food, Drink and Tobacco.							
Rice	Tons	51,035	74,195	48,515	6,406	8,641	
Tapioca, Flake, Flour and Pearl	Tons	6,436	6,979	5,547	772	831	
Coffee, Raw	Th. lbs.	2,453	1,790	918	784	504	
Pineapples, Canned	Tons	6,238	5,951	7,837	1,154	1,227	
Sugar	Tons	4,727	5,934	7,108	712	852	
Cigarettes	Th. lbs.	750	777	670	1,291	1,368	
Tobacco, Manufactured	Th. lbs.	646	648	568	563	551	
Arecanuts	Tons	2,428	1,887	1,621	596	301	
Pepper, Black, Long and White	Tons	1,995	1,812	2,443	1,797	2,248	
Other Spices	Tons	565	529	–	603	481	
Grain and Flour not specified above	Tons	4,055	6,603	–	615	887	
Rice Meal (Bran)	Tons	3,545	4,708	–	195	251	
Birds' Nests	Tons	74	96	–	379	402	
Milk, Condensed	Th. cases.	42·5	49·8	–	552	608	
Sugar Candy	Tons	5,372	1,963	–	1,014	379	
Vegetable	Tons	1,177	1,639	–	240	283	
Wines, Spirits, Malt Liquors, etc.	Th. Gals.	136	141	–	652	625	
Other Articles	–	–	–	–	2,081	1,818	
Total, Class I	–	–	–	–	20,406	22,257	
II. – Raw Materials and Articles Mainly Unmanufactured.							
Para Rubber	Tons	7,942	7,370	7,228	15,382	10,583	
Rattans	Tons	4,090	4,040	4,105	892	767	
Planks	Cub. tone of 50 c. ft.	5,045	8,223	–	323	403	}4,118
Other Wood and Timber	Cub. tone of 50 c. ft.	22,921	19,155	–	311	268	
Other Articles	–	–	–	–	1,762	1,554	
Total, Class II		–	–	–	18,670	13,575	/
OTHER BRITISH COUNTRIES (*b*)							
Exports							
III. – Articles Wholly or Mainly Manufactured.							
Tin	Tons	1,187	1,422	2,443	2,890	3,509	4,643
Cotton Piece Goods, Plain, Dyed, Printed and. Woven Coloured	Th. yds.	5,993	5,900	5,071	1,647	1,546	1,301
Gunnies	Bales of						

Particulars.		Quantities.			Values (In thousands of dollars).		
	Unit.	1926.	1927.	1928.	1926.	1927.	1928.
Hides, Tanned	Tons	1,981	1,808	1,511	2,096	1,921	1,647
Kerosene	Tons	35,504	50,841	60,336	5,156	6,555	6,436
Motor Spirit	Tons	145,761	159,060	148,778	41,204	38,674	28,209
Turpentine	Th. galls.	171	205	–	254	299	}5,851
Iron and Steel Goods	–	–	–	–	474	474	
Apparel	–	–	–	–	317	535	
Drugs and Medicines	Th. lbs.	224	222	–	189	240	
Motor Cars (Passenger)	No.	132	132	–	183	225	
Rubber Manufactures (other than Tyres and Tubes)	–	–	–	–	278	326	
Fertilisers	Tons	2,685	2,803	–	220	239	
Other Articles	–	–	–	–	3,645	3,681	
Total, Class III	–	–	–	–	58,911	58,539	48,271
Total Exports	–	–	–	–	97,987	94,371	79,123 /

) The principal imports in 19[illeg.] from different countries included under this heading were as follows: –

	$'000
AUSTRALIA	17,072
Wheat Flour	6,317
Meat	1,138
Sheep	514
Butter	967
Fresh Fruit	447
Condensed Milk	3,684
Horses and Ponies	161
Coal	524
Timber	1,075
Iron and Steel Goods	182
Machinery	187
Leather Goods	200
BRITISH NORTH BORNEO	5,867
Copra	367
Para Rubber	4,285
BRUNEI	1,359
Para Rubber	793
Cutch	320
CANADA	4,765
Motor Cars (Passenger)	2,035
Motor Cars (Commercial)	685
Motor Cars Parts and Accessories	397
Motor Vehicle Tyres Covers)	1,003
CEYLON	1,616

	$'000
Coffee	181
HONG KONG	35,847
Beans	2,082
Wheat Flour	243
Other Grain and Flour	1,444
Meat	1,001
Dried and Salted Fish	863
Dried and Preserved Fruits	1,335
Tea	1,553
Vegetables	2,522
Samsoo	327
Cigarettes	574
Manufactured Tobacco	3,319
Kachang Oil	1,731
Cement	292
Iron and Steel Goods	219
Brass and Brassware	214
Cotton Piece Goods	1,670
Woolen Goods	485
Silk Piece Goods	564
Apparel	1,138
Drugs and. Medicines	3,098
Paper and Paperware	821
Fireworks	1,252
Bamboo and Rattanware	385
Cabinetware	235
Imitation Gold and Silver Leaves	775
Mats and Matting	223
Perfumery and Cosmetics	456
SARAWAK	39,703
Sago Flour	1,424
Dried and Salted Fish	313
White Pepper	1,403
Copra	209
Jelutong	1,489
Para Rubber	14,453
Cutch	209
Kerosene	6,549
Liquid Fuel	1,612
Motor Spirit	11,000
UNION OF SOUTH AFRICA	5,351
Coal	2,420
Tin Ore	2,911 /

The principal exports in 1927 to different countries included under this heading were as follows: –

	$'000
AUSTRALIA	35,660
Pearl Tapioca	295
Black and White Pepper	1,032
Other Spices	176
Para Rubber	7,452
Kerosene	4,483
Motor Spirit	21,427
BRITISH NORTH BORNEO	5,251
Rice	1,725
Condensed Milk	187
Sugar	263
Cigarettes	393
Cotton Piece Goods	632
Kerosene	184
BRUENI	798
Rice	222
CANADA	3,644
Canned Pineapples	657
Black and White Pepper	388
Para Rubber	858
Tin	1,576
CEYLON	8,047
Peas	329
Rice	3,737
Raw Coffee	206
Para Rubber	1,979
Kerosene	254
Motor-Spirit	795
HONOKONG	10,139
Birds' Nests	402
Arecanuts	298
Black, long, and White Pepper	360
Other Spices	184
Sugar Candy	301
Wood and Timber	334
Para Rubber	292
Rattans	636
Tin	1,552
Gunnies	247
Tanned Hides	1,893
Rubber manufactures	301
Fertilisers	239
MAURITIUS	393
Planks	191

	$'000
New Zealand	5,129
Canned Pineapples	362
Black and White Pepper	249
Kerosene	255
Motor Spirit	3,896
Sarawak	10,848
Rice	2,830
Other Grain and Flour	312
Bran (Rice Meal)	184
Condensed Milk	372
Sugar	346
Wines, Spirits, &c.	453
Cigarettes	902
Manufactured Tobacco	373
Iron and Steel Goods	265
Cotton Piece Goods	779
Kerosene	749
Union of South Africa	3,072
Black and White Pepper	170
Motor Spirit	2,472 /

TRADE WITH DIFFERENT COUNTRIES – MERCHANDISE.

Particulars	Unit	Quantities.			Values (In thousands of dollars.)		
		1926.	1927.	1928.	1926.	1927.	1928.
CONTINENT OF EUROPE.							
Imports.							
I. – Animals, Food, Drink and Tobacco.							
Chocolate and Cocoa	Th. lbs.	512	580	487	417	444	321
Milk, Condensed	Th. cases.	769·1	782·2	779·4	9,530	9,263	8,893
Milk Sterilized	Th. cases.	41·4	41·6	37·5	469	457	379
Sugar	Tons	2,150	1,600	–	305	256	–
Brandy	Th. galls.	425·9	366·0	304·3	3,443	3,320	2,821
Beer and Ale	Th. galls.	491·2	515·9	526·4	1,253	1,325	1,317
Wine and other Spirituous	Th. galls.	150·2	148·7	120·9	915	992	806
Other Articles	–	–	–	–	1,430	1,301	1,230
Total, Class I		–	–	–	17,762	17,358	15,767
II. – Raw Materials and Articles Mainly Unmanufactured.							
Marble	Tons	1,026	1,017	1,406	233	230	279
Other Articles	–	–	–	–	192	137	389
Total, Class II		–	–	–	425	367	668
III. – Articles Wholly or Mainly Manufactured.							
Asbestos Manufactures	Tons	4,630	7,835	7,523	468	815	695
Cement	Tons	45,854	69,846	105,259	1,346	1,979	2,866
Glass (Plate and Sheet)	Th. sq. ft.	3,366	3,647	3,130	735	430	394

	Unit	Quantities.			Values (In thousands of dollars.)		
		1926.	1927.	1928.	1926.	1927.	1928.
	Tons	12,635	18,167	27,111	602	828	1,190
Steel Bars, Rods, Angles, Shapes and Sections	Tons	13,718	14,100	17,909	988	933	1,153
Hollow-ware (Cooking and Household Utensils)	Tons	1,710	1,360	1,367	1,042	815	671
Tubes, Pipes and Fittings	Tons	1,394	2,031	1,616	264	499	405
Other Iron and Steel Goods	–	–	–	–	4,400	3,829	3,316
	Th. doz.	237·4	166·4	184·4	724	486	435
Clocks and Watches	Thous.	221·1	110·1	109·5	870	356	483
Hardware, Implements and Instruments		–	–	–	1,073	1,117	830
Dredging Materials	–	–	–	–	–	454	3,368
Other Machinery	–	–	–	–	3,757	5,890	1,816
Cotton Piece Goods, Plain, Dyed and Printed ..	Th. yds.	11,357	10,982	10,464	4,165	3,548	3,297
Other Cotton Goods	–	–	–	–	994	790	812
Woollen Goods	–	–	–	–	693	437	421
Carried forward		–	–	–	22,121	23,206	22,152 /

CONTINENT OF EUROPE (a)

	Unit	Quantities.			Values		
Brought forward		–	–	–	22,121	23,206	22,152
Silk Piece Goods	Th. Yds.	408	1,001	140	561	713	204
cial Silk Piece Goods	Th. –	–	–	1,504	–	–	652
Haberdashery and Millinery, including Hats, Caps, etc.	–	–	–	–	2,562	1,330	835
Other Apparel	–	–	–	–	1,691	1,007	775
Acetic Acid	Tons	1,938	1,483	1,283	987	734	635
Other Chemicals	–	–	–	–	589	615	1,130
Printing Paper	Cwts.	1,849	2,332	2,531	441	527	545
Other Paper and Paperware	–	–	–	–	872	990	1,191
Motor Cars (Passenger)	No.	1,196	794	450	2,226	1,448	804
Pneumatic Tyres and Tubes – Motor Vehicles – Covers	Th.	52·9	73·2	35·2	1,294	1,522	779
Motor Vehicles – Tubes	-	42·2	64·3	27·4	309	421	131
Cycle Covers	-s	172·3	195·8	130·6	277	322	210
Fancy Goods and Toys	–	–	–	–	694	557	458
Lamp and Lampware	–	–	–	–	533	482	381
Perfumery and Cosmetics	–	–	–	–	1,103	1,093	990
Woodenware – Rubber Cases	Th.	821	1,117	1,169	969	1,334	1,207
Other Articles	–	–	–	–	6,295	5,529	7,082
Total, Class III	–	–	–	–	43,524	41,830	40,161
Total Imports	–	–	–	–	61,711	59,555	56,596 /

Particulars	Unit	Quantities.			Values (In thousands of dollars.)		
		1926.	1927.	1928.	1926.	1927.	1928.

CONTINENT EUROPE (*b*)

Exports.

I. – Animals, Food, Drink and Tobacco.

Particulars	Unit	1926.	1927.	1928.	1926.	1927.	1928.
Sago Flour	Tons	4,957	4,348	7,376	553	476	654
Tapioca, Flake and Pearl	Tons	10,823	10,678	11,513	1,194	1,276	1.626
Pineapples, Canned	Tons	1,137	887	1,631	239	206	319
Nutmegs	Tons	261	413	442	356	426	395
Pepper, Black and White	Tons	2,062	1,980	1,834	1,654	2,315	2,190
Other Articles	–	–	–	–	226	239	378
Total, Class I		–	–	–	4,222	4,938	5,562

II. – Raw Materials and Articles Mainly Unmanufactured.

Particulars	Unit	1926.	1927.	1928.	1926.	1927.	1928.
Copra	Tons	120,635	108.417	155,194	24,132	20,246	29,106
Damar	Tons	452	642	725	153	172	197
Sticklac	Tons	222	258	200	189	274	201
Para Rubber	Tons	27,588	26,378	29,380	49,033	36,813	22,740
Rattans	Tons	3,388	3,713	4,147	1,105	1,233	1,286
Other Articles	–	–	–	–	1,867	1,175	2,311
Total, Class II		–	–	–	76,479	59,913	55,841

III. – Articles Wholly or Mainly Manufactured.

Particulars	Unit	1926.	1927.	1928.	1926.	1927.	1928.
Tin	Tons	14,189	19,771	19,769	34,789	48,499	38.361
Other Articles	–	–	–	–	370	439	636
Total, Class III		–	–	–	35,159	48,938	38,997
Total Exports		–	–	–	115,860	113,789	100,400 /

(*a*) The principal imports in 1927 from different countries included under this heading were
as follows: –

	$'000
AUSTRIA	576
Paper and Paperware	362
BELGIUM	4,830
Glass (plate and sheet)	411
Steel Bars, Rods, &c.	679
Wire Nails and Staples	534
Other Iron and Steel Goods	1,344
Cotton Piece Goods	289
DENMARK	1,114
Cement	885
FRANCE	11,173
Condensed Milk	1,118
Brandy	3,218
Other Spirituous Liquors	550
Tiles	673
Tubes, Pipes and Fittings	267

Apparel	252
Motor Cars – Passenger	802
Motor Vehicle Tyres – Covers	862
Perfumery and Cosmetics	651
GERMANY	13,705
Beer and Ale	1,191
Cement	402
Hollow-ware	405
Other Iron and Steel Goods	1,409
Cutlery, Hardware, &c.	970
Machinery	1,242
Silk Lace Goods	257
Apparel	1,097
Chemicals	341
Motor Vehicle Tyres – Covers	270
Fancy Goods and Toys	446
Lamps and Lampware	451
Perfumery and Cosmetics	402
Woodware – Rubber Cases	641
ITALY	9,672
Condensed Milk	3,152
Marble	214
Asbestos Manufactures	580
Cement	272
Cotton Piece Goods	1,667
Silk Piece Goods	290
Apparel	677
Paper and Paperware	380
Motor Cars – Passengers	468
Motor Vehicle Tyres – Covers	389
NETHERLANDS	11,583
Chocolate and Cocoa	257
Condensed Milk	1,152
Iron and Steel Goods	988
Cutlery, Hardware, &c.	361
Dredging Materials	454
Other Machinery	3,952
Cotton Piece Goods	1,061
Acetic Acid	471
Other Chemicals	221
NORWAY	588
Sterilized Milk	245
SWITZERLAND	4,451
Condensed Milk	3,744 /

(b) The principle exports in 1927 to different countries included under this heading were as follows: –

	$'000
BELGIUM	1,519
Para Rubber	940
Tin	275
DENMARK	2,883
Sago Flour	242
Tapioca Pearl	217
Copra	1,919
Para Rubber	382
FRANCE	34,060
Tapioca Flake	644
Copra	1,994
Para Rubber	20,147
Rattans	457
Tin	10,042
GERMANY	16,818
Pearl Tapioca	321
Black and White Pepper	370
Copra	5,077
Sticklac	195
Para Rubber	8,690
Rattans	566
Tin	615
ITALY	13,046
Black and White Pepper	751
Para Rubber	2,673
Tin	9.246
NETHERLANDS	41,575
Nutmegs	195
Black and White Pepper	702
Copra	8,491
Para Rubber	3,756
Tin	27,825
SPAIN	2,252
White Pepper	208
Copra	1.329
Tin	432
SWEDEN	1,365
Copra	1,23 /

TRADE WITH DIFFERENT COUNTRIES – MERCHANDISE.

Particulars.	Unit	Quantities			Values (In thousands of dollars.)		
		1926.	1927.	1928.	1926.	1927.	1928.

UNITED STATES OF AMERICA.

Imports.

I. – Animals, Food, Drink and Tobacco.

Particulars.	Unit	1926.	1927.	1928.	1926.	1927.	1928.
Wheat Flour	Tons	1,558	2,989	3,607	235	418	446
Sardines	Tons	7,380	6,590	4,345	2,295	2,095	1,334
Fruits, Fresh	Tons	574	1,037	974	207	430	422
Fruits, Dried, Preserved and Canned	Tons	520	625	560	310	341	298
Milk, Condensed and Sterilized	Th. cases	46·2	49·2	70·3	446	464	672
Cigarettes	Th. lbs.	2,638	1,994	3,580	4,170	3,187	2,548
Tobacco, Manufactured		111	108	101	239	286	259
Other Articles		–	–	–	905	732	1,345
Total, Class I		–	–	–	8,807	7,953	7,324

II. – Raw Materials and Articles Mainly Unmanufactured.

Particulars.	Unit	1926.	1927.	1928.	1926.	1927.	1928.
Asphalt and Bitumen.	Tons	2,280	5,071	7,037	217	368	447
	Cwts.	5,081	11,048	15,075	105	206	218
Other Articles	–	–	–	–	58	134	121
Total, Class II		–	–	–	380	708	786

III. – Articles Wholly or Mainly Manufactured.

Particulars.	Unit	1926.	1927.	1928.	1926.	1927.	1928.
Iron, Galvanized (Corrugated and Sheet)	Tons	4,640	4,565	2,547	1,130	1,086	549
Tin Plates	Tons	1,876	3,409	1,190	431	716	284
Other Iron and Steel Goods	–	–	–	–	692	619	584
Cutlery, Hardware, Implements and Instruments	–	–	–	–	667	827	623
Electrical Goods and Apparatus	–	–	–	–	530	989	1,012
Machines and Machinery	–	–	–	–	2,206	2,302	2,072
Apparel	–	–	–	–	431	385	245
Chemicals and Drugs	–	–	–	–	284	370	375
Kerosene	Tons	12,786	10,147	12,949	2,477	1,775	1,434
Liquid Fuel	Tons	–	32,582	7,340	–	1,157	261
Lubricating Oils	Th. galls.	1,673	1,590	2,023	2,265	2,391	2,151

Particulars.	Unit	Quantities			Values (In thousands of dollars.)		
		1926.	1927.	1928.	1926.	1927.	1928.
Leather and Leather Manufactures	–	–	–	–	486	433	389
Carried forward		–	–	–	12,144	14,360	10,131 /
Brought forward		–	–	–	12,144	14,360	10,131
Paper and Paperware	–	–	–	–	320	359	341
Motor Cars (Passenger)	No.	3,858	1,514	1,465	5,927	2,322	2.337
Motor Cars (Commercial)	No.	847	586	766	1,141	835	916
Parts and Accessories: Motor Cars and Trucks	–	–	–	–	1,786	1,349	1,561
Pneumatic Tyres: Motor Vehicles-Covers	Ths.	53·6	53·7	81·6	1,167	856	1,283
Fancy Goods and Toys	–	–	–	–	383	449	259
Other Articles	–	–	–	–	2,811	2,608	2,628
Total, Class III		–	–	–	25,679	23,138	19,456
Total Imports		–	–	–	34,866	31,799	27,566

Exports.

I. – Animals, Food, Drink and Tobacco.

Particulars.	Unit	1926.	1927.	1928.	1926.	1927.	1928.
Sago Flour	Tons	2,065	1,937	2,315	307	207	207
Pineapples, Canned	Tons	557	778	1,096	98	138	178
Pepper, Black and White	Tons	552	1,646	745	618	2,167	1,167
Other Spices	Tons	317	482	473	431	547	515
Other Articles	–	–	–	–	128	106	98
Total, Class 1		–	–	–	1,582	3,165	2,166

II. – Raw Materials and Articles Mainly Unmanufactured.

Particulars.	Unit	1926.	1927.	1928.	1926.	1927.	1928.
Copra	Tons	46,992	22,120	16,859	9,416	4,039	3,080
Copal	Tons	1,292	1,261	992	565	528	400
Damar	Tons	2,582	3,263	3,616	1,031	1,217	1,235
Palm Oil	Tons	–	246	737	–	79	192
Gutta Percha	Tons	784	563	206	851	604	222
Gutta Inferior	Tons	} 7,968	{ 1,386	1,659	} 5,953	{ 941	1,108
Jelutong	Tons		5,884	4,977		3,119	2,568
Para Rubber	Tons	254,343	241,352	284,199	461,935	333,455	229,721
Para Rubber Latex	Th. galls.	2,027	1,465	804	6,480	3,298	1,148
Rattans	Tons	2,487	2,196	1,742	999	822	687
Carried forward		–	–	–	487,230	348,102	240,36.1 /
Brought forward	–	–	–	–	487,230	348,102	240,361

Particulars.	Unit	Quantities			Values (In thousands of dollars.)		
		1926.	1927.	1928.	1926.	1927.	1928.
Other Articles	–	–	–	–	811	785	738
Total, Class II		–	–	–	488,041	348,887	241,099
III. – Articles Wholly or Mainly Manufactured.							
	Tons	44,513	46,370	56,984	108,013	114,812	109,929
Other Articles	–	–	–	–	239	134	178
Total, Class III		–	–	–	108,252	114,946	110,107
Total Exports		–	–	–	597,875	466,998	353,371
JAPAN.							
Imports.							
I. – Animals, Food, Drink and Tobacco.							
Wheat Flour	Tons	3,265	1,916	631	471	244	81
Fish, Dried and Salted	Tons	4,146	3,185	1,583	2,705	2,364	1,121
Fish, Canned	Tons	322	431	256	213	279	155
Isinglass[8]	Tons	112	109	77	390	315	212
Tea	Th. lbs.	648	808	248	285	365	100
Vegetables, Preserved	Tons	582	582	376	490	569	253
Other Articles	–	–	–	–	638	814	504
Total, Class I		–	–	–	5,192	4,950	2,426
II. – Raw Materials and Articles Mainly Unmanufactured.							
Coal	Tons	236,611	200,421	147,385	2,729	2,469	1,840
Other Articles	–	–	–	–	58	132	270
Total, Class II		–	–	–	2,787	2,601	2,110
III. – Articles Wholly or Mainly Manufactured.							
Crockery and Porcelain	–	–	–	–	1,566	717	492
Cement	Tons	39,120	80,729	60,678	953	2,085	1,541
Glass and Glass-	–	–	–	–	1,133	766	429
Carried forward		–	–	–	3,652	3,568	2,462 /
Brought forward					3,652	3,568	2,462
Hollow-ware (Cooking and Household Utensils)	Tons	942	729	434	723	491	254
Iron, Galvanized (Corrugated and Sheet)	Tons	283	1,307	1,405	69	254	262
Cutlery, Hardware, Implements and Instruments	–	–	–	–	596	504	259

Particulars.	Unit	Quantities 1926.	1927.	1928.	Values (In thousands of dollars.) 1926.	1927.	1928.
Cotton Piece Goods, Plain, Dyed and Printed	Th. yds.	31,297	35,607	22,754	6,236	6,245	4,000
Cotton Blankets	Ths.	261	190	82	385	244	115
Household Cotton Goods	Th. doz.	141	122	52	452	309	144
Other Cotton Goods	–	–	–	–	483	271	298
Silk Piece Goods	Th. yds.	1,584	1,383	1,203	1,937	1,394	1,324
Artificial Silk Piece Goods	Th. yds.	–	–	1,118	–	–	644
Canvas	Th. yds.	531	559	311	287	246	126
Haberdashery and Millinery (including Hats, Caps, etc.)	–	–	–	–	560	447	262
Underwear	Th. doz.	338	276	119	1,020	692	371
Other Apparel	–	–	–	–	245	363	497
Chemicals and Drugs	–	–	–	–	760	905	428
Paints	Cwts.	9,676	10,380	5,104	196	229	88
Paper and Paper-ware	–	–	–	–	427	398	262
Parts and Accessories – Cycles	–	–	–	–	365	354	133
Rubber Tyres and Tubes	–	–	–	–	577	711	555
Fancy Goods and Toys	–	–	–	–	864	588	337
Matches	Millions	19,887	20,096	9,685	1,065	3,091	516
Mats and Matting	Cwts.	6,751	5,526	3,622	312	247	132
Woodenware – Rubber Cases	Ths.	3,950	1,481	1,452	2,602	943	793
Other Articles	–	–	–	–	3,108	2,170	1,349
Total, Class III		–	–	–	26,921	22,664	15,611
Total Imports		–	–	–	34,900	30,215	20,147
Exports.							
I. – Animals, Food, Drink and Tobacco.							
Sago Flour	Tons	2,610	1,350	992	260	142	79
Other Articles	–	–	–	–	113	101	117
Total, Class I		–	–	–	373	243	196 /
II. – Raw Materials and Articles Mainly Unmanufactured.							
Phosphates of Lime	Tons	98,325	105,666	(a)	1,504	1,811	(a)
Iron Ore	Tons	276,438	423,264	664,685	1,382	2,116	3,323

Particulars.	Unit	Quantities			Values (In thousands of dollars.)		
		1926.	1927.	1928.	1926.	1927.	1928.
Non-Ferrous Ores (other than Tin and Tungsten)	Tons	32,362	45,746	48,851	257	348	391
	Tons	219	259	113	104	107	60
Para Rubber	Tons	17,324	19,623	26,380	29,167	27,043	20,623
Rattans	Tons	2,528	1,730	1,969	741	581	617
Trocas Shells	Tons	468	403	96	356	241	50
Other Articles	–	–	–	–	689	514	433
Total Class II		–	–	–	34,200	32,761	25,497

III. – Articles Wholly or Mainly Manufactured.

	Tons	1,613	1,922	2,401	3,910	4,744	4,617
Kerosene	Tons	2,491	3,356	1,430	411	483	135
Motor Spirit	Tons	2,873	44	6,501	793	13	1,255
Other Articles	–	–	–	–	279	384	483
Total, Class III		–	–	–	5,393	5,624	6,490
Total Exports		–	–	–	39,966	38,628	32,183

NETHERLANDS INDIES.

Imports.

I. – Animals, Food, Drink and Tobacco.

Sago, Flour and	Tons	14,478	20,373	18,423	1,430	1,979	1,457
ee, Raw	Th. lbs.	18,477	18,597	14,031	6,071	5.139	4,124
Fish, Dried and Salted	Tons	2,907	2,430	3,245	1,305	1,053	1,287
Arecanuts	Tons	37,165	31,407	43,078	8,649	5,759	6,667
Pepper, Black, Long and White	Tons	12,838	8,819	11,522	10,581	11,360	14,657
	Tons	101,839	104,941	111,405	14,213	14,528	12,854
Tobacco, Manufactured	Th. lbs.	1,210	1,158	1,217	699	632	669
Carried forward		–	–	–	42,948	40,450	41,715 /
Brought forward		–	–	–	42,948	40,450	41,715
Vegetables, Preserved	Tons	2,717	2,385	2,863	352	317	370
Potatoes	Tons	6,768	9,540	–	803	1,055	} 14,029
Other Vegetables	Tons	3,509	2,657	–	432	303	
Tapioca, Flake, Flour and Pearl	Tons	7,386	6,674	–	866	764	
Other Grain and Flour	Tons	10,443	8,947	–	670	597	
	No.	113,785	102,744	–	3,060	2,897	
Birds' Nests	Tons	69	63	–	1,083	892	
Curry Stuffs	Cwts.	28,496	39,646	–	602	770	
Fish, Fresh	Tons	1,514	1,897	–	732	922	

		Quantities			Values (In thousands of dollars.)		
Particulars.	Unit	1926.	1927.	1928.	1926.	1927.	1928.
Nutmegs	Tons	2,242	2,427	–	1,483	1,273	
Other Articles	–	–	–	–	3,347	3,651	
Total, Class I		–	–	–	56,378	53,891	56,114

II. – Raw Materials and Articles Mainly Unmanufactured.

Coal	Tons	194,461	224,688	220,988	2,303	2,517	2,377
Tin Ore	Tons	23,429	27,157	28,798	40,885	48,684	46,652
Copra	Tons	68,402	50,189	73,571	12,799	8,893	12,911
Para Rubber	Tons	132,987	157,837	126,403	141,587	139,285	69,941
Gutta, Inferior	Tons	} 4,507	{ 925	1,258	} 1,732	{ 567	726
Jelutong	Tons		2,606	–		636	} 18,324
Gutta Percha	Tons	1,364	835	–	1,747	1,054	
Firewood	Cub. tons of 50 c. ft.	74,967	76,882	–	798	818	
Timber	Cub. tons of 50 c. ft.	146,848	157,775	–	3,515	2,955	
Teel or Gingelly or Sesamum.	Tons	2,500	2,264	–	435	376	
Ground Nuts	Tons	8,378	11,305	–	1,491	1,867	
Benjamin	Tons	1,561	1,625	–	915	1,022	
Copal	Tons	774	760	–	310	290	
Damar	Tons	3,537	4,239	–	783	888	
Charcoal	Tons	21,645	21,618	–	715	779	
Kapok[9]	Tons	1,307	1,436	–	646	704	
Patchouli Leaves[10]	Tons	416	1,191	–	142	519	
Rattans	Tons	19,408	18,942	–	4,236	3,787	
Mangrove Bark	Tons	16,820	15,513	–	379	356	
Other Articles	–	–	–	–	4,369	3,304	
Total, Class II		–	–	–	219,787	219,301	150,931 /

III. – Articles Wholly or Mainly Manufactured.

Cotton Piece Goods, Plain, Dyed, Printed and Woven Coloured	Th. yds.	1,636	1,366	475	628	409	145
Cotton Sarongs, Kains and Slendangs	Ths.	4,746	4,322	4,714	4,616	3,768	4,720
Kerosene	Tons	43,329	74,994	93,175	7,008	10,614	10,348
Liquid Fuel	Tons	233,522	379,378	493,735	9,379	15,761	20,116
Lubricating Oils	Th. galls.	4,330	3,908	3,250	2,395	2,100	1,822
Motor Spirit	Tons	226,556	216,420	207,196	62,525	53,075	39,998

Particulars.	Unit	Quantities 1926.	1927.	1928.	Values (In thousands of dollars.) 1926.	1927.	1928.
Turpentine	Th. galls.	263	298	–	394	447	} 2,812
Fertilisers	Tons	8,175	7,957	–	583	595	
Mats and Matting	Cwts.	36,242	23,435	–	690	470	
Other Articles	–	–	–	–	3,596	3,183	
Total, Class III		–	–	–	91,814	90,422	79,961
Total Imports		–	–	–	367,979	363,614	287,006

EXPORTS.

I. – Animals, Food, Drink and Tobacco.

Particulars.	Unit	1926.	1927.	1928.	1926.	1927.	1928.
	Tons	222,020	198,746	211,519	29,277	25,397	25,239
Fish, Dried and Salted	Tons	53,535	51,157	51,603	12,074	11,424	11,692
	Tons	3,112	2,429	2,509	457	350	314
Cigarettes	Th. lbs.	3,431	2,627	2,210	6,595	5,588	4,793
Tobacco, Manufactured	Th. lbs.	1,560	1,385	1,413	1,265	1,104	1,199
	Tons	4,627	5,503	–	598	645	} 12,569
Other Grain and Flour	Tons	6,788	6,252	–	1,383	1,293	
Rice Meal (Bran)	Tons	10,618	9,975	–	545	498	
Blachan	Tons	2,041	2,006	–	305	306	
Fruits, Dried and Preserved	Tons	2,861	2,856	–	786	805	
Milk, Condensed and Sterilized	Th. cases	153·3	130·9	–	2,024	1,654	
Sardines	Tons	1,625	1,164	–	619	404	
Biscuits	Cwts.	27,940	26,841	–	601	515	
Vegetables	Tons	11,913	13,506	–	1,920	2,103	
	Tons	1,035	1,457	–	814	924	
Coriander Seeds	Tons	1,043	1,221	–	176	327	
Other Articles	–	–	–	–	4,364	4,146	
Total, Class I		–	–	–	63,803	57,492	55,806 /

II. – Raw Materials and Articles Mainly Unmanufactured.

Particulars.	Unit	1926.	1927.	1928.	1926.	1927.	1928.
Coconut Oil	Tons	4,576	5,834	3,771	1,674	1,948	1,202
	Cub. tons of. 50 c. ft	8,130	8,477	–	433	363	} 1,539
Kachang Oil	Cwts.	9,334	9,609	–	212	207	
Other Articles	–	–	–	–	788	805	
Total, Class II		–	–	–	3,107	3,323	2,741

III. – Articles Wholly or Mainly Manufactured.

Particulars.	Unit	1926.	1927.	1928.	1926.	1927.	1928.
Kerosene	Tons	3,158	6,520	3,885	490	955	537
Liquid Fuel	Tons	5,833	13,179	15,383	244	539	673
Lubricating Oils	Th. galls.	709	965	491	613	738	406
Motor Spirit	Tons	35,086	28,559	14,313	9,656	6,617	2,721

Particulars.	Unit	Quantities			Values (In thousands of dollars.)		
		1926.	1927.	1928.	1926.	1927.	1928.
Gunnies	Bales of 100 pieces	43,295	43,515	60,218	1,623	1,504	1,752
Cotton Piece Goods, Plain, Dyed, Printed and Woven Coloured	Th. Yds.	28,591	27,353	22,585	7,175	6,761	5,434
Cotton Sarongs, Slendangs and Kains	Ths.	3,344	3,525	3,228	5,445	5,382	4,733
Other Cotton Goods	–	–	–	–	780	643	} 16,691
Crockery and Porcelain	–	–	–	–	920	721	
Other Earthen-ware, Glass and Abrasives	–	–	–	–	583	601	
Hollow-ware	Tons	817	663	–	442	340	
Iron, Galvanised (corrugated and Sheet)	Tons	3,647	2,251	–	931	532	
Other Iron and Steel Goods	–	–	–	–	1,366	998	
Cutlery, Hardware, Implements and Instruments	–	–	–	–	427	408	
Sewing Machines	No.	15,346	12,174	–	756	609	
Other Machines and Machinery	–	–	–	–	441	348	
Silk Piece Goods	Th. yds.	229	400	–	285	352	
Silk Thread	Th. lbs	62	53	–	349	229	
Twine	Tons	571	586	–	386	331	
Boots and Shoes (Leather and Other Sorts)	Doz. Prs.	52,529	69,161	–	935	1,193	
Other Apparel	–	–	–	–	1,413	1,225	
Chemicals	–	–	–	–	408	458	
Drugs and Medi-cines	Th. lbs	1,243	1,240	–	635	716	
Motor Cars (Passenger and Commercial)	No.	347	167	–	539	287	

Particulars.	Unit	Quantities			Values (In thousands of dollars.)		
		1926.	1927.	1928.	1926.	1927.	1928.
Rubber Tyres and Tubes	–	–	–	–	753	906	
Other Rubber Manufactures	–	–	–	–	273	356	
Fireworks	Cwts.	18,208	12,102	–	599	420	
Other Articles	–	–	–	–	7,074	6,296	
Total, Class III.		–	–	–	45,541	40,465	32,947
Total Exports		–	–	–	112,451	101,280	91,494 /

(a) Not included in the "Annual Summary," see note page 13. /

TRADE WITH DIFFERENT COUNTRIES – MERCHANDISE.

Particulars.	Unit.	Quantities.			Values. (In thousands of dollars,)		
		1926.	1927.	1928.	1926.	1927.	1928.
OTHER FOREIGN COUNTRIES							
Imports.							
I. – Animals, Food, Drink and Tobacco.							
Rice	Tons	193,300	620,483	593,068	66,661	78,664	72,925
Fish, Dried and Salted	Tons	46,887	44,051	43,138	10,260	10,446	10,017
Pepper, Black, Long and White	Tons	208	685	156	205	770	233
Sugar	Tons	2,941	3,251	9,247	371	453	1,091
Vegetables, Preserved	Tons	15,343	12,778	9,709	2,446	1,909	1,614
Cigarettes	Th. lbs.	3,313	3,299	2,404	4,429	4,786	3,243
Tobacco, Manufac-	Th. lbs.	5,259	1,681	1,659	3,213	885	1,037
Beans	Tons	11,938	15,457	–	1,322	1,664	} 21,392
Other Grain and	Tons	9,202	14,119	–	1,706	1,852	
Rice Meal (Bran)	Tons	85,117	95,853	–	5,217	4,456	
Cattle	No.	40,718	31,334	–	2,908	2,471	
Swine	No.	112,001	117,301	–	2,645	2,932	
Eggs, Fresh and Salted.	Th.	35,435	48,204	–	1,017	1,372	
Fruits, Fresh	Tons	5,195	6,915	–	938	1,153	
Fruits, Dried and Preserved	Tons	2,855	1,933	–	980	558	
Lard	Tons	1,342	1,170	–	725	612	
Salt	Tons	53,244	60,984	–	820	988	
Tea	Th. lbs.	4,194	1,729	–	1,875	1,264	
Vegetables (other than Preserved)	Tons	10,450	8,376	–	1,400	966	

Particulars.	Unit.	Quantities.			Values. (In thousands of dollars,)		
		1926.	1927.	1928.	1926.	1927.	1928.
Samsoo	Th. galls.	392	347	–	1,204	1,135	
Other Articles	–	–	–	–	3,191	3,048	
Total, Class I		–	–	–	113,533	122,384	111,552

II. – Raw Materials and Articles Mainly Unmanufactured.

Particulars.	Unit.	1926.	1927.	1928.	1926.	1927.	1928.
Coal	Tons	57,901	40,788	56,284	697	512	680
Tin Ore	Tons	10,064	10,928	11,199	16,252	17,961	14,768
Copra	Tons	6,090	1,436	6,803	1,137	253	1,199
Para Rubber	Tons	4,590	7,897	7,842	6,565	9,480	5,958
Asphalt and Bitumen	Tons	8,054	8,784	–	684	689	} 9,051
Planks	Cub. tons of 50 c. ft.	9,050	8,617	–	920	881	
Timber	Cub. tons of 50 c. ft.	3,634	11,445	–	220	521	
Other Wood	Cub. tons of 50 c. ft.	28,818	25,821	–	355	353	
Sticklac	Tons	901	1,559	–	717	1,562	
Kachang Oil	Cwts.	119,655	145,718	–	3,131	3,107	
Buffalo and Cow Hides	Tons	1,657	1,494	–	780	547	
Other Articles	–	–	–	–	1,867	1,428	
Total, Class II		–	–	–	33,325	37,294	31,656 /

OTHER FOREIGN COUNTRIES (*a*)

III. – Articles Wholly or Mainly Manufactured.

Particulars.	Unit.	1926.	1927.	1928.	1926.	1927.	1928.
Cement	Tons	18,080	15,682	18,425	449	384	420
Cotton Piece Goods, Plain, Dyed, Printed and Woven Coloured	Th. yds.	17,754	14,647	14,439	3,341	2,481	2,322
Cotton Sarongs, Slendangs and Kains	Ths.	1,742	1,001	1,250	2,493	1,438	1,685
Silk Piece Goods	Th. yds.	3,174	2,248	1,731	3,904	2,784	1,925
Liquid Fuel	Tons	29,519	18,741	19,056	708	454	485
Crockery and Porcelain	–	–	–	–	722	424	} 11,282
Iron and. Steel Goods	–	–	–	–	652	649	
Cotton Goods not specified above	–	–	–	–	599	405	
Silk Thread	Th. lbs.	157	113	–	888	489	
Cordage	Tons	1,361	1,458	–	894	936	
Apparel	–	–	–	–	865	636	
Drugs and Medicines	Th. lbs.	3,631	1,251	–	1,553	500	

Particulars.	Unit.	Quantities.			Values. (In thousands of dollars,)		
		1926.	1927.	1928.	1926.	1927.	1928.
Leather Boxes and Trunks	Ths.	60·9	37·5	–	589	341	
Paper and Paperware	–	–	–	–	1,077	719	
Joss Sticks and Joss	Th. Pkgs.	2,190	1,340	–	2,036	1,448	
Other Articles	–	–	–	–	9,266	4,521	
Total, Class III	–	–	–	–	30,036	18,609	18,119
Total Imports	–	–	–	–	176,894	178,287	161,327 /

Exports.

I. – Animals, Food, Drink and Tobacco.

Particulars.	Unit.	1926.	1927.	1928.	1926.	1927.	1928.
ee, Raw	Th. lbs.	4,197	5,315	3,904	1,451	1,481	1,165
Fish, Dried and Salted	Tons	877	2,020	1,164	561	547	771
Pineapples, canned	Tons	1,100	1,126	1,872	220	256	367
Arecanuts	Tons	9,034	10,595	8,126	2,782	2,808	2,043
Pepper, Black, Long and White	Tons	2,786	1,135	2,302	2,010	1,090	2,621
Sugar	Tons	11,392	8,616	9,247	1,669	1,185	1,091
Cigarettes	Th. lbs.	1,229	874	1,047	2,099	1,640	1,907
Rice	Tons	7,273	4,195	2,587	904	520	289
Tapioca, Flake, Flour and Pearl	Tons	6,781	5,261	3,434	845	629	411
Other Grain and	Tons	4,131	3,958	–	655	629	} 6,184
Sardines	Tons	737	1,213	–	299	435	
Fruits, Dried and Preserved	Tons	1,315	1,819	–	313	330	
Milk, Condensed	Th. cases	42·2	31·4	–	545	361	
Sugar Candy	Tons	2,907	3,579	–	529	691	
Vegetables	Tons	3,160	2,889	–	458	383	
Other Articles	–	–	–	–	3,547	3,129	
Total, Class I	–	–	–	–	18,887	16,114	16,849

II. – Raw Materials and Articles Mainly Unmanufactured.

Particulars.	Unit.	1926.	1927.	1928.	1926.	1927.	1928.
Coconut Oil	Tons	3,543	3,936	5,162	1,296	1,341	1,678
Para Rubber	Tons	142	169	480	290	301	512
Rattans	Tons	2,631	2,379	2,685	644	501	512
Planks	Cub. tons of 50 c.ft.	8,720	10,184	–	319	337	} 2,963
Ground Nuts	Tons	1,498	2,127	–	287	384	
Hides and Skins	Tons	289	372	–	215	216	
Mangrove Bark	Tons	7,980	5,287	–	288	198	
Gambier, Cube	Tons	573	511	–	237	161	
Other Articles	–	–	–	–	1,152	1,112	

Particulars.	Unit.	Quantities.			Values. (In thousands of dollars,)		
		1926.	1927.	1928.	1926.	1927.	1928.
Total, Class II		–	–	–	4,728	4,551	5,665 /
OTHER FOREIGN COUNTRIES (b)							
III. – Articles Wholly or Mainly Manufactured.							
Tin	Tons	1,062	1,222	1,565	2,599	3,016	3,011
Cotton Piece Goods, Plain, Dyed, Printed and Woven Coloured	Th. yds.	16,965	17,825	11,992	4,091	4,037	2,936
Cotton Sarongs, Slendangs and Kains	Ths.	602	1,032	1,044	685	1,026	1,056
Gunnies	Bales of 100 Pieces	92,766	135,593	88,629	4,002	4,841	3,251
Kerosene	Tons	18,581	25,016	38,478	2,918	3,501	4,200
Liquid Fuel	Tons	37,970	28,969	41,070	1,520	1,233	1,745
Lubricating Oils	Th. galls.	561	611	681	482	570	567
Motor Spirit	Tons	21,587	14,726	14,646	5,807	3,523	2,742
Iron, Galvanized (Corrugated and Sheet)	Tons	1,261	1,377	–	308	319	} 15,551
Other Iron and Steel Goods	–	–	–	–	1,118	1,081	
Cutlery, Hardware, Instruments and Implements	–	–	–	–	573	577	
Machines and Machinery	–	–	–	–	601	876	
Cotton Goods not Specified above	–	–	–	–	969	803	
Cordage	Tons	1,105	1,320	–	436	442	
Boots and Shoes (other than Leather)	Doz. Prs.	41,491	98,973	–	630	1,320	
Other Apparel	–	–	–	–	429	451	
Drugs and Medicines	Th. lbs.	570	558	–	371	420	
Motor Cars (Passenger and Commercial)	No.	297	308	–	387	360	
Pneumatic Tyres: Motor Vehicles – Covers	Ths.	15·9	24·5	–	444	645	

Particulars.	Unit.	Quantities.			Values. (In thousands of dollars,)		
		1926.	1927.	1928.	1926.	1927.	1928.
Rubber Manufactures (other than Tyres and Tubes)	–	–	–	–	422	478	
Other Articles	–	–	–	–	4,137	4,882	
Total, Class III		–	–	–	32,929	34,401	35,059
Total Exports		–	–	–	56,544	55,066	57,573 /

) The principal imports in 1927 from different Countries included under this heading were as follows: –

	$'000
CHINA	35,114
Beans	1,656
Other Grain and Flour	1,323
Eggs	687
Fresh Fruits	1,093
Dried and Preserved Fruits	528
Lard	575
Sugar	394
Tea	1,263
Preserved Vegetables	1,897
Other Vegetables	734
Samsoo	1,135
Cigarettes	4,674
Manufactured and Native Tobacco	510
Kachang Oil	3,107
Crockery and Porcelain	418
Cotton Piece Goods	2,314
Other Cotton Goods	393
Silk Piece Goods	2,132
Silk Thread	484
Twine	358
Drugs and Medicines	480
Paper and Paperware	713
Joss Sticks and Joss Paper	1,447
EGYPT	638
Salt	406
FRENCH INDIA	1,966
Cotton Sarongs, &c.	1,407
FRENCH INDO-CHINA	24,053
Rice	8,416
Eggs	639
Dried and Salted Fish	6,718
Cattle	453

	$'000
Swine	2,132
Tin Ore	739
Para Rubber	3,204
Iron and Steel Goods	368
PHILIPPINE Is. AND SULU	1,434
Cigars	219
Para Rubber	232
Manila Cordage	430
SIAM AND SIAMESE STATES	113,144
Rice	70,065
Other Grain and Flour	547
Bran (Rice Meal)	4,310
Cattle	1,932
Swine	758
Dried and Salted Fish	3,563
Salt	577
Black, Long and White Pepper	743
Manufactured Tobacco	609
Tin Ore	17,131
Wood and Timber	1,578
Sticklac	1,478
Buffalo and Cow Hides	512
Para Rubber	6,026
Silk Piece Goods	636 /

(*b*) The principal exports in 1927 to different countries included under this heading were as follows: –

	$'000
ARABIA	572
Raw Coffee	376
CHINA	8,589
Grain and Flour	272
Dried and Salted Fish	423
Black, White and Long Pepper	297
Sugar Candy	569
Coconut Oil	510
Para Rubber	288
Rattans	364
Mangrove Bark	196
Tin	1,625
Boots and Shoes (other than Leather)	911
Kerosene	282
Rubber Manufactures (other than Tyres and Tubes)	349
EGYPT	1,015
Liquid Fuel	591

FRENCH INDIA	1,196
Arecanuts	751
FRENCH INDO-CHINA	10,368
Arecanuts	1,168
Sugar	587
Cigarette	199
Iron and Steel Goods	309
Gunnies	2,656
Kerosene	825
Motor Spuit	2,024
PHILIPPINE ISLANDS AND SULU	1,837
Grain and Flour	386
Raw Coffee	595
SIAM AND SIAMESE STATES	29,442
Rice	237
Tapioca, Flake, Flour and Pearl	255
Other Grain and Flour	506
Raw Coffee	289
Dried and Preserved Fruits	202
Condensed Milk	357
Arecanuts	876
Sugar	539
Vegetables	211
Cigarettes	1,398
Ground Nuts	262
Coconut Oil	823
Galvanized Iron	317
Other Iron and Steel Goods	665
Cutlery, Hardware, &c.	541
Machines and Machinery	817
Cotton Piece Goods	3,798
Cotton Sarongs, &c.	763
Other Cotton Goods	653
Cordage	345
Gunnies	2,159
Boots and Shoes (other than Leather)	298
Other Apparel	393
Drugs and Medicines	217
Kerosene	2,300
Liquid Fuel	492
Lubricating Oils	460
Motor Spirit	1,495
Motor Cars	328
Pneumatic Tyres (Motor Vehicle – Covers)	622
Mats and Matting	219
SOUTH AMERICA	1,744
Black and White Pepper	627

IMPORTS AND EXPORTS OF CERTAIN IMPORTANT ARTICLES.
QUANTITIES IMPORTED FROM AND EXPORTED TO DIFFERENT
COUNTRIES AND AVERAGE VALUES PER UNIT, 1922 TO 1928.

Particulars.	1922.	1923.	1924.	1925.	1926.	1927.	1928.
TIN ORE. Imports.	Tons.	Tons.	Tons.	Tons.	Tons.	Tons.	Tons.
British India and Burma	1,387	2,002	1,473	1,832	1,802	2,226	2,307
Union of South Africa	730	1,434	1,836	1,823	1,537	1,808	1,839
Other British Countries	–	–	–	–	25	54	–
Total, British Countries	2,117	3,436	3,309	3,655	3,364	4,088	4,146
French Indo-China	–	10	123	260	358	532	734
Netherlands Indies	19,907	21,969	24,395	25,342	23,429	27,157	28,798
Siam and Siamese States	8,259	9,511	10,052	10,210	9,706	10,335	10,465
Other Foreign Countries	109	16	30	22	34	142	246
Total, Foreign Countries	28,275	31,506	34,600	35,834	33,527	38,166	40,243
Total Imports (a)	30,392	34,942	37,909	39,489	36,891	42,254	44,389
Average Value per Ton	$ 872	$ 1,189	$ 1,460	$ 1,544	$ 1,697	$ 1,736	$ 1,508
TIN. Exports.	Tons.	Tons.	Tons.	Tons.	Tons.	Tons.	Tons.
United Kingdom	11,010	10,057	16,335	13,970	11,101	9,453	12,909
British India and Burma	1,855	2,255	2,544	3,052	2,632	3,546	2,871
Hongkong	56	218	974	373	335	649	1,742
Canada	215	535	700	650	725	620	530
Other British Countries.	64	82	80	128	127	153	171
Total, British Countries	13,200	13,147	20,633	18,173	14,920	14,421	18,223
France	4,307	4,694	5,830	4,918	4,708	4,083	4,621
Germany	300	60	415	566	291	251	190
Italy	2,547	2,927	3,566	3,707	3,615	3,744	3,680
Netherlands	25	10	1,510	4,525	5,435	11,380	10,870
Other European Countries.	85	100	95	165	140	313	402
Carried forward	7,264	7,791	11,416	13,881	14,189	19,771	19,763 /
Brought forward	7,264	7,791	11,416	13,881	14,189	19,771	19,763
China	154	251	531	503	756	666	965
Japan	833	732	1,342	1,185	1,613	1,922	2,400
United States	44,765	47,820	46,195	45,120	44,513	46,370	56,985
Other Foreign Countries	41	184	557	220	343	623	716
Total, Foreign Countries	53,057	56,725	60,041	60,909	61,414	69,352	80,829
Total Exports	66,257	69,872	80,674	79,082	76,334	83,773	99,052
Average Value per Ton	$ 1,357	$ 1,714	$ 2,097	$ 2,215	$ 2,430	$ 2,466	$ 1,931
Total Imports	1,012	614	446	311	198	51	3
PARA RUBBER.	Tons.	Tons.	Tons.	Tons.	Tons.	Tons.	Tons.
Imports.							
British North Borneo	1,490	1,744	2,257	2,629	2,423	3,256	2,903
Brunei	17	99	423	346	570	612	484
Sarawak	3,609	5,433	6,803	8,701	9,206	10,942	10,092
British India and Burma	727	800	1,273	2,135	1,717	2,625	2,053
Other British Countries	–	17	9	57	17	81	1
Total, British Countries	5,843	8,093	10,765	13,868	13,933	17,516	15,533

Particulars.	1922.	1923.	1924.	1925.	1926.	1927.	1928.
TIN ORE. Imports.	Tons.	Tons.	Tons.	Tons.	Tons.	Tons.	Tons.
Netherlands Indies	27,618	59,426	93,113	138,870	132,987	157,837	126,403
Siam and Siamese States	736	1,717	2,962	5,377	4,027	5,471	4,818
Other Foreign Countries	242	40	93	79	115	177	140
Total, Foreign Countries	29,715	62,339	97,759	145,063	137,578	165,734	134,254
Total Imports	35,558	70,432	108,524	158,931	151,511	183,250	149,787
Average Value per Ton	$ 519	$ 788	$ 703	$ 1,495	$ 1,125	$ 938	$ 589 /
United Kingdom	31,306	46,801	33,503	45,698	83,998	76,398	60,994
	1,036	706	721	947	1,746	1,356	1,562
Hongkong:	288	404	1,293	293	162	177	875
	1,167	1,058	543	1,115	717	607	1,092
	1,109	1,116	2,450	2,389	5,290	5,230	3,697
Other British Countries	6	11	64	13	27	18	31
Total, British Countries	34,912	50,096	38,574	50,455	91,940	83,786	68,251
	286	720	567	864	1,152	682	1,188
	4,494	7,315	8,020	9,502	14,029	14,245	12,663
	8,076	5,472	5,078	10,381	5,845	6,429	9,398
	1,745	3,010	2,586	3,769	2,968	1,900	1,763
Netherlands	2,491	3,972	2,115	3,327	3,247	2,672	3,708
Other European Countries	103	143	470	223	347	450	656
	15,244	18,251	15,337	11,532	17,324	19,623	26,383
United States	180,340	162,888	186,701	226,530	254,343	241,352	284,203
Other Foreign Countries	194	149	258	243	142	170	480
Total, Foreign Countries	212,973	201,920	221,132	266,371	299,397	287,523	340,442
Total Exports	247,885	252,016	259,706	316,826	391,337	371,309	408,693
Average Value per Ton	$ 646	$ 1,121	$ 1,020	$ 2,355	$ 1,818	$ 1,399	$ 807
PARA RUBBER LATEX.	Thous.	Thous.	Thous.	Thous.	Thous.	Thous.	Thous.
	Galls.	Galls.	Galls.	Galls.	Galls.	Galls.	Galls.
United Kingdom	24	50	16	48	55	76	67
United States	15	20	783	2,265	2,027	1,465	804
Other Countries	1	4	4	3	6	20	49
Total Exports	40	74	803	2,316	2,088	1,561	920 /
	Tons.	Tons.	Tons.	Tons.	Tons.	Tons.	Tons.
British North Borneo	2,909	2,992	3,333	3,192	4,477	3,034	5,219
	905	777	770	781	1,266	1,179	1,633
British India and Burma	563	703	690	705	752	699	527
Other British Countries	1	4	3	232	23	1	–
Total, British Countries	4,378	4,176	4,796	4,910	6,518	4,913	7,379
	187	277	365	429	147	172	300
Netherlands Indies	55,704	57,314	56,779	56,905	68,402	50,189	73,581
Siam and Siamese States	3,631	4,904	4,482	4,363	5,846	1,140	6,470
Other Foreign Countries	2,091	2,149	892	208	97	124	33
Total, Foreign Countries	61,613	58,679	62,518	61,905	74,492	51,625	80,384

Particulars.	1922.	1923.	1924.	1925.	1926.	1927.	1928.
TIN ORE. Imports.	Tons.	Tons.	Tons.	Tons.	Tons.	Tons.	Tons.
Total Imports	65,991	58,639	67,314	66,815	81,010	56,538	87,763
Average Value per Ton	$ 164	$ 177	$ 192	$ 195	$ 187	$ 178	$ 176
Exports.	Tons.	Tons.	Tons.	Tons.	Tons.	Tons.	Tons.
United Kingdom	28,825	30,321	25,181	23,934	17,065	12,078	10,554
Other British Countries	1	14	39	–	–	34	50
Total, British Countries	28,826	30,345	25,220	23,934	17,065	12,112	10,604
Denmark	6,198	19,738	10,985	5,873	7,898	10,029	13,250
France	27,198	23,418	24,924	21,244	3,985	10,679	20,825
Germany	47,825	20,468	16,793	13,640	30,376	27,133	45,681
Italy	3,360	5,828	3,201	596	1,404	749	1,300
Netherlands	39,301	36,612	51,580	53,369	50,679	45,839	56,326
Spain	16,382	12,708	16,565	14,258	14,688	7,181	10,834
Sweden	1,101	2,304	4,801	5,620	10,594	6,501	4,427
Other European Countries	200	2,104	801	1,462	1,011	306	2,550
United States	–	–	3,453	12,945	46,992	22,120	16,859
Other Foreign Countries	95	156	726	295	712	393	198
Total, Foreign Countries	141,660	123,350	133,829	129,302	168,339	130,930	172,250
Total Exports	170,486	153,725	159,049	153,236	185,404	143,042	182,854 /
Average Value per Ton	177	190	205	210	200	186	187
RICE.	Tons.	Tons.	Tons.	Tons.	Tons.	Tons.	Tons.
Imports.							
British India and Burma	215,432	186,819	251,690	235,483	258,953	218,363	209,647
Other British Countries	313	462	389	485	1,511	131	81
Total, British Countries	215,745	187,281	252,079	235,968	260,464	218,494	209,728
French Indo-China	56,037	26,042	35,783	49,769	69,772	69,506	78,400
Siam	324,440	348,173	291,102	361,851	422,651	549,866	513,718
Other Foreign Countries	415	1,429	1,771	2,419	2,493	2,093	2,068
Total, Foreign Countries	380,892	375,644	328,656	414,039	494,916	621,465	594,186
Total Imports	596,637	562,925	580,735	650,007	755,380	839,959	803,914
Average Value per Ton	$ 117	$ 110	$ 125	$ 124	$ 130	$ 124	$ 119
Exports.	Tons.	Tons.	Tons.	Tons.	Tons.	Tons.	Tons.
British North Borneo	10,476	10,529	12,313	10,994	10,969	13,070	12,232
Sarawak	7,063	11,380	14,997	14,828	15,505	20,790	18,692
British India and Burma	356	446	480	200	205	17,105	13,960
Ceylon	4,657	2,736	2,044	2,499	21,563	37,630	16,250
Other British Countries	10,221	8,595	4,125	3,788	2,998	2,705	1,341
Total, British Countries	32,773	33,686	33,959	32,309	51,240	91,300	62,475
China	3,478	2,410	709	3,255	2,931	1,181	195
Netherlands Indies	191,122	162,013	147,672	207,168	222,020	198,746	211,519
Siam	1,413	1,470	1,331	2,192	3,463	1,919	1,638
Other Foreign Countries	4,255	1,689	2,683	2,025	879	1,095	754
Total, Foreign Countries	200,268	167,582	152,395	214,640	229,293	202,941	214,106
Total Exports	233,041	201,268	186,354	246,949	280,533	294,241	276,581
Average Value per Ton	$ 114	$ 110	$ 127	$ 126	$ 131	$ 122	$ 117
Net Imports	363,596	361,657	394,381	403,058	474,847	545,718	527,333 /

SHIPPING–FEDERATED MALAY STATES

[...]

Particulars.	Unit.	1913.	1914.	1925.	1926.	1927.	1928.
Vessels entered and cleared at Federated Malay States Ports.							
Vessels other than Native							
Entered–							
Number	No.	4,882	4,988	5,831	5,547	5,335	5,842
Tonnage	Thous. Tons	2,125	2,497	3,057	3,357	3,514	3,556
Cleared–							
Number	No.	4,877	4,983	5,828	5,546	5,342	5,830
Tonnage	Thous. Tons	2,124	2,497	3,056	3,357	3,514	3,548
Native Craft–							
Entered and Cleared–							
Number	No.	14,052	19,862	21,792	26,796	38,936	32,997
Tonnage	Thous. Tons	277	344	355	395	614	640
Ocean going Merchant Vessels calling at Port Swettenham.							
All Nationalities–							
Number	No.	107	413	481	595	652	665
Tonnage	Thous. Tons	*	*	1,899	2,349	2,500	2,542
British–							
Number	No.	*	*	*	*	492	474
Tonnage	Thous. Ton	*	*	*	*	1,940	1,903

*   Not available.

ANON., *REPORT OF SUB-COMMITTEE WITH RESPECT TO EXPORTS TO GERMANY AND AUSTRIA FROM THE STRAITS SETTLEMENTS* (1914)

Anon., *Report of Sub-Committee with respect to Exports to Germany and Austria from the Straits Settlements* (Singapore: Fraser & Neave, 1914), pp. 1–5.

e report is an attempt to gauge the economic impact of the First World War, but also throws light on the growing importance of Germany and Austria in the trade of the Straits Settlements, which continued to grow after hostilities had ceased.

Anon., *Report of Sub-Committee with respect to Exports to Germany and Austria from the Straits Settlements* (1914), extract

[...]

In considering this report we must first of all call attention to the attached figures of exports from the Straits Settlements for the year 1913, the total Export of each article being given together with individual figures of exports to the United Kingdom, Germany, Austria, Holland and Belgium.

We propose to deal with each article separately or in groups, according as they are of a similar character or are exported for a similar purpose. /

METALS.

TIN. – This is the most valuable and next to copra the largest article of export. Out of a total of 1,105,000 piculs, 11,000 piculs were shipped direct to Germany and 26,000 piculs to Austria.

e whole business in Tin is practically controlled by the London and New York Metal Exchanges.

WOLFRAM ORE. – Out of total export of 13,000 piculs, 9,000 piculs were shipped direct to Germany. Wolfram ore is used for tempering steel, and we understand is in special demand by Germany where there are special facilities for dealing with this metal.

On the contrary Wolfram ore is in little demand for United Kingdom owing to other processes being in vogue for the tempering and hardening of steel.

PRODUCE FOR CONSUMPTION.

Sago Flour. – Fine qualities are used for manufacture of confectionery, but the bulk of this article is used in the manufacture, *i.e.,* the filling of cloth and also as saccharine. Austria imports none, but Germany takes about one per cent, of total imports in direct shipments.

PEPPERS. – *Black and White.* It will be observed from the attached figures of exports that a very considerable proportion of the total exports of black and white peppers are shipped direct to German and Austrian ports. In considering this fact as also all produce shipped direct to German and Austrian ports it must be borne in mind that the bulk of such transactions are negotiated in London through British merchants.

TAPIOCAS. – It will be observed that shipments to Austria are practically nil, whilst direct shipments to Germany amounted to seven and a half per cent of the total exports. Our remarks regarding peppers apply equally with regard to tapiocas.

PINE APPLES. – Out of total exports of 751,000 cases, 21,000 were shipped direct to Germany and 4,000 cases direct to Austria. /

OIL CAKES. – The total exports amount to 118,000 piculs and of this the large proportion of 100,000 piculs were shipped direct to Germany.

Oilcake is the pressed refuse of Copra (dried cocoa–nuts) after the oil has been extracted, and is in special demand for Germany as food for cattle.

PRODUCE FOR MANUFACTURING PURPOSES.

Gambier is a tanning extract obtained from the leaves of a shrub indigenous to the Straits Settlements, and is hydraulically pressed into bales and packed in cases previous to shipment. The total exports from the Straits amount to 362,000 piculs of which 13,000 piculs were shipped direct to Germany and 5,000 to Austria. The business as regards direct shipments to Germany and Austria is chiefly negotiated in London.

Copra. – This is the most extensive article of export from the Straits. Out of total exports of 1,546,000 piculs, the very large proportion of 789,000 piculs were shipped direct to Germany and 23,000 piculs only to Austria.

Copra is the name given to dried cocoanut and the oil expressed therefrom is very valuable as same is used in the manufacture of soap and also after refining in the manufacture of nut butter. Germany encourages the latter business by putting an import duty on cocoanut oil. The consequence is none is imported. German crushing industries are therefore protected.

It is difficult to give any figures to show how much cocoa butter is consumed in Germany, but it probably amounts to 60 per cent. of the total imports. Of the remaining 40 per cent. a small proportion is forwarded to Russia to be crushed and the balance is re-exported in the shape of cocoanut oil to Great Britain and other countries.

It is therefore possible for Great Britain to purchase oil from Germany very cheaply at times.

e Maypole Dairy Co. import their supplies of cocoanut oil from Germany and Denmark, and refine it in England before making nut butter. /

RATTANS. – This is an important article of export from the Straits. Total exports amount to 492,000 piculs of which the large proportion of 146,000 piculs were shipped direct to Germany and 4,000 direct to Austria. There are various qualities of rattans which are used mainly for making seats for bent wood chairs, fancy chairs, baskets and cane work of every description. Germany and Austria make a specialty of this particular trade in which Great Britain has not hitherto competed in any serious way.

America is a large importer of rattans and has extensive factories for the manufacture of all classes of rattan and cane goods. We would suggest that an up to date catalogue be obtained from chair manufacturers, as illustrating the class of goods into which rattans are manufactured.

We forward samples of the various descriptions of rattans duly labelled with their local name and the attached memorandum describes the different purposes for which the different varieties are utilised.

Inferior Guttas, Gutta Percha, Borneo Rubber, Para Rubber, Hides, Gum
– The direct shipments of these articles to Germany and Austria are small and we have no special report to make with regard thereto.

GENERAL

e increase of late years in direct shipments to Germany and Austria, the former country in particular is in a great measure due to the increase in direct tonnage provided by foreign steamers notably of the North German Lloyd, Hamburg America, and Austrian Lloyd Steamship Companies.

In conclusion we beg to call attention to the figures of direct imports to Antwerp especially of copra, sago flour and gambier, which it will be observed are considerable. It is highly probable that a large proportion of these imports ultimately find their way to Germany.

Since the bulk of business of Straits exports is negotiated through London, we would suggest that if any further information is required it be obtained from the London Produce Brokers Association of Mincing Lane, or the London Chamber of Commerce. /

VARIETY	USED FOR
SEGAS	
BANDJERMASSIN BOOYOU	
SAMPIT BOOYOU	
COTIE PACKIRS	
PASSIR PACKIRS	Cane is cut up for seating purposes for all
PULOH LAUT PACKIRS	kinds of chairs, railway carriage seats, etc.
BROW PACKIRS	Reed is used for making fancy chairs, baskets,
JELYE LOONTIE	baby carriages, etc.
COTARINGGAN LOONTIE	
INDRAGIRI LOONTIE	
DJAMBI LOONTIE	
SANKOLERANG SEGA	
SARAWAK SEGA	
	Largely used for making into baskets for protecting live artillery shells.
ROTAN MERALL	Washed variety used for chair and basket manufacture.
PONTIANAK AND PAHANG	Used for making cheap baskets, such as coal, fish, and skip baskets used in factories.
MACASSAR ROTAN AYER, viz:–	
THOITI	These varieties yield reeds suitable for whips
GORONTALO	and chair manufacturing as well as for
TOLI TOLI	sporting goods such as cricket, hockey and
etc., etc.	racquet handles.

KIRSEPP AND BARTLETT, *REPORT OF A MISSION APPOINTED TO INVESTIGATE THE CLOVE TRADE IN INDIA AND BURMA, CEYLON, BRITISH MALAYA AND THE DUTCH EAST INDIES* (1933)

G. D. Kirsepp and C. A. Bartlett, *Report of a Mission Appointed to Investigate the Clove Trade in India and Burma, Ceylon, British Malaya and the Dutch East Indies* (London: Crown Agents, 1933), pp. 30–40, 64–5.

Cloves were used by Indians as a spice. The first part of the extract reproduced here describes the import and export of cloves to and from Malaya's two most important ports – Singapore and Penang. The second section discusses the growth of the crop in Province Wellesley and the State of Penang.

G. D. Kirsepp and C. A. Bartlett, *Report of a Mission Appointed to Investigate the Clove Trade in India and Burma, Ceylon, British Malaya and the Dutch East Indies* (1933), extract

(i) EXTENT OF TRADE.

e general character of the clove trade in British Malaya is of some complexity. Penang a field of cultivation for over a century, has a small export of cloves of local production as well as a small entrepot trade in cloves of foreign origin. Singapore has, within recent years, figured as an important clove entrepot and still operates as a distributor on a reduced scale, but with a diversity of connections. The overseas trade is concentrated entirely in these centres, from which there are also drawn the supplies required to meet the needs of the local market.

e total overseas trade handled at Penang and Singapore during the decennial period 1922 – 1931 is shown in Table XIX. Over the period referred to the combined imports averaged about 19,400 cwts. or 62,000 frasilas and the combined exports 19,100 cwts. or 61,000 frasilas.[1] Roughly 90 per cent. of this trade was represented by cloves of Zanzibar origin. Owing, however, to the conditions which now govern the redistribution of cloves from this area, the figures for the past ten years have little significance as reflecting the present position of the Malayan market or its potentialities. A correct appreciation of that position can only be obtained by a detailed examination of the trade conducted at Penang and at Singapore, each of these centres, although having certain features in common, operating for the most part an independent trade based upon separate commercial connections.

TABLE XIX.
STATEMENT SHOWING THE IMPORTS AND EXPORTS
OF CLOVE PRODUCE FOR THE TEN YEARS 1922 – 31.

Year.	Imports.		Exports.	
	cwts.	fras.	cwts.	fras.
1922	13,780	44,100	14,780	47,300
1923	17,530	56,100	15,600	49,900
1924	19,440	62,200	18,540	59,300
1925	30,690	98,200	29,300	93,800
1926	25,410	81,300	24,880	79,600
1927	34,070	109,000	32,820	105,000
1928	16,720	53,500	18,250	58,400
1929	14,810	47,400	15,220	48,700
1930	15,500	49,600	14,220	45,500
1931	5,750	18,400	7,000	22,400

(ii) PENANG.

66. *Imports.* – It will be observed from the particulars shown in Table XX that Penang imports from overseas are drawn, almost in their entirety, from Sumatra in the Dutch East Indies and from British India. The imports from Sumatra are the produce of Sumatra, while the imports from British India are the produce of Zanzibar. During the ten years under review imports from Sumatra, averaging 259 cwts. or 829 frasilas per annum, have exceeded those of Zanzibar origin which have averaged 210 cwts. or 670 frasilas per annum. Penang, however, also obtains supplies both of Zanzibar cloves and of adulterants, in the shape of exhausted clove produce, from Singapore, imports from this source not being included in the foreign trade returns. No particulars of the imports from Singapore are available, but there is no reason to suppose that they are extensive. It might perhaps be said that the Penang clove imports from all sources represent Zanzibar and Sumatra produce in about equal quantities. /

TABLE XX.
STATEMENT SHOWING THE IMPORTS OF CLOVES INTO PEN-
ANG FOR THE TEN YEARS 1922 – 31.

Year	Countries of Shipment.					
	British India (Zanzibar origin)		Sumatra (D.E.I. origin)		Other Countries	
	Cwts.	fras.	cwts.	fras.	cwts.	fras.
1922	271·5	868	301·5	964	0·62	2
1923	175·60	562	180·94	579	–	–
1924	282·80	905	154·06	483	7·81	25
1925	628·12	2,010	16·90	54	–	–
1926	567·50	1,816	327·37	1,048	·62	2

Year	Countries of Shipment.					
	British India (Zanzibar origin)		Sumatra (D.E.I. origin)		Other Countries	
	Cwts.	fras.	cwts.	fras.	cwts.	fras.
1927	26·25	84	123·43	395	–	–
1928	40·31	129	453·75	1,452	–	–
1929	89·06	285	421·25	1,348	–	–
1930	25·93	83	177 50	568	8·43	27
1931	–	–	442·81	1,417	–	–

Exports. – Particulars of the export trade in cloves from Penang, which during the period 1922 – 1931 averaged 1,148 cwts., or 3,673 frasilas, are shown in Table XXI, from which it will be seen that regular shipment is in three main directions: – (1) to the United Kingdom; (2) to China, including Hong Kong and Siam; (3) and to Sumatra.

Table XXI.

STATEMENT SHOWING THE EXPORTS OF CLOVES FROM PEN-
ANG FOR THE TEN YEARS 1922 – 31.

	Countries of Consignment.									
	United Kingdom.		Hong Kong, China Coast, Siam.		Java, Sumatra and Islands Dutch East Indies.		U.S.A.		Other Countries.	
	cwts.	fras.	cwts.	fras.	cwts.	fras.	cwts.	fras.	cwts.	fras.
1922	325·93	1,043	398·43	1,275	348·12	1,114	–	–	5·93	19
1923	572·50	1,832	409·06	1,309	355	1,136	–	–	66·56	213
1924	514·06	1,645	954·37	3,054	184·09	589	–	–	–	–
1925	105·31	337	354·37	1,134	627·10	2,007	–	–	–	–
1926	606·87	1,942	374·37	1,198	250·62	802	–	–	10·00	32
1927	530·93	1,699	264·09	845	126·56	405	–	–	30·00	96
1928	851·25	2,724	184·68	591	97·81	313	–	–	441·87	1,414
1929	585·31	1,873	254·06	813	315·31	1,009	–	–	242·18	775
1930	95·00	304	148·12	474	174·06	557	–	–	2·50	8
1931	351·87	1,126	177·18	567	110·93	355	–	–	1·25	4

Surplus of Exports over Imports. – For the ten-yearly period under review the surplus of exports over imports has averaged 675 cwts. or 2,160 frasilas per annum as follows: –

Average annual exports	1,148 cwts. 3,670 frasilas
Average annual imports	473 cwts. 1,510 frasilas
Net excess of exports	675 cwts. 2,160 frasilas

It has been noted that the import figures do not include a limited quantity of clove produce shipped coastwise from Singapore. On the other hand, the export gures omit a certain quantity of cloves sold in the local market. Ignoring these indeterminable amounts as counter-balancing factors, it may be assumed that the surplus of exports over imports, *i.e.*, 675 cwts. or 2,160 frasilas, represents very roughly the total of Penang production shipped overseas.

69. *Commercial Elements of the Trade.* –[...]While in India and Ceylon the overseas clove trade is exclusively in the hands of Indian merchants, in Penang it is shared by British, Indian and Chinese concerns. The British concerns function in one way only. They ship cloves of Penang production to the London and American markets on a consignment basis, usually on behalf of Chinese dealers. Chinese dealers are themselves exporters of Penang cloves to Hong Kong, Siam and other ports on / the China coast with which they have established trade connections. This branch of the export trade is, however, supplemented by an export of Sumatra cloves which may either be shipped as such or, more probably, as Penang cloves. While we were able to establish that Penang and Sumatra produce are bulked by these dealers, it was not possible to determine to what extent or whether the bulked article was sold exclusively to the China market. The price premium enjoyed by Penang cloves no doubt adds to the profit accruing to the trade insofar as mixing is resorted to, while the proximity of Padang and Boenkolen, the clove centres in Sumatra, and their commercial interests with Penang, through Chinese channels, explains the movement of cloves from Sumatra to Penang.

The Indian merchants interested in the trade have, as a rule, Bombay connections and deal almost exclusively in Zanzibar cloves drawn either from Bombay or Singapore. They handle Zanzibar standard quality cloves, adulterated cloves and exhausted material. In addition to supplying part of the local market they export to Sumatra, the chief importing centre there being Acheen. The Acheen importers are Indian dealers and this branch of the clove business, which has no doubt grown from the old-established trading connections between Acheen, Penang and Rangoon and the presence of Indian labour in Sumatra, accounts for the reverse movement of cloves between the two centres.

70. *Direction of Trade.* – The main features of the overseas trade of Penang during the ten years under review, as they emerge from the foregoing examinations, are: –
   (i) Exports of local production have averaged about 2,160 frasilas of which nearly 70 per cent. has been taken by the London market.
   (ii) An export trade to Siam, the China coast including Hong Kong, comprised partly of locally produced cloves, but for the most part of re-exported Sumatra cloves, the total of which has averaged 1,120 frasilas per annum.
   (iii) An import trade in Zanzibar cloves averaging about 670 frasilas per annum which in an adulterated form are sold to the local market or re-exported to Sumatra.

Quality and Price. – The factor of quality and accordingly of price in relation to the trade as it divides itself into these main channels is significant. At the time of our enquiry the prices quoted for the Penang, Sumatra and Zanzibar commodities were as follows: –

Per frasila of 35 lbs.

Penang (1st quality)	*Sumatra* (average quality)	*Zanzibar* (*via* Bombay)
Rs. 20·40	Rs. 13·94	Rs. 8·17

e premium enjoyed by Penang cloves, although dependent upon the great excellence of their quality, especially on an appearance test, would seem to arise partly from the fact that they serve a small specialised market. We are unable to believe that, in the larger markets upon which the Zanzibar industry depends, anything like so substantial a premium would be obtained. Sumatra cloves, less attractive in colour and uniformity than those of Penang production, are nevertheless of excellent quality. Both Penang and Sumatra cloves find a market in Hong Kong, Siam and other Chinese markets, which are prepared to pay for high grade cloves. The Zanzibar commodity in the adulterated form in which it is largely marketed relies upon its apparent cheapness and the existence of a class of dealers and retailers who exploit a very limited field of consumption, which a narrowing of the price premium enjoyed by the Penang and Sumatra commodities would certainly tend to reduce. Indeed, as the import figures suggest, there is reason to suspect that the market for Zanzibar cloves is already losing ground.

[...]

Other Aspects of the Trade. – Trade practice as it affects the local clove industry will be referred to at a later stage of this report, but it may be noted here that both clove stems and mother of cloves are exported to Hong Kong and that prices obtained for these commodities appear to be higher than those secured by Zanzibar exporters. In the case of stems the question of cleanness may account for the price difference.

Although Madagascar cloves are not at present imported, Marseilles quotations are received by the Indian dealers and there is no reason to suppose that the Madagascar product would be unacceptable to the class of trade which supports the Zanzibar industry. /

It may be added that the fact that Penang is a free port has contributed to its ability to share with Singapore the re-distribution trade in clove produce which is centred in Malaya.

(iii) SINGAPORE.

73. *Imports.* – Particulars of the imports of cloves into Singapore during the ten years 1922 – 1931 are shown in Table XXII. Average imports during this period have amounted to 19,000 cwts. or 61,000 frasilas per annum and practically the whole of these imports have consisted of Zanzibar cloves and cloves produced in the Dutch East Indies. The Zanzibar cloves, which represent about 95 per cent. of the imports over the period, were drawn partly from Bombay and partly from Zanzibar direct. The Dutch East Indies supplies emanated from the various centres of production in the East Indies archipelago.

TABLE XXII.
STATEMENT SHOWING THE IMPORTS OF CLOVES INTO SINGAPORE FOR THE TEN YEARS 1922 – 31.

Countries imported from.

Year	*British India.		†Other British Possessions.		§Hong Kong.		‡Dutch Eats Indies.		§Other Countries.	
	cwts.	fras.	cwts.	fras.	cwts.	fras.	cwts.	fras.	cwts.	fras.
1922	12,589·06	40,285	130·93	419	–	–	496·24	4,158	1·25	4
1923	14,536·87	46,518	2·50	8	241·56	773	2,362·49	7,560	52·18	167
1924	17,983·75	57,548	59·68	191	40·00	128	520·93	1,667	400·00	1,280
1925	29,703·75	95,952	–	–	101·87	326	216·87	694	–	–
1926	13,176·56	42,165	9,935·00	31,792	–	–	1,397·80	4,473	2·50	8
1927	4,279·68	13,695	29,058·75	92,988	–	–	543·73	1,740	9·67	31
1928	48·75	156	15,750·62	50,402	11·87	38	405·26	1,297	–	–
1929	728·43	2,331	12,949·75	41,436	–	–	624·36	1,998	–	–
1930	–	–	17,791·56	47,333	–	–	495·30	1,585	–	–
1931	1·25	5	4,625·31	14,801	–	–	684·68	2,191	–	–

   *   Zanzibar origin.
   †   From Zanzibar.
   ‡   From Sumatra, Celebes and Moluccas and other Dutch East Indies Islands.
   §   Origin doubtful

74. *Exports.* – It will be seen from the particulars shown in Table XXIII that the clove exports from Singapore have averaged about 17,900 cwts. or 57,300 frasilas per annum. The bulk of this trade has been directed to two main channels – Java and the China coast, the former having taken 87 per cent. of the total export over the period reviewed. Apart from these markets, small quantities have been shipped to Sumatra and other of the Dutch East Indies Islands, or re-distributed in what appears to be a somewhat fortuitous manner, over a wide area including the United Kingdom and the United States of America.

TABLE XXIII.
STATEMENT SHOWING THE EXPORTS OF CLOVES FROM SINGAPORE FOR THE TEN YEAR 1922 – 31.

			Countries of Consignment. Sumatra and other Dutch East Indies Islands.		Hong Kong China Coast, Siam.		Other Countries.	
	Java.							
Year	cwts.	fras.	cwts.	fras.	cwts.	fras.	cwts.	fras.
1922	12,303·12	39,370	144·37	643	863·43	2,763	361·25	1,156
1923	11,300·00	36,160	145·00	454	1,540·00	4,928	1,214·37	3,886
1924	16,098·12	51,514	174·37	558	472·50	1,512	131·87	422
1925	26,571·25	85,028	229·06	733	1,083·75	3,468	331·56	1,061
1926	20,319·06	65,021	145·00	464	2,555·31	8,177	620·31	1,985
1927	28,785·93	92,117	230·93	739	1,827·18	5,847	1,024·37	3,278
1928	14,878·43	47,611	152·18	487	555·00	1,776	1,107·18	3,543
1929	11,835·62	37,874	169·06	541	1,308·75	4,188	495·00	1,584
1930	12,342·18	39,496	115·62	370	806·56	2,581	562·81	1,801
1931	1,942·81	6,217	122·50	392	3,377·18	10,807	887·18	2,839 /

Surplus of Imports over Exports. – During the ten years 1922 – 1931 the excess of imports over exports has represented an average quantity of 1,000 cwts. or 3,200 frasilas per annum as follows: –

Average annual imports	18,900 cwts. 60,500 frasilas
Average annual exports	17,900 cwts. 57,300 frasilas
Excess of imports over exports	1,000 cwts. 3,200 frasilas

Part of this surplus was probably accounted for by carry-over stocks held in the port at the end of the period under review, and in part by the supplies shipped coastwise to Penang. The balance, the extent of which is not open to assessment, went into local consumption.

Present Position of Trade. – The tables above referred to indicate that Singapore's entrepot trade in cloves was on the increase until the year 1927, since when it has steadily declined. The rise and fall of the trade is associated with a change of direction in the movement of Zanzibar cloves attracted to the Java market. At the beginning of the decennial period reviewed practically the whole of the imports of Zanzibar cloves were obtained from Bombay, which at that time was able to monopolise the trade by reason of its shipping connections and commercial relationships with the port. The position altered in the year 1926, when Zanzibar was brought into direct steamship communication with Singapore. Thereafter the Bombay market was gradually eliminated from the trade. A further development was brought about a year or two later by the establishment of a direct steamer service from Zanzibar to Java. This trade is now, accordingly, conducted

there is a shortage of direct imports in the Java market. Anything in the nature of speculative transactions are discouraged by the fact that the freight rates by Dutch ships between Singapore and Java have been maintained on a gold parity.

Apart from the reduction effected in transport and handling charges and the elimination, first of one, and then of a second intermediary's profit which may be assumed to have benefited the Zanzibar seller as well as the Java buyer – the new routing of these supplies is of some significance in relation to the present position of the Java market.

The diversion of the Zanzibar – Java trade has resulted in the disappearance of the European element from the Singapore clove trade, which is now shared by Indian and Chinese merchants operating in much the same way as their confreres in Penang.

The imports of Dutch East Indies cloves, which are shipped from almost all the centres of Indies production, are largely re-directed to Hong Kong and the China coast ports, the trade being from Chinese to Chinese dealer. The Indian trader who handles Zanzibar cloves, usually in conjunction with exhausted material, supplies his own nationals in the local market, in Sumatra and in Hong Kong.

The total imports of Zanzibar cloves during the ten years 1922 – 1931 averaged about 18,030 cwts. or 57,700 frasilas per annum and the average exports of cloves from Singapore to Java 15,630 cwts. or 50,000 frasilas. The difference between these two figures, *i.e.,* about 8,000 frasilas a year, affords some guidance as to the quantity of Zanzibar cloves which have been absorbed by the Singapore market for disposal elsewhere during the period referred to, but as heavy stocks appear to have been held at the end of 1931 that figure may be in excess of the actual. For the reasons which apply in the case of the Penang trade the prospect of Zanzibar being able to maintain or increase its share of the clove trade handled by Singapore is not hopeful under existing conditions.

77. *Potential Trade of Port.* – Singapore, despite the advantage it enjoys in the way of communications, free port facilities and cheap handling, cannot be regarded as an essential link in the distribution of clove produce except within a very limited area. A possible development with regard to the movement of Dutch East Indies cloves to China and subsidiary markets is that it will be gradually diverted to direct shipments from the Indies ports. [...]

77A. *Complaints Regarding Zanzibar Suppliers.* – It may be observed that in the course of our investigations we received a complaint regarding the practice, commented upon elsewhere, under which Zanzibar shippers have been known to over-value consignments and subsequently refuse to liquidate their indebtedness in respect of the amounts overdrawn.

[...] (vii) CLOVE PRODUCTION IN PENANG AND PROVINCE WELLESLEY.

Extent. – The export returns of Penang trade do not distinguish between cloves being the produce of the country and those representing the re-exportation of foreign produce. Such records as do exist regarding the areas planted under cloves are of limited value. The absence of adequate statistical data, the complications affecting the export trade, and the indeterminable extent of local consumption makes it impossible to arrive at any reliable approximation of the output of cloves from Penang. Average production for export during the past ten years can, however, hardly have exceeded the 675 cwts. or 2,160 frasilas shown in paragraph 68, as the surplus of exports over imports, but may be taken roughly as being in the neighbourhood of that figure. /

Marketing. – The marketing of Penang cloves is in Chinese hands except in so far European Houses undertake the consignment of shipments to the London market on a commission basis. The producer disposes of his crop in much the same way as the Zanzibar clove grower. The Chinese produce dealer in the district townships buys the crop on the trees or the harvested crop, the transactions being to some extent complicated by credit facilities previously granted by the dealer.

Preparation and Export Packing. – The grower who harvests his own crop does not necessarily defer the sale of his cloves until after the drying process has been completed. He may sell them after only three days drying, the dealer undertaking the further drying and the cleaning and grading necessary to bring the produce into marketable condition.

Penang cloves are larger than the Zanzibar variety and are uniform in colour, which is of a light purple brown. The heads are bold and in the best quality only 5 per cent. headless cloves are allowed. The achievement of this high standard quality is the result of good cultivation and of careful preparation on the part of the producer and middleman, and also necessitates careful handling and packing at the point of export. For the London market the packing consists of a wooden container – usually a Swedish match case lined with water-proofed paper – together with an outer covering of hessian cloth. Freight to London is charged on a measurement basis at the rate of Sh. 101/- net per 50 cubic feet. The all-in charges on overseas shipments, including consignees' commission, is approximately $20 a picul or a little over Rs.8 per frasila. Overseas marketing is accordingly very much more expensive than in Zanzibar, especially as the demand for Penang cloves at the high premiums secured is seasonal. The harvesting season is usually December – January but the final disposal of shipments to London may not be affected until October when buying takes place for the Christmas market.

(viii) ASPECTS OF CULTIVATION.

84. *Historical and General.* – An excellent article on the clove and nutmeg industry in Penang and Province Wellesley, by Mr. F. R. Mason, Agriculture Field
Officer, appeared in the Malayan Agricultural Journal for January, 1931. The
following extracts from Mr. Mason's article may be quoted: –

"[...] In about 1850 there were reported to be upwards of 30 spice plantations in Penang and Province Wellesley.

"In Penang and Province Wellesley the Chinese, chiefly Khehs, restarted
the cultivation of nutmegs and cloves but before it became well established the
introduction of rubber into the country placed the cultivations of spice well in
the background, with the result that one now rarely finds a plantation of nothing
but spices. They have invariably been interplanted with or replaced by rubber.

"Both nutmegs and cloves seem to thrive best in the usual yellow loamy clay
found on the hills of Penang and at Bukit Mertajam in Province Wellesley; the
more friable the soil the better the trees seem to thrive. It is stated by Oxley that
the deeper the tinge of iron in the soil the better the plants seem to grow. He
quotes the hard ferruginous gravel found at Pringgit in Malacca where the two
spices once thrived remarkably well. The slopes of the Penang hills and the Bukit
Mertajam are in places exceedingly steep but are broken up by granite rocks
which prevent soil wash to a considerable extent; the usual practice is, however,
to build up terraces by making small walls of granite boulders, which are readily available, and filling them up with earth, this serves to support the tree and
prevent soil wash.

"In Penang and Province Wellesley cloves and nutmegs are generally cultivated
on hills from 200 to 2,000 feet above sea level and are rarely seen on the plains,
although it is said that cloves will thrive at lower altitudes provided the water table
is well below surface. It is interesting to note that at Bukit Mertajam in Province
Wellesley where every available space was once planted with cloves and nutmegs,
the limit of cultivation was reached at under 1,000 feet, above which the trees
would not grow. It is often said that nutmegs and cloves must be grown within
sight and sound of the sea: this may be an important factor as it is very noticeable
that on Bukit Mertajam hill the spices are only planted on the side facing the sea,
and also that on the Penang hill the best plantations are to be found on the slopes
facing the open sea to the / west. It is also interesting to note that few, if any, successful plantations have been established at any distance from the sea.

"In the case of both nutmegs and cloves, plants are raised from seed in beds
under shade. The seedlings are transplanted when about six inches tall. Nutmegs
are planted about 30 feet apart, while cloves should not be planted less than 20
feet apart. Cloves are very sensitive to water at the roots and any possibility of
water collecting in puddles round the young plants must be avoided.

"Manuring is an important item with both nutmegs and cloves and has always received much attention from keen growers. The usual form of manure in Penang and Province Wellesley is fish refuse, but when obtainable, prawn dust is preferred. This is the refuse from the manufacture of the well known Mayal condiment 'belachan.'[2] Manure is applied once a year, usually in a trench dug round the tree following the spread of the branches. A favourite practice amongst the Chinese on Bukit Mertajam is to dig a trench two or three times a year and fill it in with cut 'Lallang' grass.

"Clove trees begin to bear when six or seven years old. Nutmegs do not bear until the seventh or eighth year and sometimes later.

"Cloves are picked by hand but the trees are often of such a height that a light bamboo ladder has to be used to reach the top-most branches. Cloves are fit for gathering when the flower bud begins to assume a reddish colour but before the bud breaks and the small white petals have expanded. The unopen flower buds are then roughly picked over and dried in the sun. The greatest care is necessary in handling the cloves, particularly as they become dry, since the 'heads' very easily become detached and not more than five per cent. of headless cloves is allowed in a sample of first quality. In a good sample the cloves are large, not too wrinkled and a light purplish brown in colour. Too rapid drying causes them to become shrivelled and brittle. Cloves lose about 70 per cent. of their weight in drying."

85. *Economic Factors*. – We would add the following comments regarding the industry in Penang. Soil conditions and the extensive and well-distributed rainfall, contributing to the rapidity with which the clove tree comes into bearing and the high yield per tree, are certainly factors which make for successful cultivation in this area. On the other hand, the problem of soil conservation and the mortality and injury to the trees due to pests present difficulties of a nature with which the Zanzibar producer is rarely confronted.

As is indicated in the extracts quoted above terracing is resorted to for the prevention of soil wash and the maintenance of this terracing requires constant attention. One grower estimated that the cost involved on this account and in respect of general cultivation amounted to 50 $ cents or about 80 rupee cents per tree per annum.

With regard to damage by pests the species of *Loranthus* familiar in the Zanzibar plantations is very prevalent, while the ravages of a beetle borer (*Chelidonium brevicorne* Schwarzer) and a moth borer (*Paralecta antistola* Meyrick) are extensive. The Chinese cultivators are possessed of the industry and intelligence to cope with these difficulties. The prevalence of insects pests may still be a threat to successful production, but the results of careful tending and picking and particularly of manuring, more than counter-balance the natural difficulties in the way of cultivation.

The few growers whom we interviewed were emphatic in their conviction that manuring was well worth the expenditure entailed. Supplies of prawn dust are freely available at a cost which was estimated at about three rupee cent a lb. The quantity required by a fully grown tree was put at 20 lbs. yearly, younger trees requiring smaller quantities according to the stage of their development.

Slashing and hoeing of the undergrowth is practised, but care is taken not to damage the roots, a circle of carefully cultivated soil surrounding each of the trees.

86. *Revival of Interest in Industry.* – The introduction of rubber into Malaya led to the neglect·of spice cultivation; and the collapse of rubber prices is now responsible for a revival of interest in subsidiary crops including cloves. The Chinese gardeners of Penang, who rely upon mixed cultivation and readily abandon one culture for another, are being encouraged, both through official and mission agencies, to plant clove trees. The movement is of recent origin and does not yet appear to have reached any great dimensions. One authority placed new plantings at about 20 per cent. of the trees in Penang and stated that most of such plantings had taken place during the twelve months.

The persistence of this revival of interest in clove production will probably depend upon the movement of other produce prices, particularly that of rubber, and on the extent to which clove prices maintain their recent level. There is little doubt that an increase of the Penang output would lead to over-production in the specialised market which is now prepared to pay the high premiums / obtained for first quality clove spice. An expansion of Penang production or the emergence competition in the production of high grade cloves from alternative sources of supply might therefore, be expected to place an entirely different complexion upon the economics of the local industry.

The narrowing of the margin between Penang prices and those obtained for cloves from Zanzibar and elsewhere would no doubt tend to restrict the expansion of cultivation in this centre. It would however be unwise not to anticipate a fairly substantial increase in the Penang output as soon as the results of the planting now being undertaken materialise.

ANON., 'A SHORT HISTORY OF THE PORT OF SINGAPORE' IN ANON., *SINGAPORE MANUFACTURERS EXHIBITION* (1932)

Anon., 'A Short History of the Port of Singapore', in Anon., *Singapore Manufacturers Exhibition*, January 1932, National Archives, CO 273/582/3.

e following is a snapshot of the port of Singapore in 1932. The Singapore Manufacturers Exhibition, held in early January 1932, was a response to the early 1930s recession. Its aims were to 'demonstrate the enormous potentialities of [the] city as a manufacturing centre' and to bring 'before the public the extensive range of locally manufactured articles which may be purchased at very considerably lower cost than similar articles imported from Europe or America'.[1]

The Singapore Free Press and Mercantile Advertiser, 2 January 1932, p. 10.

Anon., 'A Short History of the Port of Singapore', in Anon., *Singapore Manufacturers Exhibition* (1932)

THE PORT OF SINGAPORE

STRAITS SETTLEMENTS

THE Island of Singapore is 88 miles North of the Equator and contains an area of 217 square miles, the population numbers some 566,000 persons and is probably the most cosmopolitan one in the world, about three-quarters of the people are however Chinese, and an eighth Malays, indigenous to the Country, while the Europeans total about 8,200.

ere is a continuous stream of passengers of various nationalities who land and spend a day or so in Singapore when passing through on ocean voyages or making coastal connection. The deck passengers are Chinese, Indians (including Tamils and Malabaris), Sinhalese,[1] and Javanese estate labourers, also Malay and Javanese pilgrims en route to Mecca. [...]

e Harbour is practically land-locked by islands and these afford such protection that until the reconstruction of the wharves was put in hand some twenty one years ago, the berthing accommodation consisted only of wooden wharves on wooden piles. The difference between the rise and fall of ordinary spring tides is 9 ft. / [...]

Ships. 9,130 merchant vessels, representing a tonnage of 15,908,667 tons, entered the port of Singapore in the year 1930, and of these vessels 4,645 were British, 2,384 Dutch, 539 Norwegian and 532 Japanese, the remaining 1,030 being French, German, American and other nationalities.

Small craft. A wonderful variety of vessels is to be seen in the Harbour; in addition to the large ocean going passenger and cargo steamers there may be seen at all times some hundred or so local coasting steamers, several of about 800 tons burden but mostly about 100 tons only, the adjacent Dutch Islands with their many inlets and settlements requiring a large service of small vessels for carrying food supplies and collecting produce. There are also a large number of Chinese junks, and native six-oared fishing boats propelled by oars, the crew standing facing the direction in which the boat is proceeding.

Although the majority of ocean going steamers are berthed at the Singapore Harbour Board's wharves many vessels discharge and load in the Inner and Outer Harbour necessitating a continual flow of lighters to and from the warehouses on the banks of Singapore's short and narrow river.

The Inner Harbour is protected from the North East Monsoon by a mole of granite rubble about a mile long.

Singapore is a free port, there being no customs duties, but excise duties are levied on alcoholic liquors, opium, tobacco and petroleum.

Singapore is the principal shipping and transhipment port for the Far Eastern Tropics, it being the distributing port for the Malay Peninsula, a great portion of the Netherlands East Indies and an extensive area of Indo-China.

There is also much trade with India, China, Japan and Western Australia. /

The outstanding features of trade are, however, the shipments of rubber and tin to the United States of America, and the United Kingdom, with small quantities only to the Continent. The rubber comes from the Malay States, Java and Sumatra, and the tin-ore, mined very largely in the Malay States, is smelted at Singapore and reshipped in the form of refined tin. Cotton goods from Lancashire are mostly reshipped to Singapore's neighbouring countries, and a variety of coals is imported for ships' bunkers or consumption in Singapore.

Other large imports are general cargo from Europe, Japan, China and America, from the latter motor vehicles in particular, in Singapore alone there being over 8,000 in service, rice (the main food of the country) from Rangoon and Saigon, gunny bags and opium from Calcutta, wool, flour, sandal and jarrah wood from Australia, tobacco and sugar from Java and Sumatra, matches from China and Japan, bullocks and oxen from Siam, and sheep from India and Australia. Produce transhipped at Singapore includes copra, sugar, spices (chiefly arecanuts and pepper), rattans, gums, coffee, sago flour, etc.

Regular callers at Singapore from the United Kingdom and the Continent are Alfred Holt's "Blue Funnel" Lines, and the P. & O., Glen, Ben and City Lines, Messageries Maritimes, Nippon Yusen Kaisha, Nederland Royal Mail, Rotterdam Lloyd, East Asiatic, Lloyd Triestino and Osaka Shosen Kaisha steamers.

The British India Steam Navigation Company maintain a steady service between Calcutta and Japan. Their passenger steamers, of a high order, also run regularly to Rangoon and Madras, mail train connection with Bombay being made from the latter port. Messrs. Jardine Matheson and many other companies operate to and from Chinese ports.

There is a direct cargo and passenger service monthly to the United States, Pacific Route, by the Dollar Steamship Company's steamers; a cargo service to

ere is a first-class passenger and cargo service to Australia via the East coast by Messrs. Burns Philp Co. and Messrs. Koninklyke Paketvaart Maatschappij. Regular passenger and cargo steamers also run to Fremantle via Western Australia ports.

An excellent coastal service is carried out by the Straits Steamship Company to Federated Malay States ports, also to Borneo and Bangkok, whilst the Java and Sumatra service is maintained by splendid steamers of the Koninklyke Paketvaart Maatschappij.

A brief reference to the early history of the Dock undertakings at Singapore may be of interest. In the year 1859, the first graving dock, No. 1, length 396 ft. 6 in., was completed, and the Victoria Dock, length 484 ft., was completed in the year 1868. The Dock and Wharf business was for over 40 years conducted by two Companies. The Tanjong Pagar Dock Company suffered an anxious period in its early years, and at brief intervals later, but generally both Companies flourished and steadily developed while paying dividends to their shareholders averaging nearly 12 per cent. per annum. These Companies formed a joint purse agreement in the year 1881, and amalgamated in the year 1899, when by absorption of Reserves the joint capital was doubled to $3,700,000 fully paid. The Company's undertaking was, however, by direction of the Colonial Office, expropriated by the Straits Settlements Government in the year 1905 with a view to greatly developing the Docks and Wharves, and for Government control of the Port of Singapore in Imperial interests. The Government offered $240 per share (the market value immediately prior to expropriation being about $230 per share) to the Company which was declined, and eventually had to pay some $760 per share in terms of an award by Sir Michael Hicks-Beach,[3] P.C, M.P., the Umpire (later The Right Hon'ble Michael Edward Viscount St. Aldwyn), as the result of protracted Arbitration proceedings conducted in both London and Singapore and extending over a period of twelve months, and constituting a "cause celebre" in Arbitration proceedings between a Dock Company and Government. The Government action, however, in acquiring in 1905 this hitherto privately owned undertaking and constituting a Harbour Board for the purpose of administering it has been amply justified both financially and otherwise by development on bold lines, and the provision / of additional Docks and improved Wharves in the Port of Singapore, which make Singapore second to no port in the East.

A very interesting account of the History of the Dock Undertakings in Singapore is to be found in the work, "One hundred Years of Singapore," being some account of the Capital City of the Straits Settlements from its foundation by Sir Stamford Raffles on the 6th February, 1819, to the 6th February, 1919, published in two volumes by John Murray, London, 1921.

e pilotage service, the lighting and buoying of the Harbour and the moor-

History of Dock Undertakings

"One hundred years of

THE SINGAPORE HARBOUR BOARD

The Harbour Board controls all the public wharves and dry docks in Singapore, the Estate comprising over 690 acres of land, much of which is available for future development of the docks and wharves and their adjuncts.

The Harbour Board is constituted under an enactment by the Governor of the Straits Settlements entitled Ordinance No. 130 (Ports). The Board consists of a Chairman, Deputy Chairman and 3 to 7 other members, all appointed by the Governor of the Colony.

By-laws and Rates and Charges are made by the Board subject to the approval of the Governor-in-Council.

The Board pays to Government interest at the rate of 4 per cent, per annum on the capital cost of the Undertaking and loans for New Works, and contributes to a sinking fund therefor at the rate of 1 per cent. per annum. /

The Assets and Capital Outlay of the Board at June 30th, 1931, totalled $79,462,390 *i.e.* £9,270,612 sterling (exchange being fixed by Government at 2*s*. 4*d*. per Straits Settlements dollar).

The Officers and Staff comprise about 100 Europeans, and roughly 1,900 Eurasians, Chinese, Indians, and Malays. In addition to which there are, however, over 4,000 Wharf Coolies, Chinese and Indians, and, in the Dockyard Department, over 3,000 men – skilled Chinese artizans of trades with their assistants and labourers – in all about 9,000 persons are employed directly or indirectly by the Board on its premises in busy times.

The Board has its own Police Force, and Fire Brigade fully equipped with modern motor fire floats, motor fire engines, smoke appliances, etc. The Board lights its premises throughout and controls all traffic thereon, does all road making and repairing. It also undertakes the entire sanitation and scavenging of the premises and maintains a medical staff and motor ambulance.

The following is a concise description of the Board's Wharf and Dock accommodation: –

WHARF DEPARTMENT – QUAYAGE.

POSITION.	Depth of Water at L.W.O.S.T. less than 25 feet.	Depth of Water at L.W.O.S.T. 25 feet to 30 feet.	Depth of Water at L.W.O.S.T. 30 feet.	Depth of Water at L.W.O.S.T. 33 feet. and over.
Jardines Wharf	318 ft.			
West Wharf				1,260 ft.
Main Wharf				3,152 ft.
Sheer's Wharf		330 ft.		
East Wharf	955 ft.	290 ft.		
Empire Dock (Area 24½			3,522 ft.	

Total 11,077 lineal feet of wharves. /

    e Board's standard type of transit shed (locally termed "godown") on the Main Wharf for general cargo is 200-ft. long by 100-ft. wide, of steel and corrugated iron construction, with concrete floors and ample ventilation and with projecting eaves for protection against rain in discharging or loading cargo at the wharves.

    Cold storage is provided on the Board's premises by an independent limited liability Company to whom the Board has leased land, and this Company imports regularly large quantities of meat, provisions and fruit from Australia.

    e Board has leased an area of land on the East Reclamation to the Asiatic Petroleum Co., (S.S.) Ltd., who have erected thereon tanks for the storage of fuel and diesel oil.

    e tanks are connected to the Main Wharf (sections 4, 5 and 6), the north and west walls of Empire Dock (section 7), and the West Wharf (sections 8 and 9), by means of 8" and 10" diameter pipe lines, through which vessels at these sections of the Board's premises are supplied with fuel and diesel oil.

    e following figures give an indication of the volume of the Board's operations: –

Transit sheds

Cold storage.

Fuel Oil.

	Vessels Berthed.	Nett Registered Tonnage.	INWARD. Fuel Oil. Tons.	INWARD. Coal. Tons.	INWARD. General Cargo. Tons.	OUTWARD. Fuel Oil. Tons.	OUTWARD. Coal. Tons.	OUTWARD. General Cargo. Tons.	GROSS REVENUE. Wharves. $	GROSS REVENUE. Docks. $
1914	2,685	5,795,091	–	679,198	888,598	–	650,552	566,748	3,611,105	2,056,680
1923	2,297	5,630,825	122,581	253,994	732,773	1,117	325,180	483,112	4,257,627	3,342,110
1931	3,447	10,080,436	96,437	204,126	1,031,160	105,716	215,006	849,730	4,606,902	2,780,597

All labour at the Board's Wharves and Dry Docks is supplied by the Board, and coal and general cargo are usually handled with the aid of vessels' own gear. There are 3 Quick Working Portal Electric Cranes on the Main and West Wharves, also one 15 ton Electric Crane and a stationary sheer legs capable of handling s up to 60 tons. /

Labour.

    Coal is stored under covered sheds or in the open and is owned by some dozen Steamship Owners or Merchants. It is chiefly South African, Japanese, Australian, Indian and Welsh, but there is a variety of supplies from local sources such as Borneo, Sumatra, Labuan and Sarawak.

Coal.

Coal is the only bulk cargo handled at the Board's premises, and the general cargo is of such a varied assortment that the 45 to 50 feet of quay space between the coping stone and the side of the transit shed is essential for expeditious handling and sorting.

    e special feature at the Singapore Wharves is that bunkering operations

Bunkering.

the same time as cargo is being handled, thus accelerating the despatch of steamers from the wharves and avoidance of pilotage and other costs for removal to a special bunkering wharf.

The method of handling the coal between ship and stack is for each pair of coolies to carry, by means of a bamboo pole resting on their shoulders, a basket of coal containing 160 lbs. (14 baskets to a ton). The Board pays and charges fixed rates for handling coal but the Labour Contractor pays so much per basket as it passes the scale on the wharf, the rates varying according to the volume of work on hand, the distance of the carry and the heights of the stack and ship.

The average rate of removal of coal is about 100 tons an hour, the Board's record for bunkering is 1,510 tons (21,000 baskets) placed in the bunkers of a man-of-war in five hours.

A trade peculiar to the East is the conveyance of Deck Passengers on ocean voyages and large numbers are conveyed in this manner between Singapore and both China and India, also to neighbouring ports, the larger ships carrying two to three thousand each. Further, Pilgrims to Mecca travel as Deck Passengers, and about 12,000 of them embark or disembark at the Board's Wharves annually. When embarking they take with them provisions sufficient for their requirements during the whole journey.

Licences are issued to some 600 Hawkers, Porters and Money Changers to ply their trades on the Board's Wharves. /

RATES AND CHARGES – WHARF DEPARTMENT.

There are no Port, Harbour, Dock, Town or Light dues, nor are any berths for vessels or storage places specially appropriated.

The Board charges for the use of the wharves at a rate per ton on the quantity of coal and general cargo discharged or loaded, superseded however in a few instances by a minimum charge against the vessel at a rate per day on the gross tonnage of the vessel when the combined wharfage charges on coal and general cargo do not equal the minimum charge.

The ordinary charges against steamers mainly for wharfage and stevedorage[4] on general cargo amount to about $0.95 (*2s. 2½d.*) per ton, but on coal, labour discharging only is payable by the ship, the owner of the coal paying the inward and outward wharfage and all labour on the wharf.

Free storage is allowed for goods removed from the Transit Sheds within 72 hours from the day on which the vessel completes discharge, and there are further substantial concessions for transhipment cargo.

DRY DOCKS.

–	Extreme Length. – Length on Bottom.		Breadth at Entrance.		Height of Sill above Bottom of Dock.		Depth on Sill at High Water, Ordinary Spring Tides.	
	ft.	in.	ft.	in.	ft.	in.	ft.	in.
No. 1 Dock	396	6	47	4	4	0	14	0
	380	6	45	0				
No. 2 Dock	463	0	64	0	2	0	17	0
	440	0	52	0				
Victoria Dock	484	9	64	9	2	9	20	0
	460	0	56	5				
Albert Dock	496	7	59	6	3	0	21	0
	471	0	55	9				
The King's Dock	879	0	100	0	4	6	34	0
	873	0	93	0				/

All the dry docks are closed by caissons,[5] and the King's Dock is divided by an intermediate caisson into two docks of 486 and 325 feet each, and the equipment includes a 30 ton electric travelling crane.

e Board's workshops, all of which have overhead electric cranes, are extensively equipped with up-to-date appliances, electrically driven, and are capable ecting repairs to vessels of the largest class, and their machinery, either steam or motor driven. Machines, capable of grinding either externally or internally the largest parts of motor machinery, are installed. Castings and forgings of the largest size can be made on the Board's premises. Welding, either by the oxygen-acetylene flame or by electric arc, is carried out under the supervision of ed European Welders.

e Board possesses a modern Electric Power Station with a total of 5,000 K. W. installed. The Electrical Workshops are equipped with modern electric welding and cutting plant, and all classes of electrical repairs, from small instrument work to the largest of motors or generators, are carried out.

Quarters for the Chinese artisans and native labourers are provided on the premises.

SALVAGE EQUIPMENT.

e Board's salvage equipment consists of two powerful oil burning salvage steamers, "Varuna" and "Tunda." The former is fitted with a 600 ton per hour salvage and fire pump, the latter with a 300 ton per hour pump. Both vessels tted with "Filtrators" which enables them to supply steam for an indefinite time without the necessity of refilling their water tanks; and electric searchlights. A large number of petrol, and steam driven portable pumps ranging from 4½" to

The Drydock and Repairing Department has successfully carried out many large and interesting salvage operations and damage repairs, chief among these being the Motor Vessel "Glenartney" of 13,000 tons D.W., dimensions 435-ft. by 55-ft. Fire broke out in this / vessel while she was lying alongside the Board's wharf and rapidly spread over the ship, ultimately necessitating her being submerged. She suffered serious structural damage including indentation of the ship's bottom to a depth of 8 to 10 feet, buckling of the side shell plating and frames up to the shelter deck sheer strake, and the breaking of the shafting. The vessel was lifted and put into dry dock and it was then found the heel of the stern frame was 23 inches below the base or keel line, and 14 inches to starboard, and the after body twisted. She was cut in two, all shell plates and frames renewed, and the after body brought into a true longitudinal line and the list taken out by jacking and wedge-driving until plumb with the fore body, and finally the after body was lifted and brought into true level with the keel. The vessel was made perfectly true with the lines of the hull and the two propeller bosses brought in true line with the engines. The vessel, however, suffered enormous damage through the fire alone, all cabins and passenger accommodation being burnt out, all deck fittings burnt and ironwork twisted, and the deck plating badly buckled, making it necessary to entirely strip the ship to the main deck.

In another instance, the s.s. "Unkai Maru" stranded some 30 miles from Singapore and ripped her bottom very badly necessitating under water patches being fitted before the water inside could be overcome. When the vessel lifted the pumps were kept going full force thus coping sufficiently with the water until the vessel was drydocked.

The Japanese Cruiser "Kasuga" which stranded and partially submerged in the Sunda Straits, was another difficult operation.

Another very awkward salvage job successfully carried out by the Board's Dockyard Department was that of a full-sized bucket ladder Dredger which capsized and sank in an exposed situation off the coast of Pahang, Federated Malay States, some 200 miles from Singapore. She was lifted by first hauling her up on to her keel, then cofferdamming and pumping out.

The Messageries Maritimes French Mail Steamer, "Andre Lebon," 14,368 gross tons, was also salved by the Board, the vessel having grounded and turned over on her side when at anchor off the Sultan Shoal, Singapore. /

ANON., *MEMORANDUM ON THE PROPOSED SINGAPORE HARBOUR IMPROVEMENT SCHEME DRAWN UP BY A MEMBER OF THE COMMITTEE OF THE SINGAPORE CHAMBER OF COMMERCE* (1904)

Anon., *Memorandum on the Proposed Singapore Harbour Improvement Scheme Drawn up by a Member of the Committee of the Singapore Chamber of Commerce* (Singapore: Kelly & Walsh, 1904), pp. 1–8.

In order to enable the harbour to deal with the increased trade of the port, the Tanjong Pagar Dock Co. in 1904 advocated the construction of two new docks and the reconstruction of wharves at a cost of $12,078,153. Approached for a loan, the Colonial Office referred the scheme to their Consulting Engineers, Messrs Coode Son & Matthews, whose report was highly positive. Others believed the changes to be unnecessary and overly expensive and their various arguments are summarized in the following text, which also provides interesting information on the operation of the port. In the event, as discussed in the thematic introduction, the government the following year took over the Tanjong Pagar Dock Co. and work only began on the improvements in 1908. The 879-feet wet dock (King's Dock) and the wharves were built/reconstructed by Messrs John Aird & Co. and the graving dock (Empire Dock) by Messrs Topham, Jones & Railton. Papers relating to the project can be found in the Coode archive at the Institute of Civil Engineers, London (CO/SI 001-14).[1]

1. W. Makepeace, G. E. Brooke and R. Braddell, *One Hundred Years of Singapore*, *Volume* (Singapore: Oxford University Press, 1991), pp. 11–13.

Anon., *Memorandum on the Proposed Singapore Harbour Improvement Scheme Drawn up by a Member of the Committee of the Singapore Chamber of Commerce* (1904), extract

e object of this Memorandum is: –

1. To give expression to the strong conviction which exists among a large number of business men of long local experience that the adoption of the above scheme will saddle the Colony with a heavy and totally unnecessary financial burden for many years to come.

2. To explain the grounds for the above opinion;

3. To express the hope that it may not yet be too late to modify the scheme so as to meet the real needs of the port, which are of a much less extensive nature; and that when tenders for the construction of the works now contemplated come to hand the opportunity will be taken for further seriously considering whether under any circumstances the very large expenditure involved can be regarded as justifiable or in any sense necessary; and whether even if the benefits which it is suggested will result are realized (which is doubtful) that they will be commensurate with the enormous outlay contemplated.

e scheme owes its origin to a feeling which has for some years existed in favour of the construction of a boat-harbour to relieve the congested state of the Singapore River, coupled with the fact that the berthage accommodation furnished by the Tanjong Pagar Dock Co., Ltd., was insufficient to cope with an abnormal ux of transports about four years ago, and further to the inconvenience occasionally experienced to some slight degree by local steamers working cargo from native boats, through the effects on the water in the roads of the N. E. Monsoon and occasional Sumatra Squalls. [margin note: Origin of Scheme.]

e Government asked Messrs. COODE, SON & MATTHEWS[1] to draw up a scheme which would provide for all this and, as a result, we had laid before us the original / Harbour scheme, principally consisting of a system of moles, intended to protect an "Inner Harbour" for the local shipping, with a "Reclamation" provided with wharves, quays and godowns, also intended to accommodate *local* steamers only.

The provision of shelter to such a large extent, was based upon certain evidence obtained by Mr. MATTHEWS. This evidence varied, however, a good deal, some expressing an opinion that shelter was necessary, others that it would be desirable or advantageous if it could be provided at reasonable cost and include the home shipping.

From the whole, however, Mr. MATTHEWS, who did not witness the effects of the N. E. Monsoon himself, must have concluded that same were really of such a serious nature as to require the protection of a scheme of such magnitude as he has proposed.

However, had the construction of this scheme been considerably less costly, than we are now led to expect by Mr. MATTHEWS it will be, it may be safely assumed that very little or no objection would have been raised against it by the public of Singapore.

The principal objections to the first scheme were fully expressed at a general meeting of the Chamber of Commerce by those members of the Community who had several years' close personal experience of the working of steamers in the roads, and one would have expected that their opinions, as to the actual necessity of the scheme, would have deserved at least some consideration before its construction was decided upon.

Our late Governor, however, had set his mind on the scheme and, disregarding the opinion of those who, through their business experience, are capable of forming an opinion in the matter, insisted upon it being carried through, supported by certain members of the Legislative Council, of whom it can hardly be said that they have personal experience of the actual working of steamers in the roads, and on whom the rough weather that they may have noticed at times from the Club or office-verandahs, or on an occasional trip to a departing or arriving steamer, must have made a far greater impression than it really deserved.

The late Chairman of the Chamber of Commerce, who supported the scheme, without proving the necessity thereof, gave it as his opinion that if the Government were good enough to give us such a fine harbour enclosure, the public should only be too pleased to accept it, leaving a very strong doubt as to whether he was personally convinced that the scheme was actually required.

As regards the support from the Legislative Council it is to be feared that same has been given from the same point of view and for the same reasons, as it cannot possibly be *personal experience*, with the majority of the members, that has convinced them of the necessity of the construction of the scheme.

In the meantime, experiments were made and borings taken, and we have now an Improved Harbour Scheme laid before us, which principally differs from

e objections against the present scheme are, however, practically the same as those which were raised against the first scheme, not particularly on technical grounds or the nature of its construction; but for reasons: –

1. That shelter to such an extent as is provided for by the scheme, is not actually required.
2. That there are other means of getting over the difficulties complained of, and
3. That the execution of the scheme, therefore, would incur an unwarranted expenditure of public funds, which could be far better utilized for other more pressing public purposes.

Before going into the particulars of the scheme, it should be borne in mind that Singapore, lying in the Singapore Strait, is by no means directly exposed to the full force of the N. E. Monsoon blowing down the China Sea, as would be the case if Singapore were situated at Horsburgh Light. In this respect it can in no way be compared with such places as Colombo and Madras, which are directly exposed to the S. W. and N. E. Monsoons respectively in the Indian Ocean and the Bay of Bengal, or other neighbouring ports like Samarang and Macassar, where at times all communication with the shore has to be abandoned, with the result that at Samarang cargo and passengers have to be overcarried to other ports of call. The harbour, it is true, may be rough at times with a fairly strong swell, but there is never what could be termed *a heavy sea* with *rollers* such as Mr. MATTHEWS seems to have been led to believe. Hardly ever, in fact, has an ordinary small sampan not been able to go off to any vessel in the roads.

As a most important item of evidence, the report mentions in para. 39, that Sir FRANK SWETTENHAM had personally noted that the water in the harbour was very rough, especially in the neighbourhood of Johnston's Pier, and that the monsoon beat with special violence on the wall along Collyer Quay and that a heavy swell prevailed all over the harbour for some weeks.

is may be quite true, but not to such an extent as to seriously inconvenience the shipping, which is anchored sufficiently far off the shore not to feel the effects. Besides, there is not much force required to cause water to splash high up against a straight wall, such as may be sometimes witnessed along the above named Quay. That is merely the effect of a slight swell in the harbour, not of a rough sea, and ships may be seen lying perfectly steady, working from boats alongside, and sampans plying freely in the Harbour, even when the sea is apparently beating violently on the Quay walls. A bucket of water thrown with some force against a straight wall would have the same effect.

However, although it cannot be denied that choppy water prevails in the harbour at times, it is a fact that such is hardly ever the case during a whole day, and then only on *very few days* during the year. It occurs as a rule either during

In this connection it should be pointed out that for the Local Shipping this port is not *a port of call*, where the feasibility of loading and discharging vessels would depend upon the state of the weather prevailing during the particular time of their stay in port. To almost all local steamers, Singapore is a *terminus*, where they stay as a rule 3 or 4 days, or even longer, and there has never yet been such rough weather in succession during such a long period, as not to allow these steamers ample time to handle their cargoes during the intervals when the weather was calm. The difficulty is, however, that, whenever it becomes slightly rough, the ordinary Chinese cargo boats run into the river for shelter, because they have no proper boat-harbour for temporary protection which would enable them to sail in and out conveniently. In the river they get locked up, frequently until the following day, and they are therefore unable to avail of the opportunities to work again, when the weather and sea have calmed down, which often occur immediately after a squall. It may often be noticed that steamers lie idle during a perfectly calm afternoon, simply because the cargo boats have cleared away to the river during the forenoon when the sea was a bit rough.

If a protected boat-harbour were provided, where such cargo boats could find temporary shelter, enabling them to sail in and out at any time when required, this difficulty would no longer exist. Such a boat-harbour was recommended at the time and is really all that the port actually requires as regards shelter. The local steamers themselves suffer no inconvenience worth speaking of from the swell or choppy sea, such as we get here at times and they really do not require the special protection which this costly scheme would furnish.

The scheme, in fact, can only be regarded as an absolutely "unnecessary luxury," promoted at the risk of crippling the Colony's finances and spoiling the future trade of the port. This trade has increased to its present magnitude principally owing to the *cheapness* of the port, and every effort should be directed to maintaining this feature, not only to promote development, but even to keep the trade at its present level, in view of possible outside competition. But even if the work could be constructed at small cost, the scheme, as it now stands, would neither prove a marked advantage to the port itself or to its trade and shipping, nor would it be an actual requirement. The position of the proposed moles must necessarily interfere with the present free ingress and egress during all hours of the day or night, at all times of the year, to and from a fine natural open and yet sufficiently sheltered roadstead.

The cost of construction may furthermore be safely expected to be far more than has been calculated upon in this place, with its ever growing expensive labour and material, so specially marked with regard to everything connected with building undertakings.

In para. 36 of his latest report Mr. MATTHEWS himself states that "the bottom generally is undoubtedly unfavourable for the economical construction of works of such a character as those contemplated," and it may be safely presumed that many surprises will be in store for us should the scheme be proceeded with.

As to the cost of upkeep, we have some vague promises of the high officials recently and now in charge of the Government, that the shipping will not be charged for same, but they necessarily cannot commit their successors, nor can / there be any guarantee that their successors may not be *obliged* to levy a charge, when they find that the necessary amount of revenue cannot be otherwise procured. If any part of the trade can possibly be held liable for the upkeep of harbour works it must necessarily be the Shipping, but to tax this, it is generally admitted, would be suicidal to the prospects of the port. There is no doubt that, should this charge be adopted, the principal portion would have to be borne by ocean steamers which are outside any benefits furnished by the scheme, and which are, in fact, likely to be under the disadvantage of having to anchor considerably further out from the shore to work their cargoes from lighters than they at present have to do. *(margin: Cost of Upkeep)*

As regards the scheme itself, there should be no necessity for the South and East outer moles. *(margin: Outer Moles)*

Mr. MATTHEWS himself explains in para. 56 of his Report that these outer moles could not even prevent the inner harbour from being disturbed by the ect of waves generated by strong East and North-east winds and that the construction of another expensive inner mole is required as well!

If the only protection these two outer moles can afford is that they keep out an occasional swell in the harbour, caused by the N. E. Monsoon, and which swell after all is not of frequent occurrence and hardly ever so bad as to seriously interfere with the working of steamers, then it certainly seems unjustifiable to spend such a large amount on their construction.

A good deal has been made of the fact that there occurs a certain amount of damage to goods conveyed to and from steamers in the roads, and it is only natural that insurance agents should advocate shelter so as to minimize their risks. *(margin: Damage to Cargo.)*

is damage should not, however, be altogether attributed to rough sea in the harbour. The Chinese twakows, commonly in use here, are frequently overloaded and, being as a rule uncovered and low down in the water, they offer no protection whatever against sea spray and showers of rain. *Any improvement in this respect is to be recommended.* With larger and properly covered tongkangs damage is almost unknown, and with a good boat-harbour affording shelter to the smaller craft, in case of squalls, occasional swells and choppy sea, there should be no cause for damage under normal conditions, except such as might arise through neglect and indifference on the part of the boatmen.

Referring to the intended wharf scheme at Telok Ayer for *local boats* only, *(margin: Telok Ayer Wharves.)*

so long as there is a river which leads to the centre of the town, and it may be safely said that such wharves would be availed of only to a very small extent.

The bulk of the cargo dealt with by the local shipping is of a *general* nature, the incoming cargo mostly consisting of produce which requires manipulating. The steamers engaged in these trades would have to choose between working their cargoes by boats or making use of the wharves. It would be impracticable for them to do both, by picking out those goods which are intended for, or come from the River sites and Kampong Glam, etc., and which are handled by boats, and leaving the balance for Telok Ayer to be dealt with at the wharves. Even allowing for the future expansion of the trade of this port, it is not likely / that the trade of the above-named old established centres will divert to the costly Telok Ayer Reclamation. That may be the case with a *portion* of the trade only, and the *bulk* of the goods will therefore continue to be carried to and from those parts as heretofore in *boats*. In view of this it is only reasonable to expect that the local steamers, in their own interest, will continue to work in the roads, rather than avail of the proposed wharves, thereby forcing all their constituents to deliver or receive their goods at a place which will be convenient only to a small portion of the trade, and which will incur higher expenses for handling over wharf and by cart, than it now costs.

The only exception may be with rice cargoes from Bangkok or Saigon, which require no particular manipulation, but can be stored without inconvenience to anybody. A great portion of such rice would, however, all the same be taken away by boats up the river, and the wharves would therefore practically be used only for part-cargoes and such lots as consignees occasionally do not take prompt delivery of. This could hardly be called *regular support*.

But even if there were reason to believe that the rice trade, or even part of it, and a sufficiently large share of the general local trade could be drawn to the proposed quay and wharf, so as to justify the construction thereof and the building of a costly mole scheme for its protection, it must be remembered that the proposed draft of 16 feet at low water, as provided for in para. 68 of the Report, would be altogether inadequate for the majority of the steamers engaged in these trades, and it is really a matter for surprise that Mr. MATTHEWS himself and the Government, and all those Authorities who have so readily given their support to the scheme, have not taken this most important fact into account, when recommending the building of such a costly scheme.

The majority of the steamers engaged in the Bangkok rice trade arrive here drawing from 16 feet 6 inches to 19 feet 6 inches. The Chinese Singapore-Java steamers, the Straits-China steamers and most of the Dutch local steamers load to the same draft, several to as much as 22 feet. All these vessels work their cargoes in the roads, very little being done at the wharf.

e principal carriers engaged in our local trades would therefore be excluded from the benefits which the proposed quay and wharf are supposed to furnish.

To provide the requisite depth to accommodate these as well would of course enormously increase the original cost and the subsequent expense of upkeep, while, for reasons explained elsewhere in this memorandum, the "extensive business" which Mr. MATTHEWS, in para. 83 of his Report, thinks "will certainly be drawn to the quay and wharf" is, and is likely to continue, visionary.

At any rate as the scheme stands at present, a quay and wharf are provided which will only accommodate the "mosquito" fleet and of these, as already explained, it is very doubtful whether any would ever use it except as an occasional convenience, and it may therefore be safely said that anything spent on its construction and on a costly mole scheme for its protection, will simply be money thrown away.

According to para. 83 of the Report it is further calculated that the proposed wharves would be used for cargo intended for shipment home or *vice versâ*. Any / one familiar with the trade of this port, will know that there is scarcely any direct transhipment cargo for home arriving here worth speaking of, with the exception of such regular shipments, engaged on thro' Bs/Lading, the carriage of which is in the hands of certain Home lines, which have their own local steamers and arrange their direct transhipments at the place where their Home boats take it away, *i.e.*, *Tanjong Pagar*, in order to save unnecessary expense and risk of damage by extra handling. Outward transhipment cargo, will also continue to be dealt with at *Tanjong Pagar*, where it is landed by the Home liners. For small lots it will be less expensive and easier to effect transhipment by lighter to the roads than to avail of the "overland" route, and for large quantities of transhipment cargo it pays to send the local steamers to the Tanjong Pagar wharf.

ere exists, therefore, very little prospect of the Telok Ayer wharves ever being utilized to any great extent by *local boats;* in fact, all that is required at Telok in Ayer is a quay properly fitted up for the receiving and loading of cargo *in cargo boats only*, to enable the Telok Ayer traders to load or receive their goods by lighters or kotahs for shipment to and from the steamers that work in the roads.

Shelter for such a quay by a breakwater would certainly be desirable, but such a structure need not be so far out and of such length as the present suggested inner mole. As long as it affords shelter to that part of the quay where boats are working, and a safe passage to and from Tanjong Pagar, it would answer the purpose.

e backwash from such a mole or breakwater, which Mr. MATTHEWS fears might cause some inconvenience if there existed no outer moles, would then also be considerably less than what the large inner mole, suggested by that gentleman, might cause; but besides, it can hardly be believed that this difficulty could not be overcome or at any rate, minimized by a special construction or angle of the

Transhipment.

This breakwater would thus form part of the required boat-harbour, and if a similar step was taken in the direction of Kallang, and shelter for boats be provided in that part of the roads as well, the Harbour would practically have all the improvements it requires in connection with the loading and discharging of local steamers by means of craft.

The suggested reclamation of 87 acres of land of Telok Ayer would appear to be a valuable addition to Government property, the realisation of which would also be a useful increase to the finances of the Colony. The area intended to be taken up by this reclamation is not occupied at present by any part of the shipping, as it is too shallow, and it does not therefore encroach on the berthage room in the roads. *This part of the scheme should be cordially supported.*

On recapitulation of the pros and cons of Mr. MATTHEWS' *Improved Harbour Scheme*, anyone, who has the interests of this place at heart, must agree that it is an *unnecessary luxury* which is being forced on the Mercantile Community against their will.

It is not, however, suggested that Mr. MATTHEWS is responsible for this. That gentleman was merely requested by the Government to draw up a scheme / for the protection of the Harbour, and he has done so; but whether he himself considers protection an absolute necessity is very much to be doubted.

In 1898 the River Commission made certain recommendations for the improvement of the Harbour, which were based upon the evidence given by members of the Community who had had many years' experience of the question and were therefore best able to judge as to actual requirements. If those recommendations were carried out with the addition of a protected reclamation of land at Telok Ayer, provided with quays and facilities for the handling of goods to and from boats only, and a proper boat-harbour were constructed for the protection of cargo boats, the principal improvements that our roadstead requires would be obtained and the present congestion of the river considerably reduced. This would be a prudent and economical measure and fully sufficient to satisfy the present and reasonable future requirements, far more so than to rush precipitately into a scheme the cost of which Mr. MATTHEWS himself apparently hesitates to officially and publicly estimate, and the outcome of which, in its ultimate effect in years to come on the trade of this port cannot be foreseen, but about which business men feel very dubious, however temporarily convenient it might prove in a small way.

ANON., *REPORT ON THE MARITIME TRADE AND CUSTOMS ADMINISTRATION OF BURMA FOR THE OFFICIAL YEAR 1924/5* (1925)

Anon., *Report on the Maritime Trade and Customs Administration of Burma for the Official Year 1924/5* (Rangoon: Office of the Collector of Customs, 1925).

e report describes the value of the various types of trade; its distribution among the main ports in the country, along with the number of vessels using these ports; the revenue the government earned from customs duties; and the values, prices and origins/destinations of all imports and exports. Not surprisingly, the main exports were rice and teak, the most import imports were textiles and the busiest port Rangoon. Similar reports were published annually from 1906 to 1941.

Anon., *Report on the Maritime Trade and Customs Administration of Burma for the Official Year 1924/5* (1925)

INTRODUCTION.

1. General Summary.—The following statement shows the value of the aggregate sea-borne trade of the whole province of Burma with foreign countries, with Indian ports and between Provincial ports:—

		Average value for 3 years 1920–21 to 1922–23.	1923 – 24.	1924 – 25.
I.—TRADE WITH FOREIGN PORTS.		Rs.	Rs.	Rs.
Imports, Private—Merchandise		22,70,66,252	18,25,39,623	20,94,30,923
Exports, Private {Foreign merchandise		13,56,946	13,90,080	9,88,566
{Indian merchandise		32,68,25,264	39,36,86,915	43,06,37,188
Total, Exports		32,81,82,210	39,50,76,995	43,16,2<?>,754
Total Trade, Private Merchandise		55,52,48,462	57,76,16,618	64,10,56,677
Government Stores	{Imports	37,13,911	32,54,636	26,61,993
	{Exports	12,76,812	21,01,522	25,18,331
Treasure*	{Imports	11,97,782	24,15,401	29,48,373
	{Exports	4,92,633	5,000	...
Total Trade with Foreign Ports		56,19,29,600	58,53,93,177	64,91,85,374
II: – TRADE WITH INDIAN PORTS (OUTSIDE BURMA).				
Imports, Private	{Indian merchandise	14,22,89,773	14,07,89,860	14,35,40,043
	{Foreign merchandise	2,13,32,343	1,24,71,484	1,15,96,166
Total, Imports		16,36,22,116	15,32,61,344	15,51,36,209
Exports, Private	{Indian merchandise	26,82,38,792	19,92,25,982	22,27,26,408
	{Foreign merchandise	68,84,529	58,16,755	42,60,935
Total, Exports		27,51,23,321	20,50,42,737	22,69,87,343
Total Trade, Private Merchandise		43,87,45,437	35,83,04,081	38,21,23,552
Government Stores	{Imports	52,03,906	53,49,542	29,77,309
	{Exports	36,27,644	18,34,663	26,53,484
Treasure*	{Imports	68,50,147	8,88,106	8,55,412
	{Exports	94,03,634	1,11,89,105	1,20,26,221

		Average value for 3 years 1920–21 to 1922–23.	1923 – 24.	1924 – 25.
Total Trade with Indian Ports		46,38,30,768	37,75,65,497	40,06,35,978
* For details of Treasure, *see* paragraph 2. /				
III. – TRADE BETWEEN PROVINCIAL PORTS.		Rs.	Rs.	Rs.
Imports, Private	{Indian merchandise	1,55,67,120	1,56,00,307	1,50,54,402
	{Foreign merchandise	69,38,504	72,61,780	70,48,498
Total, Imports		2,25,05,624	2,28,62,087	2,21,02,900
Exports, Private	{Indian merchandise	1,22,43,332	1,28,07,936	1,22,06,535
	{Foreign merchandise	64,49,546	70,17,299	66,29,606
Total, Exports		1,86,92,878	1,98,25,235	1,88,36,141
Total Trade, Private Merchandise		4,11,98,502	4,26,87,322	4,09,39,041
Government Stores	{Imports	10,15,297	9,30,397	9,57,404
	{Exports	12,61,867	10,98,476	7,35,770
Treasure*	{Imports	15,91,810	8,78,459	36,09,914
	{Exports	15,91,810	8,78,459	36,09,914
Total Trade between Provincial Ports		4,66,59,286	4,64,73,113	4,98,52,043
GRAND TOTAL, PRIVATE MERCHANDISE		1,03,51,92,401	97,86,08,021	1,06,41,19,270
AGGREGATE, INCLUDING TREASURE AND GOVERNMENT STORES.		1,07,24,19,654	1,00,94,31,787	1,09,96,73,395

*   For details of Treasure, *see* paragraph 2.

The balance of foreign trade in favour of Burma reached the high figure of Rs. 21·92 crores as against Rs. 21·01 crores in 1923–24. The balance of trade as against India was Rs. 8·29 crores compared with Rs. 6·29 crores.

The year was one of prosperity and progress in trade. Exports of Rice both to foreign countries, and India increased. Shipments of bran, oils, metals and ores, paraffin wax as well as timber and hides improved likewise.

On the import side, business in Cotton goods was rather brisk, and imports of metals, provisions, silk and woollen goods increased appreciably. Imports of sugar and machinery also improved to some extent. Exchange remained fairly steady and prices fell appreciably in most lines.

2. Movements of Treasure.—The following table shows the movements of treasure during the periods indicated:—

		Average value for 3 years 1920–21 to 1922–23.	1923 – 24.	1924 – 25.
TREASURE.		Rs.	Rs.	Rs.
I. – FROM OR TO FOREIGN PORTS.				
Gold – Imports, Private		11,97,782	24,15,026	29,48,227
Silver – Imports, Private		...	375	146
Gold – Exports, Private		85,574	...	...
Silver – Exports, Private		4,07,059	5,000	...
Gold and Silver (Government) – *Nil*.				/
II. – FROM OR TO INDIAN PORTS (OUTSIDE BURMA).				
Gold – Imports {Private		10,147	1,13,106	3,55,412
{Government		...	...	...
Total		10,147	1,13,106	3,55,412
Silver – Imports	{Private	6,667	...	...
	{Government	68,33,333	7,75,000	5,00,000
Total		68,40,000	7,75,000	5,00,000
Gold – Exports	{Private	...	...	...
	{Government	98,586	...	...
Total		98,586	...	...
Silver – Exports	{Private	87,60,120	1,04,56,960	1,14,47,153
	{Government	5,44,924	7,32,145	5,79,068
Total		93,05,044	1,11,89,105	1,20,26,221
III. – BETWEEN PROVINCIAL PORTS.				
Gold – Imports	{Private	...	...	...
	{Government	1,37,276	...	...
Total		1,37,276	...	...
Silver – Imports	{Private	...	...	...
	{Government	14,54,534	8,78,459	36,09,914
Total		14,54,534	8,78,459	36,09,914
Gold – Exports	{Private	...	...	...
	{Government	1,37,276	...	...
Total		1,37,276	...	...
Silver – Exports	{Private	...	...	...
	{Government	14,54,534	8,78,459	36,09,914
Total		14,54,534	8,78,459	36,09,914

NOTE—Imports of *Silver* overland from Western China represented Rs. 32·40 lakhs as against Rs. 38·36 lakhs in 1923–24.

Silver imported From Siam and exported to Western China were valued at Rs. 7·39 lakhs and Rs. 9·83 lakhs respectively. /

3. Division of Trade between the Ports.—The following table shows in what proportions the total trade in private merchandise was shared between the different ports in the Province:—

Ports.	Foreign Trade	Coasting Trade.		Foreign and Coasting Trade.	
	1924 – 25.	1924 – 25		1923 – 24.	1924 – 25.
		Indian.	Provincial.		
	Per cent.	Per cent.	Per cent.	Per cent.	Per cent.
Akyab	1·31	8·33	19·42	3·94	4·53
Moulmein	3·56	5·38	5·38	3·77	4·28
Bassein	6·86	1·01	1·35	3·74	4·55
Tavoy	·75	·02	11·59	1·14	·90
Mergui	·76	·01	16·57	1·08	1·10
Kyaukpyu	...	...	1·15	·06	·05
Victoria Point	·09	...	·49	·07	·07
Sandoway	...	·02	·98	·06	·04
Total Subordinate ports	13·33	14·77	56·93	13·86	15·52
Rangoon	86·67	85·23	43·07	86·14	84·48
GRAND TOTAL	100·00	100·00	100·00	100·00	100·00

4. Total Revenue.—The following statement shows the gross and net Customs duty, inclusive of the duty on imported salt, realised in the Province of Burma in the periods shown:—

	Average value for 3 years. 1920–21 to 1922–23.	1923–24.	1924–25.
	Rs.	Rs.	Rs.
Import duty (excluding duty on salt)	2,52,85,435	2,80,64,803	3,32,08,876
Import duty on salt	18,39,137	44,74,412	26,88,461
Export duty	72,49,891	96,39,744	99,26,992
Total, Gross duty	3,43,74,463	4,21,78,959	4,58,24,329
Refunds and Drawbacks –			
Imports	4,65,802	5,26,051	4,16,085
Exports	2,44,902	3,06,355	4,55,428
Total	7,10,704	8,32,406	8,71,513
Total, Net duty	3,36,63,759	4,13,46,553	4,49,52,816

The special feature of the year was the introduction of protective duties on certain descriptions of Iron and Steel in favour of the Indian steel industry. The duty on salt was reduced from Rs. 2–8 to Rs. 1–4 per maund and that on salted fish from 15 annas to 7½ annas per maund. There were no other changes in the rates of duty. The net import revenue rose by Rs. 34·68 lakhs to which increase it is noteworthy that cotton piece-goods contributed Rs. 17·28 lakhs, silk goods Rs. 5·76 lakhs, Sugar Rs. 4·72 lakhs and liquors / Rs. 2·01 lakhs. The revenue on

tive duties which amounted to Rs. 20·75 lakhs. The decrease in the revenue on Matches was Rs. 6·35 lakhs which is attributable partly to the overland arrivals from Siam and partly to the growth of the local match industry. The reduction in the rate of duty from Rs. 2–8 to Rs. 1–4 at the close of the preceding year mainly accounted for the heavy fall under the head "Salt Revenue." Under no other head was there any appreciable decrease except in the case of tobacco the revenue on which declined from Rs. 24·58 lakhs to Rs. 21·54 lakhs due in a great measure to imports overland.

On the export side the increase was mainly due to the duty on rice which rose from Rs. 95·57 lakhs to Rs. 98·44 lakhs.

5. Price Levels.—The following table shows the variations in the average prices of certain representative articles in the foreign trade of Rangoon, the mean of the average prices of the three years ending 1900–01 being taken as the basis for comparison and entered as 100. The British cost of living index number based on 1914 retail prices now stands between 177 and 181.

	1898–1901.	Average for 5 year 1909–10 to 1913–14.	Average for 5 years 1914–15 to 1918–19.	1921–22.	1922–23.	1923–24.	1924–25.
		IMPORTS.					
Iron and steel	100	111·8	228·9	298·9	191·8	186·9	147·8
Fish, dry, salted	100	127·5	131·8	137·1	179·3	217·8	211·9
Salt	100	86·5	206·6	133·3	167·8	137·9	121·7
Soap	100	154·2	230·6	358·1	332·6	296·6	302·3
Sugar, refined	100	87·4	128·2	168·3	157·7	174·4	145·8
Cotton—Twist and Yarn	100	153·3	246·7	347·8	309·8	288·4	288·5
„ Piece goods—grey	100	183·9	283·8	407·2	403·5	385·2	387·0
„ „ white	100	156·9	244·1	404·5	402·4	373·8	375·0
„ „ colrd., etc.	100	146·1	213·4	353·9	351·7	308·0	289·8
Silk piece-goods (pure)	100	97·1	128·0	181·7	210·2	209·4	193·5
Woollen piece-goods	100	141·9	260·2	569·9	414·7	301·1	291·5
Average Index number	100	126·6	194·6	288·8	261·9	246·1	227·4
		EXPORTS					
Rice not in the husk	100	131·0	124·9	237·2	213·4	207·7	208·2
Rice bran	100	159·1	88·4	247·4	239·0	222·4	229·3
Wood, teak	100	132·3	170·4	249·9	239·7	229·0	211·9
Hides, raw	100	145·5	205·2	89·7	89·8	93·5	102·8
Cotton, raw	100	159·6	210·1	217·4	238·8	309·5	294·6
Cutch and gambier	100	83·6	87·9	95·5	97·4	103·8	108·3
Rubber, raw	100	154·8	99·6	33·8	37·2	43·4	43·3
Lead (pig)	100	144·0	245·9	210·8	208·7	252·2	289·1
n wax	100	107·6	109·6	108·6	107·8	108·9	108·5

IMPORTS.

6. The following tables show the comparative value importance of the principal articles imported from foreign countries and India into Rangoon:—

Articles. Average value for 3 years 1920–21 to 1922–23.	1923–24.	1924–25.
Rs. Lakhs.	Rs. Lakhs.	Rs. Lakhs.
Foreign.		
Cotton manufactures including twist, etc.	5,93·50	4,51·23	6,17·75
Metals	3,15·92	1,88·13	2,01·56
Machinery and mill work	2,04·26	1,85·52	1,99·09
Sugar	81·25	85·53	85·81
Provisions	75·00	78·28	1,00·52
Hardware, etc.	90·56	55·99	68·66
Silk	59·15	33·52	50·69
Liquors	53·86	47·92	47·70
Coal, etc	45·96	24·07	15·74
Tobacco	37·39	33·46	28·01
Oils	36·62	46·04	33·85
Wool, manufactures of	39·85	36·43	59·30
Railway plant and rolling-stock	41·63	52·54	19·94
Paper and pasteboard	44·35	30·46	32·82
Building, etc., materiats, etc.	31·24	23·61	27·28
Soap	24·73	29·59	31·33
Instruments, apparatus and appliances, etc.	30·98	21·75	26·38
Earthenware, etc.	23·36	17·46	21·90
Apparel, etc.	26·30	20·07	22·31
Salt	21·08	17·35	24·48
Matches	23·91	14·29	8·66
Motor-cars, etc	41·79	30·15	30·85
Fish, etc.	15·24	24·91	27·84
Articles (not specified) imported by post	21·69	16·78	19·75
Other articles	2,78·97	2,44·73	2,74·65
Total, Merchandise	22,58·59	18,09·81	20,76·87
Indian.		
Cotton – Twist and yarn	2,36·69	1,62·29	1,59·13
Cotton, manufactures of	2,28·86	1·46·75	1,81·57
Jute, manufactures of	1,69·75	2,05·88	2,24·83
Oils	89·19	78·34	48·24
Grain and pulse	1,13·64	84·82	1,26·61
Coal	1,02·07	1,34·19	80·41
Spices	71·28	77·88	87·27
Seeds	44·59	48·40	33·77 /

	Articles. Average value for 3 years 1920–21 to 1922–23.	1923–24.	1924–25.
	Rs. Lakhs.	Rs. Lakhs.	Rs. Lakhs.
Fish	49·91	44·25	43·98
Metals	34·74	28·82	36·78
Railway plant and rolling-stock	12·52	5·20	13·35
Hardware and cutlery	25·92	14·01	20·28
Coir	17·25	14·70	17·16
All other articles	1,95·02	2,09·15	2,64·37
Total, Merchandise	1559·38	1448·36	15,51·38

and the following tables show the comparative quantity importance of certain important commodities in the past series of years.

	Articles. Average for 3 years 1920–21 to 1922–23.	1923–24.	1924–25.
	Tons.	Tons.	Tons.
Foreign.			
Coal	116,303	76,110	19,161
Metals	65,952	54,036	73,328
Salt	57,755	55,273	88,338
Oils (mineral)	41,134	60,055	57,050
Cement	23,536	26,696	37,619
Sugar	18,776	21,374	27,316
Piece-goods (cotton)	11,128	11,098	16,007
Soap	3,429	4,560	4,738
Fish	3,244	4,083	4,916
Pitch	490	536	619
Total, Foreign	3,41,747	8,13,821	329,092
Indian.			
Coal	362,355	458,547	343,979
Grain, pulse and flour	45,154	38,935	63,184
Gunny bags	31,251	34,621	33,620
Coconuts	15,718	16,396	15,806
Oils (vegetable)	11,928	12,785	7,730
Betle nuts	15,300	11,257	11,531
Oils (mineral)	15,165	3,284	253
Cotton yarn	8,461	6,947	6,558
Provisions (other sorts)	8,558	6,712	7,170
Tobacco (unmanufactured)	5,804	7,900	6,447
Total (Indian)	519,694	597,384	496,278
Total, Foreign and Indian	861,441	911,205	825,370 /

Textile–Cotton.

	Average for 3 years 1920–21 to 1922–23.		1923–24.		1924–25.	
		Rs. Lakhs.		Rs. Lakhs.		Rs. Lakhs.
FOREIGN TRADE.						
I.—Twist and Yarn— lb.						
From United Kingdom.	1,310,746	32·62	840,799	16·98	1,114,938	22·74
Japan	370,649	5·55	705,200	9·96	1,143,750	16·58
" Other countries	56,968	1·07	13,750	·24	35,997	·68
Total	1,738,363	39·24	1,559,749	27·18	2,294,685	40·00
II.—Piece-goods—						
Grey— Yds.						
From United Kingdom.	6,291,486	27·47	3,700,751	14·52	4,030,256	16·22
Japan	6,464,459	27·45	5,540,461	20·71	8,733,492	32·68
" Other countries	1,39,566	·68	245,574	·93	434,775	1·65
Total	12,895,505	55·60	9,486,786	36·16	13,198,523	50·55
White— Yds.						
From United Kingdom.	25,408,097	148·31	21,022,831	1,22·16	32,883,488	1,67·51
" Other countries	1,573,463	8·86	1,672,550	7·92	1,807,221	8·65
Total	26,931,560	1,57·17	25,695,381	1,30·08	34,690,709	1,76·16
Coloured, printed or dyed— Yds.						
From United Kingdom.	23,626,012	165·37	17,741,151	1,05·60	23,734,274	1,44·67
" Straits	804,027	8·37	2,470,153	20·06	3,128,612	25·23
" Japan	5,681,539	23·69	10,458,851	33·16	20,676,469	66·22
" Netherlands	7,407,758	57·64	4,075,520	26·96	4,675,578	29·39
" Other countries	1,448,174	13·43	1,636,312	12·79	2,511,429	18·44
Total	38,967,510	2,68·50	36,381,987	1,98·57	55,326,362	2,83·95
Total, piece–goods (including fents) and piece-goods of cotton and artificial silk Yds.	79,105,771	4,83·85	72,053,595	3,69·06	104,728,294	5,22·90
III.—Other cotton manufactures.	...	72·95	...	59·20	...	66·89
Total, cotton manufactures.	...	5,54·24	...	4,28·96	...	5,77·56
Total, cotton-goods Foreign Trade (including *raw*, *waste*, *cotton* and *twist*).	...	5,93·49	...	4,51·23	...	6,17·75 /
Textile—Cotton—*concld.*						

	Average for 3 years 1920–21 to 1922–23.		1923–24.		1924–25.	
		Rs. Lakhs.		Rs. Lakhs.		Rs. Lakhs.
COASTING TRADE (from India.)		Rs. Lakhs.		Rs. Lakhs.		Rs. Lakhs.
I—Twist and Yarn lb.	19,543,850	2,36·69	15,560,879	1,62·29	14,690,633	1,59·13
II—Piece-goods—						
Grey Yds.	13,306,732	60·56	11,538,740	42·83	14,051,729	51·33
White „	5,341,076	30·69	3,272,894	16·23	2,913,048	14·47
Coloured, printed „ etc.	20,268,774	1,14·61	13,667,845	70·88	16,540,228	87·37
Total, piece-goods „	38,916,582	2,05·86	28,479,479	1,29·94	33,505,005	1,53·17
III—Other cotton manufactures.	…	23·06	…	16·31	…	28·40
Total, cotton manufactures.	…	2,28·86	…	1,46·75	…	1,81·57
Total, cotton-goods	…	4,66·80	…	3,10·50	…	3,42·91
GRAND TOTAL, COTTON GOODS.	…	10,60·29	…	7,61·72	…	9,60·66

e import trade in piece-goods showed a distinct improvement, the total supplies from foreign countries being greater than in the "boom" year 1920–21 though a little below the pre-war figures, the average for five years of which was about 121 million yards. Japan's revival in this trade after a temporary set-back arising out of the earthquake disaster contributed largely to this result. Her supplies advanced from 16ƒ million yards valued at Rs. 54·69 lakhs to 30 million yards valued at Rs. 101·66 lakhs. Holland's contribution rose by ¼ million yards to 5½ million yards while the United Kingdom maintained her supremacy in this line as in the previous years. Larger arrivals of "Grey goods" from Bombay, "White goods" from Madras, and "coloured goods" from both mainly accounted for the increase in imports of piece-goods from India.

8. Textiles—Silk.

–	Average for 3 years 1920 – 21 to 1922 – 23.		1923 – 24		1924 – 25.	
		Rs.		Rs.		Rs.
Raw Silk— lb.		Lakhs.		Lakhs.		Lakhs.
From Straits Settlements.	725	·05	...	...	...	...
" Hongkong „	3,868	·38	...	...	...	...
" China „	84,972	8·26	2,598	·24	29,581	2·92
" Other countries	4,100	·28	...	...	...	...
Total	93,665	8·97	2,598	·24	29,581	2·92 /
Silk yarn, noils, etc, lb.	134	·02	18	·01	30	·01
Piece-goods, mixed — Yds.						
From United Kingdom.	129,844	3·63	50,906	1·14	116,167	2·38
" Other countries	12,901	·29	2,991	·07	19,376	·39
Total	142,745	3·92	53,897	1·21	135,543	2·77
Piece-goods, pure — Yds.						
From United Kingdom.	54,697	1·62	26,367	·63	21,006	·51
" Hongkong	104,478	4·35	81,878	2·36	60,138	1·14
" China	76,472	3·15	58,643	2·47	216,827	6·68
" Japan	3,383,338	36·04	2,494,656	25·70	3,742,763	35·49
" Other countries	23,863	·35	9,224	·30	19,369	·39
Total	3,642,848	45·51	2,670,768	31·46	4,060,103	44·21
Other sorts lb.	3,225	·72	2,930	·60	4,532	·79
Total value of silk	...	59·14	...	33·52	...	50·69

No raw silk was imported during the past two years except from China, her supplies showing an appreciable increase as compared with the last year. The overland arrivals of raw silk from Western China were 618,295 lbs. worth Rs. 99·50 lakhs as compared with 627,839 lbs. valued at Rs. 88·96 lakhs. The piece-goods trade also shows a substantial improvement due mainly to Japan's recovery from the serious depression caused by the earthquake. Imports from Hongkong declined, but those from China advanced nearly fourfold.

9. Textiles—Wool.

—	Average for 3 years 1920–21 to 1922–23.		1923–24.		1924–25.	
		Rs.		Rs.		Rs.
		Lakhs.		Lakhs.		Lakhs.
Yarn and knitting lb.	39,581	2·52	51,663	2·34	79,778	3·86
Carpets and rugs "	61,471	1·95	155,379	3·44	224,852	5·12
Hosiery "	40,472	4·07	59,389	3·39	32,797	1·87
Piece-goods Yds.	706,759	28·82	1,084,568	25·35	1,986,630	44·95
Shawls No.	1124	·05	8,451	·22	57,609	1·48
Other goods lb.	154,373	2·44	86,013	1·69	159,928	2·02
Total	...	39·85	...	36·43	...	59·30 /

Increases were recorded under all heads except "Hosiery" which showed a drop due to restricted arrivals from the United Kingdom. More "Carpets and rugs" as also "Shawls" received from Italy accounted for a rise under those heads. Germany was responsible for an increased imports of "Yarn and Knitting wool." The United Kingdom was the chief supplier of "Piece-goods" but the imports from Japan and Italy were also somewhat greater. The United Kingdom's share of the total trade was Rs. 36·60 lakhs as against Rs. 22·00 lakhs. Japan, Italy and Germany came next in order.

10. Metals and Ores.

		Average for 3 years, 1920–21 to 1922–23.		1923–24.		1924–25.	
			Rs. Lakhs.		Rs. Lakhs.		Rs. Lakhs.
Brass	Cwt.	2,626	3·16	2,835	2·78	2,815	2·46
Copper	"	2,630	2·55	3,129	2·67	1,718	1·26
Iron and Steel—							
Pig	Tons.	1,271	1·91	1,095	1·34	1,190	1·40
Manufactures of Iron or Steel –							
Beams, pillars, girders, etc.	"	3,093	10·29	3,265	5·07	7,706	13·63
Nails, rivets and washers.	"	1,274	7·96	1,492	7·39	1,617	6·12
Pipes and tubes and fittings.	"	19,675	1,20·30	5,400	20·46	6,307	23·26
Sheets and plates, all kinds.	"	18,971	85·72	19,835	77·89	24,053	78·46
Other manufactures.	Tons.	20,492	74·46	21,441	58·92	31,216	63·90
Total Manufactures of Iron or Steel.	"	63,505	2,98·73	51,433	1,69·73	72,089	1,86·77
Lead	Cwt.	2,289	·71	1,562	·44	2,243	·65
Quicksilver	lb.	3,159	·08	816	·02	2,102	·04
Tin	Cwt.	2,107	2·62	3,102	3·48	2,474	3·91
Zinc or spelter	"	12,035	4·30	17,578	5·19	12,794	3·27
Other sorts of Metals and Ores.	"	1,797	1·86	1,952	2·48	2,712	3·20
Total of Metals Tons and Ores.		65,952	3,15·92	54,036	1,88·13	73,328	2,01·56

Despite the fact that the protective duties were enforced during the year under report, the foreign import trade in "Iron and Steel" showed a healthy improvement. Increase was most marked under "Beams, pillars, girders," "Sheets and plates" and other manufactures (including wire nails). This increase is chiefly attributable to the extensive building scheme, which had been held in abeyance during the pendency of war, having been now put into operation. The exhorbitant house rent coupled with favourable prices of materials brought about this operation. The value of imports of all metals from the United Kingdom was Rs. 130·42 lakhs as against Rs. 140·19 lakhs and from Belgium, Germany and the United States of America, however, / advanced to Rs. 32·31, Rs. 17·40 and Rs.

10·47 lakhs respectively from Rs. 22·07, Rs. 11·33 and Rs. 6·63 lakhs respectively in 1923–24.

Imports of iron or steel of country produce from India rose from 1,517 tons valued at Rs. 3·17 lakhs to 3,199 tons worth Rs. 7·18 lakhs and of foreign manufacture from 2,483 tons valued at Rs. 8·39 lakhs to 2,803 tons worth Rs. 9·90 lakhs.

11. Hardware.—The values of the articles imported under this head were as follows:—

–	Average value for 3 years. 1920–21 to 1922–23.	1923–24.	1924–25.
	Rs. Lakhs.	Rs. Lakhs.	Rs. Lakhs.
1. Agricultural implements	5·16	2·90	1·23
2. Builders' hardware, etc.	10·03	3·65	5·44
3. Domestic hardware, etc.	3·91	2·05	1·64
4. Enamelled ironware	9·05	9·43	9·27
5. Implements and tools	16·76	12·05	13·30
6. Lamps	7·46	4·95	6·01
7. Safes	1·60	1·91	1·87
8. Other sorts	36·59	19·05	29·90
Total	90·56	55·99	68·66

The total value of imports rose by Rs. 12·67 lakhs or 23 per cent. as compared with figures for 1923–24. Of the eight sub-heads, five showed increases, the most prominent being "Other Sorts" with an increase of Rs. 10·85 lakhs or 57 per cent. As usual the United Kingdom supplied most of the "Implements and tools" as well as the miscellaneous articles under "Other Sorts." The bulk of imports of "Enamelled ironware" came from Japan. Germany's supplies were, however, valued at Rs, 2·19 lakhs as against Rs. 1·86 lakhs. Imports of "lamps" were divided almost equally between Germany and the United States of America and their supplies were valued at Rs. 2·49 lakhs and Rs. 2·76 lakhs respectively as against Rs. 1·42 lakhs and Rs. 2·74 lakhs in 1923–24.

The United Kingdom's share to the total value of imports was Rs. 31·60 lakhs as against Rs. 24·78 lakhs, Germany following with Rs. 13·06 lakhs as against Rs. 9·54 lakhs, the United States of America with Rs. 10·96 lakhs as against Rs. 10·96 lakhs and Japan with Rs. 7·26 lakhs as against Rs. 7·53 lakhs in the preceding year.

12. Machinery and Millwork.

	1923–24. Rs. Lakhs.	1924–25. Rs. Lakhs.
Prime-movers (not electrical)	10·19	10·61
Electrical machinery	28·72	19·11
Agricultural machinery	·21	1·33
Metal-working machinery (including machine tools)	3·43	2·08
Mining machinery	78·95	95·77
Oil machinery	4·78	12·02 /
Refrigerating machinery	2·55	1·68
Rice and flour machinery	5·93	6·02
Sewing and knitting machinery	9·62	8·65
Saw mill machinery	3·54	4·62
Sugar mill machinery	·01	·04
Boilers	4·28	6·00
Unenumerated	33·31	31·16
Total	1,85·52	1,99·09

ere was an increase of 7 per cent. in the total value of trade due mainly to further improvement in imports of Mining machinery. The restricted imports of "Electrical machinery" accounted for a decrease under that head. Of the total, 74 per cent. came from the United Kingdom, her usual supplies consisted mostly of Mining and oil crushing machinery and Boilers. The United States of America's portion of the trade was 19 per cent. and confined chiefly to Electrical and Mining machinery. Germany's contribution amounted to 6 per cent. which comprised of Rice milling and Oil crushing machinery.

13. Railway Plant and Rolling Stock. – Imports, almost all from the United Kingdom dropped heavily from Rs. 52·54 lakhs to Rs. 19·94 lakhs. The restricted imports of "Carriages and waggons" and "Rails, chairs, etc.," mainly accounted for this big drop. The value of the former declined from Rs. 23·80 lakhs to Rs. 8·32 lakhs and the latter from Rs. 17·32 lakhs to Rs. 2·52 lakhs.

14. Liquors.

—		Average for 3 years, 1920–21 to 1922–23.		1923–24.		1924–25.	
		Galls.	Rs. Lakhs.	Galls.	Rs. Lakhs.	Galls.	Rs. Lakhs.
Ale, Beer and Liquid Porter.		447,266	18·09	477,515	16·94	583,848	18·27
Cider and other fermented Liquors.	"	566	·04	409	·04	472	03
Spirit—							
Brandy	"	35,941	7·37	46,432	6·33	55,798	7·00
Gin	"	7,603	·89	8,708	·85	8,585	·79
Rum	"	52,821	·91	55,184	·85	61,610	·78
Whisky	"	68,836	13·17	65,084	11·95	53,801	9·37
Liqueurs	"	1,752	·47	1,821	·40	675	·11
Spirit, present in drugs, etc.,	"	7,279	2·46	7,165	2·50	9,482	3·08
Spirit, perfumed	"	2,474	3·28	2,023	2·36	2,136	2·66
Spirit, methylated	"	435	·01	31	...	12,631	·13
Other sorts of spirit.	"	34,092	3·18	24,564	3·15	18,484	2·61
Total of Spirit	"	211,233	31·74	211,012	28·39	223,202	26·53 /
Wines—							
Champagne Liquid and other sparkling wines.		2,671	1·07	2,281	·64	2,505	·61
Port	"	4,415	·81	2,920	·48	4,035	·45
Sherry, Madeira and Marsala		1,470	·21	664	·08	1,177	·12
Other sorts	"	19,964	1·89	18,024	1·35	24,585	1·69
Total of Wines	"	28,520	3·98	23,889	2·55	32,302	2·87
Total Liquors	"	687,575	53·85	712,825	47·92	839,824	47·70

Though there was a slight falling off in value due to the fluctuation in continental exchanges, an increase of 18 per cent. in volume of liquors imported during the year under review was recorded as compared with the figures of last year. The bulk of "Beer" imported, all in bottles, came as usual from the United Kingdom. Supplies of "Beer" from Germany and Japan also advanced from 133,204 and 15,461 gallons to 180,084 and 19,192 gallons respectively. The smaller arrivals of "Shamshoo" from Hongkong and China mainly accounted for a decrease under "Other sorts of Spirit." The decrease under "Whisky" was principally due to the restricted supplies from the United Kingdom but increases were recorded under Brandy, Gin and Rum. France was responsible for the more supplies of Brandy, the United Kingdom for Gin and Java for Rum. Imports of "rum" consisted as usual mainly of crude commercial alcohol and the quantity of such spirit denatured before passing from Bond totalled 54,533 gallons as compared with 49,074 gallons in 1923–24.

e increase under "Wines" was chiefly due to the larger imports of Vermouth and Gingerwine which advanced from 7,544 and 883 gallons to 10,995 and 3,360 gallons respectively and were included under "Other sorts."

At the close of the year 1,637 gallons of "Beer" 28,596 gallons of "Spirits" and 365 gallons of "Wines" remained in Bond.

15. Salt

	Average for 3 years. 1920–21 to 1922–23.		1923– 24.		1924 – 25.	
	Tons	Rs. Lakhs	Tons	Rs. Lakhs	Tons.	Rs. Lakhs
From United Kingdom	8,833	3·99	6,222	2·66	6,819	2·78
" Spain	8,272	2·81	...	...	11,625	3·06
" Aden	7,499	2·63	6,202	1·68	13,768	3·74
" Tunis	...	...	...	...	1,504	·32
" Egypt	17,605	5·34	20,605	5·70	29,668	7·17
" Germany	14,126	5·81	10,486	3·24	14,006	4·75
" Italian East Africa (Somaliland and Eritrea.)	1,415	·49	11,756	4·06	10,948	2·66
" Other countries	5	·01	2	·01	...	...
	57,755	21 08	55,273	17·35	88,338	24·48 /

ere was an appreciable increase in the foreign imports of salt which is attributable mainly to the reduction in the rate of Salt duty. Net clearances from bond amounted to 71,080 tons as against 67,476 tons. Burma salt imported into Rangoon dropped from 6,400 tons to 4,800 tons.

e following table indicates the range of prices for the various types: –

	April 1924.	February 1925.	March 1925.
United Kingdom	120	117	117
Spain	...	96	94
Aden	98	97	97
Germany	104	115	107
Egypt	96	93	93
Italian East Africa (Somaliland and Eritrea)	100	94	93

16. Sugar.

—	Average for 3 years, 1920–21 to 1922–23.		1923–24.		1924–25.	
	Rs. Tons.	Lakhs	Rs. Ton.	Lakhs	Rs. Ton.	Lakhs
REFINED SUGAR –						
(16D.S. and above).	17,761	76·9	20,751	82·40	25,104	83·56
UNREFINED SUGAR						
(15D S. and under).	...	...	...	...	...	...
Molasses	834	·83	529	·38	1,905	1·3
Confectionery	112	2·62	91	2·61	110	2·70
Saccharine	3	·59	2	·14	...	...
Beet Sugar	66	·25	1	Rs. (423)	197	·50
GRAND TOTAL, SUGAR	18,776	81·25	21,374	85·53	27,316	88·06

The direct imports from Java of refined sugar 16 D.S. and above advanced by 3,855 tons to 21,010 tons in volume and by Rs. ·92 lakh to Rs.68·19 lakhs is in value. But the supplies of such sugar from the Straits Settlements dropped from 2,811 tons valued at Rs. 11·75 lakhs to 2,640 tons valued at Rs. 9·75 lakhs. The arrivals from Hongkong were 626 tons valued at Rs.2·62 lakhs as compared with 655 tons valued at Rs. 2·80 lakhs last year. Prices ruled much lower than last year, the average figure for 23 D.S. and above being Rs. 16-8-1 as against Rs. 20-3-9 in 1923–24.

No Saccharine was imported during the year under review, the high duty having diverted the trade entirely towards land frontiers.

17. Coal. – The over-stocking of Bengal coal at the close of the preceding year brought about the reduction in imports, both from foreign countries and India during the year under review. Arrivals of coke mainly from the United Kingdom and Natal increased from 18,921 tons to 30,913 tons but those from Calcutta dropped to 13,557 tons from 21,387 tons in 1923–24

The quantity of Indian coal loaded as bunkers rose from 118,539 tons in, 1923–24 to 134,130 tons. /

The follwing table exhibits the imports of coal into Burma from Foreign Countries and India:—

	Average for 3 years, 1920–21 to 1922–23.		1923–24.		1924–25.	
		Rs.		Rs.		Rs.
Countries.	Tons.	Lakhs	Tons.	Lakhs	Tons.	Lakhs
From Foreign Countries.						
From United Kingdom	34,163	13·74	1,511	·57	3,609	1·27
" Australia	17,175	6·63	6,970	2·44	1,342	·45
" Japan	16,951	6·30	430	·15	187	·02

Countries.	Average for 3 years, 1920–21 to 1922–23.		1923–24.		1924–25.	
	Tons.	Rs. Lakhs	Tons.	Rs. Lakhs	Tons.	Rs. Lakhs
" East Africa	34,970	13·99	15,358	3·52	...	...
" Other countries	7,611	2·30	33,200	9·31	14,023	3·00
	110,870	42·96	57,469	15·99	19,161	4·74
From India.						
From Bengal	368,878	1,04·43	471,260	1,38·67	343,979	80·41
" Other provinces	738	28	300	09	...	...
	369,616	1,04·71	471,560	1,38·76	343,979	80·41
GRAND TOTAL (FOREIGN AND COASTING TRADE).	480,486	1,47·67	529,029	1,54·75	363,140	85·15

18. Tobacco.

	Average for 3 years, 1920–21 to 1922–23.	Rs. Lakhs.	1923–24.	Rs. Lakhs.	1924–25.	Rs. Lakhs.
FOREIGN TRADE—						
Unmanufactured lb.	165,281	·17	...	...	...	...
Manufactured—						
Cigars lb.	2,154	·07	178	·02	631	·04
Cigarettes „	853,567	35·67	695,427	31·31	617,813	26·02
Other sorts „	31,594	1·48	43,371	2·13	36,905	1 95
Total Tobacco (Foreign Trade).	1,052,596	37·39	758,976	33·49	655,346	28·01
COASTING TRADE—						
Unmanufactured lb.	13,066,418	40·38	17,699,464	52·81	14,441,070	38·84
Manufactured—						
Cigars lb.	29,639	·26	76,207		15,207	·15
Cigarettes „	152,025	6·85	753,455	33·96	1,228,795	46·55
Other sorts „	198,062	·90	145,875	·79	129,141	·55
Total, Tobacco, Coasting Trade.	13,446,144	48·39	18,675,001	87·91	15,814,213	86·09
GRAND TOTAL lb. (FOREIGN AND COASTING TRADE)	14,498,740	85·78	19,413,977	1,21·37	16,469,562	1,14·10 /

ere has been a substantial improvement in the import trade in Indian cigarettes, the bulk of which came from Madras. Supplies from Bengal were 71,681 lbs. valued at Rs. 2·19 lakhs as against 87,760 lbs. valued at Rs. 2·13 lakhs. In addition, 3,664 lbs. of foreign cigarettes were also imported from India as against 4,252 lbs. in the previous year. There were decreases in imports of cigarettes from

19. Mineral Oils.—Foreign imports of fuel oil advanced in volume by 621,572 gallons to 13,145,810 gallons, but the value dropped from Rs. 25·42 lakhs to Rs. 19·11 lakhs. The arrivals from Persia declined from 8,971,653 gallons valued at Rs. 19·66 lakhs to 8,221,201 gallons valued at Rs. 11·79 lakhs, but those from Borneo (Dutch) increased from 3,487,426 gallons valued at Rs. 5·59 lakhs to 4,790,698 gallons valued at Rs. 7·13 lakhs. Imports of American kerosene dropped by 705,144 gallons to 594,900 gallons and their values from Rs. 11·03 lakhs to Rs. 5·34 lakhs. The increased quantities of "Lubricating Oil" and "Other Kinds" were however received mostly from the United States of America.

20. Motor-cars and Motor-cycles.—The total number of cars imported into Burma was 1,010 as against 1,030 in 1923–24. The bulk of the trade is still shared by cheap American and Canadian cars. Imports from the United Kingdom however rose from 59 cars valued at Rs. 2·18 lakhs to 130 cars including 3 Fords, valued at Rs. 3·61 lakhs. Canadian cars including 20 Fords, numbered 296 valued at Rs. 5·37 lakhs, and 534 American cars valued at Rs. 11·45 lakhs including 197 Fords, came *via* the Atlantic Coast. Fourteen cars, of which 10 were Fords, arrived from the Straits, 25 from France and 11 from Belgium.

In addition, 30 cars valued at Rs. 1·67 lakhs were also imported from India.

Imports of motor-cycles rose from 145 to 157 and there has been an appreciable increase in the number of commercial motor-vehicles which advanced from 55 to 159, the chief source of supply being United States of America and Canada.

21. Miscellaneous—Apparel—The total value of imports which consisted largely of "Hats, caps, bonnets, etc.," from the United Kingdom advanced from Rs. 20·07 lakhs to Rs. 22·31 lakhs. There was an increase in the total quantity of "Boots and shoes" imported from 413,701 pairs to 425,188 pairs though their values fell slightly from Rs. 10·99 lakhs to Rs. 10·63 lakhs. These included 59,309 pairs of leather and 152,791 pairs of other materials from the United Kingdom as against 39,192 and 94,059 pairs respectively and their values were Rs, 4·15 and Rs. 2·07 lakhs as compared with Rs. 3·39 and Rs. 1·64 lakhs respectively in the previous year. The next important suppliers were Japan and the United States of America. The total value of "Building, etc., materials" imported rose from Rs. 23·61 lakhs to Rs. 27·28 lakhs. Larger arrivals of "Cement" mostly from the United Kingdom mainly / accounted for this rise. Imports of "Fish," of which the dry salted fish from the Straits constituted the bulk of this trade advanced from 81,682 cwts. valued at Rs. 24·91 lakhs to 98,325 cwts. valued at Rs. 27·84 lakhs. Imports of Fish, dry, unsalted, from India largely from Madras increased in quantity from 86,242 cwts. to 87,247 cwts., but the value declined from Rs. 40·01 lakhs to Rs. 39·56 lakhs. Exports of "Potatoes" to India almost all to Calcutta dropped from 18,959 tons valued at Rs. 26·20 lakhs to 12,921 tons valued at Rs. 23·71 lakhs. Larger receipts of "Electrical instruments" from the United

Kingdom and United States of America contributed chiefly to the increase in imports of Instruments, etc., from foreign countries, the value of which rose from Rs. 21·75 lakhs to Rs. 26·38 lakhs. Imports of matches declined from 1,043,822 gross of boxes valued at Rs. 14·29 lakhs to 632,616 gross of boxes valued at Rs. 8·66 lakhs. The reasons for this decline have been explained elsewhere in this report. Value of splints, veneers and logs intended for use in match making which were imported mostly from Japan amounted to Rs. 2·38 lakhs. Other items classified as "miscellaneous" showed no striking variations worthy of any comment except "Jute gunny-bags" imported into Burma from Calcutta which advanced in number from 40y millions valued at Rs. 2,06·60 lakhs to 41... millions valued at Rs. 2,37·37 lakhs.

EXPORTS.

e following tables show the value and volume of Rangoon export trade in its principal products. They indicate a more or less static state for the past year: –

Articles.	Average value for 3 years 1920–21 to 1922–23.	1923–24	1924–25.
	Rs. Lakhs.	Rs. Lakhs.	Rs. Lakhs.
Foreign.			
1. Rice, husked and unhusked	17,74·94	22,12·23	21,86·04
2. Oils—Mineral	2,06·84	1,89·38	2,49·55
3. Lead, pig	1,16·02	1,79·36	2,29·60
4. Cotton (raw)	1,31·45	1,23·39	1,65·17
5. Paraffin wax	1,17·16	1,08·30	1,30·01
6. Bran and pollard	86·89	1,01·06	1,19·98
7. Grain, pulse and flour (excluding rice)	80·64	71·93	54·23
8. Wood and timber	71·38	97·53	1,07·13
9. Oil cakes	38·71	35·62	52·40
10. Tobacco	23·01	20·19	20·52
11. Leather	16·26	14·16	11·22
12. Jadestone	17·47	8·33	7·07
13. Rubber, raw	15·87	23·42	26·78
14. Hides and skins (raw)	19·99	14·72	19·74
15. Other articles	78·76	90·30	90·20
Total, Indian Produce	27,95·39	32,89·92	34,69·64 /
Indian.			
1. Rice, husked and unhusked	10,23·00	4,76·04	5,47·32
2. Mineral oils, excluding paraffin-wax	6,67·66	6,88·85	7,74·29
3. Wood, and manufactures of	2,09·47	2,09·18	2,07·83

Articles.	Average value for 3 years 1920–21 to 1922–23.	1923–24	1924–25.
	Rs. Lakhs.	Rs. Lakhs.	Rs. Lakhs.
(excluding rice)	87·93	66·09	35·81
5. Lac	41·99	56·43	37·92
6. Railway plant and rolling-stock	28·17	9·55	17·52
7. Fruits and vegetables	20·49	26·94	25·34
8. Candles	16·86	13·75	15·15
9. All other articles	73·94	82·43	97·14
Total, Country Produce	21,69·51	16,29·26	17,58·32
Foreign.			
1.Rice	1,079,370	1,431,552	1,411,531
2. Bran	152,707	193,206	222,494
3. Oils (mineral)	69,094	67,589	89,122
4. Food grains (excluding rice)	62,842	84,379	61,183
5. Metals and ores	40,278	49,645	74,000
6. Oil cakes	38,522	41,230	56,572
7. Paraffin-wax	25,812	23,726	28,575
8. Raw cotton	12,079	8,588	12,076
9. Wood and timber	25,692	36,730	43,484
10. Seeds	3,212	1,451	878
11. Hides and skins	2,818	2,319	2,826
Total, Foreign	1,512,426	1,940,415	2,002,741
Indian.			
1. Rice	627,470	319,497	365,665
2. Oils (mineral)	485,178	617,335	653,631
3. Wood and timber	140,600	149,084	143,829
4. Food grains (excluding rice)	60,116	55,391	31,131
5. Metals and ores	2,274	2,962	3,747
6. Raw cotton	216	177	21
Total, Indian	1,315,854	1,144,446	11,98,024
Total, Foreign and Indian	2,828,280	3,084,861	3,200,765 /

23. Rice and Paddy.—The combined exports from all the ports in Burma (excluding interportal trade) will be found in the following table—

—	Average for 3 years 1920–21 to 1922–23		1923–24.		1924–25.	
	Tons.	Rs. Lakhs.	Tons.	Rs. Lakhs.	Tons.	Rs. Lakhs.
FOREIGN TRADE.						
Rice in the husk (paddy).	35,980	32·26	19,206	17·46	24,325	22·44
Rice not in the husk—						
British Empire—						
To United Kingdom	116,223	1,91·57	55,322	78·93	129,261 ( )	1,90·22

FOREIGN TRADE.	Average for 3 years 1920–21 to 1922–23		1923–24.		1924–25.	
	Tons.	Rs. Lakhs.	Tons.	Rs. Lakhs.	Tons.	Rs. Lakhs.
" Hongkong	53,112	75·27	78,065	1,03·48	31,602	34·71
" Africa	63,490	1,25·47	44,938	83·39	28,158	(*b*) 46·11
" North America	5,698	10·38	2,170	3·42	20,50	3·55
" Australasia	22,113	36·39	17,019	27·95	25,604	42·19
" Other British Possessions.	31,731	52·59	32,896	51·40	51,795	82·73
Foreign Countries—						
To Sweden	1,207	1·96	...	...	1,997	2·81
" Norway	5,19	·86	...	...	500	·85
" Denmark	2,05	·32	...	...	405	·65
" Germany	207,336	3,35·43	404,327	6,21·87	290,212	(*c*) 4,54·42
" Netherlands	31,353	46·34	51,006	76·10	84,569	(*d*) 1,24·13
" Belgium	7,397	11·32	14,906	21·10	17,824	(*e*) 24·46
" France	9,16	1·48	1,045	1·53	845	1·05
" Portugal	4,571	7·88	4,250	7·00	19,999	32·98
" Italy	6,366	9·34	10,030	14·14	22,257	35·37
" Switzerland	2,120	3·24	...	...	...	...
" Austria-Hungary	3,33	·60	...	...	...	...
" Austria	2,133	3·95	15,043	25·48	35,690	58·29
" Greece	7,49	1·38	...	...	...	...
" Egypt	48,071	81·72	39,812	66·24	140,662	(*f*) 213·51
" Turkey, Asiatic	8,647	17·01	...	...	...	...
" Sumatra	36,414	51·91	55,308	78·99	80,737	120·97
" Java	76,268	1,19·17	133,699	1,94·61	44,935	67·51
" Celebes and other Islands.	9,20	1·35	120	·19	...	...
" Philippines	5,01	·76	...	...	...	...
" China, etc.	63,034	75·99	150,850	2,48·05	47,695	71·04
" Japan	44,781	70·54	127,829	2,12·23	223,831	362·96
" Africa	2,332	4·15	6,267	9·34	2,466	4·17
" North America	27,338	46·43	85,774	1,37·08	105,304	(*g*) 175·70
" South America	1,272	2·42	4,171	6·10	8,715	14·14
" Other Foreign Countries.	8,803	15·14	21,877	36·51	29,544	47·00
Total	1,302,718	21,32·18	1,770,591	27,38·53	1,847,270	28,80·07
Total Paddy and Rice (Foreign Trade).	1,338,698	21,64·44	1,789,797	27,55·99	1,871,595	29,02·51

	Tons.	Rs. Lakhs.
(*a*) Includes United Kingdom for orders	45,725	67·37
(*b*) " Natal " "	5,31	·74
(*c*) " Germany " "	4,164	6·68
(*d*) " Netherlands " "	2,50	·30

–	Average for 3 years 1920–21 to 1922–23.		1923–24.		1924–25.	
		Rs.		Rs.		Rs.
INDIAN TRADE. (excluding Burma).	Tons.	Lakhs.	Tons.	Lakhs.	Tons.	Lakhs.
Rice in the husk (Paddy)—						
To Indian Ports	107,141	1,01·46	84,279	77·11	116,786	1,18·49
Rice not in the husk—						
To Bengal	183,817	2,81·64	23,175	33·60	69,209	1,00·53
„ Bombay	426,689	7,58·49	2,66,691	4,37·30	2,90,107	3,58·52
„ Sind, Karachi	33	·06	...	...	...	...
„ Madras	183,021	2,78·13	146,937	2,00·76	224,909	330·66
„ Indian Ports not British.	11,157	17·14	7,245	12·26	2,516	4·17
Total, Rice exports to India.	804,717	13,35·46	444,048	6,83·92	505,741	7,93·88
Total Paddy and Rice exports to India (excluding Burma ports).	911,858	14,36·92	528,327	7,61·03	622,527	912·37
GRAND TOTAL, PADDY AND RICE EXPORTS TO FOREIGN AND INDIAN PORTS (EXCLUDING BURMA PORTS).	2,250,556	36,01·36	2,318,124	35,17·02	2,494,122	38,14·88

A feature of the season under report was the comparatively small quantity of rice taken by Indian markets in spite of the fact that the Indian rice crop over-all was estimated to be some five millions tons short of the previous year. The high range of prices ruling throughout the year for Burma rice was largely responsible for this and it would seem that the people in India generally have learned from want of sufficient money with which to buy dear rice to fall back for food on cheaper grains such as wheat, jawar, dhall, gram, etc., when rice is too dear and that when prices rise above a certain level the demand from India will be small.

There was a steady shipment demand throughout the year for rice to the Straits, chiefly for small mills and Meedong qualities. Japan came out as a buyer of S. Q. during April and May and took considerable quantities of that quality. From Europe there was a good demand especially in the earlier months of the year which enabled millers to handle and dispose of the very heavy arrivals of paddy during the first half of the year. Prices for Big Mills Specials opened at Rs. 470 but rose almost immediately to Rs. 495 to drop again almost as suddenly to Rs. 455. Thereafter prices fluctuated on a gradually rising market till July when crop and an expected demand from India rushed prices up to Rs. 540 at the end of that month. After that prices declined slowly to Rs. 520 at the end of August and then fell suddenly to Rs. 480 in the middle of the September to jump again to Rs. 525 by the end of that month. Thereafter the market was dull with little demand for rice except from the Straits and prices fell away, the market closing at the end of the season weak at about Rs. 460. New season stocks came in the market at Rs. 160 on Rail and Rs. 170 on Boat but were not marketed at all freely at these rates. Supplies improved towards the end of January / but were still on a restricted scale especially on the Boat side, and prices gradually advanced till Rs. 167 for Rail and Rs. 176 for Boat was being paid at the end of the month. At these rates the market remained steady till the middle of February when the supplies improved slightly though they were small in comparison with last year. Closing prices were Rs. 170 on Rail and Rs. 178 on Boat side with an upward tendency. The rice market opened dull at the beginning of January at Rs. 405 for Big, Mills Specials with an almost entire lack of shipment demand. Later on in the month, there was a fair enquiry from Indian and Straits shippers for early milling and prices gradually advanced. Japan's demand coupled with a good enquiry locally for Europe qualities had a further hardening effect on prices. At the end of January Big Mills Specials were quoted at Rs. 425. During February the demand from India continued and owing, it is said, to the high price ruling for wheat, considerable quantities of rice were taken up for that market. Prices continued to rise up to Rs. 450 in the middle of March and then dropped to Rs. 427–8 at the close of the year.

24. Rice Bran. —The total foreign exports from the Province advanced by 37,476 tons and Rs. 25·98 lakhs to 259,549 tons valued at Rs. 1,42·86 lakhs. The United Kingdom took 200,089 tons worth Rs. 1,11·88 lakhs as against 122,957 tons valued at Rs. 66·48 lakhs. Shipments to the Straits Settlements dropped from 51,615 tons valued at Rs. 25·89 lakhs to 30,937 tons with a value of Rs, 16·50 lakhs. Germany also drew less by 13,432 tons and Rs. 7·34 lakhs to 12,240 tons valued at Rs. 7·36 lakhs. The average price slightly rose from Rs. 53 to Rs. 55 per ton.

25. Mineral Oils.

—	Average for 3 years, 1920–21 to 1922–23.		1923–24.		1924–25.	
		Rs.		Rs.		Rs.
FOREIGN TRADE —	Gals.	Lakhs.	Gals.	Lakhs.	Gals.	Lakhs.
Kerosene	6,544	·06	...	...	4,380	·02
Petroleum, dangerous flashing below 76–F. including benzene, benzol, petrol and other motor spirit.	19,600,730	204·25	16,671,048	187,55	22,053,186	2,48·10
Other kinds (*a*)	1,125,520	2·59	151,648	1·84	123,966	1·43
Total, Mineral Oils (Foreign Trade).	20,732,794	2,06·90	16,822,696	1,89·39	22,181,532	2,49·55
Costing Trade—Kerosene—						
To Bengal	58,789,184	1,99·41	63,980,727	2,14·18	66,354·076	2,23·99
„ Bombay	23,879,666	80·63	26,193,744	89·98	29,117·910	99·15
„ Sind	8,026,392	31·27	6,690,502	23·03	5,611·145	19·35
„ Madras	23,040,811	79·22	29,079,188	99·99	28,924·144	99·45
Total Presidencies	113,736·053	3,90·53	125,914,161	4,27·18	130,007·275	4,41·94
To Provincial Ports	1,608·946	5·96	1,052,176	4·46	1,011·176	4·30
„ Marmagoa	5,661,199	19·47	6,317·249	21·72	7,873·338	27·07
Total	121,006·198	4,15·96	133,313·586	4,53·36	138,891·789	4,73·31 /
Benzine and Petrol	15,785·915	2,22·92	14,735,158	2,02·55	17,787·860	2,64·82
Other kinds (*b*)	6,394·370	37·16	6,932,532	40·89	7,291·873	43·51
Total, Mineral oils (Coasting Trade).	143,186·483	6,76·04	154,981,276	6,96·80	163,971·522	7,81·64
GRAND TOTAL, MINERAL OIL (FOREIGN AND COASTING TRADE).	163,919·277	8,82·94	171,803,972	8,86·19	186,153·054	10,31·19

(*a*) "Other kinds" – *includes fuel oil, lubricating oil, etc.*
() "Other kinds" – includes lubricating oil.

The combined foreign and coasting trade advanced by 8 per cent in volume and 16 per cent in value as compared with the figures of 1923–24. The bulk of the shipments of "Benzine and Petrol" to foreign destinations went to the United Kingdom, but those to India were distributed proportionately among the Provinces, Bombay heading the list with 6, million gallons, Bengal following with 5y millions, Madras with 4 million gallons and Sind with 2 million gallons approximately as against 4y, 4 3/5, 3 2/5, and 2 million gallons in the preceding year.

26. Paraffin-wax and Candles.—The following table shows the exports from Rangoon during the periods specified:—

	Average for 3 year 1920–21 to 1922–		1923–24.		1924–25.	
	Tons.	Rs. Lakhs.	Tons.	Rs. Lakhs.	Tons.	Rs. Lakhs.
Paraffin-wax—						
Foreign	25,812	1,17·16	23,726	1,08·30	28,275	1,30·01
Coasting	608	2·82	513	2·34	677	3·08
Total	26,420	1,19·98	24,239	1,10·64	29,252	1,33·09
Candles—						
Foreign	2,358	14·88	2,236	14·14	1,719	10·84
Coasting	2,696	17·47	2,198	13·75	2,405	15·15
Total	5,054	32·35	4,434	27·89	4,124	25·99

Despite the fact that there was a heavy drop in the Chinese and Japanese demands, the trade in Paraffin-wax showed a substantial increase. This increase was attributed to a larger shipment to the United Kingdom, her takings having improved from 3,641 tons valued at Rs. 16·57 lakhs to 9,289 tons with a value of Rs. 42·25 lakhs. Chile took 1,084 tons valued at Rs. 4·93 lakhs as against none in the previous year. France, Germany and New Zealand also drew more, but the demands from China and Japan dropped from 4,701 tons and 5,190 tons valued at Rs. 21·39 lakhs and Rs. 23·81 lakhs to 855 tons and 3,559 tons valued at Rs. 3·89 lakhs and Rs. 16·19 lakhs respectively. /

27. Cotton (Raw).

	Average for 3 years, 1920–21 to 1922–23.		1923–24.		1924–25	
	Tons.	Rs. Lakhs.	Tons.	Rs. Lakhs.	Tons.	Rs. Lakhs.
To United Kingdom	3,273	38·98	2,966	42·87	2,797	38·25
„ Hongkong	413	3·38	9	·10	36	·42
„ Germany	332	3·86	180	2·79	123	1·64
„ China, etc.	1,392	14·42	776	9·53	1,233	17·00
„ Japan	6,639	70·46	4,518	66·23	7,877	1,07·73
„ Other countries	30	·35	139	1·87	10	·13
Total, Foreign Trade	12,079	1,31·45	8,588	1,23·39	12,076	1,65·17
Total, Indian Trade (excluding Burma).	281	2·54	186	2·65	86	·64
GRAND TOTAL	12,360	1,33,99	8,774	1,26·04	12,162	1,65·81

There has been no special feature in the export trade during the year under report except that Japan has again taken an increased percentage of the crop while exports to the United Kingdom are correspondingly reduced. The yield of the 1924–25 cotton crop of Burma was estimated at 12,500 tons equivalent to 70,000 bales and it is reported that the crop has been practically all marketted at the close of the year.

The quantity exported to Western China by land was 670 tons as compared with 361 tons in 1923–24.

WOOD AND TIMBER.

28. Teakwood.

	Average for 3 years, 1920–21 to 1922–23.		1923–24.		1924–25.	
		Rs.		Rs.		Rs.
To Foreign Countries.	C. Tons.	Lakhs.	C. Tons.	Lakhs.	C. Tons.	Lakhs.
To United Kingdom	14,170	40·45	20,381	60·17	22,775	61·83
„ Ceylon	2,267	3·40	3,906	5·74	5,915	7·89
„ Cape of Good Hope and Natal.	2,897	10·42	2,884	7·79	4,247	11·86
„ Mauritius	640	1·24	1,033	1·61	1,571	2·59
„ Germany	1,533	4·67	696	2·07	1,169	3·27
„ Netherlands	635	1·95	1,127	2·53	1,629	4·37
„ Portuguese East Africa.	623	1·90	1,782	4·78	2,287	6·35
„ United States of America.	838	2·56	1,572	4·72	604	1·79
„ Other Countries	1,696	4·27	2,937	7·58	2,954	6·68
Total Teakwood (Foreign Trade).	25,299	70·86	36,318	96·99	43,151	1,06·63 /
To India.						
To Bengal	41,682	64·05	43,700	65·96	41,370	62·51
„ Bombay	41,616	64·77	50,143	61·54	36,429	54·51
„ Sind	4,601	6·87	4,423	6·49	7,229	10·11
„ Madras	38,120	55·28	42,794	62·84	48,720	66·75
„ Indian Ports not British.	1,386	1·90	2,704	3·39	4,238	6·04
Total Teakwood (Indian Trade excluding Burma).	127,405	1,92·87	143,764	2,00·22	137,986	1,99·92
GRAND TOTAL (FOREIGN AND INDIA.	152,704	2,63·73	180,082	2,97·21	181,137	3,06·55

There has again been a noticeable improvement in the foreign exports, all destinations showing an increase except for the United States of America which

Kingdom was appreciably more healthy than is indicated purely by statistics as the 1924–25 total of 22,775 tons included 2,536 tons only shipped on behalf of the Local Government compared with 5,000 tons in the preceding year. Sale rates have been generally firm with a rising tendency. Exports to India however showed a slight falling off and it may be noted that this falling away would have been far more marked but for the part assumed by Burma in the supply of sleepers to the Indian Railways during the major portion of the year. Since December demand has been far more brisk and with stocks in the consuming markets down to very moderate figures, prices have been on the rise.

29. Hides and Skins.—The following table gives the exports from Rangoon to foreign ports: –

	Average for 3 years 1920–21 to 1922–23.	1923–24.	1924–25.
	Rs. Lakhs.	Rs. Lakhs.	Rs. Lakhs.
RAW HIDES {Tons	2,768 } 19·13 {	2,286 } 14·51 {	2,775 } 19·32
	423,678	325,125	405,727
RAW SKINS {Tons	26 } 56 {	12 } 12 {	23 } 36
	31,571	14,916	29,473
Total of Hides and Skins, raw (excluding cuttings of hides, etc.) {Tons	2,794 } 19·69 {	2,298 } 14·63 {	2,798 } 19·68
	455,249	340,041	435,200

ere was a further improvement in off-take by Italy and Germany which accounted for some recovery in the export trade under this head. /

Exports to India mostly to Madras also advanced from 1,194 tons valued at Rs. 7·15 lakhs in 1923–24 to 1,585 tons valued at Rs. 10·64 lakhs.

e arrivals of raw hides overland from Western China represented 242 tons valued at Rs. 1·67 lakhs as against 219 tons with a value of Rs. 1·27 lakhs in 1923–24.

30. Beans.—Foreign exports dropped from 70,182 tons valued at Rs. 57·20 lakhs to 49,778 tons with a value of Rs. 42·54 lakhs. The restricted shipments to the United Kingdom accounted for the drop. She took 8,212 tons valued at Rs. 7·68 lakhs as against 31,632 tons valued at Rs. 23·63 lakhs. Germany and Belgium drew none as against 3,495 tons and 1,250 tons valued at Rs. 3·35 lakhs and Rs. ·87 lakh respectively in the previous year. Shipments to Japan however increased from 29,442 tons valued at Rs. 24·63 lakhs. to 39,164 tons valued at Rs. 31·83 lakhs.

Exports to India, the bulk of which was absorbed by Madras, again fell from 17,882 tons valued at Rs, 19·36 lakhs to 9,474 tons valued at Rs. 12·52 lakhs.

31. Rubber.

Average for 3 years, 1920–21 to 1922–23.		1923–24.		1924–25.	
Tons.	Rs. Lakhs.	Tons.	Rs. Lakhs.	Tons.	Rs. Lakhs.
2,055	31·06	2,863	50·86	3,825	68·12

There was a further improvement in the exports of this product from Burma to foreign countries. The United Kingdom took 1,867 tons worth Rs. 35·17 lakhs as against 1,671 tons valued at Rs. 31·71 lakhs in the previous year, and the Straits Settlements 1,550 tons valued at Rs. 24·56 lakhs as against 927 tons with a value of Rs. 14·24 lakhs. Germany drew 29 tons worth Rs. ·51 lakh as against 69 tons valued at Rs. 1·42 lakhs and France 31 tons valued at Rs. ·52 lakh as against 8 tons with a value of Rs. ·01 lakh Shipments to the United States of America increased from 151 tons valued at Rs. 2·96 lakhs to 267 tons with a value of Rs. 6·11 lakhs and those to Ceylon also rose from 36 tons valued at Rs. ·50 lakh to 77 tons with a value of Rs. 1·18 lakhs.

32. Lac – Only 744 cwts. of stick lac worth Rs. ·53 lakh were exported to the United States of America as against no shipment to the foreign destinations in the preceding year. Exports to India which consisted chiefly of stick lac dropped by 5,654 cwts. and Rs. 18·52 lakhs to 59,668 cwts. valued at Rs. 37·92 lakhs. As usual Calcutta was the chief purchaser. The overland arrivals of stick lac from Western China and Shan States were 4,741 cwts. and 58,737 cwts. as against 5,742 cwts. and 59,063 cwts. respectively in 1923–24. /

33. Metals and Ores.—As usual the chief item under this head was Pig-lead, the exports of which from Rangoon to foreign destinations advanced from 42,420 tons valued at Rs. 1,79·36 lakhs to 47,374 tons valued at Rs. 2,29·60 lakhs. The United Kingdom took 24,823 tons worth Rs. 124·29 lakhs as against 21,461 tons valued at Rs. 93·36 lakhs. Shipments to Japan and Ceylon rose from 9,059 and 4,853 tons to 13,492 and 5,052 tons respectively and their values from Rs. 36·15 lakhs and Rs. 19·98 lakhs to Rs. 62·47 lakhs and Rs. 24·04 lakhs respectively. Exports to China, Hongkong and Germany declined from 3,963; 1,209 and 1,525 tons to 2,464; 785 and 450 tons respectively and their values from Rs. 16·60 lakhs, Rs. 4·86 lakhs and Rs. 7·00 lakhs to Rs. 11·58 lakhs, Rs. 3·47 lakhs and Rs. 2·28 lakhs respectively. Shipments to India mostly to Bengal rose from 2,610 tons valued at Rs. 10·55 lakhs to 3,218 tons valued at Rs. 15·05 lakhs.

There was an appreciable expansion in the foreign export trade of "Zinc" and "Lead" which advanced from 3,912 and 1,744 tons valued at Rs. 2·93 lakhs and Rs. 3·81 lakhs to 18,279 and 4,170 tons valued at Rs. 15·26 lakhs and Rs. 7·04 lakhs respectively. Belgium took the bulk of "Zinc" while Germany and the

Exports of block tin to India rose from 228 tons rained at Rs. 8·43 lakhs to 257 tons valued at Rs. 10·69 lakhs.

34 Jadestone.—Exports again fell from 3,065 cwts. valued at Rs. 8·33 lakhs to 2,766 cwts. with a value of Rs. 7·07 lakhs. As in the previous years, almost the entire output went to Hongkong. Despatches from the Mines overland to Western China totalled 212 cwts. valued at Rs. ·56 lakh as against 383 cwts. with a value of Rs. ·78 lakh in 1923–24.

DISTRIBUTION OF THE TRADE OF BURMA.

e statement below shows how the trade of Rangoon in private merchandise with foreign countries was distributed in the periods shown:—

Countries.	Average Value for 3 years 1920–21 to 1922–23. Rs. Lakhs.	1923–24. Rs. Lakhs.	1924–25. Rs. Lakhs.
Imports.			
British Empire.			
United Kingdom	12,52·55	9,85·37	10,97·55
Ceylon	3·50	3·15	2·87
Straits Settlements	96·34	1,03·68	1,13·21
Hongkong	39·66	31·17	34·00
South Africa	1·97	12·22	9·29
Zanzibar and Pema	·05	...	·01
Mauritius and Dependencies	·01	...	1·20
Australasia	15·04	9·49	9·99
Other British Possessions	8·42	10·96	10·44
Total, British Empire	14,17·54	11,56·04	12,78·56 /
Foreign Countries.			
Europe—			
Sweden	9·40	4·01	7·88
Norway	8·63	9·58	8·44
Germany	64·97	70·90	95·36
Netherlands	88·69	64·05	65·27
Belgium	31·45	31·66	45·18
France	15·18	14·80	18·05
Spain	2·96	·12	3·17
Portugal	4·06	5·74	5·27
Switzerland	12·32	8·33	13·15
Italy	13·02	13·59	29·19
Other countries	2·98	4·03	8·30
Total, Europe	2,53·66	2,26·81	2,99·26
Asia—			
Persia	22·11	19·72	11·98

Countries.	Average Value for 3 years 1920–21 to 1922–23. Rs. Lakhs.	1923–24. Rs. Lakhs.	1924–25. Rs. Lakhs.
Sumatra	·02	·14	·16
Java	55·16	73·65	76·23
Celebes and other Islands	...	·01	·01
Siam	·47	·03	·34
China, etc.	17·93	10·36	15·94
Japan	2,16·11	1,69·99	2,49·47
Other countries	3·85	8·94	7·67
Total, Asia	3,15·65	2,82·84	3,61·80
Africa—			
Egypt	5·76	6·35	7·71
Portuguese East Africa	13·99	3·53	...
Other countries	·49	4·06	2·98
Total, Africa	20·24	13·94	10·69
America—			
United States	2,51·49	1,30·16	1,26·48
Other countries	·01	·02	·08
Total, America	2,51·50	1,30·18	1,26·56
Total, Foreign Countries	8,41·05	6,53·77	7,98·31
GRAND TOTAL, BRITISH AND FOREIGN POSSESSIONS.	22,58·59	18,09·81	20,76·87
EXPORTS.			
British Empire.			
United Kingdom	5,36·58	6,14·57	7,80·36
Ceylon	4,81·13	3,51·13	3,64·50
Straits Settlements	2,95·13	3,43·79	3,49·28
Hongkong	1,39·99	1,48·81	71·02
South Africa	40·97	43·76	43·11
Zanzibar and Pemba	17·83	27·41	14·93
Mauritius and Dependencies	67·06	33·29	12·07
Australasia	38·58	21·52	35·94
Other British Possessions	49·16	57·22	94·22
Total, British Empire	16,66·43	16,41·50	17,65·43 /
Foreign Countries.			
Europe—			
Sweden	4·88	·49	2·09
Norway	5·49	·02	10·97
Germany	2,65·65	4,11·49	2,89·98
Netherlands	65·92	42·47	51·03
Belgium	26·69	43·79	51·45
France	53·82	6·15	8·85
Spain	2·66	1·90	2·77
Portugal	6·56	7·00	6·17

Countries.	Average Value for 3 years 1920–21 to 1922–23. Rs. Lakhs.	1923–24. Rs. Lakhs.	1924–25. Rs. Lakhs.
Switzerland	3·24	...	...
Italy	29·57	4·91	31·39
Austria	...	4·20	2·29
Other countries	5·51	8·76	45·01
Total, Europe	4,69·99	5,31·18	5,02·00
Asia—			
Persia	1·38	2·95	2·21
Sumatra	52·74	79·90	1,21·82
Java	1,13·51	1,95·02	67·88
Celebes and other Islands	1·35	·19	...
Siam	3·52	4·93	2·93
China, etc.	1,17·53	2,99·27	1,06·30
Japan	2,26·00	3,38·68	5,34·95
Other countries	27·55	3·76	10·19
Total, Asia	5,43·58	9,24·70	8,46·28
Africa—			
Egypt	67·89	74·03	1,56·79
Portuguese East Africa	8·09	14·74	21·38
Madagascar	...	4·06	...
Other countries	·03	·15	...
Total, Africa	76·01	92·98	1,78·17
America—			
United States	12·52	13·11	23·70
Cuba	35·14	76·12	1,32·45
Other countries	5·22	10·33	21·61
Total, America	52·88	99·56	1,77·76
Total, Foreign Countries	11,42·46	16,48·42	17,04·21
GRAND TOTAL, BRITISH AND FOREIGN POSSESSIONS.	28,08·89	32,89·92	34,69·64 /

e shares of the Provinces in India in the combined trade in private merchandise are shown in the annexed comparative table:—

Ports.	Average value for 3 years 1920–21 to 1922–23. Rs. Lakhs.	1923–24. Rs. Lakhs.	1924–25. Rs. Lakhs.
Bengal	18,24·43	16,64·40	17,40·08
Bombay	10,33·64	9,40·97	9,49·74
Madras	7,90·42	8,28·65	9,75·02
Sind	1,01·10	72·70	76·81

PROVINCIAL TRADE.

36. The following table shows the share of the interportal trade in private merchandise of each port in the Province: –

Ports.	Average value for 3 years, 1920–21 to 1922–23.		1923–24.		1924–25.	
	Imports.	Exports.	Imports.	Exports.	Imports.	Exports.
	Rs.	Rs.	Rs.	Rs.	Rs.	Rs.
Rangoon	59,62,593	1,18,77,407	48,49,331	1,31,67,006	46,62,379	1,29,69,730
Moulmein	16,73,815	11,50,787	14,54,177	15,37,127	11,37,823	10,65,589
Mergui	37,15,137	29,85,837	40,56,223	28,00,452	38,97,449	28,85,971
Tavoy	35,87,895	19,66,532	41,96,986	15,70,708	34,27,581	13,17,918
Victoria Point	1,31,166	30,460	1,68,594	37,606	1,64,329	36,296
Akyab	60,51,394	4,96,070	67,09,633	5,33,271	75,05,425	4,45,511
Kyaukpyu	6,60,819	31,248	5,87,286	23,121	4,49,500	21,069
Sandoway	1,75,543	1,04,533	3,84,503	81,431	3,60,306	40,713
Bassein	5,47,262	50,003	4,55,354	74,513	4,98,108	53,344
Total	2,25,05,624	1,86,92,877	2,28,62,087	1,98,25,235	2,21,02,900	1,88,36,141 /

SHIPPING.

37. Shipping.—The following table shows the entries and clearances of vessels engaged in the foreign and coasting trade at the various ports in the Province:—

| — | Average for 3 years 1920–21 to 1922–23. | | | | 1923–24. | |
| | Entered. | | Cleared. | | Entered. | |
	Vessels.	Tons.	Vessels.	Tons.	Vessels.	Tons.
Rangoon—						
Foreign	351	1,002,522	388	1,140,442	384	1,162,280
Coasting	1,328	2,064,142	1,293	1,919,287	1,226	2,321,254
Total	1,679	3,066,664	1,681	3,059,729	1,610	3,483,534
Akyab—						
Foreign	72	31,385	150	47,417	66	30,297
Coasting	1,833	320,088	1,127	288,914	1,728	371,559
Total	1,905	351,473	1,277	336,331	1,794	401,856
Bassein—						
Foreign	11	31,486	28	70,723	17	48,936
Coasting	231	110,317	205	67,093	205	122,073
Total	242	141,803	233	137,816	222	171,009
Moulmein—						
Foreign	35	44,886	20	24,493	40	78,186
Coasting	470	134,565	444	159,345	462	161,531
Total	505	179,451	464	183,838	502	239,717
Minor Ports—						
Foreign	48	14,592	50	14,557	58	26,779

—	Average for 3 years 1920–21 to 1922–23.				1923–24.	
	Entered.		Cleared.		Entered.	
	Vessels.	Tons.	Vessels.	Tons.	Vessels.	Tons.
Coasting	1,094	304,385	1,042	301,707	1,246	509,711
Total	1,142	318,977	1,092	316,26	1,304	536,490
GRAND TOTAL	5,473	4,058,368	4,747	4,033,978	5,432	4,832,606 /
Rangoon—						
Foreign	484	1,474,855	382	1,203,640	478	1,515,489
Coasting	1,113	2,005,493	1,190	2,467,474	1,111	2,181,278
Total	1,597	3,480,348	1,572	3,671,114	1,589	3,696,767
Akyab—						
Foreign	86	56,039	54	45,205	69	27,532
Coasting	1,455	345,387	1,769	384,376	1,584	414,785
Total	1,541	401,426	1,823	429,581	1,653	442,317
Bassein—						
Foreign	36	108,982	28	93,678	39	116,924
Coasting	202	54,866	255	106,704	255	91,202
Total	238	163,848	283	200,382	294	208,126
Moulmein—						
Foreign	13	23,328	36	86,054	14	22,693
Coasting	454	218,821	454	212,565	468	259,033
Total	467	242,149	490	298,619	482	281,726
Minor Ports—						
Foreign	66	36,630	80	49,632	85	52,932
Coasting	1,184	525,692	1,252	527,502	1,152	526,929
Total	1,250	562,322	1,332	577,134	1,237	579,861
GRAND TOTAL	5,093	4,850,093	5,500	5,176,830	5,255	5,208,797

About 71 per cent. of the number and 76 per cent. of the tonnage of vessels entering Rangoon were British or British Indian. The number of Japanese vessels rose from 91 to 109, and of Dutch, Italian and Swedish from 76, 4 and 6 to 81, 15 and 9 respectively. The number of American vessels dropped from 50 to 27 and of German and Norwegian, from 45 and 18 to 29 and 14 respectively.

ANON., *FOREIGN TRADE AND NAVIGATION OF THE PORT OF BANGKOK FOR THE YEARS 1918/9* (1919)

Anon., *Foreign Trade and Navigation of the Port of Bangkok for the Years 1918/9* (Bangkok: Department of Customs, 1919), pp. 114–18.

As discussed in the General Introduction, Siam opened itself up to foreign trade during the reign of Mongkut (1851–68). The following text reveals the extent of this trade in 1918/19, listing the value of imports/exports with Siam's trading partners, passenger traffic and the nationality and tonnage of the ships that visited its ports.

Anon., *Foreign Trade and Navigation of the Port of Bangkok for the Years 1918/9* (1919), extract

TABLE V.

Total Value of Imports and Exports from and to each Country.

	Total Imports.		Total Exports.	
	2461 (1918–19)	2462 (1919–20)	2461 (1918–19)	2462 (1919–20)
	Ticals[1]	Ticals	Ticals	Ticals
Alexandria (for orders)	...	...	...	2,479,439
Australia	460,746	296,904	42,340	63,437
Belgium	1,972	58,065	...	2,867,088
British Malay States	37,008	73,885	985,426	4,853,634
British New Guinea	...	...	8,100	...
Burmah	241,144	176,883	24,120	42,504
Canada	52,155	18,095	...	15,989
Ceylon	5,748	3,177	109,993	6,363,891
China	9,270,594	10,348,948	1,527,713	3,790,814
Cuba	1,832	1,012	294,460	...
Denmark	136,663	222,332	203,848	2,637,038
Egypt	38,885	15,911	600	9,000
Formosa	3	200,956	700	1,151
France	626,269	389,201	2,987,300	152,630
Germany	...	35,830	...	39,376
Holland	570,412	530,081	2,624,310	41,273
Hongkong	19,291,288	33,599,154	44,858,718	35,369,660
India	10,666,776	15,175,007	2,619,953	5,382,113
Indo-China	1,099,208	921,249	636,106	828,595
Italy	64,193	41,487	300	251,744
Japan	12,126,781	6,123,316	13,704,400	3,501,942
Koh Kong	249,798	496,600	146,248	149,167
Korea	7,236	10,765	...	...
Mauritius	...	...	1,700	1,082,385
Netherlands India	4,567,454	6,626,749	24,407,613	12,460,486
Penang	35,864	151,287	425,844	4,704,955
Philippine Islands	239,381	203,497	307,803	77

Countries	Total Imports.		Total Exports.	
	2461 (1918–19)	2462 (1919–20)	2461 (1918–19)	2462 (1919–20)
	Ticals[1]	Ticals	Ticals	Ticals
Port Said (for Orders)	...	...	452,599	3,580,697
Portugal	...	...	...	1,849,525
Russia	...	329	...	...
Singapore	15,131,245	28,927,369	63,818,613	69,267,653
Spain	4,573	1,607	...	...
Sweden	103,173	288,782	...	1,320,652
Switzerland	255,875	635,964	...	981,305
Union of South Africa	...	1,525	15,620	270,077
United Kingdom	21,114,776	23,703,726	1,385,057	11,980,605
U. S. of America	6,689,469	9,002,765	423,847	643,524
Rice delivered free for use on board	...	...	18,099	41,439
	103,091,917	138,439,074	162,031,430	177,300,959 /

Summary of Shipping.
FOR THE YEARS 2461 (1918–19), AND 2462 (1919–20),

Nationality.	2461 (1918–19).				2462 (1919–20).			
	With Cargo.		In Ballast.		With Cargo.		In Ballast.	
	No.	Tonnage	No.	Tonnage	No.	Tonnage	No.	Tonnage
A.–Nationality and Tonnage of Ships cleared Inwards.								
American	...	...	3	1,605	1	1,373	3	4,604
British	175	158,698	44	52,250	193	186,450	47	74,308
Chinese	30	26,408	52	49,043	...	...	...	...
Danish	2	566	1	283	12	17,504	4	6,322
Dutch	34	38,517	34	56,131	19	13,128	9	16,703
French	26	7,892	2	812	21	9,005	...	...
Japanese	41	38,183	57	61,181	50	51,302	40	44,683
Norwegian	57	52,684	19	16,563	51	44,164	13	10,935
Siamese	214	111,293	35	10,993	167	95,934	8	2,493
Swedish	...	...	...	...	...	...	1	2,482
	579	434,241	247	248,861	514	418,860	125	162,530
Aircraft, British	...	...	...	...	...	...	2	...
B.–Nationality and Tonnage of Ships cleared Outwards.								
American	4	3,879	2	1,645	...	...	2	3,592
British	222	212,595	...	...	238	258,480	2	1,241
Chinese	83	75,719	...	...	...	...	...	...
Danish	4	1,358	...	...	16	23,826	...	...
Dutch	52	89,634	14	3,812	16	26,497	14	4,536
French	27	8,404	1	300	19	5,900	...	...
Japanese	98	99,364	...	...	84	90,733	7	7,088
Norwegian	75	68,489	...	...	63	54,331	2	1,526
Siamese	241	120,163	...	...	179	100,432	2	2,459
Swedish	...	...	...	...	1	2,482	...	...

Nationality.	2461 (1918–19).				2462 (1919–20).			
	With Cargo.		In Ballast.		With Cargo.		In Ballast.	
	No.	Tonnage	No.	Tonnage	No.	Tonnage	No.	Tonnage

C.–Ships Inwards arranged according to Ports from which reported.

From	2461 (1918–19).				2462 (1919–20).			
	With Cargo.		In Ballast.		With Cargo.		In Ballast.	
	No.	Tonnage	No.	Tonnage	No.	Tonnage	No.	Tonnage
British Malay States	...	...	...	...	...	...	5	1,895
	...	...	...	...	1	649	4	5,970
	38	45,034	1	823	43	52,073	1	1,253
	...	...	...	...	...	...	1	2,482
Denmark	...	...	...	...	5	13,225	...	...
	...	...	...	...	...	...	2	5,756
Hongkong	102	108,291	23	32,495	75	82,149	8	18,098
	11	7,209	4	2,598	13	9,483	4	3,164
Indo-China	28	11,424	4	6,630	37	23,712	2	1,579
	4	3,836	6	13,767	...	...	9	19,717
Koh Kong	37	6,159	...	...	35	9,730	...	...
Netherlands India	27	28,119	21	23,257	22	19,671	6	10,173
	...	...	2	2,453	1	726	3	3,325
Philippine Islands	...	...	2	4,627	1	1,373	2	5,358
Singapore	332	224,169	184	162,211	281	206,069	78	83,760
	579	434,241	247	248,861	514	418,860	125	162,530
from United Kingdom	...	...	...	...	...	...	2	... /

D.–Ships Outwards arranged according to Ports for which cleared.

	2461 (1918–1919)).				2462 (1919–1920).			
	With Cargo.		In Ballast.		With Cargo.		In Ballast.	
	No.	Tonnage	No.	Tonnage.	No.	Tonnage.	No.	Tonnage
Australia	...	...	...	...	1	1,235	...	...
Belgium	...	...	...	...	2	5,678	...	...
British Malay States	1	55	...	...	4	5,229	...	...
	1	283	...	...	6	10,087	...	...
	19	22,866	...	...	27	34,240	...	...
Denmark	1	509	...	...	5	15,054	...	...
Formosa	...	...	...	...	1	1,341	...	...
	1	4,921	...	...	...	...	...	...
Holland	1	4,542	...	...	...	...	...	...
Hongkong	189	205,716	2	1,645	119	137,101	...	...
	18	12,687	...	...	30	22,267	...	...
Indo-China	23	6,780	1	300	29	13,387	9	8,49
	18	29,435	...	...	5	6,469	2	2,21
Koh Kong	35	5,826	...	...	37	10,249	...	...
Mauritius	...	...	...	...	1	2,658	...	...
Netherlands India	42	79,260	3	1,699	18	28,870	7	2,170
	...	...	...	...	10	10,060	1	3,131

Nationality.	2461 (1918–19).				2462 (1919–20).			
	With Cargo.		In Ballast.		With Cargo.		In Ballast.	
	No.	Tonnage	No.	Tonnage	No.	Tonnage	No.	Tonnage
Sweden	...	...	...	...	1	2,482	...	...
Union of South Africa	...	...	...	...	...	...	...	...
United Kingdom	...	...	...	...	11	26,044	...	...
U. S. of America	1	1,373	...	...	...	...	...	...
	806	679,605	17	5,757	616	562,681	29	20,442 /

Summary of Passenger Traffic by Sea.
FOR THE YEARS 2461 (1918–19) AND 2462 (1919–20).

From	Year 2461 (1918–19).		Year 2462 (1919–20).	
	Saloon.	Deck.	Saloon.	Deck.
A.–Passengers Arriving in Bangkok.				
Singapore	655	5,280	1,020	3,901
Hongkong	88	13,069	75	15,956
China	159	48,786	88	44,381
Indo-China	99	214	113	1,290
British Malay States	...	...	...	1
Denmark	...	...	7	...
Netherlands India	40	21	...	2
France	...	...	2	...
India	14	...	9	1
Ceylon	...	...	5	...
Koh Kong	28	695	16	623
Philippine Islands	4	...	2	...
	1,087	68,065	1,337	66,155
B.–Passengers departing from Bangkok.				
To	Saloon.	Deck.	Saloon.	Deck.
Singapore	825	4,226	1,093	3,972
Hongkong	284	6,260	171	14,220
China	99	26,475	165	25,146
Indo-China	98	227	87	542
Koh Kong	17	746	60	825
U. S. of America	2	...	...	...
Penang	...	...	2	...
Netherlands India	10	15	...	...
British Malay States	...	...	...	16
India	6	4	10	2
Denmark	...	...	6	...
Ceylon	5	23	...	...
United Kingdom	...	...	...	2
Japan	2	...	10	...

MAITRI (ED.), *SIAM: TREATIES WITH FOREIGN POWERS, 1920–1927* (1928)

P. K. Maitri (ed.), *Siam: Treaties with Foreign Powers, 1920–1927* (Norwood: Thailand Ministry of Foreign Affairs, 1928), pp. 123–49.

In 1917, Siam declared war on Germany largely to gain favour with the British and French governments. After the war, it used its seat at the Versailles Peace Conference to demand the repeal of previous treaties with the US, France and Britian that it believed to be unfair. While the US signed a new concordat in 1920, France and Britain delayed until 1925. The British treaty abrogated all previous agreements between the two countries, granted Siam jurisdictional and scal autonomy and incorporated the treaty of commerse and navigation, reproduced below, which laid down ground-rules for UK–Siam economic relations, and, in particular, for trade. The signing of the two treaties increased the Siam King's popularity with his people, though this gradually dissipated as discontent over his extravagance grew.[1]

---

1. F. B. Sayre, 'The Passing of Extraterritoriality in Siam', *American Journal of International Law*, 22:1 (1928), pp. 70–88. Over 80 per cent of Siam's export trade and 67 per cent of her import trade was with Britain (ibid. p. 85).

P. K. Maitri (ed.), *Siam: Treaties with Foreign Powers, 1920–1927* (1928), extract

TREATY of Commerce and Navigation between Siam and Great Britain. – Signed at London, July 14, 1925. Ratifications exchanged at London, March 30, 1926.

ARTICLE 1

ere shall be between the territories of the two contracting parties reciprocal freedom of commerce and navigation.

e subjects of each of the two contracting parties, upon conforming themselves to the laws and regulations applicable generally to native subjects, shall have liberty freely and securely to come, with their ships and cargoes, to all places and ports in the territories of the other to which subjects of that contracting party are, or may be, permitted to come, and shall enjoy the same rights, privileges, liberties, favours, / immunities and exemptions in matters of commerce and navigation as are, or may be, enjoyed by subjects of that contracting party.

ARTICLE 2

e subjects of either of the two contracting parties shall be entitled to enter, travel and reside in the territories of the other so long as they satisfy and observe the conditions and regulations applicable to the entry, travelling and residence of all foreigners.

ARTICLE 3

e dwellings, warehouses, factories and shops and all other property of the subjects of each of the two contracting parties in the territories of the other, and all premises appertaining thereto, used for purposes of residence or commerce, shall be respected. Except under the conditions and with the forms prescribed by the laws, ordinances and regulations for native subjects or for the subjects or citizens of the most favoured foreign country, no domiciliary visit shall be instituted and no search of any such buildings or premises be carried out, nor shall books, papers or accounts be examined or inspected.

ARTICLE 4

In so far as taxes, rates, customs duties, imposts,[1] fees which are substantially taxes and any other similar charges are concerned, the subjects of each of the two contracting parties in the territories of the other shall enjoy, in respect of their persons, their property, rights and interests, and in respect of their commerce, industry, professions, occupation or any other matter, in every way the same treatment as the subjects of that party or the subjects or citizens of the most favoured foreign country.

ARTICLE 5

With respect to all forestry undertakings, and to searches for minerals (including oil) and extraction (including oil wells), in Siam, British subjects and companies, partnerships and associations established in His Britannic Majesty's territories shall be entitled to treatment not less favourable / than that which is, or may hereafter be, accorded to Siamese subjects or the subjects or citizens of any other foreign country.

ARTICLE 6

The two contracting parties agree that in all matters relating to commercial or industrial pursuits or the exercise of professions or occupations, any privilege, favour or immunity which either of the two contracting parties has actually granted, or may hereafter grant, to the subjects or citizens of any other foreign country shall be extended, simultaneously and unconditionally, without request and without compensation, to the subjects of the other, it being their intention that the pursuit of commerce and industry in the territories of each of the two contracting parties shall be placed in all respects on the footing of the most favoured nation.

ARTICLE 7

The subjects of each of the two contracting parties in the territories of the other shall be at full liberty to acquire and possess every description of property, movable and immovable, which the laws of the other contracting party permit, or shall permit, the subjects or citizens of any other foreign country to acquire and possess. They may dispose of the same by sale, exchange, gift, marriage, testament or in any other manner, or acquire the same by inheritance, under the same conditions as are, or shall be, established with regard to subjects of the other contracting party, or the subjects or citizens of the most favoured foreign country.

They shall not be subjected in any of the cases mentioned in the foregoing paragraph to any taxes, imposts or charges of whatever denomination other or higher than those which are, or shall be, applicable to native subjects, or to the subjects or citizens of the most favoured foreign country.

ey shall also be permitted to export their property and their goods in general, and shall not be subjected in these matters to any other restrictions or to any other higher duties than those to which native subjects of the subjects or citizens of any other foreign country would be liable in similar circumstances. /

In all these matters British subjects shall continue to enjoy in Siam the same rights and, subject to the provisions of articles 4 and 8 of the present treaty, be subject to the same obligations as those which were provided for by article 6 of the Anglo-Siamese Treaty signed at Bangkok on the 10th March, 1909.*

ARTICLE 8

In all that relates to compulsory military service and to the exercise of compulsory judicial, administrative and municipal functions, the subjects of one of the two contracting parties shall not be accorded in the territories of the other less favourable treatment than that which is, or may be, accorded to subjects or citizens of the most favoured foreign country.

British subjects in Siamese territory shall be exempted from all compulsory military service whatsoever whether in the army, navy, air force, national guard or militia. They shall similarly be exempted from all forms of compulsory manual labour (except in cases of sudden and unexpected occurrences involving great public danger, or where Siamese law gives the option of performing such labour in lieu of the payment of taxes) and from the exercise of all compulsory judicial, administrative and municipal functions whatever, as well as from all contributions, whether in money or in kind, imposed as an equivalent for such personal service, and finally from all forced loans, whether in money or in kind, and from all military exactions or contributions. /

It is, however, understood that British subjects shall continue as heretofore to be liable to capitation tax.

ARTICLE 9

Articles produced or manufactured in the territories of one of the two contracting parties, imported into the territories of the other, from whatever place arriving, shall not be subjected to other or higher duties or charges than those

---

*   Article VI of the Anglo-Siamese Treaty of March 10, 1909, is as follows: "British subjects shall enjoy through the whole extent of Siam the rights and privileges enjoyed by the natives of the country, notably, the right of property, the right of residence and travel.

   "They and their property shall be subject to all taxes and services, but these shall not be other or higher than the taxes and services which are or may be imposed by law on Siamese subjects. It is particularly understood that the limitation in the agreement of the 20th September, 1900, by which the taxation of land shall not exceed that on similar land in Lower Burmah, is hereby removed.

   "British subjects in Siam shall be exempt from all military service, either in the army or

paid on the like articles produced or manufactured in any other foreign country. Nor shall any prohibition or restriction be maintained or imposed on the importation of any article, produced or manufactured in the territories of either of the two contracting parties, into the territories of the other, from whatever place arriving, which shall not equally extend to the importation of the like articles produced or manufactured in any other foreign country.

The only exceptions to this general rule shall be in the case of the sanitary or other prohibitions occasioned by the necessity of securing the safety of persons, or the protection of animals or plants against diseases or pests, and of the measures applicable in the territories of either of the two contracting parties with respect to articles enjoying a direct or indirect bounty in the territories of the other contracting party.

ARTICLE 10

The following articles manufactured in any of His Britannic Majesty's territories to which this treaty applies, viz., cotton yarns, threads, fabrics and all other manufactures of cotton, iron and steel and manufactures thereof, and machinery and parts thereof, shall not, on importation into Siam, be subjected to any customs duty in excess of 5 per cent, *ad valorem* during the first ten years after this treaty has come into force.

It is understood that the articles to which this provision applies shall be those included in the groups III (I), III (C) and III (G), in volume I of the Annual Statement of the Trade of the United Kingdom for 1923 compiled in the Statistical Office of the British Cusioms and Excise Department.

It is further understood that in regard to particular classes / of the above-mentioned articles customs duties may be imposed on a specific basis, provided that such specific duties do not in any case exceed in amount the equivalent of 5 per cent, *ad valorem*.

ARTICLE 11

Drawback of the full amount of duty shall be allowed upon the exportation from Siam of all goods previously imported into Siam from His Britannic Majesty's territories which, though landed, have not gone into consumption in Siam, or been subjected there to any process.

Nevertheless, His Britannic Majesty will not claim the advantages of this article in so far as exports of filled gunny bags are concerned, so long as the duty leviable on the importation of gunny bags into Siam from the territories of His Britannic Majesty shall not exceed 1 per cent, *ad valorem*.

ARTICLE 12

As soon as possible and in any case within six months of the coming into force

ARTICLE 13

Any prohibitions or restrictions, whether by the creation or maintenance of a monopoly or otherwise, which are, or may hereafter be, imposed in Siam on the importation, purchase and sale of arms and ammunition shall not be so framed or administered as to prevent British subjects, firms and companies from obtaining adequate supplies of industrial explosives for use in their industries, it being understood that nothing in this article shall preclude the Siamese Government from enforcing such reasonable regulations as may be required in the interests of public safety.

ARTICLE 14

Each of the two contracting parties undertakes to inform the other of its intention to establish any monopoly with a /

ARTICLE 20

Limited liability and other companies, partnerships and associations formed for the purpose of commerce, insurance, finance, industry, transport or any other business, and established in the territories of either party, shall, provided that they have been duly constituted in accordance with the laws in force in such territories, be entitled, in the territories of the other, to exercise their rights and appear in the courts either as plaintiffs or defendants, subject to the laws of such other party.

Each of the two contracting parties undertakes to place no obstacle in the way of such companies, partnerships and associations which may desire to carry on in its territories, whether through the establishment of branches or otherwise, any description of business which the companies, partnerships and associations of any other foreign country are, or may be, permitted to carry on.

Limited liability and other companies, partnerships and associations of either party shall enjoy in the territories of the other treatment in regard to taxation no less favourable than that accorded to the limited liability and other companies, partnerships and associations of that party.

In no case shall the treatment accorded by either of the two contracting parties to companies, partnerships and associations of the other be less favourable in respect of any matter whatever than that accorded to companies, partnerships and associations of the most favoured foreign country.

ARTICLE 21

Each of the two contracting parties shall permit the importation or exportation of all merchandise which may be legally imported or exported, and also the carriage of passengers from or to their respective territories, upon the vessels of the other, and such vessels, their cargoes and passengers shall enjoy the same privileges as, and shall not be subject to any other or higher duties, charges or

ARTICLE 22

In all that regards the stationing, loading and unloading of vessels in the ports, docks, roadsteads and harbours of the territories of the two contracting parties, no privilege or facility shall be granted by either party to vessels of any other foreign country or to national vessels which is not equally granted to vessels of the other party from whatsoever place they may arrive and whatever may be their place of destination.

ARTICLE 23

In regard to duties of tonnage, harbour, pilotage, lighthouse, quarantine or other analogous duties or charges of whatever denomination levied in the name or for the profit of the Government, public functionaries, private individuals, corporations or establishments of any kind, the vessels of each of the two contracting parties shall enjoy in the ports of the territories of the other treatment at least as favourable as that accorded to national vessels or the vessels of any other foreign country.

ARTICLE 24

The provisions of this treaty relating to the mutual concessions of national treatment in matters of navigation do not apply to the coasting trade.[2] In respect of the coasting trade, however, as also in respect of all other matters of navigation, the subjects and vessels of each of the contracting parties shall enjoy most-favoured-nation treatment in the territories of the other, in addition to any other advantages that may be accorded by this treaty.

The vessels of either contracting party may, nevertheless, proceed from one port to another port in the territories of the other contracting party, either for the purpose of landing the whole or part of their cargoes or passengers brought from abroad, or of taking on board the whole or part of their cargoes or passengers for a foreign destination.

It is also understood that in the event of the coasting trade of either party being exclusively reserved to national vessels, the vessels of the other party, if engaged in trade to or from places not within the limits of the coasting trade so reserved, shall not be prohibited from the carriage between two ports / of the territories of the former party of passengers holding through tickets or merchandise consigned on through bills of lading[3] to or from places not within the above-mentioned limits, and while engaged in such carriage these vessels and their passengers and cargoes shall enjoy the full privileges of this treaty.

ARTICLE 25

Any vessels of either of the two contracting parties which may be compelled by stress of weather or by accident to take shelter in a port of the territories of the

put to sea again, without paying any dues other than such as would be payable in a similar case by a national vessel. In case, however, the master of a merchant vessel should be under the necessity of disposing of a part of his merchandise in order to defray his expenses, he shall be bound to conform to the regulations and s of the place to which he may have come.

If any vessel of one of the two contracting parties shall run aground or be wrecked upon the coasts of the territories of the other, such vessel and all parts thereof and all furniture and appurtenances[4] belonging thereto, and all goods and merchandise saved therefrom, including any which may have been cast into the sea, or the proceeds thereof, if sold, as well as all papers found on board such stranded or wrecked vessel, shall be given up to the owners of such vessel, goods, merchandise, &c., or to their agents, when claimed by them. If there are no such owners or agents on the spot, then the vessel, goods, merchandise, &c., referred to shall, in so far as they are the property of a subject of the second contracting party, be delivered to the consular officer of that contracting party in whose district the wreck or stranding may have taken place, upon being claimed by him within the period fixed by the laws of that contracting party, and such consular

cer, owners or agents shall pay only the expenses incurred in the preservation of the property, together with the salvage or other expenses which would have been payable in the like case of a wreck of stranding of a national vessel.

e two contracting parties agree, however, that merchandise / saved shall not be subjected to the payment of any customs duty unless cleared for internal consumption.

In the case of a vessel being driven in by stress of weather, run aground or wrecked, the respective consular officer shall, if the owner or master or other agent of the owner is not present, or is present and requires it, be authorized to interpose in order to afford the necessary assistance to his fellow-countrymen.

Article 26
All vessels which, according to British law, are deemed to be British vessels, and all vessels which, according to Siamese law, are deemed to be Siamese vessels, shall, for the purposes of this treaty, be deemed British or Siamese vessels respectively.

Article 27
It shall be free to each of the two contracting parties to appoint consuls-general, consuls, vice-consuls and consular agents to reside in the towns and ports of the territories of the other to which such representatives of any other nation may be admitted by the respective Governments. Such consuls-general, consuls, vice-consuls and consular agents, however, shall not enter upon their functions until

er they shall have been approved and admitted in the usual form by the Government to which they are sent.

The consular officers of one of the two contracting parties shall enjoy in the territories of the other the same official rights, privileges and exemptions as are or may be accorded to similar officers of any other foreign country.

ARTICLE 28

In the case of the death of a subject of one of the two contracting parties in the territories of the other, leaving kin but without leaving at the place of his decease any person entitled by the laws of his country to take charge of and administer the estate, the competent consular officer of the country to which the deceased belonged shall, upon fulfilment of the necessary formalities, be empowered to take custody of and administer the estate in the manner and under / the limitations prescribed by the law of the country in which the property of the deceased is situated.

It is understood that in all that concerns the administration of the estates of deceased persons, any right, privilege, favour or immunity which either contracting party has actually granted, or may hereafter grant, to the consular officers of any other foreign country shall be extended immediately and unconditionally to the consular officers of the other contracting party.

ARTICLE 29

The consular officers of one of the two contracting parties residing in the territories of the other shall receive from the local authorities such assistance as can by law be given to them for the recovery of deserters from the vessels of the former party. Provided that this stipulation shall not apply to subjects of the contracting party from whose local authorities assistance is requested.

ARTICLE 30

The subjects of each of the two contracting parties shall have in the territories of the other the same rights as subjects of that contracting party in regard to patents for inventions, trade-marks, trade names, designs and copyright in literary and artistic works, upon fulfilment of the formalities prescribed by law.

ARTICLE 31

As soon as possible after the preponderating proportion of the imports into Siam is obtained from countries whose subjects or citizens shall have become subject to Siamese law and jurisdiction (even though still enjoying privileges under the right of evocation), the Siamese Government will promulgate and bring into operation laws for the proper regulation of the matters dealt with in article 30 and will also take the necessary measures for the regulation of merchandise marks by which imported products shall be protected from competition./

ARTICLE 32

It is hereby understood and agreed that none of the stipulations of the present treaty by which Siam grants most-favoured-nation treatment is to be interpreted as granting rights, powers, privileges or immunities arising solely by virtue of the existence of rights of exemption from Siamese jurisdiction, judicial, administrative or fiscal, possessed by other foreign countries.

ARTICLE 33

e two contracting parties agree that any dispute that may arise between them as to the proper interpretation or application of any of the provisions of the present treaty shall, at the request of either party, be referred to arbitration, and both parties hereby undertake to accept as binding the arbitral award.

e court of arbitration to which disputes shall be referred shall be the Permanent Court of International Justice at The Hague, unless in any particular case the two contracting parties agree otherwise.

ARTICLE 34

e stipulations of the present treaty shall not be applicable to India or to any of His Britannic Majesty's self-governing dominions, colonies, possessions or protectorates unless notice is given by His Britannic Majesty's representative at Bangkok of the desire of His Britannic Majesty that the said stipulations shall apply to any such territory.

Nevertheless, goods produced or manufactured in India or in any of His Britannic Majesty's self-governing dominions, colonies, possessions or protectorates shall enjoy in Siam complete and unconditional most-favoured-nation treatment so long as goods produced or manufactured in Siam are accorded in India, or such self-governing dominion, colony, possession or protectorate, treatment as favourable as that accorded to goods produced or manufactured in any other foreign country. /

ARTICLE 35

e terms of the preceding article relating to India and to His Britannic Majesty's self-governing dominions, colonies, possessions and protectorates shall apply also to any territory in respect of which a mandate on behalf of the League of Nations has been accepted by His Britannic Majesty.

ARTICLE 36

e provisions of the present treaty which apply to British subjects shall also be deemed to apply to all persons who both enjoy the protection of His Britannic Majesty and are entitled to registration in Siam in accordance with article 6 of the General Treaty signed this day.

ARTICLE 37

The present treaty shall be ratified and the ratifications shall be exchanged at London as soon as possible. It shall come into force on the same day as the General Treaty between the two contracting parties signed this day, and shall be binding during ten years from the date of its coming into force. In case neither of the two contracting parties shall have given notice to the other twelve months before the expiration of the said period of ten years of its intention to terminate the present treaty, it shall remain in force until the expiration of one year from the date on which either of the two contracting parties shall have denounced it.

It is clearly understood that such denunciation shall not have the effect of reviving any of the treaties, conventions, arrangements or agreements abrogated by former treaties or agreements or by article 5 of the General Treaty signed this day.

As regards India or any of His Britannic Majesty's self-governing dominions, colonies, possessions or protectorates, or any territory in respect of which a mandate on behalf of the League of Nations has been accepted by His Britannic Majesty to which the stipulations of the present treaty shall have been made applicable under articles 34 and 35 either of the two contracting parties shall have the right to terminate / it separately on giving twelve months' notice to that effect. Such notice, however, cannot be given so as to take effect before the termination of the period of ten years mentioned in the first paragraph of this article, except in the case of His Britannic Majesty's self-governing dominions (including territories administered by them under mandate) and the colony of Southern Rhodesia, in respect of which notice of termination may be given by either contracting party at any time.

INDUSTRY

By the end of the period, industry was limited to sectors that processed agricultural produce or minerals or used them as raw materials and provided goods/services for plantations/mines and their workforces. In Malaya, the lack of industry was largely due to the high level of cheap, quality European and Japanese imports with which indigenous firms could not compete; from the early 1900s, the rise of the rubber industry, which during upturns attracted entrepreneurial talent and resources and in busts reduced the demand for manufactures; and government apathy. British officials were generally unwilling to take any action that damaged the import of UK goods or threatened indigenous institutions and strongly believed that economic priority should be accorded to primary production, which directly benefitted British industry, and, during the inter-war period, was an important source of foreign exchange. Unfavourable local environments also played a part. Relatively low populations and incomes caused home markets to be small, high Singapore wages and electricity charges increased costs, the labour force was largely uneducated, there was little technical and management knowledge, the financial system was relatively undeveloped, and the Currency Board system magnified downturns by withdrawing cash from the economy and, during upturns, flooded the market with money, inflating production costs. Similar factors hobbled industrial development in Burma, which was additionally damaged by imports of manufactured goods from India, a culture that discouraged the accumulation of wealth and the absence of legally valid wills and the resultant division of property on death.[1]

The Processing of Agricultural Produce

e largest agricultural processing industries were those that milled rubber and rice and canned pineapples. Rubber latex after tapping had to be coagulated through the addition of acetic acid, washed and dried in the open air and milled into sheets of certain sizes and thicknesses. These sheets were then sent to a smoke house, where they were kept for four to five days in temperatures of 50–60°C, after which any blemishes were removed and they were graded accord-

estates undertook all these processes in-house, the smaller Chinese and Malay plantations sold their latex to mills. As the raw rubber could not be transported long distances, these were largely located in nearby villages and towns, though as time passed post-coagulation processes increasingly took place in plants in Singapore and Penang, and, in the inter-war period, largely in Penang. As in the other processing industries, the mills were almost wholly controlled by Chinese entrepreneurs, many of whom also owned plantations and were traders. In Burma, processing occurred along the Tenasserim coast and in the small Twante upland near Rangoon.[2]

Burmese rice was initially processed by the farmers themselves using tools powered by hand, foot or water. The husks of rice were removed through some form of friction or the rice was parboiled, steeped in boiling water and then dried, which made the husk easier to detach and produced grains that had a longer shelf life and did not become sour after cooking and were thus preferred by coolies, who cooked large pots of rice at a time. As production for export rose, mills were established in villages, thereafter besides rivers or railways, which transported the husked grain to the coast, and then in the smaller cities, and particularly in Rangoon, the main export port. Mill numbers grew from one in 1861 to 125 in 1905, 613 in 1930 and 673 in 1940. The smaller units were owned by Burmese, Indian and Chinese entrepreneurs. By 1940, 52.9 per cent of plants were operated by Burmese (346 mills employing 13,733), 15.23 per cent by the Chinese (101 mills with 2,929 employees) and 5.43 per cent by Indians (36 mills employing 18,668 workers). The mills had relatively small overheads, using cheap and efficient milling machinery, generally of German manufacture; good access to labour, the main milling period coinciding with the slack period of the agricultural year; and, because of their size, escaped the attentions of the country's overworked Factory Inspectorate. They also had close relationships with local farmers and could thus obtain good quality rice at low prices; had relatively low transport cost as compared to the larger firms based at the ports, moving the milled rice rather than the heavier unmilled crop to the coast; and, in the case of the Indian millers, had control of the Indian market.

Nonetheless, over time the smaller millers lost market share to Europeans, who in 1940 operated 27.15 per cent of mills (180 mills with 9,728 workers), most of which were located in Rangoon, Moulmein, Akyab, Bassein and Hanthawaddy and were owned by Steel Bros, which processed 75 per cent of the rice bound for Europe, the Anglo-Burma Rice Co., the Ellerman's Arakan Co. and Bulloch Co. Combining milling with the shipment of rice and operating large plants, these firms benefitted from low transaction costs and economies of scale, possessed a practical monopoly of Western markets and, with large capital reserves, could survive downturns in demand. They also rapidly adopted new

rice; in 1921 formed a buying cartel, the Bullinger pool, which allowed them to manipulate the price of rice in their own interests; and, in 1922, persuaded the British Railway Co. to raise freight rates for milled rice above those for unmilled grain, thus increasing the transport costs of up-country mills. Like their Indian and Chinese counterparts, they largely employed contractor recruited Indian workers, cheaper and supposedly more disciplined than the Burmese.[3]

Not all of the rice grown in Burma was processed within the country. Large amounts were shipped to Penang and Singapore, where, along with grain from Siam and French Indo-China, it was processed by Chinese millers, who possessed extensive kin and business networks that allowed them to purchase grain throughout South East Asia. By 1907, there were twelve such mills, six in Penang and six in Singapore, which with government-owned plants at Bagan Serai and Parit Buntar in Krian and at Temerloh in Pahang and a number of smaller up-country commercial plants also processed the harvests of Kedah, Province Wellesley and Perak.[4]

As regards the processing of pineapples, by 1936 Malaya was the world's second largest producer of canned pineapples, after Hawaii, exporting 76,403 tons of cans with a monetary value of $8.686m, 71 per cent of which went to the UK.[5] The industry was again dominated by Chinese entrepreneurs, many of whom owned plantations. By 1907, they had established eighteen factories in Singapore and, as cultivation extended into other states, plants were constructed in Johore and Selangor, which in 1938 were home to six and three factories respectively.[6] The industry had numerous problems. The crop was perishable and the factories had to work at full capacity during the May to July and November to February harvest seasons and then close down during the rest of the year. Growers seemed unable to deliver fruit at the required ripeness and in uniform shapes and sizes. The quality of the canned pineapples was thus low and variable, mechanization impossible and the sector highly labour intensive; canners avoiding the difficulties of workforce recruitment and management through the use of contractors. More significantly, profit margins were low. Growers sought to maximize fruit prices by withholding crops from the market, a strategy that also led to the delivery of overripe pineapples, while the Agency Houses that bought nal product minimized canned prices by playing off one canner against another. Forced to keep costs to a minimum, canners spent little on sanitation with the result that many tins contained putrefied fruit.[7]

Of the other smaller processing sectors, the most important were those that dealt with sugar, vegetable oil and coconuts. Vegetable oil and sugar processing took place in Burma. The extraction of vegetable oils from sessamum and groundnuts was undertaken by farmers in Myingyan, Thayetmyo and Prome, and, in 1940, Consolidated Cotton and Oil Mills Ltd, a subsidiary of Steel Bros,

Sugar refining occurred in an array of small largely Burmese-owned refineries, and, in 1940, in two factories – one at Shamaw, opened in 1926 and owned by Finely Flemming Co., and the other at Zeyawadi, Toungoo, which was established in 1934 by a group of Indian businessmen and employed 800 workers and produced 20,000 tons of sugar pa. Coconut processing, meanwhile, took place in Malaya. Coconut meat was dried in kilns, fuelled by the shells and generally located on the farms and plantations that grew the crop. Oil was extracted in Chinese mills in Singapore, which in 1914 had four plants, the largest capable of producing 130 tons of oil per week, and in Penang, the location of fifteen mills, three operated by steam and twelve by foot.[8]

The Processing of Extractive Goods

The most significant extractive processing industries were saw milling, tin smelting and, in Burma, oil refining. In 1939, Malaya possessed seventy-eight sawmills – thirteen in Singapore, which accounted for 43 per cent of total output, forty-three in the FMS, twenty in the UFMS and two in Penang. Ownership was largely in the hands of Chinese entrepreneurs, except for two European mills, one owned by Malayan Collieries Ltd, which produced pit props, one Indian mill and one Japanese mill. The Chinese sector was dominated by Singapore Steam Sawmills and, from 1913, United Sawmills Ltd, an amalgamation of Singapore mills with an authorized capital of $1m. Logs were purchased from timber concessionaires in Sumatra, Java and the Malay Peninsula, sawn using the latest technology and the resulting planks sold locally or re-exported to Siam, India and Mauritius. Elsewhere, saw milling was well established in Burma and Sarawak. Burmese mills employed almost 13,000 workers in 1940 – 6,000 in Rangoon, 2,000 in Moulmean and the remainder in Lower Chindwin, Yamethin and Toungoo – and were largely operated by the European companies that felled the wood. In the same year, Sarawak was home to sixteen mills, most producing wood for local consumption or export to Brunei and Labuan. Major plants included the Kuching Steam Sawmill (1914), the Vamco mill (1920) in Lawas district and Sarawak Oilfields mill at Bakong. There were also works at Sibu, Rajang, Pulau Selalo and Binatang.[9]

Tin smelting involves the removal from ore of non-tin materials such as iron, arsenic and antimony. The Malayan sector was dominated by two companies, the Straits Trading Co. and the Eastern Trading Co., which gradually supplanted mine smelting and took over the business of the myriad of small Chinese companies that established smelting facilities in mining towns. The Straits Trading Co. was founded in 1886 by James Sword and Herman Muhlinghaus as Sword & Muhlinghaus, and, the following year, became a limited company with a new

from the Chartered Bank of India, Australia and China, acquired from the governments of Selangor and Negri Sembilan the exclusive right to purchase ore in these States and invested in modern smelting technology that recovered a larger proportion of tin than traditional methods and used as fuel coal rather than charcoal, which due to deforestation had become expensive. Ore was bought by company branches established at Gopeng (1889), Batu Gajah (1890) and Lahat (1891) and transported by the Straits Steamship Co. to a reverbatory furnace at Telok Anson, and, when the site proved unsuitable, to a plant at Pulau Brani (1890), South of Singapore, and one at Butterworth (1901). By 1892, the company processed half of the ore from Kinta, in 1903 half of that mined in the FMS, and, by the inter-war period, smelted one third of the world's output, importing ore from the Dutch East Indies, Siam, Burma, Australia and Alaska.[10]

Its success prompted the existing Chinese firms to invest in new technology and amalgamate and attracted American interest in the sector. The foremost Chinese smelterer was Lee Chin Ho (1863–1939), who in 1898 established the Sang Kee smelting works in Penang, which in 1907 were purchased by a new company floated in that year with a share capital of $1.5m. Named the Eastern Smelting Co., it was managed by Hermann Jessen, a former employee of Behn, Meyer & Co., one of the largest tin dealers in the country, had as its directors and shareholders the leading Chinese tin mine owners and proceeded to buy up other Chinese smelting firms. Although it flourished, over time its shares gradually passed into Western hands and it essentially became a European operation.

rst American attempt to enter the industry occurred in 1901 when an American syndicate approached the Governor of the Straits Settlements regarding the erection of a smelter at Province Wellseley. It received permission, but decided to adopt a more ambitious strategy – to construct a large-scale plant at Bayonne, New Jersey, which would smelt tin from Malaya and other tin producing countries. Fearful that the smelter would decimate the Malayan sector, the government in 1903 placed a duty on the export of ore from the FMS to any country other than the Straits Settlements. When it appeared that the syndicate in retaliation would take control of the Straits Trading Co., the government let it be known that it would take a major shareholding in the company if such an attempt was made.[11]

Industries Dependent on Export Goods

In addition to industries that processed export goods, a range of sectors developed that either served the export economy or used some of its produce as raw materials. The most important support industries were electricity generation and engineering. In Malaya, the first electricity generators were purchased in

and Pahang. The generators were small and used a variety of fuels including low grade coal, local wood, charcoal, imported oil and, in Perak and Pahang, water power. As demand rose with the increased use of gravel pumps and dredges, private companies such as Huttenbachs Ltd, began to sell electricity to mines and nearby towns, and, in the Kinta Valley in 1926, local mine owners combined with the local government to set up the Perak River Hydroelectric Power Co. Public generation began in 1904 with the construction of a thermal plant at George Town, Penang. This was followed by a hydroelectric station on a stream twelve miles north-east of Kuala Lumpur (1905), the establishment of oil engine stations at Johore Bahru, Seremban, Alor Star and Malacca, and, from 1924 to 1947, the construction of a power station at Singapore. To co-ordinate generation, in 1926 the FMS Electrical Department was established, which became responsible for main town supply and oversaw generation by State Electricity Departments and the Penang Municipal Authority and the purchase of power from the private sector and the sale of electricity to mines. By 1939, Malaya generated 36.06 kilowatts per 1,000 population, 45 per cent of which in the FMS was produced by hydroelectric stations, 45 per cent by steam turbines and the remainder by diesel generators. Elsewhere in British South East Asia, the industry was well developed only in Burma, where the local government generated 3.69 kw per 1,000 population and supplied power to over a hundred towns.[12]

The Burmese engineering sector was concentrated in Rangoon and Mandalay, where the Burma Railway, the Irrawaddy Flotilla Co. and the Burmah Oil Co. workshops and dockyards employed over 4,500 workers. In Malaya, the industry was dominated by United Engineers (1881), which had plants in Singapore, Ipoh, Penang, Malacca and Seremban and provided a range of services; Thornycroft (Singapore) Ltd, specializing in the marine trade; the Singapore Harbour Board Workshop; and the Central Workshop of the Malayan Railways. There was also a vast network of small workshops and iron and brass foundries owned by Chinese entrepreneurs, many of whom had previously worked for the four dominant companies. Other support sectors were also Chinese controlled. All of the forty-four construction firms in Singapore in 1936 were Chinese owned and the Chinese dominated the barrel making sector and built and repaired almost all of the island's lighters and sea-going barges.[13]

Sectors that used export commodities as raw materials can by split by the type of good used. As regards agricultural produce, coconut and palm oil were the main raw materials of the soap industry. By 1935, there were ten soap factories in Singapore, fifteen in Penang and six in Province Wolseley, all of which were Chinese owned and sold their output on the local market and to China and the Dutch East Indies. Rubber sheet, meanwhile, was the main input in the manufacture by European and Chinese companies of rubber goods. Significant

(1900), a producer of a variety of articles ranging from plugs to tyres and belts, the American Firestone Tyre & Rubber Co., and the Czechoslovakian Bata Shoes Co. The Chinese sector was dominated by the People's Rubber Goods Manufactury, established in 1919 by the plantation owner Teo Eng Hock to produce shoes, soles, heels, corks and tubing; the Nanyang Manufacturing Co., which by 1932 was turning out 5,000 pairs of shoes per day; and Tan Kah Kee & Co. Entering the industry in 1920, the latter firm became the largest rubber manufacturer in South East Asia, producing over two hundred products sold within Malaya and exported to China, the Dutch East Indies, Europe, America and Australia. During the 1930s, the relatively underfunded Chinese industry went into a steep decline; the People's Rubber Goods Manufactury entered bankruptcy in late 1933 and Tan Kah Kee & Co. succumbed a few months later. The early 1930s recession reduced world demand for rubber goods; the sector faced strong competition in the shoe market from Japanese companies, which undercut prices; and the introduction of higher import duties by the new Chinese government decimated Chinese demand – attempts to persuade the new government to regard its goods as Chinese and thus exempt from the new duties ending in failure.[14]

As for extractive goods, teak was used by Chinese, and, to a lesser extent, Malay businesses in the manufacture of clogs, a sector superseded from the turn of the century by that producing rubber shoes, and in the production of traditional furniture such as chairs, tables and alters. A highly skilled trade, involving the creation of complex decorative carving, furniture-making was dominated by Hockchew Chinese, who established family workshops in Singapore from the 1890s, and, from the early twentieth century, were joined by a small number of Japanese practitioners. Tin, meanwhile, was used in the manufacture of cans for the pineapple canning industry, funnels, cups, pails and various bespoke ware. Tinsmiths were mostly to be found in Singapore and the sector was monopolised by Hakka Chinese from the Guangding Province of China, whose firms survived several generations.[15]

Import Substitution and Service Industries

e other significant business sectors were those that produced import substitution goods and provided services. The import substitution industries manufactured bulky articles with low ratios of value to transport costs and that possessed features that could not be easily replicated by Western competitors. Malaya produced fertilizer, earthenware, glass, paints, chemicals, bricks, largely manufactured by the Borneo Co. owned Alexandria Brickworks (1899), and cigarettes, the production of which by the Hsin Min Cigarette Factory (1932) was made possible by the introduction of an import duty on Chinese cigarettes.

(1921) was would up in 1932, fatally damaged by the 1929 collapse in cement prices, and the textile sector was decimated by competition from Japan, and, in the 1930s, from factories established in Hong Kong by Chinese companies seeking to benefit from Imperial Preference.[16] In Burma, the sector was largely concentrated in Rangoon and comprised small factories producing matches, rope, soap, maize starch and cement – the Burma Cement Co., a subsidiary of Steel Bros manufacturing 60,000 tons pa at its works at Thayetmyo. Despite imports of 180m yards of cotton goods in 1913/14, the textile industry survived. By the end of the period, there were around fifty cotton ginneries, employing between 3,500 and 4,000 workers, the majority in Meiktila, Myingyan and Sagaing, and 2,600 cotton weavers, almost 2,000 of whom worked in a factory owned by Steel Bros at Myingyan and an Indian owned works near Rangoon; the remainder operating their own looms at Hanza, Meiktila. There was also a prosperous silk weaving sector, which owed its survival largely to the production of sarongs of a design and colour that catered specifically for the local market.[17]

The most significant service industries were those meeting man's baser instincts through the provision of sex and drugs. According to official statistics, in the mid-1890s, five to six thousand women worked as prostitutes in the Straits Settlements and 1,038 in the FMS; figures that are almost certainly gross underestimates, excluding the countless thousands of females who staffed brothels and worked on a part-time basis. The large numbers of largely male immigrants in the country and the lack of alternative sport and recreation facilities created a huge demand for sex, and, at least initially, the sector was tolerated by the British authorities, confident that it helped to placate a potentially mutinous workforce. The industry was divided by gender and ethnicity. The vast majority of prostitutes were female, the demand for boys was small and largely restricted to a small enclave of Europeans. Of the female sex workers, large numbers were Chinese and Tamil and worked in brothels in towns, mines and plantations, largely owned and operated by Chinese entrepreneurs, where they served respectively a Chinese and an Indian clientele. Other significant ethnic groups were the Japanese, 1,100 of whom in 1897 officially plied their trade in the Straits; Europeans, mainly Jews from Eastern Europe, who met the needs of the European community; and Malays, who served both immigrant and indigenous males and were the preferred escorts of British District Officers and Plantation Managers. Although many had been seduced or kidnapped into the profession, or, in the case of many Chinese prostitutes, sold to pimps by their parents, the majority entered it voluntarily attracted by the relatively high incomes on offer. Like their male counterparts, Indian and Chinese workers signed indenture contracts in return for advances covering the costs of travel to Malaya, and, at the end of their

e sector prospered until the early 1920s, after which it entered a grad-
ual decline owing to a combination of supply and demand factors The British
authorities began to suppress brothels having come under great pressure to do
so from organizations such as the League of Nations, the British Social Hygiene
Council and a host of voluntary associations. It had been discovered that many
women were subjected to deprivation and cruelty, prevented from leaving the
trade by contractors increasing their debts and, despite the registration of brothels and mandatory medical examination, were infected with venereal diseases
that they transmitted to clients, reducing plantation and mine productivity. At
the same time, the demand for paid sex waned. With the westernization of towns
and the establishment of dancehalls, theatres and cinemas, alternate leisure
activities became available. It became commonplace, as the region became more
'civilized', for married European male workers to be accompanied by their wives
and families, and, more importantly, immigration policies changed. The rising
cost of imported labour prompted the government to promote the immigration
of women, who would marry, reproduce and eventually provide a cheaper supply of labour, and the 1930s recession led to the repatriation of large swathes of
immigrant workers.[18]

e distribution of opium was controlled by the government, the sole
importer of the drug. Individuals bid for the right to sell opium in a specified
area (known as a farm) for a given number of years and in return for a monthly
rent, the licence being awarded to the person who proffered the highest tender.
Almost all the bidders were Chinese entrepreneurs involved in mining, plantation agriculture or trade, who financed the purchase of the licence either with
their own funds, or, in the case of densely populated urban farms, with money
subscribed by a syndicate of investors, many of whom had interests in several
farms both in Malaya and in other South East Asian countries. On obtaining
the licence, the entrepreneur purchased the raw opium from the government at
a given price and, after processing, distributed it to a network of retail outlets,
where small quantities were sold on a takeaway basis, or to opium dens (divans),
where the drug was smoked on the premises. To halt unauthorized dealers operating in their districts, a small private security force would also generally be
assembled. Needless to say, the sector was extremely profitable, with holders of
licences selling the opium at several times the cost. Profits and investor returns
were ploughed into other ventures both in Malaya and elsewhere, including
mines, plantations, manufacturing businesses and banks.

Criticisms of the sale of opium first emerged in the 1860s when the temper-
ance movement and medical reformers in Britain and America drew attention
to the growth in opium use, a direct result of the farming system, and its impact
on addicts, many of whom overdosed and bought the drug with income that

ment dismissed these concerns. In 1906, opium contributed 53.3 per cent of the revenues of the Straits Settlements and 10.8 per cent of those of the FMS and it was argued that the halt of its sale would disrupt the indigenous way of life of both smokers and growers, have little impact on consumption, as addicts would obtain supplies illicitly, and, if this was not the case, could trigger worker mutinies. Moreover, many claimed the drug actually improved addicts' health, militating fever, dysentery and malaria, and increased their productivity, enabling them to work longer hours. By the early twentieth century, however, pressure from anti-opium societies had reached such a level that when in 1907 a network of farms operated by a syndicate of investors went bankrupt the government abandoned the farming system and began to sell the drug through public sector-owned shops and divans, arguing that this permitted greater control of consumption. More criticism followed, and, after a 1923 British government investigation into the issue, a range of policies were introduced that discouraged smoking. Opium prices were raised, public smoking regulated and opium den managers forced to sell back to the government opium dross, the material left in pipes after opium had been smoked, which would otherwise have been sold to those who could not afford to smoke the drug.[19]

Note: Information on industry can also be found in the following sources/themes:

Topic	Source	Volume/Theme
Burmese sugar refining	'Bulletin 23. Economic Survey of the Sugarcane Industry in Yamethin District'	Volume 1/Agriculture
Processing of rubber in Malaya	Eric Macfadyen, *Rubber Planting in Malaya*	Volume 1/Agriculture
Processing of coconuts in Malaya	H. L. Coghlan, *Coconut Industry in Malaya*	Volume 1/Agriculture
Malayan saw milling	*Annual Report on Forest Administration in Malaya including Brunei, 1939*	Volume 1/Agriculture
Burmese saw milling	*Burma Teak*	Volume 1/Agriculture
Malayan saw milling	'Proceedings and Report of the Commission Appointed to Inquire into the Cause of the Present Housing Difficulties in Singapore' (paragraphs 57-8)	Volume 3/Human Capital
General industry and retailing in Malaya	W. L. Blythe, *Methods and Conditions of Employment of Chinese Labour in the Federated Malay States*	Volume 3/Human Capital

Notes

1.   W. G. Huff, 'Boom-or-Bust Commodities and Industrialization in Pre-World War

Industry   355

of Malaya under British Administration', *Journal of Southeast Asian Studies*, 5:2 (1974), pp. 199–208, on p. 206; J. H. Drabble, *An Economic History of Malaysia, c. 1800–1990* (London: Macmillan, 2000), p. 136; W. G. Huff, 'Monetization and Financial Development in Southeast Asia before the Second World War', *Economic History Review*, 56:2 (2003), pp. 300–45, on p. 335; W. T. Yuen, 'Chinese Capitalism in Colonial Malaya, 1900–1941' (DPhil. dissertation, University of Hong Kong, 2010), pp. 1–130, on p. **272 [check]**; L. W. Leng, 'The Colonial State and Business: The Policy Environment in Malaya in the Inter-War Years', *Journal of Southeast Asian Studies*, 33:2 (2002), pp. 243–56, on p. 249; O. H. Spate, 'Beginnings of Industrialization in Burma', *Economic Geography*, 17:1 (1941), pp. 75–92, on pp. 87, 90–1.

2. Yuen, 'Chinese Capitalism', pp. 249–51, 254; G. Huff, 'Gateway Cities and Urbanisation in Southeast Asia before World War II', *University of Oxford Discussion Papers in Economic and Social History*, 96 (2012), pp. 1–45, on p. 23; Spate, 'Beginnings', p. 85. By 1925, Singapore had twenty-seven mills and Penang twelve mills (Yuen, 'Chinese Capitalism', p. 251).

3. A. W. King, 'Plantation and Agriculture in Malaya, with Notes on the Trade of Singapore', *Geographical Journal*, 93:2 (1939), pp. 136–48, on p. 141; S. A. Resnick, 'The Decline of Rural Industry Under Export Expansion: A Comparison among Burma, Philippines, and Thailand, 1870–1938', *Journal of Economic History*, 30:1 (1970), pp. 51–73, on p. 57; U. Khln Win, *A Century of Rice Improvement in Burma* (Manilla: International Rice Research Institute, 1991); G. Jones, *Merchants to Multinationals: British Trading Companies in the Nineteenth and Twentieth Centuries* (Oxford: Oxford University Press, 2000), p. 69; A. Fenichel and G. Huff, 'Colonialism and the Economic System of an Independent Burma', *Modern Asian Studies*, 9:3 (1975), pp. 321–35, on p. 325; A. Kaur, 'Indian Labour, Labour Standards, and Workers' Health in Burma and Malaya, 1900–1940', *Modern Asian Studies*, 40:2 (2006), pp. 425–75, on p. 448; Spate, 'Beginnings', pp. 78–84; N. Nishizawa, 'Economic Development of Burma', *Institute of Peace Studies, Hiroshima University, Japan, Research Report*, 16 (1991), pp. 1–155, on p. 133. The Indian mills were located in the Insein district, where 75 per cent of the mills were Indian owned, and along the railway west of the Pegu Yomas and into Tharrawaddy and Prome (Spate, 'Beginnings', pp. 83–4). Steel Brothers' Rangoon mill was the largest in the world (Kaur, 'Indian Labour', p. 447).

4. Yuen, 'Chinese Capitalism', pp. 264, 266; King, 'Plantation and Agriculture', p. 141.

5. Yuen, 'Chinese Capitalism', pp. 279–80. The third and fourth largest producers were Formosa and Australia.

6. By 1929, the largest canner was Tan Kah Kee, who processed 40 per cent of the country's pineapples in four plants. Unfortunately, during the early 1930s recession his extensive business empire crumbled and he was forced to sell three of his factories to Lee Kong Chian, who inherited his chief canner title (ibid., pp. 280–1).

7. Ibid., pp. 279, 280–2.

8. Ibid., p. 269; Spate, 'Beginnings', pp. 85–6; King, 'Plantation and Agriculture', p. 141; S. Thein and T. Kudo, 'Myanmur Sugar SMEs: History, Technology, Location and Government Policy', *Institute of Developing Economics Discussion Paper*, No. 147 (2008), p. 4.

9. Yuen, 'Chinese Capitalism', pp. 161–2, 270–3; Spate, 'Beginnings', p. 88; B. E. Smythies, 'History of Forestry in Sarawak', available online at http://www.happysus.com/pdf/forestry.pdf [accessed 20 December 2013] Nishizawa, 'Economic Development', p. 70. The

10. Yuen, 'Chinese Capitalism', pp. 247, 249; W. Bailey and K. Bhaopichitr, 'How Important Was Silver? Some Evidence on Exchange Rate Fluctuations and Stock Returns in Colonial-Era Asia', *Journal of Business*, 77:1 (2004), pp. 137–73, on p. 147; J. F. Hennart, 'Transaction Costs and the Multinational Enterprise: The Case of Tin', *Business and Economic History*, 16 (1987), pp. 8–9; King, 'Plantation and Agriculture', p. 147.

11. Yuen, 'Chinese Capitalism', p. 249; S. B. Saul, 'The Economic Significance of Constructive Imperialism', *Journal of Economic History*, 17:2 (1957), pp. 173–92, on pp. 184–7.

12. R. F. Kinloch, 'The Growth of Electric Power Production in Malaya', *Annals of the Association of American Geographers*, 56:2 (1966), pp. 221–3; A. Booth, 'The Transition in Open Dualistic Economies in Southeast Asia: Another Look at the Evidence', *XIV International Economic History Congress*, (2006), pp. 1–39, on p. 28; K. M. Kyi et al., *A Vision and A Strategy. Economic Development of Burma* (Stockholm: Olof Palme International Centre, 2000).

13. Spate, 'Beginnings', p. 88; Yuen, 'Chinese Capitalism', pp. 274, 278–9; S. G. Lo-Ang and C. H. Chua (eds), *Vanishing Trades of Singapore* (Singapore: University of Singapore, 1992), pp. 93–7.

14. Yuen, 'Chinese Capitalism', pp. 261–2, 270–1; H. Kuo, 'Chinese Bourgeois Nationalism in Hong Kong and Singapore in the 1930s', *Journal of Contemporary Asia*, 36:3 (2006), pp. 385–405, on pp. 388, 398–9.

15. 'Singapore Infopedia' available online at http://eresources.nlb.gov.sg/infopedia/index. htm [accessed 17 May 2014].

16. Huff, 'Boom-or-Bust', p. 1083; Yuen, 'Chinese Capitalism', pp. 271–2, 286; G. Jones and J. Wale, 'Merchants as Business Groups: British Trading Companies in Asia before 1945', *Business History Review*, 72:3 (1998), pp. 367–408, on p. 380; Kuo, 'Chinese Bourgeois', pp. 396–8; Nishizawa, 'Economic Development', p. 124; Spate, 'Beginnings', pp. 86–8.

17. Yuen, 'Chinese Capitalism', pp. 271, 286; Huff, 'Boom-or-Bust', p. 1083; Jones and Wale, 'Merchants', pp. 377, 380; Kuo, 'Chinese Bourgeois', pp. 12, 14, 17; Resnick, 'The Decline', p. 57.

18. L. Manderson, 'Colonial Desires: Sexuality, Race, and Gender in British Malaya', *Journal of the History of Sexuality*, 7:3 (1997), pp. 372–88, on pp. 374–5, 379, 383, 385–7; J. F. Warren, 'Karayuki-San of Singapore: 1877–1941', *Journal of the Malaysian Branch of the Royal Asiatic Society*, 62:2 (1989), pp. 45–80; H. C. Fischer-Tiné, 'The Greatest Blot on British Rule in the East: The "White Slave Trade" and British Colonial Rule in India ca. 1870–1920', *Leipziger Beiträge zur Universalgeschichte und Vergleichenden Gesellschaftsforschung*, 13:4 (2003), pp. 114–37; C. A. Trocki, 'Opium and the Beginnings of Chinese Capitalism in Southeast Asia', *Journal of Southeast Asian Studies*, 33: (2002), pp. 297–314, on p. 302; S. M. Lee, 'Female Immigrants and Labor in Colonial Malaya: 1860–1947', *International Migration Review*, 23:2 (1989), pp. 309–31, on p. 319; J. F. Warren, 'Prostitution and the Politics of Venereal Disease: Singapore, 1870–98', *Journal of Southeast Asian Studies*, 21:2 (1990), pp. 360–83.

19. A. L. Foster, 'Prohibition as Superiority: Policing Opium in South-East Asia, 1898–1925', *International History Review*, 22:2 (2000), pp. 253–73, on pp. 255–7, 261, 266, 269; Trocki, 'Opium', pp. 1–2, 5–7, 13–16; J. G. Butcher, 'The Demise of the Revenue Farm System in the Federated Malay States', *Modern Asian Studies*, 17:3 (1983), pp. 387–412; J. G. Butcher, *The Rise and Fall of Revenue Farming: Business Elites and the Emergence of the Modern State in Southeast Asia* (Basingstoke: Macmillan, 1993).

WINSTEDT, *MALAY INDUSTRIES.*
PART 1. ARTS AND CRAFTS (1909)

R. Winstedt, *Malay Industries. Part 1. Arts and Crafts* (Federated Malay States, 1909), pp. 8–18, 18–23, 23–6, 27–58.

Here are further extracts from R. Winstedt's book on Malay industries (see also Volume 1). His descriptions of Malay boat building, mat/basket-making and pottery production clearly display the respect held by many Europeans towards the traditional Malay way-of-life and their insistence that it be protected from the 'new economy'. Inevitably, all three sectors were damaged by the import of cheaper and better designed/quality goods from Europe, though all survived.

R. Winstedt, *Malay Industries. Part 1. Arts and Crafts* (1909), extract

BOAT-BUILDING.

[...] For up-stream above the rapids there are used only rafts, made of bamboos each some thirty feet long, lashed with rattan, cut off and fixed square in front and of tapering unequal length behind. Two or three layers of bamboo will be lashed one above the other for heavier burdens or for greater comfort; the even front ends pierced athwart and fastened together by one long wooden peg. Atop and amidship in the better-made rafts will be a platform raised a foot high on shorter lengths of bamboo and protected by a palm-leaf covering. Polers standing in front and astern manipulate long bamboo poles, and paddlers squat in front. In smooth reaches progress is slow; in rapids, however difficult, it is fairly safe – even without offering and invocation that the raftsmen make to the spirit whose narrow rock-bound home of troubled waters is to be invaded, calling upon him to open its maze "like the palm-blossom a-slip from its sheath, like the snake that / unwindeth its coils." Below the rapids, the raft will be sold to folk who have to go far a-forest for bamboo or who welcome a ready-made floating bath-house. For in the smooth lower reaches the raft is supplanted by the dug-out. /

[...]

Folk-tales give us many glimpses of the dangers and difficulties that beset the Malay boat-builder with his primitive beliefs and his primitive tools; how he has to go for days up hill and down dale in search of a tree trunk large enough; how, when at last he discovers some huge father of the forest whose foliage "sweeps the clouds above and the earth below," it is found to be inhabited by hostile jins that before felling can proceed have to be expelled with sprinkling of rice-water, smoke of incense and the assistance of jins in the service of the magician. [...]

/ Anyhow, when a trunk of hard wood of the required length of the boat but much less in diameter than the intended width has been obtained, it is hollowed by means of fire, roughly shaped and planed with an adze. The hull may

its sides and into the hollowed centre is poured water, which gradually swells the inside while the fire contracts the outside, till the width is increased and the sides expand to admit thwarts being placed under projecting ledges (cut along the inside just below the gunwale), so as to prevent the contraction consequent on drying. Sometimes this opening process is further helped by the lashing of timbers transversely below and above the hull, fastening their ends together with rattan and then straining them to serve the purpose of a press by leverage of wooden handles put into the rattan lashing: sometimes the whole business from the very beginning is done with adze alone, the builder considering that the drying of the sap by fire shortens the boat's life: sometimes two boats may be "dug out" of one large trunk, a small within a large, wedges being driven in to effect the separation. "All vessels of the dug-out class," Pitt-Rivers[1] observes in his essay on *Early Modes of Navigation*, "are necessarily long and narrow and very liable to upset; the width being limited by the size of the tree, extension can only be given them by increasing their length. In order to give greater height and width to these boats, planks are sometimes added at the sides and stitched on the body of the canoe by means of strings or cords, composed frequently of the bark or leaves of the tree of which the body is made. /

In proportion as these laced-on gunwales were found to answer the purpose of increasing the stability of the vessel, their number was increased; two such planks were added instead of one, and as the joint between the planks was by this means brought beneath the water-line, means were taken to caulk the seams with leaves, pitch, resin and other substances. Gradually the number of side planks increased and the solid hull diminished, until ultimately it dwindled into a bottom-board or keel at the bottom of the boat, serving as a centre-piece on which the sides of the vessel were built. Still she was without ribs or frame-work; ledges on the sides were carved out of the solid substance of each plank by means of which they were fastened to the ledges of the adjoining plank and the two contiguous ledges served as ribs to strengthen the boat; finally a frame-work of vertical ribs was added to the interior and fastened to the planks by cords. Ultimately the stitching was replaced by wooden pins and the side planks pinned to each other and to the ribs; and these wooden pins in their turn were supplanted by iron nails."

Malay boat-building well illustrates the truth of this sketch, though some of the steps in evolution are no longer commonly to be found. Rattan cords, for instance, have given way to wooden pegs in building strake upon strake, but are still used to stitch on the movable single plank or in-board wash-strake that is employed when it is desired to heighten the freeboard of a small dug-out and increase the carrying capacity of that bamboo grill flooring which is almost parallel with the gunwale. Another such survival is to be found in a common form of wash-strake in sea-going canoes, "formed of a strong / lacing of split bamboo knees brought up from the boat's ribs:" it is light and allows the boat to be easily righted if it has been capsized in a heavy sea. Again, despite the introduction of iron nails, conservatism has clung almost universally to the use of wooden pegs. Mast-stays are of round rattans: and the anchor a fork of wood in which a stone

xed. But to give in detail the building up of the Malay boat. /

First prepare your keel-piece, either dug-out or rarely of the European pattern.

en get ready ribs, knee-pieces and the side planking that is to come immediately above your keel-pieces – garboard strake it is called in nautical phrase; which unlike the upper strakes of planking must at all costs be of hard durable timber. Have by you wooden pegs or nails of all sizes; bark for caulking and a mixture of pitch and resin. Then place your keel-piece on stocks and shore it up straight and level with side props. Fit the ribs, approximately one every two feet apart in boats, one every four in larger vessels; near bow and stern fit a rib consisting of one forked piece of timber, to which the ends of the strakes of side-planking may be pegged fast, or in case of larger boats two or three such forked ribs. Warp the strakes of planking for the curving sides of your boat, fixing them in the required position by means of posts rattan lashings and levers, and lighting fires along them inside: plane off the sooty surface from each plank and cut a projecting ledge along its edge to fit into a similar edge on its neighbour plank – perhaps because / the smooth dug-out is the original model, all real Malay craft are carvel-built as opposed to the clinker type in which planking overlaps in ridges. Bore holes in the ledges for wooden pegs and again in those places where the planks are to be pegged on to the ribs. The ribs must never be as high as the top strake of your side-planking but must be elongated by having knees scarped on or dove-tailed into the side of them. The ends of the strakes are pegged fast to stem and stern pieces of hardwood called the "crocodiles" and outside these are nailed a false stem and stern. The knees that serve to elongate the ribs must all be cut down level. On the top of them in large vessels will be nailed a gunwale of flat planks to form a foot-way for the sailors; in boats merely a light false gunwale or wash-strake of hard wood or *nibong*. Outside the upper strakes, below the gunwale, are nailed two rubbing-strakes the breadth of a "banana." Next, horizontal timbers stretching from stem to stern are nailed to the inside of the ribs, many in larger vessels, in boats one only on each side, to support thwarts and flooring. In sailing vessels thwarts with holes are employed to support the masts. Flooring will stretch from stem to stern, except that in boats a bailing-well will be left amidships and in vessels one amidships and one astern in front of the cabin. One or two plug-holes must be bored to let out water when the boat shall be dragged ashore. Lastly, every join and crevice has to be caulked with oakum and pitch or bark and resin.

[...] The next thing is to launch the hull on the water. It has been business enough to drag the dug-out / keel-piece from its home in forest depths painfully

task has no such superstitious reverence attaching to it as the dragging of the hull down the stand to the water. The magician is again to the fore, sprinkles the boat with rice water and makes incantations and offerings. Folk-tales tell how some barks were only to be launched with one strand of a princess's hair for hawser, others only if seven pregnant women were laid down as rollers, and how the women would come out of the ordeal unscathed! The hull launched, rigging, rudder, mast and top hamper are adjusted. The Malay rudder is clearly derived from the paddle. In river dug-outs, the paddle held "on the quarter" serves for rudder as in a Canadian canoe: in big fishing-boats, a large paddle "slung at the head on a stout upright and held at the neck by a rattan lashing." Most Malay boats are propelled by the paddle, the oar being found only with decked hybrid vessels, and the paddle is handled as in a Canadian canoe; the salmon stroke of Siam, China and the gondolier being alien and practically unused. For boats working up-river, poles are employed.

The sail in the real Malay boat is of the most primitive square type and made of matting. I cannot do better than borrow Mr. Warington Smyth's expert criticism of it. "A boom along the foot of the sail is almost as necessary as the yard which spreads the head of the sail. The Malays, by the simple expedient of tilting the sail forward so as to bring the tack right back to the deck, have long converted this square-cut sail into the most powerful of lifting sails on a wind. The dipping lug is set taut along the luff by a spar / bow-line fitting in a cringle the lower end of which comes to the deck abaft the mast. The yard being too light to stand alone by the wind is invariably controlled by a vang. The unhandiness of the dipping lug in tacking is felt to the full with this sail, owing to the stiffness and weight given to it by the material of which it is made and the boom along the foot; and the operation is such a long one, that the anchor is often thrown over while the manœuvre is gone through with the two big sails . . ." A mast is always tall and light and there are never more than two./

A river-boat, to be propelled by pole and paddle, will be covered in from stem to stern with gracefully curved palm-leaf awning. A sailing boat will have a palm-leaf covered compartment at the stern.

Such in its essential features is the real Malay boat, in origin and in ultimate development a canoe. Mr. Warington Smyth has pointed out a practical reason for the survival of the original dug-out form in the shallow bars which make it impossible for deep-bodied boats to obtain shelter; and in the racing tides and baffling winds, which make imperative a boat to be easily propelled by paddles. "The Malay soon found that a long light craft, having plenty of accomodation along its sides for paddlers, was by far the best adapted to the navigation of these waters, and had the sailing vessel at its mercy nine times out of ten: moreover, the lack of the freeboard suitable for manual propulsion was not a serious danger in a locality

Malay boats, though all essentially of the canoe pattern, have many minute variations and a number of confusing names. Mr. Clifford speaks of a Kelantan river-boat, called the grasshopper's head, and adds that, "needless to say, it resembles anything in the world more closely than it does the head of any known insect." It may be presumption to question the testimony of eyes so experienced as Mr. Clifford's, but I am inclined to wager on the analogy of the universal Malay faculty for descriptive nomenclature that the Kelantan Malay has up his sleeve a species of insect not included in Mr. Clifford's study of entomology. Anyhow, many a Malay boat is named after the style of its figure-head: the "dragon" boat, the "crocodile" barge, the "cock" boat, the "horn-bill".

[...] And of course foreign influences have produced many variations of the real Malay type; influences patent in the very names of the hybrid crafts – "schooner," "pinnace," "cutter," "ketch." India, China, Portugal, Holland, England have all left their mark, occasionally in rudder and transome sterns, often in rig and sails. The rudder pivotting on metal fastenings, a pintle dropping into a gudgeon, though modern and European, has earned the nickname of "loin-cloth", as opposed to the Malay paddle type, which is called the "kicker." "The Malay more than any other oriental," says Mr. Warington Smyth, "has adopted the jib or three-cornered stay-sail. This essentially modern product of Western Europe he has adopted, not only on large traders but on the sea canoe (*kolek*) of Singapore, in which also the old Malay lug has been altogether discarded, especially for racing purposes, in favour of the sprit-sail . . ." And again, "It should be remarked that for some trades involving long voyages and calls at deep-water ports, the advantages of big-bodied craft are fully recognised by the peninsular Malays and that between Singapore and Siamese ports, for instance, fine vessels of two hundred tons built on European lines are frequently to be met with. They are rather nonde-script craft, often with overhanging clipper stems and deck-houses galore. The masts are very light and crooked-grown spars; the rigging and gear aloft make up in quantity what is lacking in quality. They are generally rigged with two nearly equal-sized masts and bowsprit on which from one to three jibs are set. The / main-sail and fore-sail are either Chinese lugs or on the European fore-and-aft plan, the gaff being a standing span controlled by vangs and the sail being set by hauling out along it and taken in by brails to the mast, topsails being used. The sails are of light material, when they are not, as in the case of regular Chinese or Malay lugs, made of matting; and they seldom set very flat." [...]

MAT AND BASKET MAKING.*

Basket and mat making must always have been part of the Malay's daily occupation. His house is made of bamboo, split, dried and wattled, or of wicker-work of palm-leaf stalks. His fishing traps are contrived of strips of split bamboo laced parallel to one another with cane. If he catches an animal in the jungle and desires to bring it home alive, he looks about for a large bamboo, splits it open down to a joint, splays out the split pieces fan-shaped, interlaces them with cane, pops his animal inside, and then laces up the one opening with cane. If he wants to carry bananas to market, he uses a large conical basket slung over the shoulder, of laced parallel canes or woven in open-work, of *bĕmban* and strengthened with cane; and for smaller parcels, he will carry in his hand an open-work *bĕmban* bag with rattan slip-cord to close its mouth. He will hang his plates in a rack of looped cane-work and have a stand of similar workmanship for his cooking-pots. If he were a man of means, he would once carry his parcels in a squat round bas-ket / and wear on his head a cap of closely woven fern-stem, though nowadays he prefers a Gladstone bag and a *topi*. In the rice-field are used open baskets regularly woven of dried strips of leaves of the common screwpine, such as is also employed for the coarsest matting. Malays produce some of the best work of its kind in the whole world, and experts speak enthusiastically of "the infi-nite variety of technical processes and their combinations, including root-work, stem-work and leaf-work; bark-work, bast-work, skin-work and spathe-work; loom-less weaving under many names; coiling in great varieties; besides wind-ing, lacing, braiding, netting knot-work and joiner-work."

[...] "Fine mats" are cited among exports from Johor by Chinese chroni-clers writing three hundred years ago. The task begins in the jungle, whither old women go to cut the green leaves of the screw-pine. They cut bundles of the leaves, bring them home, lop them an even length and strip off the thorns from the spines of the leaves. After that the leaves are dried over an ember fire, split by means of a piece of wood with metal spikes fixed in its end (like a horse-comb) into strips of the breadth required: a hollowed bamboo or piece of wood is drawn firmly down each strip to press out all moisture or the strips are tied together and pounded in a pestle. The strips are folded into short bundles and soaked in water for three days, and after they have been dried a "pretty green-ish-grey white" they are again pressed and polished with a piece of bamboo to prepare them for the plaiting. Then the plaiting begins. There are three chief methods of adornment; in mats, open-work and the interweaving of strips dyed / red, black, yellow, which latter produces graceful diaper designs; in mats, and especially in baskets, the plaiting of raised fancy stitches, called the "rice grain," "jasmine bud," the "roof-angle," and so on. For the dyed work, it is noteworthy that the coloured strands are interwoven, and not, as with the exceeding fine Batak work of Sumatra, superadded and threaded into interstices of the plaiting; also that in the north of the Peninsula there prevails, in pouches and other small objects, a debased colour scheme where crude greens, yellows, blues and reds are employed. All coloured work is practiced mainly in jungle hamlets, perhaps

Of the process of the most elaborate "mad weaving" as it is called, Mrs. Bland has written the best and fullest account. "The construction of baskets is complicated," she writes, "and much more tedious than many people imagine. It starts from a star of six strands and this produces twelve strands, for the weaving is done with both ends of every strand used. The whole basket is built up by the continual interweaving and crossing of the inner and outer strands and there is no foundation of warps round which to weave, as in English baskets: it is built up continuously round and round by weaving as in knitting a stocking. To the first star of six strands are added six more, then twelve more and so on till the size required is achieved. A six-sided shape is thus produced. The added strands are woven in always two at each corner, *buku*, or *susoh* as Malays term it, and the full mad stitch[3] is achieved after the second round. The strands that go from left to right form / the weaving strand. The weaving strands over and under which the other strands the other strands are pulled and folded are used for determining the size of the baskets. 'How many stitches?' the Malay will say when you order a basket. The crossing strands and the wrap strand are the only other names possible to mark the distinctive action in 'mad weaving.' When the size is determined on and woven, a piece of split rattan is inserted and the sides of the basket next made, and in the weaving the rattan is completely hidden. The strands of the leaf of the screw-pine are glossy on one side only; so the Malays, by carefully turning their work, arrange that the basket shall be glossy both inside and out. The sides are woven round without any adding... The height achieved, another strip of rattan, covered with *měngkuang*, is inserted: a basket ready for this second rattan has an edge that resembles a cutlet frill. The strands are then all worked back again, that is slipped over their respective duplicates till the bottom centre of the basket is reached (when they cross each other for strength and are cut off invisibly): for this tedious process the Malays use an inserter[4] of wood and brass, which resembles very much the prickers used by the American Indians in their basketry. [...]

"The pretty designs are made by twisting the strands between thumb and nger. This produces a raised ornamental twist which is very attractive. The ornamentation starts from single stitches called the 'rice-grains,' and a star of six such stitches called the 'flower of *Minusops lengi*,' and the hexagonal built round that star (by stitches joining the end of the star / together) called the 'bud.' These simple patterns are worked into large and small triangles and diamonds.... The edging round all baskets is called the 'flowery belt.' Lids are made in a similar manner and of the same number of strands as the bottoms, only woven slightly more loosely. [...]

"The women make and sell their baskets in nests of five baskets, each basting into another very nearly – there should only be the difference of two strands between various shapes and forms – square, long, oval, triangular and

ket, but with added strands to bring it to any other required shape. This is an art by itself, and many who can make hexagonal baskets cannot make other shapes; so that the hexagonal are the cheapest, fifty cents extra being asked for the fancy shapes. The long and the square are the most difficult. The women also make a basket in tiers, one on top of another, the lid of the lower basket making also the bottom of the next, and so on. Another shape is a tiered cone. They also make very coarse large ornamented baskets, which are much bought by Europeans for carrying clothes. It takes a month to make a 'nest' of very ordinary weaving, while a fine 'nest' takes from three to four months to complete, and this means daily steady work. For the ordinary hexagonal nests they earn from two dollars and fifty cents to three dollars, and for a fine one from four to five dollars."

Mrs. Bland shows that the industry is in a flourishing condition, that there is no fear of its extinction, but / much of deterioration and hurry in workmanship, owing to increased demand. [...]

Another art allied to *pandan* weaving is that of making dish covers. Sometimes they are actually woven by the "mad-weaving" method. Sometimes leaves of the rough screw-pine are dried, stretched into thin sheets, soaked and cleaned, twisted and sewn together into a conical shape like that of Chinese hats on old tea-caddies – this forms the inside lining of the cover to be made. Then the white inner sheath of bamboo is taken, torn thin, dried and placed across the bottom of a clay pot that has been inverted over embers and heated; having been so warmed, it is rubbed lightly or thoroughly with a bundle of "dragon's blood" according as a dark red or light red colour is required. Other strips of bamboo sheath are stained black. The red and black strips are cut into open-work patterns and stuck over the *mĕngkuang* lining, the background which shows through the open-work patterns being of plain white bamboo sheath or pieces of red, white, green and gilt paper or cloth. The black pieces are cut into straight strips that divide red and white triangular panels. The outer edge is woven *pandan*. This kind of cover is made in the Dindings. [...]

POTTERY.

[...] In place of the use of the potter's wheel, the whole process is done by hand.

Fine stiff clay is procured, dried, pounded, sometimes sifted even, because good clay means few breakages in burning; then mixed with water and kneaded and beaten now and again for several days. In some parts, it is said elephant's dung is mixed with it when cooking-pots are to be made, but as a rule it is left pure. The potter, generally an old woman, takes a lump of kneaded clay, places it on a plantain leaf or a wooden or earthenware plate, works it gradually with her fingers, revolving it in the process into a shape roughly resembling sometimes the base, sometimes the body of the vessel she contemplates making; leaving the upper rim of the section thinned and bent inwards to facilitate a join. When, er a few hours, the first section has hardened a little, another roughly moulded lump is built on to it; and so on, one section being adjusted to the others till the whole is completed. Shaping and welding is done by pressure of the fingers of the hand from the inside of the half-wrought vessel and by patting the outside with a wooden bat and stroking it with a knife-shaped piece of bamboo which is wetted from time to time. Rough edges, caused by the joining of the sections, are trimmed by the bamboo knife. If the vessel is to be round-bottomed, it is left to harden a while, then inverted and the outer circumference of its base pared down with the bamboo knife, after which the potter blows / into it down the mouth till at bottom swells out into the shape of the natural gourd; or instead of blowing she may make a hole in the centre, distend the bottom with her fingers to the required shape, and then close up the hole. The surface of every vessel is burnished by means of a piece of smooth stone or brass. Decoration is effected by welding ribbons of clay on the surface of the vessel to form raised ribs, by tracing lines with the point of the bamboo knife, by impressing simple patterns from carved wooden stamps. After being dried the vessels are burnt in a wide shallow pit, pieces of wood being piled beneath between and on top of them, set on fire and to burn out: a layer of earth is occasionally spread over the wood and the jars. e clay of some districts burns a terra-cotta colour, of others a bluish gray; if a black colour is desired, burnt jars are buried hot in a mass of *padi* husk or smoked over the fireplace. Resin is often employed to glaze the bottom of water-jars. [...]

Technically Malay pottery is poor and negligible, but like most wares that keep simply and closely to natural forms, it can show some graceful shapes; jugs and jars for the most part being modelled on the gourd and the coconut shell. Like so much Malay work, artistically it steals an adventitious charm from its amateurishness, its absence of uniform precision in form and patterning, its escape from monotony of colouring by what laborious ineptitude would condemn for aws of clay and burning. It has been made in all parts of the Peninsula and there are local differences of shape. In Pahang and Negri Sembilan, especially at Kuala Těmběling (which, I am told, is the head-quarters of the art), we find vessels bearing stamps of superior decorative quality, sometimes / spouted and having often *motif* of their form the short arc rather than the rounded almost circular curve. Kedah, that home of several important variations, has been credited with a rather ornamental type of water-jar decorated with running scroll patterns in which swimming fishes appear, of a darker red than the band that serves for background; but as the variation in colouring might lead one to suspect, the jars are actually of Tamil make. There are also water-jars coloured a dull brownish black and stamped deep to look like florid wood-carving; they are said to be in common use at ceremonies in Malacca, but I have been unable to discover the place of

Already the potter's art is merely a survival. Agricultural shows have stimulated native interest, it is true, and there are still kampongs down the Perak river, at Sayong and Pulau Tiga for instance, where one may see old women at work in little palm-thatched sheds under the shade of fruit trees. But alas! their wares are no longer indispensable; the hideous common blue glass decanter is ousting the gourd; Indian hardware has usurped the place of the indigenous clay cooking-pot. As a survival, however, the art may linger, may even flourish in remote districts; it is easy to learn and affords some trivial earnings to old ladies whose fingers are innocent of the superior skill required for knitting in multi-coloured Berlin wool caps and socks for the infant cradled in a tropical clime. /

METAL WORK.

TIN, BRONZE, COPPER AND BRASS.

[...] Tin is used occasionally for inlaying wooden articles like sticks and dagger-hilts. "The design is cut into the wood, care being taken that it is slightly undercut; it is then covered with clay and dried; molten tin is next poured in through a gate which has been left for the purpose; when cold, the clay is removed and the surface of the tin filed up and polished." [...]

All bronze, copper and brass work has a Sanskrit name to its metal, though *gangsa*, the word for bronze, is little known and *tĕmbaga* is applied to all the alloys with the attributes "yellow" and "red" to distinguish them. Articles are cast by the *cire perdue* process, a process obviously developed from casting simply in sand; and the Malay terminology of the art is distinct enough to deserve study. The article to be made is moulded rudely in clay and the clay mould covered with wax of the thickness desired for the metal. This wax layer is, of course, carefully moulded to the shape and thickness of the article to be cast; after which it is coated with alternate layers of fine sand and clay. When the sand and clay has dried, the mould is heated and the wax allowed to pour out through a gate left in the encircling clay. There is then a cavity formed by the melting and outflow of the wax model, a cavity of the exact shape and size of the article to be cast. Into this cavity melted metal is poured through the gate by which the wax has been allowed to flow out. When the mould has cooled, the outer shell is broken and the rough metal article is turned on a lathe to smooth its surface. "The Malay lathe is always a simple affair, and in one form of it the work is made to rotate in alternating directions by means of a cord which is attached to a flexible rod and passes round part of the work on the lathe to a treadle. When the treadle is pressed, the string is pulled and the work rotates / in one sense, while the flexible rod becomes bent; the treadle and cord are then released and the bent rod straightens itself, driving the work in the opposite sense. This appliance has also

we have examples in water-jars, bowls, basins and lamps (the exact counterpart of lamps found in India), are thick and heavy. Some, like trays and large lidded boxes, are thin and patterned with worthless florid realistic representations of butterflies, deer, flowers and birds, out-put for the most part from Palembang, which for centuries has been famous for its ware. Others, again, have petty fretted patterns chiselled or filed, such as may be seen in glass-stands and betel-trays manufactured in Penang and Singapore. Trengganu alone of native states would seem to have manufactured any quantity. [...]

IRON WORK.

[...] A palm-thatched shed, a clay furnace, a charcoal fire, piston bellows, some anvils fixed to wooden logs, a board to fend his bare shins from flying sparks, pincers, hammers, chisels and files; the stock in trade of the Malay blacksmith is ordinary and simple. But "the European cold and hot setts used for cutting pieces of iron are replaced in the Malay smithy by a tool that is simply a cold chisel, but fixed in a long wooden handle from which the chisel projects at right angles, and in use the head of the chisel is struck with a hammer, while the handle merely serves to hold it in place."

Of agricultural tools manufactured, one may infer that the adze is the most ancient. It bears a close resemblance to the celt; shaped like a small spade with a square tang which is inserted at right angles in a socket of hard wood and bound with rattan at the end of a handle, curved, bending back near the blade, about two feet long and encircled round the grip with pieces of light wood. It can serve as adze, axe, chisel or plane. / [...]

GOLD AND SILVER.

All the known styles of Malay gold and silver work are represented in the Penin-
repoussé, filigree, niello, inlay. Of these, *repoussé*[2] is the commonest, most broadly / distributed and employed for most articles. [...] For the process of *repoussé*. The craftsman first melts his gold or silver, as the case may be, in a clay crucible over a charcoal fire till it run fluid, when he adds a resinous substance to clear its colour. He chooses a mould of iron-stone or earthenware approximate in size and shape to the article in the making and pours in the melted metal: having previously oiled the mould so that the metal will not stick. As soon as the metal is cold, he removes it from the mould and gently hammers it on an anvil, large or small according to the size of the article, till the latter is thin and smooth and of the desired shape: for which operation the metal will be softened now and again by being reheated and then plunged into water. Next he fixes the prepared article upside down on a lump of molted rosin, taking care that there are no hollows between the rosin and the metal. For this process he employs a variety of chisels

according to the decoration contemplated. Most of the pattern is wrought thus from the back of the thin metal, but finishing touches are given from the front; and in case of some of the finest work done on thick metal, like the border running round the side of a large heavy bowl for example, only the pattern in highest relief can be wrought from the back, and all niceties have to be chiselled from the outside or front.

CARVALHO, *THE MANUFACTURING INDUSTRIES OF THE BRITISH EMPIRE OVERSEAS. PART 5, NEWFOUNDLAND, WEST INDIES, CEYLON, MALAYA, HONG KONG, SARAWAK, DRUNCI, BORNEO* (1931/2)

H. N. Carvalho, *The Manufacturing Industries of the British Empire Overseas. Part 5, Newfoundland, West Indies, Ceylon, Malaya, Hong Kong, Sarawak, Drunci, Borneo* (London: Erlangers Ltd, 1931/2), pp. 37–43, 47–57.

is book was published by Erlangers Ltd, the forerunner of the investment house Hill Samuel, for businessmen wishing to invest in the Empire. The first extract focuses on Malaya, and, after presenting population, occupation and production data, discusses the manufacturing and processing industries that used local agricultural, mining and forestry produce as raw materials and lists the value and country of origin of the manufactured goods imported into the country. The second extract turns the spotlight on the British protectorates on the island of Borneo (Sarawak, Brunei, British North Borneo and Labuan) and, again, provides trade data, details of customs duties and surveys of the most important economic sectors.

H. N. Carvalho, *The Manufacturing Industries of the British Empire Overseas. Part 5, Newfoundland, West Indies, Ceylon, Malaya, Hong Kong, Sarawak, Drunci, Borneo* (1931/2), extract

BRITISH MALAYA.

[...]

e area and population of these countries are as follows:–

SETTLEMENT OR STATE.	AREA. Sq. Miles.	POPULATION. 1921.	Estimated Jan., 1930.
(1) STRAITS SETTLEMENTS.			
Singapore	308	425,912	596,209
Penang, Province Wellesley and The Dindings	571	304,335	360,621
Malacca	721	153,522	205,820
	1,600	883,769	
(2) FEDERATED MALAY STATES.			
Perak	7,875	599,055	685,680
Selangor	3,195	401,009	489,262
Negri Sembilan	2,572	178,762	218,826
Pahang	14,006	146,064	168,633
	27,648	1,324,890	
(3) UNFEDERATED MALAY STATES.			
Johore	7,678	282,234	344,965
Kedah	3,648	338,558	409,828
Perlis	316	40,087	45,000
Kelantan	5,713	309,300	360,000
Trengganu	6,000	153,765	185,000
	23,355	1,123,944	
TOTAL	S.M. 52,603	3,332,603	4,069,844

[...] Under British administration and protection the trade of the Federated Malay States (as distinct from the Straits Settlements) has increased more than four-fold in the last 25 years. In the same period 639 miles of railway have been opened and 1,254 miles of excellent motor roads. Savings Bank deposits have grown from £600,000 to £4,540,300, agricultural and building land in private occupation has increased from 777,000 acres to 2,615,000 acres, and the average attendance at Malay vernacular and other schools (excluding English) rose from 12,561 to 73,265. [...]

[...] The urban population of the Straits Settlements is estimated to be 60 per cent. of the whole, of the Federated Malay States 23 per cent. and of the Unfederated Malay States 10 per cent. On this basis the urban population of Malaya would be roughly 30 per cent. of the total. The populations of the chief towns in 1930 are estimated roughly as follows:–

Singapore 500,000; Penang 180,000; Kuala Lumpur 100,000; Ipoh 44,000.

OCCUPATIONS.

According to the census of 1921 the occupations of the inhabitants were as under:–

	Straits Settlements.	F.M.S.	Unfederated Malay States.
Fishing	16,400	10,500	25,000
Agriculture	139,500	491,000	495,000
Mining and Quarrying	2,100	75,500	6,500
Industrial	62,000	46,000	34,000
Transport and Communication	69,000	31,000	13,100
Commerce and Finance	88,000	59,800	33,000
Public Administration and Defence	14,100	23,000	7,900
Profession	3,100	6,900	4,500
Sundries	86,000	87,300	19,700 /

PRODUCTION.

The value of the production of Malaya in 1929 may be estimated as under:–

	£
Agricultural products	51,000,000
Forest products	3,560,000
Mining products	16,316,000
Fishery products	4,000,000
Local factories (net output, *i.e.,* gross production less cost of raw materials)	8,000,000
	£82,876,000*

*   The Singapore Dollar is converted at 2s. 4d.

[...]

MANUFACTURING INDUSTRIES.

e main manufacturing industries are those allied to agriculture and mining. Apart from those industries which, as in the case of Ceylon, prepare raw material for export, there is a manufacture of products both for local use and export to adjacent countries, such as soap, boots, bricks, tiles, cement, rubber tyres and shoes, etc., which at present represent a comparatively small annual production, but which in course of time, especially those allied to rubber in which an excellent export business has been built up, should grow into first-class industries.

In the following list an attempt has been made to group together the various manufacturing industries of Malaya and to subdivide them into classes approximately analogous to the sub-division made in the previous monographs.

	INDUSTRY.	ESTABLISHMENT	GROUP.	INDUSTRY.	ESTABLISHMENT
TREATING RAW MATERIAL.	Copra	77	FOODSTUFF	Aerated Waters	29
	Coconut Oil	28		Banana Flour	1
	Atap[1] Depots	107		Cold Storage	6
	Rice Mills	62		Ice Factories	13
	Rubber Plantations	723		Biscuits	4
	Tallow Refinings	21		Pineapple canning	15
	Rubber Manufacturers	14		Sago Works Cigar manufacture	9 1 9
PROCESSES IN STONE.	Cement	2		Sugar refining Sugar boiling	14
		4		Tapioca Factories Fish curing (including	2
	Bricks and Tiles	59			
	Potteries	12		Blachan. Bêche de Mer,[2]	
	Concrete, Lime	1		Dried and Salt Fish) Boots and Shoes	–
	Marble Works	4	TEXTILES AND APPAREL.		3
WORKING IN WOOD.	Dredge Builders	6		Dyers	14
	Charcoal Kilns	14		Rubber shoes	5
	Matches	1		Felt and Velour Hats	1

GROUP.	INDUSTRY.	ESTAB-LISH-MENT	GROUP.	INDUSTRY.	ESTAB-LISH-MENT
	Furniture	8		Embroidery	–
	Rattan Factories	1		Lace	–
	Mat Makers	–	BOOKS AND PRINT-ING.	Printers	46
	Basket Makers	–		Bookbinders Engravers	96
	Wood cases	–		Lithographers	4
METAL AND METAL WORKS.	Iron and Brass Founders and Engineering firms	48			
	Slip Docks	3	DRUGS, SOAP AND CANDLES.	Indigo Makers	0
	Electroplating Works	1		Soap Works	24
	Shipbuilding Yards Motor Engineering	7		Essential Oils	1
		31		Gambier	1
	Smithies	190		Fertilizer Manfacturers	4
	Tin Smelting Works	10		Candle Factories	16
	Brass Works	10			
	Silver Works	–	HEAT, LIGHT AND POWER.	Electric Undertakings	5
	Jewellery	–		Gas Works	3
	Brass and White Metal Works	–	LEATHER	Tanneries	25
	Creeses³ and other Weapons	–		Hide Curing	6

In the case of the following manufactures:– Pottery, Mats, Baskets, Silver work, Jewellery, Brass ware, Creeses, Embroidery, Lace, Wood carving and weaving, no reliable statistics are available as in most cases these are purely native industries, as for instance, the weavers of Sarongs in Trengganu, who are highly skilled and have developed an extensive local market and small export trade.

The following figures are taken from the 1921 census and give an approximate idea of the number of persons engaged in these native Arts and Crafts:–

Brick Makers and Potters 3,172; Basket Makers, 3,834; Wood Carvers 94; Mat Makers, 2,978; Silversmiths 130; Goldsmiths 7,846; Brass Workers 479; Weavers 11,353; Lace Makers 219. /

(1.) AGRICULTURAL PRODUCTS.

RUBBER.

e area under rubber cultivation in Malaya in 1929* was 2,727,000 acres, of which 338,500 acres are in the Straits Settlements, 1,457,400 in the F.M.S., and 931,100 acres in the Unfederated Malay States. In 1929, 580,784 tons, valued at £50,787,800, were exported, but of this 162,109 tons, valued at £9,521,548, represented imports which were re-exported either as transhipment cargo or er processes of handling and repacking in the peninsula. The net production of rubber in Malaya in 1930, allowing for local consumption, was about 442,000 tons, against an estimated World production of 817,800 tons. The extraordinary growth of this industry can be seen from a study of the following table showing the net exports of British Malaya during the last 21 years, together with the corresponding figures for Dutch East Indies and the total world production.

Year	British Malaya. Tons.	Dutch East Indies. Tons.	World Production. Tons.	Year	British Malaya. Tons.	Dutch East Indies. Tons.	World Production. Tons.	Year	British Malaya. Tons.	Dutch East Indies. Tons.	World Production. Tons.
1910	6,500	2,400	94,000	1917	129,000	44,000	267,300	1924	183,000	149,000	428,700
1911	10,800	2,300	93,100	1918	112,000	42,000	221,400	1925	210,000	189,000	518,500
1912	20,000	3,700	112,100	1919	204,000	85,000	398,000	1926	286,000	204,000	621,900
1913	33,600	6,400	118,400	1920	181,000	80,000	353,600	1927	242,000	229,000	607,300
1914	47,000	10,400	121,700	1921	151,000	71,000	300,200	1928	299,000	229,000	656,800
1915	70,200	20,000	166,600	1922	214,000	94,000	399,700	1929	455,000	255,000	861,500
1916	96,000	33,100	210,100	1923	201,000	117,000	406,900	1930	442,700	241,000	817,800

*   The following Table shows the estimated Acreage under Rubber at the 1st January, 1931, and the production for the first seven months of 1931:–

Size of Estate.	Straits Settlements. Acres.	Federated Malay States. Acres.	Unfederated Malay States. Acres.	Total. Acres.	Estimated Production from 1st January, –31st July,1931 Tons.
Estates of 100 Acres and over Estates of	214,147	920,112	680,839	1,815,098	134,707
Less than 100 Acres	126,334	558,398	510,172	1,194,904	111,341

MANUFACTURED RUBBER GOODS.

An industry of increasing importance is being built up in the manufacture of rubber articles such as rubber soles, rubber shoes, rubber tyres, vulcanite goods, solid tyering, rickshaw mats, motor car and hall door mats, rubber floor cloths, waterproof sheeting, hose pipes and tubing, etc. In 1930 there were seven concerns manufacturing these articles on a wholesale scale and many others turning out smaller quantities by way of experiment, whose consumption of rubber was estimated at 751 tons. During the first seven months of 1931 the consumption of local factories had increased to 857 tons.

The value of this industry can be gauged from the following figures:–

	£	£
Export in 1929 of rubber shoes and soles 536,803 doz. Value		407,390
„ „ sundry rubber goods (excluding tyres)		107,762
Local consumption estimated		90,000
		605,152
Less imports rubber shoes and soles	61,694	
rubber sundries	28,573	90,267
Estimated output		£514,885

From these figures it can be seen that the local manufactures have a gross output in excess of half a million pounds of rubber goods, excluding the output of rubber tyres which to-day is only a small article of manufacture. As labour is cheap and Singapore is the central point of distribution for Eastern markets and for Australia and New Zealand, all large and growing consumers of rubber tyres, there seems a possibility of this trade increasing.

RICE.

Is the staple diet of 99 per cent. of the population, but only a third of its requirements is grown in the country. The area under cultivation is 730,000 acres. In 1929, 785,558 tons, valued at £11,137,117, were imported and 233,897 tons, valued at £3,270,330, were exported. The home production, which gives employment to about 500,000 persons, is estimated to be about 275,000 tons. The Government owns two mills, but the bulk of the milling is undertaken by private enterprise, almost entirely Chinese.

COCONUTS.

The total area under coconut cultivation is estimated at 537,000 acres. As in Ceylon, the coconut is an important article of food of the non-European population, but no approximate estimate of the home consumption can be made. In 1929, 231,288 cwts. of nuts, valued at £57,082, were exported. The trade in

to the manufacture of copra and coconut oil. Of Coconut Oil 8,731 tons, valued at £312,770, were exported and 198,638 tons of Copra, valued at £3,841,200, against an import of 86,209 tons, valued at £1,547,566. The value of production of coconut and auxiliary manufactures may be estimated at £4,200,000.

PINEAPPLES.

 e pineapple is extensively grown in Singapore, Johore and Selangor, where since 1925 the area under cultivation has increased from 24,829 acres to 47,500 in 1929. A fairly large quantity of the fruit is consumed locally, but important quantities are canned for export. In 1925, 43.208 tons were shipped, in 1926, 40,634 tons, in 1927, 40,134 tons, in 1928, 46,400 tons and in 1929, 58,692 tons, valued at £1,077,280. There are fifteen canning plants in operation, most of them run by Chinese firms. The tins in which the pineapples are exported are manufactured in the country, to meet which there is a heavy importation of Tin Plates, amounting to 21,276 tons, valued at £456,000, of which the United Kingdom supplied in 1929 87 per cent. and the United States 13 per cent.

OIL PALM.

 e cultivation of oil palm is in its infancy. The first organised effort to introduce this tree, which is indigenous to West Africa, was made about 10 years ago. In 1924, 6,544 acres were under cultivation and yielded 286 tons of palm oil and 87 tons of oil palm kernels. In 1929, 31,709 acres were under cultivation and the yield was 1819 tons of palm oil and 311 tons of oil palm kernels. The Government has reserved 100,000 acres for alienation for the cultivation of this crop. It has been found that under plantation conditions a high quality oil can be produced.

 e introduction of the oil palm into Malaya and its cultivation as a plantation crop may have results, as far as the West African product is concerned, analogous to those of the cultivation of plantation rubber on the wild rubber of Brazil. The oil palm industry, which requires capital and up-to-date machinery, should develop into a most important agricultural manufacturing industry, but at the present time the output is valued at only about £60,000.

TAPIOCA.

Has been for many years a fairly important item of export. About 33,000 acres are now under cultivation. There is an output of manufactured tapioca in the form of Flake, Flour or Pearl, amounting to about 30,000 tons. The net export in 1929 was 26,174 tons, the gross export 32,403 tons, valued at £450,000.

NIPAH.

 e Nipah Palm is a species of considerable interest; it provides not only a leaf from which a valuable roofing material "Atap" is produced but also a fruit, the stalk of which, after special treatment, yields a saccharine liquid containing from 10 per cent. to 20 per cent. of cane sugar. Since 1921 attention has been given to the nipah palm as a plantation crop with a view to the production of alcohol for use as a local motor-car fuel, and of Acetic Acid, of which large quantities are imported for use in the rubber industry. In favourable conditions this palm will fruit throughout the year and yield about 1,000 gallons of alcohol per acre per annum. The value of the manufactured products may be estimated at £250,000 in 1929.

MISCELLANEOUS AGRICULTURAL INDUSTRIES.

Amongst the minor crops, many of which yield fruits which require manufacturing treatment before local sale or export, can be numbered Coffee, Gambier, Derris (Tuba Root), Tea, Nutmeg, Pepper, Kapok, Bananas, Castor Oil, Citronella,[4] Patchouli,[5] Tobacco, Manila and Sisal Hemps, Chaulmoogra,[6] Gutta Percha, etc. The area under these crops may be estimated at approximately 75,000 acres and the annual production at £3,000,000.

(2.) MINING PRODUCTS.

The mineral production of Malaya in 1929 was approximately as under:–

		Value £
Tin		
	69,367 tons.	14,000,000
Coal	661,514 „	926,000
Gold	26,782 ounces.	110,000
Wolfram	251 tons.	17,000
Iron Ore	809,753 tons.	475,000
China Clay	3,000 "	500 000
Granite, Limestone, Laterite, Sandstone	490,000 "	
Phosphates	117,864 "	235,000
Sheelite[7]	276 "	25,000
Sundries	32,000 "	28,000
Total estimated production		£16,316,000

TIN MINING AND SMELTING.

The mining industry in Malaya gives employment to about 107,000 persons, of whom about 98 per cent. are employed in tin mining or in the tin smelting works. The export of tin (mined in Malaya) in 1929 amounted to 69,367 tons– approximately 36 per cent. of the World output.

The exports of tin for the last six years have been as follows:–

	Tons.	Percentage of World Output.
1925	48,141	33.5
1926	47,789	34.3
1927	54,323	35.4
1928	64,616	37.0

e tin ore extracted from mines in Malaya is of a remarkably high grade, averaging 72 per cent. to 73 per cent. purity. Practically every class of alluvial mining practice is used in mining the ore. Open cast mining with truck and rail or worked by hand labour only, gravel pumping with water under or without pressure, hydraulicing in all its forms, dredging, shafting, panning, all these methods are used within a comparatively restricted area. After the tin ore has been won from the mine, it is bagged and sold to a local tin ore buyer, eventually all but about 7 per cent. of the ore, which is locally smelted by the Chinese, comes into the world-renowned smelteries of the Straits Trading Company and the Eastern Smelting Co. in Singapore and Penang, who refine the ore into what is known as "Straits Tin" averaging 99.9 per cent. The tin smelting industry is of the utmost importance to Malaya: not only do these two big works smelt practically the whole of the output of the country but they attract an enormous amount of tin ore from other parts of the World.

e following tables show the import of crude tin ore and the total export of ned tin from Malaya during the last five years:–

IMPORTS OF TIN (ORE.*

	1926 Tons.	1927 Tons.	1928 Tons.	1929 Tons.	1930 Tons.
	1,802	2,226	2,307	2,321	1,974
Union of South Africa	1,537	1,808	1,839	1,651	1,032
British East Indies	23,429	27,157	28,798	29,963	26,943
	9,706	10,335	10,465	13,807	15,628
Other Countries	417	728	980	1,043	1,590
Total tons	36,891	42,254	44,389	48,785	47,167
Total value	£7,103,210	£8,558,900	£7,810,600	£7,328,300	£4,753,600

EXPORTS OF REFINED TIN.

	1926 Tons.	1927 Tons.	1928 Tons.	1929 Tons.	1930 Tons.
United Kingdom	11,101	9,453	12,908	15,392	9,398
United States	44,513	46,370	56,984	57,695	57,894
Europe	14,189	19,771	19,769	20,622	22,361
British Possessions	3,819	4,968	5,311	4,998	4,929
	1,613	1,922	2,401	2,045	1,552
Other Countries	1,099	1,289	1,679	1,272	1,080
Total tons	76,334	83,773	99,052	102,024	97,214
Total value	£21,644,700	£24,099,950	£22,315,900	£21,248,400	£14,440,000

---

*   The imports of tin ore for the first seven months of 1931 have amounted to 26,359 tons,

(3.) FOREST PRODUCTS.

The total area under forest in 1930 was estimated to be 35,145 square miles or 69 per cent. of the total area of the country, of this about 20,000 square miles is merchantable forest land.

SAW MILLS.

The major forest industry is timbering, which gives employment to about 30,000 people. There are 20 saw mills in the Straits Settlements, two at Teluk Anson, in Perak, and one at Kemaman, in Trengganu. At Krambit, in Pahang, there is a wood distillation plant. The estimated value of the raw material used in the mills and their gross output are estimated at £1,460,000 and £2,200,000 respectively.

In 1929 the imports and exports of Timber were as follows:–_

	IMPORTS.		EXPORTS.	
		Value.		Value.
	Tons.	£	Tons.	£
Timber hewn and sawn	172,241	317,912	3,069	13,560
Firewood	97,410	107,723	22,824	26,652
Planks	6,518	35,916	35,235	146,440
Sandal Wood	239	9,300	124	4,380
Teak	7,489	100,930	536	9,584
Other	12,530	25,100	275	2,064
	296,427	£596,881	62,063	£202,680

FURNITURE, BASKETS, MATS AND MATTING.

There are three furniture factories in Singapore, four in Penang and about 420 carpenters' shops throughout the country. The local Rattan furniture is popular and finds a large market. Furniture of all kinds is turned out by the factories and all sorts and conditions of woodwork, clogs, tubs, buckets, brushes and brooms by smaller manufacturers. Basket and Mat making are native industries, the centre of the industry is at Port Dickson. Interesting specimens of the local basket ware may be seen and purchased in London at the office of the Malayan Information Agency, at 57, Charing Cross.

It is difficult to appraise the value of the furniture industry and its subsidiaries. In 1929, £26,815 worth of furniture was exported and £67,100 worth of other wood articles, but the bulk of the trade is local and no approximate estimate can be arrived at. Malayan timbers are used at the railway workshops at Kuala Lumpur, where most of the coaches used on the F.M.S. railway are built. /

IMPORTS OF MANUFACTURED GOODS.

The following table gives particulars of the chief manufactured articles imported into Malaya in 1929, with countries of origin:–

	Imported.	U.K.	COUNTRIES OF ORIGIN. Other Countries.	Re-exported.
	£	%		£
Condensed Milk	1,854,533	8.3	Australia 23.3%; Switzerland 25.1%; Holland 21.8%; Italy 7.2%	246,906
Cigarettes	3,201,800	77.8	China 14.9%; U.S.A. 5%	867,675
Meats, Tinned and Canned	47,171	37.6	Other British Countries 12.9%; Europe 11.9%	10,875
Biscuits	163,775	84.1	Other British Countries 11.0%; Europe 3.6%	144,943
Chocolate and Cocoa	71,560	47.2	Europe 49.9%	6,805
Confectionery	54,700	41.9	Other British Countries 14.3%; Europe 20.7%; U.S.A. 10.5%; Japan 5.3%.	26,000
Extracts of Beef	62,297	75.3	U.S.A. 17%	1,423
Milk, Powder and Preserved	55,960	55.2	Other British Countries 39.6%	4,630
Brandy	411,222	6.9	Europe 93.1%	30,914
Whiskey	208,245	99.8	–	9,744
Beer and Ale	273,588	34.6	Europe 61.4%; Japan 3.8%	22,620
Porter and Stout	337,165	99.8	–	7,547
Manufactured Tobacco	697,940	9.7	Other British Countries 40.5%	206,604
	1,121,880	14.1	Japan 27.6%; Dutch East Indies 26.9%; South Africa 21.8%	3,180*
Cement	917,598	35.3	Europe 44.8%; Japan 10.9%	33,693
Asbestos	117,453	32.3	Europe 67.4	3,493
Crockery and Porcelain	221,990	14.4	Other British Countries 5.4%; Europe 23.8%; Japan 28.4%; Other Foreign Countries 28%	64,165
Glass and Glassware	220,093	20.0	Other British Countries 5.1%; Europe 45.5%; Japan 21.1%; Other Foreign Countries 83%	76,151
Sanitary Ware	63,441	98.7	–	293
	169,267	12.0	Europe 85.2%	3,166
Iron and Steel (all articles)	3,477,340	62.7	Europe 24.8%; U.S.A. 5.6%	474,166
Hollow-ware	315,782	18.1	Europe 55.8%; Japan 14.6%; Other Foreign Countries 11.5%	58,830
Galvanised Iron	376,756	80.7	U.S.A. 17.9%; Japan 0.4%; Others 1%	53,394
Tin Plates	456,422	86.7	U.S.A. 13.3%	49,395
Tubes, Pipes and Fittings	405,332	90.5	Europe 7.9%; Other Countries 1.6%	16,414

	Countries of Origin.			Re-exported.
	Imported. £	U.K. %	Other Countries.	£
Steel Bars, Rods, Angles, Shapes and Sections	281,128	43.4	Europe 56.2%	7,909
Steel Girders, Beams, Joists and Pillars	82,995	82.6	Europe 17.4%	901
Steel Plates and Sheets	98,264	67.7	Europe 24.7%; U.S.A. 7.5%	8,793
Steel Rails	118,621	65.0	Europe 34.6%	5,495
Wire Manufactures	214,113	28.2	Europe 68.5%	21,000
Brass and Brass Ware	161,345	37.4	Other British Countries 17.2%; Europe 20.7%; U.S.A. 1.5%; Other Foreign Countries 18.9%	35,629
Cutlery, Hardware and Implements	601,345	37.6	Europe 33.1%; Other British Countries 7.8%; U.S.A. 15.1%; Japan 1.8%	130,255
Electrical Goods and Apparatus	805,987	64.3	Europe 9.5%; U.S.A. 22%; Other 4.2%	69,435
Machinery (all articles)	2,529,191	63.5	Europe 20.8%; U.S.A. 13.6%	289,988
Cotton Yarns and Manfrs. (all articles)	6,743,453	45.0	Other British Countries 19.0%; Europe 9.2%; Japan 10.1%; Other Foreign Countries 16.1%	190,093
Woollen Goods (all articles)	309,083	56.5	Other British Countries 11.5%; Europe 29.6%; Other Foreign Counties 2.4%	28,090
Silk and Silk Mfrs. (all articles)	552,726	2.7	Other British Countries 5.3%; Europe 7.1%; Japan 38.9%; Others 46.0%	90,170
Art. Silk Piece Goods	550,204	6.2	Other British Countries 1.6%; Europe 9%; Japan 61.8%; Others 21.4%	20,356
Boots and Shoes (Leather)	61,275	72.2	Europe 14.3%	21,741
Haberdashery and Millinery	169,750	34.0	Europe 46.2%; Japan 4.1%	13,125
Hats, Caps and Other Headgear	206,204	20.9	Other British Countries 7.5%; Europe 62.1%; Japan 7.1%	38,515
Underwear	403,650	11.6	Other British Countries 32.8%; Europe 21.9%; Japan 20.3%	109,215
Chemicals	507,960	23.9	Other British Countries 5.2%; Europe 51.3%; U.S.A. 5.2%; Japan 4.8%	82,660

	Imported. £	U.K. %	COUNTRIES OF ORIGIN. Other Countries.	Re-exported. £
Drugs and Medicines	343,980	37.9	Other British Countries 20.7%; Europe 13.2%; U.S.A. 8%; Japan 8.6%; Others 11.6%	118,218
	219,905	76.3	Europe 7.7%; U.S.A. 8.2%; Others 7.8%	23,443
	349,653	76.7	Other British Countries 11.3%; Europe 5.1%; Others 6.9%	71,852
Leather and Leather Mnfrs.	273,142	8.2	Other British Countries 37.2%; Europe 4%; U.S.A. 17.3%; Others 33.3%	241,750
Paper and Paper Ware (all articles)	830,624	35.9	Other British Countries 9.9%; Europe 34.4%; U.S.A. 5.9%; Others 13.9%	100,000
Stationery	202,425	44.5	Other British Countries 10.1%; Europe 15.3%; Others 30.1%	13,168
Motor Cars (passenger)	1,056,097	39.1	Canada 12.4%; Italy 12.6%; Rest of Europe 3.4%; U.S.A. 30.7%	66,677
Motor Cars (Commercial)	281,692	24.3	Canada 32.2%; U.S.A. 43.0%; Others 0.5%	12,385
Vehicles (Parts and Axiles.)	310,747	27.5	Canada 5.8%; Europe 5%; U.S.A. 60.2%	76,140
Tyres (Motor Car, Truck and Cycle).	532,434	25.1	Other British Countries 9.7%; Europe 23.10%; U.S.A. 36.9%	171,023
Cabinet Ware and Furniture	112,765	22.8	Other British Countries 11.4%; Europe 41.6%	26,755
Woodenware (Rubber Cases)	583,480	25.0	Europe 56%; Japan 18.2%	7,080

*   Bunker coal shipped for the use of steamers engaged in foreign trade 563,066 tons valued at £1,030,583. /

[...]

SARAWAK.

[...]

e area of Sarawak is about 50,000 square miles, roughly speaking the size of England.

e total population is variously estimated at between 500,000 and 600,000. Kuching, the capital, was estimated in 1930 to have a population of 25,293 inhabitants.

[...] The inhabitants are almost entirely occupied in fishing, forestry, or agriculture, either as owners of their own plots of land or as labourers on estates. The number of Europeans is limited to a few hundreds, the bulk of the population being made up of Malays, Dyaks, Muruts and Chinese, whose immigration has been consistently encouraged. /

PRODUCTION.

[...] The following table gives a list of exports during the last 3 years:–

FOREST PRODUCE.	1928.	1929.	1930.
	£	£	£
Bees Wax	449	410	372
Birds' Nests	13,828	9,442	6,981
Camphor	125	138	342
Cutch	36,628	47,894	55,838
Damar[8]	16,677	18,200	9,247
Gutta	171,376	199,038	107,518
Illipe Nuts	27,591	181,571	1,637
Malacca Canes	4,982	1,175	2,362
Nipah Sugar and Salt	2,293	2,308	1,015
Rattans	7,229	1,953	3,103
Timber	243	9,617	11,034
Other Articles	718	798	3,015
	£282,139	**£472,544**	**£202,464**
MINERALS.			
Gold	–	4,107	14,866
Benzene	3,158,678	4,118,992	1,030,024
Crude	461,400	232,165	145,091
Kerosene	762,883	399,045	164,804
Liquid Fuel	191,405	548,993	274,305
Solar Oil[9]	–	16,736	70,513
	£4,574,366	**£5,320,038***	**£1,669,603**
PRODUCE OF CULTIVATED LAND AND MANUFACTURES.			
Betel Nuts	2,064	1,909	1,405
Copra	32,648	27,355	28,147
Plantation Rubber	961,025	1,001,000	473,831
Pepper	163,108	210,534	114,146
Sago	130,840	99,215	112,116
Tuba Roots	6,854	9,497	10,989
Other Articles	5,074	4,330	9,483
	£1,301,613	**£1,353,840**	**£750,117**
SEA PRODUCE.			
Fish	38,118	38,088	25,464
Prawns	21,134	5,577	6,574
Turtle Eggs	355	324	143

Other Articles	882	563	1,354
	£60,489	**£44,552**	**£33,535**
SUMMARY.			
Forest Produce	282,139	472,544	202,464
Minerals	4,574,366	5,320,038*	1,699,603
Agriculture and Manufactures	1,301,613	1,353,840	750,117
Sea Produce	60,489	44,552	33,535
Sundry Articles (mostly re-exports)	142,962	195,368	218,670
Exports	**£6,361,569**	**£7,386,342**	**£2,904,389**
Less revaluation of oil		3,339,187*	
		£4,047,155	
Bullion and Coin	41,754	19,916	69,387
Total Exports	**£6,403,323**	**£4,067,071**	**£2,973,776**
Estimated Production for Home Consumption	291,677	291,742	350,000
Estimated Production	**£6,695,000**	**£4,358,813**	**£3,323,776**

* The oil exports of 1929 were revalued in the supplement to the Sarawak Government *Gazette* of 16th May, 1931, where the following values were fixed: Benzene, £1,292,014; Kerosene, £163,741; Liquid Fuel, £322,118; Crude Oil, £178,273; Solar Oil, £20,598, a total of £1,976,744, against the original valuation of £5,315,931, a difference of £3,339,187. /

RUBBER.

[...] In 1910 the export of rubber from Sarawak amounted to only 10 tons, by 1916 the figure had increased to 1,000 tons, by 1919 to 2,200 tons and by 1922 to 3,800 tons. The export figures since that date have been as follows:–

1922	3,800 tons.
1923	5,700 "
1924	6,700 "
1925	9,000 "
1926	10,000 "
1927	11,000 "
1928	11,000 "
1929	11,000 "
1930	10,300 "

e cultivation of rubber has brought increased wealth both to the inhabitants and the State of Sarawak, but the facility with which the wealth was made had a deleterious effect on the agriculture of the country. The native population left the cultivation of the rice fields, was careless in maintaining the quality of the pepper and neglected the staple sago crop.

In 1922 the import of rice amounted to under 5,000 tons, valued at £105,000; by 1925 the import had increased to nearly 20,000 tons, valued at over £300,000,

ber the native population is turning once more to the cultivation of rice and other native products and it is to be hoped that the country will become once more practically self-supporting.

PEPPER.

Pepper has been produced from time immemorial and at the beginning of the nineteenth century Borneo and Sumatra were the chief producing countries of the world. Sarawak is an important producer of both black and white pepper. The plant takes about 2 years to grow, and, while maturing, the flowers appearing on the growing shoots are plucked. At the end of this period the flowers are left to seed. About 10 months after flowering the berries which form are harvested and from this white pepper is produced. Those berries which have dropped to the ground are gathered, treated and marketed as black pepper.

The quantities produced in Sarawak in the last 7 years have been as follows:–

	1924.	1925.	1926.	1927.	1928.	1929.	1930.
Pepper–White	1,172	1,152	777	845	783	1,028	1,299 tons.
Black	170	142	81	101	92	119	273 "

SAGO.

Sarawak is one of the principal sources of the world's supply.
The export during the last 7 years has been as follows:–

1924.	1925.	1926.	1927.	1928.	1929.	1930.
20,721	18,035	15,374	15,629	14,246	11,986	15,395 tons.

CUTCH.

Cutch, the solid extract from Mangrove Bark, is manufactured by the Island Trading Company, who turn out an article of uniform quality with approximately 58 to 60 per cent. of tannin content. The quantities exported have been as follows:–

1924.	1925.	1926.	1927.	1928.	1929.	1930.
3,870	2,487	2,097	660	1,929	2,530	2,498 tons.

OIL.

The striking of oil near the Brunei frontier at Miri in 1910 has been of undoubted benefit to the country. In 1909 the Anglo-Saxon Petroleum Company received a concession from the Rajah to exploit the oil resources of the country. In 1921 they transferred this concession to the Sarawak Oilfields Ltd., a company incorporated in Sarawak, now under the ægis of the Asiatic Petroleum Company. The output of oil has been as under:–

	1923.	1924.	1925.	1926.	1927.	1928.
	Tons.	Tons.	Tons.	Tons.	Tons.	Tons
Benzene	67,592	71,931	91,670	105,875	109,282	70 973
Crude	60,300	132,661	151,907	160,800	214,554	235,035
Kerosene in bulk	47,732	105,145	102,502	82,885	67,887	98,981
Liquid Fuel	325,029	262,327	203,530	332,203	217,735	196,398

e total production in 1929 was 748,194 tons. In 1930 there was a slight reduction, the production being 690,471 tons. /

COAL.

ere is abundance of coal in the country. The mines at Sadong, not far from Kuching, are at present the only producing centres. The Sadong mine supplies local needs and the Brooketon property mostly exports its output. In the Lingga district at Silantek there are large outcrops of coal.

FOREST PRODUCTS.

[...]. The trade in jelutong, gutta-percha, rattans, damar, illipe nuts, nipah palm products, camphor, etc., could all be increased. Excellent timber is to be found in the country, much of which is used for local construction work. Imports in 1930 amounted to only £3,713, against £16,920 in 1929 and £24,699 in 1928; the import of furniture amounted to £2,745 in 1930, £2,838 in 1929 and £2,375 in 1928.

TARIFF.

On the 11th October, 1930, the scale of duties on Imports was amended as follows:–

	£	s.	d.
Brandy, Whisky, Rum and other Spirituous Liquors per doz.			
Reputed quart bottles	1	8	0
„ „ „ „ „ (inferior) „ „ „	2	6	8
Beer, Cider, etc. „ „ „		3	6
Champagne and all Sparkling Wines „ „ „	1	8	0
Claret, Hock, Sherry and all Still Wines „ „ „		11	2
Gin in square bottles per case of 15 bottles	4	4	0
Gin in round stone or glass bottles of similar shape per doz., bottles, large	2	2	0
„ „ „ „ „ per doz., bottles, small	1	1	0
Gin, Old Tom, Dry Gin and similar kinds per doz. reputed quart bottles	1	8	0
Orange Curacoa in stone bottles per doz. bottles, large	2	2	0
„ „ „ per doz. bottles, small	1	1	0
Liqueurs of all kinds per doz. reputed quart bottles	1	8	0
Kerosene Oil in cases per case of 2 tins (5 cents per gallon)			11

	£	s.	d.
Liquid Fuel „			½
Benzene, Petrol, Methylated Spirit, etc. „			2
Salt, Coarse per picul = 133⅓ lbs.		3	9
Salt, Fine „ „		4	8
Tobacco – Chinese per case of 140 bundles	5	14	4
Chinese per case of 200 bundles	6	1	4
Chinese cases of other size by weight in proportion to above		–	
Java per basket of 26 2/3 ozs.	2	6	8
Pepper or "Bad" per 133 1/3 lbs.	2	6	8
Palembang[10] and other kinds „	11	13	4
Tobacco in tins and Cigarettes per pound		2	3
Cigars „		3	6
Sugar per 133 ½ lbs.		2	4
Matches per packet			¾
Fireworks and Crackers „		10%	*ad val.*
†Motor Cars, for private use		20%	„
†Motor Cars, Lorries and other Motor Vehicles, for commercial use		10%	„
†Motor Cycles		10%	„
†Motor Car and Lorry Tyres, Parts and Accessories, for private or commercial use		15%	„
†Marine and Land Engines (Steam and Motor), Boilers, Auxiliaries and Accessories, and Machinery of all descriptions		10%	„
† Marine and Land Engines (Steam and Motor), Boilers, Auxiliaries and Accessories, and Machinery of all		15%	„
Timber and Furniture		10%	„
Swine per head	1	3	4
Guns and other Firearms which may not be imported without an official permit		50%	*ad val.*
		(Max. *£2* 6s. 8d. per gun.)	
Alum[11] per 133 1/3 lbs.	1	15	0
Gypsum			
„	2	6	8
Brass Guns, Lelahs			
„		9	4
Jars (Old) each		11	8
Imitation of Old Jars, and Modern Jars selling at more than 4s. 8d.			
„		2	4

IMPERIAL PREFERENCE.

Where proof is given that imports of those articles which are marked with a † are of British Empire manufacture they are exempted from Import duty. /

IMPORTS.

In 1929 imports amounted to £2,913,970, in 1930 they had decreased by a million pounds to £1,919,869.

e principal imports during the last 2 years have been as follows:–

	1929. £	1930. £
	355,468	312,713
Bullion and Coin	262,521	4,017
Machinery	317,308	167,167
Tobacco, Cigars and Cigarettes	214,916	142,954
Manufactures of Iron and Steel	151,548	176,334
Cotton Cloth	139,920	79,699
Kerosene Oil	80,700	62,137
Cinematograph Films	60,052	43,386
	59,670	45,443
Drugs and Chemicals for manufacturing purposes	48,593	31,154
Sundry Provisions	47,761	34,049
Wines and Spirits	47,305	38,635
Milk, condensed and sterilized	44,038	35,947
Tobacco (Palembang, Java, Sarobok)	36,727	30,729
Bran and other Grains	32,493	18,831
	32,032	18,163
	30,566	24,733
Cotton Clothing	30,209	19,623
Fish, dried and salted	29,175	19,311
Cement	28,365	25,452
Drugs and Medicines	25,926	19,437
Benzene	24,880	21,789
	24,743	19,101
Crockery and Glassware	24,277	14,916
Lubricating Oil	24,195	13,502

	1929. £	1930. £
Timber	16,821	3,714
Biscuits	16,733	10,573
Soap	16,405	13,658
Salt	15,866	14,819
Matches	15,466	13,164
Motor Lorry and Car Accessories	14,939	10,667
Eggs, fresh and salted	13,085	7,253
Tea in bundles	12,711	7,940
Prawn Refuse	12,487	6,893
Paper	11,669	7,906
Vegetables, salted and preserved	11,410	9,084
Boots and Shoes	10,965	7,973
Electrical Goods	10,799	13,152
Motor Lorries and Cars	10,530	12,407
Coffee, Liberian	9,737	6,508
Furniture	9,501	4,743
Firearms	9,458	2,497
Silk and Woollen Cloth	9,121	4,429
New Gunnies	9,010	8,590
Fresh Vegetables	8,990	5,107
Cycles and Motor Cycles and parts	8,895	5,84S
Fish in tins	8,865	4,428
Lard	8,719	5,172
Iron and Steel Bars, Plates, etc.	8,423	9,199

Beans and Peas	23,241	15,833	Fresh Fruit	7,836	5,797
Chinese Tobacco			Brass and Copper		
	23,192	20,422	Ware	7,830	4,258
Twine and Thread	21,133	12,498	Manila Rope	7,719	3,430
Arrack[12]			Corrugated and		
	20,381	9,286	Galvanized Iron	7,554	6,130
Stationery and Books	20,160	10,114			
Vegetable Oil	18,930	16,774	Sundries	267,109	167,653
Paint, Varnish and Tar	17,980	19,704			
Curry Stuff and Sauce	16,912	13,024			

£2,913,970 £1,919,869

The bulk of the imports come from Singapore. In 1929 Malaya contributed £1,057,055 to the imports and £939,171 in 1930.

The trade statistics of Sarawak give no details as to the places of origin of its imports or the destination of its exports, nor is it possible to form any estimate as to these figures. There is no doubt, however, that Malaya is the main channel of trade and that direct import or export to Europe is comparatively rare.

Unfortunately, trade with the United Kingdom is very small. The following figures, taken from the annual statement of the trade of the United Kingdom, 1929, Vol. IV, give particulars of the imports and exports to and from the United Kingdom from 1925 to 1929:–

	Imports from the United Kingdom.	Exports to the United Kingdom.
	£	£
1925	88,824	120,797
1926	117,815	55,172
1927	135,974	23,555
1928	202,934	83,832
1929	145,546	61,071

In 1929 we supplied Chemicals, £1,989; Cotton Yarns and Manufactures, £6,310; Machines, £11,046; Iron and Steel and Manufactures thereof, £28,488; Soap, etc., £4,541; Ships, £18,300.

It can be said that direct trade with the United Kingdom has not been attempted. In view of the competition in cotton goods with Japan it might be useful for Lancashire manufacturers and shippers to study the question of more direct trade with Borneo, even if it means eliminating the Singapore merchant, who, by taking a profit, however small and however well deserved, is adding to the cost of the merchandise and thereby hampering the shippers and manufacturers in their fight for trade. /

BRUNEI.

[...]

e population is about 30,000. The only town of any importance is the capital, Brunei, with about 11,000 inhabitants.

PRODUCTION.

AGRICULTURAL PRODUCTS.–The cultivation of rubber, sago and rice are the main agricultural industries. As in other parts of Borneo, the low price of rubber has forced the native to turn once more to sago and his padi field. The export of rubber in 1930 fell to 870 tons, with a value of £44,092, against shipments of 1,027 tons in 1929, valued at £86,683. The export of sago in 1929 was 400,000 lbs., in 1930 the export was exactly double, in addition to which a largely increased amount was consumed locally.

FOREST PRODUCTS.–Jelutong is the main forest product, but the price is unremunerative. 100 tons were exported in 1928, 78 tons in 1929, and 48 tons in 1930.

INDUSTRIES.

CUTCH is manufactured by the Island Trading Co. Ltd., the export in 1930 amounted to 2,994 tons, valued at £25,676, against 2,085 tons, valued at £21,419, in 1929.

SILVERWARE AND BRASSWARE.–These are two interesting local industries, the skill of the silversmith of Brunei has been well known for many years. A selling centre has been opened in Singapore, where the demand for these products is increasing. The brass gongs of Brunei are local ware of particular interest.

WEAVING.–Large quantities of cotton sarongs are woven locally. The quality and dyeing is good and a small export trade has been started.

OIL.–Oil was struck at Labi, on the Sarawak border, as long ago as 1914, but the results have not as yet been satisfactory. In 1929 a field was prospected and oil struck at Seria in the Belait district.

IMPORTS AND TARIFF.

By the tariff of October, 1929, a preferential tariff of 2½per cent. was granted on British motor vehicles.

The following is a summary of the chief items of tariff:–

2½%	British Motor Cars.
5% *ad val.*	Building and House Material of all kinds; Motor Cars and all mechanically propelled road vehicles (other than British); Chemicals for use in agriculture; Coconut Oil; Copper and Copper Ware; Cordage and Rope; Fancy Goods, including Watches and Clocks, Jewellery and Sporting Goods; Haberdashery; Ready-made Clothing; Boots; Shoes; Hats; Caps; Iron; Tinware; Agricultural Implements; Lamps; Lanterns; Manufactured Rubber Goods; Tinned and Preserved Provisions of all kinds; Milk; Biscuits; Surgical and Optical Instruments.
10% *ad val.*	Chemicals, except for use in agriculture; Cloth; Bunting; Flax; Grass; Fibre or any other mixture thereof; Crockery and Earthenware; Oils; Paints and Printing Material; Silkstuffs; Timber, except house-building material.
25%	Explosives; Gunpowder; Dynamite; Squibs; Crackers.
100%	Foreign Dyestuffs.
Specific	Rifles; Guns; Revolvers, 11/8 each; Cartridges, loaded or empty, 2/4 per 100; Brass and Brassware, ¾d. per cwt.; Matches, 9/4 per tin of 120 packages; Matches for manufacture in Malaya, 2/4 per tin; Petrol, 2/8 per gallon. Brandy, Whisky, Gin, containing not less than 85% proof spirit, 21/- per gal. „ „ „ between 70% and 85% proof spirit, 16/4 per gal. „ „ „ between 40% and 70% proof spirit, 10/6 per gal. „ „ „ less than 40% proof spirit, 8/2 per gal. Manufactured Tobacco (not Chinese or Java), 16 ¾ d. per lb. /

The following is a list of imports for the years 1928, 1929 and 1930:–

	1928.	1929.	1930.
A. – **FOOD, DRINKS AND TOBACCO.**	£	£	£
Rice	27,081	23,298	24,825
Other Grains	1,602	1,396	1,007
Milk	2,209	2,525	3,523
Salt	447	539	538
Sugar	6,739	6,443	5,351
Tobacco	13,587	14,600	14,062
Provisions	12,341	11,600	12,775
Flour	2,959	2,716	2,413
Coconut Oil	2,038	1,772	1,433
Coffee	1,685	1,674	1,382
Spirit	1,981	2,364	2,313
Arrack	48	60	47
B.–**RAW MATERIALS.**			
Petroleum	7,947	7,975	8,700
Timber	1,292	790	764
Fuel Oil	–	–	3,857
C.–**MANUFACTURED ARTICLES.**			
Motor Vehicles	1,245	1,308	5,172
Dyed Cotton Goods	7,974	9,070	10,226

	1928.	1929.	1930.
Chandu	1,986	2,288	2,009
Matches	710	778	692
Miscellaneous	33,151	52,906	133,465
Coin and Bullion	2,198	3,841	30,487
	£161,670	£173,167	£295,915

ere are no statistical records of the countries of origin of imports, but it can be stated that fully 60 per cent. are shipped from Singapore. Imports from the United Kingdom are negligible–£1,033 in 1925; £858 in 1926; £1,882 in 1927; £2,142 in 1928 and £1,550 in 1929.

BRITISH NORTH BORNEO.

[...] The population in 1930 was estimated to be 294,297, an increase of about per cent. since the census of 1921 [...] The chief town is Sandakan, the capital, on the east coast, with a population in 1931 of 17,566 inhabitants, and Jesselton, in the West Coast Residency, with about 4,747 living in the town and 17,614 in the district and suburbs. It may be estimated that under 12 per cent. of the total population is urban.

OCCUPATIONS OF THE PEOPLE.

According to the census of 1921 the occupations of the people were as follows:–

PRODUCTION OF RAW MATERIALS.

Padi Cultivators	57.91% of total population.
Other Cultivators	12.00
Estate Owners and Managers	0.31
Estate Labourers	8.54
Fishermen	4.90
Jungle Produce Collectors	2.44
Forestry and Timber	1.13
Others	1.37
	88.60% /
	Carried forward 88.60%

INDUSTRIAL OCCUPATIONS.

Merchants and Traders	3.22%
Native Industries	1.70
Blacksmiths	0.14
Sawyers and Carpenters	1.07
Boat and Ship Builders	0.23
Others	1.62
	7.98%

PRODUCTION IN 1929 AND 1930.

A fair estimate of production may be arrived at by taking the exports given in the annual reports of the State and the principal crop figures given in the administration reports.

	1929.		1930.	
FOREST PRODUCTS.	£	£	£	£
Exports	388,508		365,353	
Estimated home consumption	70,000		70,000	
		458,508		435,353
MINERAL PRODUCTS.				
Exports	53,771		41,813	
Estimated home consumption	25,000		30,000	
		78,771		71,813
AGRICULTURAL PRODUCE AND MANUFACTURES.				
Exports	825,816		562,412	
Estimated home consumption including native grown rice	347,000		350,000	
		1,172,816		912,412
SEA PRODUCE.				
Exports	65,350		58,330	
Home consumption	*		*	
		65,350		58,330
SUNDRY EXPORTS	27,637			19,423
Estimated total		£1,803,082		£1,497,331

*   No estimate can be made.

[...]

The leading exports in order of value in 1928, 1929 and 1930 were rubber, timber, estate tobacco, copra, coal, dried and salt fish and cutch. If rice be added to this list, we have the main items of production of the country.

AGRICULTURAL PRODUCE.

RUBBER. – British North Borneo entered the field as a grower of plantation rubber in 1905, in 1910 she began with a modest export of 24 tons, but it was not till 1915 that she began to count amongst the world's producers. The exports since that date have been as follows:–

1915–1,050 tons.	1919–3,939 tons.	1923–4,239 tons.	1927–6,602 tons.
1916–1,938 „	1920–4,105 „	1924–4,620 „	1928–6,698 „
1917–2,444 „	1921–3,121 „	1925–5,425 „	1929–7,381 „

e area under cultivation has been as follows:-

1907	3,226 acres.	1925	70,466 acres.
1910	14,755 „	1928	96,037 „
1915	31,046 „	1929	109,000 „
1920	51,865 „	1930	108,303 „

In 1926, with an export of 6,096 tons, the value of rubber was £1,259,625, in 1930 an export of 7,105 tons was sold for only £376,450.

e distribution and destination of the rubber exports are shown in Diagram No. 32.

is the most important crop in the country and gives employment to 57 per cent. of the population. As in other parts where rubber has been cultivated, the native food crops have suffered. The area under cultivation in 1928-1929 was 40,050 acres under wet rice and 36,943 acres under dry rice. The total crop amounted to 10,640,075 gantangs* of dry and 2,308,585 gantangs of wet rice.

e country is by no means self-supporting and has to import about as much again as it grows.

TOBACCO.–The cultivation of tobacco was introduced about fifty years ago and has grown to be an industry of importance. The class of tobacco grown is similar to that cultivated in Sumatra for the outside wrappers of cigars. The industry has gone through many vicissitudes of fortune; at the present moment there is only one important tobacco estate operating. Great Britain and Holland take the bulk of the exports which have been as follows:–

	ACREAGE.	CROP.
1926	1,863	1,134,050 lbs.
1927	1,616	1,202,533 „
1928	1,142	833,200 „
1929	800	641,333 „
1930	706	809,988 „

e value of the crop exported in 1928 and 1929 was £119,344 and £97,842 respectively.

Much tobacco is grown and used locally by the natives, who make their own cigarettes, but they are now falling victims to the taste for cheap cigarettes made of American tobacco and the native industry is declining.

COCONUTS AND COPRA.–The area under cultivation in 1914 was 11,700 acres; by 1930 this figure had grown to 46,527 acres.

e export of copra in the last five years has been as under:–

		£
1926		
	4,776 tons value	90,136
1927	3,184 „ „	54,345
1928	5,915 „ „	100,679
1929	6,283 „ „	91,007
1930	6,300 „ „	72,054

OTHER PRODUCE.–Details of the export of other agricultural products can be seen on Diagram No. 32.

FOREST PRODUCTS.

TIMBER.–The real wealth of the country is in its forests. It is estimated that the area of commercial forests within easy access of the coast is in excess of 2,000,000 acres.

SERIAH or Borneo Cedar is the most widely distributed variety of timber in the country. It is a soft light wood with a reddish tinge and a well-marked grain; it is easily worked and has the characteristic odour of cedar.

KRUIN is a fairly hard wood with a heavy cross grain, dark reddish-brown in colour.

BILLIAN or Borneo Iron Wood is the most sought-after wood in the country owing to its strength and durability. Other well-known woods are the Urat Mata, Borneo Camphor and Selangan Kacha, a widely distributed wood used mostly in the construction of furniture.

In 1914 the Forestry Department was established and has done much to develop this branch of the country's wealth. In 1920 the British Borneo Timber Company was established. It has two sawmills, one a modern band mill at Sandakan. The North Borneo Trading Company, another important timber company, has a sawmill at Sandakan. There are two well-known Chinese firms in the industry, one of which owns an up-to-date electric sawmill.

The quantity and value of timber exported in the last few years have been as follows:–

	EXPORTED.	VALUE. £
1903	650,245 cubic feet	38,530
1908	975,303 „ „	60,847
1913	1,752,634 „ „	101,437
1923	2,134,321 „ „	185,627
1928	2,926,911 „ „	247,268
1929	3,497,539 „ „	291,044
1930	3,525,452 „ „	284,783

About a million cubic feet per annum is retained in the country for home con-

CUTCH, the export of which has been fairly constant up to 1930, when there was a sharp decline both in quantity and value. The export figures are as follows:–

	Tons.	Value.
		£
1926	2,478	34,994
1927	2,260	31,735
1928	2,197	31,503
1929	2,286	32,068
1930	1,633	22,015

BIRDS' NESTS.–The export of the nest of the Swift is an interesting trade. ese nests, the collection of which is apt to be dangerous, are used by the Chinese for making soup; they are formed of a glutinous substance and are built in large caves, generally several hundreds of feet above the ground. In 1928 nests to the value of £14,600 were exported, in 1929 to the value of £15,263, and in 1930 to the value of £10,935.

Full particulars of the forest products of the country can be seen in Diagram No. 32, which shows also the distribution of the timber exports.

IMPORTS.

	Value. 1928.			Value. 1929.			Value. 1930.		
	£	s.	d.	£	s.	d.	£	s.	d.
Aerated Waters	999	9	8	1,079	12	8	930	13	0
Arms and Ammunition	1,854	10	8	2,184	7	0	958	8	4
Brass and Copperware	3,221	12	8	3,025	19	8	2,344	3	8
Building Material and Timber	13,838	8	4	14,135	11	4	7,591	5	4
Cloth, Cotton, Thread, Yarns, etc.	119,352	13	8	127,221	19	4	82,329	4	4
Coal and Coke	5,812	18	4	101	10	0	75	5	0
ee	10,663	11	4	12,082	16	4	7,985	16	8
Boxes, Trunks, etc.	7,378	4	8	5,981	14	8	6,273	3	4
Bean Oil	17,362	4	4	13,589	4	4	9,462	9	8
Earthenware and Glassware	8,359	1	0	8,352	10	4	5,215	2	4
Chemicals and Dyes	6,058	14	8	6,512	4	4	5,776	8	0
Furniture	6,755	9	4	6,237	16	4	4,978	17	4
Explosives (not fireworks)	1,519	11	8	1,095	0	8	745	17	0
Hemp, Rope and Cordage	3,066	16	4	2,687	8	4	2,024	17	4
Hides and Leather and Leather Goods	2,609	14	4	2,594	15	8	1,428	14	0
Fireworks, Crackers, etc.	1,663	4	0	1,502	15	8	918	3	4
Ironware and Metalware (not Brass or Copperware)	57,629	9	8	45,175	11	0	32,206	10	8
Jewellery, Pearls, Watches, Clocks,									

	Value. 1928.			Value. 1929.			Value. 1930.		
	£	s.	d.	£	s.	d.	£	s.	d.
Kerosene Oil	26,056	2	0	28,611	9	0	23,937	8	8
Live Stock	444	17	0	546	7	0	220	10	0
Machinery	9,702	11	8	17,758	6	0	10,705	9	0
Matches	3,856	1	4	3,874	0	8	2,697	13	8
Musical Instruments	2,332	17	4	1,907	19	4	1,401	1	0
Oil, lubricating, etc., not specially classified	5,547	17	0	5,751	4	0	5,160	10	4
Opium	17,575	12	0	27,136	13	4	13,043	6	8
Petrol, Benzene, Gasolene, etc.	14,746	11	0	15,920	6	8	18,694	4	0
Paint and Paint Oils, Tar, Compositions, Polishes, etc.	6,636	18	8	7,907	18	0	5,510	5	8
Perfumery	3,350	13	4	3,867	14	8	2,331	16	4
Provisions, Fruits, Vegetables, etc.	108,492	3	8	97,238	5	8	75,014	18	4
Railway and Telegraph Materials	5,518	13	8	4,752	13	0	2,296	0	0
Rice, Flour and Grain and Paddy	256,861	3	0	233,314	13	4	201,246	19	4
Salt	4,050	4	0	4,248	13	0	3,815	2	4
Spirits and Wines	35,393	3	4	33,967	7	8	26,381	7	4
Stationery and Paper Goods	12,305	3	8	13,382	14	4	11,317	14	4
Sugar	32,711	2	4	30,291	13	8	22,086	19	8
Tea	9,305	6	8	8,444	2	0	7,090	10	8
Vehicles	7,236	19	0	7,471	18	4	3,704	3	4
Tobacco	66,610	0	4	67,475	11	4	54,104	3	4
Treasure (Bullion)	12,794	5	0	8,477	9	4	6,116	12	0
Medicines	18,348	12	8	18,012	1	0	15,533	9	4
Vessels	3,224	15	8	515	18	0	733	19	0
Coconut Oil	749	14	0	344	3	4	193	15	8
Beads, Buttons, Toys, Curios, etc.	4,618	16	8	4,504	3	0	2,822	12	8
Paper Lanterns, Fans and Jossware	2,234	5	8	2,043	1	4	1,389	12	4
Sundries	53,013	4	4	59,825	17	0	53,796	15	0
	£995,411	6	4	£964,340	8	4	£744,728	12	0 /

IMPORTS AND CUSTOMS TARIFF.

BRITISH PREFERENCE.

A preferential rebate of 25 per cent. of the import duty is granted on the following articles, when shown to the satisfaction of the Commissioners of Customs to have been consigned from and manufactured in Great Britain or Northern Ireland or Canada:–

Chemicals and dyes, cloth, clothing, haberdashery, cutlery, earthenware, crockery, porcelain, glassware, machinery and machines, metals, perfumery, timepieces, vehicles, vessels.

Unfortunately, imports from Great Britain are very limited and the British preference of 25 per cent. off the import duty cost the Customs Department only £117 in 1928, £268 in 1929, and £170 in 1930.

GENERAL TARIFF.

e following are the main items of the general tariff:–

FREE.–Aerated waters, bandages, lint, cotton wool, barbed wire, cattle, cement, disinfectants, empty bags and sacks, flour, galvanized iron, iron and steel building frames, expanded metal, asbestos and other manufactured sheetings when imported for building purposes, lamps, books, prepared manures, medicines, photographic materials, pictures, poultry, salt, soap.

5% *ad valorem.*–Building material other than that in the free list, glassware unless specially taxed, leather and paper goods or imitations thereof, unless otherwise specially taxed, provisions, stationery for printing and writing and all kinds of books of account.

10% *ad valorem.*–Beads, buttons, toys, curios, artificial flowers, feathers, umbrellas, looking glasses, combs, tinsel wares and lacquered ware, boxes, portmanteaux and trunks of any material, cloth, clothstuffs, silkstuffs, yarns, thread, cutlery, dyes and chemicals not medicinal, earthenware, crockery, porcelain, explosives other than fireworks, furniture, jewellery, chains, rings, paper lanterns, fans, joss sticks, machinery and machines, metals manufactured or unmanufactured, musical instruments, gramophones, lubricating and engine oil, paints and paint oils, tar, perfumery, timber manufactured or unmanufactured, timepieces, tobacco pipes and smoking articles, vehicles, vessels, goods or other articles chiefly comprised of manufactured timber and manufactured metal, unless otherwise taxed. Any other articles not specified in the list.

SPECIFIC DUTIES.–Coal and coke, Is. 2d. per ton; coffee, Id. per lb.; matches, 2¾ d. per 900 matches; kerosene, Is. 10½d. per 65 lbs.; petrol, 7d. per gallon; tea, Id. per lb.; Chinese tobacco, 11d. per lb.; European tobacco, 2s. 10d., cigarettes, 3s. 6d. per lb.; sparkling wines, 9s. 4d. per gallon; still wines, 4s. 8d. per gallon; spirituous liquors, 14s. per gallon.

LABUAN.

[...] The area of the island is only 30.25 square miles and its population 6,150.

[...] The population in 1921 was 5,956. Labuan imported merchandize in 1928 to the value of £79,995 from the following countries:–United Kingdom

countries £1,269. In 1929 the amount imported was £76,543, of which £3,109 came from the United Kingdom, £47,236 from British North Borneo, £19,625 from Brunei, £6,535 from Sarawak and £38 from other countries.

The exports in 1928 were valued at £192,507, and in 1929 at £200,100, all to British North Borneo, Brunei and Sarawak. Of these figures about £35,000 represent the value of imports retained for local use and £40,000 the value of exports of domestic produce.

JOHNSON, 'PRELIMINARY MEMORANDUM ON CONDITIONS IN PINEAPPLE FACTORIES IN MALAYA' (1936)

W. B. J. Johnson, 'Preliminary Memorandum on Conditions in Pineapple Factories in Malaya', National Archives, CO 273/615/4.

e pineapple industry was first regulated in 1934. The legislation required canning factories to be registered with the Registrar of Imports and Exports, who could refuse or cancel registrations if he deemed equipment or sanitary arrangements to be unacceptable and laid down various regulations regarding workers' clothing and bathing arrangements, water supply, implement cleanliness and refuse disposal. This memorandum was written two years later and describes how factory owners cut costs through inadequate or poor supervision of production lines, failure to adopt post-sterilization cooling systems etc. and the impact of these savings on the final product. It also identifies other reasons for quality failures, including the nature of the piecework system, inefficient working methods and poorly designed cans and suggests ways in which the various failings could be rectified. A Canning Officer when he wrote the report, W. B. J. Johnson in 1936 became a member of the Johore Pineapple Advisory Committee.[1]

1.   W. T. Yuen, 'Chinese Capitalism in Colonial Malaya, 1900–1941' (DPhil. dissertation, University of Hong Kong, 2010), p. 289; *The Straits Times*, 5 June 1936, p. 10.

W. B. J. Johnson, 'Preliminary Memorandum on Conditions in Pineapple Factories in Malaya' (1936)

e general impression I got was that much had been done to make the factories hygienically sound, and large quantities of money spent on the buildings, which appear to be more elaborate than necessary, whereas little or no attention had been paid to the actual process employed for improving the quality of the pack. The extra money spent in improving the appearance of the factories may be justified if pictures of these factories are used to advertise the Malayan pineapples and to help dispel the idea, which is prevalent in England and elsewhere that Malayan canned pines are packed under unhygienic conditions.

2. <u>Fresh Pines.</u> The large percentage of unripe pines being packed was particularly noticeable in all the factories, although this was less noticeable in Lees' No. 3 factory, who I understand grows his own fruit. A system similar to that employed in England might prove successful; each cannery to have an experienced fruit buyer, whose special duty is to see that the factory is kept supplied with ripe and good quality fruit; he would spend his time going round the various pineapple plantations and would give instructions when the fruit was to be picked. Outside of the canneries I noticed a heterogeneous collection of pines some of which had been obviously picked for many days and many very damaged owing to their rough handling on their devious route to the factory.

3. <u>Factory Practice.</u> There seems to be a complete lack of factory supervision. In nearly every factory I visited the Manager was away somewhere, unless it had been specially arranged that he should meet me at the factory. In one case I noticed several cans of Golden Cubes pass through the closing machine barely half full, after closing there is no method of detecting / a half filled can as the

c gravity of the syrup and fruit are fairly similar; these cans will probably be on the English market in two months time and may do a lot of harm; it is reasonable to assume that numbers of badly filled cans pass through daily, this sort of thing is absolutely inexcusable. There should definitely be a factory manager to each factory, a well paid and responsible person, whose duty it is to be on the

ble for any deficiencies in the pack. He would appoint trustworthy supervisors, one for each canning line if necessary, to watch and make certain that no faulty cans passed through. It is essential for a good pack that each can can be relied upon to be exactly similar to every other one packed under the same grade.

4. Preparation. Owing to the varying sizes and shapes of the Malayan pines and also to the cheapness and efficiency of the labour, the introduction of any preparation machinery seems completely unnecessary from an economic point of view. However the system at present employed for checking up piece work is very bad indeed, as the fruit remains standing about either in basins of water or in the cans until the quantity is sufficient to be checked off against the cutter. If the fruit stands about in the cans at this point outside contamination is inevitable, either, dust, flies or dirt scraped from the underside of the can above, get in, some fermentation takes place and all the hygienic precautions previously taken may be spoiled. If the fruit is allowed to soak in water, some of the natural juices and sugars are disolved out and a loss of flavour results. If the conditions of the cutting table are such that the fruit has to be washed before entering the can, then some type of spray washer might / be evolved, but not a soaking wash. The condition to be aimed at is, that as soon as the fruit is cut, it is filled into the can, the can is placed on a conveyor and carried direct to the syrup machine and thence through the line in the shortest possible time.

5. Processing.[1] It will be essential to adopt some form of exhaust process eventually, though exactly what form it will take I prefer not to say until I have had an opportunity of studying the effects of various exhaust processes[2] on Malayan pines. The introduction of an exhaust process will necessitate the introduction also of stationary can closing machines, either automatic or semi-automatic, as the operators would not stand to work the old revolving can type, with hot syrup flying about. Semi-automatic stationery can type closing machines are used extensively in Great Britain in conjunction with exhaust boxes.[3] A range of closing machines are made which with modifications to suit the Malayan cans would be admirably suited for the job. After examining some M.P.C. cans some time ago, the Metal Box Co. stated that the cans were so bad that no automatic closing machine could handle them efficiently, this is probably true, with the ends[4] as they are at present, but with a redesigned end and careful supervision of the body making there seems no reason whatever why automatic closing machines should not be used. With regard to the actual process to be adopted in place of the antiquated and inefficient method at present employed, I would rather wait until I have had a chance of doing some experimental work to determine the most suitable process before saying too much. There are several important points, the first is that in the new syrup machines which the United Malayan Pineapple packers have had built locally, no provision appears to have been made

for / obtaining a headspace for filling. With the adoption of an exhaust at a later date, this would counteract any benefit gained from the exhaust. At present where automatic syrupers are not employed canners seem to rely on spill to supply the headspace. Secondly there is no cooling system after sterilization, cans are stacked hot in honey comb fashion, thus keeping each other hot for many hours, this supplementary cook is probably the cause of the cloudy syrup complained of at the Cardiff Fruit Show. Another point which seams to lack attention is the amazingly rough way in which the cans are handled after leaving the closing machine, a closed can dents very easily, and after the careless way they are handled a can is very fortunate if it is not badly dented. It is a simple matter and quite cheap to supply runways for the cans consisting of two angle vans facing each other thus [image] so that when the cans do knock together the only point of contact is the seam which is rigid and will not dent easily. Dented or badly marked cans should not be exported.

A number of cans were examined at the various factories, which had been in store for some time, and a large percentage of them had developed rust spots, especially on the inside face of the end seam, this is due to the knurling[5] on the edge of the seaming chuck[6] digging into the tin-plate and actually destroying the surface coating of tin and exposing the base metal. With the stationery can type closing machines it is not necessary to have this knurling and this trouble will be eliminated. Another practice which must be deplored is the marking of the ends of the cans with a soldering iron (after closing), for identification purposes after sterilisation, this leaves a scratch on the end which usually develops into a rusty mark.

e present method of sterilising must be extremely inefficient with regard to steam consumption as well as making the working conditions very unpleasant; the steam losses due to radiation and evaporation, clouds of steam always rising, are / much greater than need be. Also the first layer of cans to enter the tank always get a considerably longer cook than the top layer, these conditions all help towards an uniform pack.

e introduction of can runways, to carry the empty cans from the can store to the filling table, and to convey the filled cans to the sterilising room and warehouse, will be a great help in saving the cans from being dented, and also will prevent a lot of unnecessary carrying especially when there is fairly limited room.

6. Labelling. A system seems to exist whereby the unlabelled cars are packed into boxes, nailed down, and stored and when an order is received the boxes are opened up again, the label attached and the boxes closed again. There seems to be no reason why the unlabelled cans should not be stacked separately in a dry well ventilated warehouse as they come from the processing line, they could then be taken straight from the pile, labeled, packed and sent off as orders come in. Faulty cans which develop hydrogen swell or bacterial spoilage after processing

can be very easily detected and removed with this method of handling. To avoid any muddle arising in the warehouse due to the cans getting mixed, the cans may be stamped with various code numbers or letters to signify the different packs and a record of these kept in the office. A very good indellible marking ink can be obtained which will withstand any mount of washing and processing and can be applied with a rubber stamp. The Identification marks could be applied to the body of the can before fillings, or alternatively to the centre of the end, this position is occupied at present by the various canners initials, I would suggest that this is only necessary on one end, say the end that is put on first, and that the other and, the one that finally closes the can, should be left plain to receive the ink stamped identification mark. Those ends / could be stamped by a small boy just before being fed late the closing machine. This method would have the additional advantage of indicating which end of the can was put on last, it is sometimes very helpful to know this if faulty seems are occurring, to check up and find which closing machine is to blame. This method of ink marking is employed in England with success, many canners prefer it to actually stamping the tin plate as this tends to destroy the tin coating unless great care is exercised. Most modern automatic closing machines are fitted with an end stamping attachment this automatically stamps each end with the code numbers as it passes to the can but many canners have dispensed with these in favour of the hand operated rubber stamp.

Labels. The actual lapels used are very poor both in design and printing. I have heard these criticised both in England and Malaya, surely something a little more attractive could be prepared (for the Golden Quality pack any way) without increasing the cost too much,. after all the label and the ends are the only part of article visible to the purchaser; an attractive exterior to a can is almost a greater inducement to buy then anything else, especially if the quality of the contents do not fall short of expectations afterwards. An enormous lot of trouble has been taken in England and America to prepare labels which are both attractive and catching to the eye. Competitions have been arranged offering monetary prizes for the best label design for each product; a lot could be learnt by studying some of the labels off English and American cans.

7. Hygienic Factory Conditions. Much good work has been done recently by the health authorities with regard to the hygienic factory conditions, by the rebuilding of factories to approved designs and water supplies etc. May I suggest that a factory routine be adopted, whereby systematic washing of the cutting / tables with water hoses after work every night; and also the sterilization of syrupers and closing machines with a steam hose be undertaken, to carry on the good work of the Health Officers. No attention seems to have been paid to the cleanliness of the inside of the can, handmade cans, I should imagine, are far from being

hygienically sound inside, a system of washing over a jet of water with the can inverted would suffice, there are several can washing machines on the market but these would probably be too expensive. However it must be remembered that hygienic factory conditions do not materially improve the contents of the can. Every can is sterilised after closing, the contents are therefore sterile and hygienically sound, if not, the can would not survive more than a few days before bacterial or mould growth would develop causing decay and bulging ends. The important point is that there should be no dirt or chemical contamination in the can which would be injurious to the appearance of the contents or to the health of the consumer; to achieve these ends it is important to have clean factor conditions. With regard to the chemical contamination there are several ways by which impurities can enter the product namely –

(1) SO_2 in sugar.
(2) Tin dissolved from the tin plate.
(3) Lead dissolved from the solder.
(4) Copper dissolved from the copper pans used during the process.
(5) Various chemicals dissolved in the water used for making up syrups.

Very rarely do any of these exceed the quantity which is injurious to health. Very bad water is apt to turn syrups cloudy, and over 5 parts per million of SO_2 tends to blacken the inside of the can. There need be no fear of cloudiness from hard water in Malaya, though I fancy, that the sugar obtained from Java / contains a fairly high quantity of SO_2; from the examination of several came I found a certain amount of blackening, this is also apt to produce a metallic taste.

8. <u>Standard Can Sizes.</u> I feel sure that the opinion expressed by the Canadian Government, that there are too many sizes of cans used in Malaya, would be supported by other buyers of Malayan canned pines. I have not been able to find out shat decided the choice of the many and varied can sizes at present used, and why they should differ from the standard sizes universally, but I can only assume that they arise through pretty individual bargaining between exporter and buyer. It would be a big step to suddenly adopt standard sizes throughout Malaya; it would cost money, at the same time it would require the agreement of all the canners to bring this about; it might even have a temporary bad effect on certain markets, but in spite of these negative effects I feel that it would benefit the industry yearly in the long run. The saving in the cost of machinery specially built to take the non-standard sizes would compensate the initial cost of the change over, and if machine made cans are adopted the saving would be much greater. The benefits gained by adapting standard sizes rather depend on whether automatic machinery is going to be used more in the future. I am inclined to think that more machinery is inevitable before long.

If standard can sizes are adopted four or five standard sizes should be sufficient, the question comes up as to whether the sizes should conform to those used in England and America, e.g. (A2. 3 7/16" × 4½", A2½ squat 4 1/16" × 3 ½", A2½. 4 1/16" × 4 11/16", A10. 6 3/16" × 6 15/16".) or to the chief sizes at present employed in Malaya namely 1½ 1b. tall, 1½ 1b. flat, 2 lb. and the gallon size. It is important that this question of / standard sizes be settled in the very near future, as it effects the purchase of any new plant, especially now that the industry is reorganizing and new machines will have to be bought. I personally am inclined to feel that the adoption of the American sizes would be beneficial in the long run, this would put Malaya on an equal footing with the rest of the canning world; the Malayan sizes are so near to the American as to make no difference to the cost of production and the benefits gained by putting on to the market a universally standard product at a lower price than anybody else, would prove to be a boon to the industry.

9. <u>Can Making.</u> The question of standard sizes has a direct bearing on the method of making cans, for if automatic machine made cans are adopted this will in itself standardise can sizes, as the cost of the plant would prohibit many sizes being used, as there has to be one complete can making line for each size of can; also it would be a point in favour of adopting American sizes, as specially made can making machinery would be very much more costly than that built to make a standard cans. Personally I would not like to recommend any individual canner to undertake automatic machine can making on his own, it is far too specialised and intricate a business. It might be worth while if the services of a skilled engineer, fully trained in can making were enlisted to run the plant, but the cost of such a plant to turn out three sizes of cans would be prohibitive to any one canner in Malaya and the output too great for one canner to handle, each line being capable of producing 150,000 can per 10 hour day. It would have to be a co-operative factory supported by all the canners, so as to ensure that each one should use the machine made cans. This may come about in time, but in the mean time there are a number of improvements which can be introduced into the present methods of can making. / With due care hand made cans can be produced with a percentage of faulty cans as low as half percent, which is the figure claimed to have been obtained by Mr. Lee Kong Chain. Unless very convincing figures are produced to show a definite saving in manufacturing costs, the old methods will survive.

The following are my criticisms of the present methods of can making and suggestions for improvement.
(1) I have reason to believe that the tin plate being used is not up to the standard required for fruit canning, there is no reason why Malayan canners should not insist on the best, they are paying top price for their tin plate. I propose

as soon as I have the necessary apparatus to carry out a complete series of tests on samples of tinplate supplied to Malayan canners to find out its qualities. I then propose to assist the canners to draw up a standard specification to safeguard their interest when ordering tinplate.

e design of the ends is such that undue strains are set up during seaming in the tin plate, I propose to go into the question of design with the canners and the manufacturers of the stamping dies in order to correct as far as possible the various faults.

(3) The use and application of rubber rings in the ends are very crude indeed, pieces of rubber get inside the can, the rings vary in thickness very greatly. Rubber solution sprayed in would correct these difficulties and would be more economical as only .08 gram of solution are required for each 2½ end, whereas the weight of rubber used in Malayan ends of the same size is in the neighbourhood of 0.3 gram. The rubber solution is applied by means of a spray in liquid form, machines are employed to do this at the rate of 80 cans per minute, the cost of such machines would be probably less than $800. After spraying / the ends are dried in an oven for 8 minutes at approx 100°. I feel sure that if one canner could be persuaded to try out this method great improvement and saving would result.

e variation in diameter of the bodies, although remarkably small considering the conditions, is too great to be certain of getting a perfect seam every time, this could probably be improved by using more carefully constructed mandrels, at present wooden mandrels[7] are being used, with a piece of metal wrapped round and nailed on.

(5) Some method of eliminating the thick lump of solder each end of the side seam must be thought out, it is at this point that leakage nearly always takes place owing to the extra thickness of solder which has to be included in the double seam. This might be removed by more careful soldering, or by a touch on a grindstone.

(6) In a number of cases canners are using thicker tinplate than is necessary, and are consequently spending money unnecessarily. Steps should be taken to determine the minimum thickness required for each size of can, in one case this has been done and a reasonable thickness arrived at, but this is not as thin as the tinplate used for similar sizes in England. The reason given for not being able to use thinner plate, was that cans were apt to crumple when exported. English canned goods imported into Malaya do not show signs of undue crumpling;

(7) The Malayan cans tend to rust fairly badly. More careful handing, better tin plate and stationery can type seeming machines without knurling on the seaming chuck will improve this. There appears to be no reason what-

ANON., 'MINUTES OF A MEETING HELD AT THE GARDENS CLUB', SINGAPORE, AT 2.30 P.M. ON APRIL 17TH, 1936, BETWEEN PINEAPPLE PACKERS AND OFFICERS OF THE AGRICULTURAL DEPARTMENT' (1936)

Anon., 'Minutes of a Meeting Held at the Gardens Club, Singapore, at 2.30 p.m. on April 17th, 1936, between Pineapple Packers and Officers of the Agricultural Department', National Archives, CO 273/615/4.

e meeting was a response to W. B. J. Johnson's memorandum (see previous source) and displays the close relationship that existed between the government and Chinese entrepreneurs. Johnson was present at the meeting, as were Dr H. A. Tempany, the Director of Agriculture, A. E. Coleman Doscas, Johore's Agricultural Officer, and representatives of the packing factories of Singapore and Johore, including Goh Hock Huat, George E. Lee and Tay Lian Teck. Although the canners rejected many of Johnson's recommendations, some progress was made.

Anon., 'Minutes of a Meeting Held at the Gardens Club, Singapore, at 2.30 p.m. on April 17th, 1936, between Pineapple Packers and Officers of the Agricultural Department' (1936)

[...]

Dr. Tempany was called upon to open the discussion. He pointed out that the meeting had been arranged in order to discuss a number of memoranda and suggestions concerning the improvement of the pineapple industry.

He then proceeded to discuss with the members the principal points arising out of the "Preliminary Memorandum on Conditions in Pineapple Factories", prepared by the Canning Officer and which had been circulated to packers. In relation to paragraph 1 of the memorandum Mr. Tay Lian Teck said that owing to the numerous local regulations relating to buildings, sanitary conditions and factory regulations, the factory buildings as a result of complying with all the regulations were more elaborate than necessary, he also emphasised the difficulty of obtaining the / sanction of the various authorities before registration could be ected, he urged that there should be more co-operation between the Agricultural Department, the Health Authorities and the Building Authorities.

He also complained that the numerous regulations with which he had to comply, when building, were not being enforced with equal stringency in factories elsewhere. Dr. Tempany replied that the question of publishing a list of standard minimum factory requirements was under discussion with the Health Authorities, he hoped that in due course it would be possible to have these requirements made uniform and published in all Administrations.

e suggestion in paragraph 2 of the Canning Officer's memorandum that an experienced fruit buyer should be provided in every factory was regarded by the meeting as being impracticable owing to the very large number of small-holdings from which the fruit it obtained by small packers.

With regard to paragraph 3, the suggestion of employing a factory manager who would be responsible for the efficient running of the factory, the opinion was generally expressed that the expense of employing such a person would not be justified by the benefits so gained, at the same time it was agreed that more supervision was necessary.

A short discussion took place on the improvements in the preparation of the pines, the Canning Officer urged the desirability of passing the cut pines through the processes in the shortest time possible so as to eliminate the possibility of outside contamination, it was pointed out that the present method of checking piece-work of the cutters made this impossible. It was mentioned that samples of conveyor belting were being obtained by the Canning Officer and would be subjected to tests under the action of pineapple juice, it was also pointed out the experiments would be made to ascertain the most efficient and practical manner of washing out the cut fruit. /

Paragraph 5. Although it was generally agreed that the inclusion of an exhaust process would be an improvement, canners expressed their intention of not installing the exhaust until it had been demonstrated to them that it would pay them to do so, especially as the exhaust would make it necessary to have new closing machines and automatic Syrupers with headspace attachments. Dr. Tempany said that he did not consider that the automatic exhauster at Goh Hock Huat's factory had been given quite a fair trial to show its value, and asked Mr. Goh Hock Huat whether he would be prepared to allow the canning officer to carry out some experiments on it. Mr. Goh Hock Huat replied that it could not be arranged before July or August owing to the canning season being in full swing.

It was also agreed that the Canning Officer should carry out demonstrations, as soon as the apparatus was available, to show the benefits of cooling cans after sterilising.

Dr. Tempany raised the question of embossing on the end of the cans the grade designation of the contents, i.e. Golden, so as to safeguard the incorrect labeling of cans later, he emphasised this point by reading extracts from a table which gave particulars of 43 different pineapple packs which had been opened and examined by the Agricultural Department [...]. Dr. Tempany pointed out that one canner was already embossing his cans in this way, and suggested that it should be compulsory for all canners to mark their cans with the grade designation by embossing or by stamping with indellible ink: he also mentioned that samples of indellible ink were being obtained for testing. To this Mr. Choy Seng replied on behalf of the older generation of packers that they did not consider it necessary to make such regulations especially as it might lead to trouble with the exporters on whom they depended for the sale of their goods. /

Mr Tay Lian Teck suggested that the three grades should be defined explicitly in the regulations, but that the marking of cans be left to the choice of the packers. The stamping of cans might be one of the requirements for Malayan

Mr Goh Hock Huat suggested that there should be a co-operative meeting of packers and exporters as soon as practicable to discuss this point and others; this suggestion received the approval of all present.

Dr. Tempany then put forward the suggestion of adopting five or six standard can sizes the same as other canning industries had done, the opinion of the meeting was divided on this point, the larger canners expressing their whole hearted approval, while the smaller ones were not in favour as they seemed afraid that it might prejudice them in the eyes of the exporters. It was proposed to discuss this point with the exporters at the forthcoming meeting.

Dr Tempany then outlined briefly the grading scheme that had been tentatively prepared and circulated to canners, he emphasized that it was entirely voluntary and would not cost the packers more than the cost of the label. The scheme met with approval.

Mr Tay Lian Teck suggested that the inclusion of an exhaust process in the requirements for fruit packed under the proposed grading scheme should not be necessary until it had been proved to be an economic unit. It was pointed out that the scheme was purely of a tentative nature at present and was open for discussion and alteration if though necessary. It was also pointed out that the scheme might prove as inducement to the smaller canners who were afraid of any further legislation, to adopt better methods of their own free will, when they realised the ts gained by packing according to the Malayan Mark standards. /

It was also suggested by Dr Tempany that any reports and technical publications made from time to time should be translated into Chinese and circulated to the packers. This suggestion gained the approval of all present.

Dr Tempany concluded by giving an account of what was being done in Kuala Lumpur in connection with the fitting up of an experimental canning laboratory and gave a brief description of the type of work which would be carried out there. He also stressed the point that the services of the Canning Officer were freely at the disposal of the packers in an advisory capacity.

Mr Lee Kong Chian said that he thought it would be better if the Canning cer were stationed in Johore and that the experimental laboratory should be situated there also, so as to be in the centre of the pineapple canning area and easily accessible to the majority of canners. The other packers agreed that this was desirable.

Dr Tempany pointed out that it was preferable for the Canning Officer to be at Headquarters for a year or so, where chemical and mycological assistance were freely available; and also that there was a good building available in Kuala Lumpur, whereas if the station were moved to Johore a new building would have to be erected and the necessary funds raised to do so.

It was agreed that the fitting up of the station in Kuala Lumpur be proceeded

sary funds being available and the decision to make the change to Johore being decided the apparatus and fittings would be designed so that a rapid change over could be made if necessary In conclusion Dr Tempany pointed out that he proposed that the Canning Officer should visit all factories in Singapore and Johore at least twice a month.

[...]

ANON., 'QUALITY PRODUCTS OF THE HO HONG MILLS', *MALAYAN TRIBUNE MEMENTO*, 2–9 JANUARY 1932 (1932)

Anon., 'Quality Products of the Ho Hong Mills', *Malayan Tribune Memento*, 2–9 January 1932, National Archives, CO 273/582/3.

Ho Hong Oil Mills Ltd was just one of the many Chinese-owned Singapore companies that processed coconuts for their oil and manufactured soap. The firm was owned by Lim Peng Siang (1872–1944), who, with his brother Lim Peng Mao, operated the Ho Hong group of companies founded in 1904. In addition to the processing of coconut oil/soap manufacture, the group had interests in shipping, through the Ho Hong Steamship Co. Ltd; rice pot-boiling; the manufacture of cement via the Ho Hong Portland Cement Works Ltd; and banking, through the Ho Hong Bank (1917), which in 1932 merged with the Chinese Commercial Bank and the Oversea-Chinese Bank to form the Oversea-Chinese Banking Corp. Siang was President of the Singapore Chinese Chamber of Commerce (1913–16), a member of the Chinese Advisory Board (1921–41) and a director of a number of public companies, including Central Engine Works Ltd and Central Motors Ltd.[1]

1. W. G. Huff, *The Economic Growth of Singapore: Trade and Development in the Twentieth Century* (Cambridge: Cambridge University Press, 1994), pp. 147, 225, 459.

Anon., 'Quality Products of the Ho Hong Mills', *Malayan Tribune Memento*, 2–9 January 1932 (1932)

e Ho Hong Oil Mills (1931), Ltd., owns the largest coconut oil mills in the Malay Peninsula. The mills are situated on the South side of Havelock Road, while the godowns for the storage of copra, oil in tins, etc., are on the North side of Havelock Road with water frontage.

e Company also acquired the "Colonial Oil Mills," situate at Teck Guan Street and Mohamed Sultan Road.

e property owned by the Company at Havelock Road is about ten acres in extent, while the actual area occupied by the oil-milling plant, tin-making plant, cooperage plant, automatic oil filling plant, godowns for storage of copra, oil cake, etc., is over three acres.

e Havelock Road Mills is divided into three distinct units, each being independent of the other. Two of these units are run on electrical energy while the third is on steam power.

e entire mills is in charge of a fully qualified English engineer, who has been with the predecessors of this Company for nearly 20 years.

e quality of the oil produced is unique and at every exhibition in Malaya where the Company's products were exhibited diplomas and medals have been awarded to the Company's predecessors for the high quality of their products.

Coconut oil for local consumption is packed in tins of six, 14, and 28 katis[1] and in order to cope with the demand for such packing, the Company has its own tin-making plant, capable of producing 100,000 tins of various sizes per month.

For export purposes the oil is packed either in steel drums or wooden barrels. The Company has its own cooperage plant capable of assembling together 12,000 barrels per month.

e coconut oil is marketed under two trade marks – "Elephant with a Palm Tree" and the "Palm Tree" – the former being known in the market as "Elephant Brand."

Special care is taken to see that the oil produced is clear, bright, and free from all oleaginous matters while the free, fatty acid content is maintained at a very

The power plant consists of four units, totalling 800 h.p., and comprises a steam unit of 300 h.p. and three electrical units aggregating 500 h.p.

The capacity of the Havelock Road Mills is about 1,000 piculs of oil per day while from the Colonial Oil Mills an output of about 120 piculs of oil per day can be obtained. Owing to the trade depression only two units of the Havelock Road Mills are in commission while the Colonial Oil Mills is not in operation.

The major portion of the coconut oil produced is exported to Siam, Dutch East Indies, and China. The Company had at considerable sacrifice secured a market for its oil in Europe, but owing to the great difference in freight rates on coconut oil between Ceylon and Europe and Singapore and Europe, it was not found possible to compete with Ceylon coconut oil, the difference in freight being about 30s. per ton of oil.

The copra cake, or poonac, which is the residue from the copra after the oil has been expressed, has a very high value as a cattle foodstuff. It is packed in rolls and exported to Europe in large quantities.

The export of coconut oil from the Colony for the year 1930 was over $2,300,000, practically all of which is exported by the Ho Hong Oil Mills.

The import of coconut oil into Singapore is negligible, amounting to about $6,000 during 1930.

It is interesting also to note that Malaya produces about 100,000 tons of copra per annum.

THE SOAP FACTORY.

The Ho Hong Soap Factory, Ltd., is situate at Havelock Road, adjoining the Ho Hong Oil Mills. /

The factory is arranged in two sections – the household soap section and the toilet soap section.

The principal machinery in the household soap section comprise two large circular soap kettles of a capacity of 40 tons each, both fitted with closed and open steam coils for boiling soap with direct and indirect steam; a jacketed circular soup crutcher[2] of 14 tons capacity, a soap cooling machine, soap forms, soap dryer, soap cutter, oil and soap pumps, etc.

The capacity of the plant is 12,000 cases of household soap per month and this output can be easily doubled at a very small additional expenditure should the necessity for expansion of the factory arise.

The principal machinery in the toilet soap section comprise two circular soap kettles of 11 tons capacity each, both fitted with closed and open steam coils, a soap drying plant, mixer, soap plodder,[3] milling machine, box and carton making machinery, etc.

e capacity of the toilet soap plant is one ton of toilet soap per day of eight

e household soap is chiefly made in bars of 2½ lbs. each bar and in tablets of various sizes.

ese soaps are marketed under the following brands: –

"Elephant," "Palm Tree," and "Ho Hong," for the bar soap, and "Elephant," "Dragon" and "Ho Hong" for the soap in single or double tablets.

Prior to the Company producing household soap, the market price of the best grade Europe-made soap was $7 per case of 20 bars, but to-day the price of the same soap is reduced to $4.80 per case. The Company's "Palm Tree" brand soap, specially manufactured for the people of Malaya, because it is made purely from vegetable oils, is retailed at only $4 per case The quality is as good as, if not better than, the best Europe-made bar soap. An additional advantage of purchasing "Palm Tree" brand soap is that each bar is wrapped in a specially waxed paper to keep off the dust from the soap, while the net weight is 2½ lb. per bar. In view of the fact that "Palm Tree" brand soap is made from vegetable oils only, the Mohamedans and Indians are able to use this soap freely.

e toilet soap produced has not sold as well as might be expected owing to the prejudice against locally produced soap, but after considerable propaganda work this prejudice is being gradually overcome.

[...]

Practically all the raw materials used for the manufacture of household and toilet soap have to be imported with the exception of coconut oil and palm oil.

ANON., 'WORLD'S BIGGEST TIN SMELTERS. GROWTH OF STRAITS TRADING CO.', *THE SINGAPORE FREE PRESS EXHIBITION SUPPLEMENT* (1932)

Anon., 'World's Biggest Tin Smelters. Growth of Straits Trading Co.', *The Singapore Free Press Exhibition Supplement*, 2 January 1932, National Archives, CO 273/582/3.

e following text provides a description of the Straits Trading Co., the operations of which are discussed in the thematic introduction. The plant at Pulau Brani was destroyed prior to the Japanese Occupation in February 1942, but was rebuilt after the Second World War. Today, the firm is an investment holding company owned by the Tecity Group with interests in tin mining and smelting (through its subsidiary Malaysia Smelting Corp.), real estate (via Straits Developments Ltd), hospitality (Rendezvous Hospitality Group), advertising and fund management.

Anon., 'World's Biggest Tin Smelters. Growth of Straits Trading Co.', *The Singapore Free Press Exhibition Supplement* (1932)

e Straits Trading Co., Ltd., Singapore, was founded in the year 1887, with a capital of $150,000, to acquire the business of tin ore smelters and general merchants carried on at that time by Messrs. James Sword and Herman Muhlinghaus in the States of Sungei Ujong and Selangor.

e first reduction of the ore was done by a small reverberatory furnace[1] in a shed at Teluk Anson, Perak, but the results were very disappointing. Shortly erwards, however, the Company erected smelting works at Pulau Brani, Singapore, and they exist there to this day, though changes out of all recognition from their original layout and in regard to type of plant installed.

e Company possesses a second smelting plant at Butterworth, Province Wellesley, which was originally started in 1902 to keep pace with increasing business. This plant was completely modernised a few years ago.

e Company's capital has been increased from $150,000 at its formation by successive stages to $15,000,000 authorised ($9,000,000 paid up). Since then, by refunds of capital to shareholders, the figures have respectively become $1,500,000 authorised and $900,000 paid up. This was coincident with a steadily growing business, and with important developments and progress in metallurgical practice that give the Company to-day first place among the tin smelters of the world.

e primitive Chinese methods of tin-ore smelting in small shaft furnaces, with charcoal as fuel and reducing agent, were replaced by smelting in small reverberatory furnaces. The latter in their turn gave way to large modern regenerative reverberatory furnaces, gas fired, with modern fume recovery attachments. This progress in smelting practice has resulted in larger recoveries of metal from the ore, with benefit alike to the tin mining industry and the prosperity of Malaya in general.

e Company's properties cover an area of over seventy acres, and the combined smelting plants at Pulau Brani and Penang are the largest and most up-to-date in the world. They have a total smelting capacity up to 60,000 tons of refined tin per annum.

The product of the Straits Trading Co., Ltd.'s smelteries is the world-renowned "Straits Tin," the ore supplies coming mainly from the Federated Malay States. The following table shows the total exports of tin and tin in ore from the Federated Malay States for a period of thirty years:

Years.	Tin Piculs.	Tin in Tin Ore Piculs.	Total Exports Piculs.	Tons.
1901	364,364	420,879	785,243	46,741
1902	335,601	445,267	780,868	46,480
1903	345,589	494,158	839,647	49,979
1904	333,044	533,193	853,237	50,966
1905	308,288	548,372	856,660	50,992
1906	306,746	510,036	816,782	48,618
1907	234,157	579,479	813,636	48,431
1908	147,608	708,457	854,065	50,837
1909	180,585	638,301	818,886	48,743
1910	166,316	570,583	736,899	43,863
1911	167,422	574,276	741,698	44,149
1912	174,784	638,688	813,472	48,421
1913	85,502	756,627	842,129	50,127
1914	61,179	762,730	823,909	49,042
1915	73,405	712,265	785,670	46,766
1916	80,245	656,770	737,015	43,870
1917	90,966	578,231	669,197	39,833
1918	74,741	553,074	627,815	37,370
1919	86,298	534,220	620,518	36,936
1920	67,884	519,020	586,904	34,935
1921	76,708	502,724	579,432	34,490
1922	98,852	493,954	592,806	35,286
1923	98,384	534,135	632,519	37,650
1924	113,267	626,656	739,923	44,043
1925	123,620	647,940	771,560	45,926
1926	92,390	679,519	771,909	45,947
1927	63,553	813,067	876,620	52,180
1928	49,044	991,461	1,040,505	61,935
1929	16,706	1,109,598	1,126,304	67,042
1930	8,124	1,034,567	1,042,691	62,065

[A Straits picul equals 133 1/3 lbs. or 16.80 piculs equals 1 ton].

It will be noted that the introduction of modern methods of tin smelting has gradually resulted in the bulk of the ore being exported to the European smelters at Singapore and Penang for conversion into refined tin. The Straits Trading Co., Ltd. smelt the preponderating part of the output of tin ore from Malaya, with the result that it is the most important seller of Straits refined tin in the

East. The following statement of its sales of Straits tin at Singapore and Penang will be of interest:

Year.		Tons.
1907	–	40,205
1908	–	47,768
1909	–	40,297
1910	–	35,346
1911	–	38,252
1912	–	36,489
1913	–	43,017
1914	–	41,718
1915	–	47,249
1916	–	43,504
1917	–	37,887
1918	–	36,241
1919	–	37,315
1920	–	28,294
1921	–	27,759
1922	–	39,690
1923	–	45,514
1924	–	48,160
1925	–	45,856
1926	–	41,014
1927	–	48,042
1928	–	59,518
1929	–	62,372
1930	–	52,137

e Straits Trading Co. Ltd.'s head office is at Singapore, and it possesses buying agencies throughout the whole of Malaya, at which points the ore is received from producers for transport to the Company's smelting plants. The technical and commercial organisations of the Company are of a high order, and improvements in existing smelting method and processes by metallurgical research are constantly aimed at.

e uses of tin are so well known as to require no comment here. "Straits Tin" is world-renowned, and finds consumers in all parts of the globe, the biggest demand coming from the United States of America.

e Straits Trading Co., Ltd.'s brand of "Straits Tin" analyses over 99.85% pure and possesses the physical characteristics so much desired by consumers; its ness is unexcelled and it is uniform in quality. It is shipped in ingots weighing 100lbs.

ANON., 'TAMPENIS CEMENT TILE WORKS', *MALAYAN TRIBUNE MEMENTO*, 2–9 JANUARY 1932 (1932)

Anon., 'Tampenis Cement Tile Works', *Malayan Tribune Memento*, 2–9 January 1932, National Archives, CO 273/582/3.

e following is a very brief account of the operations of the Tampenis Cement Tile Works Ltd, one of numerous small Chinese firms producing products for the regional market, in this case Malaya, Siam, Burma, China and India. Further information on the works can be found in *The Singapore Times*, 2 January 1932, p. 10.

Anon., 'Tampenis Cement Tile Works', *Malayan Tribune Memento*, 2–9 January 1932 (1932)

One of the most interesting series of exhibits will be that of the Tampenis Cement Tile Works, Ltd., a firm which was probably the first in the field with this line of product. The firm had a very modest beginning in Sungei Road, where it was under German control. About the year 1916, possibly 15 years after its flotation, its possibilities were envisaged by a local business man, who acquired a controlling interest and turned the firm into a limited liability company. No expense was spared to make the business not only a paying concern but a credit to the city; the interests of the workers were considered simultaneously with those of the principals and the original theory that the best article is produced by the best-conditioned workmen has been amply justified.

When the factory was transferred from Sungei Road to its present site in Serangoon Road, special quarters were erected for the workmen. These houses were constructed under hygenic principles and the workers are probably as contented as those employed by any firm in the East. The number of employees at the moment is about 100, consisting of Chinese, Malays, Javanese, and Boyanese.[1] This number, owing to such factors as the trouble in China, has had unfortunately to be reduced from something like 300.

Only the finest material obtainable goes in to the making of these tiles and the most up-to-date electrical machinery is in use. There is a great variety of designs and colours and prospective customers are sure to find an article to suit their taste. One of the most attractive designs is in a fascinating mosaic effect.

e dyes used are specially imported and are unfadable, whilst the completed titles are firm and durable. /

e methods of producing the completed tile are of interest. The work is supervised by Mr. Khoo Tiam Hock, the manager and a recognised expert, who has been employed by the firm since its inception. After the cement and sand – the latter of the finest white quality – has been mixed the composition is pressed by means of hydraulic screw presses and is then coloured by means of stencils and by free hand work. The tile is then polished. Wall tiles are also produced in many varieties of colours and designs. The works can turn out as many as 6,000 tiles per day.

ANON., 'STEEL CASTINGS FOR ALL PURPOSES. MACHINERY MAKING IN THE TROPICS', *THE SINGAPORE FREE PRESS EXHIBITION SUPPLEMENT*, 2 JANUARY 1932 (1932)

Anon., 'Steel Castings for all Purposes. Machinery Making in the Tropics', *The Singapore Free Press Exhibition Supplement*, 2 January 1932. National Archives, CO 273/582/3.

United Engineers was formed in 1912 by the amalgamation of Riley Hargreaves & Co. (1865) and Howarth Erskine & Co. (1875). Soon afterwards, it acquired the Federated Engineering Co. of Kuala Lumpur to become the largest supplier of heavy equipment in the region, operating in Thailand, Hong Kong and China as well as in Malaya. Today, the group employs 5,000 workers and has a presence in twelve Asian countries and revenues of $2,012m (31 December 2013).[1]

1. Anon., 'United Engineers Ltd. Company History', available online at http://uel.com.sg/corp_profile/co_history.htm [accessed on 28 March 2014].

Anon., 'Steel Castings for all Purposes. Machinery Making in the Tropics', *The Singapore Free Press Exhibition Supplement*, 2 January 1932 (1932)

ose who are familiar with the iron and steel centres at home, and have had a glimpse into the workshops where these industries are carried out cannot fall to have been impressed with the sights they saw. The furnaces in which the metals are melted radiate bright lights and fierce heat, and streams of molten metal are poured into moulds, while workmen bathed in perspiration work in relays at their arduous tasks.

It is difficult to realize a similar form of industry in this tropical country, yet it exists. Once a week or so at the United Engineers' workshops at Damar Road may be seen Malaya's only steel foundry in operation. Here steel castings are made varying in weight from a few ounces to several tons. The Bessemer process is used, which consists of melting special pig iron and scrap steel of known analysis in a cupola furnace[1] and transferring this molten metal to a converter[2] where by blowing a current of air over it a series of chemical actions take place, which, by oxidation, purify the iron and generate intense heat. When this operation, known as blowing, is complete various alloy additions are made to produce a steel of the desired quality.

Castings for such a variety of purposes are required that the quality of steel best suited to each type is carefully studied. Constant analyses of the steel are made in the laboratory and physical tests in bars of the steel produced are made to indicate its actual strength. At the steel foundry stall at the Exhibition there will be seen the machines on which these tests are made. It is impossible to have at the Exhibition anything like a representative variety of the castings manufactured. Those displayed include a large wearing tread ring for a dredge screen roller path; numerous gears and pulleys; special high carbon-chrome steel teeth for excavating machinery; and various castings in the rough and finished machined state, most of which are repairs and renewals for tin dredges. The Steel Foundry Department forms an essential part of the firm's activities. It commenced in 1923, when complete dredges were designed and built in Singapore.

Besides supplying parts for the maintenance of dredges all over the country, its field of service has greatly extended, and wherever a steel casting is required for any purpose it can be obtained from this local foundry. Casting have been supplied to all parts of British Malaya, to Burma, Siam, Borneo, Sarawak, East Indies, Hong Kong and Shanghai.

When part of a machine of any description breaks down in this country and material stronger than cast iron is required to replace it, this can be made in steel in Singapore, and in a few weeks the castings can be accurately finished and machined ready for replacement, whereas several months would pass before such a service could be performed by a home firm. These advantages are becoming widely recognised and this pioneer steel foundry in Malaya forms a place of importance among Singapore manufacturers.

MACHINERY.

It may come as a surprise to many to learn that tin dredges are made in Singapore. That, however, is the case. The United Engineers, who have secured for this purpose the services of a member of an experienced British dredge building firm, have built an appreciable number of the tin dredges operating Malaya.

Dredges have been built by United Engineers for the following tin dredging companies; Klang River, Rawang Tin, Malim Nawar, Petaling Tin, Penawat Tin, Tanjong Tin, and Thabawleik Tin, whilst two dredges for the Teja Malaya Tin Dredging Co, were reconstructed by this Singapore firm.

The dredges are built in the workshop in River Valley Road. The only parts that have to be imported ready made are the prime movers such as main engines and electrical machinery, also certain special alloy steel wearing parts. Everything else is locally constructed from imported raw material, a steel casting department of the firm having been brought into operation for the purpose of supplying the dredge construction department with steel castings.

The existence of the dredge building department of United Engineers reduces by the period occupied by the transport from England the time in which a spare part may be replaced on any Malayan dredge. It also considerably expedites the time occupied in building a new dredge. Penawat Tin was built within 16½ months of the date of the placing of the order with United Engineers.

Dredge machinery and parts, although taking a very big place in the firm's manufacturing activities, by no means complete the field. The firm manufactures a complete line of rubber machinery, and designs, fabricates and erects rubber factories in entirety.

Supported by a strong list of agency representations, united Engineers are able to equip completely, from building to plant, any type of manufacturing industry possible in Malaya. They are manufacturers for manufacturers.

ARNOLD, *ON COTTON FABRICS AND THE COTTON INDUSTRY OF BURMA* (1897)

G. F. Arnold, *On Cotton Fabrics and the Cotton Industry of Burma* (Rangoon: Government Printing Office, 1897), pp. 1–20.

George Frederick Arnold was the Deputy Secretary to the Government of India Legislative Department and Acting Divisional Judge at Prome, Burma. A man of many and varied interests, he was the first writer to apply psychology to the study of the legal process. His paper on the Burmese cotton industry concentrates on the manufacture of cotton fabrics, though also touches on the cultivation of cotton and the cotton trade. As discussed in the thematic introduction, his conclusion that the sector was in terminal decline was overly pessimistic in that both the domestic and factory industry survived.[1]

1. B. H. Bornstein and S. D. Penrod, 'Hugo Who? G. F. Arnold's Alternative Early Approach to Psychology and Law', *Applied Cognitive Psychology*, 22:6 (2008), pp. 759–68.

G. F. Arnold, *On Cotton Fabrics and the Cotton Industry of Burma* (1897), extract

Reports have been submitted from nearly all the districts in Burma and also from the Shan States. On certain points their unanimity is so complete that it will suffice to state the conclusion merely; on others, where a few only disagree with the majority, the dissentient view will be quoted in each case.

II. – The present condition of the cotton industry in Burma.

Statistics have not been given, though in some districts a rough estimate of the number of looms has been made; but the returns of the last and the preceding census have been available, and some of the annual and triennial trade reports have also been consulted.

It would appear that cotton is cultivated in almost every district in Upper Burma, and in about half the Lower Burma districts. In most of these latter only very little is now grown, in out-of-the-way parts, for home consumption, and the area of cultivation is yearly contracting. Not that it is a case of resorting to the more productive sources and receding from the less, in obedience to the fall of prices or the variations in demand, but cotton, alike in fertile and unfertile regions, is / going out of cultivation because the demand for cotton goods is being wholly supplied from imported sources, except where lack of communication and length of way cut

the more distant villages from the march of civilisation. Indeed, in such parts as it is now grown, the conditions are of a kind that are wholly unaffected by trade and to which the principles of political economy do not apply.

A few people still continue to sow their own cotton and weave their own garments because they have done so from time immemorial, and have not yet come

ciently in contact with the outer world to break the custom which they have always followed.

It is more a pastime than an industry, the weaving being done by the daughters and wives, who supply the household raiment, but seldom offer any articles for sale.

Any surplus over the wants of the family is not aimed at when sowing the cotton, but should there be any, it is disposed of in its raw condition to the nearest purchaser who will take it.

In Lower Burma, then, there is no manufacture of cotton fabrics that can be termed an industry: what does exist is a survival that becomes rarer and rarer as the years go on.

Much of this is true also of the Upper Province, but here the conditions are slightly different. In some districts, *e.g.*, in Meiktila and Myingyan, cotton is grown largely and exported raw to China and India; there are also more weavers, men and women alike pursuing the trade, though the imported yarn, ready dyed, is used largely in preference to the native homespun.

This, however, is not everywhere the case. It is recognized in some parts, *e.g.*, in the Mogôk district and the Shan States, that the coarser native yarn makes a cheaper and more durable material: in others, especially among the Kachins and Shans of Hsenwi and Kēngtūng, there exists a national costume woven from home-grown sources, and the people wear no other, since either such is their will, or foreign manufacturers have not yet produced the patterns of their choice. In Upper Burma also while the physical features of the land are more favourable to cotton cultivation, there are more regions as yet only partially opened to trade and to which the journeyman clothes-seller does not penetrate with his wares. Here cotton is much grown and weaving flourishes, protected from competition, temporarily at least, by nature's barriers. In yet a few districts, even where there is no difficulty of access, / the home industry appears to hold its own against foreign manufacutures: thus it is reported from Mandalay, Mônywa, and Tagaung that the local trade has been scarcely, if at all, affected by importations of yarn and ready-made goods.

The cases, however, are few in number in which this is stated without qualification, and they may be taken merely as particular instances: as a general principle, wherever the imported fabric, whether in the form of yarn or goods, meets the home production, it rapidly ousts its rival from the field. Its greater brilliancy of colour attracts the people, who are glad moreover to avoid the labour involved in weaving and dyeing clothes by the long and tedious native process.

The above conclusions may be established in two ways – by quotations from the various district reports, and by deductions from the census and trade returns.

Every District Officer in Lower Burma records either that the weaving industry does not exist now, or that, where it still lingers, it is rapidly dying out on account of the influx of foreign goods. A few of these statements have been selected as examples.

From Kyaukpyu it is reproted that "there is no manufacture of cotton fabrics as an industry. The ordinary process of weaving used is so very slow that the work is hardly paying. In the Cheduba township there is only one woman engaged in it."

In Hanthawaddy "out of 80,000 houses about 8,500 have looms. Imported yarn is now rapidly displacing the native product, and very little yarn-spinning

used to do, as imported fabrics are brought to their doors by clothes-sellers from Rangoon. It takes, on an average, a single person five days to make fabrics which realize Rs. 2."

In Northern Arakan "the villagers do not weave any clothes, but buy them from the bazaar locally. In former years the people used to weave and make their clothes in their own houses."

In Tharrawaddy "hand-made yarns are made only near the hills and at a distance from the railway line. There are no professional weavers, and the importation of Manchester goods is fast crushing the local industry."

e Deputy Commissioner of Henzada remarks: "The art of weaving is fast dying out in the Henzada district, and the yarn used is generally imported and not locally spun. The / same influences which ensured the destruction of the home spinning and weaving in England are now operating in Burma. The industry is moribund, the wages earned by a weaver are not sufficient ordinarily to support a family, and the weavers rarely, if ever, live entirely on their earnings. Weaving is a useful employment for the unmarried girls only of the family. In the hills and remoter parts of the jungle the Karens and hillmen still spin and weave their own clothing for home consumption only."

In the Pyapôn subdivision of the Ma-ubin district "before the annexation of Pegu every Burmese house had a loom, and a girl of that time was not considered accomplished unless she knew how to weave. Since then foreign goods came in oods, and their cheapness and superior quality secured for them a better sale in the market and more popularity than the local production; consequently the number of looms has dwindled down: there are now about 923 looms, and the workers are, without exception, females."

In the Yandoon subdivision "the manufacture of cotton cloths is being superseded by the silk industry, which pays better and is less troublesome. Now a man feels ashamed to go to a festival with cotton clothes unless he is very poverty-stricken."

In the Shwegyin subdivision of the Toungoo district "there are about 800 looms, but most of them are not used. The Burmans only use them when they have nothing more profitable to do."

In Upper Burma more cotton is grown and the manufacture of cotton goods ourishes in some parts. As a whole, however, the conclusion to be drawn is to the same effect. *(ii) In Upper Burma.*

In the Kyauksè district no cotton fabric industry exists.

At Taungdwingyi "more than three-fourths of the cotton now manufactured is made from imported yarn. There is about one loom to three houses, but before imported yarn and cloth became so cheap, there was a large proportion of the population devoted entirely to weaving."

From Pyinmana in the Yamèthin district it is reported that "the industry is said to have been greater here in Burmese times, the restrictions of the Forest Department being assigned as the cause of the decline." What these restrictions are is not explained, but they appear to have reference to dyeing materials, which are mostly obtained from the bark of trees. /

In Pakôkku at only one village of the Yesagyo township is weaving carried on, imported cotton fabrics being preferred, and in Yawdwin it exists for domestic use only and not for trade.

In Katha "the Kachin and Kadus still very generally make their own clothing. Weaving is carried on for home use only, the instruments being very rude and the method laborious. The threads made from home-grown cotton are being rapidly ousted by the common threads of European manufacture. Threads equally cheap and dyed more brilliantly can be had in nearly all the bazaars."

In the Upper Chindwin "there can be no question that the local industry, which was never on a large scale, is being rapidly supplanted by the importation of fabrics from abroad. The fact of the industry surviving in any shape must be largely attributed to the difficulty of communication which prevails in this district."

The Deputy Commissioner of Bhamo writes: "The cotton-manufacturing industry is now passing out of that primitive phase where every household man-ufactured its own garments and cloths from the crop grown on its own piece of ground. This state of affairs was general in the Bhamo district only fifteen years ago, and, in the hills, the Kachins, and, to a lesser extent, the Shans are still in the same stage of development. In Bhamo itself there are few indications left of this condition of things. Material and prepared thread are more cheaply obtained from the steamer flats, and by consequence the local industry is rapidly giving way to imported fabrics."

There are, however, one or two reports that differ somewhat in their tone.

Thus in the Lower Chindwin the industry is said to be large and to employ a large number of families; though it is added that the cultivator finding his jowar and paddy-fields give him a more satisfactory outurn, usually relegates his cotton to the inferior classes of soil.

In the Ruby Mines district the industry is confined to supplying home wants, and there is occasional enterprise in local, but not export, trade. Further, more cotton was grown and more looms employed formerly than now; but the cause of the fall-off is not apparent, as it is said that "the influence of imported fabrics on the local industry may be set down at almost *nil*, for at present the effect is not calculated to make the Burman abandon producing what he believes and knows to be both cheaper and more durable." And again, "it is probable / that it will always be a domestic industry, unless and until, which is very unlikely, the imported manufactures are brought to the doors of the people at from 25 to 50

In Mandalay the industry is resorted to only by the poorer classes for domestic use and not for the purposes of trade. Professional weavers generally work in silk, but occasionally take to cotton when the price of silk falls. Cotton is bought ready spun and dyed at Rs. 5 per hundred bundles, a bundle containing seven skeins.[2]

It is remarked, however, that "imported fabrics do not in any way influence the local industry: those who can afford it indulge in them in preference to those of local manufacture, which provides material only to the poorer class." It is perhaps doubtful, as will be seen later on, whether, under these circumstances, the uence of imported fabrics can be so completely discounted.

From Meiktila the raw cotton is exported to Myingyan, and from thence to Bhamo and Rangoon. "The bulk of the yarn used for weaving purposes in the district is made locally, only a comparatively small proportion being imported, while the consumption of ready-made cotton clothing in the form of *pasos*,[3] *lungyis*, &c., of European manufacture is of quite unimportant dimensions. There has probably been an increase since the annexation in the amount of European ready-made clothing imported into the district, but the increase has been chiefly ned to Meiktila and some of the larger towns. Apart from this, there is little evidence to show that imported fabrics are ousting locally made materials, except perhaps in the finer qualities. Imported yarn is some 3½ times dearer than locally made white and dyed yarn." In Thayetmyo it is stated that in the past 12 years there has been a certain amount of progress in the industry owing to the introduction of mill-made goods, with which the Burmans have to compete. During the last three years also a trade has been opened up with the Chinese from Bhamo, who buy the white cloth and dye it and make it into clothes in China.

e declension of the industry does not therefore seem so rapid or so marked in the Upper Province, though it is not difficult to see that, even where the reports are most favourable, there are signs of the coming change.

In the Southern Shan States a considerable quantity of cotton is exported in pressed bales to Yunnan, and caravans from China coming round with wares, collect cotton and European and Indian cotton / fabrics for their return journey. *(iii) The Southern Shan States.*

ese latter are bought principally in Burma, but the raw cotton is obtained from the hill villages and local bazaars at the rate of Rs. 25 per 100 viss. Sometimes one, sometimes two, trips are made in the year. In the Kēngtūng State cotton is grown almost exclusively by the hill tribes. They make their clothes of it and sell their surplus to the Shans of the villages and to the Chinese caravans. In Shan villages nearly every house has a loom, and the women clean, dye, spin and weave their own cotton. The hill people, the Shans of the more remote villages, and generally the poorer sort, still wear clothing of home manufacture: there can be no doubt, however, as to the popularity of the finer imported stuff. Indian and Manchester white cotton cloth is likewise imported, dyed locally,

of imported cotton fabrics, their use will be largely extended. Further, money is by no means plentiful. With more ready money larger purchases of imported fabrics may be looked for.

Speaking of the effect of customs on the people, it is stated:

"In Kēngtūng State tribal custom prescribes a certain style of dress, and especially the women have a distinctive costume, as have also the Shan-Chinese community, and the Lü men and women. Such dresses are now homespun, but custom will only delay, not prevent, the use of imported fabrics, as soon as traders can sell them at a less cost.

"Already the people of the Kēngtūng valley have adopted imported stuff for turbans, and the Lü women freely use imported fabrics for their jackets, after dyeing them to their own taste. So far, the Shan-Chinese have adhered to their homespun, but this is due as much to economy as to conservatism. When imported stuff is as cheap and as good as the native cloth, they will probably buy it."

In the Hsipaw State the villages on the main roads used to weave their cloth, but now most people buy the cotton goods which come up from below. There was formerly a finer sort of *hpyin* manufactured for making jackets and *thingans*,[4] but now that the finer cloth can be easily obtained in every bazaar, only the coarse *hpyin* is woven. There is a considerable amount of cotton cultivation round Lashio, but clothes are often made from imported calico of Manchester manufacture, and the cotton yarn used for weaving is not always locally produced. / There can be little doubt that, as the Shan States are opened up, European goods will eventually drive the Shan articles from the market. The Palaungs of Taungbaing buy their threads already dyed from the hawkers, or traders, or in a bazaar. Imported fabrics have certainly reduced the amount of weaving done, and as the country becomes more civilized the weaving will still further decrease.

The locally made cloth being infinitely more durable, it is cheaper to wear clothes made from it, but the richer Palaungs of Namsan and surrounding villages that are nearer civilization, prefer some thing finer in appearance. It is only amongst the poorer classes that weaving is now done.

How far are these conclusions borne out by the census returns of 1881 and 1891?

It will be seen by a reference to the introduction written by Mr. Eales to the latter report that there were 229,185 persons engaged in the cotton industry in all Burma in 1891, of whom 39,142 were males and 190,043 were females. It is, he says, essentially an occupation pursued by women, chiefly in the rural tracts, as shown by the local returns, and notwithstanding the excess of population in Lower Burma, far fewer weavers are found there than in the Upper Province.

For the year 1881 we have only census returns for Lower Burma, and Mr. Eales points out that, owing to the difference of classification in the two reports, the female population, the number of women weavers in Lower Burma may be calculated to have decreased by 13.19 per cent. during the last decade, the total number in Lower Burma being only 35,412 in 1891. These figures include silk-weavers also; but as he is further of opinion that the Burmans were largely giving up cotton for silk garments, the ratio of decrease among the cotton-weavers would be still greater.

It is interesting also to further examine some of the district reports now received in the light of the census of 1891.

In Bassein and Tavoy, it is said, there is now no cotton industry; but the census of 1891 gives a total of 9,983 persons engaged in the cotton industry the Tavoy and 3,728 in Bassein. Similarly in Upper Burma, in the Kyauksè district there were 5,935 persons employed thus in 1891, now there are reported to be none. The census was taken in November 1891. If then these latter reports are accurate, all this has happened within five years – a declension so rapid as to be scarcely credible. /

Again, from the Kindat subdivision it is reported that "thousands and thousands who earned a living by the cotton industry have been thrown out of employment with the advent of goods of European manufacture." The total population, however, of the whole Upper Chindwin district in 1891 was only 75,785 persons, and it is further said in the report that "the local cotton industry was never on a large scale in this district," so that the statement above referred to must be exaggerated. In Mandalay the census returns show that in 1891 there were 37,469 people engaged in the cotton industry, being over 16 per cent. of the total male and over 33 per cent. of the total female population of the district, and in the Lower Chindwin district there were 24,307 similarly employed, being 4 per cent. of the male and 26 per cent. of the female population. It is now, however, reported from Mandalay that the industry is resorted to only by the poorer classes for domestic use, and not for the purposes of trade, and from the Lower Chindwin that the industry is a large one and employs a large number of families.

What is the inference to be drawn? Either that there has been a decline in the industry in Mandalay, and not in the Lower Chindwin, within the last five years, or else a widely different view has been taken in each case of the position of the trade. But Mandalay is just one of those districts which reports that "imported fabrics do not in any way influence the local industry," if then there has been a decline, to what is it due? Possibly to a larger consumption of silk clothing, or perhaps imported fabrics have had a larger influence than has been recognized.

It will thus be seen that the main conclusions arrived at are entirely supported by the census figures, though some of the reports seem open to correction on certain points.

A few quotations from the trade returns will further give some idea of the extent of the present importations and the general position of the Burma cotton trade.

Turning, then, to the report on the trade and navigation of Burma for the year 1895-96, we find that among the most notable increases in imports is recorded cotton twist and yarn 18½ lakhs, and coloured cotton piece-goods[5] 15½ lakhs, during the year, though there were indications that the trade was somewhat overdone. /

The following figures are given: –

	Rs.
Imported from the United Kingdom during the year 8,934,339 lbs. of cotton twist and yarn, valued	45,87,322
From other foreign countries 226,360 lbs.	1,46,342
Total 9,160,699 lbs. valued at	47,33,664

In the previous year the total was –

	Rs.
3,830,594 lbs. valued at	28,99,925
In 1893-94 3,923.365 lbs. valued at	31,55,691

The value of the cotton piece-goods imported was Rs. 1,04,21,954 as against Rs. 87,53,277 of the year before, and Rs. 1,26,73,323 of 1893-94.

There was also a large increase in the importations of cotton twist, yarn and piece-goods from Bengal, Madras, and Bombay. These country yarns are said to have competed successfully with the foreign article, and sometimes to have replaced it, but it is doubtful whether this will be so now that the import duties on the latter have been removed. The importations of country yarn were –

	1895-96. lbs.	1894-95. lbs.
From Bengal	2,531,748	1,624,763
From Bombay	3.163,290	2,976,084
From Madras	2,431,600	1,279,700

– a substantial advance in each case.

The figures relating to cotton piece-goods from Bombay, Madras, Bengal, Sind, and the other Indian ports tell the same tale, except with regard to white bleached goods only, the imported quantity of which has fallen off.

The following statistics from the report on the trade of Burma with the adjoining countries will illustrate how the cotton trade stands in relation to neighbouring States.

Indian piece-goods were imported to the amount of Rs. 13,519 from the

kind of manufactured cotton, except European twist and yarn, there was a most marked advance in the quantity exported.

The totals exported in the two triennial periods were as follows: –

	1893–96.	1890–93.
	lbs.	lbs.
Indian twist and yarn	1,053,826	282,906
European twist and yarn	493,100	506,810
Indian piece-goods	249,630	28,916
European piece-goods	4,813,899	2,749,295 /

e countries that have received these exportations are West China, the Northern and Southern Shan States, Siam, Zimmè and Karenni.

As these figures only include the exports sent by land, it is quite clear that yarn and cotton goods are conveyed largely through Burma to China, &c., and with the opening of the Mandalay-Kunlôn Railway a further increase may be anticipated.

Prominent among the reasons of the decline of the cotton trade is the slow and laborious native method of spinning and weaving as compared with the machinery used in the European and Indian mills. Below is a description of the process, as carried on in the Shwebo district, which is typical of the whole country: – *III. – Description of cotton weaving and spinning.*

"The cotton boll having been gathered, is separated from the pod, and picked by hand: it is then put in the basket. It is next separated from the seeds, which is done by pressing the boll between two small wooden revolving rollers, worked by hand. After pressing it, cotton is placed in a basket which is funnel shaped, with the mouth towards the worker. This basket is made to revolve and the cotton is caught up on the string of a bow. By pulling and loosening this bow-string the cotton fabrics are separated out, and it becomes ready for preparing thread. Wound about small sticks, the cotton is now made into a cylinder with a small aperture.

"with a spinning-jenny these small cylinders are converted into thread. A small piece of thread is attached to the roller, and the loose end held to the cotton cylinder, which winds off in thread.

"As the small balls of thread are wound off they are put into a basket. The cotton has now to be cleaned.

It is thoroughly soaked in rice-water, and pressed out on a flat board, and then placed in the sun to dry.

After cleansing, the cotton thread is wound on a frame consisting of two horizontal bars, and combed to make it less coarse. The comb used is the inside of the fruit called 'sat-thwa-bin,' which, when dried, is not unlike a dry hand sponge. The skein being thus roughly combed is wound on to a revolving circular frame, and thence on to hand-reels. The web is next prepared by winding the skein off two hand-reels round posts. The entanglement at the corner posts is of course intentional, / as when the web is attached to the loom one set of threads must fall and the other rise.

[...] The shuttle is a small hollow piece of wood, containing a ball of thread which is thrown across between the two lines of thread composing the warp. A small pedal is attached to each of the two bars of the loom, and these are pulled down by the foot alternately, as the shuttle is thrown across."

The Shans use much the same instruments as the Burmans; the Chins, have a different process called "*gyat*-weaving," but no description of it has been sent. The Karen method, as practised in the Toungoo district, is of a very primitive character. The thread is prepared in the same manner as by the Burmese, but no loom is used. The two ends of the warp are simply fastened to some convenient fixture, and the loops in the middle passed round a rod of about 1 inch in diameter, the threads being arranged one by one to the full breadth of the warp, which is generally about 18 inches. The rod is fastened to the weaver's body by a cord fixed at each end of it and going round the body. The weaver sits on the ground pulling the warp tight towards him, and manipulates the shuttle and *gyat-thwa*.

The process is much slower than the Burmese method, but the cloth is of higher value, being thicker and more durable.

Of the dyeing nothing need be said, except that here also the foreign dyes, being cheaper and more brilliant, are entirely displacing the native ones. [...]

It must now be abundantly plain that the cotton fabric industry has no immediate future before it in Burma. To quote the words of the Sub-divisional Officer of Shwebo: "Commercially speaking, the industry is quite unimportant, and it is rather from the quaint character of the manufacturing implements, some of them almost identical with those in vogue in Homeric Greece, from the glimpse it gives us of the state of trade in pre-British times – in short, it is as a survival rather than as a living industry that cotton fabric manufacture of this description derives its interest." /

A retrospect of what has been written shows that the reasons of this decay are the introduction of imported articles, the length and tediousness of the native method, and its un-remunerative character, and these are but three aspects of the same cause. Probably the imported articles are cheaper, though the quotations made from some of the reports would appear to contradict this. Most, however, state it definitely, and in those in which the contrary is alleged, what seems really meant is that the native cloth being coarser and thicker, is more durable, and that the poorer classes do not purchase the foreign imported cloth since they have not money to do so, while they have sufficient means to buy the cotton seed and utilize their own labour in the manufacture of clothes. But this is no proof that the home article is really the cheaper, unless the cost of labour is to be counted in one case and not in the other, and how much more expensive the division of labour among the operatives. When one worker goes through every process of the task, he cannot accomplish it quickly: it takes days to do; and so it has come about that the men have neglected weaving and spinning, and it is now left entirely to women.

Nor does there appear as yet to be any prospect of mills being erected and machinery introduced into Burma. Labour is too scarce at present, and paddy planting is at once more profitable and affords more leisure: the Burman would not be content to work in a mill for wages that would enable the mill-owner to compete with outside manufactories.

Perhaps, as the population grows and coolie labour is imported in increasing quantities from India, mills may some day be established in Rangoon, but the time seems distant yet, unless the State should first be the pioneer with its supply of convict labour. Much would also depend on the amount and quality of the raw cotton to be obtained in Burma.

Cotton is grown in several of the Upper Burma districts, especially round Myingyan and Meiktila and also in the Northern Arakan tract of Lower Burma, for trade purposes. It is exported to India by sea, and to Western China, either up the river to Bhamo and from thence overland to Yunnan, or down the river to Rangoon, whence it is shipped *viâ* the Straits to the ports on the Chinese sea-board.

V. – The raw cotton trade in Burma.

is trade is almost entirely in the hands of Chinese agents resident in Burma, some in Rangoon, some in Myingyan, &c. / They learn from friends in China the price of cotton in the various markets there, and thus decide whether they are likely to realize more profit by shipping it from Rangoon to South China, or by sending it from Bhamo to Yunnan. That sent down by steamer is pressed before shipment by English firms in hydraulic pressing machines, of which there are said to be two only at present in Rangoon. It sometimes happens that cotton which has been despatched to Rangoon, after lying there some weeks, is finally taken up again to Bhamo and sent by the land route to China in obedience to the latest intelligence.

e trade returns show that 8,555 cwt. of raw cotton were exported by sea in 1895-96, as against 4,489 cwt. in the preceding year, though in 1892-93 the gures reached 20,434 cwt. Most of this went to China and the Straits Settlements, there being a decrease in the shipments to Bengal.

By land 111,983 maunds were sent to Western China and the Northern Shan States in the years between 1893-94 and 1895-96, as against 126,926 maunds in the preceding triennial period.

ere were 242,196 maunds sent from Upper to Lower Burma, and 15,306 maunds from Lower to Upper Burma during 1893-94 to 1895-96, and in each case the amounts far exceed those of the previous years. This up and down traf-c is probably partly due to the reason given above, and now that the Railway

Department have reduced their rates for cotton, a further stimulus will doubtless be given to the trade.

The figures are some index of the surplus raw cotton production in Burma, as there were no importations from outside, except an insignificant amount of 39 maunds from the Northern Shan States. To obtain the total outturn must further be reckoned the amount grown and consumed on the spot by the women weavers of the house, for which there are no figures.

It would appear then that, if mills were established in Burma, there would be no difficulty in obtaining cotton, and that there is a better prospect for a raw-cotton industry than for the manufacture of cotton fabrics in Burma, as now carried on.

[...]

From the artistic side there is little to be said of the cotton fabrics of Burma. *Pasos, tameins, lungyis,* jackets, bags, blankets and *culagas* or curtains are the chief articles made by the Burmese, and there is not much variety in the patterns. Most are either stripes or checks, in which the tints are nicely blended, and they use all colours, uniting the imported red yarn with their own home made. But the best and brightest patterns are in the silk garments, and sometimes a cotton *paso* is shot with threads of silver or gold silk. The most elaborate designs are found in the curtains or *culagas* used for hanging on walls. Here the art advances to the pictorial stage, various scenes, figures, &c., being represented. Dark blue and indigo colours are those fancied by the Shans and hill tribes, but their sombreness is generally relieved by trimmings of red or some bright hue. Among the Shans of the Hsenwi State some curious sleeping-mats or cloths are made. They are described as being of a zig-zag or diamond shaped pattern, woven usually in black or red on a white ground, and carried out with the nicest exactness and regularity of detail.

Still more intricate is the Kachin work, both in the adornment of bags or pockets and the female costume. The ground work is usually dark blue with longitudinal blue stripes, but is sometimes seen all white, or made of equal stripes of red, white and blue, into which are woven at intervals little stars, crosses, or squares of various colours and irregular shapes.

The Lü women of the Southern Shan States wear a turban fashioned like a tea-cosy.[6] It is always dark blue and ornamented with real or imitation gold and silver thread, which is interwoven with the cotton, and, when on the head, the ornamental protion is outside and to the front. Hitherto this has been preserved; but in the weaving of their embroidered petticoats and the border on the trousers of the Lü men pieces of coloured imported stuff are now added.

The attempts of English manufacturers to imitate such garments have been very few and not sufficiently like the original to satisfy the people. But there are signs that, struck by the brilliant dyed foreign stuffs, even these hill races are beginning to purchase them and introduce them into their native dress. Thus the tribal costumes will soon be wholly modified. If this should come about rapidly, the foreign manufacturer will not trouble to imitate what he foresees is not likely to be required; / he will have set a new fashion with his imported goods, and will be largely responsible for the disappearance of the traditional raiment.

MORRIS, 'THE LACQUERWARE INDUSTRY OF BURMA', *JOURNAL OF THE BURMA RESEARCH SOCIETY* (1919)

A. P. Morris, 'The Lacquerware Industry of Burma', *Journal of the Burma Research Society*, 9:1 (1919), pp. 1–14.

e lacquerware sector was one of the few industries that expanded during the period largely owing to increased European demand for its products. After a section on the tapping of the thitsi tree, which produced the material used on the surface of lacquerware, the article discusses the traditional and modern lacquering processes, different types of lacquerware and the future of the sector.

A. P. Morris, 'The Lacquerware Industry of Burma', *Journal of the Burma Research Society* (1919)

THITSI, THE MATERIAL USED IN LACQUER WARE.

[...] The material used in the production of the shiny surface of lacquered wares is procured from more than one plant. The Japanese obtain their material from the sumach (Rhus vernicifera), and the Burmans theirs from the *thitsi* tree (melanorrhoea usitata). In both cases the material is obtained by making incisions in the bark of the tree, whence there issues a greyish sticky liquid which hardens on exposure to a jet black solid. The composition of the Japanese and Burmese materials is similar consisting, in the case of *thitsi*, of about 85 per cent. of urushic acid, the balance being diastatic matter, oils and gums. Urushic acid, by the way, derives its name from "urushi," the Japanese word for lacquer. Hardening takes place by the action of the diastatic matter on the urushic acid, and unlike varnishes lacquer ware needs moisture when drying and sets better in the dark; in fact it will not set properly in direct sunlight, while a temperature above 120 degrees Fahr. is bad for it.

e *thitsi* tree is a fine upstanding tree found particularly in the drier forests of the province up to 3,500 feet. The timber is a very beautiful dark red with yellowish streaks, hard and durable and takes a good polish. With age the colour acquires a deeper tone and the wood / is very suitable for high class furniture. It is however with the lacquer material that we are concerned, this is known as

. In a monograph on the tree prepared by the Forest Department, (Indian Forest Records Vol. VI, Part III) Mr. Blandford is quoted as follows: –

"Method of Tapping. – The usual method of tapping is to make two deep notches to form a V. The notches are eight to ten inches long, and about two inches deep. At the base of the V, small bamboo cups are placed, with an edge stuck into a small horizontal cut just at the base of the V, in such a way that the oil which exudes from the V-shaped notch flows into the cup. The oil can only be collected in fairly dry weather, as when it rains the oil is either washed away or is too diluted in the cups to be of any use. If only a little rain water is mixed with the *thitsi*, it becomes of a reddish colour. The number of cups that can be put on one tree depends on the size of the tree, and whether the tree is to be tapped for a large temporary outturn or for a regular yearly outturn. It is usual to have notches, one above the other, as high as a man can reach. About four or five can be made in a slanting direction, one above the other. Once the tree has been tapped in any one place, it must be left at least four, if not five, years to allow the original notches to heal over completely before being tapped again.

"It thus follows that, if a line of notches is made each year and the tree is big enough to allow of five lines being made, the tree can be tapped every year; for, as soon as the total available surface has been tapped, the old blazes will have healed up completely and notching can be continued. The notching appears to have no effect on the life of a tree, and trees that are covered with scars appear to be as healthy as those which have not been tapped. Trees of all sizes can be tapped, but of course – only trees of some size (about six feet breast-girth) can be tapped every year for the reasons specified above."

The bulk of the present Burma supplies come from Katha and the Shan States and it is estimated that the total output is about 200 tons a year. Bad methods of tapping threaten the future supplies, and the question of preserving the tree and regulating tapping is under consideration. At present the right to tap trees is subject to forest licences, but there is no attempt to ensure scientific and safe methods.

DEVELOPMENT OF LACQUER WARE

To a forest dweller the value of *thitsi* as a material would soon become evident, and probably *thitsi* was first used as a waterproofing on basket ware. The material is so used wherever the tree is found, and an example of this simple application of *thitsi* is shewn among the exhibits.

The next step was the production of a smooth surface. Probably this was first obtained on basket ware by the addition of several coats of the *thitsi*. This would fill up the interstices and give a coating more or less shiny but still showing the nature of the framework. From this to a really smooth surface is a fairly long step. The method by which ordinary simple lacquer ware, done on coarse basket work, is given a smooth shiny surface is as follows. The basket is first of all treated with a mixture / of *thitsi* and clay which fills in the larger interstices without using up very much *thitsi*. This, after hardening, is smoothed and a second coating is applied which is smoothed again. The second coating is generally of a finer material made by mixing *thitsi* with ash as a diluent, the object being to obtain a smooth surface with as little expenditure of *thitsi* as possible. The finer the work the finer is the powdered ash used; in high class work the ash is obtained from cow-dung, paddy husk, or bones. This ash in fact also seems to shorten the period of setting, and as each coat has to set before another can be applied quick setting is of some importance. The rest of the process is purely one of smoothing and coating with *thitsi* turn and turn about. As the article comes near a finish the smoothing is more carefully done. Nature provides a suitable "sand paper" in the leaf of the *dahat* tree, or in some cases the object is polished with paddy husk and water, while for the very finest work the fossil wood commonly found in the dry zone is powdered and used, this latter generally on the finer circular wares which can be turned on the primitive lathe which you will see in use in the balcony. The polishing agent varies with the quality of finish and the availability of materials.

Often part of the article is coloured a brilliant red by painting it with a mixture of *hinthapada* and *thitsi*. Hinthapada is obtained from China and is mercuric sulphide or cinnabar; it is exported from China to Europe as Chinese vermilion. Mixed with a small amount of *thitsi* and *shansi* (an oil from the Shan States) and applied to lacquer wares its brilliant red colour shows in spite of the darkening of the *thitsi*, though in course of time it does tone somewhat and a very beautiful colour it is too.

Generally the framework is of bamboo as described, but occasionally, as in the case of boxes, the craftsmen use wood. This naturally gives a smooth surface more readily and soft woods to which *thitsi* will adhere are preferred, such woods as "Baing" (Tetrameles nudiflora) and "didu" (Bombax insigne).

is is the method of manufacture of the ordinary simple lacquer wares of the Province. The main centres of production are at present Maungdaung and Kyaukka in the Lower Chindwin district.

[...]

Method of Production of Modern Pagan Ware.

e characteristic of the "yun" work is that a pattern is worked on to the lacquer surface by a method of successive incisions filled with colouring matter. The process has reached its highest development in / Pagan and a description of the method by which the highest grades of Pagan ware are produced will perhaps be of interest.

We will take for our example a cup. After a series of coatings has brought the surface up to the condition of the plain lacquered ware already described, the cup is handed to a craftsman skilled in "yun" work. He takes the cup and proceeds to outline his figures by making a series of scratches with a sharp pointed iron style. The figures drawn are more or less conventionalised, but the skill exhibited is very considerable. One cannot but admire the neat way in which a design is started on a circular surface such as a cup and the draughtsman, without making any apparent calculations or guide marks, starts from one point and works round till he arrives again at the starting point, and yet, when the design

rately has the spacing been done. If you want evidence of the skill required to do this successfully try it for yourselves and you see how hard it is. The case with which the draughtsman proceeds and the rapidity with which he works are well worth some observation. The starting point for a figure is apparently the eye. The scratches having been made a mixture of *hinthapada* and *thitsi* and *shansi* is rubbed over the surface of the cup filling the scratches with colour. When this has set the cup is again put on the lathe and polished, all colour being removed from the surface except that which fills the scratches, and we then have the out-lines left in red on a black surface. A new series of scratches is made and the process is repeated. To obtain yellow lines they use orpiment as their pigment, to obtain green they mix together orpiment[1] and indigo and for orange they use realgar.[2] With these four pigments, hinthapada, orpiment, realgar and indigo, the patterns are produced, each different shade being worked in by a separate series of scratches, so that in the fine work the article is alternately scratched and polished a large number of times. Now each application of *thitsi* and each coating of colour takes some four or five days to set. This setting is carried out in cellars, for as I have already stated damp and darkness aid in the setting of *thitsi*. In a good piece of work in which the separate processes may be as many as 26, the time between start and finish is often as much as six months. This explains the delay which occurs between the giving of an order and the delivering of an article and while purchasers may fret at this delay and blame the craftsman they can only secure a shortening of the time by accepting inferior work. Visitors some-times do not understand the prices quoted by the craftsmen for wares, two boxes of apparently about the same size varying by 300 per cent. in price. The explana-tion lies in the amount of work and the number of coatings of colour put on; for apart from the actual quantity of labour the time between start and completion of the work is an important factor. In the case of a good piece of work the mean time between the expenditure of labour and the completion of the work is three months and for this period the craftsman has to await payment for his labour; hence he must charge a greater rate for the labour than for similar labour which can earn a return in a shorter period. I do not / claim for it that this fine work is the most attractive, personally I think that less ornament rather than more orna-ment is desirable, but the difference in price is certainly justified by the greater length of time and the greater amount of labour spent on the fine work.

At Pagan there has been a tendency to produce a very light ware, and conse-quently the best work in the manufacture of modern betel boxes or bowls has been done on finer framework than in the old ware. The difference is purely one of the framework, which is made of very fine woven bamboo, or in the case of the very thinnest articles, the warp is of bamboo and the woof of hair, generally horse hair. The lightness of the ware is an attraction in its way, and it exhibits the remarkable

ibility and you cannot crush the material as you would a Panama hat. I have one or two good specimens of the ware, but I always prefer to show off this flexibility myself rather than let visitors to whom I am showing it handle my property. If you crack the cup or whatever you are handling it cannot be repaired.

[...]

GILT LACQUER WARE.

In real gold leaf work this covering of a surface rather than the filling in of scratches is more common. And in passing one may remark that in practically all Burmese gilding work *thitsi* is used as the medium for sticking the gold leaf to the article which is to be gilded.

Kengtung in the Southern Shan States has a particular type of lacquer ware which is represented by a small collection kindly sent in by Mr. Grose. The chief article of manufacture in Kengtung, apart from plain wares, is a peculiar type of basket ware bowl, covered with lacquer, and gilded. Some of these have a smooth surface, some have an embossed surface. Of the latter I shall speak later. Curiously enough, although Kengtung is nearer the Lao area, that is to say the area from which the "yun" work originates, the makers of these Kengtung bowls apparently claim to be the descendants of Laikkha people, and to have learned the use of *thitsi* as an ornamental ware from their Laikkha ancestors. At the same time the Kengtung type of bowl is their invention and while Laikkha men produce the Kengtung bowl this is a very modern development and is due to the enthusiasm of the Assistant Superintendent of the Shan States. I think it was Mr. Gahan who first induced the Laikkha people to make "Kengtung" bowls.

e gilt lacquer ware of the Province reached a high degree of excellence at Prome, one Saya Pa, now dead, having been a master of the craft. In consequence gilt lacquer has become associated with the name of Prome town although the work was done in other places and as a matter of fact since the death of Saya Pa the industry has died in Prome. So much can a master craftsman do for the credit of his craft.

e process by which the Burmese workers produce the gilded figure work on lacquer ware is as follows. After the surface has been treated with excessive coats of lacquer until a high degree of polish is obtained, the artist paints in a design with a paint made of orpiment and gum water. When completed and before the *thitis* is absolutely hard the whole surface / is treated with gold leaf.

e surface is then allowed to harden in the usual way and is afterwards washed with water. On the surface to which the orpiment paint has been applied the gold washes away leaving a jet black surface and the pattern stands out in black and gold. The pattern that is painted on is therefore a negative of the final design.

The Prome designs are usually rather of the "Willow-pattern" type, surrounded by floral scrolls. A fine example is exhibited. This is a replica of some tables which are at Government House; these tables were much admired by Sir Harcourt Butler and he wished to have more made. The industry at Prome was dead, but careful photographs were taken and the tables were reproduced at Pagan by Saya Khan.

Mandalay has at present a few workers in this particular branch of craft. Every year you will see some of their caskets at the Art Exhibition, this being the particular line in which they excel. But they also make large chests for holding the Buddhist scriptures and such chests from Mandalay, Pagan, Prome and elsewhere will be found all over the country. As a rule the figures are drawn in line in the manner already described and appear therefore in black lines on a gold ground. The old Prome ware of the type associated with the name of Saya Pa is bolder in design and consequently more attractive in many ways than the rather finicky designs from Mandalay. It has been a rather unfortunate general tendency of Burmese art ware during the last twenty years or so that it has forsaken the bold designs of the older masters and has taken rather to crowded detail, very skilfully executed, but lacking the artistic merit of the older work. [...]

Moulded Work.

We now turn to another form of lacquer ware, the moulded work made with a putty prepared from *thitsi* and ash. I have already mentioned that to fill the interstices in the basket framework the craftsman mixed *thitsi* with other substances. For the finer work the mixture, known as "thayo", is made of *thitsi* and bone of paddy husk ash. This mixture gives a fine plastic material which readily lends itself to manipulation, and it can be applied and made to adhere to plain surfaces, such as the side of boxes, by means of *thitsi*. After a few days it becomes hard and the general appearance is that of polished ebony, and in fact it is in some ways superior to carved wood being less liable to fracture. The craftsman in working this material uses a small moulding board, which he sprinkles with ash much as a pastry cook sprinkles his pastry with flour to prevent its adhering to the board and rolling pin. The putty itself is also constantly sprinkled with ash. The moulding is done / with fingers and a small tool, usually made of horn. With great dexterity he rapidly forms sprays and flowers, a touch with the fingers giving the leaves that curve which renders them lifelike. Each small piece as it is finished is stuck on the box, or whatever surface is to be ornamented, by means of *thitsi*, and after the whole has dried it is generally painted over with *thitsi* to make sure that it adheres properly. In this way, large boxes for manuscripts, the bases of shrines, and other articles, are ornamented. Smaller running patterns are moulded in place instead of on the moulding board. The result is an embossed jet black surface. Generally this is gilded, though speaking for oneself, the ungilt work often seems more attractive. There are standard patterns in the floral work which have generally accepted names. Some small panels of the work are to be found in the exhibit, several of them illustrate the "Yodaya" design which is distinguished, not by the type of foliage, but by the general outline. Another panel shows the thaminbye or "running stag" design. The reason for the name may not be very apparent, it is an undulating design and the idea is that this undulating motive represents the path which a stag in flight takes through the jungle. This type of work has a quarter assigned to it in Mandalay, Sadaiktan being so called from the "sadaiks" or manuscript chests which are made there, and the trade in these articles is still very considerable. Some of the Kengtung bowls exhibit the same kind of ornament.

As an extension of this craft we have the "hmansi shwekya", or glass mosaic work. In this work in addition to "thayo" moulding the the articles are ornamented with small pieces of coloured glass or mica set in "thayo". For the bases of shrines this type of ornament is common and some of the tazaungs of the Shwe Dagon contain fine example of the work. For small articles it is not so attractive, but with large objects at a distance in bright sunlight the work is very effective.

[…]

Properties of Thitsi, and the Future of the Lacquer Industry.

So much for the industry as it stands, what of its future? Before making any attempt to discuss this I should like to say a few words more on the properties *thitsi*. Some two years ago I asked Mr. Raikes, electrical inspector, to test the electrical properties of *thitsi* putty and he gave this material a good deal of his attention. He found that it had high insulting values, and it seemed possible that it might be useful for the moulding of small switch bases and other electrical apparatus. It takes a long time to set however and while the addition of ferric oxide accelerates hardening, experiments have not gone much further in that direction. Mr. Raikes found that tape dipped in *thitsi* and wound on wires served as a useful insulation, here again there does not seem much room for development except in its use for temporary work locally, the price of *thitsi* is fairly high and *thitsi*-soaked tape is not likely to replace the usual insulating materials. As a paint it gives a ne black finish, and as already noted it is very flexible and therefore not likely to ake off. It is not acted on by strong alkalis or acid and might be useful as a paint for corrugated iron roofs of engine sheds and other similar structures liable to be attacked by acid. Except for such special purposes its price precludes its use.

If the tapping of trees is subjected to regulation as suggested, the price of *thitsi* will probably rise anyhow for a good many years to come. But unless precautions are taken to regulate tapping the supply is liable to decrease, so we may expect some advance in price either way.

That the price does preclude the export of the material is perhaps fortunate. As it is all the material produced is used within the country in the manufacture of finished articles. Were the price such as to secure export orders the effect would be to kill an industry and that certainly would not benefit the Province as a whole.

It does not follow however that changes cannot advantageously be made in the state of the industry. At present lacquered wares are found in practically every Burman household, but there is a tendency in many cases for these wares to be replaced by metal work. If the material used / in the coarser lacquer wares can be deflected to wares of a higher quality or to wares which bring in a greater daily wage to the workers it will all be to the good. At present the value of the imports of lacquered wares to Burma amounts to ½ lakh per year. There is no reason why the Burman workers should not capture all this trade and have a large share in the lacquer were trade of India as well. All that is needed is some experiment, a certain amount of instruction, and improved organisation; rather much has to be done perhaps, but it is not an impossible proposition.

ANON., *MEMORANDUM ON BUSINESS METHODS AND TRADING REGULATIONS IN SIAM* (1917)

Anon., *Memorandum on Business Methods and Trading Regulations in Siam* (London: Board of Trade, 1917), pp. 1–15.

e memorandum was compiled from information collected by the Board of Trade's Department of Commercial Intelligence and provided by T. H. Lyle, H.M. Consul-General at Bangkok. Lyle was appointed British Vice Consul at Nan in 1896 and became Consul at Chiang Mai in 1907. He achieved limited fame during the Shan Rebellion when he negotiated with the rebels and persuaded many of them to lay down their arms and go home. He left Chiang Mai in 1913 and was subsequently knighted. The report covers every aspect of doing business in Siam.

Anon., *Memorandum on Business Methods and Trading Regulations in Siam* (1917), extract

BUSINESS METHODS.

CHANNELS THROUGH WHICH BUSINESS IS DONE.

[...] The *most growing channel to-day* is that of European firms in Siam buying goods through their own firms or agents in Europe on their own account for sale in Siam. Prior to the war, the most growing channel was that of large native dealers or retail stores in Siam buying from Europe direct through agents in Europe, for there was an increasing tendency on the part of native indentors to order direct from suppliers through agents in Europe. *It is fully expected that this tendency will develop after the war.*

Special reference may be made to the important piece goods trade. In this trade the first channel indicated above is followed, and European firms in Siam buy in Europe on account of dealers in Siam. These dealers usually indent for particular "chops" or brands. The successful European firms have their own "chops" or marks for particular lines of goods; such "chops" become known and popular in the Bazaar, and it is for goods of a particular "chop" or mark that the Bazaar dealer asks.

If a manufacturer desires to open and cultivate business in Siam he should endeavour to be represented there by a good firm who will push business. This is much more important than a visit from a smart traveller at rare intervals, although periodical visits by travellers are most valuable if made in conjunction with a capable agent on the spot. Should the traveller be acting alone, it is recommended that business be transacted on "documents against payment" terms, the usual usance being from sight to thirty days.

AGENCY CONDITIONS, ETC.

Commission

e rates of commission usually paid to agents in Siam for the sale of imported articles vary according to the nature of the goods, and according to the risk of *del

agent in Siam taking orders from dealers the commission is payable on all orders executed, and it is usual to pay the agent a commission on orders placed direct with the manufacturers, the amount of which varies but probably averages 2½ per cent.

In the case of the European manufacturer's agent in Siam selling from stock goods consigned by his principal, the rule varies, but / frequently there is a stipulation that the goods have to be paid for by the agent within twelve months, sold or unsold. As a rule the agent takes the *del credere* risk for an additional consideration of about 2½ per cent.

As regards the special terms and conditions under which the agent is usually employed by an overseas principal, the manufacturer generally gives the agent commission upon all orders, whether placed through him or not, and frequently refers the same to the agent to be dealt with; conversely, the agent usually, but not always, binds himself to the manufacturer in respect of the latter's line of goods. Occasionally manufacturers have two or more lines, for which they have more than one agent.

Generally speaking, contracts are made in the name of the agent (unless he is merely managing a branch in Siam for an overseas principal), but of course disclosing the name of the principal.

There are occasions, however, when important contracts, such as for machinery, railway material, etc., are made in the name of the principals, and this generally applies in the case of Government contracts.

The legal responsibility of the agent of an overseas firm in Siam to his principal will depend largely upon the nationality of the agent.

The principle of extra-territoriality prevails in Siam, and although several nations have surrendered this privilege, other nations still retain the right whereby their subjects are governed by their own laws, administered by Consular Courts.

The United Kingdom has to all intents abandoned extra-territoriality in Siam, and the responsibility of a British agent dwelling in Siam representing a British manufacturer would be governed by the Siamese law of principal or agent, and decided in a Siamese Court.

Denmark and France (as regards her Asiatic subjects and protégés only) have also agreed to their subjects being justiciable in the Siamese Courts.

Should the agent in Siam be other than a Siamese subject, a British subject, a Danish subject, or a French Asiatic subject, his responsibilities would depend upon the views held in such matters by the Consular Court of the nationality to which he belonged. *It is, therefore, highly advisable that British principals should endeavour to confine their agencies in Siam to individuals or firms of British nationality.*

There are no trading fees or special trade taxes payable in respect of opera-

applied to dealings in "Arms and Ammunition" and "Wines and Spirits," and licences are necessary to trade in these goods. The amount of the licence fee varies in accordance with the nature of the business carried on, but no distinction is made in respect of the nationality of the dealer.

One highly important point relating to agencies in Siam is that referred to above, viz., the differentiation in the law applicable where a British exporter appoints as agent one who is the subject of a nation which has not foregone its extra-territorial rights. In / the event of the principal suing his agent, the latter, if a foreigner other than Danish, Siamese, or French Asiatic, will be justiciable only in the Consular Court of his own nationality. It might happen, therefore, that the views held by a foreign Consular Court in respect of an action brought by a principal against his agent in Siam would be totally at variance with the judgment given in a Siamese Court in a counter action brought on the same subject and on the same facts against the principal by the agent.

is differentiation would, of course, not apply where the agent sues on behalf of his principal; in this event the agent, despite his foreign nationality, would be governed, as regards the privileges and obligations of his principal, by the latter's nationality.

Terms of Payment, Credit, etc.

Where the agent in Siam of an overseas principal takes orders from dealers he usually pays cash against documents in Europe, and receives cash discounts; and in this case he usually arranges the terms of credit granted to the dealer. *Terms credit.*

In the case of an overseas firm's agent in Siam selling from stock goods consigned by his principal, the latter usually agrees to the terms of credit recommended by the agent, who almost invariably takes the *del credere* risk with the dealer. The credit period is usually three months, promissory notes[2] being taken on delivery. Discount for cash is usually 3 per cent. In default of any stipulation to the contrary, there is no limit of time in which the goods consigned are to be disposed of, payment being remitted by the agent on completion of the sale. *Terms of*

In the case of European manufacturer's agents in Siam taking orders from *payment.* dealers, there are two modes of payment, viz.:

(1) The agent pays the principal against shipping documents and receives cash discounts (see above); this is much the more usual course.

(2) The manufacturer draws on the dealer direct, the agent appearing "in case of need." In this case the draft[3] would be drawn through a bank either at 60 or 90 days sight. Bills are practically invariably drawn in sterling, payable at the bank's selling rate for drafts. On the subject of bills and promissory notes generally, it may be said that credit to native dealers granted by Continental firms has been

Where the principal draws directly on the dealer, the goods are usually sold c.i.f.

Where the agent acts as principal to the dealer he sells on "delivered" terms, generally in sterling on a commission basis, and sometimes on an inclusive tical price basis.[4] Makers' invoices must show weights of all goods – including piece goods[5] – as this is required by the Customs.

In the case of dispute between buyer and seller the arbitrator is now usually appointed by the local International Chamber of / Commerce. This Chamber comprises individuals of all nationalities, and includes in its membership practically all the important European firms.

Recovery of Debts.

[N.B. – In framing answers to the questions under this heading, opinions have been obtained from a legal as well as from a commercial point of view. Where the opinions differ, the mercantile point of view, which for practical purposes is no doubt the more useful, will appear preceded by (M) and the legal view by (L).]

(M). – There is no established local procedure for recovering debts. The merchant usually makes every endeavour to settle a debt without bringing an action in the local courts, owing to the time such actions take, and, in many cases, the possibility of the disappearance of the debtor or of his assets before judgment can be obtained.

The minimum sum it is worth while bringing an action to recover, may be put at 250 ticals (approximately £19).

(M). – To the query whether actions for recovery of debt are decided promptly, commercial opinion responds with a curt negative.

(L). – From a judicial source the following outline of local procedure has been obtained:

There is a summary procedure for claims under 200 ticals (approximately £15), viz.: the plaintiff makes a statement, either written or verbal, upon which the Court issues a summons, stating the amount claimed. After service of the summons the defendant must make either a verbal or written statement within 8 days. A day for hearing is fixed forthwith, and the proceedings are quite short, a prompt decision being arrived at. The Court costs in such a case would be approximately 15 ticals (23s.), exclusive of expenses of witnesses and lawyer.

In cases where the amount claimed is 200 ticals or over, more formality is necessary, the claim and defence consisting of written statements; the evidence must be taken down in detail, and a written judgment delivered.

Cases, however, in which there is no substantial defence are, as a rule, quickly

In cases founded upon promissory notes, which are still in the keeping of the plaintiff, and on which the signature is admitted, the Court will not hear evidence to prove payment.

A fee of 2½ per cent. is charged on the amount claimed, on entry of the case.

It is difficult to state what is the minimum sum it is worth while bringing an action to recover, but many small claims are brought in the Courts, which may. be evidence that the litigants find it advantageous to have recourse thereto.

In bankruptcy the procedure is much the same as in England, but the time occupied by the proceedings is very much greater and a great deal of debt passes unpunished. The Siamese Law of Bankruptcy was promulgated in 1912; the essentia] points are as follows: – Bankruptcy.

One creditor with a liquidated claim of 1,000 ticals (about £77), or any two or more creditors the aggregate amount of whose claims / amount to that sum, may put in a petition upon depositing 50 ticals (£3 17s.) and becoming liable for the costs and expenses incurred in the proceedings.

An interim receiver is then appointed and the petition served upon the debtor.

Upon the hearing of the petition it is necessary to prove:

1. The debt of the petitioning creditor.
2. Suspension of payment by the debtor.
3. The service of the petition.

ere are no "Acts of Bankruptcy" as in English law.

e foregoing remarks apply solely to proceedings in Siamese Courts. As previously stated it should be borne in mind that extra-territoriality[6] exists in Siam, and that, if the defendant be other than Siamese, British, Danish, or French Asiatic, the proceedings against him must be taken in the Consular Court of his nationality – *vide* Agency Conditions on pp. 4 – 5. It is, therefore, very advisable not to engage in direct dealings with native or Continental European dealers, but rather to endeavour to appoint or be represented by a local agent of British nationality, who will be in a position to meet the various technical points which arise from the mixture of nationalities and jurisdictions prevailing in Siam.

MARKING OF IMPORTED ARTICLES.

ere are no requirements as to marking of imported articles to show country of origin, etc., and goods need not be marked "imported by," followed by the name of the importer. The words "imported by" would only be evidence of the genuineness of the articles, and would not of themselves protect an unregistered mark; even registration of a mark is not necessarily conclusive evidence of the

It is to be regretted that the enforcement of a Siamese enactment for the registration and protection of trade marks, which has been brought forward of recent years at the urgent request of the foreign mercantile community, will probably have to be abandoned owing to the opposition of certain European nations whose extra-territorial privileges the law is alleged to infringe.

PACKING.

In considering the subject of packing, the Customs requirement that invoices must show weights should not be forgotten.

It is advisable also that consignors should realize that practically everything is opened and examined by the Customs in Bangkok, usually on an open wharf or in a cargo boat, and that the breaking open of cases for examination is not performed carefully or skilfully. Due allowance for this rough handling should be made by the packers.

Goods are usually preferred packed in cases, and there is no statutory limit of weight; with regard, however, to the question of weight of heavy packages such as machinery, etc., manufacturers and exporters should bear in mind the fact that the facilities in Bangkok for handling such are exceedingly poor. Attention should / also be directed to the necessity of most careful packing of all goods of a fragile or damageable nature, in view of the notoriously rough handling of goods which occurs during transhipment at Singapore.

It is difficult to lay down a broad rule to cover the question of packing, as much depends upon the nature of the goods; but the following remarks in regard to piece goods may be helpful, particularly as the packing, etc. of many lines of piece goods is peculiar to the Siamese market: –

Yarns, grey shirtings, and low quality cotton blankets are usually packed in bales. Most other piece goods are packed in cases which are usually tin lined, with the exception of *higher quality blankets* the cases containing which are lined with oil cloth.

Voiles, prints, art silk fancies are packed one piece each in a paper parcel.

Papoons, yarn dyed – finest quality, one piece in tissue paper, then in a carton; *medium quality*, one corge or occasionally half a corge in a carton; *lower quality*, each corge in white mull or printed handkerchief containing either whole, half, or quarter corge.[7]

Papoons, piece dyed – usually in tissue paper and one piece cartons, sometimes ten or twenty pieces in a carton.

Woven Sarongs – one corge in white mull or printed handkerchief. Sarongs of this class come forward in pairs.

Pakamas – one corge in white mull; sometimes in pairs but usually in single pieces.

White cambrics,[8] *lawns, etc.* – five or ten piece cartons or parcels.

Blankets, good quality – five or ten piece cartons.

Lower quality – five or ten piece parcels; sometimes not in parcels.

Shawls – six or twelve piece cartons or parcels.

During the war some temporary modifications in regard to packing are being made; for instance – some pakamas are being forwarded in bales instead of in cases. Possibly this method of packing these goods may be continued if found satisfactory. Some khaki drills are also packed in bales. With regard to the make-up of piece goods generally, this is always stipulated at the time of ordering.

A printed Import and Export List has been issued by the Siamese Customs, showing the designations and denominations by which articles of merchandise are to be distinguished when imported into or exported from Bangkok. This List, a copy of which may be consulted by British manufacturers and shippers of British goods at the Department of Commercial Intelligence of the Board of Trade, 73, Basinghall Street, London, E.C.2, may provide useful reference for packing goods or for drawing up invoices of contents. /

CATALOGUES.

Catalogues should be in English, as the use of the Siamese language in catalogues involves more trouble than it is worth. Manufacturers are advised to exercise discretion as to sending catalogues to entirely unknown people. It is not unusual for clerks earning but a small monthly salary to send off their twenty post cards in a mail for catalogues; as often as not the chief motive seems to be a hope of pictures to amuse their children.

It would be useful if catalogues gave particulars of packing, weights, and measurements, so that where c.i.f. prices are not stated the same could be approximately calculated.

Identifying numbers to items in a catalogue enable repeat orders to be made with greater ease: it is desirable also that the numbers should be constant and not varied with each edition of the catalogue issued.

ADVERTISING.

ere are several local newspapers – English, Siamese and Chinese – which offer facilities for advertising, but the rates are exceedingly costly, and the necessity of publishing an advertisement in three different languages increases the expense. A few posters are resorted to by one or two enterprising firms. On the whole, however, advertising in Siam is as yet neither satisfactory nor effective, though

For local purposes two directories are published in Siam, viz.:

"The Directory for Bangkok and Siam," published by the "Bangkok Times Press, Ltd.," and obtainable in the United Kingdom from F. Algar, 11, Clement's Lane, Lombard Street, E.C. 4, price 9s.

"The Siam Directory" published at the "Siam Observer Press, Ltd.," Oriental Avenue, Bangkok, price 7.50 ticals.

In addition to the Bangkok directories, business houses in Siam are generally provided with the Singapore Directory, and with the Directory and Chronicle of Hongkong.

Kelly's Directory of Merchants, Manufacturers and Shippers is available for reference at His Majesty's Consulate-General at Bangkok.

Stamp Taxes.

There are no stamp taxes[9] of any description levied in Siam on either documents or goods. Where medicines or drugs are concerned, it would be well, where such drugs contain or are likely / to contain morphia or cocaine, to state the fact that these elements are or are not present, and the proportion thereof, as this statement may save trouble under the Siamese Morphine Act.

CONSULAR INVOICES, BILLS OF LADING.

There are no requirements under Siamese laws or regulations as to Consular invoices or bills of lading.

Certificates of origin for imported goods are not required under any circumstances by the Royal Siamese Customs.

CUSTOMS TARIFF AND REGULATIONS.

The rate of Customs duty on all goods imported into Siam is 3 per cent. *ad valorem, i.e.*, 3 per cent. of the wholesale price landed in Bangkok. On wines and beers the duty is 5 per cent.; on spirits the charge is 2 ticals (tical = 1s. 6½d. approx.) per gallon of 50 degrees "*pure*" spirit (not "proof" spirit), with an additional duty of 4 cents (·72d.) for every gallon per degree over 50.

It should be borne in mind that the Customs require makers' invoices to show *weights* of all goods.

---

*   Names of importers of and dealers in various classes of goods in Siam, furnished by H.M. Consul-General at Bangkok, may be obtained by British manufacturers and shippers of British goods on application to the Department of Commercial Intelligence of the

As regards damaged goods the rule is that if goods arrive damaged, or short through leakage, etc., the Customs require the goods to be exhibited before delivery is taken from their custody; otherwise no claim for remission of duty on the damaged or lost portion is entertained. But an understanding with the Customs exists that in case of articles of value, the opening or exhibition of which on a wharf might cause risk of damage or loss, a Customs officer is allowed to go to the merchant's premises and see the case opened there. For this service a small fee is charged.

REGULATIONS AFFECTING COMMERCIAL TRAVELLERS.

No special regulations exist in Siam affecting the operations of commercial trav-

No duty is levied on samples having no commercial value, but samples of value are dutiable as ordinary goods. Duty on samples or on any goods not sold may, however, be deposited, and will be refunded if re-exportation takes place within two years. A list of the samples must be given by the traveller to the Customs so that they may be identified on re-exportation. If any samples are sold, the duty leviable on such samples is deducted from the amount to be refunded. /

BRITISH BANKS IN SIAM.

e undermentioned British banks have established agencies or branches in Bangkok, through which city practically all the overseas trade of Siam is transacted: –

Chartered Bank of India, Australia and China.

Head Office: 38, Bishopsgate, London, E.C.2.

Hongkong and Shanghai Banking Corporation.

London Office: 9, Gracechurch Street, E.C.3.

Mercantile Bank of India, Ltd. (Siam Forest Company, Ltd., Bangkok Agents).

Head Office: 15, Gracechurch Street, London, E.C.3.

SHIPPING FACILITIES.

e following is a list of the British steamship companies carrying cargo for Bangkok, *via* Singapore: –

e Ocean Steamship Co., Ltd., and the China Mutual Steam Navigation Co., Ltd. (Joint Service), from Birkenhead, Glasgow and Bristol Channel ports – Alfred Holt & Co., India Buildings, Liverpool.

Colin Scott & Co., 94, Hope Street, Glasgow (Ocean Steamship Company).

J. & A. Roxburgh, 69, Buchanan Street, Glasgow (China Mutual).

Jones, Heard & Co., 107, Dock Street, Newport, Mon.

The Atlantic Transport Co., Victoria Chambers, Swansea (China Mutual).

Burgess & Co., Ltd., Swansea (Ocean Steamship Company).

Peninsular and Oriental Steam Navigation Co., from Middlesbrough, Immingham and London –

Peninsular and Oriental Steam Navigation Co., 122, Leadenhall Street, London, E.C.3.

Escombe, McGrath & Co., 3, East India Avenue, London, E.C.3; Zetland Buildings, Middlesbrough; Albert Square, Manchester; and Immingham.

"Glen" and "Shire" Lines Joint Service of steamers, from Middlesbrough, Immingham, Hull, and London –

The Royal Mail Steam Packet Company's "Shire" Line Service –

McGregor, Gow & Holland, Ltd., 4, Fenchurch Avenue, London, E.C.3; Northern Assurance Buildings, Manchester; Paragon Buildings, Hull; and Immingham.

Andrew Weir & Co., Middlesbrough. /

"Glen" Line Service –

Glen Line, Ltd., 1, East India Avenue, London, E.C.3.

McGregor, .Gow & Holland, Ltd., 4, Fenchureh Avenue, London, E.C.3; Northern Assurance Buildings, Manchester; Paragon Buildings, Hull; and Immingham.

T. A. Bulmer & Co., Queen's Square, Middlesbrough.

The "Ben" Line (Wm. Thomson & Co., Leith), from Leith, Middlesbrough and London –

Killick, Martin & Co., 7, Fen Court, Fenchureh Street, London, E.C.3.

T. A. Bulmer & Co, Queen's Square, Middlesbrough.

The "Mogul" Line, from Middlesbrough, Glasgow and Birkenhead –

Gellatly; Hankey & Co., Dock House, Billiter Street, London, E.C.3, 82, Mitchell Street, Glasgow, and 22, Water Street, Liverpool.

CURRENCY.

The monetary unit is the silver tical, weighing 16 grammes, 900 fine.

By the Siamese Gold Standard Act of 1908 the Government undertakes to give ticals in Bangkok against gold deposited with their bankers in London at the rate of 13 ticals per £1. The local banks' rates, however, vary somewhat from this figure, and fluctuate slightly according to the exigencies of local trade.

The local silver currency is backed by gold reserve held in London, which in

e paper currency consists of notes of different values, ranging from 5 ticals to 1,000 ticals. According to the Siamese paper currency law, which has been amended recently, not more than 50 per cent. of the value of the notes in circulation may be invested by the Treasury, and not more than 25 per cent. may be held in gold coin or bullion or in silver bullion, while a balance of at least 25 per cent. must be held in silver ticals for the due encashment of the notes. The amount of the notes in circulation in February, 1917, was about 48,000,000 ticals.

EDITORIAL NOTES

Wray, *Notes on Perak with a Sketch of its Vegetable, Animal and Mineral Products*

wind furnaces: furnaces powered by the wind.
dwts.: deadweight tons.
Galena: a gray mineral, the principal ore of lead.

Greig, *Mining in Malaya*

lodes: A lode is a vein of mineral ore deposited between clearly demarcated layers of rock.
Pulsometers: A Pulsometer is a pump without pistons which operates by means of pulsed condensation of steam.
annular: shaped like or forming a ring.
shieves: A shieve is a grooved disc in a pulley.
terne: an alloy of lead containing tin (10–20 per cent) and antimony (1.5–2 per cent).
conchoidal: of, relating to, or being a surface characterized by smooth, shell-like convexities and concavities.
Pelton wheels: The Pelton wheel is a water impulse turbine invented by Lester Allan Pelton in the 1870s. It extracts energy from the impulse of moving water, as opposed to its weight like the traditional overshot water wheel.

Anon., 'Report on Mining in Malaya, 1939'

Ilmenite: a titanium ore, $FeTiO_3$.
quinquennium: a period of five years.
gneiss: a common and widely distributed type of rock formed by high-grade regional metamorphic processes from pre-existing formations that were originally either igneous or sedimentary rocks.
kaolinised granite: granite that has become clay.

Noetling, *Report on the Petroleum Industry in Upper Burma from the End of the Last Century up to the Beginning of 1891*

Yule: Sir Henry Yule (1820–89), a Scottish Orientalist.

Anon., *Report on the Mineral Production of Burma 1939*

1. *gangue*: commercially worthless material that surrounds, or is closely mixed with, a wanted mineral in an ore deposit.
2. *flumes*: A flume is an open artificial channel or chute carrying a stream of water.

Chhibber, 'The Salt Industry of Amherst District'

1. *Beaume*: the scale of Baume's hydrometer invented by the French chemist Antoine Baumé (1728–1804).
2. *Beaume's hydrometer*: provides scientific measurements for the density of liquids.
3. *maunds*: A maund is unit of mass equal to 82.28 lbs.
4. *deliquescent*: To deliquesce is to dissolve and become liquid by absorbing moisture from the air.

Cowie Harbour Coal Co. Ltd, 'Report on the Silimpopon Coal Mines and Property, 1926'

1. *airways*: ventilation shafts.

Anon., *Return of Imports and Exports, Straits Settlements, 1889*

1. *Slendangs*: A Slendang is a long narrow scarf.
2. *Specie*: coin.
3. *Gram*: the seed of several plants, including the chickpea, consumed as food.
4. *Dholl*: the seed of the leguminous shrub, Cajanus cajan, consumed as food.
5. *Fishmaws*: A fish maw is the stomach of a fish. Consumed as food.
6. *Beche-de-mer*: sea cucumbers. Marine animals of the class Holothuroidea used in fresh or dried form in cooking.
7. *Cubebs*: the dried berries of the Cubeb (Piper cubeba) plant.
8. *Gamboge*: a partially transparent deep saffron to mustard yellow pigment.
9. *Tamarind*: the edible pod-like fruit of the tamarind tree.
10. *Mace*: an aromatic spice.
11. *Dragon's blood*: a bright red resin that is obtained from various plants in the genera *Croton, Dracaena, Daemonorops, Calamus rotang* and *Pterocarpus*.

Alexander, *British Malaya: Malayan Statistics*

1. *Ghee*: a class of clarified butter.
2. *Arecanuts*: betal nuts.
3. *Arrack*: a distilled alcoholic drink.
4. *Samsoo*: or Samsu: a locally distilled potent spirit.
5. *Damar*: a resin produced by the Dipterocarpaceae family of trees.
6. *Sticklac*: resin-like substance secreted by certain lac insects used in varnishes and sealing wax.
7. *Gunnies*: sacks.
8. *Isinglass*: a transparent, almost pure gelatin prepared from the air bladder of the sturgeon

Kapok: a silky fibre obtained from the fruit of the silk-cotton tree and used for insulation and as padding in pillows, mattresses and life preservers.

Patchouli leaves: the leaves of a small South East Asian shrub that yields a fragrant oil used in the manufacture of perfumes.

Kirsepp and Bartlett, *Report of a Mission Appointed to Investigate the Clove Trade in India and Burma, Ceylon, British Malaya and the Dutch East Indies*

asilas: A frasila is approximately 35 pounds.

belachan: shrimp paste.

Anon., 'A Short History of the Port of Singapore'

Sinhalese: an ethnic group native to the island of Sri Lanka.

Mole: a large, usually stone wall constructed in the sea, used as a breakwater to enclose or protect an anchorage or a harbour.

Sir Michael Hicks-Beach: Michael Edward Hicks Beach, first Earl St Aldwyn (1837–1916). A British Conservative politician, who served as Chancellor of the Exchequer (1885–6 and 1895–1902) and led the Conservative Party in the House of Commons (1885–6).

stevedorage: the cost of employing labour to unload cargo.

caisson: a floating structure used to close off the entrance to a dock.

Anon., *Memorandum on the Proposed Singapore Harbour Improvement Scheme Drawn up by a Member of the Committee of the Singapore Chamber of Commerce*

Messrs. COODE, SON & MATTHEWS: The firm, a partnership between Sir William Matthews (1844–1922) and Sir John Coode (1816–92), concentrated on the construction and inspection of harbours and docks and built works at Dover, Singapore, Colombo and Valletta and undertook inspections in Cape Colony, Ceylon, Cyprus, Hong Kong and Malta.

Anon., *Foreign Trade and Navigation of the Port of Bangkok for the Years 1918/19*

Ticals: The silver tical was the monetary unit of Siam. The government exchange rate in Bangkok, governed by the Siamese Gold Standard Act of 1908, was 13 ticals per £1. Local banks' rates fluctuated around this figure depending on the exigencies of local trade.

Maitri (ed.), *Siam: Treaties with Foreign Powers, 1920–1927*

imposts: An impost is a tax or duty that is imposed

coasting trade: trade between Siam ports.

3. *bills of lading*: A bill of lading is a document issued by a carrier to a shipper, listing and acknowledging receipt of goods for transport and specifying terms of delivery.
4. *appurtenances*: equipment used for a specific purpose or task.

Winstedt, *Malay Industries. Part 1. Arts and Crafts*

1. *Pitt Rivers*: Augustus Henry Lane-Fox Pitt Rivers (1827–1900), an English army officer, ethnologist and archaeologist.
2. *repoussé*: metal shaped or decorated with patterns in relief formed by hammering and pressing on the reverse side of the metal.

Carvalho, *The Manufacturing Industries of the British Empire Overseas . Part 5, Newfoundland, West Indies, Ceylon, Malaya, Hong Kong, Sarawak, Drunci, Borneo*

1. *Atap*: the leaves of the nipa palm.
2. *Bêche de Mer*: large sea cucumber, which is boiled, dried and used in Asian cuisine. See Anon., *Return of Imports and Exports, Straits Settlements, 1889*, n. 6.
3. *creeses*: A creese is a Malay dagger.
4. *Citronella*: a tropical Asian grass from which an oil is extracted that is used in perfumery and in some insect repellents.
5. *Patchouli*: a small South East Asian shrub from the leaves of which an oil is extracted that is used in perfumery.
6. *Chaulmoogra*: a tropical Asian tree of the genus *Hydnocarpus*, whose seeds contain an oil formerly used to treat skin lesions caused by leprosy and other diseases.
7. *Sheelite*: a product produced from coal tar.
8. *Damar*: a hard tree resin.
9. *Solar oil*: a petroleum fraction that has undergone purification. Used in marine diesel engines and the tanning industry.
10. *Palembang*: a form of tobacco.
11. *Alum*: a colourless soluble hydrated double sulphate of aluminium and potassium used in the manufacture of pigments and in dressing leather and sizing paper.
12. *Arrack*: a distilled alcoholic drink. See Alexander, *British Malaya*, note 3 above.

Johnson, 'Preliminary Memorandum on Conditions in Pineapple Factories in Malaya'

1. *Processing*: the heating of the can after it is sealed to cook the contents and to prevent their spoilage by microorganisms.
2. *exhaust process*: the conveyance of cans through an exhaust box to raise their temperature and to expel air and other gases from the product.
3. *exhaust boxes*: The exhaust box may consist of a hot-water bath through which the cans are conveyed, partially immersed, or a conveyor belt to carry the cans through a blanket of steam.

ends: an end is the top or bottom of a can.
knurling: small ridges or grooves.
chuck: a clamp that holds a tool.
mandrels: A mandrel is a metal/wood rod or bar around which material, such as metal or glass, may be shaped.

Anon., 'Quality Products of the Ho Hong Mills'

katis: a unit of mass equal to 604.8 grammes.
crutcher: a mixing machine.
soap plodder: used to extrude soap into ropes, which are then cut and pressed.

Anon., 'World's Biggest Tin Smelters. Growth of Straits Trading Co.'

reverberatory furnace: a metallurgical or process furnace that isolates the material being processed from contact with the fuel, but not from contact with combustion gases.

Anon., 'Tampenis Cement Tile Works'

Boyanese: people from Bawean, an Indonesian island located approximately 150 km north of Surabaya in the Java Sea.

Anon., 'Steel Castings for all Purposes. Machinery Making in the Tropics'

cupola furnace: a cylindrical shaft type of blast furnace used for re-melting metals, usually iron, before casting.
converter: a furnace in which pig iron is converted into steel by the Bessemer process.

Arnold, *On Cotton Fabrics and the Cotton Industry of Burma*

lungyis: cloth, often brightly coloured, which is used as a piece of clothing.
skeins: a length of thread or yarn wound in a loose long coil.
pasos: a form of sarong.
thingans: small robes.
piece-goods: fabrics made and sold in standard lengths.
tea-cosy: a covering for a teapot to keep the contents hot.

Morris, 'The Lacquerware Industry of Burma'

orpiment: arsenic trisulfide, As_2S_3, a yellow mineral used as a pigment.
realgar: a soft orange-red arsenic ore, As_2S_2, used in pyrotechnics and tanning and as a pigment.

Anon., *Memorandum on Business Methods and Trading Regulations in Siam*

1. *risk of del credere*: that the purchaser will not pay for the goods.
2. *promissory notes*: a written promise to pay or repay a specified sum of money at a stated time or on demand.
3. *draft*: A bill/draft of exchange is a written order directing that a specified sum of money be paid to a specified person in a specified time period.
4. *tical price basis*: the payment is made in ticals, the former standard monetary unit of Thailand, replaced by the baht in 1928.
5. *piece goods*: fabrics made and sold in standard lengths.
6. *extra-territoriality*: exemption from local legal jurisdiction.
7. *corge*: a unit of twenty.
8. *cambrics*: A cambric is a finely woven white linen or cotton fabric.
9. *stamp taxes*: A stamp tax is a tax collected by requiring a stamp to be purchased and attached to a good/document.

LIST OF SOURCES

	Source
L. Wray Jr, *Notes on Perak with a Sketch of its Vegetable, Animal and Mineral Products* (1886)	British Library, shelfmark T 29790(i)
Golden Raub: A Series of Articles on the Raub Gold Mines and their Prospects (1897)	British Library, shelfmark 07108.k.15
G. E. Greig, *Mining in Malaya* (1924)	LSE, Government Publications, shelfmark 595 (24)
Anon., 'Report on Mining in Malaya, 1939'	National Archives, shelfmark CO 717/132/9
F. Noetling, *Report on the Petroleum Industry in Upper Burma from the End of the Last Century up to the Beginning of 1891* (1892)	Natural History Musuem Library, Mineralogy Collection, shelfmark (591) NOE
Report on the Mineral Production of Burma 1939 (1939)	British Library, shelfmark ST 117
H. L. Chhibber, 'The Salt Industry of Amherst District', *Journal of the Burma Research Society* (1929)	British Library, shelfmark SV 66
Cowie Harbour Coal Co. Ltd, 'Report on the Silimpopon Coal Mines and Property, 1926' (1926)	National Archives, shelfmark CO 874/160
'Labuan. Lease of Coal Mines in the Island of Labuan dated 14th November, 1889' (1889)	National Archives, shelfmark CAOG 14/162
Return of Imports and Exports, Straits Settlements, 1889 (1890)	LSE, Government Publications, shelfmark 595 (R35)
C. S. Alexander, *British Malaya: Malayan Statistics* (1928)	LSE, Government Publications, shelfmark 595 (119)
Report of Sub-Committee with respect to Exports to Germany and Austria from the Straits Settlements (1914)	LSE, Pamphlet Collection, shelfmark P 17507
G. D. Kirsepp and C. A. Bartlett, *Report of a Mission Appointed to Investigate the Clove Trade in India and Burma, Ceylon, British Malaya and the Dutch East Indies* (1933)	LSE, Government Publications, shelfmark 6781 (33)
Anon., 'A Short History of the Port of Singapore', in Anon., *The Singapore Manufacturers Exhibi-* (1932)	National Archives, shelfmark CO 273/582/13

Anon., *Memorandum on the Proposed Singapore Harbour Improvement Scheme Drawn up by a Member of the Committee of the Singapore Chamber of Commerce* (1904) — British Library, General Reference Collection, shelfmark 8776.h.41.(6.)

Anon., *Report on the Maritime Trade and Customs Administration of Burma for the Official Year 1924/5* (1925) — British Library, shelfmark IOR V/24/488

Anon., *Foreign Trade and Navigation of the Port of Bangkok for the Years 1918/9* (1919) — LSE, Government Publications, shelfmark 593 (R2)

P. K. Maitri (ed.), *Siam: Treaties with Foreign Powers, 1920–1927* (1928) — LSE, Government Publications, shelfmark 593 (6)

R. Winstedt, *Malay Industries. Part 1. Arts and Crafts* (1909) — British Library, shelfmark V 10064

H. N. Carvalho, *The Manufacturing Industries of the British Empire Overseas. Part 5, Newfoundland, West Indies, Ceylon, Malaya, Hong Kong, Sarawak, Drunci, Borneo* (1931/2) — National Library of Wales, shelfmark HC246 E69

W. B. J. Johnson, 'Preliminary Memorandum on Conditions in Pineapple Factories in Malaya' (1936) — National Archives, shelfmark CO 273/615/4

Anon., 'Minutes of a Meeting Held at the Gardens Club, Singapore, at 2.30 p.m. on April 17th, 1936, between Pineapple Packers and Officers of the Agricultural Department' (1936) — National Archives, shelfmark CO 273/615/4

Anon., 'Quality Products of the Ho Hong Mills', *Malayan Tribune Memento*, 2–9 January 1932 (1932) — National Archives, shelfmark CO 273/582/3

Anon., 'World's Biggest Tin Smelters. Growth of Straits Trading Co.', *The Singapore Free Press Exhibition Supplement*, 2 January 1932 (1932) — National Archives, shelfmark CO 273/582/3

Anon., 'Tampenis Cement Tile Works', *Malayan Tribune Memento*, 2–9 January 1932 (1932) — National Archives, shelfmark CO 273/582/3

Anon., 'Steel Castings for all Purposes. Machinery Making in the Tropics', *The Singapore Free Press Exhibition Supplement*, 2 January 1932 (1932) — National Archives, shelfmark CO 273/582/3

G. F. Arnold, *On Cotton Fabrics and the Cotton Industry of Burma* (1897) — British Library, shelfmark IOR/V/27/631/39

A. P. Morris, 'The Lacquerware Industry of Burma', *Journal of the Burma Research Society* (1919) — British Library, shelfmark SV 66

Anon., *Memorandum on Business Methods and Trading Regulations in Siam* (1917) — LSE, Government Publications, shelfmark 42 (588/1–21)